8/20/48

For your

leisure moments,

if any.

Claire + Tillie

P.S. Bon Voyage

Maureen Carlson
apt. 3D

THE NOBEL PRIZE TREASURY

The NOBEL PRIZE Treasury

Edited by
MARSHALL McCLINTOCK

DOUBLEDAY & COMPANY, INC.

Garden City, N.Y. 1948

ACKNOWLEDGMENTS

"His Widow's Husband" from *Plays—First Series* by Jacinto Benavente; by permission of Charles Scribner's Sons; copyright, 1917, 1945, by John Garrett Underhill. "Why Do We Laugh?" from *Laughter* by Henri Bergson; reprinted by permission of The Macmillan Company, N. Y. "Between the Battles" by Björnstjerne Björnson; reprinted by permission of *Folk Lore* and Joseph E. Weingarten; copyright, 1941, by *Folk Lore*. "Wang Lung" from *The First Wife and Other Stories* by Pearl S. Buck; copyright, 1933, by Pearl S. Buck; Permission of The John Day Company, N.Y. publishers. "The Gentleman from San Francisco" from *The Gentleman from San Francisco* by Ivan Bunin; copyright, 1923, by Alfred A. Knopf, Inc.; reprinted by permission of the publisher. Five poems by Giosué Carducci; reprinted by permission of Kegan Paul, Trench, Trubner & Co., Ltd. "The Shoes" by Grazia Deledda, from *The Copeland Translations*; by permission of Charles Townsend Copeland and Charles Scribner's Sons. "Confidence Africaine" by Roger Martin du Gard; copyright, 1943, by *Accent* magazine; reprinted by special permission of the author and translator. "Lucifer" from *The Well of St. Clare* by Anatole France and "Sylvestre Bonnard Finds Jeanne" from *The Crime of Sylvestre Bonnard* by Anatole France; reprinted by permission of Dodd, Mead & Company, Inc. "Salvation of a Forsyte" from *Caravan* by John Galsworthy; copyright, 1925, by Charles Scribner's Sons. Pages from *The Journals of André Gide*; copyright, 1947, by Alfred A. Knopf, Inc.; reprinted by permission of the publisher. "Kamanita and Vasitthi" from *The Pilgrim Kamanita* by Karl Gjellerup; by permission of William Heinemann, Ltd. "Isak and Inger" from *Growth of the Soil* by Knut Hamsun; copyright, 1921, by Alfred A. Knopf, Inc.; reprinted by permission of the publisher. "The Sunken Bell" by Gerhart Hauptmann; copyright, 1899, by Robert Howard Russell; copyright, 1899, 1914, by Doubleday & Company, Inc. "Two Worlds" from *Demian* by Hermann Hesse; copyright, 1923, by Hermann Hesse; copyright, 1948, by Henry Holt & Company, Inc. "Snake Song," "Summer Dancing," and "Eden" by Erik Axel Karlfeldt, from *Arcadia Borealis*; translated by Charles Wharton Stork; copyright, 1938, by the University of Minnesota Press. "The Way Through the Woods" from *Rewards and Fairies* by Rudyard Kipling; copyright, 1910, by Rudyard Kipling, and "The Strange Ride of Morrowbie Jukes" from *Under the Deodars* by Rudyard Kipling; copyright, 1899, 1927, by Rudyard Kipling, both by permission of Mrs. George Bambridge and Doubleday & Company, Inc. "The Outlaws" from *Invisible Links* by Selma Lagerlöf; copyright, 1899, by Pauline Bancroft Flach, renewed 1926; reprinted by permission of Doubleday & Company, Inc. "Travel Is So Broadening" from *The Man Who Knew Coolidge* by Sinclair Lewis; copyright, 1928, by Harcourt, Brace and Company, Inc. "Interior" by Maurice Maeterlinck, by special permission of the author. "Little Hanno" from *Buddenbrooks* by Thomas Mann; copyright, 1924, by Alfred A. Knopf, Inc.; reprinted by permission of the publisher. "The Prayer" by Gabriela Mistral from *An Anthology of Contemporary Latin-American Poetry*; edited by Dudley Fitts; copyright, 1942, 1947, by New Directions. "To the Children," "The Lamp," and "Little Feet" by Gabriela Mistral, from *Some Spanish-American Poets*; translated by Alice Stone Blackwell; reprinted by permission of the University of Pennsylvania Press. "The Mares of the Camargue" by Frédéric Mistral, from *The Poetical Works of George Meredith*; copyright, 1912, by Charles Scribner's Sons; copyright, 1940, by William M. Meredith; by permission of Charles Scribner's Sons. "Desire Under the Elms" by Eugene O'Neill; copyright, 1931, by Eugene O'Neill; by permission of Random House, Inc. "The Haunted House" from *The Medals and Other Stories* by Luigi Pirandello; copyright, 1939, by E. P. Dutton & Co., Inc. "Our Lord of the Ship" from *The One-Act Plays of Luigi Pirandello*; copyright, 1928, by E. P. Dutton & Co., Inc. "Death" by Ladislas Reymont from *Selected Polish Tales*; by permission of Oxford University Press, London. "Lightning Strikes Christophe" from *Jean-Christophe* by Romain Rolland; copyright, 1910, 1911, 1913, 1938, by Henry Holt and Company, Inc. "Bartek the Conqueror" from *Laughing Truths* by Henryk Sienkiewicz; by permission of Basil Blackwell & Mott, Ltd. "Anniversary Celebrations" from *Laughing Truths* by Carl Spitteler; by permission of G. P. Putnam's Sons, New York, and Putnam & Company, Ltd., London. "Hylas and Kaleidusa Over Hill and Vale" from *Selected Poems of Carl Spitteler*; by permission of Putnam & Company, Ltd., London. Eleven poems from *The Crescent Moon* by Rabindranath Tagore; by special permission of the Trustees of Rabindranath Tagore, The Macmillan Company, New York, and Macmillan & Co., Ltd., London. "Young Olav and Ingunn" from *The Master of Hestviken* by Sigrid Undset; copyright, 1928, by Alfred A. Knopf, Inc.; reprinted by permission of the publisher. "The Land of Heart's Desire" from *Plays and Controversies* by William Butler Yeats, "Down by the Salley Gardens," and "The Lake Isle of Innisfree" from *Collected Poems* by William Butler Yeats; reprinted by permission of The Macmillan Company, New York, Macmillan & Co., Ltd., London, and Mrs. W. B. Yeats. "Synnöve's Song" and "Over the Lofty Mountains" by Björnstjerne Björnson, from *An Anthology of Norwegian Lyrics*; copyright, 1942, by The American-Scandinavian Foundation. "The Call of Life" by Knut Hamsun from *Told in Norway*; copyright, 1927, by The American-Scandinavian Foundation. "Ann and the Cow" by Johannes V. Jensen, from *Denmark's Best Stories*; copyright, 1928, by The American-Scandinavian Foundation. "At Memphis Station" by Johannes V. Jensen from *A Book of Danish Verse*; copyright, 1922, by The American-Scandinavian Foundation. "A Bathing Girl" by Johannes V. Jensen from *A Second Book of Danish Verse*; copyright, 1927, by The American-Scandinavian Foundation. "Dreams and Life" and "My Forefathers" by Erik Axel Karlfeldt and "Invocation and Promise" by Verner von Heidenstam, from *A Book of Swedish Verse*; copyright, 1930, by The American-Scandinavian Foundation. "A Clean White Shirt" by Verner von Heidenstam from *Sweden's Best Stories*; copyright, 1928, by The American-Scandinavian Foundation. "Little Ahasuerus" by Johannes V. Jensen from *The American-Scandinavian Review*; copyright, 1923, by The American-Scandinavian Foundation. "A Fisher Nest" by Henrik Pontoppidan from *The American-Scandinavian Review*; copyright, 1927, by The American-Scandinavian Foundation. "Taavati Antila" by Frans Eemil Sillanpää, from *The American-Scandinavian Review*; copyright, 1940, by The American-Scandinavian Foundation.

Foreword

Foreword

T**HE PERSON** who shall have produced in the field of literature the most distinguished work of an idealistic tendency."

That is the definition, according to the will of Alfred Nobel, of the author to whom the Nobel prize in literature should be given each year. The selection of that author is no easy task, especially when one recalls another provision of the will, that "no consideration whatever shall be paid to the nationality of the candidates." Thus all of world literature is to be judged by the small group of men called upon to select "the most distinguished." It is obvious that no choice could fail to raise some objections; it is amazing only that a storm of protest has not arisen after most announcements of prize winners.

The fact is that criticism of the awards has been rare and mild. As the Nobel prizes approach their fiftieth anniversary, they remain the outstanding literary awards, the only ones of true international importance, carrying far more prestige than any other honor that an author may achieve. The material advantages are considerable, too, for the sales of a prize winner's books are increased throughout the world and the prize itself now amounts to more than $40,000. Until moving-picture companies went into the business of giving literary prizes, the Nobel award carried the largest monetary value.

When the list of winners is studied, one can understand why the Nobel prize has retained, and even increased, its prestige and importance. True, there are a few names rarely heard any more, and a few others that never have been widely known in America. Sometimes the small American public of an author may be explained by difficulties of translation, especially of poetry. Of those authors who were once widely read here but whose books now sit without frequent disturbance on library shelves, the playwrights seem to be in the majority. Somehow a play gets an old-fashioned air about it much sooner than a prose work, but many of these playwrights still make good reading, even if not good staging.

In the main, it is the American public that is the loser in not knowing and reading more of the Nobel prize winners. For there is no denying that these are all great authors, with something important to say and an interesting way of saying it. If the reader makes some discoveries for himself in this volume, in addition to enjoying the writing of authors he already knows he likes, then the editor will feel that he has done a double good turn.

The Nobel prizes were instituted by the will of Alfred Nobel, Swedish inventor of dynamite, who died in 1896 leaving nine million dollars in a fund the interest of which was to be used as prizes in five fields of endeavor. Awards are given "to those persons who shall have contributed most materially to benefit mankind" in physics, chemistry, medicine, and peace, and also in literature for the most distinguished idealistic work, as defined above. The literature awards are made by the Swedish Academy, which appoints a committee from its own eighteen members to carry out this work. The Nobel will provides that an award may be shared by two winners, or that no award at all may be given in any year. Although the will implied that the prize was to be given for a work published in the preceding year, the committee has disregarded this completely, making the award always for the whole body of an author's work, no matter when it was written. In some cases the prize winner has produced nothing at all for several years before receiving the prize, and often a specific work cited by the committee was published many years before.

The Swedish Academy is not expected to do its own screening of all possible winners. Nominations or recommendations are welcomed from universities, recognized academies, and similar institutions of standing throughout the world. Authors who have already won the prize may also make nominations. The Academy no doubt calls upon scholars and critics for opinions to help make the final decision, but no one has ever suggested that anyone but the committee itself really make the choice in all honesty and to the best of its ability.

Since the first award was made in 1901, forty-two authors have received the prize. No awards were given in 1914, 1918, 1935, 1940, 1941, 1942, or 1943. In two years—1904 and 1917—the award was shared by two authors. Of the forty-two winners, twenty-three were primarily writers of fiction, nine were poets, seven dramatists, two philosophers, and one a historian. Some of these classifications are arbitrary, as several authors were prominent in more than one field, but usually the labeling of an author's chief work is obvious.

Seventeen nationalities are represented among the award winners. The French lead with seven, the Germans come next with five; England has five, also, if you count Shaw as English rather than Irish, which seems to be the accepted practice, even by Mr. Shaw. There have been three winners each from the United States, Italy, Norway, Sweden, and Denmark, two each from Spain, Poland, and Switzerland. (Hermann Hesse, although born a German, has been a Swiss citizen for almost thirty years and is so counted here.) One winner each comes from Ireland, Belgium, India, Chile, Finland, and Russia. The Russian representative is Ivan Bunin, who has lived in France for about the length of time that Hesse has lived in Switzerland, so perhaps consistency should dictate his classification as French.

These statistics of nationality bring up the provision in Alfred Nobel's will barring any consideration of this factor in making the awards. Has that provision been carried out faithfully? Some criticism has been made that the Scandinavian countries have received an undue share of the prizes. Norway,

Sweden, Denmark, and Finland have a total of ten winners. But two of the Danes shared one award, and only two or three of the other winners would be questioned by even the most carping critic as worthy of the prize; they might not question at all if they were more familiar with those authors' works. Some of the prize winners with the largest American publics have been Scandinavian—Sigrid Undset, Knut Hamsun, Björnstjerne Björnson, Selma Lagerlöf. Considered seriously, the suggestion of Scandinavian favoritism seems to hold little water.

Another criticism, however, carries much more weight. This is the charge that the Swedish Academy has an anti-Russian prejudice. This prejudice, if it exists, is not just anti-Communist, for there is as much evidence of it before the Bolshevik Revolution as since. Russian literature has been rich and deeply significant for a long time; it has produced many truly great writers. But only one Russian has been given the Nobel prize, and he was a voluntary exile from his country for twenty years when he got it. Meanwhile, what great Russian writers were being overlooked by the Nobel committee? One is regarded as among the greatest authors the world has known, in any language, at any time—Leo Tolstoy. He lived until 1910, so was passed over nine times for authors like Sully-Prudhomme, Théodor Mommsen, José Echegaray, Frédéric Mistral, and Rudolf Eucken. Now, these authors are important. Their work was certainly distinguished, even if not, perhaps, "the most distinguished." But they cannot compare in influence, popularity, significance, or even "idealistic tendencies" with Tolstoy. Nor can Sully-Prudhomme and Mommsen compete with Chekhov, who lived until 1904. Other Russian authors of international importance who have been skipped by the prize givers are Leonid Andreev, Maxim Gorki, and Mikhail Sholokhov, to mention only the most prominent.

Examination of the record would thus indicate that nationality *has* been considered—if it is Russian nationality—in the awarding of Nobel prizes. This may be an unconscious prejudice on the part of the awarding committee, whose record of honesty and impartiality has in general been unblemished.

However, there are other indications that nationality has entered the thoughts of the committee members. Except for 1935, all the years in which the prize was omitted were war years. Yet many very great authors were living in those years, some of whom, a year or two later, were thought worthy of the prize without having written any more books. The committee no doubt thought that the giving of a prize to any citizen of a warring nation might be construed as taking sides in the war—and Sweden was fortunately one of the few nations that succeeded in keeping out of *both* world wars. It is significant, perhaps, that in the war year 1916 the prize went to the Swede, Verner von Heidenstam, in 1917 to Gjellerup and Pontoppidan, two neutral Danes. In 1915 the award was a courageous one, given to Romain Rolland, a Frenchman who was fighting for peace despite attacks on him from all sides. But the Nobel prizes remained neutral, for Rolland was in voluntary exile in Switzerland, crying a plague on both warring houses and working for war prisoners of all nations.

There was one war, however, in which the committee did not hesitate to take sides, a very small war with only two contestants. In 1939 the Nobel prize was given to Frans Eemil Sillanpää, a Finn, during the course of the Russian-Finnish war. Sillanpää was almost unknown outside the Scandinavian countries, but the Nobel committee has often chosen winners of great merit but slight international reputation. An examination of Sillanpää's writings reveals a great ability and charm, a talent certainly the equal of that possessed by many another Nobel winner. Still, those who think they have detected anti-Russian bias in the awarding of the Nobel prizes felt some confirmation in this single departure from neutrality in wartime.

It is always easy, of course, to think of some other author who should have won the prize rather than the one who did win. It is hard not to be outraged that your favorite author is neglected by the committee. A pleasant pastime can be made out of thinking of authors who should have won the prize but didn't. Among Americans there is Mark Twain, who lived nine years after the prizes began, and Carl Sandburg, Theodore Dreiser, Willa Cather, and others any reader can think of. English authors who failed to win are Thomas Hardy, Joseph Conrad, H. G. Wells, Algernon Charles Swinburne, George Meredith, G. K. Chesterton, Arnold Bennett, John Masefield, Aldous Huxley, Somerset Maugham, D. H. Lawrence, James Joyce (or is he Irish?), and T. S. Eliot (American?). The last of these was said to be a runner up in 1947 and will probably win if he lives a few more years.

Despite the high French score among prize winners, there are several of first rank who failed. Emile Zola lived until 1902 and so had a brief chance; others are Marcel Proust, Jules Romains, Paul Bourget, Paul Claudel, and François Mauriac (also said to have been seriously considered in 1947). Germans who missed are Heinrich Mann, Rainer Maria Rilke, Hermann Sudermann. There are even three great Scandinavian authors who surely merited the award—Henrik Ibsen, who died in 1906, Georg Brandes, alive until 1927, and Martin Andersen Nexö, who is still alive. The Italian, Benedetto Croce, and the Czech, Karel Čapek, might have been excellent choices. The committee could bestow a prize on the Orient, perhaps, through Lin Yutang. And if they allowed nationality to enter their thoughts just a little bit, they might strike a blow for tolerance by rewarding Sholom Asch or another distinguished Yiddish author.

This speculation, though interesting, is really beside the point. The important things are the winners of the Nobel prize and the writing they did. Even though some good authors have not won the prize, this does not alter the fact that the winners are great authors whose writings are enjoyable and instructive. The common criticism that they are too old, past their creative peak, seems to me to carry little weight. The objection has frequently been made that the Nobel prize has gone to authors so successful that they needed neither the prestige nor the money, that it failed to stimulate or make possible more and greater writing. But Alfred Nobel did not say that the prize should help pay the rent and food bills so an author could devote all of his time to writing. He wanted "the most distinguished work" rewarded, and such work is usually sure to come from an author of great reputation and ability. It is true that a great many old men have won the Nobel prize. Eight winners were in their seventies, two in their eighties, when the honor came to them. Only six winners have been in the forties, and of these three were Americans. The average age of winners is sixty-one, but there have been

Shaw from a friend or the public library. I am sorry that he would not join such distinguished company as may be found here.

Shaw reminds me of copyright. I wish to express my thanks to authors, agents, and publishers who kindly granted permission to reprint copyrighted material in this volume. Every effort has been made to find the owners of rights to all selections used; if any acknowledgments have been omitted or any rights overlooked, it is by accident. Forgiveness is asked and the assurance given that any necessary correction will be made when possible.

Finally I want to thank those who have made suggestions for this collection, and especially my wife, Inez Bertail, who has read many volumes to give me the benefit of her opinions and reactions, which proved of inestimable value in making final choice among so many tempting treasures.

MARSHALL McCLINTOCK

Contents

Contents

THE NOBEL PRIZE TREASURY

André Gide

PAGES FROM THE JOURNAL

[1909]

THE DEATH OF CHARLES-LOUIS PHILIPPE

No! NO, it wasn't the same thing. . . . This time, he who disappears is a *real* man. We were counting on him; we were dependent on him; we loved him. And suddenly he ceases to be there.

On the way to Cérilly

I am writing this in the train—where I am still chatting with him. Oh, already confused recollections! If I did not fix them today, tomorrow, already utterly crushed, I should get them all mixed up.

Saturday evening a note from Marguerite Audoux tells me that Philippe is ill.

Sunday morning I rush to his place, on the Quai Bourbon; his concierge sends me to the Dubois hospital; he is unknown there. I learn that three persons came to ask for him the day before, who went away as uninformed as I. Mme Audoux's card bears no indication. . . . What shall I do? . . . Doubtless Francis Jourdain can give me some news; I write him. The telegram I receive from him on Tuesday morning already deprives me of all hope; I rush to the address he gives me.

At the end of the corridor in the Velpeau hospital a room door remains open. Philippe is there. Ah, what does it matter now that the long windows of that room open directly into a big bright garden! It would have been good for his convalescence; but already he has lost consciousness; he is still struggling, but has already left us.

I approach the bed where he is dying; here are his mother, a friend whom I don't know,[1] and Mme Audoux, who recognizes and welcomes me. I lead her out to the parlor for a minute.

Philippe has been here a week. At first the typhoid fever seemed very mild and, in the beginning, of so ill-defined a character that it was treated as a mere grippe. Then, for several days, Philippe was treated as typhoid cases are treated today; but the regime of cold baths was very impractical in his little lodging on the Quai Bourbon. Tuesday evening he was carried to the Velpeau hospital; nothing alarming until Sunday; then suddenly meningitis sets in; his heart beats wildly; he is lost. Dr. Élie Faure, his friend, who,

[1] Léon Werth. [A.]

against all hope, carries on and will continue to surround him with care, from time to time risks an injection of spartein or of camphorated oil; but already the organism has ceased to react.

We return to the bedside. Yet how many struggles still and with what difficulty this poor suffering body resigns itself to dying! He is breathing very fast and very hard—very badly, like someone who has forgotten how.

The muscles of his neck and of the lower part of his face tremble; one eye is half open, the other closed. I rush to the post office to send some telegrams; almost none of Philippe's friends is informed.

At the Velpeau hospital again. Dr. Élie Faure takes the invalid's pulse. The poor mother queries: "How is the fever developing?" Through her suffering she is careful to speak correctly; she is a mere peasant, but she knows who her son is. And during these lugubrious days, instead of tears, she sheds floods of words; they flow evenly, monotonously, without accent or melody, in a somewhat hoarse tone, which at first surprises as if it didn't properly interpret her suffering; and her face remains dry.

After lunch I come back again; I cannot realize this loss. I find Philippe only slightly weaker, his face convulsed, shaken; struggling with slightly less energy against death.

Wednesday morning

Chanvin was waiting for me in the parlor. We are led, on the right side of the courtyard, to a little secret room, with an entrance on an angle—hiding as if ashamed. The rest of the establishment does not know of its existence, for we are in a *house of health*,[2] which you enter only to be cured, and this is the chamber of the dead. The new guest is led into this room at night, when the rest of the house is asleep; on the wall a notice specifies: "not before 9 p.m. or after 7 a.m." And the guest will leave here only by way of that low door, the bolted door I see over there at the end of the room, opening directly on the other street. . . .

There he is: very small on a large shroud; wearing a brownish suit; very erect, very rigid, as if at attention for the roll call. Hardly changed, moreover; his nostrils somewhat pinched; his little fists very white; his feet lost in big white socks rising up like cotton nightcaps.

A few friends are in the room, weeping silently. The mother comes toward us, unable to weep, but moaning. Each time another person comes in she begins a new complaint like a professional mourner of antiquity. She is not speaking to us but to her son. She calls him; she leans over him, kisses him: "Good little boy!" she says to him. . . . "I knew all your little habits. . . . Ah, close you in now! close you in forever. . . ."

At first this sorrow surprises one, so eloquent it is; no expression in the intonation, but an extraordinary invention in the terms of endearment . . . then, turning toward a friend, without changing her tone, she gives an exact indication as to the funeral charges or the time of departure. She wants to take her son away as quickly as possible, take him away from everybody, have him to herself, down in their country: "I'll go and see you every day, every day." She caresses his forehead. Then turning toward us again: "Pity me, gentlemen! . . ."

[2] In French *maison de santé* is one of the expressions for "hospital."

Marguerite Audoux tells us that the last half-hour was horrible. Several times everyone thought all was over; the frightful breathing stopped; the mother would then throw herself onto the bed: "Stay with us a bit more, my dear! Breathe a bit more; once more! just once more!" And as if "the good little boy" heard her, in an enormous effort all his muscles could be seen to tighten, his chest to rise very high, very hard, and then fall back. . . . And Dr. Élie Faure, seized with despair, would exclaim sobbing: "But I did everything I could. . . ."

He died at nine p.m.

At the *Mercure de France,* where the edition of the works of Lucien Jean, for which he was to write the preface, is in abeyance; while I talk with Vallette, Chanvin is writing some letters of mourning. The mother wants to take the body away this very night; at eight o'clock a brief ceremony will gather together a few friends, either at the hospital or at the station. I shall not go, but want to see Philippe once more. We go back there. Léautaud accompanies us.

Here we are again in the mortuary room. Bourdelle has come to take the death-mask; the floor is littered with splashes of plaster. Yes indeed, we shall be happy to have this exact testimony; but those who know him only through it will never imagine the full expression of this strapping little fellow, whose whole body had such a special significance. Yes, Toulouse-Lautrec was just as short as he, but deformed; Philippe was upright; he had small hands, small feet, short legs; his forehead well formed. Beside him, after a short time, one became ashamed of being too tall.

In the courtyard a group of friends. In the room, the mother, Marguerite Audoux (oh, how beautiful the quality of her grief seems to me!), Fargue; Léautaud, very pale against his very black beard, is swallowing his emotion. The mother is still moaning; Fargue and Werth are examining a time-table; it is agreed that we shall meet tomorrow morning at the Quai d'Orsay station for the eight-fifteen train.

Thursday, 8 o'clock

Quai d'Orsay station, where Chanvin and I arrive, fortunately well ahead of time, for there we discover that the eight-fifteen train leaves from the Gare de Lyon. Alas, how many friends, ill informed as we were, will not have time to get to the other station as we do at once! We don't see one in the train. Yet several had promised to come.

All night long it rained and there was a strong wind; now the air, somewhat calmed, is warm; the countryside is drenched; the sky is uniformly desolate.

We have taken tickets to Moulins. From the time-table that I buy in Nevers, I discover that to reach Cérilly it still takes three or four hours from Moulins in a little dawdling train, plus a long ride in the stagecoach; and that the little train will have left when we arrive. Can we make that leg of the trip in a carriage?

In Moulins we get refusals from three hacksters; the distance is too great: we shall need an automobile. And here it is! We light out into the country.

The air is not cold; the hour is beautiful. In a moment the wind wipes away our fatigue, even our melancholy, and speaking of Philippe, we say: if you are watching us from some part of heaven, how amused you must be to see us racing after you along the road!

Beautiful country ravaged by winter and the storm; on the lavender edge of the sky how delicate are the greens of the pastures!

Bourbon-l'Archambault. This is where your twin sister and your brother-in-law, the pastry-cook, live. Ah! here is the hearse coming back from Cérilly. . . . Evening is falling. We enter the little village just before nightfall. The auto is put in the coach-house of the hotel where we have left our bags. Here we are on the village square. We are moving about in one of Philippe's books. We are told the way to his house. It is there on the road halfway up the hill, past the church, almost opposite the house of *Père Perdrix.*[3] On the ground floor the shutters of the only window are closed like the eyelids of someone plunged in meditation; but the door is ajar. Yes, this is the right place: someone opens the door as he leaves, and in the narrow room opposite the entrance, between lighted candles, we see the coffin draped with black cloth and covered with wreaths. The mother rushes toward us, is amazed to see us; was her child so much loved! She introduces us to some village people who are there: friends come from Paris on purpose; she is proud of it. A woman is sobbing in a corner; it is his sister. Oh, how she resembles him! Her face explains our friend's, which was slightly deformed by a scar on the left side of the jaw which the beard did not quite hide. The brother-in-law cordially comes up to us and asks if we don't want to see Charles-Louis's room before more people come.

The whole house is built on his scale; because it was very small he came out of it very small. Beside the bed-sitting-room, which is the one you enter, the bright empty room where the maker of sabots, his father, used to work; it gets its light from a little court, as does Philippe's room on the second floor. Small, unornamented room; on the right of the window, a little table for writing; above the table, some shelves with a few books and the high pile of all his school notebooks. The view one might have from the window is cut short by two or three firs that have grown right against the wall of the courtyard. That is all; and that was enough. Philippe was comfortable here. The mother does the honors of the place:

"Look carefully, gentlemen; this is all important if you are going to talk about him."

In the front of the house, the best parlor, in which is collected the little luxury of this humble dwelling: decorated mantel, framed portraits, draperies; this is the room that is never used.

"Even though we are poor people, you see that we are not in dire poverty."

She intends that at the hotel where we are staying we should consider ourselves as her guests as long as we remain in Cérilly.

"Do you want to see Papa Partridge's house?" asks the brother-in-law; "it should interest you."

And we go with him to the last house in the village; but the room in which we are received has been redone. As we are leaving, the brother-in-law leans toward us:

[3]*Papa Partridge,* a novel by Charles-Louis Philippe.

"The man you see over there is Jean Morantin; you know, the *lord of the village*. When Louis spoke of him in his book, people wanted to get him worked up. He said: no, no, I know little Philippe! He's a good boy; he certainly didn't intend to say anything bad about me."

We return to the hotel, where we find Valery Larbaud, just arrived from Vichy, and we spend the evening with him.

The funeral takes place Friday morning at ten o'clock. No other friend has come; yes, Guillaumin, the author of *La Vie d'un simple;*[4] he lives on a farm thirteen kilometers from here. We still "hope" for a quarter of an hour more; Cérilly lies between several railroad lines and can be reached from several different directions. Finally the short procession starts moving.

Small gray and brown romanesque church, filled with shadow and sound counsel. The deacon comes toward us where we remain grouped around the coffin:

"This way, gentlemen! Come this way, where we have a big fire."

And we approach a brazier near the apse. Twice during the ceremony the brother-in-law comes toward us; the first time to tell us that Marcel Ray has just arrived from Montpellier with his wife; then, the second time, leaning toward us:

"You should visit the Chapel of the Saints; my brother-in-law spoke of that too in his books."

The ceremony ends; we walk toward the cemetery. The sky is overcast. Occasionally a low moving cloud befogs the distant landscape. Here is the open grave. On the other side of the grave, opposite me, I watch the sobbing sister, who is being supported. Is it really Philippe that we are burying? What lugubrious comedy are we playing here? A village friend, decorated with lavender ribbon,[5] a shopkeeper or functionary of Cérilly, steps forward with some manuscript pages in his hand and begins his speech. He speaks of Philippe's shortness, of his unimpressive appearance, which prevented him from attaining honors, of his successive failures in the posts he would have liked to hold: "You were perhaps not a great writer," he concludes, "but . . ." Nothing could be more stirring than this naïve reflection of the modesty Philippe always showed in speaking of himself, by which this excellent man was doubtless taken in. But some of us feel our hearts wrung; I hear someone whisper near me: "He's making a failure out of him!" And I hesitate a moment to step up before the grave and say that only Cérilly could speak so humbly of Philippe; that, seen from Paris, Philippe's stature seems to us very great. . . . But, alas, wouldn't Philippe suffer from the distance thus established between him and those of his little village, from which his heart never wandered?

Moreover, Guillaumin follows the other speaker; his speech is brief, full of measure and tact, very moving. He speaks of another child of Cérilly who went away like Philippe and died at thirty-five like him, just a century ago:

[4] *The Life of a Simple Man.*
[5] The insigne of the Palmes Académiques, a minor distinction awarded by the state.

the naturalist Perron. A little monument on the square immortalizes him. I shall copy the pious and touching inscription:

PERRON
DRIED UP LIKE
A YOUNG TREE
THAT SUCCUMBS
UNDER THE WEIGHT
OF ITS OWN FRUIT

Another side of the monument bears a bronze relief showing François Perron seated under a mangrove dotted with cockatoos in an Australian landscape peopled with familiar kangaroos.

An automobile stops at the gate of the cemetery; it is Fargue arriving just as the speeches are ending.

I am happy to see him here; his grief is very great, like that of all who are here; but it seems, besides, that Fargue represents a whole group of absent friends among the very best and that he comes bearing their homage.

We return to the hotel, where Mme Philippe invites us to dinner; her son-in-law, M. Tournayre, represents her. I am seated beside him; he tells me certain details of his brother-in-law's early childhood:

"Already at the age of five or six little Louis used to play 'going to school'; he had made up little notebooks, which he would put under his arm and then say: 'Good-by, Mamma; I am going to school.'

"Then he would sit down in a corner of the other room, on a stool, turning his back to everything. . . . Finally, a quarter of an hour later, the class being over, he *would come home:* 'Mamma, school is over.'

"But one fine day, without saying a word to anyone, slipping out, he really went to school; he was only six; the teacher sent him home. Little Louis came back again. Then the teacher asked: 'What have you come here for?' 'Why—to learn.'

"He is sent home again; he is too young. The child insists so much that he gets a dispensation. And thus he begins his patient education."

O "good little boy," I understand now what made you like so much, later on, *Jude the Obscure*. Even more than your gifts as a writer, than your sensitivity, than your intelligence, how much I admire that wondering application which was but one form of your love!

We leave.

And during the whole return trip I think of that article which I had promised him to write, that I was getting ready to write, on the appearance of his book, which Fasquelle is to publish any moment now—that article which he was waiting for. I fix the various points in my mind.

Philippe's death cannot make me exaggerate my praise in any regard; at most by bending me more sadly over that stirring figure and by allowing me to study him better (in the papers he left behind), it will strengthen my admiration by sharpening the contours.

Some people only half knew him because they saw only his pity, his affection, and the exquisite qualities of his heart; with that alone he could not have become the wonderful writer that he was. A great writer meets more than one requirement, answers more than one doubt, satisfies various appetites. I have only moderate admiration for those who cannot be seen from all sides, who appear deformed when looked at from an angle. Philippe could be examined from all sides; to each of his friends, of his readers, he seemed very unified; yet no two of them saw the same Philippe. And the various praises addressed to him may well be equally justified, but each one taken alone does not suffice. He has in him the wherewithal to disorient and surprise—that is to say, the wherewithal to endure.

[1911]

6 January

Every evening I read for Dominque Drouin from eight thirty to nine o'clock. Read the first evening Töpffer's *Le Col d'Anterne,* then *"Kanut"* and *"Aymerillot,"* both of which struck me as very bad; then *"Oceano Nox"* and the end of *"Les Malheureux"* and other bits of *Les Contemplations,* which plunged me into the deepest admiration. Yesterday *"Les Djinns";* this evening Turgenyev's short story "The Dog."[1]

Then, withdrawing into the little recess in the hallway, I read an hour of English before going to bed (*Robinson Crusoe* and Macaulay's study on the *Life of Byron*).

Leaving the Palais de Justice, where I had gone so that Fargue could not suspect my zeal. (He had come the evening before, panic-stricken, to beg me to intercede for a friend whose signature had been misused by some scoundrels—and the worst of it is that Fargue himself was not there, at the Palais de Justice. . . . He wanted me to intercede with Judge Flory; fortunately Marcel Drouin, whom I went to consult in the morning about the advisability of such a step, pointed out how contrary it was to all decency—and I was aware of this myself; but nothing is harder for me than an act that seems to be a side-stepping of responsibility; that is why I felt myself obliged to go to the Palais!) In the VIIIth Court I had seen only a few vague robbers appear. I had left Auteuil very early, hoping to stop at the Louvre on the way; but my fear of missing Fargue made me get there à half-hour too early. (I didn't tell him this in my letter this evening, in order not to seem to be complaining; I wrote that I had waited for him from noon until one o'clock; in reality I was there at eleven thirty.)

But, upon leaving, I went to the Louvre and, going up by the staircase of the Assyrians, went through all the galleries of drawings. I felt unresponsive and the light was as dull as possible. Saw the Thony-Thiéry collection without any pleasure; admired at length the Persian and Hispano-Moresque enam-

[1] "Kanut or the Parricide" and "Aymerillot" are both narrative poems from Hugo's *Légende des siècles;* "Night over the Ocean," "The Unfortunates," and "The Jinns" are also poems by Victor Hugo, as is the collection of *Les Contemplations.*

els—particularly a white bowl of the twelfth century (?). Had no real emotion except in front of Rembrandt's drawings. Naked body of a young man lying down; lord offering a flower (every line in perspective is suppressed—*absent* suggestion of the shoulder, which is seen from the front—wonderful; foreknowledge or forefeeling of the effect, which makes each suggestion eloquent). After that I couldn't look at anything; hurried through the rooms and the big gallery to reach the Chauchard collection. In the big Rubens gallery met Freegrove-Wenzer, of whom I just happened to be thinking. He drags me to his place and shows me his albums and sketches for paintings; but in his library I notice an album by his young friend from Brunswick, illustrations of the most delectable sort of *Les Liaisons dangereuses;*[2] he suggests my taking the album away with me to show it, as I did the drawings by both of them. His friend's studio is in rue des Beaux-Arts; he has the key; he wants to take me there, although the friend is not back yet. We go there, but impossible to open the door. On the way (rue de Seine) the window of a small shop attracts us; a Guérin and a Naudin are exhibited in it. We go in; a little woman in a dark dress, very young and attractive-looking, asks me after a moment if I am not M. Gide and tells me that I must have received, the day before, a letter from her husband. I realize that I am at Vildrac's. From this moment on I begin to have *too good* a time; that is, the curiosity of this new amusement makes me forget every other consideration and I begin to act like a madman. Having discovered that Vildrac is at Rouveyre's, who is to give a portrait or a caricature of me to the *Mercure,* I jump into a carriage with my Englishman and give the coachman Rouveyre's address. At Rouveyre's I find Vildrac and his business associate, whom I mistake for Rouveyre; then, my infirmity getting worse, when Rouveyre himself appears I confuse him so completely with the other that I think I have already shaken hands with him. (Impossible to explain this; on occasion now I *cease* to recognize the person with whom I am talking; and this lasts several minutes— enough, in any case, to fill me with a sort of anguish.)

To all three of them I must have seemed mad; I wanted to appear at ease, so that I talked too much and too loud. Meanwhile Rouveyre kept leaning over on one side as if he had the colic; Vildrac disappeared in his beard; the business associate alone, whom I didn't know, smiled at me with excessive affability; the Englishman effaced himself, or at least remained outside the circle that we formed; he leaned against a mantel and I could no longer understand myself why I had brought him. And no one understood or could give any reason for my sudden visit, flanked by this unknown person. I pretended for a moment to have come to show Rouveyre the drawings for *Les Liaisons dangereuses,* which I was carrying under my arm; and all together we looked at them. Then I took leave of them and departed, leaving them dazed.

When shall I have ahead of me days to be filled only with reading, meditation, and work!

Getting home, wrote to Ruyters; good piano-practice. First and third ballades by Chopin, which I am beginning to play *as I wish to;* as I think they are meant to be played.

[2]*Dangerous Relations,* the famous eighteenth-century novel by Choderlos de Laclos, which Gide has often praised.

February

A letter from Jammes even more distant than his silence was and unfortunately more obviously inspired by the pleasure caused him by my praise of his latest poems than by a resurgence of friendship. This letter convinces me that there is more than a mere misunderstanding between us; that is to say, just as I feared, much literature, and offended literature.

27 March

Saw Vielé-Griffin yesterday; charming cordiality. He accuses some writers or other of not knowing French and of writing, for instance, "fallow land" (*friche*) where they should have said "plowed land" (*guéret*);—but he himself writes *"opprobe"* and *"frustre"* (*passim*).[3]
He forgives Régnier nothing; as if he suffered from still liking him, he cannot refrain from talking of him every time I go to see him or meet him.

Lunched with Barrès (at Blanche's). Great anxiety about the figure he cuts; he knows how to maintain silence in order to say nothing but important things. He has changed greatly since almost ten years ago when I last saw him; but he has kept his very active charm, though constantly holding back and knowing how to keep his reserve. What prudence! What economy! He is not a great intelligence, not a "great man," but *clever,* using everything in him until he achieves the appearance of genius. Especially using circumstances, and knowing how to take advantage of what he has, to the point of hiding what he lacks.

8 May

At the studio of R. B., a painter and engraver, perhaps a Jew, certainly a Russian—who wants to do a portrait of me. This is a kind of flattery that will always get me. This portrait (dry-point) is to figure in an album together with a very few others: Rodin, Bartholomé, both sculptors; two painters, Besnard and Renoir; two musicians, Debussy and Bruneau; two philosophers, Bergson and Poincaré, etc. . . . Finally Verhaeren, who introduced him to my *Porte étroite* and has sent him to me.
It is in Montmartre, rue V. You ring at the third-floor apartment but have to go down an inside staircase to reach the studio, on the level of the second floor or even between the first and second, for I fancy that the house has two studios for every three floors. A universal man, B. indulges—with the same genius and no shame whatever—in sculpture, engraving, and oil painting. Right now he would like to make stage sets for R. Like many today, he proves to himself that he is a colorist by using only the crudest colors; he has a cruel eye. He intends to achieve mystery by neglecting drawing. You can recognize in a large clay woman, half-naked, the same model as in a big portrait reproducing the harmonies of a wild parrot (buttercup background, aspidistra-green dress, tomato-colored book in her hand): his wife.
Considerable time is spent in seeking the pose I am to take. As soon as I am settled, I like the long silence of this study; I, usually so easily distracted by some muscular impatience, I find that this forced immobility invites my thought to roam; but B. wants to talk. I foresee even worse: twice, smiling at

[3]Instead of the correct forms *opprobre* and *fruste*.

the sheet of metal he is cutting into, he said: "There is someone upstairs who is burning to meet you." Suddenly, starting at a little sound from the upper floor—which must be a signal:

"Véra! Véra! You know that Monsieur Gide is here. We are expecting you!"

The woman of the portrait comes down the steps smiling at my reflection in a large mirror in front of which I am posing.

Mme B. was born on Réunion Island, whence the sparkle of her lips and the languor in her eyes. Without a corset, the points of her well-formed breasts can be seen through the tussah silk of her dress; voluptuous face and body; auburn hair arranged in a turban. A little more familiarity with women would have warned me that the beautiful Véra wrote and that she planned to take advantage of my pose in order to inflict a reading on me. The conversation (for which, moreover, I was as little as possible responsible, for fear of breaking my pose) had no other purpose than to lead up to that reading. But they had to attack the subject from a distance. B. told me his desire to add two women to his album. "Probably Madame Curie . . . and, on the other hand, Madame de Noailles." But this first attempt not having started anything, the conversation was falling off when, at some turning or other, after we had talked of the husband's universal gifts, quite innocently I asked:

"And you, madame, what do you do?"

"I? Oh, nothing," she replied in haste.

A silence during which B., leaning over his sheet of metal, smiles with a knowing air, then, cupping his hand as if to keep his voice from anyone but me:

"She writes."

Whereupon Véra: "Will you be quiet! How absurd he is! Monsieur Gide, don't listen to him. . . . Can it be called 'writing' when all you do is set down on paper a few poems that you can't keep to yourself? . . . When I read them to Verhaeren, he wouldn't believe that I was not accustomed to writing. . . . But why should I write? This is what I ask myself every day in front of my sheet of paper: Who would be interested in this?" (And repeating her sentence with an accent on each syllable): "Who would be interested in this?—Who could be interested in it? . . ." (Obviously she is waiting for me to reply: "Why—perhaps I would," but since I remain silent, she becomes more precise): "Come, Monsieur Gide, I ask you."

Then B., coming to her aid: "When the emotion is sincere . . ."

And she: "Oh, as for the sincerity! . . . In fact it's very odd: I begin without knowing what I shall write; when I reread, it's always lines of poetry; I write in rhythm despite myself; yes, I can't do anything about it, everything I write is in rhythm. M. Gide, I wish you would tell me: do you think it's possible to achieve anything by work and pruning? . . ."

Here, somewhat stupidly, I try to establish a distinction between the two words, suggesting that *"work* does not necessarily imply *pruning."* But I am not understood and it is better to skip it. The conversation starts off again on a new track.

"Do you know Verhaeren very well? What a charming conversationalist! Have you heard him tell stories? Ah! the other day at Saint-Cloud we spent the whole day telling each other stories. . . . Indeed, that is one of the things that have encouraged me to write. 'It would be criminal not to write up these recollections!' he told me. That was after I had just told him about my grandfather's death. . . . Just imagine, two coffins had been ordered! Yes, two coffins; the maid had made a mistake. . . . That morning two dealers arrived, each one with his coffin; of course there followed a heated dialogue; you can guess that, despite the circumstances, each one could hardly keep from laughing. One was pointing out the quality of the wood, the other the comfort of his cushions. Finally I remember that my uncle managed to get rid of one of them, who said to him as he left: 'I'll take the coffin away, but I see that you will need it soon.' Do you too think that I ought to write this up? . . . Verhaeren claims that in Brittany he saw this sign in a shop window: 'Hygienic coffins. . . .' But X." (I don't remember what important name she used), "who was with us, exclaimed: 'With poets you never know where reality ends. . . .' It's like this other memory he liked so much. . . . Just imagine that I had got into the habit of buying a bouquet of flowers every morning from a little Paris urchin of about fourteen who was always in the same spot. According to the season it was violets or mimosa. . . . This lasted two years. Finally one day I was unable to go out, but a friend of mine who knew the urchin gave him my address so that he could take the bouquet to me. I see the urchin arrive and, as soon as the door is open, he throws the bouquet at me across the room, shouting: 'Ah, you think urchins don't feel anything! Yes, every day for the past two years, when you pass you look at me and you don't see that I am also looking at you. . . . Ah! you think that Paris urchins don't feel anything because they haven't the right to say anything? . . .' And, slamming the door, he dashes away. I never saw him again. . . ."

I: "He killed himself."

She, dreamily: "Perhaps. . . . Oh, I have many recollections of that kind!"

I: "And that is what you write?"

She: "No. But it comes to the same thing; what I write is, after all, made up of memories. For instance, I read Verhaeren a poem he liked very much—that is, he thought the form wasn't perfect, but the feeling was there all right."

He: "That's the important thing!"

Etc. . . . etc. . . .

"My hair is coming down," she said, stepping in front of the mirror; "I must go up and fix it."

She disappears, and reappears a moment later.

"Let's see, M. Gide, if you have any Sherlock Holmes in you. Guess what I have in my right hand?" (She is holding her hands behind her back.)

It is her poems, unimaginably dull, and decidedly I have to endure the reading of them.

Then, in the vast silence that immediately follows, she plays her last trump, desperately.

"And suppose I told you that now I am writing a play!"

I: "Ahem!!!" (I take out my watch.) "Why, it's much later than I thought. Will it take you much longer?"

He: "Twenty minutes."

I, resigned: "All right! And what is your play about?"

She: "No, I don't want to talk about it. I haven't yet told it to anyone," etc.
Yet, since I don't ask any questions, she makes up her mind:
She: "Well, here it is! I start out from the observation that in contemporary literature the women characters are always very ordinary, even shameful. I want to show a woman who gradually feels a maternal love taking the place of her conjugal love. Do you understand?"
I: "Not at all."
She: "Yes, she has married someone rather ordinary, and little by little she feels developing for him a sort of maternal love. To begin with, she raises him to her level; she gives him wings and eventually he rises above her. . . . Tell me what you think of it." Etc.

Nine days in Bruges

At Verbeke's printing-house to correct the proofs of *L'Otage,* of *La Mère et l'enfant,* of *Isabelle,* of *Corydon* and of the June issue of the review.[4]

The issue appears with Saint-Léger's *Éloges* bristling with printer's errors.[5] The experience makes me ill and, to divert my mind from it, I imagine what might have happened the first time Debussy was played:

The conductor attached great importance to the music; unfortunately he had against him the theater manager and the organizer of the concerts; at least they did not approve it, so that in the beginning he had to struggle to get the new composition accepted on his program.

He knew, moreover, that he was going to displease his public, but it was a point of honor with him to prefer pleasing the composer and himself; indeed, he felt that he had become a conductor solely for this reason: to make possible the presentation, beside the most classic harmonies, of the newest harmonies.

Debussy himself, who feared an imperfect execution, would have preferred not to be played; to convince him, it took the conductor's insistence and the urging of a few rare friends.

An unfortunate precaution that Debussy had thought it necessary to take made everyone wait some time for the scores, so that this composition, especially difficult because of its originality, could not be rehearsed by the whole orchestra together. The players arrived quite green before their sheets of music the day of the concert and played in defiance of common sense. The conductor had any amount of courage to fight against the ill will of the public, but not to betray a musician he liked, who was hissing with the public and was right to hiss. He himself would have liked to hiss and then to explain. . . . Someone said to him on the way out, when he was attempting an explanation, an excuse: "With music like that what does one note matter in place of another? This simply proves that you are wrong to include it on

[4]The *N.R.F.,* following the custom of most French literary reviews, had founded a publishing house under the name of Librairie Gallimard—Éditions de la Nouvelle Revue Française. Among the first books issued over this imprint were Claudel's drama *The Hostage,* Charles-Louis Philippe's novel *The Mother and Child,* and Gide's novel *Isabelle. Corydon* appeared in a very limited private edition the same year, anonymous as to author and publisher, as *C.R.D.N.* Verbeke directed the St. Catherine Press, Ltd., of Bruges, which printed the first issues of the *N.R.F.* and is still known for fine work.

[5]The statesman Saint-Léger Léger has always written under the pseudonym of St.-J. Perse. His first published work was formed of the beautiful lyric poems of *Praises.*

your program; it deserved such an execution—which, as far as I am concerned, didn't seem so bad." It was this that put the finishing touch to the conductor's despair; he fell ill that very evening; the next day he swallowed his baton and died.

Between oneself and the world raise a barrier of simplicity.
Nothing so baffles them as naturalness.

I prefer the friendship, esteem, and admiration of one gentleman to that of a hundred journalists. But since each journalist, all alone, makes more noise than a hundred gentlemen, you must not be astonished if my books are surrounded by a little silence, or much unkind noise.

NOVEL
His simple decency—and a certain scruple about the quality of the arms he deigned to use against his adversaries (a scruple he could not get over) gave his adversaries a terrible advance over him. Handicap.

NOVEL
The man who begins to drink. Very harmonious family; eight children.
The wife dies. The father unable to keep an eye on the children. Collapse and complete abandon. The old boarder (with spectacles) rapes one of the daughters whom the father is obliged to leave at home while he goes to work. He suspected him, however, but didn't dare accuse him before. Sudden outbursts of rage. He struggles. He ends up by drinking with the old man. Moral decay.

NOVEL
X. has a generous, even chivalrous character; somewhat utopian. He is vying with Christian feelings (he is a Jew); generosity without morality. He offers his wife to Y., his unfortunate friend who has been eating his heart out for the last five years. Y. and the wife do not consummate the adultery; but in a theater during a rehearsal when they think they are protected by the darkness in their box, the band of actors sees them in each other's arms. The tale is immediately spread abroad and commented on. . . . There begins, for the husband, a struggle with the phantom; he cannot maintain the nobility of his attitude; the viciousness of the environment lowers him to the level of common cuckolds.

Cuverville

The bad weather and my work keep me from observing this year, as I did for three successive years, the finches that live in my garden. Now that they are more numerous it is harder to observe them. In the beginning a single couple nested in the bush near the bench where I was accustomed to sit. Couple? No, it was a triangular arrangement. For a long time I refused to accept the evidence, considering as accepted and indubitable the hatred of rival males; yet I was forced to admit it: the two males that I saw attending to the same female, feeding the same nest, got along perfectly together.

And if it is not the same trio that I saw the following year, then these customs must be current among finches.

What inclines me to believe this is that I encountered them at Arco, in the Italian Tyrol. At the end of the winter season—that is, at nesting-time—from the hotel terrace, almost deserted at that season, during a fortnight we were able to observe some rather tame finches that the hotel-keeper was protecting. There were three of them, a female and two males, very easily distinguishable one from the other but equally solicitous in regard to the female and equally good providers for the nest.

Not claiming to be the only one to have noticed these strange customs among finches or other birds, for a long time I planned to write Henry de Varigny, who was then writing for *Le Temps* an interesting column on rural life, was glad to answer unknown correspondents, and on occasion even would launch a little inquiry. But wouldn't such a subject seem to him to belong to the novel rather than to natural history?

Cuverville, 3 July

X. (I later on) was accustomed to say that age had not forced him to give up a single pleasure of which he did not just happen to be on the point of getting tired.

After *Robinson Crusoe* I read *Tom Jones,* and in the intervals *Olalla* and *The Bottle Imp* by Stevenson, numerous *Essays* by Lamb, then aloud with Mlle Siller *The Mayor of Casterbridge,* and *The End of the Tether* by Conrad; some Milton (*Samson Agonistes*), Thomson (*Evolution of Sex*—the first four or five chapters); Stevenson, *Weir of Hermiston.*[6]

Les Sources, 15 October

A Friday the 13th, I couldn't have missed it.

Traveled beside a bespectacled little tart who kept the whole compartment awake until one thirty a.m. to read *Baiser de femme,*[7] which she began when we were still in the Paris station and devoured at one sitting. Too annoyed with her to be able to go to sleep afterward; and especially annoyed not to have dared say something cutting to her because of the corpulent protector who was snoozing opposite her.

Worked on *Les Caves.* Probably Lafcadio had already met Protos before his adventure in the train.[8]

Rain outside. But on changing trains at Avignon, the exquisite quality of the air refreshed me.

I was no sooner settled in my new compartment than there entered, half supported by his wife, a corpse. She is in deep mourning—you might think it was already in his honor—her face somewhat swollen, somewhat yellow, somewhat shiny; rather insignificant, effacing herself before him. Very tall; one might rather say: very long; a face that must have been rather handsome (he can't be more than forty-five), but which has lost every expression

[6]These titles are all given in English in the original. "Olalla" is one of the stories in Stevenson's *The Merry Men.*

[7]*A Woman's Kiss.*

[8]Indeed, in the finished novel that fantastic encounter gains piquancy from the fact that Lafcadio and Protos had been classmates and intimate friends in Paris.

save that of suffering and anguish; not the waxlike color of dead men, but an ashen, leaden hue. . . . His gestures are broad and lacking in co-ordination, and while his wife says to him: "Don't be afraid: the conductor promised me not to do the coupling until you would be settled" (she repeats this several times), he tumbles into the corner seat (we are in first class) and throws one leg up much higher than he needs to in order to cross it over the other. Occasionally he moans weakly. His wife says, as if speaking to someone behind the scenes or by way of sympathy:

"From Nancy to Dijon it was all right, but it was from Dijon on that *I* began to be so tired. And yet we had been promised that we would have to change only once. . . ."

Then he, very quickly, as if fearing to run out of breath, and in an angry voice:

"I told you we hadn't taken the right train. It's that employee in Dijon who made a mistake. . . . Hm! hm!"

At this moment a brakeman goes down the passageway (the train hasn't started yet). The wife asks once more if this is the right train for *Amélie-les-Bains*. What diseases is that little dump supposed to cure? I haven't yet succeeded in discovering what is the matter with *him*.

I look at my time-table. It is barely eight o'clock. The train does not reach Amélie-les-Bains until four o'clock; *he* will never make it!

His nose is constantly running, and as he wipes it once more:

"Take out your other handkerchief," his wife says; "you can see that you already used this one when you had your chocolate."

And indeed the handkerchief is repulsive; but he doesn't give a damn. His cap slips onto one side; his wife straightens it; she spreads a little Scotch plaid over his pointed knees; then helps him slip on a pair of black cotton gloves; very painful; his extraordinarily thin and long hand is out of joint; his middle fingers fall backward like a doll's fingers. What is his disease? Suppose I should catch it! But I cannot take my eyes off him. (The only other traveler, in the corner opposite me, is resolutely hiding behind *Les Pirates de l'Opéra*—and doesn't raise his eyes during the whole trip.) The invalid says:

"It's the jolts that have shaken up my guts like this."

He tries to cough but chokes, while his wife reassures him:

"You know it always does you good to sneeze."

She calls that "sneezing"! On my word, he is beginning the death rattle; he can't catch his breath; she herself becomes a bit worried and in a rather loud voice, as much, I think, for us as for him:

"There's nothing to worry about; everyone knows that it's nervous."

Finally, having caught his breath, he says:

"Ah! I am very low. . . ."

And then she begins to lament not having taking advantage of the stop at Avignon to give him an injection. (She gives him one at Tarascon, shortly afterward.)

"That's right! I hadn't thought of it a moment. Do you want a little piece of sugar? Do you . . . ? How do you feel?"

He says nothing. I see a thread of liquid dripping onto his vest; I think he is crying; but no, it comes from the corner of his mouth.

We are coming to Nîmes. She says to him:
"Nîmes: the Tour Magne!"
Oh, go to hell! . . . But this is where I get off.

Hermann Hesse

TWO WORLDS

I WILL BEGIN my story with an event of the time when I was ten or eleven
years old and went to the Latin school of our little town. Much of the
old-time fragrance is wafted back to me, but my sensations are not un-
mixed, as I pass in review my memories—dark streets and bright houses and
towers, the striking of clocks and the features of men, comfortable and homely
rooms, rooms full of secrecy and dread of ghosts. I sense again the atmosphere
of cozy warmth, of rabbits and servant-girls, of household remedies and dried
fruit. Two worlds passed there one through the other. From two poles came
forth day and night.

The one world was my home, but it was even narrower than that, for it
really comprised only my parents. This world was for the most part very well
known to me; it meant mother and father, love and severity, good example
and school. It was a world of subdued luster, of clarity and cleanliness; here
were tender friendly words, washed hands, clean clothes and good manners.
Here the morning hymn was sung, and Christmas was kept.

In this world were straight lines and paths which led into the future; here
were duty and guilt, evil conscience and confession, pardon and good resolutions, love and adoration, Bible texts and wisdom. To this world our future
had to belong, it had to be crystal-pure, beautiful and well ordered.

The other world, however, began right in the midst of our own household,
and was entirely different, had another odor, another manner of speech and
made different promises and demands. In this second world were servant-girls
and workmen, ghost stories and breath of scandal. There was a gaily colored
flood of monstrous, tempting, terrible, enigmatical goings-on, things such as
the slaughter house and prison, drunken men and scolding women, cows in
birth-throes, plunging horses, tales of burglaries, murders, suicides. All these
beautiful and dreadful, wild and cruel things were round about, in the next
street, in the next house. Policemen and tramps passed to and fro, drunken
men beat their wives, crowds of young girls flowed out of factories in the
evening, old women were able to bewitch you and make you ill, robbers
dwelt in the wood, incendiaries were rounded up by mounted policemen—
everywhere seethed and reeked this second, passionate world, everywhere,

except in our rooms, where mother and father were. And that was a good thing. It was wonderful that here in our house there were peace, order and repose, duty and a good conscience, pardon and love—and wonderful that there were also all the other things, all that was loud and shrill, sinister and violent, yet from which one could escape with one bound to mother.

And the oddest thing was, how closely the two worlds bordered each other, how near they both were! For instance, our servant Lina, as she sat by the sitting-room door at evening prayers, and sang the hymn with her bright voice, her freshly washed hands laid on her smoothed-out apron, belonged absolutely to father and mother, to us, to what was bright and proper. Immediately after, in the kitchen or in the woodshed, when she was telling me the tale of the headless dwarf, or when she quarreled with the women of the neighborhood in the little butcher's shop, then she was another person, belonged to the other world, and was enveloped in mystery. It was the same with everything and everyone, especially with myself. To be sure, I belonged to the bright, respectable world, I was my parents' child, but the other world was present in everything I saw and heard, and I also lived in it, although it was often strange and foreign to me, although one had there regularly a bad conscience and anxiety. Sometimes I even liked to live in the forbidden world best, and often the homecoming into the brightness—however necessary and good it might be—seemed almost like a return to something less beautiful, to something more uninteresting and desolate. At times I realized this: my aim in life was to grow up like my father and mother, as bright and pure, as systematic and superior. But the road to attainment was long, you had to go to school and study and pass tests and examinations. The road led past the other dark world and through it, and it was not improbable that you would remain there and be buried in it. There were stories of prodigal sons to whom that had happened—I was so passionately fond of reading them. There the return home to father and to the respectable world was always so liberating and so sublime, I quite felt that this alone was right and good and desirable. But still that part of the stories which dealt with the wicked and profligate was by far the most alluring, and if one had been allowed to acknowledge it openly, it was really often a great pity that the prodigal repented and was redeemed. But one did not say that, nor did one actually think it. It was only present somehow or other as a presentiment or a possibility, deep down in one's feelings. When I pictured the devil to myself, I could quite well imagine him down below in the street, openly or in disguise, or at the annual fair or in the public house, but I could never imagine him with us at home.

My sisters also belonged to the bright world. It often seemed to me that they approached more nearly to father and mother; that they were better and nicer mannered than myself, without so many faults. They had their failings, they were naughty, but that did not seem to me to be deep-rooted. It was not the same as for me, for whom the contact with evil was strong and painful, and the dark world so much nearer. My sisters, like my parents, were to be treated with regard and respect. If you had had a quarrel with them, your own conscience accused you afterwards as the wrongdoer and the cause of the squabble, as the one who had to beg pardon. For in opposing my sisters I offended my parents, the representatives of goodness and law. There were secrets which I would much sooner have shared with the most depraved street urchins than with my sisters. On good, bright days when I had a good conscience, it was often delightful to play with my sisters, to be gentle and nice to them, and to see myself under a halo of goodness. That was how it must be if you were an angel! That was the most sublime thing we knew, to be an angel, surrounded by sweet sounds and fragrance like Christmas and happiness. But, oh, how seldom were such days and hours perfect! Often when we were playing one of the nice, harmless, proper games I was so vehement and impetuous, and I so annoyed my sisters that we quarreled and were unhappy. Then when I was carried away by anger I did and said things, the wickedness of which I felt deep and burning within me, even while I was doing and saying them. Then came sad, dark hours of remorse and contrition, the painful moment when I begged pardon, then again a beam of light, a peaceful, grateful happiness without discord, for minutes or hours.

I used to go to the Latin school. The sons of the mayor and of the head forester were in my class and sometimes used to come to our house. They were wild boys, but still they belonged to the world of goodness and of propriety. In spite of that I had close relations with neighbors' boys, children of the public school, whom in general we despised. With one of these I must begin my story.

One half-holiday—I was little more than ten at the time—I went out with two boys of the neighborhood. A public-school boy of about thirteen years joined our party; he was bigger than we were, a coarse and robust fellow, the son of a tailor. His father was a drunkard, and the whole family had a bad reputation. I knew Frank Kromer well, I was afraid of him, and was very much displeased when he joined us. He had already acquired manly ways, and imitated the gait and manner of speech of the young factory hands. Under his leadership we stepped down to the bank of the stream and hid ourselves from the world under the first arch of the bridge. The little bank between the vaulted bridge wall and the sluggishly flowing water was composed of nothing but trash, of broken china and garbage, of twisted bundles of rusty iron wire and other rubbish. You sometimes found there useful things. We had to search the stretch under Frank Kromer's direction and show him what we found. He then either kept it himself or threw it away into the water. He bid us note whether the things were of lead, brass or tin. Everything we found of this description he kept for himself, as well as an old horn comb. I felt very uneasy in his company, not because I knew that father would have forbidden our playing together had he known of it, but through fear of Frank himself. I was glad that he treated me like the others. He commanded and we obeyed; it seemed habitual to me, although that was the first time I was with him.

At last we sat down. Frank spat into the water and looked like a full grown man; he spat through a gap in his teeth, directing the sputum in any direction he wished. He began a conversation, and the boys vied with one another in bragging of schoolboy exploits and pranks. I was silent, and yet, if I said nothing, I was afraid of calling attention to myself and inciting Kromer's anger against me. My two comrades had from the beginning turned their backs on me, and had sided with him; I was a stranger among them, and I felt my clothes and manner to be a provocation. It was impossible that

Frank should like me, a Latin schoolboy and the son of a gentleman, and the other two, I felt, as soon as it came to the point, would disown me and leave me in the lurch.

At last, through mere fright, I also began to relate a story. I invented a long narration of theft, of which I made myself the hero. In a garden by the mill on the corner, I recounted, I had one night with the help of a friend stolen a whole sack of apples, and those none of the ordinary sorts, but russets and golden pippins, the very best. In the danger of the moment I had recourse to the telling of this story which I invented easily and recounted readily. In order not to have to finish off immediately, and so perhaps be led from bad to worse, I gave full scope to my inventive powers. One of us, I continued, always had to stand sentinel, while the other was throwing down apples from the tree, and the sack had become so heavy that at last we had to open it again and leave half the apples behind; but we returned at the end of half an hour and took the rest away with us.

I hoped at the end to gain some little applause. I had warmed to my work and had let myself go in my narration. The two small boys waited quiet and expectant, but Frank Kromer looked at me penetratingly through half-closed eyes and asked me in a threatening tone:

"Is that true?"

"Yes," I said.

"Really and truly?"

"Yes, really and truly," I asserted defiantly, though inwardly I was stifling through fear.

"Can you swear to it?"

I was terribly frightened, but I answered without hesitation: "Yes."

"Then say: 'I swear by God and all that's holy'!"

I said: "I swear by God and all that's holy!"

"Aw, gwan!" said he and turned away.

I thought that everything was now all right, and was glad when he got up and made for the town. When we were on the bridge I said timidly that I must now go home. "Don't be in such a hurry," laughed Frank, "we both go the same way." He dawdled on, and I dared not tear myself away, especially as he was actually taking the road to our house. As we arrived, I looked at the heavy brass-knocker, the sun on the window and the curtains in my mother's room, and I breathed a sigh of relief. Home at last! What a blessing it was to be at home again, to return to the brightness and peace of the family circle!

As I quickly opened the door and slipped inside, ready to shut it behind me, Frank Kromer forced his way in as well. He stood beside me in the cool, dark stone corridor which was only lighted from the courtyard, held me by the arm and said softly: "Not so fast, you!"

Terrified, I looked at him. His grip on my arm was one of iron. I tried to think what he had in his mind, whether he was going to maltreat me. I wondered, if I should scream, whether anyone would come down quickly enough to save me. But I gave up the idea.

"What's the matter?" I asked. "What d'you want?"

"Nothing much. I only want to ask you something—something the others needn't hear."

"Well, what do you want me to tell you? I must go upstairs, you know."

"You know, don't you, whose orchard that is by the mill on the corner?" said Frank softly.

"No, I don't know; I think it's the miller's."

Frank had wound his arm round me, and he drew me quite close to him, so that I had to look up directly into his face. His look boded ill, he smiled maliciously, and his face was full of cruelty and power.

"Now, kid, I can tell you whose the garden is. I have known for a long time that the apples had been stolen, and I also know that the man said he would give two marks to anyone who would tell him who stole the fruit."

"Good heavens!" I exclaimed. "But you won't tell him anything?" I felt it was useless to appeal to his sense of honor. He came from the other world; for him betrayal was no crime. I felt that for a certainty. In these matters people from the "other" world were not like us.

"Say nothing?" laughed Kromer. "Look here, my friend, d'you think I am minting money and can make two shilling pieces myself? I'm a poor chap, and I haven't got a rich father like yours, and when I get the chance of earning two shillings I must take it. He might even give me more."

Suddenly he let me go free. Our house no longer gave me an impression of peace and safety, the world fell to pieces around me. He would report me as a criminal, my father would be told, perhaps even the police might come for me. The terror of utter chaos menaced me, all that was ugly and dangerous was aligned against me. The fact that I had not stolen at all did not count in the least. I had sworn to it besides. Oh, dear! Oh, dear!

I burst into tears. I felt I must buy myself off. Despairingly I searched all my pockets. Not an apple, not a penknife, absolutely nothing. All at once I thought of my watch. It was an old silver one which wouldn't go. I wore it for no special reason. It came down to me from my grandmother. I drew it out quickly.

"Kromer," I said, "listen, you mustn't give me away, that wouldn't be nice of you. Look here, I will give you my watch; I haven't anything else, worse luck! You can have it, it's a silver one; the mechanism is good, there is one little thing wrong, that's all, it needs repairing."

He smiled and took the watch in his big hand. I looked at his hand and felt how coarse and hostile it was, how it grasped at my life and peace.

"It's silver," I said, timidly.

"I wouldn't give a straw for your silver and your old watch!" he said with deep scorn. "Get it repaired yourself!"

"But, Frank," I exclaimed, quivering with fear lest he should go away. "Wait a minute. Do take the watch! It's really silver, really and truly. And I haven't got anything else." He gave me a cold and scornful look.

"Very well, then, you know who I am going to; or I can tell the police. I know the sergeant very well."

He turned to go. I held him back by the sleeve. I could not let that happen. I would much rather have died than bear all that would take place if he went away like that.

"Frank," I implored, hoarse with emotion, "please don't do anything silly! Tell me it's only a joke, isn't it?"

"Oh, yes, a joke, but it might cost you dear."

"Do tell me, Frank, what to do. I'll do anything!" He examined me critically through his screwed-up eyes and laughed again.

"Don't be silly," he said with affected affability. "You know as well as I do. I've got the chance of earning a couple of marks, and I'm not such a rich fellow that I can afford to throw it away, you know that well enough. But you're rich, why, you've even got a watch. You need only give me just two marks and everything will be all right."

I understood his logic. But two marks! For me that was as much, and just as unobtainable, as ten, a hundred, as a thousand marks. I had no money. There was a money box that my mother kept for me, with a couple of ten and five pfennig pieces inside which I received from my uncle when he paid us a visit, or from similar sources. I had nothing else. At that age I received no pocket-money at all.

"I have nothing," I said sadly. "I have no money at all. But I'll give you everything I have. I've got a book about red Indians, and also soldiers, and a compass. I'll get that for you."

But Kromer only screwed up his evil mouth, and spat on the ground.

"Quit your jawing," he said commandingly. "You can keep your old trash yourself. A compass! Don't make me angry, d'you hear? and hand over the money!"

"But I haven't any. I never get money. I can't help it."

"Very well, then, you'll bring me the two marks in the morning. I shall wait for you in the market after school. That's all. If you don't bring any money, look out!"

"Yes; but where shall I get it, then? Good Lord! if I haven't any—"

"There's enough money in your house. That's your business. Tomorrow after school, then. And I tell you: If you don't bring it—"

His eyes darted a terrible look at me, he spat again and vanished like a shadow.

I could not go upstairs. My life was ruined. I wondered if I should run away and never come back, or go and drown myself. But these thoughts were not clearly formulated. I sat crouched in the dark on the bottom step and I surrendered myself to my misfortune. There Lina found me in tears as she came down with a basket to get wood.

I begged her to say nothing on her return and I went up. My father's hat and my mother's sunshade hung on the rack near the glass door. All these things reminded me of home and tenderness, my heart went out to them imploringly and, grateful for their existence, I felt like the prodigal son when he looked into his old homely room and sensed its familiar atmosphere. All this, the bright father-and-mother world, was mine no longer, and I was buried deeply and guiltily in the strange flood, ensnared in sinful adventures, beset by enemies and dangers, menaced by shame and terror. The hat and sunshade, the good old sandstone floor, the big picture over the hall cupboard, and the voice of my elder sister in the living-room, all this was dearer and more precious to me than ever, but it was no longer consolation and secure possession. All of it was now a reproach. All this belonged to me no more, I could share no more in its cheerfulness and peace. I carried mud on my shoes that I could not wipe off on the mat, I brought shadows in with me, of which the home-world had no knowledge. How many secrets had I already had, how many cares—but that was play, a mere nothing compared with what I was bringing in with me that day.

Fate was overtaking me, hands were stretched out after me, from which even my mother could not protect me, of which she was to be allowed no knowledge. It was all the same, whether my offense was thieving, or a lie (had I not taken a false oath by God?). My sin was not this or that, I had tendered my hand to the devil. Why did I follow him? Why had I obeyed Kromer, more than ever I did my father? Why had I falsely invented the story of the theft? Why had I plumed myself on having committed a crime, as if it had been a deed of heroism? Now the devil had me by the hand, now the evil one was pursuing me.

For a moment I felt no further dread of the morrow, but I had the terrible certainty that my way was leading me further and further downhill and into the darkness. I realized clearly that from my wrongdoing other wrongdoings must result, that the greetings and kisses I gave to my parents would be a lie, that a secret destiny I should have to conceal hung over me.

For an instant confidence and hope came to me like a lightning flash as I gazed at my father's hat. I would tell him everything, would accept his judgment and the punishment he might mete out; he would be my confidant and would save me. Confession was all that would be necessary, as I had made so many confessions before—a difficult bitter hour, a serious, remorseful plea for forgiveness.

How sweetly that sounded! How tempting that was! But nothing came of it. I knew that I should not do it. I knew that I had now a secret, that I was burdened with guilt for which I myself would have to bear the responsibility alone. Perhaps I was at this very moment at the cross-roads, perhaps from this hour henceforth I should have to belong to the wicked, forever share secrets with the bad, depend on them, obey them, and become as one of themselves. I had pretended to be a man and a hero, now I had to take the consequences.

I was glad that my father, as he entered, found fault with my wet boots. It diverted his attention from something worse, and I allowed myself to suffer his reproach, secretly thinking of the other. That gave birth to a peculiar new feeling in me, an evil cutting feeling like a barbed hook. I felt superior to my father! I felt, for an instant's duration, a certain scorn of his ignorance; his scolding over the wet boots seemed to me petty. "If you only knew!" I thought, and looked upon myself as a criminal who is being tried for having stolen a loaf of bread, while he ought to confess to having committed murder. It was an ugly and repugnant feeling, yet strong and not without a certain charm, and it chained me to my secret and my guilt more securely than anything else. Perhaps Kromer has already gone to the police and given me away, I thought, and a storm is threatening to break over my head, while here I am looked upon as a mere child!

This was the important and permanent element of the whole event up to this point of my narration. It was the first cleft in the sacredness of parenthood, it was the first split in the pillar on which my childhood had reposed, and which everyone must overthrow, before he can attain to self-realization. The inward, fundamental basis of our destiny is built up from these events, which no outsider observes. Such a split or cleft grows together again, heals up and is forgotten, but in the most secret chamber of the soul it continues to live and bleed.

I myself felt immediate terror in the presence of this new feeling, I would have liked to embrace my father's feet there and then, to beg his forgiveness. But one cannot beg pardon for something fundamental, and a child knows and feels that as well and as deeply as any adult.

I felt the need to think over the affair and to consider ways and means for the morrow; but I did not get around to it. My whole evening was taken up solely in accustoming myself to the changed atmosphere of our living-room. Clock and table, Bible and looking-glass, bookcase and pictures seemed all to be saying good-by to me. With freezing heart I had to stand by and watch my world, the good happy time of my life, sever itself from me, to be relegated to the past. I was forced to realize that I was being held fast to new sucking roots in the darkness of the unfamiliar world outside. For the first time I tasted death, and death tasted bitter, for it is birth, with the terror and fear of a formidable renewal.

I was glad to be lying at last in bed. But first I had passed through purgatory in the form of evening prayers, and we had sung a hymn, one of my favorite ones. Alas! I did not join in, and each note was gall and poison for me. I did not join in the common prayer, either, when my father gave the blessing, and when he finished: "Be with us all!" I tore myself convulsively from the circle. The grace of God was with them all, but with me no longer. Cold and very tired, I went away.

After I had lain awhile in bed, wrapped around in warmth and safety, my troubled heart strayed back once again, and fluttered uneasily in the past. Mother had wished me good-night, as she always did, her step sounded yet in the room, the light of her candle gleamed through the crack in the door. Now, I thought, now she will come back again—she has felt my need, she will give me a kiss and will ask, in tones kind and full of promise, what is the matter. Then I can weep, the lump in my throat will melt away, I will throw my arms about her and will tell her, and everything will be right—I shall be saved! And when the crack in the door had become dark again I still listened for a while and thought—she must come, she must.

Then I came back to reality, and looked my enemy in the face. I saw him clearly, he had one eye closed, his mouth laughed uncouthly. While I gazed at him and the inevitable gnawed at my heart, he became bigger and more ugly, and his wicked eye lit up devilishly. He was close beside me, until I dropped off to sleep. But I did not dream of him, nor of the day's events. I dreamed instead that we were in a boat, my parents, my sisters and I, lapped in peace and the brightness of a holiday. I woke up in the middle of the night, with the after taste of bliss. I still saw the white summer dresses of my sisters glistening in the sun, and then fell from my paradise back to reality, and the enemy with the wicked eye stood opposite me.

I looked ill when mother came in quickly in the morning and told me how late it was and wanted to know why I was still in bed, and when she asked what was the matter with me, I vomited.

But I seemed to have gained a point. I rather liked to be somewhat ill and to be allowed to spend the morning in bed drinking camomile tea, to listen to mother clearing-up in the next room, and to hear Lina outside in the corridor opening the door to the butcher. To stay away from morning school was rather like a fairy-story, and the sun which played in the room was not the same you saw through the green curtains at school. But today all this had lost its charm for me. It had a false ring about it.

If I had died! But I was only slightly ill, as I had often been before, and nothing was gained by that. It prevented me from going to school, but it did not protect me in any way from Kromer, who would be waiting for me in the market at eleven o'clock. And mother's friendliness was this time without comfort; it was burdensome and painful. I soon pretended to be asleep again, and thought the matter over, but all to no purpose—I had to be in the market at eleven o'clock. For that reason I got up at ten, and said that I was better. As usual in such cases I was told that either I must go back to bed or go to school in the afternoon. I said I would rather go to school. I had formed a plan.

I dared not go to Kromer without money. I had to get possession of the little savings-box which belonged to me. There was not enough money in it, far from enough, I knew; but it was still a little, and something told me that a little was better than nothing; for at least Kromer had to be appeased.

I felt horrible as I crept in my socks into my mother's room and took my box from her writing table; but it was not so horrible as the previous day's experience. My heart beat so fast I nearly died, and it was no better when I found, at the first look, down below on the stairs, that the box was locked. It was easy to break it open, it was only necessary to cut through a thin plate of tin; but the action caused me pain, for only in doing this was I committing theft. Up to then I had only taken lumps of sugar and fruit on the sly. Now I had stolen something, although it was my own money. I realized I had taken a step nearer Kromer and his world, that I was slipping gradually downwards—and I adopted an attitude of defiance. The devil could run away with me if he liked, there was no way out. I anxiously counted the money, it had sounded so much in the box, now in my hand it was miserably little. There were sixty-five pfennigs. I hid the box in the basement, held the money in my closed fist and went out of the house, with a feeling different from any with which I had ever left the portal before. Someone called to me from above, I thought, but I went quickly on my way.

There was still plenty of time. I sneaked by a roundabout way through the streets of a changed town, beneath clouds I had never seen before, by houses which seemed to spy on me, and people who suspected me. On the way I recollected that one of my school friends had once found a thaler in the cattle market. I would have liked to pray to God to work a miracle and allow me to make such a treasure-trove. But I had no longer the right to pray. And even then the box would not be made whole again.

Frank Kromer saw me in the distance. However, he came along very slowly and seemed not to be looking out for me. As he approached me he beckoned me commandingly to follow. He passed on tranquilly, without once looking round, went down Straw Street and over the bridge, and stopped on the outskirts of the town in front of a new building. No one was working there, the walls stood bare, without doors or windows. Kromer looked round and then went through the doorway. I followed him. He stepped behind the wall, beckoned to me and stretched out his hand.

"That makes sixty-five pfennigs," he said and looked at me.

"Yes," I said timidly. "That's all I have—it's too little, I know, but it's all. I haven't any more."

"I thought you were cleverer than that," he exclaimed, blaming me in what were almost mild terms. "Between men of honor there must be honest dealing. I will not take anything from you, except what is right. You know that. Take your pfennigs back, there! The other—you know who—doesn't try to beat me down. He pays."

"But I have absolutely nothing else. That was my money-box."

"That's your affair. But I don't want to make you unhappy. You still owe me one mark thirty-five pfennig. When can I have it?"

"Oh, you will soon have it, certainly, Kromer. I don't know yet—perhaps tomorrow, or the day after, I shall have some more. You understand that I can't tell my father, don't you?"

"That's no concern of mine. I don't want to harm you. If I liked, I could get the money before noon, you see, and I'm poor. You wear nice clothes, and you get something better to eat for dinner than I do. But I won't say anything. I am willing to wait a few days. The day after tomorrow, in the afternoon, I will whistle for you, then you will bring it along. You can recognize my whistle?"

He gave me a whistle that I had often heard before.

"Yes," I said, "I know it."

He went away, as if I didn't belong to him. It had been only a transaction between us, nothing further.

Even today, I believe, Kromer's whistle would terrify me if I heard it again suddenly. From then on I heard it often. It seemed I heard it continually and always. No place, no game, no work, no idea in which this whistle would not sound. I was dependent on it, it was now the messenger of my fate. On mild, glowing autumn afternoons I was often in our little flower garden, which I loved dearly. A peculiar impulse made me take up again boyish games which I had played formerly. I played, as it were, that I was a boy who was younger than I, who was still good and free, innocent and secure. But in the middle of the game, always expected and yet always terribly disturbing and surprising sounded Kromer's whistle, destroying the picture my imagination had painted.

Then I had to go, I had to follow my tormentor to evil and ugly places, had to render an account and let myself be dunned. The whole business may have lasted a few weeks, but it seemed to me like a year, or an eternity. I seldom had money—a five or ten pfennig piece stolen from the kitchen table when Lina left the market basket standing there. Each time I was blamed by Kromer, and heaped with abuse; it was I who deceived him and kept back what was his due, it was I who robbed him and made him unhappy! Seldom in life has need so appressed me, seldom have I felt a greater helplessness, a greater dependence.

I had filled up the savings box with toy money—no one made any enquiries. But that as well could be discovered any day. I was even more afraid of mother than of Kromer's harsh whistle, especially when she stepped up to me softly—was she not going to ask me about the money-box?

As I presented myself to my evil genius several times without money he began to torment and to make use of me after a different fashion. I had to work for him. He had to see to various things for his father. I did that for him or he made me do something more difficult, hop on one leg for ten minutes, or fasten a scrap of paper on to the coat of a passer-by. Many nights these torments realized themselves in my dreams, and I wept and broke out in a cold sweat in my nightmare.

For a time I was ill. I often vomited and felt cold, but at night I lay in a fever, bathed in perspiration. Mother felt that something was wrong and displayed much sympathy on my behalf, but this tortured me because I could not respond by confiding in her.

One evening, after I had already gone to bed, she brought me a piece of chocolate. This action was a souvenir of former years when, if I had been good, I was often rewarded in this way before going off to sleep. Now she stood there and held the piece of chocolate out to me. This so pained me that I could do nothing but shake my head. She asked what was the matter with me and stroked my hair. I could only sob out: "Nothing! nothing! I won't have anything." She put the chocolate on my bed table and went away. When she wished subsequently to question me on the matter I made as if I knew nothing about it. Once she brought the doctor to me, who examined me and prescribed cold ablutions in the morning.

My state at that time was a sort of insanity. I was shy and lived in torment like a ghost in the midst of the well-ordered peace of our house. I had no part in the others' lives, and could seldom, even for as much as an hour, forget my miserable existence. In the presence of my father, who often took me to task in an irritated fashion, I was reserved and wrapped up in myself.

2

Deliverance from my troubles came from quite an unexpected quarter, and with it something new entered into my life, which has up to the present day exercised a strong influence.

A short time before we had had a new boy at our Latin school. He was the son of a well-to-do widow who had moved to our town. He was in mourning and wore a crape band round his sleeve. His form was above mine, and he was several years older, but I soon began to take notice of him, as did all of us. This remarkable boy impressed one as being much older than he looked. He made on no one the impression of being a mere schoolboy. With us childish youngsters he was as distant and as mature as a man, or rather, as a gentleman. He was by no means popular, he took no part in the games, much less in the fooling. It was only the self-conscious and decided tone which he adopted towards the masters that pleased the others. His name was Max Demian.

One day it happened, as it occasionally did in our school, that for some cause or other, another class was sent into our large schoolroom. It was Demian's form. We little ones were having Biblical history, the big ones had to write an essay. While we were having the story of Cain and Abel knocked into us, I kept looking across at Demian, whose face fascinated me strangely, and saw his wise, bright, more than ordinarily strong features bent attentively and thoughtfully over his task. He did not look at all like a schoolboy doing an exercise, but like a research worker solving a problem. I did not find him really agreeable. On the contrary, I had one or two little things against him. With me he was too distant and superior, he was much too provokingly sure of himself, and the expression of his eyes was that of an adult—which children never like—rather sad with occasional flashes of scorn. Yet I could not resist looking at him, whether I liked him or not. But the minute he looked in my direction I looked away, somewhat frightened. If today I consider what he looked like as a schoolboy, I can say that he was in every respect different from the others, and bore the stamp of a striking personality and therefore attracted attention. But at the same time he did everything to prevent himself from being remarked—he bore and conducted himself like a disguised prince who finds himself among peasant boys and makes every effort to appear like them.

He was behind me on the way home from school. When the others had run on, he overtook me and said: "Hello!" Even his manner of greeting, although he imitated our schoolboy tone of voice, was polite and like that of a grown-up person.

"Shall we go a little way together?" he questioned in a friendly way. I was flattered and nodded. Then I described to him where I lived.

"Oh, there?" he said laughingly. "I know the house already. There is a remarkable work of art over your door, which interested me at once."

I did not guess immediately to what he was referring, and was astonished that he seemed to know our house better than I did. There was indeed a sort of crest which served as a keystone over the arch of the door, but in course of time it had become faint and had often been painted over. As far as I knew, it had nothing to do with us, or with our family.

"I don't know anything about it," I said timidly. "It's a bird, or something like it; it must be very old. They say that the house at one time belonged to the abbey."

"Very likely," he nodded. "We'll have another good look at it. Such things are often interesting. It is a hawk, I think."

We continued our way. I was considerably embarrassed. Suddenly Demian laughed, as if something funny had struck him.

"Oh, I was present at your lesson," he said with animation. "The story of Cain, who carried the mark on his forehead, was it not? Do you like it?"

Generally I used not to like anything of all the things we had to learn. But I did not dare to say so—it was as though a grown-up person were talking to me. I said I liked the story very much.

Demian tapped me on the shoulder. "No need to impose on me, old fellow. But the story is really rather remarkable. I think it is much more remarkable than most of the others we get at school. The master didn't say very much about it, only the usual things about God and sin, et cetera. But I believe—" he broke off, smiled, and questioned: "But does it interest you?

"Well," he continued, "I think one can conceive this story of Cain quite differently. Most things we are taught are certainly quite true and right, but one can consider them all from a different standpoint from the master's, and most of them have a much better meaning then. For instance, we can't be quite content with the explanation given us with regard to this fellow Cain and the mark on his forehead. Don't you find it so, too? It certainly might happen that he should kill one of his brothers in a quarrel, it is also possible that he should afterwards be afraid, and have to come down a peg. But that he should be singled out into the bargain with a decoration for his cowardice, which protects him and strikes terror into everyone else, that is really rather odd."

"Certainly," I said, interested. The case began to interest me. "But how else should one explain the story?" He clapped me on the shoulder.

"Quite simply! The essential fact, and the point of departure of the story, was the sign. Here was a man who had something in his face which terrified other people. They did not dare to molest him, he made a big impression on them, he and his children. Perhaps, or rather certainly, it was not really a sign on his forehead like an office stamp—things are not as simple as that in real life. I would sooner think it was something scarcely perceptible, of a peculiar nature—a little more intelligence and boldness in his look than people were accustomed to. This man had power, other people shrank from him. He had a 'sign.' One could explain that as one wished. And one always wishes what is convenient and agrees with one's opinions. People were afraid of Cain's children, they had a 'sign.' And so they explained the sign not as it really was, a distinction, but as the contrary. The fellows with this sign were said to be peculiar, and they were courageous as well. People with courage and character are always called peculiar by other people. That a race of fearless and peculiar men should rove about was very embarrassing. And so people attached a surname and a story to this race, in order to revenge themselves on it, in order to compensate themselves more or less for all the terror with which it had inspired them. Do you understand?"

"Yes—that means to say, then—that Cain was not at all wicked? And the whole story in the Bible isn't really true?"

"Yes and no. Such ancient, primitive stories are always true, but they have not always been recorded and explained in the proper manner. In short, I mean that Cain was a thundering good fellow, and this story got attached to his name simply because people were afraid of him. The story was merely a report, something people might have set going in a gossiping way, and it was true in so far as Cain and his children did actually wear a sort of 'sign' and were different from most people."

I was much astonished.

"And do you believe then, that the affair of the murder is absolutely untrue?" I asked, much impressed.

"Not at all! It is certainly true. The strong man killed a weak one. One may doubt of course whether it was really his brother or not. It is not important, for, in the end, all men are brothers. A strong man, then, has killed a weak one. Perhaps it was a deed of heroism, perhaps it was not. But in any case the other weak people were terrified, they lamented and complained, and when they were asked: 'Why don't you simply kill him as well?' they did not answer, 'Because we are cowards,' but they said instead: 'You can't. He has a sign. God has singled him out!' The humbug must have arisen something after this style— Oh, I am keeping you from going in. Good-by, then!"

He turned into Old Street and left me alone, more astonished than I had ever been before. Scarcely had he gone when everything that he had said seemed to me quite unbelievable! Cain a noble fellow, Abel a coward! Cain's sign a distinction! It was absurd, it was blasphemous and infamous. What was God's part in the matter? Had he not accepted Abel's sacrifice, did he not love Abel? Demian's story was nonsense! I suspected him of making fun of me and of wishing to mislead me. The devil of a clever fellow, and he could talk, but—well—

Still, I had never thought so much about any of the Biblical or other stories before. And for some time past I had never so completely forgotten Frank Kromer, for hours, for a whole evening. At home I read through the story once again, as it stands in the Bible, short and clear. It was quite foolish to try to find a special, secret meaning. If it had one, every murderer could look upon himself as a favorite of God! No, it was nonsense. But Demian had a nice way of saying such things, so easily and pleasantly, as if everything were self-evident—and then his eyes!

My ideas were certainly a little upset, or rather they were very much confused. I had lived in a bright, clean world, I myself had been a sort of Abel, and now I was so firmly fixed in the other and had sunk so deeply, but really what could I do to help it? What was my position now? A reminiscence glowed in me which for the moment almost took away my breath. I remembered that wretched evening, from which my present misery dated, when I looked for an instant into the heart of my father's bright world and despised his wisdom! Then I was Cain and bore the sign; I imagined that it was in no way shameful, but a distinction, and in my wickedness and unhappiness I stood on a higher level than my father, higher than good and pious people.

It was not in such a clear-thinking way that my experience then presented itself to me, but all this was contained therein. It was only a flaming up of feeling, of strange emotions which caused me pain and yet filled me with pride.

When I considered the matter, I saw how strangely Demian had spoken of the fearless and the cowards! How curiously he had explained the mark on Cain's forehead. How singularly his eyes had lit up, those peculiar eyes of a grown person! And indistinctly it shot through my brain: Is not he himself, this Demian, a sort of Cain? why did he defend him, if he did not feel like him? Why had he this force in his gaze? Why did he speak so scornfully of the "others," of the fearsome, who are really the pious and the well-considered of God?

This thought led me to no definite conclusion. A stone had fallen into the well, and the well was my young soul. And this business with Cain, the murderer and the sign, was for a long, a very long, time the point from which my seekings after knowledge, my doubts and my criticisms took their departure.

I noticed that the other boys also occupied themselves a good deal with Demian. I had not told anyone of his version of the story of Cain, but he appeared to interest the others as well. At least, many rumors concerning the "new boy" became current. If only I still knew all of them, each would help to throw fresh light on him, each would serve to interpret him. I only remember the first rumor was that Demian's mother was very rich. It was also said that she never went to church, nor the son either. Another rumor had it that they were Jews, but they could just as easily have been, in secret,

Mohammedans. Furthermore, tales were told of Max Demian's strength. So much was certain, that the strongest boy in his form, who challenged him to a fight, and who at his refusal branded him coward, suffered a terrible humiliation at his hands. Those who were there said that Demian had simply taken him by the nape of the neck with one hand and had brought such a pressure to bear that the boy went white and afterwards crawled away, and that for several days he was unable to use his arm. For a whole evening a rumor even ran that he was dead. For a time everything was asserted and believed, everything that was exciting and wonderful. Then there was a satiety of rumors for a while. A little later new ones circulated, which asserted that Demian had intimate relations with girls and "knew everything."

Meanwhile my affair with Frank Kromer took its inevitable course. I could not get away from him, for although he left me in peace for days together, I was still bound to him. In my dreams he lived as my shadow, and thus my fantasy credited him with actions which he did not, in reality, do; so that in dreams I was absolutely his slave. I lived in these dreams—I was always a deep dreamer—more than in reality. These shadowy conceptions wasted my strength and my life force. I often dreamed, among other things, that Kromer ill-treated me, that he spat on me and knelt on me and, what was worse, that he led me to commit grave crimes—or rather I was not led, but simply forced, through his powerful influence. The most terrible of these dreams, from which I woke up half mad, presented itself as a murderous attack on my father. Kromer whetted a knife and put it in my hand, as we were standing behind the trees of a lane, and lying in wait for someone—whom I knew not; but when someone came along and Kromer through a pressure of the arm informed me that this was the man, whom I was to stab, it turned out to be my father! Then I woke up.

With all these troubles, I still thought a great deal about Cain and Abel, but much less about Demian. It was, strangely enough, in a dream that he first came in contact with me again. I dreamed once more, of assault and ill-treatment which I suffered, but instead of Kromer, this time it was Demian who knelt upon me. And, what was quite new and profoundly impressive, everything that I suffered resistingly and in torment at the hands of Kromer, I suffered willingly from Demian, with a feeling which was composed as much of joy as of fear. I had this dream twice, then Kromer occupied his old position in my thoughts.

For a long time I have not been able to separate what I experienced in these dreams from what I underwent in reality. But in any case my evil relation with Kromer took its course, and was by no means at an end, when I had at last, by petty thefts, paid the boy the sum owed. No, for now he knew of these thefts, as he always asked me where the money came from, and I was more in his hands than ever. He frequently threatened to tell my father everything, and my terror then was scarcely as great as the profound regret that I had not myself done that in the beginning. However, miserable as I was, I did not repent of everything, at least not always, and sometimes felt, I thought, that things could not have helped being as they were. The hand of fate was upon me, and it was useless to want to break away.

I conjecture that my parents suffered not a little in these circumstances.

A strange spirit had come over me, I no longer fitted into our community which had been so intimate, and for which I often felt a maddening home-sickness, as for a lost paradise. I was treated, particularly by mother, more like a sick person than like a miserable wretch. But the actual state of affairs I was able to observe best in the conduct of my two sisters. It was quite evident from their behavior, which was very considerate and which yet caused me endless pain, that I was a sort of person possessed, who was more to be pitied than blamed for his condition, but yet in whom evil had taken up residence. I felt that I was being prayed for in a different way from formerly, and realized the fruitlessness of these prayers. I often felt burning within me an intense longing for relief, an ardent desire for a full confession, and yet I realized in advance that I should not be able to tell everything to father and mother properly, in explanation of my conduct. I knew that I should be received in a friendly way, that much consideration and compassion would be shown me, but that I should not be completely understood. The whole affair would have been looked upon as a sort of backsliding, whereas it was really the work of destiny.

I know that many people will not believe that a child scarcely eleven years old could feel thus. But I am not relating my affairs for their benefit. My narration is for those who know mankind better. The grown-up person who has learned to convert part of his feelings into thoughts, feels the absence of these ideas in a child, and comes to believe that the experiences are likewise lacking. But they have seldom been so vivid and not often in my life have I suffered as keenly as then.

One rainy day I was ordered by my tormentor to Castle Place, and there I stood, waiting and digging my feet in the wet chestnut leaves, which were still falling regularly from the black, dripping branches. Money I had none, but I had brought with me two pieces of cake that I had stolen in order at least to be able to give Kromer something. I had long since been accustomed to stand about in any odd corner waiting for him often for a very long time, and I put up with the unalterable.

Kromer came at last. That day he did not stay long. He poked me several times in the ribs, laughed, took the cake, and even offered me a moldy cigarette, which however I did not accept. He was more friendly than usual.

"Oh," he said, as he went away, "before I forget—next time you can bring your sister along, the elder one. What's her name? Now tell the truth."

I did not understand, and gave no answer. I only looked at him wonderingly.

"Don't you get me? You must bring your sister along."

"But, Kromer, that won't do. I mustn't do that, and besides she wouldn't come."

I thought this was only another pretext for vexing me. He often did that, requiring me to do something impossible, and so terrifying me. And often, after humiliating me, he would by degrees become more tractable. I then had to buy myself off with money or with some other gift.

This time he was quite different. He was really not at all angry at my refusal.

"Well," he said airily, "you'll think about it, won't you? I should like to make your sister's acquaintance. It will not be so difficult. You simply take her out for a walk, and then I come along. Tomorrow I'll whistle for you, and then we can talk more about it."

When he had gone, a glimpse of the meaning of his request dawned on me. I was still quite a child, but I knew by hearsay that boys and girls, when they were somewhat older, did things which were forbidden, things of a secret and scandalous nature. And now I should also have to—it was suddenly quite clear to me how monstrous it was! I immediately resolved never to do that. But I scarcely dared think of what would happen in that case and how Kromer would revenge himself on me. A new torment began, I had not yet been tortured enough.

I walked disconsolately across the empty square, my hands in my pockets. Fresh torments, a new servitude!

Suddenly a fresh, deep voice called to me. I was terrified and began to run on. Someone ran after me, a hand gripped me from behind. It was Max Demian.

I let myself be taken prisoner. I surrendered.

"It's you?" I said uncertainly. "You frightened me so!"

He looked at me, and never had his glance been more like that of an adult, of a superior and penetrating person. For a long time past we had not spoken with one another.

"I am sorry," he said in his courteous and at the same time very determined manner. "But listen, you mustn't let yourself be frightened like that."

"Oh, that can happen sometimes."

"So it appears. But look here: If you shrink like that from someone who hasn't hurt you, then this someone begins to think. It makes him curious, he wonders what can be the matter. This somebody thinks to himself, how awfully frightened you are, and he thinks further: one is only like that when one is terrified. Cowards are always frightened; but I believe you aren't really a coward. Aren't I right? Of course, you aren't a hero either. There are things of which you are afraid. There are also people of whom you are afraid. And that should never be. No one should ever be afraid of other people. You aren't afraid of me? Or are you, perhaps?"

"Oh no, of course not."

"There, you see. But there are people you are afraid of?"

"I don't know . . . let me go, what do you want of me?"

He kept pace with me—I was going quicker with the idea of escaping—I felt his look directed on me from the side.

"Just assume," he began again, "that I mean well with you. In any case you needn't be afraid of me. I would very much like to try an experiment with you—it's funny, and you can learn something that's very useful. Listen: I often practice an art which is called mind-reading. There's no witchcraft in it, but it seems very peculiar if one doesn't know how to do it. You can surprise people very much with it. Well, let us try it. I like you, or I interest myself in you, and I would like to find out what your real feelings are. I have already made the first step towards doing that. I have frightened you—you are, then, easily frightened. There are things and people of which and of whom you are afraid. Why is it? One need be afraid of no one. If you fear somebody then it is due to the fact that he has power over you. For example, you have done something wrong, and the other person knows it—then he has power over you. D'you get me? It's clear, isn't it?"

I looked helplessly into his face, which was serious and prudent as always, and kind as well, but without any tenderness—his features were rather severe. Righteousness or something akin lay therein. I was not conscious of what was happening; he stood like a magician before me.

"Have you understood?" he questioned again.

I nodded. I could not speak.

"I told you mind-reading looked rather strange, but the process is quite natural. I could for example tell you more or less exactly what you thought about me when I once told you the story of Cain and Abel. But that has nothing to do with the matter in hand. I also think it possible that you have dreamed of me. But let's leave that out! You're a clever kid, most of 'em are so stupid. I like talking now and then with a clever fellow whom I can trust. You have no objections, have you?"

"Oh, no! Only I don't understand."

"Let's keep to our old experiment! We have found that: the boy S. is easily frightened—he is afraid of somebody—he apparently shares a secret with this other person, which causes him much disquietude. Is that about right?"

As in a dream I lay under the influence of his voice, of his personality. I only nodded. Was not a voice talking there, which could only come from myself? Which knew all? Which knew all in a better, clearer way than I myself?

Demian gave me a powerful slap on the shoulder.

"That's right then. I thought so. Now just one question more: Do you know the name of the boy who has just gone away?"

I sank back, he had the key to my secret, this secret which twisted back inside me as if it did not want to see the light.

"What sort of a fellow? There was no one there, except myself."

He laughed.

"Don't be afraid to tell me," he said laughingly. "What's his name?"

I whispered: "Do you mean Frank Kromer?"

He nodded contentedly.

"Bravo! You're a smart chap, we shall be good friends yet. But now I must tell you something else: this Kromer, or whatever his name is, is a nasty fellow. His face tells me he's a rascal! What do you think?"

"Oh yes," I sobbed out, "he is nasty, he's a devil! But he mustn't know anything! For God's sake, he mustn't know anything. D'you know him? Does he know you?"

"Don't worry! He's gone, and he doesn't know me—not yet. But I should like to make his acquaintance. He goes to the public school?"

"Yes."

"In which class?"

"In the fifth. But don't say anything to him! Please, don't say anything to him!"

"Don't worry, nothing will happen to you. I suppose you wouldn't like to tell me a little more about this fellow Kromer?"

"I can't! No, let me go!"

He was silent for a while.

"It's a pity," he said, "we might have been able to carry the experiment still further. But I don't want to bother you. You know, don't you, that it is not right of you to be afraid of him? Such fear quite undermines us, you must get rid of it. You must get rid of it, if you want to become a real man. D'you understand?"

"Certainly, you are quite right . . . but it won't do. You don't know . . ."

"You have seen that I know a lot, more than you thought. Do you owe him any money?"

"Yes, I do, but that isn't the essential point. I can't tell, I can't!"

"It won't help matters, then, if I give you the amount you owe him? I could very well let you have it."

"No, no, that is not the point. And please: don't say anything to anybody! Not a word! You are making me miserable!"

"Rely on me, Sinclair. Later you can share your secrets with me."

"Never, never!" I exclaimed vehemently.

"Just as you please. I only mean, perhaps you will tell me something more later on. Only of your own free will, you understand. Surely you don't think I shall act like Kromer?"

"Oh no—but you don't even know anything about it!"

"Absolutely nothing. But I think about it. And I shall never act like Kromer, believe me. Besides, you don't owe me anything."

We remained a long time silent, and I became more tranquil. But Demian's knowledge became more and more of a puzzle to me.

"I'm going home now," he said, and in the rain he drew his coat more closely about him. "I should only like to repeat one thing to you, since we have gone so far in the matter—you ought to get rid of this fellow! If there is nothing else to be done, then kill him! It would impress me and please me, if you were to do that. Besides, I would help you."

I was again terrified. I suddenly remembered the story of Cain. I had an uncanny feeling and I began to cry softly. So much that was weird seemed to surround me.

"All right," Max Demian said, smilingly. "Go home now! We will put things square, although murder would have been the simplest. In such matters the simplest way is always the best. You aren't in good hands, with your friend Kromer."

I came home, and it seemed to me as if I had been away a year. Everything looked different. Between myself and Kromer there now stood something like future freedom, something like hope. I was lonely no longer! And then I realized for the first time how terribly lonely I had been for weeks and weeks. And I immediately recollected what I had on several occasions turned over in my mind: that a confession to my parents would afford me relief and yet would not quite liberate me. Now I had almost confessed, to another, to a stranger, and as if a strong perfume had been wafted to me, sensed the presentiment of salvation!

Still my fear was far from being overcome, and I was still prepared for long and terrible menial wrestlings with my evil genius. So it was all the more remarkable to me that everything passed off so very secretly and quietly.

Kromer's whistle remained absent from our house for a day, two days, three days, a whole week. I dared not believe my senses, and lay inwardly on the watch, to see whether he would not suddenly stand before me, just at that moment when I should expect him no longer. But he was, and remained, away! Distrustful of my new freedom, I still could not bring myself to believe in it wholeheartedly. Until at last I met Frank Kromer. He was coming down the street, straight in my direction. When he saw me, he drew himself together, twisted his features in a brutal grimace, and turned away without more ado, in order to avoid meeting me.

That was a wonderful moment for me! My enemy ran away from me! My devil was afraid of me! Surprise and joy shook me through and through!

In a few days Demian showed himself once again. He waited for me outside school.

"Hullo," I said.

"Good morning, Sinclair. I only wanted to hear how you're getting on. Kromer leaves you in peace, doesn't he?"

"Did you manage that? But how did you do it? How? I don't understand it. He hasn't come near me."

"Splendid. If he should come again—I don't think he will, but he's a cheeky fellow—then simply tell him to remember Demian."

"But what does it all mean? Have you had a fight with him and thrashed him?"

"No, I'm not so keen on that. I simply talked to him, as I did to you, and I made it clear to him that it is to his own advantage to leave you in peace."

"Oh, but you haven't given him any money?"

"No, kid. You have already tried that way yourself."

I attempted to pump him on the matter, but he disengaged himself. The old, embarrassed feeling concerning him came over me—an odd mixture of gratitude and shyness, of admiration and fear, of affection and inward resistance.

I had the intention of seeing him again soon, and then I wanted to talk more about everything, about the Cain affair as well. But I did not see him. Gratitude is not one of the virtues in which I believe, and to require it of a child would seem to me wrong. So I do not wonder very much at the complete ingratitude which I evinced towards Max Demian. Today I believe positively that I should have been ruined for life if he had not freed me from Kromer's clutches. At that time also I already felt this release as the greatest event of my young life—but I left the deliverer on one side as soon as he had accomplished the miracle.

As I have said, ingratitude seems to me nothing strange. Solely, the lack of curiosity I evinced is odd. How was it possible that I could continue for a single day my quiet mode of life without coming nearer to the secrets with which Demian had brought me in contact? How could I restrain the desire to hear more about Cain, more about Kromer, more about the thought-reading?

It is scarcely comprehensible, and yet it is so. I suddenly saw myself extricated from the demoniacal toils, saw again the world lying bright and cheerful before me. I was no longer subject to paroxysms of fear. The curse was broken, I was no longer a tormented and condemned creature, I was a schoolboy again. My temperament sought to regain its equilibrium and tranquillity as quickly as possible, and so I took pains above all things to put behind me all that had been ugly and menacing, and to forget it. The whole, long story of my guilt, of my terrifying anxiety, slipped from my memory wonderfully quick, apparently without having left behind any scars or impressions whatsoever.

The fact that I likewise tried as quickly to forget my helper and deliverer, I understand today as well. Instinctively my mind turned from the damning recollection of my awful servitude under Kromer, and I sought to recover my former happy, contented mental outlook, to regain that lost paradise which opened once more to me, the bright father-and-mother world, where my sisters dwelt in the fragrant atmosphere of purity, in loving kindness such as God had extended to Abel.

On the very next day after my short conversation with Demian, when I was at last fully convinced of my newly-born freedom and feared no longer a relapse to my condition of slavery, I did what I had so often and so ardently desired to do—I confessed. I went to mother and showed her the little savings-box with the broken lock, filled with toy mark pieces instead of with real money, and I told her how long I had been in the thrall of an evil tormentor, through my own guilt. She did not understand everything, but she saw the money-box, she saw my altered look and heard my changed voice—she felt that I was healed, that I had been restored to her.

And then with lofty feelings I celebrated my readmission into the family, the prodigal son's return home. Mother took me to father, the story was repeated, questions and exclamations of wonder followed in quick succession, both parents stroked my hair and breathed deeply, as in relief from a long oppression. It was all lovely, like the stories I had read, all discords were resolved in a happy ending.

I surrendered myself passionately to this harmonious state of affairs. I could not have enough of the idea that I was again free and trusted by my parents. I was a model boy at home and played more frequently than ever with my sisters. At prayers I sang the dear, old hymns with the blissful feeling of one converted and redeemed. It came straight from my heart, it was no lie this time.

And yet it was not at all as it should have been. And this is the point which alone can truly explain my forgetfulness of Demian. I ought to have made a confession *to him!* The confession would have been less touching and less specious, but for me it would have borne more fruit. I was now clinging fast to my former paradisaical world, I had returned home and had been received in grace. But Demian belonged in no wise to this world, he did not fit into it. He also—in a different way from Kromer—but nevertheless he also was a seducer, he too bound me to the second, evil, bad world, and of this world I never wanted to hear anything more. I could not now, and I did not wish to give up Abel and help to glorify Cain, now when I myself had again become an Abel.

So much for the outward correlation of events. But inwardly it was like this: I had been freed from the hands of Kromer and the devil, but not through my own strength and effort. I had ventured a footing on the paths of the world, and they had been too slippery for me. Now that the grasp of a friendly hand had saved me, I ran back, without another glance round, to mother's lap, to the protecting, godly and tender security of childhood.

I made myself younger, more dependent on others, more childlike than I really was. I had to replace my dependence on Kromer by a new one, since I was powerless to strike out for myself. So I chose, in the blindness of my heart, the dependence on father and mother, on the old, beloved, "bright world," on this world which I knew already was not the sole one. Had I not done this, I should have had to hold to Demian, to entrust myself to him. The fact that I did not, appeared to me then to be due to justifiable distrust of his strange ideas; in reality it was due to nothing else than fear. For Demian would have required more of me than did my parents, much more. By stimulation and exhortation, by scorn and irony he would have tried to make me more independent. Alas, I know that today: nothing in the world is so distasteful to man as to go the way which leads him to himself!

Gabriela Mistral

THE PRAYER

THOU knowest, Lord, with what flaming boldness,
my word invokes Thy help for strangers.
I come now to plead for one who was mine,
my cup of freshness, honeycomb of my mouth,
lime of my bones, sweet reason of life's journey,
bird-trill to my ears, girdle of my garment.
Even those who are no part of me are in my care.
Harden not Thine eyes if I plead with Thee for this one!

He was a good man, I say he was a man
whose heart was entirely open; a man
gentle in temper, frank as the light of day,
as filled with miracles as the spring of the year.

Thou answerest harshly that he is unworthy of entreaty
who did not anoint with prayer his fevered lips,
who went away that evening without waiting for Thy sign,
his temples shattered like fragile goblets.

But I, my Lord, protest that I have touched,—
just like the spikenard of his brow,—
his whole gentle and tormented heart:
and it was silky as a nascent bud!

Thou sayest that he was cruel? Thou forgettest, Lord, that
    I loved him,
and that he knew my wounded heart was wholly his.
He troubled for ever the waters of my gladness?
It does not matter! Thou knowest: I loved him, I loved him!

And to love (Thou knowest it well) is a bitter exercise;
a pressing of eyelids wet with tears,
a kissing-alive of hairshirt tresses,
keeping, below them, the ecstatic eyes.

The piercing iron has a welcome chill,
when it opens, like sheaves of grain, the loving flesh.
And the cross (Thou rememberest, O King of the Jews!)
is softly borne like a spray of roses.

Here I rest, Lord, my face bowed down
to the dust, talking with Thee through the twilight,
through all the twilights that may stretch through life,
if Thou art long in telling me the word I await.

I shall weary Thine ears with prayers and sobs;
a timid greyhound, I shall lick Thy mantle's hem,
Thy loving eyes cannot escape me,
Thy foot avoid the hot rain of my tears.

Speak at last the word of pardon! It will scatter
in the wind the perfume of a hundred fragrant vials
as it empties; all waters will be dazzling;
the wilderness will blossom, the cobblestones will sparkle.

The dark eyes of wild beasts will moisten,
and the conscious mountain that Thou didst forge from stone
will weep through the white eyelids of its snowdrifts;
The whole earth will know that Thou hast forgiven!

TO THE CHILDREN

MANY years hence, when I am a little heap of silent dust, play with me,
with the earth of my heart and of my bones!
    If a mason gathers me up, he will make me into a brick, and I
shall remain fast forever in a wall; and I hate quiet niches. If they make me
a brick in a prison, I shall grow red with shame when I hear a man sob; and

if I am a brick in a school, I shall still suffer, because I cannot sing with you in the early mornings.

I would rather be the dust with which you play, on the country roads. Clasp me, for I have been yours; unmake me, for I made you; trample upon me, because I did not give you the whole of beauty and the whole of truth! Or only sing and run above me, so that I may kiss your beloved feet.

When you hold me in your hands, recite some beautiful verse, and I shall rustle with delight between your fingers. I shall rise up to look at you, seeking among you the eyes, the hair of those whom I taught.

And when you make any image out of me, break it every moment; for every moment the children broke me, with tenderness and grief!

THE LAMP

Blessed be my lamp! It does not overwhelm me, like the blaze of the sun, and it has a softened glance, of pure gentleness, of pure sweetness.

It burns in the middle of my room; it is its soul. Its subdued reflection hardly makes my tears glitter, and I do not see them as they run over my breast.

According to the dream that is in my heart, I change its little crystal head. For my prayer, I give it a blue light, and my room becomes like the depths of the valley—now that I no longer raise my prayer from the bottom of the valleys. For my sadness, it has a violet crystal, and makes things suffer with me. It knows more of my life than the breasts on which I have reposed. It is alive, because it has touched my heart so many nights. It has the soft warmth of my inner wound, which now does not burn—which, because it has lasted so long, has become very soft.

Perhaps at nightfall, the dead, who have no power of sight, come to seek it in the eyes of the lamps. Who can that dead man be who is gazing at me with so much silent gentleness?

If it were human it would grow weary in the presence of my suffering, or else, full of solicitude, it would wish to be with me still when the mercy of sleep comes. Then it is perfection.

It cannot be perceived from without, and my enemies who pass believe I am alone. To all my possessions, as small as it, as divine as it, I give an imperceptible brightness, to defend them from the thieves of happiness.

Enough for me is what its halo of light illumines. It has room for my mother's face and the open book. Let them leave me only what this lamp bathes in its light; they may dispossess me of all beside!

I ask of God that tonight no sad soul may lack a soft lamp to dim the brightness of its tears!

LITTLE FEET

O TINY feet of children,
    Blue with the cold, unshod!
How can they see, nor cover you—
    O God!

O little feet, sore wounded
    By every stone and brier,
Chilled by the snows in winter,
    Defiled by mire!

Man, blind, knows not that where you go,
    In valley or on height,
You always leave behind a flower
    Of living light—

That where your little bleeding soles
    You set, O childish feet!
The tuberose in her snowy bloom
    Becomes more sweet.

Since in straight paths day after day
    Ye travel bare,
Be as heroic, little feet,
    As ye are fair!

Two little suffering jewels,
    Doomed to a bitter lot!
How can the people pass you by
    And see you not?

Johannes V. Jensen

ANN AND THE COW

IN THE cattle-pen at Hvalpsund Fair stood an old woman with her cow. She stood off a little to one side with her solitary cow, either because she was modest or because she wanted to attract more attention. She stood there so tranquilly, her head-dress drawn slightly down over her forehead on account of the sun, and knitted on a stocking which was already long enough to be turned back into a thick roll. She was dressed in a quaint, old-fashioned style, with a blue skirt that smelled in a home-like way of the dye-pot, and a brown knitted shawl crossed over her flat chest. The head-dress was faded and wrinkled after its long sojourn in the drawer; the wooden shoes were flat-bottomed, but she had polished them. In addition to the four needles she plied so swiftly with her worn hands, she had an extra one stuck in her gray hair. She stood with one ear toward the music which came from the booths, but she also looked now and again at the people and animals that traded and crowded beside her. All about her and coming from all directions were noises and confusion: the neighing from the horsestalls, the bustle of boats on the beach, the crashing of drums and loud cries from the clowns; but she stood there in the sunshine, oh, so calmly, and knitted on her stocking.

By her side with its head near her elbow stood the cow, bored and stiff-legged, chewing its cud. It was an old cow, but a good one, with a healthy-looking coat of hair and a really noble bearing. It was, to be sure, somewhat knobby in the hind-quarters and along the backbone, but that was the worst that could be said about it; the udder bulged soft and hairy beneath its belly, and there were not too many rings on the pretty black and white horns. It stood with moist eyes, chewing for the second time its cud. The lower jaw moved steadily from left to right and when it had swallowed, it turned its head and looked about, again to stand with motionless jaws while the next ball of cud rose through the gullet and up into its mouth. The insides of it sang vibrantly, like the deep notes of an organ, each time it breathed, and it drooled contentedly at the mouth. It was a sound, healthy cow, which had experienced what can happen to cows, and arrived at years of discretion. It had given birth to calves without even seeing them or getting a chance to lick them, and had then consumed its fodder and given its milk in good faith. And now it chewed its cud here as willingly as anywhere else and swung its tail in stiff spirals at the flies. The tether hung carefully twined about one horn, for the cow did not care to play the vagabond or run loose. The yoke was old and smooth-worn, without either iron over the nose or inturned pegs, for this cow had really no need of such contrivances. It may be noted that it wore its new rope to-day, not the old thin worn one with which it usually grazed. Old Ann wished that she, that is to say the cow, should look her best.

Since it was a good cow and obviously ripe for slaughter, it was not long before a man came over, looked at it, and ran his fingers along the well-groomed hide—a familiarity which the cow resented but not enough to become vexed about.

"How much for the cow, granny?" asked the man, transferring his stern look from the cow to Ann. Ann kept on knitting.

"It is not for sale," she replied. Then, as if to put a courteous period to the conversation, she dropped the needles out of one hand and with it wiped herself industriously under the nose. The man hesitated, but at length walked away; he seemed to find it difficult to take his eyes off the cow.

Not long thereafter a dapper and smooth-shaven butcher flicks his cane against the cow's horns and lets his plump hand glide quickly over the smooth flesh.

"How much for the cow?"

Old Ann looks first at her cow, now piously regarding the same, then turns her head and appears to find something interesting to look at far off in the distance.

"It is not for sale."

Done. Our cattle-dealer walks off in his blood-stained duster. But almost immediately afterwards there comes another man desirous of making a purchase. Old Ann shakes her head.

"The cow is not for sale."

When she had in this manner turned away many men, of course she became known; they began to gossip about her. A man who had once before tried to buy the cow and had been refused now returned and made a bid that was more than tempting. Old Ann said "No" in a very firm voice, but she seemed to be worried.

"*Is* it sold, then?" asked the man.

No, it certainly was not sold.

"Yes, but why in all the world do you stand here, then, and parade the cow?"

Old Ann hung her head, but stubbornly kept on knitting.

"What? Why do you stand here with the cow?" asked the man, who now felt himself positively insulted. "Is it your *own* cow?"

Yes, it certainly was that. It certainly was Ann's cow. She added that, really, she had had it since it was a calf; yes, really she had. If talk could appease the man, thought Ann, it should not be lacking. But he interrupted her.

"Do you stand here and make fun of people?"

Mercy! Ann is silent under this blow. She knits as if she were delirious. She knows not where to *look*, she is so bewildered. And the man, angrily, persists—

"I say, are you come to the Fair to make fun of people?"

It is then that Old Ann stops knitting. And as she loosens the tether from the cow's horn in preparation for the homeward trip, she fastens her wide-open eyes beseechingly on the man.

"It is such a lonely cow," she says confidingly. "It is *such* a lonely cow! It is the only one I have on my little farm, and it so very seldom gets out among other cattle. And so I thought I'd bring her to the Fair, so that she could mingle with her own kind, and enjoy herself a bit; yes, really, that's what I thought. And I meant well; it couldn't do any harm to any one, and—and so it was that we came here. But we aren't for sale, and so we may as well be on our way. And *I'm sorry,* I should have said. And good-bye. And thank you."

LITTLE AHASUERUS

T HE Manhattan East Side—the slum of New York—is full of children of all nationalities, a mass of little creeping things who have either been born in the New World or been dragged over there as infants by their emigrant parents. They are now going to become Americans, regardless of their language, origin, or past.

Children enjoy a privileged position in America; already as tiny babies they are treated with marked consideration as the American citizens of to-morrow. Who knows, it may be a future President who shows you the honor of throwing a snowball at you! Nowhere else do children enjoy their free-dom so thoroughly as in America; they are allowed to do anything they like; the Republic is theirs. Everybody is watching them, but they may go wher-ever they like. They may sit in a street car, singing to beat the band; it can't be helped. They are not rebuked and are therefore apt to become a pest, but their parents can afford it. In America the bashful child with a finger in his mouth and a numb feeling all over his body is an unknown species. They get a chance to use their lungs and are on the go as soon as they can walk. Nor do you anywhere else find children who of their own accord commence at such an early age to find work for themselves!

They often start their career as newsboys; no sooner can they speak plainly than you see them air their fringed comforters in the draught below the stairs that lead to the Brooklyn Bridge, where street cars come swinging in a curve, making their deafening clangor on the track, while the L trains keep thundering overhead; and here, where you can't hear your own voice, where people are busy but must have their paper, here in this whirlpool, the shout-ing mite of five or six summers is floating about with a bundle of newspapers under his arm, fresh and inky from the press—and he doesn't keep silent; he is not going to wait until somebody gets sentimental and lets the sweet little chap make money; no, he is on the job with the energy of a Zulu warrior, he butts like a small sized ram, and a constant jagged yell comes out of his throat: *"Journ'l! Wourld! All about horrible murder!"*

With one hand, black as a funeral from the printer's ink, he tears a paper out of the bundle, shoves it up to the man on the moving street car, and with the other little child's fist, already hard from the coppers of New York, he catches the cents, and immediately disappears; darting across the street for a new chance, he barely misses a passing street car; then crossing between the legs of a pair of horses and out-maneuvring a grown-up competitor, by now himself blue and hard in the face, he trips up a "friend" with whom he used to play marbles. *"Journ'l! Wourld!"* The tenderness is not out of his limbs yet; he still has all his milk-teeth, and yet he is already so far with all his tiny person that not only is he one of those who add to the fever of the metropolis, but he forces it; he outspeeds the busy ones; you can almost see the sparks he strikes from everything. And he is very cold-blooded at that—otherwise he would have no long life ahead of him; but he knows he has to act to be seen. The paper in his hand, the news, must quiver—horrible, horrible—and in this way the little Americans of the future from their very childhood get a natural training in the endurance of a tension that would be enough to kill any average European. He is like a wholesome piece of insanity—in other words, a perfect devil—when, standing on the curb with not a single customer in sight, he suddenly hurls his war-cry out in the air— *"Wourld!"* He is possessed. But the man of the future is exactly the one who is mad and knows how to carry it. Sometimes he gets invalided at an early age by having a leg run off, but if there is a skip left in the other one, you can see him, balancing his seven or eight years on a crutch, take up the competition in the surf in Park Row; you cannot break him so long as you do not pity him.

Edison started as a newsboy.

And as a newsboy you can find little Ahasuerus on the curb outside the City Hall turned towards the multitude of people and vehicles over there under the towering World Building. He is just an ordinary newsboy to look at, but he surely is the very smallest in size—the size you could show for money: *the smallest newsboy in the world.* The whole mite may be perhaps four years. His little arm can scarcely reach around the newspapers which he carries folded in a parcel, a single paper in his other hand ready for sale. It would be more reasonable to imagine that this little chap was playing at being a newsboy, and had taken his position according to all the rules of the game merely to enjoy the feeling of what it was like, while his big brother worked the real thing out where the fight was hot; but no, he is a big brother himself, and this is dead serious. Once in a while when the traffic gets to be particularly crowded and the noise outgrows itself, he also thinks that he ought to make himself felt and makes a step forward to the edge of the sidewalk, handing a paper out towards the crowd in general; *"Wourld!"* he yells again, and makes an effort to bark like an old experienced newsboy, and his little chest is tightening all the way down to his stomach, making him shrivel forward: *"Wourld!"* Naturally his tender child's voice is drowned by the thunder of the noise, but he has announced what he had to announce and again goes back one step, sticks to his post, meeting every demand, and, like a regular business man, "always aiming at giving everybody a square deal." Now and then some one gets the idea of buying a paper from this very boy, perhaps because he is so tiny that he makes a record, and then he must get a copy up as quick as a flash, get the cent in his hand, and immediately tear a fresh copy out of the bundle, ready for another immediate sale, as he has seen the others do: *"Wourld!"* And if he should reach the bottom of his supply he has been instructed to apply at a certain railing in the neighborhood where a man, who never says anything, quickly counts out another small bundle for him. And in this way the day must pass until daddy or mother comes and settles with the man and fetches the little one.

Otherwise he is left entirely to New York. He knows a few English words by heart which he is supposed to use in case he should get lost; they explain that his name is Leo with a Slavonic surname, that he lives in the Bowery and then a number that's awfully hard to say. What else Leo might have to communicate to himself while he stands there, thinking his little childish thoughts, takes the form of Yiddish, his mother tongue, of which he speaks a more personal dialect with his sister at home, little Marya, who is still younger. Leo misses her every day; she is as dear to him as the mother's milk he once drank and since forgot. The longing for his sister sticks like a pain in his tiny body, which is warm as a budding flower; he misses Sis so much on this hard job of his. And everything else that Leo can think of contributes to this inner swelling and gnawing like a growing sprout that lies bursting under ground; his whole being is one vague craving, his heart so full and big with wants that are already old.

For this is not where he belongs; he was born immensely far from here in a city called Lodz; and the world that was his starts with a back yard and a wall with a factory chimney sticking up, the smoke from which makes the daylight down in the back yard change like a constant restless procession of shadows, a bit of sky and then again gloom. In this migratory light Leo gained consciousness in a window sill filled with rainwater, in which he dipped one of his fingers and then put it to his tongue—his first chance of tasting the moisture of the heavens blended with the dust of the earth, bitter, but unforgettable as the primal ocean of creation. Later on he was promoted to familiarity with wet flag stones and a sink outflow, through which raw potato peel would now and again be washed out into a grating, a mystery of height and depth to which he will never find the key and which will for ever remain buried in his recollection. And there he also used to help Marya build puff-puff trains out of firewood on the floor.

Then he knows something about a doorway leading to the street—the street that everything comes from; and he remembers a day when it was roaring with people and horsemen fighting the crowd and drawn swords; shooting and tramping that shook the earth, the end of the world with everybody running in and out, the air filled with doleful shrieks, broken windows and people with bleeding heads reeling through the door. Then Leo got on the real big puff-puff and remembers nothing but hard times for daddy and mother, always traveling, always on the road, until they got on board the steamer and saw nothing but water day after day. They kept on sailing and sailing, and to Leo this trip on the ocean will never end; he will always remain faithful to it because that is how his life started; his child's brain clings to the ship and the heavy rolling of the sea as to a home he has come from but will never see again.

The sun grinned through the clouds towards dusk, and on the foc's'le head where the emigrants crowded together and looked towards the vacant horizon, a baby face stuck out of a rough blanket and was swung high into the sky as the stem of the vessel rose; this was little Leo on his mother's arm, the youngest lookout on board, the fairy-tale of the ship. The steamer forced her way on, slowly thumping and heaving; heavy seas came down on the ship like naked warriors, their swords in their teeth; they were crushed and reduced to foam which was flung into the air and stayed there for the fraction of a second, reflecting the everlasting sign of the rainbow in its salt spray before it disappeared. In this play some of Leo's soul remains; that is where he is from.

Yes, Leo early became a stranger to his own childhood, an exile before he could walk, a searcher of eternity like the homeless wind. Now the back yard with the sink outflow and the wandering shadows has gone; the waves are no more; now it is the Bowery, high up following many black stairs, with no end of colored washing hanging to dry on lines outside the window, a battle of colors exposed to wind and weather. And here where Leo has been put to work stand the dizzy tall buildings, white steam floating out of their tops towards the sunshine, glaring with thousands of windows, while shafts of shadow-like ladders to heaven lean from the roofs precipitously down to the streets. And Leo is selling newspapers and longing, longing—for a past that never quite existed.

Life has only taught him a certain yearning. He is like a deep dream. But if trials have already put a personal mark on the little man, a still deeper fate lies in his blood—the uncertainties and wanderings of his ancestors. His little head with his oriental features is formed like a mask in which are reflected and lie dormant all the ups and downs which have bent and hardened the people of Israel. The ghostly large eyes shine with all the mysteriousness of remote Asian antiquity, thousands of years before Abraham broke up his camp in the country between the rivers and went to Canaan; they are still dewed with the sweetness of a herdsman's life that takes no note of time. Certain soft features around the wings of his nose are suggestive of Egyptian works of art and call to memory the days when Israel was making bricks along the Nile and met the sunny daughters of Osiris in the rushes in the evening. The crispy blackamoor's hair and a certain play of the features tells of a beautiful Nubian slave-girl, whose blood has entered the race at some time, and the square Assyrian mouth points to the weeping years by the waters of Babylon that surely did not lack any pastimes either. He resembles the portraits from Fayum, half Greek, half African, and yet Jewish. And now, as a matter of fact, he stands in New York as a little Polish emigrant, who can hardly blow his own nose, and sells *The World*.

He cannot yet read and does not know what he is saying; therefore, from his mouth, it may easily be taken as unintentionally symbolic, a brave and painfully comic challenge to the ungenial world in which he has become a derelict, when now and again he gathers all his breath to hurl a cry of "*Wourld!*" over the street noise. This is little Ahasuerus.

One day the father remained absent from the little miserable room in the Bowery, where the window to the street was darkened every three minutes by an L train that thundered by and set the entire house jarring. Day after day passed, and the father did not come back. The mother cried her eyes out over the two little ones, who kept asking questions which they answered themselves, looking so wise, but understanding nothing.

The husband's disappearance, in a way never fully explained, was linked with an event in the Jewish world of New York, the big demonstration that took place on the anniversary of some Russian massacre.

One hundred and fifty thousand fugitive Jews on that day paraded through the streets of New York, an historical performance which was meant to petrify the world, but as a matter of fact only formed one more ripple in the human whirlpool of Manhattan. They assembled over in the poor sections of darkest Brooklyn and went across the Williamsburg Bridge into East Side New York, all the way feeding on new supporters from the Ghetto until, like a human ocean, they turned into Broadway and filed in full marching order up through the city.

At intervals there would be brass bands in the procession, playing mournful melodies, the distance between each band being not so great but that one heavy dirge could be heard to mingle its wailings in glaring discord with those of another. Ancient Hebrew hymns, strangely gloomy and pregnant, dragged themselves along in a most unmerciful dissonance with the tones of Chopin's inevitable funeral march. And in this nightmare in the middle of the day through the modern streets of New York, where the doleful music created the effect of a procession of ancient ghosts, under this torn sky they came wandering six by six, one silent rank after another, wandering and wandering, all wearing stiff bowler hats that fell deep down over the back of their heads, as you will find it in whatever part of the world the Jews have been swept away to, every one of them with a long frock coat dragging at his heels, clothes that had been worn by bigger people before them, every one of them big-footed and flat-footed. That is how they file past with bent backs, their faces thrust forward in which the features may differ, as if borrowed from all the other peoples of the world, but in which the stamp is always Jewish, hard and smouldering; thus they come marching by, out of step, each of them lonesome, but today apparently in agreement on one purpose—for how long?

On lower Broadway the parade is lost in the bottom of the canyon formed by the skyscrapers on both sides and in the usual week-day traffic. The crowd is packed closer together on both sidewalks, and the police have to direct the vehicles through other channels, otherwise the parade creates no particular sensation; they are used to parades on Broadway; that is not enough to make them drop their work. Up on the huge frontages you can see a few people step out on the broad cornices high up below the window sills and look down upon the street. Pedestrians stand still for a moment to find out what it's all about: "I see, the Jews are having a parade, eh?"

In here between the closed cliff-like house fronts the sounds of the music are thrown back still more blaringly, and with doubled discord, now near by, now roaring in hollow tones at a distance like a subterranean uproar suggestive of doomsday, a sound as if the dead were coming! As always happens when music is mixed together, distorted and barbaric tones leapt up in the air, shrieks emanated from space as from invisible beings, loud flute-like notes that didn't come from any instrument but came about through interference, strange, naked, piercing shrieks that suggested the immediate vicinity of dead bodies, the air filled with weeping souls.

The parade did not get so far as to fulfill its purpose: that of having a monster meeting with speeches and resolutions. Having dragged its living protest in good order and to the tunes of the entire pre-historic mass of music up through Broadway, where colossal signs with mammoth letters in gold—Stern Bros., Haurowitz & Co.—glared from the skyscrapers of the merchant princes down on the current of drooping heads—it closed up in Union Square and broke into a panic. In a few minutes the legions had fled on all sides and disappeared, leaving no more traces behind them than does a dandelion when scattered by the wind.

How the panic started and what caused it nobody ever found out; there seemed to have been nothing in particular; it was probably a fit of what might be called "the Jewish fear," a sudden insanity at being so many people together in one spot. A lot of filings loaded with the same sort of electricity could not have dispersed more effectively than did this mob. It started as the people in the parade commenced to circle round in the open square, when suddenly some were seized with a terror that spread like an explosive infection; the masses crowded together, and as more kept on coming and everybody wanted to be in the center, it was as if a tornado struck down over the closely-packed, panic-deranged heads, and swept them all off the square before you could say Jack Robinson.

A few death cries sounded; otherwise the mob was horribly silent, moved mutely like the tide and with the force of an earthquake. On a certain spot in the square there was a pretty big wooden shed; that was overturned, pushed out of its place and rocked as if by a hurricane, now with one corner down, now with another; a man who had been up there with a moving picture camera fell down with his box and tripod, and kept swimming for some time on the waving heads before sinking to the bottom. Lamp posts and railings gave way like so many straws; policemen were being trampled to death. At first the masses churned around irresolutely, but suddenly threw a section over towards the northern gap of Broadway; so sudden, indeed, that several people were literally squashed up on the corner walls; other waves separated to the various corners of the universe, and soon the masses dissolved in a topsy-turvy, blind flight on all sides. It was as if a black wave of people had been washed up towards the wall of Manhattan and was being crushed into a foam that passed on and refracted the daylight in all the seven flash-colors of terror.

Nobody who participated in this new destruction of Jerusalem will ever forget that he saw the rainbow of hell.

But Leo's father did not return from this parade. The next day the place near a lamp post in Twenty-third Street, which he used to lean against—with a bunch of shoe laces around his neck for sale, dressed in long Russian boots and fur cap—was vacant and could be filled by another peddler. A chair in the Astor library remained empty for a couple of days, the librarian wondering what had happened to the Russian who came every evening to study American social economics. But apart from that he was missed only in the little home in the Bowery. Here he was grieved over as only Jews, who have been taught it by their strict God, know how to grieve.

It broke the mother down. She was ill already; for a long time she had been coughing badly and suffering from a heavy feeling in her legs as if some one were trying to pull her down into the ground. Now her cough, mingled with an incessant weeping, soon broke her heart. It was as if a strange inhuman being barked out of her when she fought with her rough and jarring cough until the blood came, and tears furrowed her poor, despairing face. The mother had been so pretty, and her raven-black, girlish hair still stood about her head like a tornado, but her lovely eyes had become wild, and the seal of death was burning below her pointed cheek-bones. She leaned forward now, and seemed to have a deep hollow under her breast as if somebody had run the butt end of a heavy log into her heart region. Her legs tied her down to the floor; she could not walk any more. Towards dark and during the night she lost her reason and was delirious; and during the day every time the trains rushed by and darkened the window, a glimpse of insanity came into her eyes. She had commenced to die and felt it every time darkness approached her.

But she still preserved the unconquerable smile with which she had met all misfortunes, a certain mocking mood that raised her above the accidents of life, as if everything that happened were not her fate at all. She was one of those who would laugh when everything was at its worst. And when dusk lighted the light of irresponsibility in her deep, grim eyes, with broad, shadowing eyelashes—the Fayum eyes that Leo had inherited—terror was opposed by a mysterious, hardy smile, a reserve of cheerfulness in spite of everything. Even when she wept, and she wept without ceasing after her husband had disappeared, her pain was mingled with laughter and inarticulate mockery; she herself could perish, but her nature could not die.

"Go home," she finally whispers on the last day, an almost inaudible wheezing, and she looks at the children with large cadaverous eyes. She lies, rattling feebly in her throat, but cannot pass away so long as the two little mites are with her; the agony of seeing them keeps her alive. The delirium has left her, and her clear reason has returned; she weeps no more; this must be the end.

"Go home, go," she begs again earnestly of Leo and Marya who are standing at the door, doubtful and holding each other's hands. She can only smile with her eyes; her mouth and nose have stiffened, but they recognize her from her wonderful motherly eyes, which laugh like stars and embrace them in a world of love and light. Otherwise they don't know what to think, that almost isn't mother any more, she has changed so much, just as if that barking beast within her, that has made her so strange to them lately, had now completely taken her place; but no, those eyes are still mother's eyes. And finally they feel they have to do what mother tells them to do and turn to leave. They do not grasp the meaning of it, but as she is so good to them they cannot act against her wishes. The mother's eyes hang on them as they stand there, lost and obedient, fumbling the door and stretching on their toes; they still hesitate and look back . . .

"Go," she moans. And they leave, tripping well-behavedly and blocking each other's way, still holding hands, over the doorstep and close the door noiselessly. Then there is a silent chuckle in her chest because they are so sweet, a lonely flickering sob of happiness, that passes over into the last unconscious fight with darkness.

Leo and Sister proceeded slowly up the street, hand in hand, past the fine Bowery pawn-shops with revolvers and knuckle-dusters in the windows, and past the many sinister saloons, the mirrored swing-doors of which seemed to throw half the street, with buildings, sky, sun and everything, around in space and drop it beyond the edge of the world, every time anybody pushed them open. The surroundings altogether showed themselves in a pretty dazzled and refracted glimmering to the two orphans who saw them through tears.

But they were children and wept no longer than the weeping lasted. Sister comforted herself and commenced to eat an onion, the last gift her mother had put into her hands. Leo, who showed more foresight, kept his. But when he had finished weeping he commenced to think seriously of his problem. They were to go home, mother said, and as Marya was so tiny and didn't understand anything, it was for him to shoulder the responsibility.

What was meant by home, was not quite obvious to Leo. He had a faint conception of the ocean, waving in a circle, and of an infinity of lands and countries dancing in rounds outside the car window. He had a vision of in-hospitable fourth class waiting rooms in Germany, which had once been his home, desolate and lofty, always perambulated by the common people moving from one place to another, bringing the draught in with them and leaving the doors wide open behind them. He tried to rest his thoughts in the stalls on Ellis Island, with a mass of people brooding over their bundles on the floor. There his particular stronghold had been a certain bundle in the corner, where mother was, and he remembered how she would get a warm coloring in her eyes if he roamed too far away. One conception was fixed; that of the old window sill; where the daylight had been changed continually by a draught of pulsating factory smoke, and then the dear old sink outflow and the grating down in the back yard; but this picture which lay in the middle, as it were, had shrunk and become so distant that it felt more like a faint recollection of having belonged to some undefined, vague far away place, out there in the wide world. And guided by this instinct Leo started on his way, grabbed Marya firmly by the hand, and passed along. The main thing was that he was not to get separated from Marya, most of his homesickness being associated with Sister. Now, therefore, it was a question of obeying mother, and taking Sis and himself back home to safety.

It was all very easy for Marya; she was gnawing her onion, and was only too pleased to be promenading the streets with Leo. She was not yet three years old, and still lived in that happy dreamland which we bring with us from before our birth; she looked so vigorous and had the rose-colored chub-biness under both eyes which marks a sound sleeper. Weeping had only salted her mouth more red and given her an appetite. Sister was not dark like Leo but had turbulent red hair, as if it might be ferruginous. Her eyes were bright with a whitish ring and black eyelashes. Medusa eyes, and her skin was like goat's milk, greyish and pure. The little sleepy face was a smile in itself; otherwise she was very self-possessed and dignified. In this was Sister kept strutting along holding Leo's hand, her "tummy" curving out like a tiny Salome, extremely gentle and quite silent from sheer good health.

They walked far. It was a sunny day, but the air was cold, and the little ones commenced to get that stiff fatness in their faces which accompanies an inner stupor when one is cold. Leo had lost his bearings long ago and only followed the old law not to leave the sidewalk. When they came to a street crossing they skipped across and continued on their way on the other side, and in this way they came high up on Manhattan. More than once it happened that some big driver would shout loud curses at them from the top of his load and lying back on his reins would bring a pair of huge horses to an abrupt stop, rearing over the heads of the children; this might happen when, in spite of all his talent as a strategist, Leo fell from one danger into another, but somehow they always got off with nothing worse than a fright; somebody would always look after them when their own heedfulness failed. In this way several hours passed that almost seemed like an eternity to Leo's childish imagination, and the determination to get home more and more took the form of a flight, a run for life. But gradually, as they grew tired, the excitement turned into silent grief.

After a while they stopped, exhausted and numb. There was some kind of a little building, entirely built of metal, decorated in green, which looked friendly, and there they took shelter. Having rested a bit, Leo gave the house a glance and discovered that one end was wide open as a door and that a deep flight of stairs led down, farther than he could see. Many people walked down the stairs which must therefore lead to some nice place. Warm air came up the stairway, there was a peculiar burnt smell about it, and Leo thought there might be some big kitchen or a bakery down there, the very place where all food came from. Without long consideration, Leo made signs to Sister to follow him and commenced to descend; this, apparently, was the way home. Sister turned round and took the steps backwards, on all fours. In order not to be too much in the way, they kept close to the tiled wall and let the busy people who had to get down have the middle of the stairs. After a lot of crawling, which was particularly exhausting to Sister, who every little while put her hands on her skirt and got in her own way, they landed down in the Subway. And this is where the adventurous trip started, which got into all the papers the following morning and for a moment made the two children prominent in New York, the noisiest and most forgetful city in the world.

Deep down where the stairs ended, it was like a fine palace with tiled floors and only white plate-like bricks on the walls. But there was no indication of food; this only appeared to be a large lobby where people were waiting; even here they had electric light but otherwise no conveniences, and people stood at a stall which had papers and picture books for sale, or were fidgeting about as if they might be hungry, sending one another hostile looks. Don't tell me there is a train coming! But that's just what happened. Suddenly there was a puff in the air, a peculiar wide draught that was familiar to Leo, and out from the dark earth came a train, consisting of many cars that jarred and stopped so suddenly that people standing up in them behind the windows swayed and had to catch hold of straps. A crowd of people swarmed out, another lot crowded in, chased by the shoutings of the conductors, the iron gates at the end of the cars were closed with a bang, and immediately the train moved on and disappeared into the earth in the opposite direction. Quite a lot got on that train; good for them! Leo and Sister were looking on for a long time without hope of getting a seat, while one train left after another. They didn't dare to get into the crowding around the cars, and besides, you needed a ticket and they didn't have any at all.

But Leo didn't want always to be amongst those who waited; he wanted to get on, and here, no doubt, was the way. Having gradually been forced up all the way to where the black tunnel went into the ground and where the train disappeared, he determined to insure his own and Sister's admittance, even though they might have to walk; he therefore let himself slide from the low platform down on the track. Sister turned around, lay down on her stomach, and also went sliding. Nobody had noticed them; not a single soul looked any other way than in the direction of the next incoming train. And without hesitation they therefore walked into the depth of the earth, Leo first and Sister close on his heels. Between the rails and the walls, there was a little footpath of oily gravel, almost twelve inches wide. They walked leisurely and found that it wasn't all dark; ahead at a distance there were two bulbs in the wall. But suddenly the air began to whirl and press upon them; the singing and jarring in the earth rose to a keen roaring that came closer, and they saw a green eye grow out of the earth. Leo and Sister stood pressed close against the wall, feeling nothing until it was all over. *The train had passed them,* only a couple of inches away; the pressure of air had tugged at their clothes, and they had been swallowed up in a glaring sound, a shaking and a shriek of iron against iron. But now it was all over, they only tasted some nasty dust on their lips and felt a bit scorched, otherwise everything was all right. They walked along cheerfully, and when again they noticed the green eye and felt the pressure of the air through the tunnel, they were already used to it and stood with their backs against the wall until it was over. They walked and walked and finally came to the next station. But as it didn't satisfy them as the end of their expedition, they passed it without being seen—goodness knows how—and kept on traveling. Not two feet from where they tumbled around in the half dark was the "third rail" where the current was strong enough to pulverize them if they only touched it with a finger. But destiny was probably busy lifting the hasp on a fourth floor window some place where little children were alone at home, and at least let the two mites' little feet remain where it was safe for them to walk. They faced bigger dangers than that; they got unmolested through the subterranean railroad labyrinth at Grand Central Terminal where the Subway passes through, and on a long way through the large tunnel on the other side until they were found at last.

If you can believe the newspapers that carried the story next day, the children walked all the way from Thirty-third Street to Forty-second Street through the Subway. How they ever got through Grand Central without being hurt is beyond any man's power of explanation. But a railroad worker saw them strolling out of the tunnel at Forty-second Street and raised a yell of terror. It might almost have caused the death of the children. Trains were approaching from different sides, and when Leo heard that he had been found out and that it was terrible, he lost his head and commenced to cry. Of course they must have been in danger if a big fellow yelled as badly as that. The two mites stood, their arms around each other's neck, when the workman came in mad jumps and snapped them away right in front of the light on an engine. He escaped back to a light-platform, a small island in the middle of the rail-ocean, where he walloped each of the kids and fainted merely from the strain he had been through. Great drama—one man fainted, two kids howling over him partly from fear, partly from the spanking they had had. The firm little Marya possessed a truly heavenly scale of notes, once she got started. But not a sound was heard in the tunnel among all the trains, and to some engine driver, who might perhaps observe the group under the light of his lantern, the whole thing looked like a mysterious but in itself very eloquent pantomime.

But the catastrophe put an end to the wanderings of the two little orphans. The monster that had grabbed them, both cried and laughed as soon as he recovered; he kept on thumping them and giving them coppers, a man, apparently, whose personality contained crude self-contradictions, and finally turned them over to a wonderful big cop up in the street, who carried Sister on his arm towering high over all traffic and street noise, and left it to Leo to follow them by holding on to the end of his club.

It was getting dark and the lights were turned on up and down, mingling their faint light with the radiance of the evening sky over New York. The city rested in its fairy light, airy like a dream, a beautiful fata morgana, and yet more real than any other city in the world. At one place Leo noticed a tall, narrow palace towering over the street with thousands of lighted windows until it was lost in the clear, greenish sky. It faced the street as the tall bow of a ship, and high up, where it formed a sort of landing, it went over into a still taller tower-like continuation. This wonder, which he would never forget, was the *New York Times* building. And as he saw New York that evening, with a dawning confidence in his heart, the first foundation was laid of an adventurous mood that did not beckon him farther away; little Ahasuerus was getting home.

Theirs was a triumphant walk to the nearest orphans' home, and there the two "baby tramps" were received with the greatest festivity, like long expected acquaintances, and right away they were put to playing visitors with a lot of other children who had also got lost. Leo, of his own accord, went over in a corner with Sister and shared his onion, which he still kept, with her. Now he felt that conservation of provisions was no longer required.

Oh no, they were extremely well taken care of with food and everything. It ought to be known, however, that the people to whom they had been brought turned out to be regrettably particular about cleanliness, taking the trouble, as they did, of pulling them in and out of one unnecessary tubful of water after another. But we have to accept the bad things with the good things in this world.

Not having been called for before nine o'clock that evening, they were taken in a fine-looking carriage to the headquarters of the orphans' home and billeted there, each in a nice little bed with rails and white linen. Now that they were asleep, nature demanded its rights; but they were not alone at that. All around them sounded lamentations from other babies, who also called and called for mother until their cries faded and died away, now here, now there, and sleep showered mercy on them all.

Leo and Sister now became children of New York. There they are going to take root, and there they are going to bloom. In this wild forest, where only the rules of growth and warmth count, they will shoot right up in the air, like faultless palms. Leo, who made his first steps in the new world as a promising newspaper man, no doubt will develop into a great editor, who will some day put still another section on some newspaper palace, another shining thousand-eyed tower higher up in the transparent atmosphere of New York.

But Marya, with the Medusa eyes and the prominent little stomach, will become—time passes quickly and she is almost there now—a world renowned star tragedienne, who shines on the stage with the boundless wealth of pain of her personality, framed in a glory of blood-red curls, a rare and forceful impersonator of all sufferings on earth.

And when she feels like basking her genius in the rainbow-colored sunlight of comedy, she will be seen with a luxuriantly curved Salome figure and bewitching eyes wandering over the stage, a wholesome smile on her face, and with the decapitated head of a theatrical critic on a charger.

AT MEMPHIS STATION

HALF-AWAKE and half-dozing,
in an inward seawind of danaid dreams,
I stand and gnash my teeth
at Memphis Station, Tennessee.
It is raining.

The night is so barren, extinguished,
and the rain scourges the earth
with a dark, idiotic energy.
Everything is soggy and impassable.

Why are we held up, hour upon hour?
Why should my destiny be stopped here?
Have I fled rain and soul-corrosion
in Denmark, India, and Japan,
to be rain-bound, to rot, in Memphis,
Tennessee, U.S.A.?

And now it dawns. Drearily light oozes
down over this damp jail.
The day uncovers mercilessly
the frigid rails and all the black mud,
the waiting-room with the slot-machine,
orange peels, cigar- and match-stumps.
The day grins through with spewing roof-gutters,
and the infinite palings of rain,
rain, say I, from heaven and to earth.

How deaf the world is, and immovable!
How banal the Creator!

And why do I go on paying dues
at this plebeian sanatorium of an existence!

Stillness. See how the engine,
the enormous machine, stands calmly and seethes;
shrouding itself in smoke, it is patient.
Light your pipe on a fasting heart,
damn God, and swallow your sorrow!

Yet go and stay in Memphis!
Your life, after all, is nothing but
a sickening drift of rain, and your fate
was always to be belated
in some miserable waiting-room or other—
Stay in Memphis, Tennessee!

For within one of these bill-shouting houses,
happiness awaits you, happiness,
if you can only gulp down your impatience—
and here there is sleeping a buxom young girl
with one ear lost in her hair;
she will come to encounter you
some fine day on the street,
like a wave of fragrance,
looking as though she knew you.

Is it not spring?
Does the rain not fall richly?
Is there not the sound of an amorous murmur,
a long, subdued, conversation of love
mouth to mouth
between the rain and the earth?
The day began so sadly,
but now, see the rainfall brighten!
Do you not allow the day its right of battle?
So now it is light. And there is a smell of mould
from between the rusting underpinning of the platform
mingled with the rain-dust's rank breath—
a suggestion of spring—
is that no consolation?

And now see, see how the Mississippi
in its bed of flooded forest
wakes against the day!
See how the titanic river revels in its twisting!
How royally it dashes through its bends, and swings the rafts
of trees and torn planks in its whirls!
See how it twirls a huge stern-wheeler
in its deluge-arms

like a dancer, master of the floor!
See the sunken headland—oh, what immense, primeval peace
over the landscape of drowned forests!
Do you not see how the current's dawn-waters
clothe themselves mile-broad in the day's cheap light,
and wander healthily under the teeming clouds!

Pull yourself together, irreconcilable man!
Will you never forget that you have been promised Eternity?
Will you grudge the earth its due, your poor gratitude?
What would you do, with your heart of love?

Pull yourself together, and stay in Memphis;
announce yourself in the market as a citizen;
go in and insure yourself among the others;
pay your premium of vulgarity,
so that they can know they are safe, as regards you,
and you will not be fired out of the club.
Court the damosel with roses and gold rings,
and begin your saw-mill, like other people.
Yank on your rubbers regularly . . .
Look about you, smoke your sapient pipe
in sphinx-deserted Memphis . . .

Ah! there comes that miserable freight-train
which has kept us waiting six hours.
It rolls in slowly—with smashed sides;
it pipes weakly; the cars limp on three wheels;
and the broken roof drips with clay and slime.
But in the tender, among the coals,
lie four still forms
covered with bloody coats.

Then our huge express-locomotive snorts;
advances a little; stops, sighing deeply;
and stands crouched for the leap. The track is clear.

And we travel onward
through the flooded forest
under the rain's gaping sluices.

A BATHING GIRL

Even, I think, when you're bathing,
  Girl, you make love to the billows,
  Innocent-hearted as they are,
Practising ever caresses.

With tickling girl-hands you catch at
The curly heads of the breakers,
As, you remember, Europa
Riding (How fearsome!) the bull.

What are those lithe swimming antics,
What but incipient embraces?
Why do you turn on your back, too,
When comes the wave, whitely seething?

Kissed on your whole lovely body,
Tumbled about by the billows,
You are reborn of the foam—
Oh, but your feet in the air, though!

Ask not for grace with your legs!
That has brought many to ruin.
No, turn your back to the spoiler—
Not that that always will save you.

Ocean beleaguers you, bather,
Like a vast buffalo herd;
When was so little a thing
Striven for so mightily? Seldom.

When, too, you stand in your shift
Out in the breeze,
Surely some god of air
Smiles at such ill-covered limbs.

These are not evil thoughts;
I love you.
And the salt taste on your lips,
That is my soul, my darling!

Frans Eemil Sillanpää

TAAVETTI ANTILA

WHAT is big, what little in this world of ours? At the inn tonight we were talking about some quite unknown hero who had fallen like a true man and a soldier.

Immediately Taavetti Antila comes to my mind; that man of whom we spoke would have been his counterpart, had he been old. This Taavetti was a capable, trustworthy worker who was contented with the wages of the neighborhood and who had no interest in seeking out places where the pay was higher. Mattock and ax were his weapons in the struggle for existence, weapons with which he veritably achieved mastery over life. For all of him, the birch stumps might be ever so full of knots. When the workmen had given them up after trying without avail to get at them from different angles, Taavetti would take over the job of splitting cord-wood for the farmer with the understanding that he must cut up these unruly stumps as well. And cut them up he did. Swinging his ax in a wide circle he made first a deep notch, then drove in the wedge. The wood fibers cried out angrily at first when Taavetti's wedge tore them apart, but it availed them nothing; they had finally to loosen their hold on the trunk structure. Loosen it, too, at the place Taavetti wished, so that in the end, for all their knottiness, they matched in appearance and size those that a light ringing blow had hewn from a fine, clean trunk.

At clearing land and digging ditches Taavetti Antila was also in a class by himself. Whether or not the land be good and adapted to cultivation—the farmer in any case so pictures it when he negotiates with Taavetti about his wages. But it is all the same to Taavetti. He goes no further into the matter; he asks the same pay which he has received for clearing another similar piece of land and which to the best of his knowledge other workmen ask. But the seemingly inoffensive brushwood, low and scraggly though it is, nevertheless conceals a plenty of both those evils which are a real test of the strength and limbs of the clearer of land—rocks and stumps. There are old pine stumps, which have been soaked through and through with tar and still have no will to rot. When such a stump with all its roots has been pulled out, it turns out to be a huge monster, beside which the land clearer, despite all his strength, seems like a dwarf, quite like those men in pictures from distant lands who are standing next to a giant tree they have just felled. And then the rocks! A rock, too, may look quite unobtrusive—nothing more than an innocent hump on the earth's surface. Strike it with the iron bar, it rings quite soft and yielding, as if it were sticking only a little way into the ground and all that was needed was to push the bar under it and pry a bit . . . But even for our Taavetti, who is not only powerful but also canny as a result of much experience, this means quite a piece of work.

But what of that farmer from Kutinperä who was so incredibly close-fisted and had refused to give Taavetti the contract for his clearing? Taavetti himself cared not a whit about the whole affair after he had discovered for himself something of the character of the miserly fellow.—Well, the farmer and his hired men set to work clearing the land in time taken from the ordinary work of the farm. There were malicious rocks sticking deep in the ground, just as Taavetti had said, but the farmer worked at them with dogged frenzy. When in the evening the dinner bell rang and the day laborers put down their tools, he stayed out in the fields and kept toiling away. It was a Saturday evening. On one's own land fortunately one doesn't need to stop at the stroke of the bell. For hours he had been working with his men on an especially big rock, without its budging or giving an inch. Now the farmer was trying single-handed to tip the rock in the direction he wanted it. He pushed, kicked, and threw his weight against it; finally in angry desperation he attempted it with his bare hands. These hands were lean and sinewy, with bulging nails. And these hands, pressed against the sides of the rock, were all that was to be seen of the man, when they finally went out to search for him. . . . In its own time the rock had loosened slowly but surely and had pushed the man under it, as a strong-willed, forceful adult little by little bends a stubborn child to his will.

"I knew it and I told him, too, that the rocks out there are devilish fellows," said Taavetti Antila, when he learned of the accident. But when Taavetti returns from a clearing job which has been to his liking and in which he has established his mastery over the fields with that determined posture of the head peculiar to him and a tense expression in his furrowed face—yes, when he comes back from such a labor, he will carry a splendid bundle of pine chips on his back. This is a little gift for Miina, his wife. Which means as much as this: he merely throws the chips into a corner out in the woodshed. Miina will find them. They burn like powder! With his family Taavetti is the master of the house, cares for everything, gives all the orders. And it would occur to nobody to challenge him.

Taavetti Antila is still living. To be sure, he hurt his foot badly. He dislocated the joint in the cleft of a tree trunk and was laid up for a long time. Since then he hasn't been altogether the same; he favors this foot when walking. Yet he has no idea that there is any such thing in existence as accident insurance. Much going about is painful for him, especially when he must carry anything, and sometimes the wound breaks open. But he does a pretty good job still at his work. Whenever I think of what the future may hold for Taavetti, I can be sure of only so much: that if there is a way around it, he will never accept aid from the community.

Taavetti Antila is altogether a man and knows what he is about. But why should I talk for so long around the point that occurred to me tonight when I thought of him. Or rather, I thought of Taavetti when we were talking about typical Finns—for what I wish to say is that he is the very prototype of the Finnish character among older men.

Once in a while I used to go out in an hour of leisure, purely for the pleasure I found in it, to where Taavetti was working, and watch him for a time without his noticing me; then I would go up and chat with him. He has known me from the days when I was still in swaddling clothes. We have been on intimate terms from the ground up, so to speak. I approach him therefore quite differently from the self-conscious city dweller on vacation whose notions of such an upright and somewhat ingenuous woodman—were one able to extract them from his head and spread them out on the table— might prove quite exhilarating. This city gentleman might in his fashion be quite fascinated by Taavetti, might even later on in the autumn talk about him enthusiastically to his friends at the club and the office as a "splendid type" or the like. But essentially he considers him a dull, backward man of nature, though not quite "naïve," since Taavetti Antila, who ordinarily doesn't laugh without occasion, cannot suppress a smile in spite of himself, when such a puny little fellow stands next to him and attempts in real earnest to give him—Taavetti—expert instructions in the elementary principles of lifting rocks and stumps from the ground.

When Taavetti comes back home at night, he is usually ill-humored and taciturn at the evening meal. Work like his is tiring and oftentimes he is annoyed, too, with his "old woman." But after such a day Taavetti laughs with gusto even at his meal. At the moment when he has dipped his potato in the sauce and is raising it vertically—when he must open wide his mouth anyway—one can drop a word about the stimulating experiences with the gentleman from the city. And when his mouth is full, one can proceed a little further with the subject. It isn't just anything that may be said appropriately at this moment, but a story like this—just the thing!

"Well, now, what kind of a gentleman was he?" asks Miina.

"Devil only knows," Taavetti answers, as he guides another load to his mouth, "but can you think of anything more foolish? An excuse for a man like that has the nerve to talk when sensible people are discussing problems."

Thank goodness, I stand on quite a different footing with Taavetti—he knew my father well and still considers me no more than a boy. No, he wouldn't make sport of me behind my back with his answers, if I should ask questions about his work. He understands that I am simply not conversant with such matters. On the other hand, when he needs help with something that must be written out and comes therefore to me, he has occasion then, perhaps, to admire the flourish with which this proceeds from my hand— nor is he averse to the fact that it costs him nothing and that he can count on a cup of coffee afterwards and once in a while, if it happens to be a holiday, on a drop of stronger brew.

But out where he works, I have the feeling, when I am beside him, of being hopelessly unessential, for I have neither physical nor mental capabilities with which to make a showing.

For my last vignette of him I should like to add to this simple recollection a delightful experience. Once again I was out on the clearing with Taavetti. I was walking about, looking around, and out of curiosity making an estimate of the area. Then it struck me that here and there were little patches that had not been cleared. At first I suspected there must be technical grounds for the neglect. Yet when I examined more closely I found no especially big rocks or stumps, but only a leafy shrub or two or a clump of moss. Then I risked asking Taavetti, though not quite without the painful feeling that I was being like "the excuse for a man."

"No, that isn't anything so special," he answered, "only a couple of nests of little birds, and the older ones are flying back and forth with food for the young. I didn't want to disturb them, so I cleared around them. I thought to myself, these few bushes and clumps can wait; later on in the autumn I can take them out when the birds are gone. Go on up and see for yourself how nice they are."

And Taavetti's mouth opens revealing traces of chewing tobacco as he warns me with a sh . . . sh . . . to approach quietly.

Strength, solidity—and a heart.

Pearl Buck

WANG LUNG

W ANG LUNG was the son of Wang the Farmer. All his life he had lived in the Wang village on the borders of the city of Nanking, and, since he daily carried green vegetables into the city to sell, he was no common, ignorant fellow. He knew, for instance, sooner than anyone else in the village, when the Emperor finally relinquished the throne. Indeed, the event could not have taken place more than a year before he heard of it. He at once informed his father, who told his uncle, and his uncle, who was the village letter-writer, told all the villagers who came to beg him to write to their relatives, and in a short time everyone knew of it.

For three days at least they all spoke in whispers, being much distressed and hourly expecting catastrophe. No one, of course, had ever seen the Emperor, but still each person had felt him to be a supporting, eternal power, the Son of Heaven, who arranged matters with the magistrates in the upper regions. In short, one could leave both the welfare of the nation and one's own little sins to the Emperor while one tended garden and took vegetables in the spring and ducks in the autumn to sell in the market-place. Now, with the Emperor gone, no one dared to leave the village. Indeed, Wang the Grandfather, who perfectly remembered the time of the Taipings, immediately expected looting and robbery. So he gathered together certain family valuables, such as the deed to the land, a coat of goatskin, dingy from generations of use and yet good for several more, and some bits of silver, and secreted them in the hollow mud wall of the house. Three days he sat stroking his sparse, yellow-white beard, his eyes fixed on the loosened earth, and at night he ordered his bed moved out and slept beneath it.

But, since nothing happened by the end of the fourth day, he took the treasure from its hiding-place, grumbling and a bit disappointed, and people began to go about their business again, although at first a little fearfully. At last, however, they no longer felt any need of the Emperor, and, as time passed, they even began to rejoice that he was gone, since their crops were as good every year as if he had intervened for them with Heaven.

Indeed, one day in the tea-shop in the city Wang Lung heard a young man cry in a loud voice over his tea-bowl that emperors were but idle fellows and cost the nation a great deal of money. Wang Lung was struck with cold horror at this speech and at such disdain of the honorable dead, and he watched for a long time to see whether a tile would not fall from the roof upon the young man or whether he would not choke over his tea and die. But, when nothing of the sort occurred, Wang Lung, after reflecting with some effort, because thinking was never easy, decided that the young man must have spoken the truth, so that the gods did not dare to rebuke him. He gazed respectfully at the young man.

The young man wore a long gown of dark blue cloth neither heavy nor light but perfectly suited to the season, which was the third month of spring. His hair was cut very close to his head and oiled as smoothly as a woman's. "This man must be from southern parts," Wang murmured to himself, "since I have not seen his like before."

The young man was talking rapidly and casting quick eyes over the crowd in the tea-shop. When he saw Wang Lung staring at him, he smoothed back his brow with his long, pale hands and raised his voice a little. "We Chinese have more people than any other country in the world, and all foreign countries should fear us. Nevertheless they despise us because we have no fire-wagons and fighting-ships. Yet these are simple things. In the ancient times did not our wise men ride upon clouds of fire and upon dragons breathing out smoke? What has been done, can be done again. Now we are a republic and the Emperor is dead. All things are possible."

Wang Lung had come nearer, and, stooping, he picked up the hem of the young man's gown and inquired politely, "May I ask how much this gown cost?" With the fine, soft cloth still between his thumb and forefinger he felt of it again and muttered: "Ah, what is this stuff? It feels like cloud material. Sir, is this foreign goods, and how much does it cost?"

But the young man became suddenly angry and snatched the garment away with a quick movement. "Do not soil it with your fingers, filthy one," he cried. "I paid two dollars a foot for it, and it is good English woolen cloth!"

Two dollars a foot! Wang's mouth gaped suddenly like a fish's mouth. He did not see two dollars in a month of labor. How many feet would it take for such a gown as this, swinging to the ankles and clinging about the throat, even to the very ears? While the young man continued to speak of republics, Wang Lung reflected carefully upon the amount of blue cotton cloth he had bought for his wedding garment six years before. Five feet for the front, five for the back, five for the sleeves—say, a ten-foot length and a half—say, a bit of extra thrown in, as was the custom when one bought ten feet of cloth at the shop. It would all come to not less than twenty-eight rounds of silver. He was aghast at such wealth. Twenty-eight dollars, a year's income, wrapped about the fragile body of this short-haired youth! "It is very dear," he murmured.

The young man turned to him complacently. "It is foreign goods grown upon the backs of English sheep and woven especially for the black-haired people by the hands of English slaves," he explained. Then, seeing Wang Lung's astonishment and admiration, he went on in a fluent, oracular manner: "As I was saying, we no longer need the Emperor. Our great nation may now be governed as our ancient sage has said, by the people, for the people and of the people. Even you, my poor fellow, may have a share in deciding who is to be our president."

"I?" said Wang, suddenly drawing back. "I have my father and old grandfather to support and my wife and three slaves, since she has given me only girls and no son yet. Their empty mouths are forever stretched wide around me. I have no time. Please, sir, attend to this matter for me."

The young man laughed loudly at this and struck the table with the flat of his hand, so that everyone in the tea-shop looked up and Wang, embarrassed to be so much seen, turned his face away.

"How ignorant you are, you fellow!" cried the young man. "You have only to write a name upon a bit of paper and drop it into a box."

"Sir, I cannot write," pleaded Wang anxiously.

"Get someone to write for you then. Oh, how ignorant you are!" said the young man, swallowing the last of his tea and throwing two pennies upon the table.

"Sir, I am a worm," replied Wang. "But what shall I write?"

"Write the name of the man you wish to be president," said the young man.

He spoke with such impatience that Wang Lung did not dare to ask, further, what "president" might mean.

By this time many people were listening to the conversation, and the young man, turning on the threshold and resuming his former manner, said with great emphasis: "Therefore, my countrymen, the time of prosperity is near. The rich will become poor and the poor will become rich."

Wang pricked up his ears. How was this—the poor become rich? He ventured timidly, fearing the young man's wrath. "Sir, how shall this be?"

"In all republics it is so," said the young man. "In America all men live in palaces, and only the rich are compelled to work. As soon as emperors are put away and the Revolution comes, these things happen. That is why my hair is cut off. It is to show that my spirit is free. I am a revolutionist. I and the other revolutionists will save the nation and uplift the poor and oppressed!"

He bowed and turned to go. Wang Lung still squatted upon his carrying-pole, whither he had withdrawn when the young man had been angry. He sat there now, in front of the door, staring as in a dream, and the young man could not pass because of him. "Out of my way, you!" the young man cried, and scornfully he pushed the pole with his foot.

Wang Lung rose hurriedly, removed his baskets into the street and then stood watching the young man as he walked away, his blue gown swaying from side to side.

Of everything said, Wang had really heard only this, that the poor would become rich. This hope he had cherished all his life, but of late years he had given it up as unrealizable. His ancestors had worked upon the bit of land he was cultivating, and none had ever become rich. But now it all seemed really true; now that the Emperor was dead, anything might happen.

He stared down the street, thinking, seeing the blue gown glow out of the gray distance. If he should become rich, he would have just such a gown as that, soft and bright and warm. He looked down his body upon his patched, yellowish trousers and upon his brown bare feet. He saw himself clothed with that warmth and brightness. But, as he bent his head, his queue fell down, rusty from sun and wind and uncombed for many days. "How can I wear my new gown with a head like this?" he muttered.

It seemed to him that the gown was already buttoned about him with the very same kind of small gilt buttons that had been on the young man's. So, although he had sold only a little green stuff, he counted his coins carefully and, going down the street to a traveling barber's stand, he shouted, "Shave my head entirely, and I will pay you ten copper pieces."

Thus Wang Lung became a revolutionist.

But he himself was not aware of the fact. When he returned to the village at evening, the villagers, idling about on the threshing-floors before the houses, saw him shaven like a priest and began to laugh. No one knew what to say except Wang Liu's only son, who went daily to school in the city and therefore understood more than the others. He cried now: "He is a revolutionist! My teacher says only revolutionists cut off their hair."

Wang Lung was very much embarrassed to hear this. He knew nothing of revolutionists, and he was afraid because he had inadvertently become that which he knew not. So he put down his carrying-pole with a loud noise, that he might not appear disturbed or unlike himself, and shouted to his wife as he did every evening: "Now then, Mother of Slaves, where is the rice? I have spent my precious breath all day to buy you food and, coming home at night in exhaustion, find not even a bowl of tea ready."

The villagers at once saw that he was acting as usual and dispersed from his door, merely marveling among themselves at his appearance. Nevertheless, the idle name clung to him. He was called "Wang the Revolutionist" from that day, and gradually the name ceased to have any meaning at all except as attached to him.

As for Wang, he thought for a long time of the blue gown he would have when he became rich. At first he daily expected this miracle to happen, and, as his hair grew, he kept it smooth with two fingers wet in bean-oil. But summer followed spring, and autumn died into winter, and the year gave birth to the new year, and his life was the same as ever. He still was compelled to work from morning until night, and he still had no sons. At last he became angry to the depths of his spirit, so that at night he could not sleep upon his bed.

It was not that any one thing overwhelmed him. Rather he was beset with many vexations, which augmented his rebellion at being destined, seemingly, to have no leisure in his old age. This idea made him so angry that he reviled his wife three times each day, saying, "Cursed is earth full of useless seed!"

Whenever he heard that other women had given birth to sons, he felt himself ill used and ground his teeth together. He was angry when the price of cloth and oil and fuel rose, while he could not wrest more produce from the land. He was angry every day in the city because he saw men idling along the streets in satin and velvet and sleeping over the tables in the tea-shop and gambling on the counters of shops, while he, on his way to the market, must bend his bare back under the load to feed them. In the end, the least thing angered him; a fly, settling on his sweaty face, made him shout and leap as if at a mad dog, so that, seeing him, people cried, "This is a madman who roars at a fly!" And the secret symbol of all his wrath was the blue gown he could never buy.

One day in the city he passed, as was his custom, through the Street of the Confucian Temple, and there upon a wooden box stood a young man, talking loudly. He was a mere white-faced lad, and he wore a long black cotton gown. He moved his thin, childish hands and looked restlessly over the heads of the people gathering around him. Wang Lung said to himself that he was tired and would therefore stop to hear this new thing. He sat down upon his pole and wiped his face with the towel that hung from his belt.

At first he could not understand what it was all about. He expected to hear something of emperors and republics, but instead this youth spoke of foreigners. He had a small voice, which cracked when he tried to speak loudly, and he cried: "They have killed us and trodden upon us. They are imperialists—robbers of all nations!"

Wang Lung listened, astonished. He knew nothing of foreigners. He had, it is true, always rather enjoyed seeing them; for they were strange to look upon and were a marvel to speak of in the village. But what manner of men they might really be, it had not entered his mind to inquire. He was not specially interested even now, and so he felt for his small bamboo pipe. At any rate he would blow a little tobacco before going on. And then he heard the lad scream in his high, wavering voice: "These riches are ours. Houses and lands and gold and silver they have taken from us. They live like kings while we are their slaves. Steam-wagons and music-machines, clothes of blue and red and yellow satin—like kings! Down with the capitalists! A thousand thousand years to the Revolution, when the poor shall become rich and the rich become poor!"

Wang Lung started forward and dropped his pipe. The poor become rich? Again? He pressed to the lad's side and asked with a sort of surly timidity, "Sir, when shall these things be?"

The youth turned fiery, unseeing eyes on him and answered: "Now, now! When the revolutionists enter the city, everything is yours. Take what you like. Comrade, you are a revolutionist?"

"I am called 'Wang the Revolutionist,'" answered Wang Lung simply.

But the youth was not listening to him. He was screaming again, "Down with the capitalists, down with the foreigners, down with religion, down with imperialism! A thousand thousand years to the Revolution, when the poor shall become rich and the rich become poor!"

When Wang Lung heard these words, he knew suddenly what revolution meant. Capitalism, imperialism, religion, these words meant nothing, but he understood that the poor should become rich and the rich become poor. Ah, he was a revolutionist, then.

He stood staring at the young man and, even as he stared, a policeman suddenly appeared with a fixed bayonet and, before anyone knew what he was about, placed it at the young man's back. "Off to jail then, young revolutionist," he said in a loud, gruff voice, "and let us see how quickly you will become rich!" The young man, suddenly turned into a yellow-faced wraith, descended without a word and walked away, the policeman propelling him gently from behind with his bayonet. The crowd disappeared like a cloud before the sun, and Wang Lung in great terror and confusion of mind picked up his baskets and trotted rapidly toward the market.

He was very much frightened, and he said nothing all day to anyone. In the evening, instead of sleeping over a bowl of green tea as he usually did, he harnessed the water-buffalo to the plow and plowed the sweet-potato field until the moon sank behind the willow-trees and he could no longer see the furrows.

The next morning he rose at an early hour to go to the market. When he approached the city gates, he saw that upon them were pasted large fresh sheets of paper covered with characters. At these he stared for a long time, wondering what they meant, but, since he had never been able to read a character in his life, he could make nothing of them. At last he asked an aged man who was passing to read them for him, discerning by the great horn spectacles and slow walk that this was a man of learning. The scholar stopped and read every word with great care, and Wang Lung waited patiently, although the sun rose higher and higher until its rays crept into the deep arch of the gate itself. At last the old man turned to Wang and said: "These words concern others than you, my poor fellow. They announce that revolutionists have been found in the city and have been beheaded."

"Beheaded?" gasped Wang Lung.

"Yes, indeed," answered the scholar, looking very profound. "And furthermore it says that, if you go to the Bridge of the Three Sisters, you will see their heads in a row. Our Governor will have none of these Cantonese rebels." And the scholar walked on, his skirts swaying from side to side in excess of dignity.

Wang Lung stood gazing at the crooked letters, sick with fear. Was he not called "Wang the Revolutionist"? He cursed the blue gown that had brought him to this pass. His desire for riches was quite forgotten, and some terrible dread drew him toward the Bridge of the Three Sisters. He left his baskets at the hot-water shop of an eighth cousin on his mother's side and went to the bridge, which was a mile away, although he could ill spare the time with his vegetables drying up in the heat of noon.

He saw that what the old scholar had said was true. There at the bridge, upon seven bamboo poles, were seven bleeding heads, bent on ragged, severed necks; heads with fringes of black hair hanging over their dull, half-closed eyes. One head had its mouth open and its tongue thrust out, half bitten off between set white teeth. Looking more closely at this head, Wang Lung saw with a leap of fear at his heart that this was the head of the lad to whom he had listened the day before. But then they were all the heads of very young men.

About the place stood a jeering crowd. An old man with broken teeth spat upon the ground and cried, "See what happens to revolutionists!"

Wang started at the word. Revolutionists? Suppose some who knew him should pass and call out, as his acquaintances so often did, "Ha, Wang the Revolutionist! Have you eaten?" It was an idle salutation, meaning nothing on other days but today meaning anything. He hurried off.

Thereafter he worked very hard indeed and spoke little. He did not even complain to his wife, so that finally she went in alarm to the blind sooth-sayer of the village and asked whether her husband was going to be ill. But the whole trouble was that Wang Lung continually beheld in his imagination an eighth head hanging beside the seven already there on the Bridge of the Three Sisters. In the evening, when he could no longer work, he saw very clearly his own dead face with half-shut eyes and drawn gray lips. When his third cousin passed the door and cried gaily, "What has Wang the Revolu-tionist heard today in the city?" Wang Lung strode to the door and cursed him a thousand years and would not listen to his words of astonishment. The hardest thing was the impossibility of telling anyone of his fear. To speak would have been to invite the knife to his neck.

From that day he hated everything. He hated the land that ate up his life and demanded increasing toil. He hated those neighbors of his, to whom he could not explain his fear; he despised the villagers, who were content to remain as their ancestors had been, clothed in coarse cotton and eating brown rice forever. He hated the city with its streets full of careless, idle people.

As his hatred grew, his fear lessened. He heard no more of revolutions and was all the angrier because he saw now no way for the poor to become rich. He thought about the rich and he hated them. He knew what these rich were like. Once a year he went to pay his respects to the gentry in the village, as the custom was, and there he saw satin curtains at the doors and satin cushions on the carved chairs. Even the servants were decked out in silk. As for him, he had never touched silk in all his life except furtively at a cloth-shop, that he might know its smoothness.

And the foreigners—the lad had said they were the richest of all. Some-times he heard in the tea-shops about them now. They sat upon chairs of gold and at tables of silver. They walked upon lengths of velvet as carelessly as he walked upon the wild grass at the side of the country roads. On their beds were covers of brocade embroidered with jewels. Riches! He grew to hate the foreigners more than anything else, because it was wrong that for-eigners should live like kings so long as there was one Chinese as poor as he. At first he had only longed for the poor to become rich, but, thinking of all the wrongs he endured, he longed equally for the rich to become poor.

Turning these matters over in his mind incessantly, he ceased to work so hard. Since he was not accustomed to so much puzzling, he found it impos-sible to hoe and to think at the same time. He was obliged therefore to stop when his thoughts became too much for him. Since he accomplished less than of old in one day, he became poorer and poorer until his wife cried at him: "I cannot say where the cotton wadding for our winter clothes is to come from. We shall not be able to feed our bodies within and clothe them without at the same time." This speech made him very angry, so angry that he ground his teeth together without knowing why.

One day in great heaviness of spirit he cast down his baskets carelessly at the tea-shop and determined not to work that day, come what might, since all his work brought him no nearer riches. He sat down at the table nearest the door and ordered a bowl of tea. There was another man at the table, a youngish man in a long black cotton gown, with short hair brushed straight up from his forehead. As he wiped his wet face on his towel, he looked at Wang Lung and said softly, "You work too hard, my comrade."

"I do indeed, sir," replied Wang Lung, sighing and pulling over his shoulders the patched gray coat he had taken off in the heat of the walk. "But how can it be helped? With rice what it is and a house full of idle women to feed, my flesh is torn from my bones in the day's toil."

"You are poor, bitterly poor," whispered the young man, bending toward him, "and you should be rich."

Wang Lung shook his head. He would not allow himself to be disturbed again by that word "rich" in the mouth of a young man. He poured himself a bowl of tea and sipped it loudly, thankful for its heat in his rapidly chilling body.

"You work and starve while others play and eat," continued the young man.

"That is true," said Wang Lung suddenly.

"Yet you are a good man and deserving of far more than they."

Wang Lung shook his head again, smiling a little.

"Yes, this is true," the young man insisted. "I can see it in your honest face. Allow me to pour you more tea." Rising, he poured tea into Wang Lung's bowl as courteously as if Wang's coat were whole and new.

Wang Lung rose to thank him, and to himself he said: "How wise this young man is! He discerns my quality at once." Aloud he said, "Sir, where is your honorable palace?"

But the young man answered: "Oh, I am a poor man, too. But I am come to tell you and your friends that you will soon be rich. When the revolutionists come into the city—"

Wang rose hastily to his feet. "I am no revolutionist!" he declared.

"No, no," said the young man soothingly; "you are a good man. I can see it."

Wang Lung sat down again. By now the sharp air felt icy upon his sweat-dampened skin. He pulled his garment more closely about him.

"You are too poor," said the young man. "I pity you with all my heart."

Wang Lung felt very sorry for himself. No one had ever pitied him before. Indeed some had even considered him fortunate, since, though burdened with a family of women and compelled to work hard, he was his father's only son and would some day own the six acres of family land and the three-roomed, mud-plastered house. So now, at the thought that somebody realized how very poor and hard-worked and pitiable he was, tears welled up into his eyes. "It is true," he said in a broken voice.

"And it is very wrong," the young man continued. "You are a clever man. I can see it. You deserve to be rich. I say it again. But your chance is coming. When the revolutionists enter the city, the poor will become rich and the rich will become poor."

"How?" asked Wang Lung, bending forward to catch the answer, since they were speaking very softly indeed.

The young man cast a hasty glance about. "The foreigners are surfeited with riches beyond anyone," he replied in a whisper. "They throw away silver as of no account, caring only for gold. The very walls of their houses are filled with gold—gold they have stolen from us Chinese. Else why do they remain in this country? Why do they not return to their own land? They take the gold from us so that you and I have none. It belongs to us. When the revolutionists come, be ready!" And immediately the young man rose and left the tea-shop.

Wang Lung, remembering the heads he had seen, did not like even to recall the young man's words. Only, when he thought of the gold possessed by others, especially the foreigners who had no right to it, he grew very bitter within. He said to himself, "Doubtless they have whole boxes of blue gowns like mine"; and suddenly he seemed to see the blue gown again in all its first beauty, and he was sick for its warmth and brightness.

Not more than a month later he heard that the revolutionists were approaching the city. He had not forgotten what the young man said: it must be that all the years of talk about the Revolution were coming true at last. In the market one day, when he was haggling with a customer over a pound of cabbage, someone whispered in his ear, "In ten days be ready!"

Turning quickly, Wang Lung saw the young man who had pitied him. Though he would have spoken, the man did not stay and the customer cried impatiently, "Now then, son of a robber, two coppers!"

Wang Lung was compelled to answer as usual, "Never! May I starve if I let it go for less than four!"

To himself he said, "Ten days? Well, we shall see it when it comes."

Thus he waited, half skeptical, half afraid. But it became evident soon that something was about to happen. Into the city poured silently like dark water from the river thousands and thousands of soldiers. He marveled, staring at the endless procession as it went by the tea-shop. "Are these revolutionists?" he asked the waiter.

But the waiter cast him a fiery look and hissed at him: "Be silent, O double fool! Do you want us all to be beheaded? Can you not see the coarse bones of these men and hear the rattling of the words in their throats and the way in which they swallow bread and refuse rice? These are Northerners, anti-revolutionists, and the heads of many fools like you hang at the bridge." Then, bending over Wang Lung to take his cup, he whispered, "In seven days be ready!" and he went quickly away.

Those words again! Wang Lung started. Ready for what? He was by this time wholly bewildered and, not daring to speak to anyone all that day, he went doggedly about his business, avoiding the main streets where the great stream of gray-clad figures continued to pass.

Then, on the evening of the next day, a terrific noise began to descend out of the sky. Thunder roared back and forth, and the very earth shook. They were eating their supper around the table, he and his father and his grandfather, while his wife and daughters waited on them. Putting down his chopsticks to listen the better, he discerned two noises, one a loud, intermittent bellow and the other a frantic pup-pup-pup, which he disliked very much because he had never heard any noise like it before. He rose to go out and investigate and then was afraid and turned to his wife. "Go and see what this is," he commanded.

She crept slowly along the wall and peered out. Something struck the earth at her feet and made her fall back; a fan-shaped spray of earth flew into the room and was scattered into the food and over the table. They were all smitten with horror; Wang Lung rushed to the wooden door, flung it across the opening and barred it tight. They sat there then in the darkness, not daring to light even the bean-oil lamp, hearing the earth as it struck upon the roof and the incessant broken noises that came out of the night. To himself Wang Lung said in dismay: "Is this the Revolution? We shall all be dead of it, and my life will be gone for a blue gown."

But the next morning the noise had died into the distance. Wang Lung peered forth from his door and at once grew very angry. His plots of vegetables were ruined with holes and buried under earth. He ran out and cursed Heaven, forgetting his fears of the night before in the catastrophe that had now befallen him. He collected a few heads of the remaining cabbage. There were not enough to fill one of his baskets. He went slowly into the house.

"It is the end of my days," he said mournfully to his wife. "The turnips do not mature for another month. What shall we eat?"

His wife sat down upon a wooden bench and rocked back and forth, wiping her eyes. "I am as good as dead," she sobbed. "Nothing but evil all my days! Nevertheless, sell the cabbage. It will bring something, and, that gone, we must starve until the turnips swell at the roots."

Wang Lung went therefore toward the city in great dejection. But, before he had gone a third of a mile, he stopped in horror. A corpse lay across the road! He stared, unbelieving. The man's blood spread over the dust, and the edges of the pool curled over. It was not well to be seen beside a dead body. Lifting his eyes to pass on, Wang Lung noted to his astonishment a dozen or more sprawling shapes and beyond these others. Had all the inhabitants of the city been killed by the wrath of Heaven on the preceding night? He ran breathless through the gates and found in the street a surging, singing, yelling mob.

"What is it, what is it?" he cried, speaking to the nearest men. But they were as people insane, struggling and pushing, and Wang Lung found himself swept on, unanswered, into the midst of the crowd. "What is it, what is it?" he continued to call loudly. But no one told him, and he could walk neither forward nor backward of his own will. He began to be afraid. "Why did I not send the Mother of Slaves this morning to the market?" he muttered to himself.

Then he heard a hoarse voice cry: "This way to the rich man's house! This way to the foreigners!" Instantly he knew what was happening. It was the Revolution. As his heart began to beat quickly, he gave himself to the multitude, only struggling to keep from being trampled. In the midst of the mob were soldiers, but not soldiers like the dead ones on the roadside. These were short, slender men, and they kept shouting in a sort of rhythm, "On—on—riches—riches!"

He grew dizzy. He did not know what it was all about, or what had happened. But he rushed on with the others until they came before a tall gate set in a brick wall. It was in a part of the city that he could not recognize. Ordinarily he would not have dreamed of entering such a gate as this. But today the wild daring of the crowd caught him, and he felt he had a right to anything.

Two soldiers struggled forward and pounded on the gate with the butts of their guns. He stared at them and saw that their faces were flushed as if with wine and their eyes terrible and glittering like glass. They beat against the gate again and again until at last a board gave way. Then they turned to the mob. "All is yours, now," they cried. "The poor shall become rich and the rich become poor. A thousand years to the Revolution!"

But the mob halted an instant, wavering. Then the boldest of those excited men and women crept through the hole and unbarred the gate, and afterward they all passed slowly in. Wang Lung was upon the outskirts, and, when he had crawled through the gate, he straightened himself and looked curiously about him for an instant at a square of smooth grass edged with trees and a row of many-colored flowers. It was very clean and quiet, and there was no one to be seen.

The crowd straggled toward the two-story house set at the end of a brick wall. No one seemed to know quite what to do. But the two soldiers sprang upon the steps and pounded against the door. Someone unlocked it instantly. Wang Lung had a glimpse of a tall, strangely clothed figure and a white, calm face.

Then the crowd suddenly gathered itself and surged into the house, with a loud, prolonged murmur like the howl an animal gives above its prey. Hearing it, Wang Lung was filled with a lust stronger than lust for food. He suddenly became fiercer than a wild dog and, snarling like the others, he rushed ahead, pushing and fighting through the narrow doorway. Once within, they halted; then they swept up a flight of stairs.

There the mob broke to pieces, becoming merely separate beasts that fought over a common booty. Wang Lung fought with the rest, although at no time did he see clearly for what he was fighting. Through his hands passed many things: cloth, glass, paper, wood. Once he caught the gleam of a bit of silver and laid hold on that, but, when it was snatched from him, forgot it to seize something else. He stopped to look at nothing, seeing always in other hands an object more desirable.

His eyes burned and blurred with his beating blood, and like the others he yelled incessantly without knowing that he made any noise. He was possessed of a greed so great that it left room for nothing else in his mind. Whenever a fresh closet or fresh drawer was opened, a score of struggling men fell upon it, fighting, pulling, tearing. Though his arms were full of things, he dropped them all and pressed to seize on what was newly discovered.

And then, swiftly, like a gale passing on a summer's day, the crowd swept out. Since he had been among the first to come into the house, he was now among the last to leave. He found himself alone at the end, and, like a man who wakes from a sleep, he looked around him. The room was bare of everything except two broken chairs, a small table and a chest of drawers with gaping holes where the drawers had been pulled out.

He came then to his right mind. What was he doing here? This was a foreigner's house. He looked at the chairs. They were of common wood. The table, too, was of cheap wood and not of gold, as they had told him. The walls were whitewashed and bare, and the floor was of rough, painted wood.

For the first time he looked curiously at the things in his hands. They were a child's garment of white cotton cloth, a large leather shoe, two stiff-backed books, full of strange characters, and a small, worn purse containing a dollar and some copper money. There was nothing even remotely like the blue gown.

He sighed and felt all at once very tired, and then he knelt and packed everything securely in the garment and turned to go downstairs. He had come up those stairs quickly and easily, but now he found them difficult and strange, since he had never been on stairs before that day. He shifted his bundle and clung to a railing and went stiffly down. He was quite exhausted.

Down-stairs there were still a few women, picking up articles that others had dropped in their haste. Wang Lung stopped, thinking he might see something of value. But there were only many books scattered about and one or two wooden chairs, another wooden table, a picture torn and trampled —nothing of any value anywhere. He saw a bit of gray cloth and stooped and, as he did so, caught sight of a little group in the inner room.

They were people such as he had never seen before—a man, a woman, two children, standing close together. Their clothes were torn and soiled and their upper clothes were entirely gone. The woman had drawn a piece of cloth about her shoulders. On the man's forehead was a cut, and a rill of blood was trickling down the side of his white face. Wang Lung had never seen blood so red.

He stared at them, and they looked steadfastly back at him in silence, even the children uttering no sound. He found this gaze difficult to endure at last. He looked away and then back again, and the man said something in a strange tongue. The woman smiled a little bitterly, and they all continued to look at him with their shining, steady eyes. "These people are not afraid!" Wang Lung said aloud, and then, hearing his own voice, he was suddenly ashamed and ran quickly out of the gate.

The streets were deserted, but in the distance he could hear the howling noise of the mob. After a moment's hesitancy, he turned and walked steadily toward his home. Still the dead soldiers lay on the road, and flies were beginning to gather from the hot sunshine. Country people were hurrying along toward the city. They asked Wang Lung many times what was taking place there, but he only shook his head. He was very tired of everything. He cared for nothing in the world.

When he reached home, he put his bundle on the table and said to his wife, "There is my share of the Revolution."

Then he went into the inner room and threw himself on the bed. He remembered nothing definitely except the strange clear gaze of those foreign eyes. "They were really not afraid," he muttered to himself. And then, turning over, he said, "I do not believe they were even rich people."

In the other room he heard his wife exclaiming, "These books are fit for nothing but to make shoe soles, but at least this dollar will feed us until the turnips can be eaten."

Roger Martin Du Gard

CONFIDENCE AFRICAINE

May, 1930

My dear friend:

You have urged me very flatteringly to give you "something" for your
readers. I was about to reply once more that everything that I have
to say passes automatically into my *Thibaults,* when it occurred to me
that I might copy out for you some pages from an old diary of mine. The subject is a conversation—a confidence, rather. It was told to me last summer on
the steamer coming back from Africa. My companion spoke without any regard for literary or moral considerations and I set down his story exactly as I
heard it. Perhaps you will not find it as interesting as it seemed to me then.
I wonder, too, whether you will see fit to offer your readers a narrative
which I admit is likely to shock some good people. Whatever may become
of these pages, I shall have given you proof of my good will and constant
sympathy.

But as I begin to copy them I see that they will hardly be intelligible without a few words of introduction.

Three years ago, in the course of an automobile trip in the Midi, I was
obliged to make a detour and stop at Font-Romeu, where little Frantz H.
was finishing his cure. I decided to speak to his physician and find out
on the spot if my pupil was really well and if he could safely return to Paris
to continue his studies. I was pleased to find Frantz in excellent condition.
He was waiting impatiently for the day of his departure, and I arranged to
spend a fortnight with him in order to take him on some excursions in the
surrounding region—one of the most beautiful in all France.

There were not many guests at the *Pension des Roches.* Frantz introduced
me to a youngish, dark-skinned man—an Italian—with a cordial expression
and mild, absent-minded eyes. His name was—for your readers, I shall call
him Leandro Barbazano. He had been there for six months, at the bedside
of his nephew—let us call him Michele Luzzati—a lad of sixteen who could
no longer get up at all, so near was the end: indeed, he died before the
end of my stay. Frantz spent a few minutes every morning and evening
in Michele's room; he was the only person the doctor allowed to visit him.
I myself had only one glimpse of Michele alive. I remember him better as
he lay in death—no more than a skeleton, but with the beauty of a Persian
prince. The window curtains were closed; no crucifix, no candles; not even
flowers: nothing that pertains to a funeral. In the dusk of the room, his
profile was outlined on the white pillow with a chiseled perfection that
would have seemed unearthly but for the smooth and gleaming skin of the
face, in which there still remained an indefinable appearance of life and

youth. The mute, animal intensity of the uncle's grief was agonizing to see. It surprised the professional attendants, who had been anticipating every day for five or six weeks the inevitable death of the boy.

Frantz's friendship with the nephew had brought me into daily contact with the uncle. People become acquainted quickly in health resorts. I liked Barbazano's simple and straightforward character at once. He was the son of a bookseller in a large city of Northern Africa which I shall designate only by the letter Y (Oran, Algiers, Constantine, or Tunis, as you choose), and he was continuing his father's business in partnership with his brother-in-law Luzzati, the father of Michele. The Barbazano-Luzzati firm, he told me, was the leading book store of Y. Leandro himself was a little crude, being of common origin, but he had a sufficiently cultivated mind, thanks to his reading and travels. He had served his apprenticeship in book stores in France, Switzerland and Italy; he spoke several languages and was familiar with the main currents of European literature. This formed the subject of our first conversations. Later he began to talk to me about himself and his nephew. I had been touched from the first by the maternal attentions which he lavished on Michele. I learned that he had left his home and his business three years before to attempt this rescue; he knew every little sanatorium in the Alps, the Jura, the Vosges; all treatments, all climates had been tried— in vain. Although all the doctors agreed that the boy had been tuberculous to the marrow from infancy and could never have been cured, Barbazano reproached himself for not having attempted to save Michele's health sooner, and this unjustified remorse was frequently the subject of frank talks between us, which did more to bring us together than all our literary discussions.

I was with Leandro during the slow passing of Michele. Those three days of waiting created a temporary but active bond of friendship between us. When the boy died I put my car at Barbazano's service for the necessary errands and formalities. Contrary to our expectations, Michele's body was not taken back to Africa: the Luzzatis wired Leandro to have their son buried in the little cemetery of Font-Romeu. I was struck by one detail: Barbazano had the watch, fountain pen, cuff links and other trinkets that had belonged to his nephew put into the coffin with him; then he had his linen and all his clothes burned in the incinerator of the pension. He was capable of tenderness, but he was not sentimental.

Frantz and I accompanied Barbazano in the funeral procession as if we had been his oldest friends. The burial was soon over: the passage from the hotel to the cemetery was brief, and there was no religious service. The next day we took Leandro to the station at Perpignan and, touched to the heart, saw him leave for Marseilles with only a tourist's suitcase in his hand and not a single souvenir of the child he was leaving behind him.

I resumed my trip north a few days later.

Barbazano wrote to me as soon as he had arrived in Africa. We exchanged two or three letters and a few cards; then our chance connection began to lapse. However, I had word from him the next year. He reminded me of a conversation we had had about the Fascist regime, repeated his wish to become a French citizen, and asked for my assistance. I did what I could for him, and a few months later he informed me that he had been naturalized.

Last summer when circumstances brought me to North Africa and to Y itself, I immediately thought of Barbazano. I let him know that I was coming. He met me at the wharf and greeted me in his usual fashion—undemonstratively, but with a masculine cordiality that was altogether authentic. He scarcely resembled the bowed, feverish, care-worn man from whom I had parted three years earlier at Perpignan. His pure Roman face, precisely modeled in spite of a slight fleshiness, had a serene and happy expression. On seeing him again I was struck with his resemblance to the death mask of little Michele, the extraordinary nobility of which, I believe, will always remain in my memory.

During the six weeks I spent at Y, Leandro Barbazano put himself out in a thousand ways to remove all difficulties from my path and make my visit enjoyable. I even had a little trouble in declining some of his proposals. He wanted to introduce me to the various groups of local writers and even had the notion of having me give a lecture in the muncipal theater. When I assured him that I was incapable of speaking in public and that I had absolutely no message to give to the people he wanted to assemble in my honor, I remember that he shrugged his shoulders and replied with a disarmingly authoritative air: "Come, now! You will do as your colleagues do. All the authors who come here give a lecture. The historians on history, the poets on poetry, the novelists on the novel. They talk about themselves, their works, their method of writing, their hobbies, their diet. And no matter how well they have taken care to stock the stores with their books, everything is sold out inside of a week." I nearly had to lose my temper and scowl at him for several days in order to escape this ritual exhibition.

But I am digressing. I will only add a word about the Barbazano-Luzzati book store. It was evidently one of the best in the city. Situated on one of the busiest corners, it was filled with customers all day long. At noon and at seven o'clock in the evening, a clerk lowered the iron shutter across the front of the store, leaving only a low, empty doorway: the store then ceased to be a bookshop and became a little gathering-place where men of letters, teachers, journalists, and students met when their work was over; there for an hour the latest minor publications from Paris were passed religiously from hand to hand. I too should have come willingly to the room behind the store for a daily chat with Leandro; but he always wanted me to stay for lunch or dinner, and rather than share those noisy and overabundant family meals I preferred to eat at the cook-shops I chanced upon while strolling through the native quarter. For Leandro lived with his brother-in-law and his sister. He did not appear to mind it in the least, and this surprised me, for they seemed very different from him.

Ignazio Luzzati was a very old man, with round shoulders and a puffy Levantine face; but behind his steel-rimmed glasses gleamed a pair of steady, determined, and very watchful eyes. He sat all day, like a buddha, on a dais at the back of the shop; too fat to climb the ladder or even come and go through the galleries of books, he had erected this overseer's platform from which he conducted all sales by himself, calling out remarkably exact orders to the young Jewish and Italian clerks, who had been trained to obey him like hunting dogs.

The sister of Leandro had such a gracious name that I cannot bring myself to change it—all the more as it was her sole adornment. She was called Amalia. Although much younger than her husband (indeed, he seemed more like her father), she too had a decidedly oriental corpulence. Certainly she wasn't beautiful: I should even say that her creased turtle-like eyes, her fat face, her oily complexion and her pear-shaped body, flabby and distorted from pregnancies and nursing, were calculated to make her a sovereign remedy against concupiscence. I understood her appearance better after seeing her gorge herself with a compote of figs steeped in fresh cream and honey. In addition to the platefuls of macaroni which she consumed at meal times, she munched sweets from morning to night, and nearly always talked with her mouth full. Her cash drawer was full of stuffed pistachios, dates, loukoums, and the change was always sticky. In justice I must add that there was something passionate and imperious about her gluttony that took away most of its repugnance. This voracity seemed to be the outlet, the last resort, of all a woman's ardor; it was almost pathetic.

About her swarmed a half-dozen little Luzzatis of both sexes, from fifteen years old down to two, all fat and dumpy, with chubby cheeks and round bottoms, and flabby as frogs; they were afflicted with hoarse voices and thick mops of hair and were all unspeakably vulgar. The thought that they were the brothers and sisters of the admirable Michele did not at first enter my mind; but when it finally dawned on me, the effect was stupefying.

When I was first introduced to the Luzzatis I thought it proper to say a word about the son whom I had virtually seen die three years before. "He had long been doomed," sighed Mme. Luzzati. I was disagreeably impressed by this conventional expression of sorrow. "Adipose tissue," I reflected, "retards all activities and even paralyzes the most natural feelings." The mother's indifference surprised me all the more when I turned to old Luzzati and saw that he was in tears. Thereafter I avoided mentioning Michele's name. But two or three times, perhaps, in the course of my visits and the meals I was obliged to take with the Luzzatis, Leandro or I referred to our meeting at Font-Romeu, and each time the eyes of Papa Luzzati silently filled with tears. There could be no doubt that Michele had been his father's favorite child.

I was recalled to France without having had an opportunity to go farther south. In any case, the season (it was the beginning of August) was unfavorable. To compensate for this, Barbazano offered to show me some of the sites along the coast. We devoted the last week of my stay to this excursion. Leandro was a well-informed guide, a sensible and congenial companion. I like these simple and candid people who are what they are and have no false pretensions. Leandro had a practical mind, trained by experience, direct and adaptable and free of all mysticism. His natural good sense reminded me of a mountain stream, cold, a little rough, but clear and lively. He was not obsessed by general ideas and he talked undogmatically, as a sincere man who had often had to change his opinions; but on most questions he had sound views, formed by contact with facts rather than by thumbing books. His conversation—and he spoke only when he actually had something to say—was always refreshing. His presence counted for a great deal in the happy memory which I have of that tour along the African shore.

Consequently, I was glad to learn on our return to Y that he had to go to Marseilles for a few days on business and that if I chose to wait for a later boat we could go together.

The crossing was ideal. Only a few passengers. Not a breath of wind, not an eddy in the water. When night fell, it was so mild and balmy that we did not have the heart to go below and sleep in our cabin but decided to wait for sunrise on deck, stretched out side by side in our canvas chairs.

It was there in that incomparable isolation, that Leandro spoke to me for the first time about his past, in words which I have scrupulously preserved and which I now copy down for you.

August 24

—Arrived at Marseilles yesterday morning. Said good-bye to Leandro after a last dinner together at the Vieux-Port. I, rather moved at leaving him. He, not at all: cordial, natural, as always, and perfectly matter-of-fact.

Shall be in Paris this evening, but shan't reach Beleme until Friday. Should like to take advantage of this railroad trip to set down the story Leandro told me on deck that fine evening of the 21st.

Had exchanged desultory remarks about modern literature—the timid progress of psychology in the contemporary French novel, the boldness of certain German and English novelists, etc. He mentioned the article in the *Revue des deux Mondes* in which I was criticized for having dealt with "questionable" subjects in my book—subjects that were deemed utterly "unlikely." He then made a vague remark, something like this, but in an unexpectedly irritated tone: "I don't know how people are made, Monsieur du Gard! Everything always seems unlikely to them. Isn't life made up almost entirely of unusual details?" The conversation dropped. Then he said, rather abruptly: "Look, Monsieur du Gard, this is the first time I've ever felt like telling this to anyone . . . You have seen our life at the store— Amalia, old Luzzati, their swarm of children. At first sight what could be less unusual, you think. Well, who ever knows? . . . If I were sure I wouldn't spoil this fine evening for you with my talk . . ."

My only response was to draw my deck chair up to his.

Now that I have decided (he said), I will tell you the whole thing crudely, just as it happened. But I must go back twenty years. And even farther, for the beginning. To our childhood.

We were brought up by our father—my sister and I. My mother died when I was three: I don't remember her. Amalia, who is four years older than I, was seven then. My father was extremely harsh and domineering. We didn't love him. You see—I warned you that I would be frank. He was the son of an Italian who had kept a newspaper stall. He himself had long since taken over this little business. He made money little by little and then opened this book store. He was almost illiterate. He had had a hard life. When he was married for the second time, to our mother, he was already aging. My sister and I never knew him except as an old man with a white goatee and decayed teeth and a hard skin that had gradually become lined with creases— just like a piece of wet parchment, you know, that has been left to shrivel in the sun. We never kissed him.

Very well. A little while after my mother died we moved to an old building at the entrance to the Jewish quarter. I must describe it to you because of what came later. It was at the corner of two streets. The book store on the ground floor was in a good location for selling. Behind it there was a back room and then a big kitchen that opened on a court. From the back room you went up by a little winding staircase—I can see it still—to the room on the second floor. It was fairly large but it was only one room. For several years all three of us lived there. I remember only a little about that time. I slept in my father's bed and my sister on a mattress in a corner. Amalia was probably eight or nine years old. She took her role of big sister seriously. She looked after me—got me up in the morning, washed my face, took me to paddle in the gutter in the court, and I believe she used to slap me, with permission.

A little later—I was beginning to go to school, I was about eight and Amalia twelve—there was a considerable change in our lives. We stopped sleeping in the room on the second floor. Our father said that he had attacks of asthma at night and was waking us up. I believe this was true. But Amalia later pointed out to me that this recurrence of asthma had coincided with the arrival of a serving woman who had been hired to do the cooking and gradually began to keep house for us. Not that it matters. Business was not going badly. Father had money. He rented a room for my sister and me on the fourth floor, on the same level as the terrace. We reached it by the main stairway for tenants. It was bright and cool enough, with white marble flagstones and glazed tile on the lower walls. It was quite deep, for Father had been able to divide the back part of the room with a sort of low partition made out of planks and old packing-cases. This gave each of us a long, narrow cell shut off by a curtain: just enough room for a bed, a night table, and a chair. The washstand was in front of the window, in the undivided part of the room; my sister and I took turns using it.

It was there that we grew up. We were very free, you understand. There was no one to oversee us on our top floor. But we did not abuse this freedom. The difference in our ages seemed to fade away year by year. We got along with each other perfectly. All the more because we had to endure Father's ill-temper together, storming from morning to night down on the first floor.

That period passed quickly. I was twelve—fourteen—sixteen. When I think of it, it must seem strange to you, a girl of twenty sharing her bedroom with a brother of sixteen. But I assure you, Monsieur du Gard, it surprised no one there. In the first place we had always shared the same room. And then that low partition between us gave us each a little nook of his own. And besides, in those days, families used to be crowded together any which way in those old tenements. Promiscuity like ours was quite commonplace.

Very well. Like all girls of her age, Amalia had a sweetheart. She was pretty enough, God knows. Her sweetheart was a boy of the neighborhood, an Italian like us, the son of a grain dealer. They would meet for five minutes at nightfall, at the corner of the alley behind the house, whenever my sister could find an excuse to go on an errand. Often too, thanks to me, they would meet on Sundays at the soccer match, when my sister was allowed to go with me. Amalia had no secrets from me. In our room in the evening, while we were undressing and long after we had gone to bed, we would talk endlessly about ourselves through the wooden partition. She would tell me about her

handsome Stefano and how she was going to marry him as soon as he had
done his army service. For my part, I didn't hesitate to enlighten her on my
first schoolboy sprees and my little affairs with the girls of the neighborhood.
We were really like two sworn friends. Don't imagine that I am telling you
all this simply to rehearse old memories. It is necessary for a full understanding.
Anyway, I am now coming to what I wanted to tell you.

Very well. I was seventeen years old. I had just taken my degree. That
rather impressed my father. Nevertheless, he refused to let me continue my
studies. He had put me to work in the store. But he did allow me to take
a few courses at the University, so that I had more freedom than an ordinary
clerk. I made good use of it. I was a healthy young fellow and God knows
I was interested in women. I had a lot of little adventures in the neighborhood; but momentary adventures—love affairs of twenty minutes, without
an aftermath. Sometimes on Saturdays when Amalia went upstairs to bed,
she found the water jar placed in a certain way which meant: "Don't worry,
I won't be in till midnight." But this didn't happen very often.

Then, that year at Easter, or perhaps Pentecost, the daughter of one of our
neighbors, a tenant on the third floor, came home for a vacation. Her name
was Ernestina. She was a swarthy little Italian, thin and wiry, a real alley-cat.
She was two years younger than Amalia and so two years older than I.
She had been our playmate in the old days and even as a child had drawn
me into corners to kiss. But we hadn't seen her for several years; her mother
had sent her away to work for an uncle who had an export business in the
south. I realized on our first meeting that Ernestina had learned other things
down there besides bookkeeping. The very day after her arrival she let me
take her up to the terrace of our house. There was a little wooden shed
there to pile the laundry in when it was dry. All told, it made a very satisfactory nook for a boy of seventeen and a girl of nineteen bent on having
a good time together. Ernestina was evidently determined to make the most
of her vacation and to have me make the most of it with her. The only idea
in our heads was to be together as much as possible. We had to invent ruses.
Her mother kept her in in the evenings. Several times, when Amalia was at
the cashier's desk in the store, I was able to take Ernestina to our room.
But that wasn't enough. We were becoming more and more avid. We
dreamed of having a whole night in each other's arms. It was she who found
the way: the last day, I don't know how, she managed to make a false departure, and while her mother thought she was on the way to the train, she
came in and hid in my room in order to spend the night there with me. I was
to take her to the station at dawn.

Naturally we had to tell my sister, and that seemed perfectly simple to
Ernestina. I remember saying to her: "Since you think it's so simple, settle it
with Amalia yourself; I don't want to talk to her about it." My sister had
known about our affair from the beginning. Just the same, I must admit it
embarrassed me to bring my mistress to the room where my sister was
sleeping and make love a few feet away from her. But we had talked freely
about such things for years. Besides, I didn't know for sure what experience
she herself had had; Ernestina said that Amalia knew as much as she did.
And then, there was that famous partition. And above all, the desire I had for

Ernestina did not leave much room for scruples . . . You see, I am telling you all this without embellishment.

To tell the truth, Amalia did not fall in with the scheme very gladly. I wasn't present when they discussed it, and Ernestina would tell me nothing; but all that day I could see from my sister's attitude that she was annoyed. Perhaps without entirely knowing why herself. I suppose that if she could have spent the night elsewhere she would have done so. I suppose. I am not absolutely sure; she may have been a little curious too.

It had been terribly hot that day. Ernestina had been in the room on the fourth floor since six o'clock in the evening, and I had gone up several times to kiss her and bring her something to eat. After dinner my father and Lucia sat out in front of the shop, as they often did, for a breath of air. Lucia was the housekeeper, who now lived with us. I sat down beside them so as not to give the impression of slipping away too soon. I wondered what had become of Amalia. Had she gone upstairs already? At dinner she had said she had a headache. By nine o'clock I was so impatient that I said good night and had the audacity to go off and leave the closing of the shutters to my father, contrary to all our habits. My father did not take such matters lightly.

Very well. I expected to find the two girls gossiping upstairs. Not at all. It was dark as night in the room and completely silent. I groped my way to my bed. Ernestina was there. She whispered to me: "Don't make any noise, Amalia is sleeping. She has a headache." Her breathing could be heard on the other side of the partition; she appeared to be asleep. But it was hardly nine o'clock, and her falling off to sleep seemed unnatural, after a day like that.

I admit I had something else to think of than Amalia's sleep, and that both of us very soon forgot that she was so near us. At the end of a few minutes we had abandoned even the most elementary discretion. It was quite a night, Monsieur du Gard, and Ernestina had no reason to regret missing her train. . . .

It was necessary for her to leave the first thing in the morning. As soon as it was dawn we had to dress hastily and slip out of the house. Amalia was still asleep. Ernestina did not say good-bye to her.

She was still asleep, or pretending to be, when I returned from the station. It wasn't more than five o'clock. I was tired and went back to bed. Then I got up again as usual at seven. A little later Amalia also got up as usual. I heard her putting on her shoes behind the curtain as I washed myself. She said good morning as if nothing had happened. But when she came out of her alcove I could see from her appearance that she hadn't slept a wink. I had finished washing. As usual, I made room for her and then went down to open the shop. Not a word about Ernestina.

We didn't get along very well the next few days. There were spats over trifles; and instead of laughing in a moment, as we used to do, we would remain hostile and sulk at each other the rest of the day.

Amalia seemed determined to be disagreeable to me. She trumped up all sorts of grievances. Thus, she took it into her head to get up as soon as she heard me getting out of bed and monopolize the washstand before me. She said: "Turn about's fair play—I'm tired of pouring out your dirty water."

It was absurd. There was no need for her to be downstairs before eight o'clock; whereas I had to have opened the shutters of the store by then and got the milk and bought the morning paper, if I didn't want to have a row with Father. He always had me read the paper aloud to him at breakfast. The first time, I let her have her way and went downstairs without washing. Very well. But the next day, when she started to do it again, I lost my temper. She was already in front of the basin, in her slip and petticoat. When she saw me coming, she splashed water at me. I am purposely telling you this in detail. Sometimes we used to scuffle in fun, but this time I was in no mood for fooling. I caught her from behind, lifted her up on my knee and carried her to her bed. She was heavy and kicked about like a fiend. I had my hands on her breast, and her buttocks were squirming against me. All this is very clear in my memory: I have often relived that ridiculous scene; moreover, it was that morning, that moment, in that transit from washstand to bed, that it first dawned on me that my sister was a woman made like other women, and even that she was infinitely more desirable than Ernestina. I threw her on her bed, cursing as if I were still furious with her. I remember that she suddenly ceased to struggle: I strode haughtily back to the washstand. I washed and dressed. When I left the room, she was still lying across the bed in the same position.

Very well. Let me go on. I had the habit of reading rather late at night. Amalia had never made any objection. Anyway, the partition separating us kept my little candle-end from bothering her. But she seemed absolutely bent on upsetting my ways. Now she got the notion of making me put out the light, on the pretext she was tired and I was keeping her awake. Naturally, I refused. Then she climbed up very quietly on her chair and blew out the light by waving a petticoat over the partition with her outstretched arm. I relighted it immediately. She began again. I can still see her over the partition, her hair tumbling down and a look of malice in her eyes. I am sure that she hated me that night and sincerely wished me ill. Decidedly, Ernestina's vacation had spoiled a number of things.

The next evening I had taken care to protect the flame, and when I saw her ineffectually shaking her petticoat over the partition, I burst out laughing without interrupting my reading. I heard her lie down again. I thought that that childish prank was over. But not at all! I was reading peacefully: suddenly I saw her leap towards me and upset the candlestick with her hand. Then it all happened in a minute. I lost my head completely. In two seconds I was on my feet and had her around the waist. Just what did happen? I am trying to remember everything as distinctly as I can. It was dark. I was wild with fury. So was she. She was a husky girl. I tried to overcome her, to throw her on the floor, with the fixed intention of thrashing any desire for further tricks out of her. We were pressed together in the dark, both in our nightgowns, and struggling like two madmen. Finally I lifted her off her feet. She clutched the back of my neck with her fingernails. I inhaled that scent of flesh still warm from the bed—the same odor that I had breathed all one night on the body of Ernestina. With a sudden movement, I bent her over backwards on my mattress. In the same instant I found myself caught between her two bare legs, which she closed behind me. I swayed. I fell on her. There wasn't much left of my anger, I confess—just enough to sharpen my desire. I sought her lips, furiously. I believe that she was awkwardly holding them out. . . .

And there you are.

You see how naturally things like that can happen. It's very simple even, when you think about it and trace everything back step by step.

Well, it went on for four years. Four years. Even a little longer. And I am not ashamed to tell you, Monsieur du Gard: they were the four happiest years—the only really happy years—of my life!

Amalia was a virgin when I took her. But she was—what shall I say—passionately inexperienced. I was seventeen, and except for Ernestina I had had only lucky escapades, often enough without even a bed—between two doors, in the corner of a cellar, beneath the trees in a park, in the fields. I didn't know what a continuous, daily union was. It is incredible how much love is augmented by the habits that grow up between two bodies. And then, of course, we were both ardent and quite insatiable, as one is at that age. This wasn't all. Looking back, I believe I can distinguish still another thing. When a man and wife are on good terms and have lived together a long time and become utterly used to each other's nearness, they are united by a very deep feeling, a wordless, internal understanding of which they are scarcely aware and which is quite indescribable. It is this that makes them a couple. Young people have no idea what it is like. Well, thanks to our seventeen years together, our intimacy of brother and sister, and to our having the same blood in our veins, we gained immediately that kind of secret understanding that settled couples have . . . But you will analyze all this much better than I can, Monsieur du Gard.

The strangest part is that no one around us ever suspected a thing. To be sure, we were careful to ward off suspicion. From time to time, on Saturday nights, I would ask my father for a little money to go and "shoot pool"; and the next day Amalia would tease me openly at the table for looking tired. For her part she broke off with the grain dealer's son and let herself be courted publicly by one of our neighbors, a rather stupid fellow who was satisfied to meet her occasionally in the street—just what was needed to create a little neighborhood gossip.

Well, it went on for four years. And no doubt it would have gone on still longer. But two things intervened about which we could do nothing.

The first was the approach of my military service. I had already taken a medical examination at the Italian consulate. At the end of the year I was to join a Sicilian regiment and spend two years in Italy. No way of getting out of it. I swear many a time I thought of deserting! If it hadn't been for my father, I might have done it. What a stupid trick that would have been!

The other thing came from my father. He was nearly seventy, and he had decided that Amalia should marry. Some time before, to better the business, he had hired a former bookseller from Naples, a hard worker, with age and experience, who was beginning to make our store one of the best places in the city. You have met him: it was Luzzati, my brother-in-law. He was about fifty years old then. He had saved up a pretty little nestegg. And he had a passion for my sister, silent but stubborn and intense, like himself. Father thought it an excellent match: at one stroke he would assure his own future and that of his children. Luzzati was going to purchase half of the business and get the daughter of the house into the bargain; and he promised to accept me as partner when my term of service was over. Thanks to this arrangement, my father, who was getting old and more and more asthmatic, could retire and live on his income without waiting until I was old enough to manage the store.

There was only one obstacle: the attitude of Amalia. Oh, she did not dare say no to Father. But she was evasive and kept putting off her reply to gain time. From the day Luzzati entered the household she had taken a dislike to him. Between ourselves she always called him "the old pig." She found him obsequious, repulsive. She heaped insults on him. She said to me: "I would rather kill myself."

Looking back, I have an unhappy memory of that year. It was the first time Father had encountered such opposition in his own family. You could see that he was boiling with suppressed anger. But I believe he would have turned his daughter out into the streets sooner than give up his plan. The months passed. Amalia held firm. In our room we forgot all that. Our passion was only intensified by those threats and by my approaching service. I was to embark at the beginning of October. Father's rage became terrible. He scarcely spoke at all to Amalia.

In the mountains towards the south, about a hundred kilometers away, there was a well-known vocational school in a sort of convent. It was managed by nuns; young girls were sent there for two or three years to learn all sorts of manual trades. Sometimes Father would speak of it significantly at the table while looking at Luzzati, who took his noon meal with us. One Sunday evening as Amalia started up to bed he followed her to the staircase and said, looking her full in the eyes: "If you don't consent by next Sunday I will take you to the vocational school, and you shall stay there as long as necessary." We knew very well that he would do as he said. You may object that Amalia was of age. But that was our way of life, Monsieur du Gard, and it never occurred to us that we could throw off our father's authority, no matter how old we were.

Amalia cried for several days. I did not know what to say to her. The thought of her marrying "the old pig" was as unbearable to me as it was to her. But the idea that we might be deprived of the three months we had left before my departure, was still more horrible. That was what decided her. She was heroic. She consented, but on the condition that the marriage should not take place before the end of the year and that until then Luzzati should not treat her as his fiancée or say a word to her about it. Father was beside himself. But Luzzati accepted; he even seemed happy. Amalia told me: "It's all the same to me, I will kill myself as soon as you are gone." And she was capable of it, Monsieur du Gard. It made me sweat to think of it. Finally I overcame my repugnance and told her: "Accept him. I shall be back in two years, and we will go to France together." She didn't even answer me. I am sure I would never have convinced her. But suddenly she had an idea of her own. An entirely unexpected idea. "Yes, I will marry him; but only if you will arrange to make me pregnant before then." You see? Since there was no way out, she consented to sleep with Luzzati and to be his wife for two years, if she was sure of having a child by me and of not having one by him. Very well. We "arranged" matters, and sure enough two months later we knew what we wanted. I was satisfied. I knew now that Amalia would not commit suicide and that she would wait for me.

I am reaching the end of my story—or nearly. But what I have left to say is not very cheerful.

I left for Sicily in October and they were married.

Seven months later Amalia had a child. A boy. As you have already guessed, it was Michele. He was only just alive, as if he really had been born prematurely: in the first year alone they nearly lost him a dozen times.

During all that year Amalia wrote ardent letters to me in secret. In every one she talked about my coming home and our running away together. I thought of nothing else myself, but naturally I could only write to her about trivialities. And then, little by little . . . the tone of her letters changed. One day she announced that she was pregnant again. Only that. I was more surprised than jealous. Frankly, I was beginning to think less about her myself. You will understand that: to enter into a new life at twenty is an intoxicating experience; and besides, there were pretty girls in Sicily. Then her letters became fewer. Finally I had a telegram announcing my father's death. In a word, when my service was over and I came home, I found Amalia heavier and full of her own life, with her two children— Michele always pale and sickly, and Giustina, that fat girl you've seen, who never made any difficulties about living and already appeared to be the elder. The first few days Amalia avoided being alone with me, I believe. Before her husband she did not seem at all embarrassed to see me. I was the one who looked like a fool. Did she consider the past mere childishness? Or had she simply forgotten how she felt then? You will believe this or not, as you choose, Monsieur du Gard, but *there was never anything between us again.*

Anyway, I stayed with them only a short while that time. The store was doing very well. I wasn't needed there. I persuaded my brother-in-law that it would be a good thing to let me go and study the book trade in France. And so I left. I served a stage of apprenticeship in Marseilles, another in Lyon, another in Geneva, and a fourth in Paris. I was there when the war broke out.

I returned to Italy. I worked for another stage in a book store in Rome. But not long. The Italian mobilization compelled me to rejoin my regiment. Ten months later I was a second lieutenant. I went through a lot. I don't say that to boast, I did no more than many another. But it helps to explain what happened afterwards.

When I found myself at home again in 1919, safe and sound, and home with them all at the Barbazano-Luzzati store—well, in spite of everything, Monsieur du Gard, life seemed pretty wonderful! My brother-in-law, who was feeling his age, gave me the heartiest welcome. Amalia, mother of a family now, seemed happy. I can see her as she was then. I can see the four children, sturdy and noisy and tumbling over each other from morning to night, around Michele's armchair. He would smile at them gently . . . Poor little fellow . . . Monsieur du Gard, telling this to you now, I should like to be able to say that it was solely because of him that I stayed there and settled down with them. And it is certainly true that I adored the child. But no, it wasn't because of him that I accepted their family life so easily. It was congenial to me. The past was far off and had no effect on me. The war had made a great break. My sister, Luzzati's wife, always pregnant or nursing a baby, with her fat little children and her old husband never reminded me—*has never since reminded me*—of the Amalia of my youth. That is the absolute truth.

And then, that store of ours had an attraction for me that no other book-shop could possibly have. Luzzati has always treated me as his employer. You have seen him there: he keeps the selling end, all the dull routine work, for himself. He has let me do a little publishing. I started that review. I built up those collections I showed you. I felt that I was happy. I was.

There was only one dark spot in that life—Michele's health. Even about that I deceived myself for a long time. He was never really sick. I would say to myself: "It's the heat, the climate . . ." or else: "It's only a phase—he'll grow out of it." I didn't see how he was fading away. I was hurt, though, to see that Amalia obviously cared more for his brothers and sisters. Oh, quite without thinking: it was simply that only the healthy ones were her true children. You imagine perhaps that Michele was a sort of living remorse for her, for the two of us? No. It might have been so. But it wasn't. I must confess one thing to you: it wasn't until very late that I myself realized my guilt in the matter. Very late: at Font-Romeu, and a little be-fore . . . Suddenly I told myself that I was responsible, after all, for that birth, that sickness, that martyrdom. And yet— Responsible? How can one know? As for my sister, I will swear she never thought of it. For her—without her realizing it, of course—Michele's death was a relief. Yes. And at bottom, Monsieur du Gard, it was for me too. In spite of the grief I felt, I am happy now. I am even more happy, more tranquil, than before. We are all happy. All of us together.

That is the way it happened, and nothing can change it.

He stopped. And it all seemed so simple to me that night that I had noth-ing to say.

(Here followed some notes of a professional nature, in case I might want to use this story some time as literary material. I shall not copy them all for you, my dear friend. I shall only set down these few lines in closing.)

. . . It would be necessary also to change the ending, as from the return from Sicily; and above all not breathe a word of my recollections of the obese Amalia of forty, enthroned behind the cashier's desk in the midst of her brats—or gobbling her honeyed figs—or letting her imposing breast flow out of her jacket to humor her last-born, a fat-cheeked urchin nearly two years old and still unweaned, who ate at the table with us and then at the end of the meal greedily scrambled up into his mother's lap to suck a few gulps of stale milk by way of dessert.

Eugene O'Neill

DESIRE UNDER THE ELMS

CHARACTERS

EPHRAIM CABOT

SIMEON

PETER } *His sons*

EBEN

ABBIE PUTNAM

Young Girl, Two Farmers, The Fiddler, A Sheriff, and other folk from the neighboring farms.

THE action of the entire play takes place in, and immediately outside of, the Cabot farmhouse in New England, in the year 1850. The south end of the house faces front to a stone wall with a wooden gate at center opening on a country road. The house is in good condition but in need of paint. Its walls are a sickly grayish, the green of the shutters faded. Two enormous elms are on each side of the house. They bend their trailing branches down over the roof. They appear to protect and at the same time subdue. There is a sinister maternity in their aspect, a crushing, jealous absorption. They have developed from their intimate contact with the life of man in the house an appalling humaneness. They brood oppressively over the house. They are like exhausted women resting their sagging breasts and hands and hair on its roof, and when it rains their tears trickle down monotonously and rot on the shingles.

There is a path running from the gate around the right corner of the house to the front door. A narrow porch is on this side. The end wall facing us has two windows in its upper story, two larger ones on the floor below. The two upper are those of the father's bedroom and that of the brothers. On the left, ground floor, is the kitchen—on the right, the parlor, the shades of which are always drawn down.

PART ONE–SCENE ONE

Exterior of the Farmhouse. It is sunset of a day at the beginning of summer in the year 1850. There is no wind and everything is still. The sky above the roof is suffused with deep colors, the green of the elms glows, but the house is in shadow, seeming pale and washed out by contrast.

A door opens and EBEN CABOT

comes to the end of the porch and stands looking down the road to the right. He has a large bell in his hand and this he swings mechanically, awakening a deafening clangor. Then he puts his hands on his hips and stares up at the sky. He sighs with a puzzled awe and blurts out with halting appreciation.

EBEN. God! Purty! (*His eyes fall and he stares about him frowningly. He is twenty-five, tall and sinewy. His face is well-formed, good-looking, but its expression is resentful and defensive. His defiant, dark eyes remind one of a wild animal's in captivity. Each day is a cage in which he finds himself trapped but inwardly unsubdued. There is a fierce repressed vitality about him. He has black hair, mustache, a thin curly trace of beard. He is dressed in rough farm clothes.*

He spits on the ground with intense disgust, turns and goes back into the house.

SIMEON *and* PETER *come in from their work in the fields. They are tall men, much older than their half-brother* [SIMEON *is thirty-nine and* PETER *thirty-seven*], *built on a squarer, simpler model, fleshier in body, more bovine and homelier in face, shrewder and more practical. Their shoulders stoop a bit from years of farm work. They clump heavily along in their clumsy thick-soled boots caked with earth. Their clothes, their faces, hands, bare arms and throats are earth-stained. They smell of earth. They stand together for a moment in front of the house and, as if with the one impulse, stare dumbly up at the sky, leaning on their hoes. Their faces have a compressed, unresigned expression. As they look upward, this softens*).

SIMEON (*grudgingly*). Purty.

PETER. Ay-eh.

SIMEON (*suddenly*). Eighteen year ago.

PETER. What?

SIMEON. Jenn. My woman. She died.

PETER. I'd fergot.

SIMEON. I rec'lect—now an' agin. Makes it lonesome. She'd hair long's a hoss' tail—an' yaller like gold!

PETER. Waal—she's gone (*This with indifferent finality—then after a pause*) They's gold in the West, Sim.

SIMEON (*still under the influence of sunset—vaguely*). In the sky?

PETER. Waal—in a manner o' speakin'—thar's the promise. (*Growing excited*) Gold in the sky—in the West—Golden Gate—Californi-a!—Goldest West!—fields o' gold!

SIMEON (*excited in his turn*). Fortunes layin' just atop o' the ground waitin' t'be picked! Solomon's mines, they says! (*For a moment they continue looking up at the sky—then their eyes drop*).

PETER (*with sardonic bitterness*). Here—it's stones atop o' the ground—stones atop o' stones—makin' stone walls—year atop o' year—him 'n' yew 'n' me 'n' then Eben—makin' stone walls fur him to fence us in!

SIMEON. We've wuked. Give our strength. Give our years. Plowed 'em under in the ground,—(*he stamps rebelliously*)—rottin'—makin' soil for his crops! (*a pause*) Waal—the farm pays good for hereabouts.

PETER. If we plowed in Californi-a, they'd be lumps o' gold in the furrow!

SIMEON. Californi-a's t'other side o' earth, a'most. We got t' calc'late—

PETER (*after a pause*). 'Twould be hard fur me, too, to give up what we've 'arned here by our sweat. (*A pause.* EBEN *sticks his head out of the dining-room window, listening*).

SIMEON. Ay-eh. (*A pause*) Mebbe —he'll die soon.

PETER (*doubtfully*). Mebbe.

SIMEON. Mebbe—fur all we knows —he's dead now.

PETER. Ye'd need proof.

SIMEON. He's been gone two months—with no word.

PETER. Left us in the fields an evenin' like this. Hitched up an' druv off into the West. That's plum onnateral. He hain't never been off this farm 'ceptin' t' the village in thirty year or more, not since he married Eben's maw. (*A pause. Shrewdly*) I calc'late we might git him declared crazy by the court.

SIMEON. He skinned 'em too slick. He got the best o' all on 'em. They'd never b'lieve him crazy. (*A pause*) We got t' wait—till he's under ground.

EBEN (*with a sardonic chuckle*). Honor thy father! (*They turn, startled, and stare at him. He grins, then scowls*) I pray he's died. (*They stare at him. He continues matter-of-factly*) Supper's ready.

SIMEON *and* PETER (*together*). Ay-eh.

EBEN (*gazing up at the sky*). Sun's downin' purty.

SIMEON *and* PETER (*together*). Ay-eh. They's gold in the West.

EBEN. Ay-eh (*Pointing*). Yonder atop o' the hill pasture, ye mean?

SIMEON *and* PETER (*together*). In Californi-a!

EBEN. Hunh? (*Stares at them indifferently for a second, then drawls*) Waal—supper's gittin' cold. (*He turns back into kitchen*).

SIMEON (*startled—smacks his lips*). I air hungry!

PETER (*sniffing*). I smells bacon!

SIMEON (*with hungry appreciation*). Bacon's good!

PETER (*in same tone*). Bacon's bacon! (*They turn, shouldering each other, their bodies bumping and rubbing together as they hurry clumsily to their food, like two friendly oxen toward their evening meal. They disappear around the right corner of house and can be heard entering the door*).

CURTAIN

SCENE TWO

The color fades from the sky. Twilight begins. The interior of the kitchen is now visible. A pine table is at center, a cookstove in the right rear corner, four rough wooden chairs, a tallow candle on the table. In the middle of the rear wall is fastened a big advertising poster with a ship in full sail and the word "California" in big letters. Kitchen utensils hang from nails. Everything is neat and in order but the atmosphere is of a men's camp kitchen rather than that of a home.

Places for three are laid. EBEN takes boiled potatoes and bacon from the stove and puts them on the table, also a loaf of bread and a crock of water. SIMEON and PETER shoulder in, slump down in their chairs without a word. EBEN joins them. The three eat in silence for a moment, the two elder as naturally unrestrained as beasts of the field, EBEN picking at his food without appetite, glancing at them with a tolerant dislike.

SIMEON (*suddenly turns to EBEN*). Looky here! Ye'd oughtn't t' said that, Eben.

PETER. 'Twa'n't righteous.

EBEN. What?

SIMEON. Ye prayed he'd died.

Eugene O'Neill

EBEN. Waal—don't yew pray it? (*A pause*).

PETER. He's our Paw.

EBEN (*violently*). Not mine!

SIMEON (*dryly*). Ye'd not let no one else say that about yer Maw! Ha! (*He gives one abrupt sardonic guffaw.* PETER *grins*).

EBEN (*very pale*). I meant—I hain't his'n—I hain't like him—he hain't me!

PETER (*dryly*). Wait till ye've growed his age!

EBEN (*intensely*). I'm Maw—every drop o' blood! (*A pause. They stare at him with indifferent curiosity*).

PETER (*reminiscently*). She was good t' Sim 'n' me. A good Stepmaw's scurse.

SIMEON. She was good t' everyone.

EBEN (*greatly moved, gets to his feet and makes an awkward bow to each of them—stammering*). I be thankful t' ye. I'm her—her heir. (*He sits down in confusion*).

PETER (*after a pause—judicially*). She was good even t' him.

EBEN (*fiercely*). An' fur thanks he killed her!

SIMEON (*after a pause*). No one never kills nobody. It's allus somethin'. That's the murderer.

EBEN. Didn't he slave Maw t' death?

PETER. He's slaved himself t' death. He's slaved Sim 'n' me 'n' yew t' death—on'y none o' us hain't died—yit.

SIMEON. It's somethin'—drivin' him —t' drive us!

EBEN (*vengefully*). Waal—I hold him t' jedgment! (*Then scornfully*) Somethin'! What's somethin'?

SIMEON. Dunno.

EBEN (*sardonically*). What's drivin' yew to Californi-a, mebbe? (*They look at him in surprise*) Oh, I've heerd ye! (*Then, after a pause*) But ye'll never go t' the gold fields!

PETER (*assertively*). Mebbe!

EBEN. Whar'll ye git the money?

PETER. We kin walk. It's an a'mighty ways—Californi-a—but if yew was t' put all the steps we've walked on this farm end t' end we'd be in the moon!

EBEN. The Injuns'll skulp ye on the plains.

SIMEON (*with grim humor*). We'll mebbe make 'em pay a hair fur a hair!

EBEN (*decisively*). But t'aint that. Ye won't never go because ye'll wait here fur yer share o' the farm, thinkin' allus he'll die soon.

SIMEON (*after a pause*). We've a right.

PETER. Two-thirds belongs t'us.

EBEN (*jumping to his feet*). Ye've no right! She wa'n't yewr Maw! It was her farm! Didn't he steal it from her? She's dead. It's my farm.

SIMEON (*sardonically*). Tell that t' Paw—when he comes! I'll bet ye a dollar he'll laugh—fur once in his life. Ha! (*He laughs himself in one single mirthless bark*).

PETER (*amused in turn, echoes his brother*). Ha!

SIMEON (*after a pause*). What've ye got held agin us, Eben? Year arter year it's skulked in yer eye—somethin'.

PETER. Ay-eh.

EBEN. Ay-eh. They's somethin'. (*Suddenly exploding*) Why didn't ye never stand between him 'n' my Maw when he was slavin' her to her grave—t' pay her back fur the kindness she done t' yew? (*There is a long pause. They stare at him in surprise*).

SIMEON. Waal—the stock'd got t' be watered.

PETER. 'R they was woodin' t' do.

SIMEON. 'R plowin'.

PETER. 'R hayin'.

SIMEON. 'R spreadin' manure.

PETER. 'R weedin'.

SIMEON. 'R prunin'.

PETER. 'R milkin'.

EBEN (*breaking in harshly*). An' makin' walls—stone atop o' stone—makin' walls till yer heart's a stone ye heft up out o' the way o' growth onto a stone wall t' wall in yer heart!

SIMEON (*matter-of-factly*). We never had no time t' meddle.

PETER (*to* EBEN) Yew was fifteen afore yer Maw died—an' big fur yer age. Why didn't ye never do nothin'?

EBEN (*harshly*). They was chores t' do, wa'n't they? (*A pause—then slowly*) It was on'y arter she died I come to think o' it. Me cookin'—doin' her work—that made me know her, suffer her sufferin'—she'd come back t' help—come back t' bile potatoes—come back t' fry bacon—come back t' bake biscuits—come back all cramped up t' shake the fire, an' carry ashes, her eyes weepin' an' bloody with smoke an' cinders same's they used t' be. She still comes back—stands by the stove thar in the evenin'—she can't find it nateral sleepin' an' restin' in peace. She can't git used t' bein' free—even in her grave.

SIMEON. She never complained none.

EBEN. She'd got too tired. She'd got too used t' bein' too tired. That was what he done. (*With vengeful passion*) An' sooner'r later, I'll meddle. I'll say the thin's I didn't say then t' him! I'll yell 'em at the top o' my lungs. I'll see t' it my Maw gits some rest an' sleep in her grave! (*He sits down again, relapsing into a brooding silence. They look at him with a queer indifferent curiosity*).

PETER (*after a pause*). Whar in tarnation d'ye s'pose he went, Sim?

SIMEON. Dunno. He druv off in the buggy, all spick an' span, with the mare all breshed an' shiny, druv off

clackin' his tongue an' wavin' his whip. I remember it right well. I was finishin' plowin', it was spring an' May an' sunset, an' gold in the West, an' he druv off into it. I yells "Whar ye goin', Paw?" an' he hauls up by the stone wall a jiffy. His old snake's eyes was glitterin' in the sun like he'd been drinkin' a jugful an' he says with a mule's grin: "Don't ye run away till I come back!"

PETER. Wonder if he knowed we was wantin' fur Californi-a?

SIMEON. Mebbe. I didn't say nothin' and he says, lookin' kinder queer an' sick: "I been hearin' the hens cluckin' an' the roosters crowin' all the durn day. I been listenin' t' the cows lowin' an' everythin' else kickin' up till I can't stand it no more. It's spring an' I'm feelin' damned," he says. "Damned like an old bare hickory tree fit on'y fur burnin'," he says. An' then I calc'late I must've looked a mite hopeful, fur he adds real spry and vicious: "But don't git no fool idee I'm dead. I've sworn t' live a hundred an' I'll do it, if on'y t' spite yer sinful greed! An' now I'm ridin' out t' learn God's message t' me in the spring, like the prophets done. An' yew git back t' yer plowin'," he says. An' he druv off singin' a hymn. I thought he was drunk—'r I'd stopped him goin'.

EBEN (*scornfully*). No, ye wouldn't! Ye're scared o' him. He's stronger—inside—than both o' ye put together!

PETER (*sardonically*). An' yew—be yew Samson?

EBEN. I'm gittin' stronger. I kin feel it growin' in me—growin' an' growin'—till it'll bust out—! (*He gets up and puts on his coat and a hat. They watch him, gradually breaking into grins. EBEN avoids their eyes sheepishly*) I'm goin' out fur a spell—up the road.

PETER. T' the village?

SIMEON. T' see Minnie?

EBEN (*defiantly*). Ay-eh!

PETER (*jeeringly*). The Scarlet Woman!

SIMEON. Lust—that's what's growin' in ye!

EBEN. Waal—she's purty!

PETER. She's been purty fur twenty year!

SIMEON. A new coat o' paint'll make a heifer out of forty.

EBEN. She hain't forty!

PETER. If she hain't, she's teeterin' on the edge.

EBEN (*desperately*). What d'yew know—

PETER. All they is . . . Sim knew her—an' then me arter—

SIMEON. An' Paw kin tell yew somethin' too! He was fust!

EBEN. D'ye mean t' say he . . . ?

SIMEON (*with a grin*). Ay-eh! We air his heirs in everythin'!

EBEN (*intensely*). That's more to it! That grows on it! It'll bust soon! (*Then violently*) I'll go smash my fist in her face! (*He pulls open the door in rear violently*).

SIMEON (*with a wink at* PETER—*drawlingly*). Mebbe—but the night's wa'm—purty—by the time ye git thar mebbe ye'll kiss her instead!

PETER. Sart'n he will! (*They both roar with coarse laughter.* EBEN *rushes out and slams the door—then the outside front door—comes around the corner of the house and stands still by the gate, staring up at the sky*).

SIMEON (*looking after him*). Like his Paw.

PETER. Dead spit an' image!

SIMEON. Dog'll eat dog!

PETER. Ay-eh. (*Pause. With yearning*) Mebbe a year from now we'll be in Californi-a.

SIMEON. Ay-eh. (*A pause. Both yawn*) Let's git t'bed. (*He blows out the candle. They go out door in rear.*

EBEN *stretches his arms up to the sky—rebelliously*).

EBEN. Waal—thar's a star, an' somewhar's they's him, an' here's me, an' thar's Min up the road—in the same night. What if I does kiss her? She's like t'night, she's soft 'n' wa'm, her eyes kin wink like a star, her mouth's wa'm, her arms're wa'm, she smells like a wa'm plowed field, she's purty . . . Ay-eh! By God A'mighty she's purty, an' I don't give a damn how many sins she's sinned afore mine or who she's sinned 'em with, my sin's as purty as any one on 'em! (*He strides off down the road to the left*).

SCENE THREE

It is the pitch darkness just before dawn. EBEN *comes in from the left and goes around to the porch, feeling his way, chuckling bitterly and cursing half-aloud to himself.*

EBEN. The cussed old miser! (*He can be heard going in the front door. There is a pause as he goes upstairs, then a loud knock on the bedroom door of the brothers*) Wake up!

SIMEON (*startedly*). Who's thar?

EBEN (*pushing open the door and coming in, a lighted candle in his hand. The bedroom of the brothers is revealed. Its ceiling is the sloping roof. They can stand upright only close to the center dividing wall of the upstairs.* SIMEON *and* PETER *are in a double bed, front.* EBEN'S *cot is to the rear.* EBEN *has a mixture of silly grin and vicious scowl on his face*) I be!

PETER (*angrily*). What in hell's-fire . . . ?

EBEN. I got news fur ye! Ha! (*He

gives one abrupt sardonic guffaw).

SIMEON (*angrily*). Couldn't ye hold it 'til we'd got our sleep?

EBEN. It's nigh sunup. (*Then explosively*) He's gone an' married agen!

SIMEON *and* PETER (*explosively*) Paw?

EBEN. Got himself hitched to a female 'bout thirty-five—an' purty, they says . . .

SIMEON (*aghast*). It's a durn lie!

PETER. Who says?

SIMEON. They been stringin' ye!

EBEN. Think I'm a dunce, do ye? The hull village says. The preacher from New Dover, he brung the news —told it t'our preacher—New Dover, that's whar the old loon got himself hitched—that's whar the woman lived—

PETER (*no longer doubting—stunned*). Waal . . . !

SIMEON (*the same*). Waal . . . !

EBEN (*sitting down on a bed—with vicious hatred*). Ain't he a devil out o' hell? It's jest t' spite us —the damned old mule!

PETER (*after a pause*). Everythin'll go t' her now.

SIMEON. Ay-eh. (*A pause—dully*) Waal—if it's done—

PETER. It's done us. (*Pause—then persuasively*) They's gold in the fields o' Californi-a, Sim. No good a-stayin' here now.

SIMEON. Jest what I was a-thinkin'. (*Then with decision*) S'well fust's last! Let's light out and git this mornin'.

PETER. Suits me.

EBEN. Ye must like walkin'.

SIMEON (*sardonically*). If ye'd grow wings on us we'd fly thar!

EBEN. Ye'd like ridin' better—on a boat, wouldn't ye? (*Fumbles in his pocket and takes out a crumpled sheet of foolscap*) Waal, if ye sign this ye kin ride on a boat. I've had

it writ out an' ready in case ye'd ever go. It says fur three hundred dollars t' each ye agree yewr shares o' the farm is sold t' me. (*They look suspiciously at the paper. A pause*).

SIMEON (*wonderingly*). But if he's hitched agen—

PETER. An' whar'd yew git that sum o' money, anyways?

EBEN (*cunningly*). I know whar it's hid. I been waitin'—Maw told me. She knew whar it lay fur years, but she was waitin' . . . It's her'n —the money he hoarded from her farm an' hid from Maw. It's my money by rights now.

PETER. Whar's it hid?

EBEN (*cunningly*). Whar yew won't never find it without me. Maw spied on him—'r she'd never knowed. (*A pause. They look at him suspiciously, and he at them*) Waal, is it fa'r trade?

SIMEON. Dunno.

PETER. Dunno.

SIMEON (*looking at window*). Sky's grayin'.

PETER. Ye better start the fire, Eben.

SIMEON. An' fix some vittles.

EBEN. Ay-eh. (*Then with a forced jocular heartiness*) I'll git ye a good one. If ye're startin' t' hoof it t' Californi-a ye'll need somethin' that'll stick t' yer ribs. (*He turns to the door, adding meaningly*) But ye kin ride on a boat if ye'll swap. (*He stops at the door and pauses. They stare at him*).

SIMEON (*suspiciously*). Whar was ye all night?

EBEN (*defiantly*). Up t' Min's. (*Then slowly*) Walkin' thar, fust I felt 's if I'd kiss her; then I got a-thinkin' o' what ye'd said o' him an' her an' I says, I'll bust her nose fur that! Then I got t' the village an' heerd the news an' I got madder'n hell an' run all the way t' Min's not knowin' what I'd do— (*He pauses—then sheepishly but more defiantly*) Waal—when I seen her, I didn't hit her—nor I didn't kiss her nuther—I begun t' beller like a calf an' cuss at the same time, I was so durn mad—an' she got scared —an' I jest grabbed holt an' tuk her! (*Proudly*) Yes, sirree! I tuk her. She may've been his'n—an' your'n, too— but she's mine now!

SIMEON (*dryly*). In love, air yew?

EBEN (*with lofty scorn*). Love! I don't take no stock in sech slop!

PETER (*winking at* SIMEON). Mebbe Eben's aimin' t' marry, too.

SIMEON. Min'd make a true faithful he'pmeet! (*They snicker*).

EBEN. What do I care fur her— 'ceptin' she's round an' wa'm? The p'int is she was his'n—an' now she b'longs t' me! (*He goes to the door —then turns—rebelliously*) An' Min hain't sech a bad un. They's worse'n Min in the world, I'll bet ye! Wait'll we see this cow the Old Man's hitched t'! She'll beat Min, I got a notion! (*He starts to go out*).

SIMEON (*suddenly*). Mebbe ye'll try t' make her your'n, too?

PETER. Ha! (*He gives a sardonic laugh of relish at this idea*).

EBEN (*spitting with disgust*). Her —here—sleepin' with him—stealin' my Maw's farm! I'd as soon pet a skunk 'r kiss a snake! (*He goes out. The two stare after him suspiciously. A pause. They listen to his steps receding*).

PETER. He's startin' the fire.

SIMEON. I'd like t' ride t' Californ-a—but—

PETER. Min might o' put some scheme in his head.

SIMEON. Mebbe it's all a lie 'bout Paw marryin'. We'd best wait an' see the bride.

PETER. An' don't sign nothin' till we does!

SIMEON. Nor till we've tested it's good money! (*Then with a grin*) But if Paw's hitched we'd be sellin' Eben somethin' we'd never git no-how!

PETER. We'll wait an' see. (*Then with sudden vindictive anger*) An' till he comes, let's yew 'n' me not wuk a lick, let Eben tend to thin's if he's a mind t', let's us jest sleep an' eat an' drink likker, an' let the hull damned farm go t' blazes!

SIMEON (*excitedly*). By God, we've 'arned a rest! We'll play rich fur a change. I hain't a-going to stir outa bed till breakfast's ready.

PETER. An' on the table!

SIMEON (*after a pause—thoughtfully*). What d'ye calc'late she'll be like—our new Maw? Like Eben thinks?

PETER. More'n' likely.

SIMEON (*vindictively*). Waal—I hope she's a she-devil that'll make him wish he was dead an' livin' in the pit o' hell fur comfort!

PETER (*fervently*). Amen!

SIMEON (*imitating his father's voice*). "I'm ridin' out t' learn God's message t' me in the spring like the prophets done," he says. I'll bet right then an' thar he knew plumb well he was goin' whorin', the stinkin' old hypocrite!

SCENE FOUR

Same as Scene Two—shows the interior of the kitchen with a lighted candle on table. It is gray dawn outside. SIMEON *and* PETER *are just finishing their breakfast.* EBEN *sits before his plate of untouched food, brooding frowningly.*

PETER (*glancing at him rather irritably*). Lookin' glum don't help none.

SIMEON (*sarcastically*). Sorrowin' over his lust o' the flesh!

PETER (*with a grin*). Was she yer fust?

EBEN (*angrily*). None o' yer business. (*A pause*) I was thinkin' o' him. I got a notion he's gittin' near—I kin feel him comin' on like yew kin feel malaria chill afore it takes ye.

PETER. It's too early yet.

SIMEON. Dunno. He'd like t' catch us nappin'—jest t' have somethin' t' hoss us 'round over.

PETER (*mechanically gets to his feet.* SIMEON *does the same*). Waal —let's git t' wuk. (*They both plod mechanically toward the door before they realize. Then they stop short*).

SIMEON (*grinning*). Ye're a cussed fool, Pete—and I be wuss! Let him see we hain't wukin'! We don't give a durn!

PETER (*as they go back to the table*). Not a damned durn! It'll serve t' show him we're done with him. (*They sit down again.* EBEN *stares from one to the other with surprise*).

SIMEON (*grins at him*). We're aimin' t' start bein' lilies o' the field.

PETER. Nary a toil 'r spin 'r lick o' wuk do we put in!

SIMEON. Ye're sole owner—till he comes—that's what ye wanted. Waal, ye got t' be sole hand, too.

PETER. The cows air bellerin'. Ye better hustle at the milkin'.

EBEN (*with excited joy*). Ye mean ye'll sign the paper?

SIMEON (*dryly*). Mebbe.

PETER. *Mebbe.*

SIMEON. We're considerin'. (*Peremptorily*) Ye better git t' wuk.

EBEN (*with queer excitement*). It's Maw's farm agen! It's my farm! Them's my cows! I'll milk my durn fingers off fur cows o' mine! (*He goes out door in rear, they stare after him indifferently*).

SIMEON. Like his Paw.

PETER. Dead spit 'n' image!

SIMEON. Waal—let dog eat dog! (*EBEN comes out of front door and around the corner of the house. The sky is beginning to grow flushed with sunrise.* EBEN *stops by the gate and stares around him with glowing, possessive eyes. He takes in the whole farm with his embracing glance of desire*).

EBEN. It's purty! It's damned purty! It's mine! (*He suddenly throws his head back boldly and glares with hard, defiant eyes at the sky*) Mine, d'ye hear? Mine! (*He turns and walks quickly off left, rear, toward the barn. The two brothers light their pipes*).

SIMEON (*putting his muddy boots up on the table, tilting back his chair, and puffing defiantly*). Waal—this air solid comfort—fur once.

PETER. Ay-eh. (*He follows suit. A pause. Unconsciously they both sigh*).

SIMEON (*suddenly*). He never was much o' a hand at milkin', Eben wa'n't.

PETER (*with a snort*). His hands air like hoofs! (*A pause*).

SIMEON. Reach down the jug thar! Let's take a swaller. I'm feelin' kind o' low.

PETER. Good idee! (*He does so—gets two glasses—they pour out drinks of whisky*) Here's t' the gold in Californi-a!

SIMEON. An' luck t' find it! (*They drink—puff resolutely—sigh—take their feet down from the table*).

PETER. Likker don't pear t' sot right.

SIMEON. We hain't used t' it this early. (*A pause. They become very restless*).

PETER. Gittin' close in this kitchen.

SIMEON (*with immense relief*). Let's git a breath o' air. (*They arise briskly and go out rear—appear around house and stop by the gate. They stare up at the sky with a numbed appreciation*).

PETER. Purty!

SIMEON. Ay-eh. Gold's t' the East now.

PETER. Sun's startin' with us fur the Golden West.

SIMEON (*staring around the farm, his compressed face tightened, unable to conceal his emotion*). Waal—it's our last mornin'—mebbe.

PETER (*the same*). Ay-eh.

SIMEON (*stamps his foot on the earth and addresses it desperately*). Waal—ye've thirty year o' me buried in ye—spread out over ye—blood an' bone an' sweat—rotted away—fertilizin' ye—richin' yer soul—prime manure, by God, that's what I been t' ye!

PETER. Ay-eh! An' me!

SIMEON. An' yew, Peter. (*He sighs—then spits*) Waal—no use'n cryin' over spilt milk.

PETER. They's gold in the West—an' freedom, mebbe. We been slaves t' stone walls here.

SIMEON (*defiantly*). We hain't nobody's slaves from this out—nor no thin's slaves nuther. (*A pause—restlessly*) Speakin' o' milk, wonder how Eben's managin'?

PETER. I s'pose he's managin'.

SIMEON. Mebbe we'd ought t' help—this once.

PETER. Mebbe. The cows knows us.

SIMEON. An' likes us. They don't know him much.

PETER. An' the hosses, an' pigs, an' chickens. They don't know him much.

SIMEON. They knows us like brothers—an' likes us! (*Proudly*) Hain't we raised 'em t' be fustrate, number one prize stock?

PETER. We hain't—not no more.

SIMEON (*dully*). I was fergittin'. (*Then resignedly*) Waal, let's go help Eben a spell an' git waked up.

PETER. Suits me. (*They are starting off down left, rear, for the barn when Eben appears from there hurrying toward them, his face excited*).

EBEN (*breathlessly*). Waal—har they be! The old mule an' the bride! I seen 'em from the barn down below at the turnin'.

PETER. How could ye tell that far?

EBEN. Hain't I as far-sight as he's near-sight? Don't I know the mare 'n' buggy, an' two people settin' in it? Who else . . . ? An' I tell ye I kin feel 'em a-comin', too! (*He squirms as if he had the itch*).

PETER (*beginning to be angry*). Waal—let him do his own unhitchin'!

SIMEON (*angry in his turn*). Let's hustle in an' git our bundles an' be a-goin' as he's a-comin'. I don't want never t' step inside the door agen arter he's back. (*They both start back around the corner of the house. Eben follows them*).

EBEN (*anxiously*). Will ye sign it afore ye go?

PETER. Let's see the color o' the old skinflint's money an' we'll sign. (*They disappear left. The two brothers clump upstairs to get their bundles. Eben appears in the kitchen, runs to window, peers out, comes back and pulls up a strip of flooring in under stove, takes out a canvas bag and puts it on table, then sets the floorboard back in place. The two brothers appear a moment after. They carry old carpet bags*).

EBEN (*puts his hand on bag guardingly*). Have ye signed?

SIMEON (*shows paper in his hand*). Ay-eh. (*Greedily*) Be that the money?

EBEN (*opens bag and pours out pile of twenty-dollar gold pieces*). Twenty-dollar pieces—thirty on 'em. Count 'em. (*Peter does so, arranging them in stacks of five, biting one or two to test them*).

PETER. Six hundred. (*He puts them in bag and puts it inside his shirt carefully*).

SIMEON (*handing paper to* EBEN). Har ye be.

EBEN (*after a glance, folds it carefully and hides it under his shirt—gratefully*). Thank yew.

PETER. Thank yew fur the ride.

SIMEON. We'll send ye a lump o' gold fur Christmas. (*A pause.* EBEN *stares at them and they at him*).

PETER (*awkwardly*). Waal—we're a-goin'.

SIMEON. Comin' out t' the yard?

EBEN. No. I'm waitin' in here a spell. (*Another silence. The brothers edge awkwardly to door in rear—then turn and stand*).

SIMEON. Waal—good-by.

PETER. Good-by.

EBEN. Good-by. (*They go out. He sits down at the table, faces the stove and pulls out the paper. He looks from it to the stove. His face, lighted up by the shaft of sunlight from the window, has an expression of trance. His lips move. The two brothers come out to the gate*).

PETER (*looking off toward barn*). Thar he be—unhitchin'.

SIMEON (*with a chuckle*). I'll bet ye he's riled!

PETER. An' thar she be.

SIMEON. Let's wait 'n' see what our new Maw looks like.

PETER (*with a grin*). An' give him our partin' cuss!

SIMEON (*grinning*). I feel like raisin' fun. I feel light in my head an' feet.

PETER. Me, too. I feel like laffin' till I'd split up the middle.

SIMEON. Reckon it's the likker?

PETER. No. My feet feel itchin' t' walk an' walk—an' jump high over thin's—an'. . . .

SIMEON. Dance? (*A pause*).

PETER (*puzzled*). It's plumb on-nateral.

SIMEON (*a light coming over his face*). I calc'late it's 'cause school's out. It's holiday. Fur once we're free!

PETER (*dazedly*). Free?

SIMEON. The halter's broke—the harness is busted—the fence bars is down—the stone walls air crumblin' an' tumblin'! We'll be kickin' up an' tearin' away down the road!

PETER (*drawing a deep breath—oratorically*). Anybody that wants this stinkin' old rock-pile of a farm kin hev it. T'ain't our'n, no sirree!

SIMEON (*takes the gate off its hinges and puts it under his arm*). We harby 'bolishes shet gates, an' open gates, an' all gates, by thunder!

PETER. We'll take it with us fur luck an' let 'er sail free down some river.

SIMEON (*as a sound of voices comes from left, rear*). Har they comes! (*The two brothers congeal into two stiff, grim-visaged statues.* EPHRAIM CABOT *and* ABBIE PUTNAM *come in.* CABOT *is seventy-five, tall and gaunt, with great, wiry, concentrated power, but stoop-shouldered from toil. His face is as hard as if it were hewn out of a boulder, yet there is a weakness in it, a petty pride in its own narrow strength. His eyes are small, close together, and extremely near-sighted, blinking continually in the effort to focus on objects, their stare having a straining, ingrowing quality. He is dressed in his dismal black Sunday suit.* ABBIE *is thirty-five, buxom, full of vitality. Her round face is pretty but marred by its rather gross sensuality. There is strength and obstinacy in her jaw, a hard determination in her eyes, and about her whole personality the same unsettled, untamed, desperate quality which is so apparent in* EBEN).

CABOT (*as they enter—a queer strangled emotion in his dry cracking voice*). Har we be t' hum, Abbie.

ABBIE (*with lust for the word*). Hum! (*Her eyes gloating on the house without seeming to see the two stiff figures at the gate*) It's purty—purty! I can't b'lieve it's r'ally mine.

CABOT (*sharply*). Yewr'n? Mine! (*He stares at her penetratingly. She stares back. He adds relentingly*) Our'n—mebbe! It was lonesome too long. I was growin' old in the spring. A hum's got t' hev a woman.

ABBIE (*her voice taking possession*). A woman's got t' hev a hum!

CABOT (*nodding uncertainly*). Ay-eh. (*Then irritably*) Whar be they? Ain't thar nobody about—'r wukin' —r' nothin'?

ABBIE (*sees the brothers. She returns their stare of cold appraising contempt with interest—slowly*). Thar's two men loafin' at the gate an' starin' at me like a couple o' strayed hogs.

CABOT (*straining his eyes*). I kin see 'em—but I can't make out. . . .

SIMEON. It's Simeon.

PETER. It's Peter.

CABOT (*exploding*). Why hain't ye wukin'?

SIMEON (*dryly*). We're waitin' t' welcome ye hum—yew an' the bride!

CABOT (*confusedly*). Huh? Waal—this be yer new Maw, boys. (*She stares at them and they at her*).

SIMEON (*turns away and spits contemptuously*). I see her!

PETER (*spits also*). An' I see her!

ABBIE (*with the conqueror's conscious superiority*). I'll go in an' look

at *my* house. (*She goes slowly around to porch*).

SIMEON (*with a snort*). Her house!

PETER (*calls after her*). Ye'll find Eben inside. Ye better not tell him it's *yewr* house.

ABBIE (*mouthing the name*). Eben. (*Then quietly*) I'll tell Eben.

CABOT (*with a contemptuous sneer*). Ye needn't heed Eben. Eben's a dumb fool—like his Maw—soft an' simple!

SIMEON (*with his sardonic burst of laughter*). Ha! Eben's a chip o' yew —spit 'n' image—hard 'n' bitter's a hickory tree! Dog'll eat dog. He'll eat ye yet, old man!

CABOT (*commandingly*). Ye git t' wuk!

SIMEON (*as* ABBIE *disappears in house—winks at* PETER *and says tauntingly*). So that thar's our new Maw, be it? Whar in hell did ye dig her up? (*He and* PETER *laugh*).

PETER. Ha! Ye'd better turn her in the pen with the other sows. (*They laugh uproariously, slapping their thighs*).

CABOT (*so amazed at their effrontery that he stutters in confusion*). Simeon! Peter! What's come over ye? Air ye drunk?

SIMEON. We're free, old man—free o' yew an' the hull damned farm! (*They grow more and more hilarious and excited*).

PETER. An' we're startin' out fur the gold fields o' Californi-a!

SIMEON. Ye kin take this place an' burn it!

PETER. An' bury it—fur all we cares!

SIMEON. We're free, old man! (*He cuts a caper*).

PETER. Free! (*He gives a kick in the air*).

SIMEON (*in a frenzy*). Whoop!

PETER. Whoop! (*They do an absurd Indian war dance about the old man who is petrified between rage and the fear that they are insane).*

SIMEON. We're free as Injuns! Lucky we don't skulp ye!

PETER. An' burn yer barn an' kill the stock!

SIMEON. An' rape yer new woman! Whoop! (*He and* PETER *stop their dance, holding their sides, rocking with wild laughter).*

CABOT (*edging away).* Lust fur gold—fur the sinful, easy gold o' Californi-a! It's made ye mad!

SIMEON (*tauntingly).* Wouldn't ye like us to send ye back some sinful gold, ye old sinner?

PETER. They's gold besides what's in Californi-a! (*He retreats back beyond the vision of the old man and takes the bag of money and flaunts it in the air above his head, laughing).*

SIMEON. And sinfuller, too!

PETER. We'll be voyagin' on the sea! Whoop! (*He leaps up and down).*

SIMEON. Livin' free! Whoop! (*He leaps in turn).*

CABOT (*suddenly roaring .with rage).* My cuss on ye!

SIMEON. Take our'n in trade fur it! Whoop!

CABOT. I'll hev ye both chained up in the asylum!

PETER. Ye old skinflint! Good-by!

SIMEON. Ye old blood sucker! Good-by!

CABOT. Go afore I . . . !

PETER. Whoop! (*He picks a stone from the road.* SIMEON *does the same).*

SIMEON. Maw'll be in the parlor.

PETER. Ay-eh! One! Two!

CABOT (*frightened).* What air ye . . . ?

PETER. Three! (*They both throw, the stones hitting the parlor window with a crash of glass, tearing the shade).*

SIMEON. Whoop!

PETER. Whoop!

CABOT (*in a fury now, rushing toward them).* If I kin lay hands on ye—I'll break yer bones fur ye! (*But they beat a capering retreat before him,* SIMEON *with the gate still under his arm.* CABOT *comes back, panting with impotent rage. Their voices as they go off take up the song of the gold-seekers to the old tune of "Oh, Susannah!"*

"I jumped aboard the Liza ship,
  And traveled on the sea,
  And every time I thought of home
  I wished it wasn't me!
Oh! Californi-a,
  That's the land fur me!
I'm off to Californi-a!
  With my wash bowl on my knee."

(*In the meantime, the window of the upper bedroom on right is raised and* ABBIE *sticks her head out. She looks down at* CABOT—*with a sigh of relief).*

ABBIE. Waal—that's the last o' them two, hain't it? (*He doesn't answer. Then in possessive tones).* This here's a nice bedroom, Ephraim. It's a r'al nice bed. Is it my room, Ephraim?

CABOT (*grimly—without looking up).* Our'n! (*She cannot control a grimace of aversion and pulls back her head slowly and shuts the window. A sudden horrible thought seems to enter* CABOT'S *head)* They been up to somethin'! Mebbe—mebbe they've pizened the stock—'r somethin'! (*He almost runs off down toward the barn. A moment later the kitchen door is slowly pushed open and* ABBIE *enters. For a moment she stands looking at* EBEN. *He does not notice her at first. Her eyes take him in penetratingly with a calculating appraisal of his strength as against hers. But under this her desire is dimly awakened by his youth and good looks. Suddenly he becomes conscious of her presence and looks up. Their eyes meet. He leaps to his feet, glowering at her speechlessly).*

ABBIE (*in her most seductive tones which she uses all through this scene*). Be you—Eben? I'm Abbie— (*She laughs*) I mean, I'm yer new Maw.

EBEN (*viciously*). No, damn ye!

ABBIE (*as if she hadn't heard—with a queer smile*). Yer Paw's spoke a lot o' yew. . . .

EBEN. Ha!

ABBIE. Ye mustn't mind him. He's an old man. (*A long pause. They stare at each other*) I don't want t' pretend playin' Maw t' ye, Eben (*Admiringly*). Ye're too big an' too strong fur that. I want t' be frens with ye. Mebbe with me fur a fren ye'd find ye'd like livin' here better. I kin make it easy fur ye with him, mebbe. (*With a scornful sense of power*) I calc'late I kin git him t' do most anythin' fur me.

EBEN (*with bitter scorn*). Ha! (*They stare again, EBEN obscurely moved, physically attracted to her—in forced stilted tones*) Yew kin go t' the devil!

ABBIE (*calmly*). If cussin' me does ye good, cuss all ye've a mind t'. I'm all prepared t' have ye agin me—at fust. I don't blame ye nuther. I'd feel the same at any stranger comin' t' take my Maw's place. (*He shudders. She is watching him carefully*) Yew must've cared a lot fur yewr Maw, didn't ye? My Maw died afore I'd growed. I don't remember her none. (*A pause*) But yew won't hate me long, Eben. I'm not the wust in the world—an' yew an' me've got a lot in common. I kin tell that by lookin' at ye. Waal—I've had a hard life, too—oceans o' trouble an' nuthin' but wuk fur reward. I was a orphan

early an' had t' wuk fur others in other folks' hums. Then I married an' he turned out a drunken spreer an' so he had to wuk fur others an' me too agen in other folks' hums, an' the baby died, an' my husband got sick an' died too, an' I was glad sayin' now I'm free fur once, on'y I diskivered right away all I was free fur was t' wuk agen in other folks' hums, doin' other folks' wuk till I'd most give up hope o' ever doin' my own wuk in my own hum, an' then your Paw come. . . . (CABOT *appears returning from the barn. He comes to the gate and looks down the road the brothers have gone. A faint strain of their retreating voices is heard: "Oh, Californi-a! That's the place for me." He stands glowering, his fist clenched, his face grim with rage*).

EBEN (*fighting against his growing attraction and sympathy—harshly*). An' bought yew—like a harlot! (*She is stung and flushes angrily. She has been sincerely moved by the recital of her troubles. He adds furiously*) An' the price he's payin' ye—this farm—was my Maw's, damn ye!—an' mine now!

ABBIE (*with a cool laugh of confidence*). Yewr'n? We'll see 'bout that! (*Then strongly*) Waal—what if I did need a hum? What else'd I marry an old man like him fur?

EBEN (*maliciously*). I'll tell him ye said that!

ABBIE (*smiling*). I'll say ye're lyin' a-purpose—an' he'll drive ye off the place!

EBEN. Ye devil!

ABBIE (*defying him*). This be my farm—this be my hum—this be my kitchen—!

EBEN (*furiously, as if he were going to attack her*). Shut up, damn ye!

ABBIE (*walks up to him—a queer coarse expression of desire in her face and body—slowly*). An' upstairs

—that be my bedroom—an' my bed! (*He stares into into her eyes, terribly confused and torn. She adds softly*) I hain't bad nor mean—'ceptin' fur an enemy—but I got t' fight fur what's due me out o' life, if I ever 'spect t' git it. (*Then putting her hand on his arm—seductively*) Let's yew 'n' me be frens, Eben.

EBEN (*stupidly—as if hypnotized*). Ay-eh. (*Then furiously flinging off her arm*) No, ye durned old witch! I hate ye! (*He rushes out the door*).

ABBIE (*looks after him smiling satisfiedly—then half to herself, mouthing the word*) Eben's nice. (*She looks at the table, proudly*) I'll wash up *my* dishes now. (EBEN *appears outside, slamming the door behind him. He comes around corner, stops on seeing his father, and stands staring at him with hate*).

CABOT (*raising his arms to heaven in the fury he can no longer control*). Lord God o' Hosts, smite the undutiful sons with Thy wust cuss!

EBEN (*breaking in violently*). Yew 'n' yewr God! Allus cussin' folks—allus naggin' 'em!

CABOT (*oblivious to him—summoningly*). God o' the old! God o' the lonesome!

EBEN (*mockingly*). Naggin' His sheep t' sin! T' hell with yewr God! (CABOT *turns. He and* EBEN *glower at each other*).

CABOT (*harshly*). So it's yew. I might've knowed it. (*Shaking his finger threateningly at him*) Blasphemin' fool! (*Then quickly*) Why hain't ye t' wuk?

EBEN. Why hain't yew? They've went. I can't wuk it all alone.

CABOT (*contemptuously*). Nor noways! I'm wuth ten o' ye yit, old's I be! Ye'll never be more'n half a man! (*Then, matter-of-factly*) Waal—let's git t' the barn. (*They go. A last faint note of the "Californi-a" song is heard from the distance.* ABBIE *is washing her dishes*).

CURTAIN

PART TWO—SCENE ONE

The exterior of the farmhouse, as in Part One—a hot Sunday afternoon two months later. ABBIE, *dressed in her best, is discovered sitting in a rocker at the end of the porch. She rocks listlessly, enervated by the heat, staring in front of her with bored, half-closed eyes.*

EBEN *sticks his head out of his bedroom window. He looks around furtively and tries to see—or hear—if anyone is on the porch, but although he has been careful to make no noise,* ABBIE *has sensed his movement. She stops rocking, her face grows animated and eager, she waits attentively.* EBEN *seems to feel her presence, he scowls back his thoughts of her and spits with exaggerated disdain—then withdraws back into the room.* ABBIE *waits, holding her breath as she listens with passionate eagerness for every sound within the house.*

EBEN *comes out. Their eyes meet. His falter, he is confused, he turns away and slams the door resentfully. At this gesture,* ABBIE *laughs tantalizingly, amused but at the same time piqued and irritated. He scowls, strides off the porch to the path and starts to walk past her to the road with a grand swagger of ignoring her existence. He is dressed in his store suit, spruced up, his face shines from soap and water.* ABBIE *leans forward on her chair, her eyes hard and angry now, and, as he passes her, gives a sneering, taunting chuckle.*

EBEN (*stung—turns on her furiously*). What air yew cacklin' 'bout?

ABBIE (*triumphant*). Yew!

EBEN. What about me?

ABBIE. Ye look all slicked up like a prize bull.

EBEN (*with a sneer*). Waal—ye hain't so durned purty yerself, be ye? (*They stare into each other's eyes, his held by hers in spite of himself, hers glowingly possessive. Their physical attraction becomes a palpable force quivering in the hot air*).

ABBIE (*softly*). Ye don't mean that, Eben. Ye may think ye mean it, mebbe, but ye don't. Ye can't. It's agin nature, Eben. Ye been fightin' yer nature ever since the day I come —tryin' t' tell yerself I hain't purty t'ye. (*She laughs a low humid laugh without taking her eyes from his. A pause—her body squirms desirously—she murmurs languorously*) Hain't the sun strong an' hot? Ye kin feel it burnin' into the earth— Nature—makin' thin's grow—bigger 'n' bigger—burnin' inside ye—makin' ye want t' grow—into somethin' else—till ye're jined with it—an' it's your'n—but it owns ye, too—an' makes ye grow bigger—like a tree— like them elums— (*She laughs again softly, holding his eyes. He takes a step toward her, compelled against his will*) Nature'll beat ye, Eben. Ye might's well own up t' it fust 's last.

EBEN (*trying to break from her spell—confusedly*). If Paw'd hear ye goin' on. . . . (*Resentfully*) But ye've made such a damned idjit out o' the old devil. . .! (ABBIE *laughs*).

ABBIE. Waal—hain't it easier fur yew with him changed softer?

EBEN (*defiantly*). No. I'm fightin' him—fightin' yew—fightin' fur Maw's rights t' her hum! (*This breaks her spell for him. He glowers at her*) An' I'm onto ye. Ye hain't foolin' me a mite. Ye're aimin' t'

swaller up everythin' an' make it your'n. Waal, you'll find I'm a heap sight bigger hunk nor yew kin chew! (*He turns from her with a sneer*).

ABBIE (*trying to regain her ascendancy—seductively*). Eben!

EBEN. Leave me be! (*He starts to walk away*).

ABBIE (*more commandingly*). Eben!

EBEN (*stops—resentfully*). What d'ye want?

ABBIE (*trying to conceal a growing excitement*). Whar air ye goin'?

EBEN (*with malicious nonchalance*). Oh—up the road a spell.

ABBIE. T' the village?

EBEN (*airily*). Mebbe.

ABBIE (*excitedly*). T' see that Min, I s'pose?

EBEN. Mebbe.

ABBIE (*weakly*). What d'ye want t' waste time on her fur?

EBEN (*revenging himself now— grinning at her*). Ye can't beat Nature, didn't ye say? (*He laughs and again starts to walk away*).

ABBIE (*bursting out*). An ugly old hake!

EBEN (*with a tantalizing sneer*). She's purtier'n yew be!

ABBIE. That every wuthless drunk in the country has. . . .

EBEN (*tauntingly*). Mebbe—but she's better'n yew. She owns up fa'r 'n' squar' t' her doin's.

ABBIE (*furiously*). Don't ye dare compare. . . .

EBEN. She don't go sneakin' an' stealin'—what's mine.

ABBIE (*savagely seizing on his weak point*). Your'n? Yew mean—my farm?

EBEN. I mean the farm yew sold yerself fur like any other old whore —my farm!

ABBIE (*stung—fiercely*). Ye'll never live t' see the day when even a stinkin' weed on it 'll belong t' ye! (*Then in a scream*) Git out o' my sight! Go on t' yer slut—disgracin' yer Paw 'n' me! I'll git yer Paw t' horsewhip ye off the place if I want t'! Ye're only livin' here 'cause I tolerate ye! Git along! I hate the sight o' ye! (*She stops, panting and glaring at him*).

EBEN (*returning her glance in kind*). An' I hate the sight o' yew! (*He turns and strides off up the road. She follows his retreating figure with concentrated hate. Old* CABOT *appears coming up from the barn. The hard, grim expression of his face has changed. He seems in some queer way softened, mellowed. His eyes have taken on a strange, incongruous dreamy quality. Yet there is no hint of physical weakness about him—rather he looks more robust and younger.* ABBIE *sees him and turns away quickly with unconcealed aversion. He comes slowly up to her*).

CABOT (*mildly*). War yew an' Eben quarrelin' agen?

ABBIE (*shortly*). No.

CABOT. Ye was talkin' a'mighty loud. (*He sits down on the edge of porch*).

ABBIE (*snappishly*). If ye heerd us they hain't no need askin' questions.

CABOT. I didn't hear what ye said.

ABBIE (*relieved*). Waal—it wa'n't nothin' t' speak on.

CABOT (*after a pause*). Eben's queer.

ABBIE (*bitterly*). He's the dead spit 'n' image o' yew!

CABOT (*queerly interested*). D'ye think so, Abbie? (*After a pause, ruminatingly*) Me 'n' Eben's allus fit 'n' fit. I never could b'ar him noways. He's so thunderin' soft—like his Maw.

ABBIE (*scornfully*). Ay-eh! 'Bout as soft as yew be!

CABOT (*as if he hadn't heard*). Mebbe I been too hard on him.

ABBIE (*jeeringly*). Waal—ye're gittin' soft now—soft as slop! That's what Eben was sayin'.

CABOT (*his face instantly grim and ominous*). Eben was sayin'? Waal, he'd best not do nothin' t' try me 'r he'll soon diskiver. . . . (*A pause. She keeps her face turned away. His gradually softens. He stares up at the sky*) Purty, hain't it?

ABBIE (*crossly*). I don't see nothin' purty.

CABOT. The sky. Feels like a wa'm field up thar.

ABBIE (*sarcastically*). Air yew aimin' t' buy up over the farm too? (*She snickers contemptuously*).

CABOT (*strangely*). I'd like t' own my place up thar. (*A pause*) I'm gittin' old, Abbie. I'm gittin' ripe on the bough. (*A pause. She stares at him mystified. He goes on*) It's allus lonesome cold in the house—even when it's bilin' hot outside. Hain't yew noticed?

ABBIE. No.

CABOT. It's wa'm down t' the barn—nice smellin' an' warm—with the cows. (*A pause*) Cows is queer.

ABBIE. Like yew?

CABOT. Like Eben. (*A pause*) I'm gittin' t' feel resigned t' Eben—jest as I got t' feel 'bout his Maw. I'm gittin' t' learn to b'ar his softness—jest like her'n. I calc'late I c'd a'most take t' him—if he wa'n't sech a dumb fool! (*A pause*) I s'pose it's old age a-creepin' in my bones.

ABBIE (*indifferently*). Waal—ye hain't dead yet.

CABOT (*roused*). No, I hain't, yew bet—not by a hell of a sight—I'm sound 'n' tough as hickory! (*Then moodily*) But arter three score and ten the Lord warns ye t' prepare. (*A pause*) That's why Eben's come in my head. Now that his cussed sinful brothers is gone their path t' hell, they's no one left but Eben.

ABBIE (*resentfully*). They's me, hain't they? (*Agitatedly*) What's all this sudden likin' ye've tuk to Eben? Why don't ye say nothin' 'bout me? Hain't I yer lawful wife?

CABOT (*simply*). Ay-eh. Ye be. (*A pause—he stares at her desirously—his eyes grow avid—then with a sudden movement he seizes her hands and squeezes them, declaiming in a queer camp meeting preacher's tempo*) Yew air my Rose o' Sharon! Behold, yew air fair; yer eyes air doves; yer lips air like scarlet; yer two breasts air like two fawns; yer navel be like a round goblet; yer belly be like a heap o' wheat. . . . (*He covers her hand with kisses. She does not seem to notice. She stares before her with hard angry eyes*).

ABBIE (*jerking her hands away—harshly*). So ye're plannin' t' leave the farm t' Eben, air ye?

CABOT (*dazedly*). Leave. . . ? (*Then with resentful obstinacy*) I hain't a-givin' it t' no one!

ABBIE (*remorselessly*). Ye can't take it with ye.

CABOT (*thinks a moment—then reluctantly*). No, I calc'late not. (*After a pause—with a strange passion*) But if I could, I would, by the Etarnal! 'R if I could, in my dyin' hour, I'd set it afire an' watch it burn—this house an' every ear o' corn an' every tree down t' the last blade o' hay! I'd sit an' know it was all a-dying with me an' no one else'd ever own what was mine, what I'd made out o' nothin' with my own sweat 'n' blood! (*A pause—then he adds with a queer affection*) 'Ceptin' the cows. Them I'd turn free.

ABBIE (*harshly*). An' me?

CABOT (*with a queer smile*). Ye'd be turned free, too.

ABBIE (*furiously*). So that's the thanks I git fur marryin' ye—t' have ye change kind to Eben who hates ye, an' talk o' turnin' me out in the road.

CABOT (*hastily*). Abbie! Ye know I wa'n't. . . .

ABBIE (*vengefully*). Just let me tell ye a thing or two 'bout Eben! Whar's he gone? T' see that harlot, Min! I tried fur t' stop him. Disgracin' yew an' me—on the Sabbath, too!

CABOT (*rather guiltily*). He's a sinner—nateral-born. It's lust eatin' his heart.

ABBIE (*enraged beyond endurance—wildly vindictive*). An' his lust fur me! Kin ye find excuses fur that?

CABOT (*stares at her—after a dead pause*). Lust—fur yew?

ABBIE (*defiantly*). He was tryin' t' make love t' me—when ye heerd us quarrelin'.

CABOT (*stares at her—then a terrible expression of rage comes over his face—he springs to his feet shaking all over*). By the A'mighty God—I'll end him!

ABBIE (*frightened now for Eben*). No! Don't ye!

CABOT (*violently*). I'll git the shotgun an' blow his soft brains t' the top o' them elums!

ABBIE (*throwing her arms around him*). No, Ephraim!

CABOT (*pushing her away violently*). I will, by God!

ABBIE (*in a quieting tone*). Listen, Ephraim. 'Twa'n't nothin' bad—on'y a boy's foolin'—'twa'n't meant serious—jest jokin' an' teasin'. . . .

CABOT. Then why did ye say—lust?

ABBIE. It must hev sounded wusser'n I meant. An' I was mad at thinkin'—ye'd leave him the farm.

CABOT (*quieter but still grim and cruel*). Waal then, I'll horsewhip him off the place if that much'll content ye.

ABBIE (*reaching out and taking his*

hand). No. Don't think o' me! Ye mustn't drive him off. 'Tain't sensible. Who'll ye get to help ye on the farm? They's no one hereabouts.

CABOT (*considers this—then nodding his appreciation*). Ye got a head on ye. (*Then irritably*) Waal, let him stay. (*He sits down on the edge of the porch. She sits beside him. He murmurs contemptuously*) I oughtn't t' git riled so—at that 'ere fool calf. (*A pause*) But har's the p'int. What son o' mine'll keep on here t' the farm—when the Lord does call me? Simeon an' Peter air gone t' hell—an' Eben's follerin' 'em.

ABBIE. They's me.

CABOT. Ye're on'y a woman.

ABBIE. I'm yewr wife.

CABOT. That hain't me. A son is me —my blood—mine. Mine ought t' git mine. An' then it's still mine— even though I be six foot under. D'ye see?

ABBIE (*giving him a look of hatred*). Ay-eh. I see. (*She becomes very thoughtful, her face growing shrewd, her eyes studying* CABOT *craftily*).

CABOT. I'm gettin' old—ripe on the bough. (*Then with a sudden forced reassurance*) Not but what I hain't a hard nut t' crack even yet—an' fur many a year t' come! By the Etarnal, I kin break most o' the young fellers' backs at any kind o' work any day o' the year!

ABBIE (*suddenly*). Mebbe the Lord'll give *us* a son.

CABOT (*turns and stares at her eagerly*). Ye mean—a son—t' me 'n' yew?

ABBIE (*with a cajoling smile*). Ye're a strong man yet, hain't ye? 'Tain't noways impossible, be it? We know that. Why d'ye stare so? Hain't ye never thought o' that afore? I been thinkin' o' it all along. Ay-eh—an' I been prayin' it'd happen, too.

CABOT (*his face growing full of joyous pride and a sort of religious ecstasy*). Ye been prayin', Abbie?— fur a son?—t' us?

ABBIE. Ay-eh. (*With a grim resolution*) I want a son now.

CABOT (*excitedly clutching both of her hands in his*). It'd be the blessin' o' God, Abbie—the blessin' o' God A'mighty on me—in my old age—in my lonesomeness! They hain't nothin' I wouldn't do fur ye then, Abbie. Ye'd hev on'y t' ask it—anythin' ye'd a mind t'!

ABBIE (*interrupting*). Would ye will the farm t' me then—t' me an' it. . . ?

CABOT (*vehemently*). I'd do anythin' ye axed, I tell ye! I swar it! May I be everlastin' damned t' hell if I wouldn't! (*He sinks to his knees pulling her down with him. He trembles all over with the fervor of his hopes*) Pray t' the Lord agen, Abbie. It's the Sabbath! I'll jine ye! Two prayers air better nor one. "An' God hearkened unto Rachel"! An' God hearkened unto Abbie! Pray, Abbie! Pray fur him to hearken! (*He bows his head, mumbling. She pretends to do likewise but gives him a side glance of scorn and triumph*).

SCENE TWO

About eight in the evening. The interior of the two bedrooms on the top floor is shown. EBEN *is sitting on the side of his bed in the room on the left. On account of the heat he has taken off everything but his undershirt and pants. His feet are bare. He faces front, brooding moodily, his chin propped on his hands, a desperate expression on his face.*

In the other room CABOT *and* ABBIE *are sitting side by side on the edge of their bed, an old four-poster with feather mattress. He is in his night shirt, she in her nightdress. He is still in the queer, excited mood into which the notion of a son has thrown him. Both rooms are lighted dimly and flickeringly by tallow candles.*

CABOT. The farm needs a son.

ABBIE. I need a son.

CABOT. Ay-eh. Sometimes ye air the farm an' sometimes the farm be yew. That's why I clove t' ye in my lonesomeness. (*A pause. He pounds his knee with his fist*) Me an' the farm has got t' beget a son!

ABBIE. Ye'd best go t'sleep. Ye're gittin' thin's all mixed.

CABOT (*with an impatient gesture*). No, I hain't. My mind's clear's a well. Ye don't know me, that's it. (*He stares hopelessly at the floor*).

ABBIE (*indifferently*). Mebbe. (*In the next room* EBEN *gets up and paces up and down distractedly.* ABBIE *hears him. Her eyes fasten on the intervening wall with concentrated attention.* EBEN *stops and stares. Their hot glances seem to meet through the wall. Unconsciously he stretches out his arms for her and she half rises. Then aware, he mutters a curse at himself and flings himself face downward on the bed, his clenched fists above his head, his face buried in the pillow.* ABBIE *relaxes with a faint sigh but her eyes remain fixed on the wall; she listens with all her attention for some movement from* EBEN).

CABOT (*suddenly raises his head and looks at her—scornfully*). Will ye ever know me—'r will any man 'r woman? (*Shaking his head*) No. I calc'late 't wa'n't t' be. (*He turns away.* ABBIE *looks at the wall. Then, evidently unable to keep silent about*

his thoughts, without looking at his wife, he puts out his hand and clutches her knee. She starts violently, looks at him, sees he is not watching her, concentrates again on the wall and pays no attention to what he says) Listen, Abbie. When I come here fifty odd year ago—I was jest twenty an' the strongest an' hardest ye ever seen—ten times as strong an' fifty times as hard as Eben. Waal—this place was nothin' but fields o' stones. Folks laughed when I tuk it. They couldn't know what I knowed. When ye kin make corn sprout out o' stones, God's livin' in yew! They wa'n't strong enuf fur that! They reckoned God was easy. They laughed. They don't laugh no more. Some died hereabouts. Some went West an' died. They're all under ground—fur follerin' arter an easy God. God hain't easy. (*He shakes his head slowly*) An' I growed hard. Folks kept allus sayin' he's a hard man like 'twas sinful t' be hard, so's at last I said back at 'em: Waal then, by thunder, ye'll git me hard an' see how ye like it! (*Then suddenly*) But I give in t' weakness once. 'Twas arter I'd been here two year. I got weak—despairful—they was so many stones. They was a party leavin', givin' up, goin' West. I jined 'em. We tracked on 'n' on. We come t' broad medders, plains, whar the soil was black an' rich as gold. Nary a stone. Easy. Ye'd on'y to plow an' sow an' then set an' smoke yer pipe an' watch thin's grow. I could o' been a rich man— but somethin' in me fit me an' fit me—the voice o' God sayin': "This hain't wuth nothin' t' Me. Git ye back t' hum!" I got afeerd o' that voice an' I lit out back t' hum here, leavin' my claim an' crops t' whoever'd a mind t' take 'em. Ay-eh. I actoolly give up what was rightful mine! God's hard, not easy! God's in the stones! Build my church on a rock—out o' stones an' I'll be in them! That's what He meant t' Peter! (*He sighs heavily—a pause*) Stones. I picked 'em up an' piled 'em into walls. Ye kin read the years o' my life in them walls, every day a hefted stone, climbin' over the hills up and down, fencin' in the fields that was mine, whar I'd made thin's grow out o' nothin'—like the will o' God, like the servant o' His hand. It wa'n't easy. It was hard an' He made me hard fur it. (*He pauses*) All the time I kept gittin' lonesomer. I tuk a wife. She bore Simeon an' Peter. She was a good woman. She wuked hard. We was married twenty year. She never knowed me. She helped but she never knowed what she was helpin'. I was allus lonesome. She died. After that it wa'n't so lonesome fur a spell. (*A pause*) I lost count o' the years. I had no time t' fool away countin' 'em. Sim an' Peter helped. The farm growed. It was all mine! When I thought o' that I didn't feel lonesome. (*A pause*) But ye can't hitch yer mind t' one thin' day an' night. I tuk another wife—Eben's Maw. Her folks was contestin' me at law over my deeds t' the farm—my farm! That's why Eben keeps a-talkin' his fool talk o' this bein' his Maw's farm. She bore Eben. She was purty—but soft. She tried t' be hard. She couldn't. She never knowed me nor nothin'. It was lonesomer 'n hell with her. After a matter o' sixteen odd years, she died. (*A pause*) I lived with the boys. They hated me 'cause I was hard. I hated them 'cause they was soft. They coveted the farm without knowin' what it meant. It made me bitter 'n wormwood. It aged me—them covetin' what I'd made fur mine. Then this spring the call come—the voice o' God cryin' in

my wilderness, in my lonesomeness —t' go out an' seek an' find! (*Turning to her with strange passion*) I sought ye an' I found ye! Yew air my Rose o' Sharon! Yer eyes air like. . . . (*She has turned a blank face, resentful eyes to his. He stares at her for a moment—then harshly*) Air ye any the wiser fur all I've told ye?

ABBIE (*confusedly*). Mebbe.

CABOT (*pushing her away from him—angrily*). Ye don't know nothin'—nor never will. If ye don't hev a son t' redeem ye. . . . (*This in a tone of cold threat*).

ABBIE (*resentfully*). I've prayed, hain't I?

CABOT (*bitterly*). Pray agen—fur understandin'!

ABBIE (*a veiled threat in her tone*). Ye'll have a son out o' me, I promise ye.

CABOT. How kin ye promise?

ABBIE. I got second-sight mebbe. I kin foretell. (*She gives a queer smile*).

CABOT. I believe ye have. Ye give me the chills sometimes. (*He shivers*) It's cold in this house. It's oneasy. They's thin's pokin' about in the dark—in the corners. (*He pulls on his trousers, tucking in his night shirt, and pulls on his boots*).

ABBIE (*surprised*). Whar air ye goin'?

CABOT (*queerly*). Down whar it's restful—whar it's warm—down t' the barn. (*Bitterly*) I kin talk t' the cows. They know. They know the farm an' me. They'll give me peace. (*He turns to go out the door*).

ABBIE (*a bit frightenedly*). Air ye ailin' tonight, Ephraim?

CABOT. Growin'. Growin' ripe on the bough. (*He turns and goes, his boots clumping down the stairs.* EBEN *sits up with a start, listening.* ABBIE *is conscious of his movement and stares at the wall.* CABOT *comes out of the house around the corner and stands by the gate, blinking at the sky. He stretches up his hands in a tortured gesture)* God A'mighty, call from the dark! *(He listens as if expecting an answer. Then his arms drop, he shakes his head and plods off toward the barn.* EBEN *and* ABBIE *stare at each other through the wall.* EBEN *sighs heavily and* ABBIE *echoes it. Both become terribly nervous, uneasy. Finally* ABBIE *gets up and listens, her ear to the wall. He acts as if he saw every move she was making, he becomes resolutely still. She seems driven into a decision—goes out the door in rear determinedly. His eyes follow her. Then as the door of his room is opened softly, he turns away, waits in an attitude of strained fixity.* ABBIE *stands for a second staring at him, her eyes burning with desire. Then with a little cry she runs over and throws her arms about his neck, she pulls his head back and covers his mouth with kisses. At first, he submits dumbly; then he puts his arms about her neck and returns her kisses, but finally, suddenly aware of his hatred, he hurls her away from him, springing to his feet. They stand speechless and breathless, panting like two animals).*

ABBIE *(at last—painfully).* Ye shouldn't, Eben—ye shouldn't—I'd make ye happy!

EBEN *(harshly).* I don't want t' be happy—from yew!

ABBIE *(helplessly).* Ye do, Eben! Ye do! Why d'ye lie?

EBEN *(viciously).* I don't take t'ye, I tell ye! I hate the sight o' ye!

ABBIE *(with an uncertain troubled laugh).* Wall, I kissed ye anyways—an' ye kissed back—yer lips was burnin'—ye can't lie 'bout that! *(Intensely)* If ye don't care, why did ye kiss me back—why was yer lips burnin'?

EBEN *(wiping his mouth).* It was like pizen on 'em. *(Then tauntingly)* When I kissed ye back, mebbe I thought 'twas someone else.

ABBIE *(wildly).* Min?

EBEN. Mebbe.

ABBIE *(torturedly).* Did ye go t' see her? Did ye r'ally go? I thought ye mightn't. Is that why ye throwed me off jest now?

EBEN *(sneeringly).* What if it be?

ABBIE *(raging).* Then ye're a dog, Eben Cabot!

EBEN *(threateningly).* Ye can't talk that way t' me!

ABBIE *(with a shrill laugh).* Can't I? Did ye think I was in love with ye—a weak thin' like yew? Not much! I on'y wanted ye fur a purpose o' my own—an' I'll hev ye fur it yet 'cause I'm stronger'n yew be!

EBEN *(resentfully).* I knowed well it was on'y part o' yer plan t' swaller everythin'!

ABBIE *(tauntingly).* Mebbe!

EBEN *(furious).* Git out o' my room!

ABBIE. This air my room an' ye're on'y hired help!

EBEN *(threateningly).* Git out afore I murder ye!

ABBIE *(quite confident now).* I hain't a mite afeerd. Ye want me, don't ye? Yes, ye do! An' yer Paw's son'll never kill what he wants! Look at yer eyes! They's lust fur me in 'em, burnin' 'em up! Look at yer lips now! They're tremblin' an' longin' t' kiss me, an' yer teeth t' bite! *(He is watching her now with a horrible fascination. She laughs a crazy triumphant laugh)* I'm a-goin' t' make all o' this hum my hum! They's one room hain't mine yet, but it's a-goin' t' be tonight. I'm a-goin' down now an' light up! *(She makes him a mocking bow)* Won't ye come courtin' me in the best parlor, Mister Cabot?

EBEN (*staring at her—horribly confused—dully*). Don't ye dare! It hain't been opened since Maw died an' was laid out thar! Don't ye. . . ! (*But her eyes are fixed on his so burningly that his will seems to wither before hers. He stands swaying toward her helplessly*).

ABBIE (*holding his eyes and putting all her will into her words as she backs out the door*). I'll expect ye afore long, Eben.

EBEN (*stares after her for a while, walking toward the door. A light appears in the parlor window. He murmurs*). In the parlor? (*This seems to arouse connotations for he comes back and puts on his white shirt, collar, half ties the tie mechanically, puts on coat, takes his hat, stands barefooted looking about him in bewilderment, mutters wonderingly*) Maw! Whar air yew? (*Then goes slowly toward the door in rear*).

SCENE THREE

A few minutes later. The interior of the parlor is shown. A grim, repressed room like a tomb in which the family has been interred alive. ABBIE *sits on the edge of the horsehair sofa. She has lighted all the candles and the room is revealed in all its preserved ugliness. A change has come over the woman. She looks awed and frightened now, ready to run away.*

The door is opened and EBEN *appears. His face wears an expression of obsessed confusion. He stands staring at her, his arms hanging disjointedly from his shoulders, his feet bare, his hat in his hand.*

ABBIE (*after a pause—with a nervous, formal politeness*). Won't ye set?

EBEN (*dully*). Ay-eh. (*Mechanically he places his hat carefully on the floor near the door and sits stiffly beside her on the edge of the sofa. A pause. They both remain rigid, looking straight ahead with eyes full of fear*).

ABBIE. When I fust come in—in the dark—they seemed somethin' here.

EBEN (*simply*). Maw.

ABBIE. I kin still feel—somethin'. . . .

EBEN. It's Maw.

ABBIE. At fust I was feered o' it. I wanted t' yell an' run. Now—since yew come—seems like it's growin' soft an' kind t' me. (*Addressing the air—queerly*) Thank yew.

EBEN. Maw allus loved me.

ABBIE. Mebbe it knows I love yew, too. Mebbe that makes it kind t' me.

EBEN (*dully*). I dunno. I should think she'd hate ye.

ABBIE (*with certainty*). No. I kin feel it don't—not no more.

EBEN. Hate ye fur stealin' her place—here in her hum—settin' in her parlor whar she was laid— (*He suddenly stops, staring stupidly before him*).

ABBIE. What is it, Eben?

EBEN (*in a whisper*). Seems like Maw didn't want me t' remind ye.

ABBIE (*excitedly*). I knowed, Eben! It's kind t' me! It don't b'ar me no grudges fur what I never knowed an' couldn't help!

EBEN. Maw b'ars him a grudge.

ABBIE. Waal, so does all o' us.

EBEN. Ay-eh. (*With passion*) I does, by God!

ABBIE (*taking one of his hands in hers and patting it*). Thar! Don't git riled thinkin' o' him. Think o' yer

Maw who's kind t' us. Tell me about yer Maw, Eben.

EBEN. They hain't nothin' much. She was kind. She was good.

ABBIE (*putting one arm over his shoulder. He does not seem to notice—passionately*). I'll be kind an' good t' ye!

EBEN. Sometimes she used t' sing fur me.

ABBIE. I'll sing fur ye!

EBEN. This was her hum. This was her farm.

ABBIE. This is my hum! This is my farm!

EBEN. He married her t' steal 'em. She was soft an' easy. He couldn't 'preciate her.

ABBIE. He can't 'preciate me!

EBEN. He murdered her with his hardness.

ABBIE. He's murderin' me!

EBEN. She died. (*A pause*) Sometimes she used to sing fur me. (*He bursts into a fit of sobbing*).

ABBIE (*both her arms around him —with wild passion*). I'll sing fur ye! I'll die fur ye! (*In spite of her overwhelming desire for him, there is a sincere maternal love in her manner and voice—a horribly frank mixture of lust and mother love*) Don't cry, Eben! I'll take yer Maw's place! I'll be everythin' she was t' ye! Let me kiss ye, Eben! (*She pulls his head around. He makes a bewildered pretense of resistance. She is tender*) Don't be afeered! I'll kiss ye pure, Eben—same 's if I was a Maw t' ye —an' ye kin kiss me back 's if yew was my son—my boy—sayin' goodnight t' me! Kiss me, Eben. (*They kiss in restrained fashion. Then suddenly wild passion overcomes her. She kisses him lustfully again and again and he flings his arms about her and returns her kisses. Suddenly, as in the bedroom, she frees himself from her violently and springs to his feet. He is trembling all over, in a strange state of terror.* ABBIE *strains her arms toward him with fierce pleading*) Don't ye leave me, Eben! Can't ye see it hain't enuf—lovin' ye like a Maw—can't ye see it's got t' be that an' more—much more—a hundred times more—fur me t' be happy—fur yew t' be happy?

EBEN (*to the presence he feels in the room*). Maw! Maw! What d'ye want? What air ye tellin' me?

ABBIE. She's tellin' ye t' love me. She knows I love ye an' I'll be good t' ye. Can't ye feel it? Don't ye know? She's tellin' ye t' love me, Eben!

EBEN. Ay-eh. I feel—mebbe she— but—I can't figger out—why—when ye've stole her place—here in her hum—in the parlor whar she was—

ABBIE (*fiercely*). She knows I love ye!

EBEN (*his face suddenly lighting up with a fierce, triumphant grin*). I see it! I sees why. It's her vengeance on him—so's she kin rest quiet in her grave!

ABBIE (*wildly*). Vengeance o' God on the hull o' us! What d'we give a durn? I love ye, Eben! God knows I love ye! (*She stretches out her arms for him*).

EBEN (*throws himself on his knees beside the sofa and grabs her in his arms—releasing all his pent-up passion*) An' I love yew, Abbie!—now I kin say it! I been dyin' fur want o' ye—every hour since ye come! I love ye! (*Their lips meet in a fierce, bruising kiss*).

SCENE FOUR

Exterior of the farmhouse. It is just dawn. The front door at right is opened and EBEN *comes out and walks around to the gate. He is dressed in his working clothes. He seems changed. His face wears a bold and confident expression, he is grinning to himself with evident satisfaction. As he gets near the gate, the window of the parlor is heard opening and the shutters are flung back and* ABBIE *sticks her head out. Her hair tumbles over her shoulders in disarray, her face is flushed, she looks at* EBEN *with tender, languorous eyes and calls softly.*

ABBIE. Eben. (*As he turns—playfully*) Jest one more kiss afore ye go. I'm goin' to miss ye fearful all day.

EBEN. An' me yew, ye kin bet! (*He goes to her. They kiss several times. He draws away, laughingly*) Thar. That's enuf, hain't it? Ye won't hev none left fur next time.

ABBIE. I got a million o' 'em left fur yew! (*Then a bit anxiously*) D'ye r'ally love me, Eben?

EBEN (*emphatically*). I like ye better'n any gal I ever knowed! That's gospel!

ABBIE. Likin' hain't lovin'.

EBEN. Waal then—I love ye. Now air yew satisfied?

ABBIE. Ay-eh, I be. (*She smiles at him adoringly*).

EBEN. I better git t' the barn. The old critter's liable t' suspicion an' come sneakin' up.

ABBIE (*with a confident laugh*). Let him! I kin allus pull the wool over his eyes. I'm goin' t' leave the shutters open and let in the sun 'n' air. This room's been dead long enuf. Now it's goin' t' be my room!

EBEN (*frowning*). Ay-eh.

ABBIE (*hastily*). I meant—our room.

EBEN. Ay-eh.

ABBIE. We made it our'n last night, didn't we? We give it life—our lovin' did. (*A pause*).

EBEN (*with a strange look*). Maw's gone back t' her grave. She kin sleep now.

ABBIE. May she rest in peace! (*Then tenderly rebuking*) Ye oughtn't t' talk o' sad thin's—this mornin'.

EBEN. It jest come up in my mind o' itself.

ABBIE. Don't let it. (*He doesn't answer. She yawns*) Waal, I'm a-goin' t' steal a wink o' sleep. I'll tell the Old Man I hain't feelin' pert. Let him git his own vittles.

EBEN. I see him comin' from the barn. Ye better look smart an' git upstairs.

ABBIE. Ay-eh. Good-by. Don't ferget me. (*She throws him a kiss. He grins—then squares his shoulders and awaits his father confidently.* CABOT *walks slowly up from the left, staring up at the sky with a vague face*).

EBEN (*jovially*). Mornin', Paw. Star-gazin' in daylight?

CABOT. Purty, hain't it?

EBEN (*looking around him possessively*). It's a durned purty farm.

CABOT. I mean the sky.

EBEN (*grinning*). How d'ye know? Them eyes o' your'n can't see that fur. (*This tickles his humor and he slaps his thigh and laughs*) Ho-ho! That's a good un!

CABOT (*grimly sarcastic*). Ye're feelin' right chipper, hain't ye? Whar'd ye steal the likker?

EBEN (*good-naturedly*). 'Tain't likker. Jest life. (*Suddenly holding out his hand—soberly*) Yew 'n' me is quits. Let's shake hands.

CABOT (*suspiciously*). What's come over ye?

EBEN. Then don't. Mebbe it's jest as well. (*A moment's pause*) What's come over me? (*Queerly*) Didn't I feel her passin'—goin' back t' her grave?

CABOT (*dully*). Who?

EBEN. Maw. She kin rest now an' sleep content. She's quits with ye.

CABOT (*confusedly*). I rested. I slept good—down with the cows. They know how t' sleep. They're teachin' me.

EBEN (*suddenly jovial again*). Good fur the cows! Waal—ye better git t' work.

CABOT (*grimly amused*). Air yew bossin' me, ye calf?

EBEN (*beginning to laugh*). Ay-eh! I'm bossin' yew! Ha-ha-ha! See how ye like it! Ha-ha-ha! I'm the prize rooster o' this roost. Ha-ha-ha! (*He goes off toward the barn laughing*).

CABOT (*looks after him with scornful pity*). Soft-headed. Like his Maw. Dead spit 'n' image. No hope in him! (*He spits with contemptuous disgust*) A born fool! (*Then matter-offactly*) Waal—I'm gittin' peckish. (*He goes toward door*).

CURTAIN

PART THREE— SCENE ONE

A night in late spring the following year. The kitchen and the two bedrooms upstairs are shown. The two bedrooms are dimly lighted by a tallow candle in each. EBEN is sitting on the side of the bed in his room, his chin propped on his fists, his face a study of the struggle he is making to understand his conflicting emotions. The noisy laughter and music from below where a kitchen dance is in progress annoy and distract him. He scowls at the floor.

In the next room a cradle stands beside the double bed.

In the kitchen all is festivity. The stove has been taken down to give more room to the dancers. The chairs, with wooden benches added, have been pushed back against the walls. On these are seated, squeezed in tight against one another, farmers and their wives and their young folks of both sexes from the neighboring farms. They are all chattering and laughing loudly. They evidently have some secret joke in common. There is no end of winking, of nudging, of meaning nods of the head toward CABOT who, in a state of extreme hilarious excitement increased by the amount he has drunk, is standing near the rear door where there is a small keg of whisky and serving drinks to all the men. In the left corner, front, dividing the attention with her husband, ABBIE is sitting in a rocking chair, a shawl wrapped about her shoulders. She is very pale, her face is thin and drawn, her eyes are fixed anxiously on the open door in rear as if waiting for someone.

The musician is tuning up his fiddle, seated in the far right corner. He is a lanky young fellow with a long, weak face. His pale eyes blink incessantly and he grins about him slyly with a greedy malice.

ABBIE (*suddenly turning to a young girl on her right*). Whar's Eben?

YOUNG GIRL (*eying her scornfully*). I dunno, Mrs. Cabot. I hain't seen Eben in ages. (*Meaningly*) Seems like he's spent most o' his time t' hum since yew come.

ABBIE (*vaguely*). I tuk his Maw's place.

YOUNG GIRL. Ay-eh. So I've heerd. (*She turns away to retail this bit of gossip to her mother sitting next to her. ABBIE turns to her left to a big stoutish middle-aged man whose*) *flushed face and starting eyes show the amount of "likker" he has consumed*).

ABBIE. Ye hain't seen Eben, hev ye?

MAN. No, I hain't. (*Then he adds with a wink*) If yew hain't, who would?

ABBIE. He's the best dancer in the county. He'd ought t' come an' dance.

MAN (*with a wink*). Mebbe he's doin' the dutiful an' walkin' the kid t' sleep. It's a boy, hain't it?

ABBIE (*nodding vaguely*) Ay-eh—born two weeks back—purty's a picter.

MAN. They all is—t' their Maws. (*Then in a whisper, with a nudge and a leer*) Listen, Abbie—if ye ever git tired o' Eben, remember me! Don't fergit now! (*He looks at her uncomprehending face for a second —then grunts disgustedly*) Waal—guess I'll likker agin. (*He goes over and joins* CABOT *who is arguing noisily with an old farmer over cows. They all drink*).

ABBIE (*this time appealing to nobody in particular*). Wonder what Eben's a-doin'? (*Her remark is repeated down the line with many a guffaw and titter until it reaches the fiddler. He fastens his blinking eyes on* ABBIE).

FIDDLER (*raising his voice*). Bet I kin tell ye, Abbie, what Eben's doin'! He's down t' the church offerin' up prayers o' thanksgivin'. (*They all titter expectantly*).

A MAN. What fur? (*Another titter*).

FIDDLER. 'Cause unto him a—(*He hesitates just long enough*) brother is born! (*A roar of laughter. They all look from* ABBIE *to* CABOT. *She is oblivious, staring at the door.* CABOT, *although he hasn't heard the words, is irritated by the laughter and steps forward, glaring about him. There is an immediate silence*).

CABOT. What're ye all bleatin' about

—like a flock o' goats? Why don't ye dance, damn ye? I axed ye here t' dance—t' eat, drink an' be merry —an' thar ye set cacklin' like a lot o' wet hens with the pip! Ye've swilled my likker an' guzzled my vittles like hogs, hain't ye? Then dance fur me, can't ye? That's fa'r an' squar', hain't it? (*A grumble of resentment goes around but they are all evidently in too much awe of him to express it openly*).

FIDDLER (*slyly*). We're waitin' fur Eben. (*A suppressed laugh*).

CABOT (*with a fierce exultation*). T'hell with Eben! Eben's done fur now! I got a new son! (*His mood switching with drunken suddenness*) But ye needn't t' laugh at Eben, none o' ye! He's my blood, if he be a dumb fool. He's better nor any o' yew! He kin do a day's work a'most up t' what I kin—an' that'd put any o' yew pore critters t' shame!

FIDDLER. An' he kin do a good night's work, too! (*A roar of laughter*).

CABOT. Laugh, ye damn fools! Ye're right jist the same, Fiddler. He kin work day an' night too, like I kin, if need be!

OLD FARMER (*from behind the keg where he is weaving drunkenly back and forth—with great simplicity*). They hain't many t' touch ye, Ephraim—a son at seventy-six. That's a hard man fur ye! I be on'y sixty-eight an' I couldn't do it. (*A roar of laughter in which* CABOT *joins uproariously*).

CABOT (*slapping him on the back*). I'm sorry fur ye, Hi. I'd never suspicion sech weakness from a boy like yew!

OLD FARMER. An' I never reckoned yew had it in ye nuther, Ephraim. (*There is another laugh*).

CABOT (*suddenly grim*). I got a lot in me—a hell of a lot—folks don't know on. (*Turning to the fiddler*) Fiddle 'er up, durn ye! Give 'em somethin' t' dance t'! What air ye, an ornament? Hain't this a celebration? Then grease yer elbow an' go it!

FIDDLER (*seizes a drink which the* OLD FARMER *holds out to him and downs it*). Here goes! (*He starts to fiddle "Lady of the Lake." Four young fellows and four girls form in two lines and dance a square dance. The* FIDDLER *shouts directions for the different movements, keeping his words in the rhythm of the music and interspersing them with jocular personal remarks to the dancers themselves. The people seated along the walls stamp their feet and clap their hands in unison.* CABOT *is especially active in this respect. Only* ABBIE *remains apathetic, staring at the door as if she were alone in a silent room*).

FIDDLER. Swing your partner t'the right! That's it, Jim! Give her a b'ar hug! Her Maw hain't lookin'. (*Laughter*) Change partners! That suits ye, don't it, Essie, now ye got Reub afore ye? Look at her redden up, will ye? Waal, life is short an' so's love, as the feller says. (*Laughter*).

CABOT (*excitedly, stamping his foot*). Go it, boys! Go it, gals!

FIDDLER (*with a wink at the others*). Ye're the spryest seventy-six ever I sees, Ephraim! Now if ye'd on'y good eye-sight . . . ! (*Suppressed laughter. He gives* CABOT *no chance to retort but roars*) Promenade! Ye're walkin' like a bride down the aisle, Sarah! Waal, while they's life they's allus hope, I've heerd tell. Swing your partner to the left! Gosh A'mighty, look at Johnny Cook high-steppin'! They hain't goin' t'be much strength left fur howin' in the corn lot t'morrow. (*Laughter*).

CABOT. Go it! Go it! (*Then suddenly, unable to restrain himself any*

longer, he prances into the midst of the dancers, scattering them, waving his arms about wildly*) Ye're all hoofs! Git out o' my road! Give me room! I'll show ye dancin'. Ye're all too soft! (*He pushes them roughly away. They crowd back toward the walls, muttering, looking at him resentfully*).

FIDDLER (*jeeringly*). Go it, Ephraim! Go it! (*He starts "Pop, Goes the Weasel," increasing the tempo with every verse until at the end he is fiddling crazily as fast as he can go*).

CABOT (*starts to dance, which he does very well and with tremendous vigor. Then he begins to improvise, cuts incredibly grotesque capers, leaping up and cracking his heels together, prancing around in a circle with body bent in an Indian war dance, then suddenly straightening up and kicking as high as he can with both legs. He is like a monkey on a string. And all the while he intersperses his antics with shouts and derisive comments*). Whoop! Here's dancin' fur ye! Whoop! See that! Seventy-six, if I'm a day! Hard as iron yet! Beatin' the young 'uns like I allus done! Look at me! I'd invite ye t' dance on my hundredth birthday on'y ye'll all be dead by then. Ye're a sickly generation! Yer hearts air pink, not red! Yer veins is full o' mud an' water! I be the on'y man in the county! Whoop! See that! I'm a Injun! I've killed Injuns in the West afore ye was born—an' skulped 'em too! They's a arrer wound on my backside I c'd show ye! The hull tribe chased me. I outrun 'em all— with the arrer stuck in me! An' I tuk vengeance on 'em. Ten eyes fur an eye, that was my motter! Whoop! Look at me! I kin kick the ceilin' off the room! Whoop!

FIDDLER (*stops playing—exhaust-*

edly). God A'mighty, I got enuf. Ye got the devil's strength in ye.

CABOT (*delightedly*). Did I beat yew, too? Waal, ye played smart. Hev a swig. (*He pours whisky for himself and* FIDDLER. *They drink. The others watch* CABOT *silently with cold, hostile eyes. There is a dead pause. The* FIDDLER *rests.* CABOT *leans against the keg, panting, glaring around him confusedly. In the room above,* EBEN *gets to his feet and tiptoes out the door in rear, appearing a moment later in the other bedroom. He moves silently, even frightenedly, toward the cradle and stands there looking down at the baby. His face is as vague as his reactions are confused, but there is a trace of tenderness, of interested discovery. At the same moment that he reaches the cradle,* ABBIE *seems to sense something. She gets up weakly and goes to* CABOT).

ABBIE. I'm goin' up t' the baby.

CABOT (*with real solicitation*). Air ye able fur the stairs? D'ye want me t' help ye, Abbie?

ABBIE. No. I'm able. I'll be down agen soon.

CABOT. Don't ye git wore out! He needs ye, remember—our son does! (*He grins affectionately, patting her on the back. She shrinks from his touch*).

ABBIE (*dully*). Don't—tech me. I'm goin'—up. (*She goes.* CABOT *looks after her. A whisper goes around the room.* CABOT *turns. It ceases. He wipes his forehead streaming with sweat. He is breathing pantingly*).

CABOT. I'm a-goin' out t' git fresh air. I'm feelin' a mite dizzy. Fiddle up thar! Dance, all o' ye! Here's likker fur them as wants it. Enjoy yerselves. I'll be back. (*He goes, closing the door behind him*).

FIDDLER (*sarcastically*). Don't hurry none on our account! (*A suppressed*

laugh. He imitates ABBIE) Whar's Eben? (*More laughter*).

A WOMAN (*loudly*). What's happened in this house is plain as the nose on yer face! (ABBIE *appears in the doorway upstairs and stands looking in surprise and adoration at* EBEN *who does not see her*).

A MAN. Ssshh! He's li'ble t' be listenin' at the door. That'd be like him. (*Their voices die to an intensive whispering. Their faces are concentrated on this gossip. A noise as of dead leaves in the wind comes from the room.* CABOT *has come out from the porch and stands by the gate, leaning on it, staring at the sky blinkingly.* ABBIE *comes across the room silently.* EBEN *does not notice her until quite near*).

EBEN (*starting*). Abbie!

ABBIE. Ssshh! (*She throws her arms around him. They kiss—then bend over the cradle together*) Ain't he purty?—dead spit 'n' image o' yew!

EBEN (*pleased*). Air he? I can't tell none.

ABBIE. E-zactly like!

EBEN (*frowningly*). I don't like this. I don't like lettin' on what's mine's his'n. I been doin' that all my life. I'm gittin' t' the end o' b'arin' it!

ABBIE (*putting her finger on his lips*). We're doin' the best we kin. We got t' wait. Somethin's bound t' happen. (*She puts her arms around him*) I got t' go back.

EBEN. I'm goin' out. I can't b'ar it with the fiddle playin' an' the laughin'.

ABBIE. Don't git feelin' low. I love ye, Eben. Kiss me. (*He kisses her. They remain in each other's arms*).

CABOT (*at the gate, confusedly*). Even the music can't drive it out—somethin'. Ye kin feel it droppin' off the elums, climbin' up the roof, sneakin' down the chimney, pokin' in the corners! They's no peace in houses, they's no rest livin' with folks. Somethin's always livin' with ye. (*With a deep sigh*) I'll go t' the barn an' rest a spell. (*He goes wearily toward the barn*).

FIDDLER (*tuning up*). Let's celebrate the old skunk gittin' fooled! We kin have some fun now he's went. (*He starts to fiddle "Turkey in the Straw." There is real merriment now. The young folks get up to dance*).

SCENE TWO

A half hour later—Exterior— EBEN *is standing by the gate looking up at the sky, an expression of dumb pain bewildered by itself on his face.* CABOT *appears, returning from the barn, walking wearily, his eyes on the ground. He sees* EBEN *and his whole mood immediately changes. He becomes excited, a cruel, triumphant grin comes to his lips, he strides up and slaps* EBEN *on the back. From within comes the whining of the fiddle and the noise of stamping feet and laughing voices.*

CABOT. So har ye be!

EBEN (*startled, stares at him with hatred for a moment—then dully*). Ay-eh.

CABOT (*surveying him jeeringly*). Why hain't ye been in t' dance? They was all axin' fur ye.

EBEN. Let 'em ax!

CABOT. They's a hull passel o' purty gals.

EBEN. T' hell with 'em!

CABOT. Ye'd ought t' be marryin' one o' 'em soon.

EBEN. I hain't marryin' no one.

CABOT. Ye might arn a share o' a farm that way.

EBEN (*with a sneer*). Like yew did, ye mean? I hain't that kind.

CABOT (*stung*). Ye lie! 'Twas yer Maw's folks aimed t' steal my farm from me.

EBEN. Other folks don't say so. (*After a pause—defiantly*) An' I got a farm, anyways!

CABOT (*derisively*). Whar?

EBEN (*stamps a foot on the ground*). Har!

CABOT (*throws his head back and laughs coarsely*). Ho-ho! Ye hev, hev ye? Waal, that's a good un!

EBEN (*controlling himself—grimly*). Ye'll see!

CABOT (*stares at him suspiciously, trying to make him out—a pause—then with scornful confidence*). Ay-eh. I'll see. So'll ye. It's ye that's blind—blind as a mole underground. (*EBEN suddenly laughs, one short sardonic bark: "Ha." A pause. CABOT peers at him with renewed suspicion*) Whar air ye hawin' 'bout? (*EBEN turns away without answering. CABOT grows angry*) God A'mighty, yew air a dumb dunce! They's nothin' in that thick skull o' your'n but noise—like a empty keg it be! (*EBEN doesn't seem to hear. CABOT's rage grows*) Yewr farm! God A'mighty! If ye wa'n't a born donkey ye'd know ye'll never own stick nor stone on it, specially now arter him bein' born. It's his'n, I tell ye— his'n arter I die—but I'll live a hundred jest t' fool ye all—an' he'll be growed then—yewr age a'most! (*EBEN laughs again his sardonic "Ha." This drives CABOT into a fury*) Ha? Ye think ye kin git 'round that someways, do ye? Waal, it'll be her'n, too—Abbie's—ye won't git 'round her—she knows yer tricks—she'll be too much fur ye—she wants the farm her'n—she was afeerd o' ye—she told me ye was sneakin' 'round tryin' t' make love t' her t' git her on yer side . . . ye . . . ye mad fool, ye! (*He raises his clenched fists threateningly*).

EBEN (*is confronting him, choking with rage*). Ye lie, ye old skunk! Abbie never said no sech thing!

CABOT (*suddenly triumphant when he sees how shaken* EBEN *is*). She did. An' I says, I'll blow his brains t' the top o' them elums—an' she says no, that hain't sense, who'll ye git t'help ye on the farm in his place—an' then she says yew'n me ought t' have a son—I know we kin, she says —an' I says, if we do, ye kin have anythin' I've got ye've a mind t'. An' she says, I wants Eben cut off so's this farm'll be mine when ye die! (*With terrible gloating*) An' that's what's happened, hain't it? An' the farm's her'n! An' the dust o' the road —that's you'rn! Ha! Now who's hawin'?

EBEN (*has been listening, petrified with grief and rage—suddenly laughs wildly and brokenly*). Ha-ha-ha! So that's her sneakin' game—all along! —like I suspicioned at fust—t' swaller it all—an' me, too . . . ! (*Madly*) I'll murder her! (*He springs toward the porch but* CABOT *is quicker and gets in between*).

CABOT. No, ye don't!

EBEN. Git out o' my road! (*He tries to throw* CABOT *aside. They grapple in what becomes immediately a murderous struggle. The old man's concentrated strength is too much for* EBEN. CABOT *gets one hand on his throat and presses him back across the stone wall. At the same moment,* ABBIE *comes out on the porch. With a stifled cry she runs toward them*).

ABBIE. Eben! Ephraim! (*She tugs at the hand on* EBEN'S *throat*) Let go, Ephraim! Ye're chokin' him!

CABOT (*removes his hand and flings* EBEN *sideways full length on the grass, gasping and choking. With a cry,* ABBIE *kneels beside him, trying to take his head on her lap, but he pushes her away.* CABOT *stands looking down with fierce triumph*). Ye needn't t've fret, Abbie, I wa'n't aimin' t' kill him. He hain't wuth hangin' fur—not by a hell of a sight! (*More and more triumphantly*) Seventy-six an' him not thirty yit—an' look whar he be fur thinkin' his Paw was easy! No, by God, I hain't easy! An' him upstairs, I'll raise him t' be like me! (*He turns to leave them*) I'm goin' in an' dance!—sing an' celebrate! (*He walks to the porch—then turns with a great grin*) I don't calc'late it's left in him, but if he gits pesky, Abbie, ye jest sing out. I'll come a-runnin' an' by the Etarnal, I'll put him across my knee an' birch him! Ha-ha-ha! (*He goes into the house laughing. A moment later his loud "whoop" is heard*).

ABBIE (*tenderly*). Eben. Air ye hurt? (*She tries to kiss him but he pushes her violently away and struggles to a sitting position*).

EBEN (*gaspingly*). T'hell—with ye!

ABBIE (*not believing her ears*). It's me, Eben—Abbie—don't ye know me?

EBEN (*glowering at her with hatred*). Ay-eh—I know ye—now! (*He suddenly breaks down, sobbing weakly*).

ABBIE (*fearfully*). Eben—what's happened t' ye—why did ye look at me 's if ye hated me?

EBEN (*violently, between sobs and gasps*). I do hate ye! Ye're a whore— a damn trickin' whore!

ABBIE (*shrinking back horrified*). Eben! Ye don't know what ye're sayin'!

EBEN (*scrambling to his feet and following her—accusingly*). Ye're nothin' but a stinkin' passel o' lies! Ye've been lyin' t' me every word ye spoke, day an' night, since we fust—done it. Ye've kept sayin' ye loved me. . . .

ABBIE (*frantically*). I do love ye! (*She takes his hand but he flings hers away*).

EBEN (*unheeding*). Ye've made a fool o' me—a sick, dumb fool—a-purpose! Ye've been on'y playin' yer sneakin', stealin' game all along—gittin' me t' lie with ye so's ye'd hev a son he'd think was his'n, an' makin' him promise he'd give ye the farm and let me eat dust, if ye did git him a son! (*Staring at her with anguished, bewildered eyes*) They must be a devil livin' in ye! T'ain't human t' be as bad as that be!

ABBIE (*stunned—dully*). He told yew . . . ?

EBEN. Hain't it true? It hain't no good in yew lyin'.

ABBIE (*pleadingly*). Eben, listen—ye must listen—it was long ago—afore we done nothin'—yew was scornin' me—goin' t' see Min—when I was lovin' ye—an' I said it t' him t' git vengeance on ye!

EBEN (*unheedingly. With tortured passion*). I wish ye was dead! I wish I was dead along with ye afore this come! (*Ragingly*) But I'll git my vengeance too! I'll pray Maw t' come back t' help me—t' put her cuss on yew an' him!

ABBIE (*brokenly*). Don't ye, Eben! Don't ye! (*She throws herself on her knees before him, weeping*) I didn't mean t' do bad t'ye! Fergive me, won't ye?

EBEN (*not seeming to hear her—fiercely*). I'll git squar' with the old skunk—an' yew! I'll tell him the truth 'bout the son he's so proud o'! Then I'll leave ye here t' pizen each other—with Maw comin' out o' her grave at nights—an' I'll go t' the gold fields o' Californi-a whar Sim an' Peter be!

ABBIE (*terrified*). Ye won't—leave me? Ye can't!

EBEN (*with fierce determination*). I'm a-goin', I tell ye! I'll git rich thar an' come back an' fight him fur the farm he stole—an' I'll kick ye both out in the road—t' beg an' sleep in the woods—an' yer son along with ye —t' starve an' die! (*He is hysterical at the end*).

ABBIE (*with a shudder—humbly*). He's yewr son, too, Eben.

EBEN (*torturedly*). I wish he never was born! I wish he'd die this minit! I wish I'd never sot eyes on him! It's him—yew havin' him—a-purpose t' steal—that's changed everythin'!

ABBIE (*gently*). Did ye believe I loved ye—afore he come?

EBEN. Ay-eh—like a dumb ox!

ABBIE. An' ye don't believe no more?

EBEN. B'lieve a lyin' thief! Ha!

ABBIE (*shudders—then humbly*). An' did ye r'ally love me afore?

EBEN (*brokenly*). Ay-eh—an' ye was trickin' me!

ABBIE. An' ye don't love me now!

EBEN (*violently*). I hate ye, I tell ye!

ABBIE. An' ye're truly goin' West—goin' t' leave me—all account o' him being born?

EBEN. I'm a-goin' in the mornin'—or may God strike me t' hell!

ABBIE (*after a pause—with a dreadful cold intensity—slowly*). If that's what his comin's done t' me—killin' yewr love—takin' yew away—my on'y joy—the on'y joy I ever knowed —like heaven t' me—purtier'n heaven—then I hate him, too, even if I be his Maw!

EBEN (*bitterly*). Lies! Ye love him! He'll steal the farm fur ye! (*Brokenly*) But t'ain't the farm so much—not no more—it's yew foolin' me—gittin' me t' love ye—lyin' yew loved me—jest t' git a son t' steal!

ABBIE (*distractedly*). He won't steal! I'd kill him fust! I do love ye! I'll prove t' ye . . . !

EBEN (*harshly*). T'ain't no use lyin' no more. I'm deaf t' ye! (*He turns away*) I hain't seein' ye agen. Good-by!

ABBIE (*pale with anguish*). Hain't ye even goin' t' kiss me—not once— arter all we loved?

EBEN (*in a hard voice*). I hain't wantin' t' kiss ye never agen! I'm wantin' t' forgit I ever sot eyes on ye!

ABBIE. Eben!—ye mustn't—wait a spell—I want t' tell ye. . . .

EBEN. I'm a-goin' in t' git drunk. I'm a-goin' t' dance.

ABBIE (*clinging to his arm—with passionate earnestness*). If I could make it—'s if he'd never come up between us—if I could prove t' ye I wa'n't schemin' t' steal from ye—so's everythin' could be jest the same with us, lovin' each other jest the same, kissin' an' happy the same's we've been happy afore he come—if I could do it—ye'd love me agen, wouldn't ye? Ye'd kiss me agen? Ye wouldn't never leave me, would ye?

EBEN (*moved*). I calc'late not. (*Then shaking her hand off his arm —with a bitter smile*) But ye hain't God, be ye?

ABBIE (*exultantly*). Remember ye've promised! (*Then with strange intensity*) Mebbe I kin take back one thin' God does!

EBEN (*peering at her*). Ye're gittin' cracked, hain't ye? (*Then going towards door*) I'm a-goin' t' dance.

ABBIE (*calls after him intensely*). I'll prove t' ye! I'll prove I love ye better'n. . . . (*He goes in the door, not seeming to hear. She remains standing where she is, looking after him—then she finishes desperately*). Better'n everythin' else in the world!

SCENE THREE

Just before dawn in the morning— shows the kitchen and CABOT's *bedroom. In the kitchen, by the light of a tallow candle on the table,* EBEN *is sitting, his chin propped on his hands, his drawn face blank and expressionless. His carpetbag is on the floor beside him. In the bedroom, dimly lighted by a small whale-oil lamp,* CABOT *lies asleep.* ABBIE *is bending over the cradle, listening, her face full of terror yet with an undercurrent of desperate triumph. Suddenly, she breaks down and sobs, appears about to throw herself on her knees beside the cradle; but the old man turns restlessly, groaning in his sleep, and she controls herself, and, shrinking away from the cradle with a gesture of horror, backs swiftly toward the door in rear and goes out. A moment later she comes into the kitchen and, running to* EBEN, *flings her arms about his neck and kisses him wildly. He hardens himself, he remains unmoved and cold, he keeps his eyes straight ahead.*

ABBIE (*hysterically*). I done it, Eben! I told ye I'd do it! I've proved I love ye—better'n everythin'—so's ye can't never doubt me no more!

EBEN (*dully*). Whatever ye done, it hain't no good now.

ABBIE (*wildly*). Don't ye say that! Kiss me, Eben, won't ye? I need ye t' kiss me arter what I done! I need ye t' say ye love me!

EBEN (*kisses her without emotion —dully*). That's fur good-by. I'm a-goin' soon.

ABBIE. No! No! Ye won't go—not now!

EBEN (*going on with his own thoughts*). I been a-thinkin'—an' I hain't goin' t' tell Paw nothin'. I'll leave Maw t' take vengeance on ye. If I told him, the old skunk'd jest be stinkin' mean enuf to take it out on that baby. (*His voice showing emotion in spite of him*) An' I don't want nothin' bad t' happen t' him. He hain't t' blame fur yew. (*He adds with a certain queer pride*) An' he looks like me! An' by God, he's mine! An' some day I'll be a-comin' back an' . . . !

ABBIE (*too absorbed in her own thoughts to listen to him—pleadingly*). They's no cause fur ye t' go now—they's no sense—it's all the same's it was—they's nothin' come b'tween us now—arter what I done!

EBEN (*something in her voice arouses him. He stares at her a bit frightenedly*). Ye look mad, Abbie. What did ye do?

ABBIE. I—I killed him, Eben.

EBEN (*amazed*). Ye killed him?

ABBIE (*dully*). Ay-eh.

EBEN (*recovering from his astonishment—savagely*). An' serves him right! But we got t' do somethin' quick t' make it look s'if the old skunk'd killed himself when he was drunk. We kin prove by 'em all how drunk he got.

ABBIE (*wildly*). No! No! Not him! (*Laughing distractedly*) But that's what I ought t' done, hain't it? I oughter killed him instead! Why didn't ye tell me?

EBEN (*appalled*). Instead? What d'ye mean?

ABBIE. Not him.

EBEN (*his face grown ghastly*). Not —not that baby!

ABBIE (*dully*). Ay-eh!

EBEN (*falls to his knees as if he'd been struck—his voice trembling with horror*). Oh, God A'mighty! A'mighty God! Maw, whar was ye, why didn't ye stop her?

ABBIE (*simply*). She went back t'

her grave that night we fust done it, remember? I hain't felt her about since. (*A pause.* EBEN *hides his head in his hands, trembling all over as if he had the ague. She goes on dully*) I left the piller over his little face. Then he killed himself. He stopped breathin'. (*She begins to weep softly*).

EBEN (*rage beginning to mingle with grief*). He looked like me. He was mine, damn ye!

ABBIE (*slowly and brokenly*). I didn't want t' do it. I hated myself fur doin' it. I loved him. He was so purty—dead spit 'n' image o' yew. But I loved yew more—an' yew was goin' away—far off whar I'd never see ye agen, never kiss ye, never feel ye pressed agin me agen—an' ye said ye hated me fur havin' him—ye said ye hated him an' wished he was dead —ye said if it hadn't been fur him comin' it'd be the same's afore between us.

EBEN (*unable to endure this, springs to his feet in a fury, threatening her, his twitching fingers seeming to reach out for her throat*). Ye lie! I never said—I never dreamed ye'd— I'd cut off my head afore I'd hurt his finger!

ABBIE (*piteously, sinking on her knees*). Eben, don't ye look at me like that—hatin' me—not after what I done fur ye—fur us—so's we could be happy agen—

EBEN (*furiously now*). Shut up, or I'll kill ye! I see yer game now— the same old sneakin' trick—ye're aimin' t' blame me fur the murder ye done!

ABBIE (*moaning—putting her hands over her ears*). Don't ye, Eben! Don't ye! (*She grasps his legs*).

EBEN (*his mood suddenly changing to horror, shrinks away from her*). Don't ye tech me! Ye're pizen! How could ye—t' murder a pore little critter— Ye must've swapped yer soul t' hell! (*Suddenly raging*) Ha! I kin see why ye done it! Not the lies ye jest told—but 'cause ye wanted t' steal agen—steal the last thin' ye'd left me—my part o' him— no, the hull o' him—ye saw he looked like me—ye knowed he was all mine—an' ye couldn't b'ar it—I know ye! Ye killed him fur bein' mine! (*All this has driven him almost insane. He makes a rush past her for the door—then turns—shaking both fists at her, violently*) But I'll take vengeance now! I'll git the Sheriff! I'll tell him everythin'! Then I'll sing "I'm off to Californi-a!" an' go—gold—Golden Gate—gold sun— fields o' gold in the West! (*This last he half shouts, half croons incoherently, suddenly breaking off passionately*) I'm a-goin' fur the Sheriff t' come an' git ye! I want ye tuk away, locked up from me! I can't stand t' luk at ye! Murderer an' thief 'r not, ye still tempt me! I'll give ye up t' the Sheriff! (*He turns and runs out, around the corner of house, panting and sobbing, and breaks into a swerving sprint down the road*).

ABBIE (*struggling to her feet, runs to the door, calling after him*). I love ye, Eben! I love ye! (*She stops at the door weakly, swaying, about to fall*) I don't care what ye do—if ye'll on'y love me agen— (*She falls limply to the floor in a faint*).

SCENE FOUR

About an hour later. Same as Scene Three. Shows the kitchen and CABOT's *bedroom. It is after dawn. The sky is brilliant with the sunrise. In the kitchen,* ABBIE *sits at the table, her body limp and exhausted, her head bowed down over her arms, her face hidden. Upstairs,* CABOT *is still asleep but awakens with a start. He looks toward the window and gives a snort of surprise and irritation—throws back the covers and begins hurriedly pulling on his clothes. Without looking behind him, he begins talking to* ABBIE *whom he supposes beside him.*

CABOT. Thunder 'n' lightin', Abbie! I hain't slept this late in fifty year! Looks 's if the sun was full riz a'most. Must've been the dancin' an' likker. Must be gittin' old. I hope Eben's t' wuk. Ye might've tuk the trouble t' rouse me, Abbie. (*He turns —sees no one there—surprised*) Waal—whar air she? Gittin' vittles, I calc'late. (*He tiptoes to the cradle and peers down—proudly*) Mornin', sonny. Purty's a picter! Sleepin' sound. He don't beller all night like most o' 'em. (*He goes quietly out the door in rear—a few moments later enters kitchen—sees* ABBIE *with satisfaction*) So thar ye be. Ye got any vittles cooked?

ABBIE (*without moving*). No.

CABOT (*coming to her, almost sympathetically*). Ye feelin' sick?

ABBIE. No.

CABOT (*pats her on shoulder. She shudders*). Ye'd best lie down a spell. (*Half jocularly*) Yer son'll be needin' ye soon. He'd ought t' wake up with a gnashin' appetite, the sound way he's sleepin'.

ABBIE (*shudders—then in a dead voice*). He hain't never goin' t' wake up.

CABOT (*jokingly*). Takes after me this mornin'. I hain't slept so late in . . .

ABBIE. He's dead.

CABOT (*stares at her—bewilderedly*). What. . . .

ABBIE. I killed him.

CABOT (*stepping back from her—aghast*). Air ye drunk—'r crazy—'r . . . !

ABBIE (*suddenly lifts her head and turns on him—wildly*). I killed him, I tell ye! I smothered him. Go up an' see if ye don't b'lieve me! (CABOT *stares at her a second, then bolts out the rear door, can be heard bounding up the stairs, and rushes into the bedroom and over to the cradle.* ABBIE *has sunk back lifelessly into her former position.* CABOT *puts his hand down on the body in the crib. An expression of fear and horror comes over his face*).

CABOT (*shrinking away—tremblingly*). God A'mighty! God A'mighty (*He stumbles out the door—in a short while returns to the kitchen—comes to* ABBIE, *the stunned expression still on his face—hoarsely*) Why did ye do it? Why? (*As she doesn't answer, he grabs her violently by the shoulder and shakes her*) I ax ye why ye done it! Ye'd better tell me 'r . . . !

ABBIE (*gives him a furious push which sends him staggering back and springs to her feet—with wild rage and hatred*). Don't ye dare tech me! What right hev ye t' question me 'bout him? He wa'n't yewr son! Think I'd have a son by yew? I'd die fust! I hate the sight o' ye an' allus did! It's yew I should've murdered, if I'd had good sense! I hate ye! I love Eben. I did from the fust. An' he was Eben's son—mine an' Eben's—not your'n!

CABOT (*stands looking at her dazedly—a pause—finding his words with an effort—dully*). That was it—what I felt—pokin' round the corners—while ye lied—holdin' yerself from me—sayin' ye'd a'ready conceived—(*He lapses into crushed silence—then with a strange emotion*) He's dead, sart'n. I felt his heart. Pore little critter! (*He blinks back one tear, wiping his sleeve across his nose*).

ABBIE (*hysterically*). Don't ye! Don't ye! (*She sobs unrestrainedly*).

CABOT (*with a concentrated effort that stiffens his body into a rigid line and hardens his face into a stony mask—through his teeth to himself*). I got t' be—like a stone—a rock o' jedgment! (*A pause. He gets complete control over himself—harshly*) If he was Eben's, I be glad he air gone! An' mebbe I suspicioned it all along. I felt they was somethin' onnateral—somewhars—the house got so lonesome—an' cold—drivin' me down t' the barn—t' the beasts o' the field. . . . Ay-eh. I must've suspicioned—somethin'. Ye didn't fool me—not altogether, leastways—I'm too old a bird—growin' ripe on the bough. . . . (*He becomes aware he is wandering, straightens again, looks at* ABBIE *with a cruel grin*) So ye'd liked t' hev murdered me 'stead o' him, would ye? Waal, I'll live to a hundred! I'll live t' see ye hung! I'll deliver ye up t' the jedgment o' God an' the law! I'll git the Sheriff now. (*Starts for the door*).

ABBIE (*dully*). Ye needn't. Eben's gone fur him.

CABOT (*amazed*). Eben—gone fur the Sheriff?

ABBIE. Ay-eh.

CABOT. T' inform agen ye?

ABBIE. Ay-eh.

CABOT (*considers this—a pause—then in a hard voice*). Waal, I'm thankful fur him savin' me the trouble. I'll git t' wuk. (*He goes to the door—then turns—in a voice full of strange emotion*) He'd ought t' been my son, Abbie. Ye'd ought t' loved me. I'm a man. If ye'd loved me, I'd never told no Sheriff on ye no matter what ye did, if they was t' brile me alive!

ABBIE (*defensively*). They's more to it nor yew know, makes him tell.

CABOT (*dryly*). Fur yewr sake, I hope they be. (*He goes out—comes around to the gate—stares up at the sky. His control relaxes. For a moment he is old and weary. He murmurs despairingly*) God A'mighty, I be lonesomer'n ever! (*He hears running footsteps from the left, immediately is himself again.* EBEN *runs in, panting exhaustedly, wild-eyed and mad looking. He lurches through the gate.* CABOT *grabs him by the shoulder.* EBEN *stares at him dumbly*) Did ye tell the Sheriff?

EBEN (*nodding stupidly*). Ay-eh.

CABOT (*gives him a push away that sends him sprawling—laughing with withering contempt*). Good fur ye! A prime chip o' yer Maw ye be! (*He goes toward the barn, laughing harshly.* EBEN *scrambles to his feet. Suddenly* CABOT *turns—grimly threatening*) Git off this farm when the Sheriff takes her—or, by God, he'll have t' come back an' git me fur murder, too! (*He stalks off.* EBEN *does not appear to have heard him. He runs to the door and comes into the kitchen.* ABBIE *looks up with a cry of anguished joy.* EBEN *stumbles over and throws himself on his knees beside her—sobbing brokenly*).

EBEN. Fergive me!

ABBIE (*happily*). Eben! (*She kisses him and pulls his head over against her breast*).

EBEN. I love ye! Fergive me!

ABBIE (*ecstatically*). I'd fergive ye all the sins in hell fur sayin' that! (*She kisses his head, pressing it to her with a fierce passion of possession*).

EBEN (*brokenly*). But I told the Sheriff. He's comin' fur ye!

ABBIE. I kin b'ar what happens t' me—now!

EBEN. I woke him up. I told him. He says, wait 'til I git dressed. I was waiting. I got to thinkin' o' yew. I got to thinkin' how I'd loved ye. It hurt like somethin' was bustin' in my chest an' head. I got t' cryin'. I knowed sudden I loved ye yet, an' allus would love ye!

ABBIE (*caressing his hair—tenderly*). My boy, hain't ye?

EBEN. I begun t' run back. I cut across the fields an' through the woods. I thought ye might have time t' run away—with me—an' . . .

ABBIE (*shaking her head*). I got t' take my punishment—t' pay fur my sin.

EBEN. Then I want t' share it with ye.

ABBIE. Ye didn't do nothin'.

EBEN. I put it in yer head. I wisht he was dead! I as much as urged ye t' do it!

ABBIE. No. It was me alone!

EBEN. I'm as guilty as yew be! He was the child o' our sin.

ABBIE (*lifting her head as if defying God*). I don't repent that sin! I hain't askin' God t' fergive that!

EBEN. Nor me—but it led up t' the other—an' the murder ye did, ye did 'count o' me—an' it's my murder, too, I'll tell the Sheriff—an' if ye deny it, I'll say we planned it t'gether—an' they'll all b'lieve me, fur they suspicion everythin' we've done, an' it'll seem likely an' true to 'em. An' it is true—way down. I did help ye—somehow.

ABBIE (*laying her head on his—sobbing*). No! I don't want yew t' suffer!

EBEN. I got t' pay fur my part o' the sin! An' I'd suffer wuss leavin' ye, goin' West, thinkin' o' ye day an' night, bein' out when yew was in—(*Lowering his voice*) 'r bein' alive when yew was dead. (*A pause*) I want t' share with ye, Abbie—prison 'r death 'r hell 'r anythin'! (*He looks into her eyes and forces a trembling smile*) If I'm sharin' with ye, I won't feel lonesome, leastways.

ABBIE (*weakly*). Eben! I won't let ye! I can't let ye!

EBEN (*kissing her—tenderly*). Ye can't he'p yerself. I got ye beat fur once!

ABBIE (*forcing a smile—adoringly*). I hain't beat—s'long's I got ye!

EBEN (*hears the sound of feet outside*). Ssshh! Listen! They've come t' take us!

ABBIE. No, it's him. Don't give him no chance to fight ye, Eben. Don't say nothin'—no matter what he says. An' I won't neither. (*It is* CABOT. *He comes up from the barn in a great state of excitement and strides into the house and then into the kitchen.* EBEN *is kneeling beside* ABBIE, *his arm around her, hers around him. They stare straight ahead*).

CABOT (*stares at them, his face hard. A long pause—vindictively*). Ye make a slick pair o' murderin' turtle doves! Ye'd ought t' be both hung on the same limb an' left thar t' swing in the breeze an' rot—a warnin' t' old fools like me t' b'ar their lonesomeness alone—an' fur young fools like ye t' hobble their lust. (*A pause. The excitement returns to his face, his eyes snap, he looks a bit crazy*) I couldn't work today. I couldn't take no interest. T' hell with the farm! I'm leavin' it! I've turned the cows an' other stock loose! I've druv 'em into the woods whar they kin be free! By freein' 'em, I'm freein' myself! I'm quittin' here today! I'll set fire t' house an' barn an' watch 'em burn, an' I'll leave yer Maw t' haunt the ashes, an' I'll will the fields back t' God, so that nothin' human kin never touch 'em! I'll be a-goin' to Californi-a—t' jine Simeon an' Peter—true sons o' mine if they

be dumb fools—an' the Cabots'll find Solomon's Mines t'gether! (*He suddenly cuts a mad caper*) Whoop! What was the song they sung? "Oh, Californi-a! That's the land fur me." (*He sings this—then gets on his knees by the floor-board under which the money was hid*) An' I'll sail thar on one o' the finest clippers I kin find! I've got the money! Pity ye didn't know whar this was hidden so's ye could steal. . . . (*He has pulled up the board. He stares—feels —stares again. A pause of dead silence. He slowly turns, slumping into a sitting position on the floor, his eyes like those of a dead fish, his face the sickly green of an attack of nausea. He swallows painfully several times—forces a weak smile at last*) So—ye did steal it!

EBEN (*emotionlessly*). I swapped it t' Sim an' Peter fur their share o' the farm—t' pay their passage t' Californi-a.

CABOT (*with one sardonic*). Ha! (*He begins to recover. Gets slowly to his feet—strangely*) I calc'late God give it to 'em—not yew! God's hard, not easy! Mebbe they's easy gold in the West but it hain't God's gold. It hain't fur me. I kin hear His voice warnin' me agen t' be hard an' stay on my farm. I kin see his hand usin' Eben t' steal t' keep me from weakness. I kin feel I be in the palm o' His hand, His fingers guidin' me. (*A pause—then he mutters sadly*) It's a-goin' t' be lonesomer now than ever it war afore—an' I'm gittin' old, Lord—ripe on the bough. . . . (*Then stiffening*) Waal—what d'ye want? God's lonesome, hain't He? God's hard an' lonesome! (*A pause. The Sheriff with two men comes up the road from the left. They move cautiously to the door. The Sheriff knocks on it with the butt of his pistol*).

SHERIFF. Open in the name o' the law! (*They start*).

CABOT. They've come fur ye. (*He goes to the rear door*) Come in, Jim! (*The three men enter.* CABOT *meets them in doorway*) Jest a minit, Jim. I got 'em safe here. (*The Sheriff nods. He and his companions remain in the doorway*).

EBEN (*suddenly calls*). I lied this mornin', Jim. I helped her to do it. Ye kin take me, too.

ABBIE (*brokenly*). No!

CABOT. Take 'em both. (*He comes forward—stares at* EBEN *with a trace of grudging admiration*) Purty good —fur yew! Waal, I got t' round up the stock. Good-by.

EBEN. Good-by.

ABBIE. Good-by. (*Cabot turns and strides past the men—comes out and around the corner of the house, his shoulders squared, his face stony, and stalks grimly toward the barn. In the meantime the Sheriff and men have come into the room*).

SHERIFF (*embarrassedly*). Waal— we'd best start.

ABBIE. Wait. (*Turns to* EBEN) I love ye, Eben.

EBEN. I love ye, Abbie. (*They kiss. The three men grin and shuffle embarrassedly.* EBEN *takes* ABBIE's *hand. They go out the door in rear, the men following, and come from the house, walking hand in hand to the gate.* EBEN *stops there and points to the sunrise sky*) Sun's a-rizin'. Purty, hain't it?

ABBIE. Ay-eh. (*They both stand for a moment looking up raptly in attitudes strangely aloof and devout*).

SHERIFF (*looking around at the farm enviously—to his companion*). It's a jim-dandy farm, no denyin'. Wished I owned it!

CURTAIN

Luigi Pirandello

THE HAUNTED HOUSE

MICE are never aware of the trap when they fall into one. Would they ever be caught if they knew that one had been laid for them? And even when they have been caught, they seem unable to realize where they are, and keep scuttling madly right and left, poking their whiskered little noses through the bars, squeaking and squealing in desperate endeavor to find a way out.

On the other hand, when a man starts litigation, he knows perfectly well that he is walking into a trap. But while the mouse struggles the man stays quiet—quiet of course with his body; inside—that is, mentally—he behaves exactly like the mouse, if not worse.

This was, in fact, what was happening to the crowd of clients who, covered with perspiration and eaten alive by the flies and the boredom, were sitting on that sweltering August morning in the waiting-room of the lawyer Zummo, awaiting their turn to consult him.

None of them moved from their seats but the glances of wild hatred exchanged between them could leave no doubt as to their thoughts. Each would have liked the lawyer exclusively to himself, and each felt that, with so many clients to interview in the same morning, there would be little time available for them all. Besides, with that big crowd to handle, with that frightful heat of ninety degrees in the shade, with so many different points to argue, would the lawyer's mind still be as clear as the case required?

Every time that the clerk, who was sitting at a desk copying notes at a frantic speed, glanced at the clock, two or three clients would sigh for boredom, while others, exhausted from the heat and the long wait, would keep their eyes glued on the big, dusty bookcases overloaded with legal papers—the scourge and ruin of so many unhappy families. Others still, trying to look indifferent, would peer through the green shutters of the window into the street where people were walking happy and careless whilst they . . . Phew! —and with a furious gesture of the hand they would flick off the flies made wilder and more aggressive than ever through the heat and the heavy perspiration.

Even more troublesome than the flies was the lawyer's little son, a brat of ten, barefooted and unkempt, who had obviously run away from the adjoining house to cheer up papa's clients.

"What's your name?" "What's that locket?" "How does it open?" "What's inside?" "A lock of hair?" "Whose hair is it?" "Why do you keep it?"

Then, hearing papa nearing the door to escort some important client, he would suddenly dive beneath the table, and hide himself between the legs of the clerk.

Everyone in the waiting-room would rise to his feet, each client looking beseechingly at the lawyer, who would raise both hands, saying: "Patience, my friends, one at a time."

The lucky one would follow him obsequiously, shutting the door behind him while the others would sit down again to their exasperating and oppressive wait.

Three clients only, who seemed to be husband, wife and daughter, showed no sign of impatience. The husband—a man in his sixties—had a gloomy, almost mournful appearance. He had obstinately refused to remove a ruffled, greenish, wide-brimmed top-hat which no doubt he considered the most appropriate accessory to the heavy, old-fashioned frock-coat stinking of naphthaline. It was quite obvious that this dress had been chosen out of deference for the occasion, an official interview with a lawyer.

Yet he was not perspiring.

Pale to the extreme, he looked almost bloodless, his jaw and cheeks being thinly covered with a layer of mouldy greyish fur. His light grey eyes, set close to a massive nose, had a squint, and, bent on his chair, with his head drooping and his thin hands resting on a stick, he looked almost crushed by some intolerable load. At his side, with a defiant look of flashing stupidity, sat his wife.

Stout and thriving, with a pronounced bust, she seemed unable to unglue from the ceiling a pair of beautiful jet-black eyes staring from her somewhat whiskered red face.

Next to her sat their daughter—thin, pale and squinting like her father—almost a cripple. It nearly looked—watching them together—as if only the presence of the stout woman between father and daughter could prevent them from falling to the ground.

The three had aroused the intense curiosity of the other clients, for three times the poor things had allowed newcomers to take their turn, alleging that their case was so important that it would require a very long interview with the lawyer.

What could have happened to them? Who was threatening them? Perhaps a vendetta or a murder? Perhaps financial ruin?

No, it could not be financial ruin. The wife was loaded with gold; large ear-rings dangled from her ears; a double chain was choking her neck; a large golden locket was going up and down on her bosom: a long gold chain was securing her fan, and valuable rings covered her stumpy fingers. What then had brought them there to consult the lawyer Zummo?

Little by little all the clients were being received by the lawyer, but the three would remain sitting there—motionless and disinterested—deeply absorbed in their own thoughts. Only every now and then the wife would make use of her fan or the man would lean forward to the child to remind her:

"Tinina . . . remember the thimble."

Some of the clients tried hard to push the lawyer's brat towards the three, but even the child—scared by those mournful faces—would have nothing to do with them.

And when—it was about noon—all the clients had gone, the three were still sitting there, motionless and dumb like statues, glued to their chairs.

"Well, have you fallen asleep? Why are you waiting to go in?" shouted the clerk, raising his head and getting impatient.

"May we?" asked the man apologetically while the three rose to their feet.

"Of course you may; you should have gone in before," reproached the clerk. "Don't you know that it's nearly lunch time? And, by the way, what's your name?"

The man at last removed his top-hat, uncovering at the same time the torture which the heavy gear had been causing him. From his pink, smoking cranium came rivers of sweat, covering his bloodless, ghastly face. Bending forward to the clerk he whispered ceremoniously:

"Piccirilli Serafino."

The lawyer—thinking his morning work at an end—was tidying up his desk and making ready to go when he was faced by the three unknown clients:

"Who are you?" he said with bad grace.

"Piccirilli Serafino," the man breathed with a deep bow as he watched the two women curtseying to the ground as he had instructed them to do.

"Sit down," said the lawyer staring at the unusual clients, "but be quick, as I am expected at lunch."

The three sat in a row facing the desk, fearfully embarrassed. Piccirilli tried to smile but his face was pitiful. Obviously he had forgotten how to smile.

"You see . . ." he began.

"We have come to ask . . ." broke in the daughter.

"Unbelievable things . . ." puffed the mother, her eyes glued to the ceiling.

"Speak one at a time," frowned the lawyer. "I told you I am in a hurry. What is it you want of me?"

"It's like this," said Piccirilli with a gulp. "We have been served with a summons."

"Murder, sir, murder," burst in the wife.

"Mama, please," said the daughter, trying to calm her.

Piccirilli looked at his wife and with as much authority as his miserable physique would allow he begged:

"Let me speak, Mararo."

Then turning to the lawyer:

"We have received a summons. We have been forced to leave the house we were occupying because . . ."

"I understand," broke in the lawyer. "Order to quit."

"No, sir," said Piccirilli apologetically. "Not at all; on the contrary it was we who left; we were forced to go even against the will of the landlord. Now he claims damages for breach of contract and because he said we had given the house a bad name . . ."

"But how?" said Zummo, his face darkening and turning this time to the wife. "You left the house, you have given the house a bad name and now the landlord. . . . Let's be clear; you can talk to a lawyer like to a priest. . . . Did you use the house for some immoral trade, for instance?"

"Certainly not," hurried Piccirilli, crossing both hands on his chest. "Nothing of the kind. No trade, whatever. We are not in business. True, my wife lends from time to time a trifle of money . . . privately . . . at reasonable rate. . . ."

"I understand," said the lawyer, "the usual terms."

"Absolutely," confirmed the man; "terms of which even the Church would approve, but this has nothing to do with our case. Signor Granella—the landlord—says that we have defamed his house because during the three months we have lived in it we have seen strange things which make me shiver every time I think of them."

"May God ever prevent his worst sinners witnessing what we have seen," burst out the wife with a loud sigh, rising to her feet and making the sign of the cross.

"Persecution, a real persecution," muttered the daughter.

"Quite right, nothing else but persecution," added the father. "There is no other word. For three months we have been the victims of a persecution in that house."

"Persecution by whom?" yelled the lawyer, losing his patience.

"By . . . by ghosts," whispered Piccirilli after a long pause, leaning towards the desk and hiding his mouth with his hand for fear of speaking too loud. "Yes, ghosts, sir."

"By whom? . . ." said the lawyer, thinking he had heard wrong.

"Ghosts, ghosts!" shouted the wife, waving her arm in defiance.

The lawyer jumped to his feet—furious.

"Nonsense—don't make me laugh! Persecuted by ghosts! Get out! Let me go to lunch, don't waste my time."

But the three, jumping from their chairs, drew nearer the desk, imploring:

"Don't go, don't go! You don't believe us, but we have seen them with our own eyes, we have seen them and heard them—they have persecuted us for three months."

They were all talking together, in an awful pandemonium which made the lawyer even more furious.

"Enough," he thundered, "you are crazy: you should see a specialist for mental diseases, not a lawyer."

"But I have been served with a writ," implored Piccirilli, his hands clasped as in prayer.

"Quite right, too," shouted Zummo in his face.

"Is this your advice, then?" said the wife, pushing the others aside. "Is this the way you deal with people needing help? You would not talk like this if you had been persecuted as we have been, if you had seen the ghosts as we have seen them."

"So you have really seen them, have you?" sneered the lawyer.

"Of course I have seen them," broke in the father. "With my own eyes."

"And I with mine," added the daughter.

"Yes, very likely with *those* eyes," exploded the lawyer, pointing at their squints.

"Then what about mine?" screamed the wife, stretching her right hand on her breast and opening her large black eyes as wide as she could. "These are straight, by God, and big enough to see! And they have seen those ghosts as clearly as they see you now."

"You are sure, are you?" said Zummo, mockingly.

"Quite sure," sighed the woman. "But if you still don't believe us we can produce witnesses, people who will come and tell what they have seen too. . . ."

The lawyer frowned, obviously impressed.

"Witnesses, you said?"

"Yes, sir, people who have seen and heard."

"Seen what, for instance?"

"Seen chairs moving about without anyone touching them."

"Chairs?"

"Yes, sir, chairs."

"What, ordinary chairs like the one in that corner?"

"Precisely, an ordinary chair going head-over-heels round the room like boys in the street and then—what shall I say—an orange-shaped pincushion made by my daughter being flung into the face of my husband as if thrown by an invisible hand. Oh! and a wardrobe trembling and squeaking as in a fit which from inside . . . from inside . . . (my flesh creeps at the mere thought of it) . . . shouts of laughter would break through."

"Shouts of laughter," added the daughter.

"Shouts of laughter," confirmed the father.

But the wife, without losing time, went on.

"Dozens of neighbors have seen all this and would be ready to give evidence, as I told you, while we three have seen and heard even more."

"Tinina, the thimble," broke in the father.

"Yes," began the child with a sigh. "I had a little silver thimble, a present from my grandmother (God bless her soul!). I was terribly fond of the little thing, but one day it disappeared. I searched the whole house for three days and could not find it until, one night, as I was sleeping under my mosquito net. . . ."

"It's full of mosquitoes, too, that accursed house," broke in the mother.

"And what a size the mosquitoes are," confirmed the father, shaking his head.

"I heard the noise of something jumping on the roof of the net," continued the daughter.

"It was like a rubber ball bouncing from the floor," interrupted the father, stopping the child with a gesture.

"Then suddenly the small object—it was my thimble—was thrown violently against the ceiling and fell to the ground—dented!"

"Dented," confirmed the mother.

"Dented," repeated the father.

"I got out of bed, trembling, to pick it up, and just as I was bending down, from the ceiling came . . ."

"Shouts of laughter, shouts and shouts of laughter . . ." ended the mother.

The lawyer stood silent for a while, his head bent and his hands behind his back.

"Playful ghosts!" he said after a while, scratching his head with a finger and trying to scrutinize the truth of this unbelievable tale. "Go on, go on; it's most amusing."

"Playful? Not playful at all, sir," retorted the woman. "Infernal, you mean. Ghosts that snatch the sheets from our beds, sit on our stomachs at night, clasp us by the shoulders, seize our arms, shake our furniture, ring the bells as if an earthquake had burst out, poison our food, throw ashes in the pans, is that your idea of playful? Not even the priest with his holy water could stop them; and when we told Granella d'you know what he had the cheek to answer? 'Nonsense, eat well and cure your nerves.' We begged him to come and see for himself but he would not listen. In fact, he even threatened us. 'Be careful how you talk or I'll finish you'—his very words."

"And he has finished us," concluded the husband bitterly. "Now, sir, we are in your hands. You can believe us. We are respectable people, and we shall know how to repay you."

The lawyer, as usual, pretended not to catch the last sentence. For a long while he stood by the desk, tugging at his moustache, deep in thought. Then he looked at the clock. It was nearly one. His people had been waiting for him for almost an hour and his lunch was long overdue.

"It is a peculiar case," he said at last. "You quite understand that I cannot accept your story of the ghosts: all you say may be mere imagination . . . mere gossip . . . but I am considering the legal side of the question. You say you have seen . . . hm! I don't like the word ghost . . . you have seen something . . . we shall say—and you have witnesses to prove that it was impossible for you to continue to live in the house because of . . . er . . . of a kind of . . . shall we say . . . er . . . peculiar persecution. . . . I must agree the case is novel and interesting . . . I may feel inclined to take it on. . . . Perhaps it will be possible to find some legal argument in your favour. Let me think it over before I decide. It's late now, but if you call again to-morrow I will let you know what I can do for you!"

Almost unconsciously the thought of this strange case was turning and turning in the lawyer's mind like a windmill. At lunch he couldn't eat: after lunch—when he lay on the bed for a nap as he used to do during the summer months—he couldn't get to sleep.

"Ghosts," he would say to himself with a sneer, while the vision of the three comic figures who swore over and over again of having seen them was flashing back to his mind.

Many times as a child he had been told stories about ghosts which had terrified him and made him spend sleepless nights.

"The soul," he sighed, stretching up his arms beneath the mosquito net and letting them fall back heavily on the bed. "The soul . . . the immortal soul. . . ." Of course, to believe in ghosts, he admitted, one must believe in the immortality of the soul, it's obvious, but did he believe in it or not? He had always said that he didn't and how could he now admit even a doubt? Could he go back on his own belief? He knew that one often lied to oneself, that people are often afraid of exploring their own selves for fear of discovering that they are so different from those they believe themselves to be or from those for whom they want to be known. But how many had ever given a serious thought to the question of the soul? Life was so absorbing that one hardly had time to think over these matters; yet they should be more important than all others. A friend dies and—like obstinate animals—we refuse to think of him beyond the moment of death, fully satisfied with the recollection of the past, and merely lighting a cigar to dispel our distress. Even science, as it happens, does not go beyond human existence, ignoring death and refusing to consider it. "Do not worry about death"—says science—"carry on your daily duties, think of your present life, of your work, of your profession." Quite right. The lawyer, too, so far, had refused to be worried about death, but here it was: the immortal soul—or ghosts—as it happened, knocking at his door, forcing him to be bothered with them. "You want to ignore us"—they seemed to tell him. "You wanted to ignore death but here we come, from the kingdom of the dead knocking at the doors of those who are still alive, making fun of you, making chairs and tables dance round your room, frightening your clients, laughing at them from the depths of an old wardrobe, puzzling you today—my learned lawyer —and puzzling to-morrow a body of equally learned judges who will have to try the most novel action ever heard in any court, an action for damages against ghosts!" Could he still ignore them?

Jumping from his bed, full of excitement, Zummo went back to his study and to his books of reference.

Articles 1575 and 1577 of the Civil Code seemed to offer some ground for his case.

They laid down—"inter alias"—that the lessee of a house was entitled to the "peaceful enjoyment" of the property during the period of the lease and that "the lessor was responsible to him for any undisclosed nuisance which might reduce or hinder the full enjoyment of the tenancy."

The law was clear, but—here was the crux of the case—it was necessary to prove the existence of ghosts and their presence in that house.

He had statements and witnesses to corroborate his clients' story, but to what extent was the evidence reliable? How could he quote scientists to substantiate these statements?

Having again questioned the Piccirilli family, the lawyer promised to accept the case and to work on it with the best of his skill.

He first read a general history of spiritualism, from the origins of mythology to the present day; next he consulted Jacolliot's book on the wonders of fakirism; and he then read everything written on the matter by the greatest and most reliable experts, from Crookes to Wagner, from Aksafof to Gibier and Zoellner, from Janet to de Rochas, from Richet to Morselli. He thus learnt—much to his astonishment—that even the most sceptical men of science had declared that the so-called "spiritual phenomena" could not be put in doubt.

He was elated. "Now"—he said to himself—"things begin to look much brighter." So long as these phenomena had been reported by people of no importance, like the Piccirillis, he, a man of sound education and grounded in positive science, had a good right to laugh at them. Even if he had seen them with his own eyes he could have believed them to be the result of some hallucination. But when men of science like Lombroso or Richet had acknowledged their existence the matter was entirely different.

Forgetting his clients and his case, he gave himself up, with ever-increasing conviction, to the study of spiritualism. For a long time his past work— yet so flourishing and so remunerative—had failed to give the intellectual satisfaction for which he had been craving. Lost in that little town where so little could be found to satisfy his hunger for the higher outlets of the brain, he now found that a new opening had been revealed to him by those books on the great problem of the after-death. Could then the great problem of death be solved? Could the soul of a dead person come back for an instant and "materialize"? Could it come back to him, who had been so blind, shake his hand and say: "Zummo, don't worry. Don't trouble about your petty existence on earth. There is something else, a much better life awaiting you one day!! Forward! Don't fear!"

Almost every day Piccirilli, either with his wife or his daughter, was coming to see him and to discuss the case.

"I am still working on the case: don't worry: I am not forgetting you," the lawyer would say. But, to tell the truth, he had completely forgotten everyone, putting off as many cases as he could and even refusing to interview new clients. At last, however, out of gratitude to the poor Piccirillis, who had unconsciously shown him the way to light, he decided to go carefully into their case.

A grave difficulty met him at the very outset.

In all experiments of which he had read, the presence of ghosts had been revealed through a medium. No doubt, then, one of the three Piccirillis—

even without knowing it—must be a medium and—in this case—the nuisance of the ghosts was due to the tenants and not to the house. This would mean the collapse of the whole case. On the other hand why—if one of the Piccirillis was a medium—had the ghosts ceased to appear in the new home? Why had they never appeared in any of the houses where they had lived before? Obviously there must be something in the popular belief that ghosts only live in certain houses, and if this could be proved his case would stand. Furthermore, had not the witnesses corroborated his clients' statement? This alone should disprove the explanation given by some scientists that ghosts are only seen by certain persons. Medium or no medium—he thought—ghosts have their own existence and to make doubly sure he would call on the Piccirillis and find out the truth for himself by holding a séance and watching results.

Frightened at this suggestion the Piccirillis refused to have anything to do with the experiment, but the lawyer insisted that the test was useful—even essential—for the case, and a séance was held. Tinina was found at once to be a powerful medium and Zummo—mad with joy—was thus able to witness almost all those astonishing revelations of which, so far, he had only been acquainted through his book. The Piccirillis' case—it is true—was collapsing, but his own knowledge of the after-death was widening to such an extent that he could not help feeling mad with joy. "Let Granella win his case, my friends. . . . What does it matter? Don't you see that here, before us, stands the revelation of the immortal soul?"

But how could the Piccirillis share their lawyer's enthusiasm for the immortal soul? They thought he had gone mad. They refused to believe that these experiments were anything else but infernal practices of which they were the victims. They had escaped from Granella's ghosts to fall amongst their lawyer's demons. Could anything be worse? Was he going to ruin them for ever? That would be the result of the case if somebody got to know what was going on at their place.

"Don't be afraid," the lawyer would say contemptuously. "Do you take me for a babe? Here you see me as a friend, not as a lawyer. When the case will come up for hearing, I shall know how to plead the mysterious nuisance of the house!"

And he did, in fact, plead that the nuisance was due to the house, not to the presence there of some extraordinary medium, but his pleadings were so unconvincing that his case was lost from the beginning.

On the contrary he amazed the court, his colleagues and the public with an unexpected and bombastic profession of faith, describing Allan Kardech as the "New Messiah," speaking of spiritualism as "The new religion of humanity," and showing how the tree of life had been practically dried up by science but was now likely to be revived under the warmth of new faith. "The mystery of death"—he said—"would soon be revealed: the veils of darkness would soon be lifted while quaint shadows are already creeping through the space to warn us about a world beyond. . . ."

And here he proceeded to speak of the most astonishing phenomena of spiritualism with such dramatic eloquence that the audience—carried away by his words—was enthralled and spellbound. The court, however—more practically minded and less inclined to follow the lawyer in his sublime heights—refused to give a verdict for his clients. Modern science—they said —had not yet accepted the still uncertain theories arising out of spiritualism. Besides, how could the lessor be held responsible for ghosts, for wandering shadows with no material substance? And how could ghosts be called "undisclosed nuisances" as specified by the law? Besides, was not the control of ghosts beyond the physical power of man and, if so, how could the landlord be asked to be responsible for them? No, the court could not agree with the lawyer's brilliant defence, and "judgment for the plaintiff" was their only possible verdict.

The public—still crystallized by the amazing and absorbing defence—greeted the verdict with unmistakable signs of disapproval. The lawyer himself—unable to restrain a flood of indignation which almost caused his arrest—rushed out of the room dragging after him his three dismal clients whom he pointed out to the cheering crowd as the "martyrs of a new religion."

Across the piazza, Signor Granella—the owner of the house—stout and blustering—was watching the crowd, with his hands in his pockets, letting it be well heard by those round him that he would not be scared to spend the night alone in the haunted house. He would sleep there that very night alone—he said—without a servant, as the Piccirillis had so ruined the reputation of the house that not even his most trusted servant would accompany him. Yes, this was what the Piccirillis had done to him, he said. It had become a lost house, a house in ruins. But now that the court had given their judgment and restored the reputation of the house he would go there himself and sleep there alone, not afraid of facing those ridiculous ghosts.

Ah! Ah! He would have something to tell them if they ever dared to show themselves. . . .

Granella's house was built on the highest point of the town at the very top of the hill, not far from the "Gate of the Winds." It stood there alone, on a large open space only facing a ruined shed where an occasional carman would shelter for the night while keeping an eye on his mule and cart.

Only a grim oil lamp would provide a glimmer of light over the square on moonless nights, but a few yards below—on the other side of the gate—life would start again with its endless rows of thickly populated dwellings so that—although somewhat lonely and gloomy at night—it was an ideal residence with plenty of air and freedom, full with comforts which could seldom be found in other residences of the same town.

It had been fully re-papered and re-painted since the Piccirillis' departure. Granella had lavished money freely in cleaning it up from top to bottom, but although so many visitors had come to inspect it—perhaps out of curiosity—nobody had made an offer and no tenant had yet been found for it.

"Well," repeated Granella to those near him, "I'll sleep there to-night," and, having brought to the place an iron bedstead, a chest of drawers, a washing stand and a few chairs—enough to furnish one room—he kept to his word and walked to the house at dusk, taking good care to let his neighbors know what he was doing.

"But why those two pistols?" commented the neighbors, watching the two large-sized firearms hanging at his belt.

If gangsters had threatened the house those pistols might have been useful, but what use could firearms be against ghosts?

Was Granella afraid? Of course he was not; he had been laughing and sneering all through the trial and there was no reason to be afraid now; but somehow—a queer feeling—why had that confounded lawyer been talking so much about ghosts and spiritualism? Why had he been allowed to talk of "proofs" and of scientific backing, thus staggering the audience and allowing even respectable people to admit that there might be some truth, after all, in what he said? In fact, hadn't one of the judges even admitted to Zummo in confidence—immediately after the trial—that his speech had shattered his opinions and that it was only out of respect for the present state of legislation that he had to concur with the other judges in the verdict? It was that swaggering Zummo who—with his speech—had carried away the whole town and was now making him feel lonely and disgruntled as though his friends had let him down, like cowards.

There wasn't a soul on the wide ground upon which the house stood. How bare, how dismal the place looked. Even the tiny flame of the street lamp seemed to flicker and tremble as though frightened by the thick darkness of the surrounding valley. He let himself into the house. . . . Why was the flame of the candle fluttering as if someone were blowing on it? (It was his own excitement causing him to puff through his nostrils.)

Crossing several empty rooms to reach the one he had furnished, his eyes were glued on the flame which he sheltered with his hand to avoid seeing the shadow of his own body monstrously enlarged on the walls. The bed, the chest of drawers, the basin, the chairs, all seemed lost in the darkness of the room. He placed the candle on the chest of drawers and could go no further. His heart was pounding. He was bathed in sweat. . . . And now what next? He must bolt the door as he used to do at home; but before doing that why not try to open the window just a tiny bit and get out on the balcony? . . . It was so hot inside. The fresh paint was stinking. Yes, he would let some fresh air come in while he made up his bed. He took out a sheet from a bundle he had brought and laid it on the mattress. A knock seemed to come from the door. A shiver ran through his loins hitting him like the stroke of a razor. Who is it? A knob of his iron bed must have knocked against the wall. He waited, terrified. . . . Silence. Yet that silence, somehow, seemed alive. . . .

He pulled himself together and got hold of one of his pistols. Holding the candle in the other hand he pushed the door and shouted:

"Who's there?"

Nothing. Silence. Charily he pushed the door a little wider. Nothing in the room but a ladder left behind by the decorator. No doubt the knock was due to the knob of the bed. He returned to his room and went out on the balcony.

"Shrr. . . ."

Curse that bat. It had been attracted by the light of the candle of course, and Granella laughed, watching the little animal flutter in the darkness, but a new squeak from the bedroom made him jump again.

Nonsense, it was the newly pasted paper on the walls trying to make fun of him. He laughed again, but looking inside the room something terrible caught his eyes; an enormous white tongue stretching itself along the floor from the adjoining room.

Curse that roll of wallpaper left behind by the workmen on top of the steps and now unrolling itself through the door like a devil's tongue.

Granella had had enough. He shut the window and, seizing hat and candle, flew down the stairs. Not a soul outside the house. He carefully let himself out and sliding along the wall of the house he swiftly dwindled through the darkness into town.

A night in the open would do him good, he thought. After all, why risk his health for that wretched house?

He had been silly. It was a mistake to go there that night without first getting used to it. He would try again to-morrow night. . . .

But somebody had watched him in his flight from the house. A carman sheltered by the ruined shed had seen him creeping along the walls and had spoken to the neighbours who in their turn had informed the lawyer.

Zummo was thrilled.

"I knew it! I knew it!" he shouted, mad with joy. "I swear to you that I had foreseen all this. I knew that sooner or later Granella's own evidence would be in our favour. Now let's all work together and waste no time."

The trap was set for the same night. The lawyer and five or six trusted men—no more—would collect the evidence they required. Let them all hide in the shed and watch. Above all not a word to anyone, for God's sake.

"Swear."

"We swear."

No professional triumph in Zummo's career could have been greater than on that night when—after a long watch with his friends—he saw Granella, barefooted, shivering and terror-stricken grasping his shoes in one hand, and holding with the other hand the trousers which he had not had time to button. He was creeping from the house like a thief, trying to escape.

Springing from the shadow, Zummo was on him like a tiger.

"Good evening, Signor Granella. Enjoying a quiet walk, eh?"

It all happened in a flash: five or six men were round poor Granella laughing and sneering, pushing him against the wall.

"Now, old fool, do you believe in the immortal soul? Blind justice has given you the verdict, but who was right? Tell us, tell us, what did you see? . . . Speak . . . what did you see?"

It was all in vain, for poor Granella, crying and trembling, was unable to answer. He had simply lost his speech.

OUR LORD OF THE SHIP

PRINCIPAL CHARACTERS

A SCHOOLMASTER. A DOCTOR (*called the Master Doctor*). A CATERER. A WAITER (*to the Caterer*). SIGNOR LAVACCARA. HIS WIFE. SERAFINA, their daughter. TOTÒ, *their son.* A BUTCHER. AN OLD SAILOR (*with a Young Sailor*).

OTHER PARTS

A BAKER, AN ICE CREAM PEDDLER, A MELON VENDOR, A FISHMONGER, AN ERRAND BOY (*to the caterer*), TWO DRUMMERS, THREE WOMEN IN SHAWLS (*carrying flour*), TWO BOYS (*with flowers*), A PROSTITUTE, TWO LABORERS (*who are with her*), A CLERK, HIS WIFE, THEIR TWO DAUGHTERS, A FRIEND (*of the Clerk's family*), THREE OTHER SAILORS (*saved by miracle*), A MAN WITH AN ACCORDION, TWO PROSTITUTES, A SERVANT GIRL, A SOLDIER, TWO YOUNG MEN (*students*), TWO PICKPOCKETS, THE LAWYER, THE LAWYER'S WIFE, THE NOTARY, THE NOTARY'S WIFE, FOUR CARD PLAYERS, AN AGED MAN (*alone*), AN OLD MAN AND AN OLD WOMAN, *brother and sister, with* ANOTHER OLD MAN, THREE PRIESTS, TOWNSPEOPLE, THE CHURCH CONGREGATION.

The production of "Our Lord of the Ship" requires a passage connecting the floor of the theatre with the stage. The people who come to attend the festival enter the door at the rear of the theatre, proceed down the centre aisle, and reach the stage across a sort of gangplank.

The stage itself represents a section of the open space in front of a little rural church. This edifice stands at the back, set at a rather high elevation, with a flight of steps, these worn and grass-grown, leading to the entrance. The entire façade and the bell tower need not necessarily be visible: it is sufficient for the audience to have a view of the portal.

Among the trees that line both sides of the square are little booths with counters draped with waving covers and hung with bright-colored bunting. There, eatables of all kinds are being offered for sale—cakes, sweets, more solid refreshments. An open-air café with tables, seats, barrels of wine.

The passage down the centre aisle is really just a by-way leading to the church. The greater number of people who are attending the festival are supposed to have arrived by other streets. From behind the scenes, Right and Left, come voices, noises, commotions, as indicated in the course of the play.

As the curtain rises, a beating of drums is heard. It comes, however, not from the stage, but from the back of the theatre, behind the audience.

CATERER (*very fat, with a paper cap on his head; he is in his shirt-sleeves—the cuffs rolled up to his elbows—and he is wearing a rough apron with blue-and-white stripes*). Oh, Libè-è, I'm talking to you! Get busy! Spread the table cloths! People are beginning to come already!

(*Behind the scenes, Right and Left, and at varying distances, the singsong cries of vendors are repeated from time to time. This continues all through the performance, but not so loud as to distract attention from what is going on on the stage. Some of the cries are indicated here; others may be added—they should be varied in tone and cadence*).

BAKER. Cakes and cookies! Cakes and cookies!

ICE CREAM MAN. Ice cream! Ice cream! A penny a cone!

MELON MAN. Fresh melon! Iced melon!

FISHMONGER. Fresh mullet and cod! Fresh mullet and cod!

(*Amid the general bustle, off stage, the tinkling of mandolins, and the clinking of toys that are being sold by vendors.*)

CATERER (*seeing a Boy come up the passage, panting, with a barrel on his shoulders*). Look out, there! Don't you see how you're shaking that barrel? Man alive—the wine will turn to vinegar! (*Meantime, the Waiter comes in*).

WAITER. Here I am! Here I am! (*He leaps behind the counter and takes out the covers*). Here are the tablecloths! (*He begins to spread them on the tables. His sleeves are rolled up; he is wearing a little cap,*

a red carnation tucked over his right ear. Whistling, he sets the tables: cheap knives and forks, thick, heavy glasses, rough earthenware plates that are painted with splotches of red and blue, supposedly flowers. The golden light of a warm autumn afternoon falls upon the stage. As the play goes on, the light turns to a bright red, and finally to a misty purple*).

BUTCHER (*appearing behind his counter and addressing the caterer. He has a coarse red face with a heavy mustache; powerful muscular arms, bare; on his head a rough cap; and tied around his waist, a leather apron*). What about this doctor that hasn't come yet?

CATERER. He'll be here, all right! I invited him myself.

BUTCHER. Yes, but if he doesn't come, I can't begin my slaughter!

CATERER. The others can't begin yet either, so don't get excited! (*Speaking to the Boy who has come on stage with the barrel, and helping him to put it down*). Is this the last, or are there more?

BOY (*taking off the sack which he has been wearing to protect his neck and shoulders*). The last one! The last, thank Heaven!

(*From the Rear, the drum beat grows more distinctly audible, "Brm, brm, brm." Two Drummers come in. They are old men, with swarthy faces and short grizzly beards. They are wearing old pointed hats with dangling tassels, velvet coats much worn and faded (the one green and the other dark brown), knickerbockers, coarse cotton stockings (blue), and rough hob-nailed boots. Behind them, two Sailors, who have been miraculously saved by Our Lord of the Ship, one old, the other young. The Old Sailor is tall, but rather bent, with a dark, stolid face, grey hair that is coarse and smooth, a beard*

*also grey, and hard, wrathful eyes.
The Young Sailor, thickset, sturdy,
has a broad, smiling countenance.
They are both barefoot, with white
cloth trousers rolled up to their knees
and fastened at the waist by gay red
sashes. They are in their shirt sleeves,
their blue shirts open over their
chests. Each one carries, hung from
around the neck, a votive tablet with a
crude painting: a bright blue sea in
storm, a shipwrecked boat, its name
written on the stern in such large letters as to be easily legible; in a rift in
the clouds appears Our Lord of the
Ship, the worker of the miracle. Besides these tablets the two rescued
Sailors are bringing, as gifts to the
church, piles of wax tapers on trays
covered by embroidered cloths. They
carry the trays under one arm each
half supported by a gaudy ribbon that
is slung across the chest and over one
shoulder. Following the sailors come
three women with shawls over their
heads—they are carrying sacks of
flour—and two little boys, awkwardly dressed in their best clothes,
each carrying flowers).*

YOUNG SAILOR. Hail to Our Lord of
Grace, good Christians!

THE WOMEN AND THE OLD SAILOR.
Hail! Hail!

CATERER *(taking off his cap and
waving it).* Hail! Hail!

*(The little procession traverses the
audience to the stage, crosses the
latter, and goes up the steps of the
church leaving the two Drummers
outside. The drums fall silent as the
procession disappears inside the edifice. The Drummers go out, Left,
hoping to find other rescued seafarers
to escort to the church in the same
manner. A woman of the streets
rushes out of the church with two
laborers, one of these decent, respectable, with a guitar slung around his
neck; the other a rough, slovenly*

*person. The Prostitute, disgustingly
fat and heavily rouged, is already
drunk; the two Laborers are trying
to control her).*

WOMAN. Come come! Let's sit
down here!

SECOND LABORER *(running after
her).* No! Not so near the church!

WOMAN *(throwing herself down on
a seat, her legs wide apart, and opening her arms).* Oh, I feel just grand!

SECOND LABORER *(pulling at her in
an effort to drag her along).* Come,
come! Come away! This is no place
for us!

FIRST LABORER. Easy now! Easy!
She'll come, of her own accord!

WOMAN *(getting up and throwing
her arms around his neck).* Darling,
play for me, play! You play, and I'll
sing!

SECOND LABORER *(to the First, leading him aside, Left).* No, for heav-
en's sake! Such a voice! When she
starts singing everyone else starts
running! *(The Woman follows them,
laughing boisterously, as they go out,
Left.)*

CATERER. It's just as well they found
out for themselves that this was no
place for them.

*(The Schoolmaster and the Doctor
come on stage by way of the theatre.
They are talking together. The
Schoolmaster, a pale, thin, blond-
haired youthful individual is dressed
in black. Faced by the ironies and
obscene brutalities of daily life, he
has kept, as a poet at heart, an un-
shaken faith in human nature and
in the ideals of human life. The
Doctor is a sprightly old man, badly
dressed, with a dirty straw hat on his
head, and with a shepherd's crook
for a cane).*

SCHOOLMASTER. You come to this
festival regularly every year?

DOCTOR. I don't come for the pleasure of it, my boy. It's a matter of

work with me! Whenever I'm in this part of the country—where I am known as the Master Doctor—it's my official duty to be present at the annual slaughter of the hogs. It takes place every year in connection with the festival of Our Lord of the Ship.

SCHOOLMASTER. Connection? What connection can there be between the slaughter of hogs and the festival of Our Lord of the Ship?

DOCTOR. Ah that, I can't imagine! (*They have reached the stage and the Caterer comes to meet them*).

CATERER. Good day, sir. A seat at one of these tables?

BUTCHER. Oh, the doctor at last! And he must be pretty hot! A litre for him at my expense—from the best barrel—wherever he chooses to sit! ... To the health of the Master Doctor!

DOCTOR. Thanks, my good man, thanks! But I never drink on an empty stomach!

CATERER. Remember, doctor! This year you promised me the honor of serving you a plate of giblets, cooked the way I cook them!

DOCTOR. And I'll keep my promise, the moment I'm through with what I have to do!

CATERER. As you see, they've given me a place here, near the church. If there's any rough play, we won't be in it!

BUTCHER. But we'll do a good business just the same, and don't you forget it! Gentlemen here, the tough ones and the brawlers over there! Besides, people who are screeching all the time don't eat so much!

WAITER (*to the Schoolmaster*). Won't you have a chair?

SCHOOLMASTER. Why, to tell the truth, I have a place reserved for me somewhere—if you could tell me which one it is.

WAITER. Reserved? Under what name?

SCHOOLMASTER. Lavaccara, Signor Lavaccara.

WAITER. Oh, that's the table there! (*He points to a table near the front of the stage, Right*). Here you are, sir! Do sit down! Signor Lavaccara will be here soon.

BUTCHER. Lavaccara is the man who sold me the pig! (*The two sit down at the table*).

WAITER. Just a little something in the meantime?

SCHOOLMASTER. Thanks! I think I'll wait.

(*Down the centre aisle to the gangway walk a humble Clerk, his Wife, their Two Daughters, and a Young Man, a friend of the family. The clerk has squeezed himself into an old frock-coat which is buttoned up to his chin. He is wearing a shabby silk hat, cocked a little to one side, and a ready-made bow-tie. His sleek mustaches have been carefully combed, waxed, and turned up at the ends. The wife and daughters are fat creatures, all dressed in summer attire. The young man is in a straw hat and in spats much too large for his ankles. His old-fashioned starched cuffs are a source of much anxiety to him. They keep catching on the sleeves of his coat, and he seems to be afraid they will come off*).

CLERK (*starting across the gangway and addressing the young man*). Oh, you ought to have seen the dust there used to be in the streets when the women wore long skirts! They kept stirring it all up! (*In confidence*). What their legs must have looked like, underneath! Hee-hee!

WIFE. Martino! Martino! The girls can hear you!

CLERK (*reaching the stage*). We might sit down right here!

A DAUGHTER. Heavens, no, papa! Not here! We can't see anything from here!

WAITER. You can see when the procession comes out of the church! Sit down! Sit down!

CLERK (*politely*). No, thanks! We really came, you know, more to get the air than to eat. (*He bows and tips his hat. They go out, Right*).

SCHOOLMASTER (*turning to the Doctor*). In view of this name, Our Lord of the Ship, there is probably some legend in which swine had a part. (*Meantime, the two Sailors, with the women and boys, have come out of the church. The Old Sailor hears the last words of the Schoolmaster and grows indignant*).

OLD SAILOR. What do you mean, sir? What have hogs got to do with Our Lord of the Ship? No blasphemy, sir! The Lord of the Ship is a sailor. He belongs to us seafaring men! What have hogs got to do with it?

SCHOOLMASTER (*embarrassed, trying to excuse himself*). Oh, no! I didn't mean that! I was just wondering . . .

WAITER (*aggressively to the sailors*). Speak with respect to your betters! No one meant any offence!

OLD SAILOR. But it is an offence. All of you insult us, feasting and guzzling here in front of the church where we come every year from the sea to bring offerings and to make thanksgiving for being saved from a terrible death by Our Lord of the Ship! (*The younger of the two women comes forward and humbly, sadly, stretches out an arm to lead the old man away*).

WOMAN. Come, father, come!

OLD SAILOR (*tearing himself away and angrier than ever*). No, let me alone! I have been wanting to shout this in someone's face for a long time! (*Turning to the Schoolmaster*).

Have you ever seen that Christ in the church there? Well, go and see Him! Go and see Him!

WAITER. That's true! What an image! Enough to scare anyone!

CATERER. As near like Christ Himself as anything possibly could be.

DOCTOR. It looks as the real body of Christ must have looked when the Jews got through with Him, praise His name! (*Making the sign of the Cross*). But it was the sculptor that did it. He went to work with real vim. He didn't leave an ounce of flesh that wasn't a wound or a bruise.

BUTCHER. He wanted to show us what he could do!

WAITER. All the same. He works miracles! The church is full of tablets, tapers, all kinds of vows. (*The roll of drums is heard again from the Left, off the stage*). Oh look! Here come some more that have been saved!

(*Three more Sailors come in, dressed much like the first two, and preceded by the same two Drummers. They are followed by a crowd of women with shawls and capes over their heads*).

A SAILOR. Hail to Our Lord of Grace, good Christians!

(*The first two Sailors, with the women and boys, kneel and join in the cry: "Hail! Hail!" The other bystanders take off their hats. The new procession goes into the church, leaving the two Drummers outside. Again they go away. The Old Sailor, rising from his knees with the others, begins to speak immediately*).

OLD SAILOR. I saw it myself when I was just a boy. He was first carried into this church by a crew of sailors, foreigners they were, running along like crazy men, shouting and weeping, holding the image on high, with their arms. We found out about it afterwards! It was an old crucifix they had nailed up in the hatchway of a ship—she came from down Eastward, from the Levant. Well sir, the sea had split that ship in two like a nut, and there the crew was, struggling in the water, and what should they find but this crucifix floating in their midst. The Christ had broken loose from the ship all by Himself, and they clung to Him, and He brought them to safety, every soul of them, swimming along on His Holy Cross with His arms stretched out and looking up to heaven—like this!

DOCTOR. But, my good man, I don't think anyone here means to offend Him in any way.

OLD SAILOR (*interrupting angrily*). Even when you choose His day to slaughter your hogs? (*He seizes the two women by the arm*). Let's go, let's go! We'll lose our faith among these heathen! (*He starts to go off with the others across the gangway, when, from the back of the theatre, comes the long drawling wail of an accordion which is being badly played by a young man with a bushy shock of hair. The man is wearing a smart little jacket over loose baggy trousers. He is in company with Two Girls of the Streets. The Old Sailor turns quickly away, urging his women, the Young Sailor and the little boys after him, across the stage. They disappear, Right, the Old Sailor crying*): This way! This way!

YOUNG MAN (*as the Two Girls, laughing boisterously, try to take the accordion from him*). Give it to me, I tell you! Anyone can push the thing in and out, but it's a different matter to handle your fingers—like this—pressing on the keys—like this. (*Swaying pirouetting about, to the beat of the accordion, they come on stage and disappear, Right*).

DOCTOR (*to the Schoolmaster*).

Things are getting a little gay! Well, the connection, if there be any, is just a matter of the season, I imagine. Pork is supposed to be harmful in summer, so it's taboo! But by this season of the year, the early autumn, the weather should begin to be cooler (it never is!) so they wait for this first Sunday in September to make their first slaughter. Now that Sunday happens to be the festival of Our Lord of the Ship! (*He gets up*). The slaughter is where I come in! I boss the job!

BUTCHER. You boss the job! I should like to know how you boss the job!

CATERER. Oh yes, they bring the pigs to him, all washed and combed, perfumed with powder on their noses, and blue tassels tied to their tails! (*A pretty young Servant Girl steps lightly along the gangway, and with her an awkward sentimental Soldier in uniform*).

SERVANT GIRL. Yes, I do all the cooking, and besides that, I clean up, I sweep, and do the ironing—great big baskets like this! You see there are four children! (*They move along, talking, and are soon on the stage. The Servant Girl recognizes the Doctor, and smiles at him without, however, halting*).

SERVANT GIRL. Good day, Master Doctor!

DOCTOR. Be careful, my dear, when you're out with soldiers!

SERVANT GIRL (*going off, Left*). No danger! He's going away on leave in three days!

DOCTOR (*to the Butcher*). Come, let's get along with our business.

BUTCHER. Master Doctor, you'll see what a fine animal we have this year!

DOCTOR. I'm sure it is, if it's that one Lavaccara had.

BUTCHER. My, but he cried when he sold it to me!

CATERER. And they say he's still groaning about it!

BUTCHER. We'll see how he acts, when he comes to get the head, and the half of the liver we agreed on!

CATERER (*to the Schoolmaster*). If you are invited, sir . . .

SCHOOLMASTER. Oh, I am! I'm invited! . . .

CATERER. . . . you won't have a very good time!

DOCTOR. Perhaps Lavaccara invited you here just to console him for his pig.

SCHOOLMASTER. Just possible! Because, so far as eating is concerned, I never touch meat of any kind— never! I teach the humanities to signor Lavaccara's son. I belong to the old school, and, to tell the truth, I'm very sorry to have the boy come to a festival like this,—I really don't understand it at all.

DOCTOR. Oh, for that matter, I don't believe the others will understand it, after they've been here a while!

BUTCHER (*taking a knife and a whet stone from the counter and beginning to sharpen the knife*). Come, Master Doctor! It's getting late. I have everything ready!

SCHOOLMASTER (*jumping to his feet*). Oh, my God! Surely they aren't going to do the slaughtering right here before our eyes!

BUTCHER (*sticking at the air with the knife in truculent mirth*). Right here! Right here! We stick them this way! And then—we take out the insides, and then—we skin them, and then we quarter them! . . . Well, well, what do you think of that? He turns pale just to hear me talk about it!

SCHOOLMASTER. But it's horrible! You might at least do the killing away from the crowd!

DOCTOR. So you teach the humanities according to the old school?

BUTCHER. You'll see what a clean job I do on a liver, all shiny, quivering! . . .

DOCTOR. Without this business of slaughtering, don't you see, the festival would lose part of its traditional character. Who knows?—it might even lose its original religious significance!

SCHOOLMASTER. Ah, yes! . . . The blood sacrifice!

DOCTOR. You should remind your pupil of Maia, mother of Mercury, from whom this animal takes its noblest Latin name: *maia, maialis.* (*To the Butcher*). Come, let's get on! (*He disappears behind the counter with the Butcher*).

SCHOOLMASTER (*still standing, his hands on the table top, gazing upward as if inspired*). Yes, of course, Maia! *Maia, maialis!* (*From behind the curtain come the voices of the men who are getting ready for the slaughter, and the first grunts of the pig. The Schoolmaster trembles, but makes an effort to control himself*). It's true—quite true, that with the progress of civilization—(*A squeal from the pig makes him turn cold: he shivers*)—oh, my God! . . . man grows weaker; he loses ground though he is ever striving to regain . . . (*Another squeal as above. The Schoolmaster unable to control his horror*) . . . oh, my God! . . . to regain his ancient religious feeling!

(*Signor Lavaccara comes down the center aisle to the gangway, holding his son by the hand and followed by his Wife and Daughter. He is an enormously fat and rosy individual, his flesh trembling as he walks. Heavy eyebrows under a bulging forehead seem to lend a touch of sadness to his coarse, puffy, stupid face. He seems to be bursting out of a new dark blue coat and a pair of white canvas trousers. He has a bright red tie and a massive gold watch chain, and dangling from the chain a piece of coral and other charms against the Evil Eye. He is carrying a stout bamboo cane with a horn handle. Totò, the little boy, about ten, should be made up to look like a little pig in a sailor's suit. The Wife, in a green dress with many puffs, is just as fat, as awkward, as vulgar as her husband. The Daughter, however, Serafina, by name, is attired as a nun of the Madonna Addolorata: a purple robe, a cape edged in black, and around her waist, a black cord. Tall, thin, of sallow complexion, she always keeps her large troubled eyes downcast. She speaks in a harsh masculine voice).*

WAITER. Ah, here he is at last! Signor Lavaccara and his family!

LAVACCARA (*panting, almost out of breath, calling from afar to the Waiter*). Say, have they killed him yet? Have they killed him yet?

WAITER (*hearing above the distant roll of drums and the faint sound of the accordion, the squeal of the pig behind the Butcher's curtain and the cries of the men who are holding the animal down*). There! They're killing him now!

LAVACCARA (*quickly, making a desperate effort to run, and shouting to the Waiter*). No! Run and tell them not to kill him! I'll give him back his money! I'll give him back his money!

WIFE (*talking at the same time and stopping her ears*). Heavens! Poor Nicola!

TOTÒ (*crying, running along with his father*). Nicò! Nicò! (*The pig's squeals grow louder*).

LAVACCARA (*now on the stage, with his hands in his hair*). No! No!

WAITER (*The squeals suddenly cease. From behind the curtain, ex-*

cited voices from the men who are holding the animal). There, it's done!

LAVACCARA (*falling into a chair and covering his face with his hands*). Oh! Oh!

SERAFINA (*bending over him*). This will help expiate your sins, father!

WIFE (*at his other side, very much distressed*). Come away! Come away! You're all in a sweat!

SCHOOLMASTER (*to Totò, who, curious and frightened, is trying to see behind the curtain*). Here, Totò! What are you doing, Totò? Don't go in there!

LAVACCARA (*mourning the pig, and eulogizing as if it were some late-departed relation*). Everything but talk, he would do, everything but talk! Why you could carry on a regular conversation! Totò would call to him "Nicò! Nicò!" And Nicò would come running to eat bread out of his hand! Just like a puppy! Just like a puppy! And more intelligent, oh I should say so, more intelligent than a human being!

SCHOOLMASTER (*gasping, lean as he is himself*). Lean, therefore, lean! He could not have been very fat?

LAVACCARA (*surprised and almost insulted, turning quickly to look at him*). Lean? Lean? He weighed three hundred if he weighed an ounce!

SCHOOLMASTER (*with an ecstatic smile, clasping his hands*). Excuse me, but if he was fat, how do you think he could have been intelligent?

LAVACCARA. Why not? Does fatness preclude intelligence, according to you? What about me, then?

SCHOOLMASTER. Oh, where do you come in, signor Lavaccara?

LAVACCARA. I weigh more than two hundred, myself!

SCHOOLMASTER. That's all right! But you belong to another species.

You're a man, signor Lavaccara, and that means, if you stop to consider . . . Listen: when you eat, and may God send you a good appetite . . . ! you eat for yourself—you're not getting fat for other people!

WAITER (*entering into the conversation with the idea dawning on him*). Of course! Of course! The pig thinks he's eating for himself, but as a matter of fact he's being fattened for someone else!

SCHOOLMASTER. Let's suppose that you, with all your fine intelligence, were . . .

WAITER (*interested, and continuing to insert a remark from time to time*). Yes—begging pardon—a hog—

SCHOOLMASTER. . . . Well, would you eat?

WAITER. *I* wouldn't! When I saw them bringing me a pail of swill, I'd . . . I'd give a grunt . . .

SCHOOLMASTER (*quickly, in his turn*), . . . of disgust!—

WAITER. 'Nix! Thanks, just the same, gentlemen, but you'll have to eat me lean!

SCHOOLMASTER. There you are! So if a hog is fat, it's a sign he hasn't thought much! Come, signor Lavaccara, console yourself with the reflection that . . .

WAITER. . . . we aren't saying it wasn't a fine pig. . . .

SCHOOLMASTER. . . . but you can't say it was intelligent!

LAVACCARA (*rising in a rage*). What are you talking about? How can a poor beast know that people are making him eat in order to eat him fatter themselves?

WIFE (*in approval*). There you are! There you are!

LAVACCARA (*continuing*). He thinks he's eating for himself too! And isn't he? Why, it's nonsense, of course he is! And to say that he oughtn't to eat, just so that the people who feed him will have to eat him lean—why . . .

WIFE (*backing him up*). Nonsense! Nonsense!

LAVACCARA. . . . such an idea would never enter a pig's head!

SCHOOLMASTER. Ah, there we're agreed! But then, don't you see? It doesn't enter a pig's head! But it does enter a man's head! And a man, therefore, as regards the luxury of eating . . .

WAITER (*quickly*) . . . like a hog . . .

SCHOOLMASTER. . . . Yes, he can indulge himself. . . .

WAITER. . . . knowing that, in the end, even if he gets fat, he isn't going to be slaughtered! But a pig, no! An intelligent pig . . .

SCHOOLMASTER. . . . to keep from being slaughtered, or at least to get even with the people who are to slaughter him. . . .

WAITER. . . . ought to keep lean, by eating daintily, like a lady with no appetite. Sure! As clear as can be!

SCHOOLMASTER. Therefore, go ahead, signor Lavaccara! Eat your spaghetti in peace!

CATERER. So say I, and I'll bring you a troughful, this big, with a sauce that tastes like—like the blood of a dragon! You're dying to have some spaghetti, I can read it in your eyes! (*He withdraws behind the curtain*).

WAITER. Console yourself with your spaghetti, signor Lavaccara!

LAVACCARA. Console the devil! I hoped to get here in time to save him! You know? I really did!

WIFE. Dead! The poor thing! Dead!

LAVACCARA (*turning angrily on the Schoolmaster*). You don't seem to take account of this—that that poor beast ate without the slightest suspicion that as soon as he got fat he would be slaughtered!

WIFE. Poor Nicola! He trusted us! He trusted the people who fed him!

SCHOOLMASTER. Trust! You call it trust? I'd call it stupidity! Trust!

LAVACCARA. Why stupidity?

SCHOOLMASTER. Because ever since the world began, man has been showing these hogs that he has an appetite for their flesh!

WAITER. Hasn't he, though! Why sometimes people even sample their ears and tails while they're still alive!

CATERER (*coming back with a big dish of spaghetti piping hot*). All ready! To table! To table! (*The Waiter runs to take the dish from the Caterer's hands and sets it on the table. The little boy cannot restrain himself*).

WAITER. Here you are! Eat! Eat!

TOTÒ. Me first, papa! Give me some! Me first, papa!

LAVACCARA (*pounding his fist on the table*). Totò, sit down! I won't stand this! What a pig! And his greediness! Look, it sticks right out of his eyes! I ought to have sold *him!* I ought to have sold him—instead of Nicola!

WIFE. Oh, now that, Saverio! . . . He's a boy!

LAVACCARA (*serving small portions to all, and keeping the rest for himself*). Nicola had better manners! (*Then to the Schoolmaster, still irritated*). No use looking at me like that, Professor! You don't convince me! You don't convince me! Everything else today I eat, but not Nicola —not a mouthful of Nicola!

SCHOOLMASTER. Permit me to remark that you are wrong! Let's be fair, do let's be fair! If you ought not to eat Nicola, what obligation would a man be under to raise such an unclean beast in the first place— to raise him, feed him, look after him? . . . Man, baptized flesh—why should a man take a pig to pasture?

What service does the pig render in return for the food he eats? . . .

WAITER. No, you can't deny that as long as a pig lives, he lives well.

SCHOOLMASTER. . . . and, considering the life that he has led, even if he is slaughtered afterwards, he ought to be satisfied—because you can't deny either that . . .

WAITER. . . . pig that he is . . . he didn't deserve it!

SCHOOLMASTER. Why all you have to do is . . . just to look at one! *That*—an intelligent beast? With that snout?

WAITER. . . . with those ears?

SERAFINA (*who is not eating*). . . . with those eyes!

WAITER. . . . and that funny little thing, you know, signorina, curled up behind! . . . (*The daughter, throwing back her head, bursts into shrieks of laughter*).

WIFE (*reprovingly*). Serafina! Serafina!

SCHOOLMASTER. Let her laugh, signora! She's right. And would they grunt like that . . . ? (*A great grunting is heard from back stage as if a whole drove of hogs were arriving on the run*). There! There! Do you hear them? . . . Those, intelligent beasts? Their grunt is the very voice of hoggishness! (*To Lavaccara*). And now look, just look at the people who have come to this festival! Here, these that are coming now! (*Other merrymakers come from the back of the theatre, now one at a time, now by twos and threes, or even in larger groups. They cross the gangway, then the stage, and disappear Right or Left, conversing among themselves. First, two young men, well dressed, students perhaps*).

FIRST YOUNG MAN. Oh yes, women! When they want to tell you a lie, they just cry about it, and anything seems true!

SECOND YOUNG MAN. Oh, I know how to deal with women! "Aren't you ashamed to act like that with me?" So I shouted at her! And she didn't say a word, not a word! She just kept on crying! . . . (*They go out*).

SCHOOLMASTER. How different, observe, how different those boys from your Nicola! The divine gift of intelligence appears even in their slightest gesture! (*Two tough looking customers, pickpockets, come in*).

FIRST PICKPOCKET. Just before dark; or rather it was dark, you might say! Someone who knew us could have said it was us, but anyone who didn't, couldn't have seen anything!

SECOND PICKPOCKET. He was standing there?

FIRST PICKPOCKET. Yes! The cross-eyed girl was combing her hair in the window, and I caught him in the act—he was throwing a flower up to her from down below! Hah, hah, hah! (*They disappear laughing, but they will return later*).

LAVACCARA. But they are a couple of rogues! At least, my dear fellow, when a pig goes wrong, you can say he's innocent!

SCHOOLMASTER. No, you can't—not innocent! Never! You can't call him guilty, perhaps, but you can't call him innocent! Never! A pig is just stupid, signor Lavaccara! That's all you can be sure of!

BUTCHER (*coming back on stage and calling from behind his counter*). Magnificent! A fine hog! How about the head? Shall I bring the head, signor Lavaccara?

LAVACCARA (*howling, his arms in the air*). Don't let me see it! Don't let me see it!

BUTCHER. All right! All right! I'll have it taken to the kitchen.

SCHOOLMASTER. Look, look! Our friend the lawyer, and the notary,

with their wives! (*These enter from the Left. The Lawyer fat, ruddy, freckled, is near-sighted and wears blue glasses. A short thick beard is scattered over his chin. He is carefully dressed in an old gray coat and a white vest, already soiled. He stands with a fat paunch thrust far forward, his hands in his trousers pockets. The Notary is a tall, lean man with a gloomy, chocolate-colored face, sharp angular shoulders, and long dangling arms. He is dressed in black. The Lawyer's Wife is a thin, blonde woman with a greenish, bilious-looking countenance. The Notary's Wife, short, dark-haired, very plump, with a double chin, is a stupid, prosperous person, good-natured toward everybody. Both women are in their best clothes, which they wear pretentiously without grace*).

LAWYER. Ah, my dear Lavaccara! So you have sought refuge here too? What a crowd over there! You just can't get through! Oh, your servant, signora, signorina! Ah, my dear Professor! With your permission. . . . (*He sits down at a near-by table, turning his back to them. The ladies greet each other, scarcely bowing. The Waiter immediately runs to take their order and talks to them while serving*).

BUTCHER (*to the Lawyer*). I have just slaughtered signor Lavaccara's hog. A most unusual piece of pork! How about a slice?

LAWYER. And why not, if it's signor Lavaccara's?

LAVACCARA (*confidentially, to the Schoolmaster*). That fellow over there is a lawyer, but I can assure you he's more of a pig than my pig that he's going to eat!

SCHOOLMASTER. Don't say that, signora Lavaccara! A pig is a pig, and that's all; whereas that fellow over there—not meaning to contradict you

—may be a pig, but he's also a lawyer! And that other one there, he is a pig but also a notary; and this one coming now, he's a pig but also a watchmaker. Yes, behind him, a pig but also a druggist. A difference, sir, quite a difference!

(*Other merrymakers drift in by degrees from Left and Right, for the most part ordinary humanity of varying aspects, of various ages—shopkeepers, clerks, professional men, blacksmiths, merchants. They talk quietly among themselves, as they sit down at the tables. The two Pickpockets return, and walk about among the tables, spying around furtively. Four men, Card-players, sit down at one of the tables. They throw aside the tablecloth, order wine, and begin to play with a pack of cards which one of them takes from his pocket. Meantime An Old Man, noticeably tall, has been coming silently, and very slowly, up the passage. He has a ghastly face with a set smile. He is wearing a black overcoat, green with age and too short in the sleeves. In one hand he is carrying a handkerchief, and in the other, a cane. He crosses the stage and disappears, Right. He has hardly gone, when An Old Man and An Old Woman reach the gangway, talking together. They are brother and sister, both dressed in heavy mourning. He is a thin frail individual with a white goatee, and a stiff, square-topped hat; she, a rather stout, placid-faced woman. With them Another Old Man, a friend, who is listening to them sympathetically*).

SISTER. She was with us here, at the festival, just a year ago!

BROTHER. Thin as a rail, poor thing! A shadow of herself!

SISTER. But just the same—do you remember?—whatever you said to her, she always had an answer ready!

BROTHER. Just think what it must mean to believe in God! Her death for me, well—just look at me! It has worn me down to nothing; but she, she believes—and just look at her! It hasn't done a thing to her! She is sure that some day she is going to see her in heaven!

FRIEND (*reaching the stage and finding the tables filled*). But there aren't any places left here!

BROTHER. Well, we'll find room a little farther along, over there. (*He points to the left*).

SISTER. No, we must go to church first! They are beginning to sing, do you hear? The procession will be out soon. (*They move along and enter the church. From the church, faintly, comes a slow nasal chant accompanied by an organ*).

SCHOOLMASTER. Those two, for example! Did you see them? That's real human nature! They are thinking of a relative who was alive and happy with them at this festival last year!

LAVACCARA. Yes, a fine thought! They ought to be ashamed of themselves! Going around dressed in black that way, in all this song and gayety!

SCHOOLMASTER. But first, notice, they went to church!

(*At this point, the din behind the scenes begins to grow louder, until little by little it becomes an uproar —the uproar of a bestial orgy: squeals of pigs being slaughtered mingle with the calls of street vendors, the voices of caterers inviting people to their tables, the cries of butchers calling their pork, a tumult of drunken, quarrelsome, boisterous laughter, and of jangling music from the instruments of wandering musicians. The Schoolmaster still continues to defend humanity against Lavaccara, notwith-*

*standing the way it is slaughtering
itself before his very eyes; but in the
end he wavers, terrified, and yields
before the impressively obscene spectacle of triumphant bestiality).*

LAVACCARA (*getting to his feet,
threateningly, slightly drunk*). But
they did wrong to go to church! Stop
defending this humanity of yours!
To these bigots I prefer anybody
that comes here to prove himself
more of a pig than a pig itself! Just
look at them there! Can't you hear
them grunting?

SCHOOLMASTER. Exactly! Exactly!
Cries that seem torn from them by
the violence of some great grief!
Without knowing it, their voices
have the very tones of the poor beasts
that are being slaughtered! And that
is sensibility! That is humanity! In
that again I recognize man!

(*As he finishes, a quarrel starts at
the Card-players' table. Three of the
men jump to their feet, shouting,
cursing, overturning chairs. They set
upon the fourth, who also rises, and
all four begin to scuffle, producing
general excitement*).

CARDPLAYERS (*together*). Thief!
Cheat! You're cheating! Get him!
Carrion! I didn't! Let me go! My
cards! Give me my cards! Cheat!
Thief! (*The two Pickpockets take
advantage of the confusion to jostle
the lawyer's wife and tear off her
necklace*).

LAWYER'S WIFE (*shrieking*). My
necklace! My necklace! Two thieves!
Stop them! My necklace! (*To her
husband*). Run! Run! Thief! Thief!
(*The Lawyer tries to break through
the crowd to follow the two thieves,
who disappear, Left. His wife keeps
on screaming but nobody pays any
attention to her. The Card-player
who has been accused of cheating
draws a knife! Terrified cries of
women and children. Men try to*

*break up the fight. Meantime the
Clerk, wild-eyes, howling, comes in
from the Left*).

CLERK. They've run off! They've
run off, My wife! My daughter! Run
off! While I was asleep! (*No one
pays any attention to him. The fight
is broken up amid an increasing tumult: tables are overturned; women,
drunken, dishevelled, and men
flushed with desire, pour in from
Left and Right. To the strains of a
discordant music played by a little
band of wandering musicians a wild
and disorderly dance begins. At this
point the light on the stage should
be a bright red. The Schoolmaster
has fallen into a state of desperate
depression. Lavaccara shouts to him
in triumph*):

LAVACCARA. Humanity? Humanity?
There's humanity for you! There!
You still recognize it?

(*All at once a great bell rings,
sepulchral, solemn, resonant. As if
the sun had suddenly set, the light
turns violet. The dancing stops, as
if people were frightened; the shouting becomes a kind of bestial wailing, a whine of contrition as it were.
Again the great bell! From inside the
church, the peal of the organ, and
the singing of faithful worshippers!
The twin doors of the church swing
open, and a tall Priest in robes and
stole appears. He stops like a spectre
on the threshold, holding aloft Our
Lord of the Ship, a large crucifix,
ghastly, blood-stained. Two Other
Priests, equally ghostly, stand beside
him, and two more kneeling before
him, move censers to and fro. The
people, panting, groaning, wailing,
fall to their knees and beat their
breasts. Slowly the priest descends
the steps, followed by a praying congregation from within the church,
and preceded by other priests, bearing lighted lamps aloft on the ends*

of long black staffs. The procession turns to the Left and disappears, reappearing presently at the rear of the theatre. The people rise and follow it, staggering, beating their breasts. The wailing gradually becomes louder. The Schoolmaster and Lavaccara are left alone on the stage, stunned. The Schoolmaster rises slowly and points to the weeping crowd).

SCHOOLMASTER. No, no, don't you see? They are weeping! They are weeping! A moment ago they were like beasts! They were drunk! But now see them, weeping, behind their bleeding Christ! Could any tragedy be greater than this? (*The procession finishes its match around the theatre, returns to the stage, and re-enters the church. The tolling of the bell ceases*).

CURTAIN

Ivan Bunin

THE GENTLEMAN FROM SAN FRANCISCO

"Alas, alas, that great city Babylon, that mighty city!"—
—Revelation of St. John.

THE Gentleman from San Francisco—neither at Naples nor on Capri could any one recall his name—with his wife and daughter, was on his way to Europe, where he intended to stay for two whole years, solely for the pleasure of it.

He was firmly convinced that he had a full right to a rest, enjoyment, a long comfortable trip, and what not. This conviction had a two-fold reason: first he was rich, and second, despite his fifty-eight years, he was just about to enter the stream of life's pleasures. Until now he had not really lived, but simply existed, to be sure—fairly well, yet putting off his fondest hopes for the future. He toiled unweariedly—the Chinese, whom he imported by thousands for his works, knew full well what it meant,—and finally he saw that he had made much, and that he had nearly come up to the level of those whom he had once taken as a model, and he decided to catch his breath. The class of people to which he belonged was in the habit of beginning its enjoyment of life with a trip to Europe, India, Egypt. He made up his mind to do the same. Of course, it was first of all himself that he desired to reward for the years of toil, but he was also glad for his wife and daughter's sake. His wife was never distinguished by any extraordinary impressionability, but then, all elderly American women are ardent travelers. As for his daughter, a girl of marriageable age, and somewhat sickly,—travel was the very thing she needed. Not to speak of the benefit to her health, do not happy meetings occur during travels? Abroad, one may chance to sit at the same table with a prince, or examine frescoes side by side with a multi-millionaire.

The itinerary the Gentleman from San Francisco planned out was an extensive one. In December and January he expected to relish the sun of southern Italy, monuments of antiquity, the tarantella, serenades of wandering minstrels, and that which at his age is felt most keenly—the love, not entirely disinterested though, of young Neapolitan girls. The Carnival days he planned to spend at Nice and Monte-Carlo, which at that time of the year is the meeting-place of the choicest society, the society upon which depend all the blessings of civilization: the cut of dress suits, the stability of thrones, the declaration of wars, the prosperity of hotels. Some of these people passionately give themselves over to automobile and boat races, others to roulette, others, again, busy themselves with what is called flirtation, and others shoot pigeons, which soar so beautifully from the dove-cote, hover a while over the emerald lawn, on the background of the forget-me-not colored sea, and then suddenly hit the ground, like little white lumps. Early March he wanted to devote to Florence, and at Easter, to hear the Miserere in Paris. His plans also included Venice, Paris, bull-baiting at Seville, bathing on the British Islands, also Athens, Constantinople, Palestine, Egypt, and even Japan, of course, on the way back. . . . And at first things went very well indeed.

It was the end of November, and all the way to Gibraltar the ship sailed across seas which were either clad by icy darkness or swept by storms carrying wet snow. But there were no accidents, and the vessel did not even roll. The passengers,—all people of consequence—were numerous, and the steamer, the famous "Atlantis," resembled the most expensive European hotel with all improvements; a night refreshment-bar, Oriental baths, even a newspaper of its own. The manner of living was a most aristocratic one; passengers rose early, awakened by the shrill voice of a bugle, filling the corridors at the gloomy hour when the day broke slowly and sulkily over the grayish-green watery desert, which rolled heavily in the fog. After putting on their flannel pajamas, they took coffee, chocolate, cocoa; they seated themselves in marble baths, went through their exercises, whetting their appetites and increasing their sense of well-being, dressed for the day, and had their breakfast. Till eleven o'clock they were supposed to stroll on the deck, breathing in the chill freshness of the ocean, or they played table-tennis, or other games which arouse the appetite. At eleven o'clock a collation was served consisting of sandwiches and bouillon, after which people read their newspapers, quietly waiting for luncheon, which was more nourishing and varied than the breakfast. The next two hours were given to rest; all the decks were crowded then with steamer chairs, on which the passengers, wrapped in plaids, lay stretched, dozing lazily, or watching the cloudy sky and the foamy-fringed water hillocks flashing beyond the sides of the vessel. At five o'clock, refreshed and gay, they drank strong, fragrant tea; at seven the sound of the bugle announced a dinner of nine courses. . . . Then the Gentleman from San Francisco, rubbing his hands in an onrush of vital energy, hastened to his luxurious state-room to dress.

In the evening, all the decks of the "Atlantis" yawned in the darkness, shone with their innumerable fiery eyes, and a multitude of servants worked with increased feverishness in the kitchens, dish-washing compartments, and wine-cellars. The ocean, which heaved about the sides of the ship, was dreadful, but no one thought of it. All had faith in the controlling power of the captain, a red-headed giant, heavy and very sleepy, who, clad in a uniform with broad golden stripes, looked like a huge idol, and but rarely emerged, for the benefit of the public, from his mysterious retreat. On the forecastle, the siren gloomily roared or screeched in a fit of mad rage, but few of the diners heard the siren: its hellish voice was covered by the sounds of an excellent string orchestra, which played ceaselessly and exquisitely in a vast hall, decorated with marble and spread with velvety carpets. The hall was flooded with torrents of light, radiated by crystal lustres and gilt chandeliers; it was filled with a throng of bejeweled ladies in low-necked dresses, of men in dinner-coats, graceful waiters, and deferential maîtres-d'hôtel. One of these,— who accepted wine orders exclusively—wore a chain on his neck like some lord-mayor. The evening dress, and the ideal linen made the Gentleman from San Francisco look very young. Dry-skinned, of average height, strongly, though irregularly built, glossy with thorough washing and cleaning, and moderately animated, he sat in the golden splendor of this palace. Near him stood a bottle of amber-colored Johannisberg, and goblets of most delicate glass and of varied sizes, surmounted by a frizzled bunch of fresh hyacinths. There was something Mongolian in his yellowish face with its trimmed silvery moustache; his large teeth glimmered with gold fillings, and his strong, bald head had a dull glow, like old ivory. His wife, a big, broad and placid woman, was dressed richly, but in keeping with her age. Complicated, but light, transparent, and innocently immodest was the dress of his daughter, tall and slender, with magnificent hair gracefully combed; her breath was sweet with violet-scented tablets, and she had a number of tiny and most delicate pink dimples near her lips and between her slightly-powdered shoulder blades. . . .

The dinner lasted two whole hours, and was followed by dances in the dancing hall, while the men—the Gentleman from San Francisco among them—made their way to the refreshment bar, where Negroes in red jackets and with eyeballs like shelled hard-boiled eggs, waited on them. There, with their feet on tables, smoking Havana cigars, and drinking themselves purple in the face, they settled the destinies of nations on the basis of the latest political and stock-exchange news. Outside, the ocean tossed up black mountains with a thud; and the snow-storm hissed furiously in the rigging grown heavy with slush; the ship trembled in every limb, struggling with the storm and ploughing with difficulty the shifting and seething mountainous masses that threw far and high their foaming tails; the siren groaned in agony, choked by storm and fog; the watchmen in their towers froze and almost went out of their minds under the superhuman stress of attention. Like the gloomy and sultry mass of the inferno, like its last, ninth circle, was the submersed womb of the steamer, where monstrous furnaces yawned with red-hot open jaws, and emitted deep, hooting sounds, and where the stokers, stripped to the waist, and purple with reflected flames, bathed in their own dirty, acid sweat. And here, in the refreshment bar, carefree men, with their feet, encased in dancing shoes, on the table, sipped cognac and liqueurs, swam in waves of spiced smoke, and exchanged subtle remarks, while in the dancing-hall everything sparkled and radiated light, warmth and joy. The couples now turned around in a waltz, now swayed in the tango; and the music, sweetly shameless and sad, persisted in its ceaseless entreaties. . . . There were many persons of note in this magnificent crowd; an ambassador, a dry, modest old man; a great millionaire, shaved, tall, of an indefinite age, who, in his old-fashioned dress-coat, looked like a prelate; also a famous Spanish writer, and an international belle, already slightly faded and of dubious morals. There was also among them a loving pair, exquisite and refined, whom everybody watched with curiosity and who did not conceal their bliss; he danced only with her, sang—with great skill—only to her accompaniment, and they were so charming, so graceful. The captain alone knew that they had been hired by the company at a good salary to play at love, and that they had been sailing now on one, now on another steamer, for quite a long time.

In Gibraltar everybody was gladdened by the sun, and by the weather which was like early Spring. A new passenger appeared aboard the "Atlantis" and aroused everybody's interest. It was the crown-prince of an Asiatic state, who traveled incognito, a small man, very nimble, though looking as if made of wood, broad-faced, narrow-eyed, in gold-rimmed glasses, somewhat disagreeable because of his long moustache, which was sparse like that of a corpse, but otherwise—charming, plain, modest. In the Mediterranean the breath of winter was again felt. The seas were heavy and motley like a peacock's tail and the waves stirred up by the gay gusts of the tramontane, tossed their white crests under a sparkling and perfectly clear sky. Next morning, the sky grew paler and the skyline misty. Land was near. Then Ischia and Capri came in sight, and one could descry, through an opera-glass, Naples, looking like pieces of sugar strewn at the foot of an indistinct dove-colored mass, and above them, a snow-covered chain of distant mountains. The decks were crowded, many ladies and gentlemen put on light-fur-coats; Chinese servants, bandy-legged youths—with pitch black braids down to the heels and with girlish, thick eyelashes,—always quiet and speaking in a whisper, were carrying to the foot of the staircases, plaid wraps, canes, and crocodile-leather valises and handbags. The daughter of the Gentleman from San Francisco stood near the prince, who, by a happy chance, had been introduced to her the evening before, and feigned to be looking steadily at something far-off, which he was pointing out to her, while he was, at the same time, explaining something, saying something rapidly and quietly. He was so small that he looked like a boy among other men, and he was not handsome at all. And then there was something strange about him; his glasses, derby and coat were most commonplace, but there was something horse-like in the hair of his sparse moustache, and the thin, tanned skin of his flat face looked as though it were somewhat stretched and varnished. But the girl listened to him, and so great was her excitement that she could hardly grasp the meaning of his words, her heart palpitated with incomprehensible rapture and with pride that he was standing and speaking with her and nobody else. Everything about him was different; his dry hands, his clean skin, under which flowed ancient kingly blood, even his light shoes and his European dress, plain, but singularly tidy—everything hid an inexplicable fascination and engendered thoughts of love. And the Gentleman from San Francisco, himself, in a silk-

hat, gray leggings, patent leather shoes, kept eyeing the famous beauty who was standing near him, a tall, stately blonde, with eyes painted according to the latest Parisian fashion, and a tiny, bent peeled-off pet-dog, to whom she addressed herself. And the daughter, in a kind of vague perplexity, tried not to notice him.

Like all wealthy Americans he was very liberal when traveling, and believed in the complete sincerity and good-will of those who so painstakingly fed him, served him day and night, anticipating his slightest desire, protected him from dirt and disturbance, hauled things for him, hailed carriers, and delivered his luggage to hotels. So it was everywhere, and it had to be so at Naples. Meanwhile, Naples grew and came nearer. The musicians, with their shining brass instruments had already formed a group on the deck, and all of a sudden deafened everybody with the triumphant sounds of a ragtime march. The giant captain, in his full uniform appeared on the bridge and like a gracious Pagan idol, waved his hands to the passengers,—and it seemed to the Gentleman from San Francisco,—as it did to all the rest,—that for him alone thundered the march, so greatly loved by proud America, and that him alone did the captain congratulate on the safe arrival. And when the "Atlantis" had finally entered the port and all its many-decked mass leaned against the quay, and the gangplank began to rattle heavily,—what a crowd of porters, with their assistants, in caps with golden galloons, what a crowd of various boys and husky ragamuffins with pads of colored postal cards attacked the Gentleman from San Francisco, offering their services! With kindly contempt he grinned at these beggars, and, walking towards the automobile of the hotel where the prince might stop, muttered between his teeth, now in English, now in Italian—"Go away! Via . . ."

Immediately, life at Naples began to follow a set routine. Early in the morning breakfast was served in the gloomy dining-room, swept by a wet draught from the open windows looking upon a stony garden, while outside the sky was cloudy and cheerless, and a crowd of guides swarmed at the door of the vestibule. Then came the first smiles of the warm roseate sun, and from the high suspended balcony, a broad vista unfolded itself: Vesuvius, wrapped to its base in radiant morning vapors; the pearly ripple, touched to silver, of the bay, the delicate outline of Capri in the skyline; tiny asses dragging two-wheeled buggies along the soft, sticky embankment, and detachments of little soldiers marching somewhere to the tune of cheerful and defiant music.

Next on the day's program was a slow automobile ride along crowded, narrow, and damp corridors of streets, between high, many-windowed buildings. It was followed by visits to museums, lifelessly clean and lighted evenly and pleasantly, but as though with the dull light cast by snow;—then to churches, cold, smelling of wax, always alike; a majestic entrance, closed by a ponderous, leather curtain, and inside—a vast void, silence, quiet flames of seven-branched candlesticks, sending forth a red glow from where they stood at the farther end, on the bedecked altar,—a lonely, old woman lost among the dark wooden benches, slippery grave-stones under the feet, and somebody's "Descent from the Cross," infallibility famous. At one o'clock—luncheon, on the mountain of San-Martius, where at noon the choicest people gathered, and where the daughter of the Gentleman from San Francisco

once almost fainted with joy, because it seemed to her that she saw the Prince in the hall, although she had learned from the newspapers that he had temporarily left for Rome. At five o'clock it was customary to take tea at the hotel, in a smart *salon,* where it was far too warm because of the carpets and the blazing fireplaces; and then came dinner-time—and again did the mighty, commanding voice of the gong resound throughout the building, again did silk rustle and the mirrors reflect files of ladies in low-necked dresses ascending the staircases, and again the splendid palatial dining hall opened with broad hospitality, and again the musicians' jackets formed red patches on the estrade, and the black figures of the waiters swarmed around the maître-d'hôtel, who, with extraordinary skill, poured a thick pink soup into plates. . . . As everywhere, the dinner was the crown of the day. People dressed for it as for a wedding, and so abundant was it in food, wines, mineral waters, sweets and fruits, that about eleven o'clock in the evening chamber-maids would carry to all the rooms hot-water bags.

That year, however, December did not happen to be a very propitious one. The doormen were abashed when people spoke to them about the weather, and shrugged their shoulders guiltily, mumbling that they could not recollect such a year, although, to tell the truth, that it was not the first year they mumbled those words, usually adding that "things are terrible everywhere"; that unprecedented showers and storms had broken out on the Riviera, that it was snowing in Athens, that Aetna, too, was all blocked up with snow, and glowed brightly at night, and that tourists were fleeing from Palermo to save themselves from the cold spell. . . .

That winter, the morning sun daily deceived Naples; toward noon the sky would invariably grow gray, and a light rain would begin to fall, growing thicker and duller. Then the palms at the hotel-porch glistened disagreeably like wet tin, the town appeared exceptionally dirty and congested, the museums too monotonous, the cigars of the drivers in their rubber raincoats, which flattened in the wind like wings, intolerably stinking, and the energetic flapping of their whips over their thin-necked nags—obviously false. The shoes of the signors, who cleaned the street-cars tracks, were in a frightful state, the women who splashed in the mud, with black hair unprotected from the rain, were ugly and short legged, and the humidity mingled with the foul smell of rotting fish, that came from the foaming sea, was simply disheartening. And so, early-morning quarrels began to break out between the Gentleman from San Francisco and his wife; and their daughter now grew pale and suffered from headaches, and now became animated, enthusiastic over everything, and at such times was lovely and beautiful. Beautiful were the tender, complex feelings which her meeting with the ungainly man aroused in her,—the man in whose veins flowed unusual blood, for, after all, it does not matter what in particular stirs up a maiden's soul: money, or fame, or nobility of birth. . . . Everybody assured the tourists that it was quite different at Sorrento and on Capri, that lemon-trees were blossoming there, that it was warmer and sunnier there, the morals purer, and the wine less adulterated. And the family from San Francisco decided to set out with all their luggage for Capri. They planned to settle down at Sorrento, but first to visit the island, tread the stones where stood Tiberius's palaces, examine the fabulous wonders of the Blue Grotto, and listen to the bagpipes of Abruzzi, who

roam about the island during the whole month preceding Christmas and sing the praises of the Madonna.

On the day of departure—a very memorable day for the family from San Francisco—the sun did not appear even in the morning. A heavy winter fog covered Vesuvius down to its very base and hung like a gray curtain low over the leaden surge of the sea, hiding it completely at a distance of half a mile. Capri was completely out of sight, as though it had never existed on this earth. And the little steamboat which was making for the island tossed and pitched so fiercely that the family lay prostrated on the sofas in the miserable cabin of the little steamer, with their feet wrapped in plaids and their eyes shut because of their nausea. The older lady suffered, as she thought, most; several times she was overcome with sea-sickness, and it seemed to her then she was dying, but the chambermaid, who repeatedly brought her the basin, and who for many years, in heat and in cold, had been tossing on these waves, ever on the alert, ever kindly to all,—the chambermaid only laughed. The lady's daughter was frightfully pale and kept a slice of lemon between her teeth. Not even the hope of an unexpected meeting with the prince at Sorrento, where he planned to arrive on Christmas, served to cheer her. The Gentleman from San Francisco, who was lying on his back, dressed in a large overcoat and a big cap, did not loosen his jaws throughout the voyage. His face grew dark, his moustache white, and his head ached heavily; for the last few days, because of the bad weather, he had drunk far too much in the evenings.

And the rain kept on beating against the rattling window panes, and water dripped down from them on the sofas; the howling wind attacked the masts, and sometimes, aided by a heavy sea, it laid the little steamer on its side, and then something below rolled about with a rattle.

While the steamer was anchored at Castellamare and Sorrento, the situation was more cheerful; but even here the ship rolled terribly, and the coast with all its precipices, gardens and pines, with its pink and white hotels and hazy mountains clad in curling verdure, flew up and down as if it were on swings. The rowboats hit against the sides of the steamer, the sailors and the deck passengers shouted at the top of their voices, and somewhere a baby screamed as if it were being crushed to pieces. A wet wind blew through the door, and from a wavering barge flying the flag of the Hotel Royal, an urchin kept on unwearyingly shouting "Kgoyal-al! Hotel Kgoyal-al! . . ." inviting tourists. And the Gentleman from San Francisco felt like the old man that he was,— and it was with weariness and animosity that he thought of all these "Royals," "Splendids," "Excelsiors," and of all those greedy bugs, reeking with garlic, who are called Italians. Once, during a stop, having opened his eyes and half-risen from the sofa, he noticed in the shadow of the rock beach a heap of stone huts, miserable, mildewed through and through, huddled close by the water, near boats, rags, tin-boxes, and brown fishing nets,—and as he remembered that this was the very Italy he had come to enjoy, he felt a great despair. . . . Finally, in twilight, the black mass of the island began to grow nearer, as though burrowed through at the base by red fires, the wind grew softer, warmer, more fragrant; from the dock-lanterns huge golden serpents flowed down the tame waves which undulated like black oil. . . . Then, suddenly, the anchor rumbled and fell with a splash into the water, the fierce yells of the boatman filled the air,—and at once everyone's heart grew easy. The electric lights in the cabin grew more brilliant, and there came a desire to eat, drink, smoke, move. . . . Ten minutes later the family from San Francisco found themselves in a large ferry-boat; fifteen minutes later they trod the stones of the quay, and then seated themselves in a small lighted car, which, with a buzz, started to ascend the slope, while vineyard stakes, half-ruined stone fences, and wet, crooked lemon-trees, in spots shielded by straw sheds, with their glimmering orange-colored fruit and thick glossy foliage, were sliding down past the open car windows. . . . After rain, the earth smells sweetly in Italy, and each of her islands has a fragrance of its own.

The Island of Capri was dark and damp on that evening. But for a while it grew animated and let up, in spots, as always in the hour of the steamer's arrival. On the top of the hill, at the station of the *funiculaire,* there stood already the crowd of those whose duty it was to receive properly the Gentleman from San Francisco. The rest of the tourists hardly deserved any attention. There were a few Russians, who had settled on Capri, untidy, absent-minded people, absorbed in their bookish thoughts, spectacled, bearded, with the collars of their cloth overcoats raised. There was also a company of long-legged, long-necked, round-headed German youths in Tyrolean costume, and with linen bags on their backs, who need no one's services, are everywhere at home, and are by no means liberal in their expenses. The Gentleman from San Francisco, who kept quietly aloof from both the Russians and the Germans, was noticed at once. He and his ladies were hurriedly helped from the car, a man ran before them to show them the way, and they were again surrounded by boys and those thickset Caprean peasant women, who carry on their heads the trunks and valises of wealthy travelers. Their tiny, wooden, foot-stools rapped against the pavement of the small square, which looked almost like an opera square, and over which an electric lantern swung in the damp wind; the gang of urchins whistled like birds and turned somersaults, and as the Gentleman from San Francisco passed among them, it all looked like a stage scene; he went first under some kind of mediaeval archway, beneath houses huddled close together, and then along a steep echoing lane which led to the hotel entrance, flooded with light. At the left, a palm tree raised its tuft above the flat roofs, and higher up, blue stars burned in the black sky. And again things looked as though it was in honor of the guests from San Francisco that the stony damp little town had awakened on its rocky island in the Mediterranean, that it was they who had made the owner of the hotel so happy and beaming, and that the Chinese gong, which had sounded the call to dinner through all the floors as soon as they entered the lobby, had been waiting only for them.

The owner, an elegant young man, who met the guests with a polite and exquisite bow, for a moment startled the Gentleman from San Francisco. Having caught sight of him, the Gentleman from San Francisco suddenly recollected that on the previous night, among other confused images which disturbed his sleep, he had seen this very man. His vision resembled the hotel keeper to a dot, had the same head, the same hair, shining and scrupulously combed, and wore the same frock-coat with rounded skirts. Amazed, he almost stopped for a while. But as there was not a mustard-seed of what is called mysticism in his heart, his surprise subsided at once; in passing the corridor of the hotel he jestingly told his wife and daughter about this strange coincidence of dream and reality. His daughter alone glanced at him with alarm, longing suddenly compressed her heart, and such a strong feeling of solitude on this strange, dark island seized her that she almost began to cry. But, as usual, she said nothing about her feeling to her father.

A person of high dignity, Rex XVII, who had spent three entire weeks on Capri, had just left the island, and the guests from San Francisco were given the apartments he had occupied. At their disposal was put the most handsome and skillful chambermaid, a Belgian, with a figure rendered slim and firm by her corset, and with a starched cap, shaped like a small, indented crown; and they had the privilege of being served by the most well-appearing and portly footman, a black, fiery-eyed Sicilian, and by the quickest waiter, the small, stout Luigi, who was a fiend at cracking jokes and had changed many places in his life. Then the maître-d'hôtel, a Frenchman, gently rapped at the door of the American gentleman's room. He came to ask whether the gentleman and the ladies would dine, and in case they would, which he did not doubt, to report that there was to be had that day lobsters, roast beef, asparagus, pheasants, etc., etc.

The floor was still rocking under the Gentleman from San Francisco—so sea-sick had the wretched Italian steamer made him—yet, he slowly, though awkwardly, shut the window which had banged when the maître-d'hôtel entered, and which let in the smell of the distant kitchen and wet flowers in the garden, and answered with slow distinctiveness, that they would dine, that their table must be placed farther away from the door, in the depth of the hall, that they would have local wine and champagne, moderately dry and but slightly cooled. The maître-d'hôtel approved the words of the guest in various intonations, which all meant, however, only one thing; there is and can be no doubt that the desires of the Gentleman from San Francisco are right, and that everything would be carried out, in exact conformity with his words. At last he inclined his head and asked delicately:

"Is that all, sir?"

And having received in reply a slow "Yes," he added that to-day they were going to have the tarantella danced in the vestibule by Carmella and Giuseppe, known to all Italy and to "the entire world of tourists."

"I saw her on post-card pictures," said the Gentleman from San Francisco in a tone of voice which expressed nothing. "And this Giuseppe, is he her husband?"

"Her cousin, sir," answered the maître-d'hôtel.

The Gentleman from San Francisco tarried a little, evidently musing on something, but said nothing, then dismissed him with a nod of his head.

Then he started making preparations, as though for a wedding: he turned on all the electric lamps, and filled the mirrors with reflections of light and the sheen of furniture, and opened trunks; he began to shave and to wash himself, and the sound of his bell was heard every minute in the corridor, crossing with other impatient calls which came from the rooms of his wife and daughter. Luigi, in his red apron, with the ease characteristic of stout people, made funny faces at the chambermaids, who were dashing by with tile buckets in their hands, making them laugh until the tears came. He rolled head over heels to the door, and, tapping with his knuckles, asked with feigned timidity and with an obsequiousness which he knew how to render idiotic:

"Ha sonata, Signore?" (Did you ring, sir?)

And from behind the door a slow, grating, insultingly polite voice, answered:

"Yes, come in."

What did the Gentleman from San Francisco think and feel on that evening forever memorable to him? It must be said frankly; absolutely nothing exceptional. The trouble is that everything on this earth appears too simple. Even had he felt anything deep in his heart, a premonition that something was going to happen, he would have imagined that it was not going to happen so soon, at least not at once. Besides, as is usually the case just after sea-sickness is over, he was very hungry, and he anticipated with real delight the first spoonful of soup, and the first gulp of wine; therefore, he was performing the habitual process of dressing, in a state of excitement which left no time for reflection.

Having shaved and washed himself, and dexterously put in place a few false teeth, he then, standing before the mirror, moistened and vigorously plastered what was left of his thick pearly-colored hair, close to his tawny-yellow skull. Then he put on, with some effort, a tight-fitting undershirt of cream-colored silk, fitted tight to his strong, aged body with its waist swelling out because of an abundant diet; and he pulled black silk socks and patent-leather dancing shoes on his dry feet with their fallen arches. Squatting down, he set right his black trousers, drawn high by means of silk suspenders, adjusted his snow-white shirt with its bulging front, put the buttons into the shining cuffs, and began the painful process of hunting up the front button under the hard collar. The floor was still swaying under him, the tips of his fingers hurt terribly, the button at times painfully pinched the flabby skin in the depression under his Adam's apple, but he persevered, and finally, with his eyes shining from the effort, his face blue because of the narrow collar which squeezed his neck, he triumphed over the difficulties—and all exhausted, he sat down before the pier-glass, his reflected image repeating itself in all the mirrors.

"It's terrible!" he muttered, lowering his strong, bald head and making no effort to understand what was terrible; then, with a careful and habitual gesture, he examined his short fingers with gouty callosities in the joints, and their large, convex, almond-colored nails, and repeated with conviction, "It's terrible!"

But here the stentorian voice of the second gong sounded throughout the house, as in a heathen temple. And having risen hurriedly, the Gentleman from San Francisco drew his tie more taut and firm around his collar, and pulled together his abdomen by means of a tight waistcoat, put on a dinner-coat, set to rights the cuffs, and for the last time he examined himself in the mirror. . . . This Carmella, tawny as a mulatto, with fiery eyes, in a dazzling dress in which orange-color predominated, must be an extraordinary dancer, —it occurred to him. And cheerfully leaving his room, he walked on the carpet, to his wife's chamber, and asked in a loud tone of voice if they would be long.

"In five minutes, papa!" answered cheerfully and gaily a girlish voice. "I am combing my hair."

"Very well," said the Gentleman from San Francisco.

And thinking of her wonderful hair, streaming on her shoulders, he slowly walked down along corridors and staircases, spread with red velvet carpets,— looking for the library. The servants he met hugged the walls, and he walked by as if not noticing them. An old lady, late for dinner, already bowed with years, with milk-white hair, yet bare-necked, in a light-gray silk dress, hurried at top speed, but she walked in a mincing, funny, hen-like manner, and he easily overtook her. At the glass door of the dining hall where the guests had already gathered and started eating, he stopped before the table crowded with boxes of matches and Egyptian cigarettes, took a great Manilla cigar, and threw three liras on the table. On the winter veranda he glanced into the open window; a stream of soft air came to him from the darkness, the top of the old palm loomed up before him afar-off, with its boughs spread among the stars and looking gigantic, and the distant even noise of the sea reached his ear. In the library-room, snug, quiet, a German in round silver-bowed glasses and with crazy, wondering eyes—stood turning the rustling pages of a newspaper. Having coldly eyed him, the Gentleman from San Francisco seated himself in a deep leather arm-chair near a lamp under a green hood, put on his pince-nez and twitching his head because of the collar which choked him, hid himself from view behind a newspaper. He glanced at a few headlines, read a few lines about the interminable Balkan war, and turned over the page with an habitual gesture. Suddenly, the lines blazed up with a glassy sheen, the veins of his neck swelled, his eyes bulged out, the pince-nez fell from his nose. . . . He dashed forward, wanted to swallow air—and made a wild, rattling noise; his lower jaw dropped, dropped on his shoulder and began to shake, the shirt-front bulged out,—and the whole body, writhing, the heels catching in the carpet, slowly fell to the floor in a desperate struggle with an invisible foe. . . .

Had not the German been in the library, this frightful accident would have been quickly and adroitly hushed up. The body of the Gentleman from San Francisco would have been rushed away to some far corner—and none of the guests would have known of the occurrence. But the German dashed out of the library with outcries and spread the alarm all over the house. And many rose from their meal, upsetting chairs, others growing pale, ran along the corridors to the library, and the question, asked in many languages, was heard: "What is it? What has happened?" And no one was able to answer it clearly, no one understood anything, for until this very day men still wonder most at death and most absolutely refuse to believe in it. The owner rushed from one guest to another, trying to keep back those who were running and soothe them with hasty assurances, that this was nothing, a mere trifle, a little fainting-spell by which a Gentleman from San Francisco, had been overcome. But no one listened to him, many saw how the footman and waiters tore from the gentleman his tie, collar, waistcoat, the rumpled evening coat, and even—for no visible reason—the dancing shoes from his black silk-covered feet. And he kept on writhing. He obstinately struggled with death, he did not want to yield to the foe that attacked him so unexpectedly and grossly. He shook his head, emitted rattling sounds like one throttled, and turned up his eye-balls like one drunk with wine. When he was hastily brought into Number Forty-three,—the smallest, worst, dampest, and coldest room at the end of the lower corridor,—and stretched on the bed,—his daughter came running, her hair falling over her shoulders, the skirts of her dressing-gown thrown open, with bare breasts raised by the corset. Then came his wife, big, heavy, almost completely dressed for dinner, her mouth round with terror.

In a quarter of an hour all was again in good trim at the hotel. But the evening was irreparably spoiled. Some tourists returned to the dining-hall and finished their dinner, but they kept silent, and it was obvious that they took the accident as a personal insult, while the owner went from one guest to another, shrugging his shoulders in impotent and appropriate irritation, feeling like one innocently victimized, assuring everyone that he understood perfectly well "how disagreeable this is," and giving his word that he would take all "the measures that are within his power" to do away with the trouble. Yet it was found necessary to cancel the tarantella. The unnecessary electric lamps were put out, most of the guests left for the beer-hall, and it grew so quiet in the hotel that one could distinctly hear the tick-tock of the clock in the lobby, where a lonely parrot babbled something in its expressionless manner, stirring in its cage, and trying to fall asleep with its paw clutching the upper perch in a most absurd manner. The Gentleman from San Francisco lay stretched in a cheap iron bed, under coarse woolen blankets, dimly lighted by a single gas-burner fastened in the ceiling. An ice-bag slid down on his wet, cold forehead. His blue, already lifeless face grew gradually cold; the hoarse, rattling noise which came from his mouth, lighted by the glimmer of the golden fillings, gradually weakened. It was not the Gentleman from San Francisco that was emitting those weird sounds; he was no more,—someone else did it. His wife and daughter, the doctor, the servants were standing and watching him apathetically. Suddenly, that which they expected and feared happened. The rattling sound ceased. And slowly, slowly, in everybody's sight a pallor stole over the face of the dead man, and his features began to grow thinner and more luminous, beautiful with the beauty that he had long shunned and that became him well. . . .

The proprietor entered. "Gia e morto," whispered the doctor to him. The proprietor shrugged his shoulders indifferently. The older lady, with tears slowly running down her cheeks, approached him and said timidly that now the deceased must be taken to his room.

"O no, madam," answered the proprietor politely, but without any amiability and not in English, but in French. He was no longer interested in the trifle which the guests from San Francisco could now leave at his cash-office. "This is absolutely impossible," he said, and added in the form of an explanation that he valued this apartment highly, and if he satisfied her desire, this would become known over Capri and the tourists would begin to avoid it.

The girl, who had looked at him strangely, sat down, and with her handkerchief to her mouth, began to cry. Her mother's tears dried up at once, and her face flared up. She raised her tone, began to demand, using her own language and still unable to realize that the respect for her was absolutely gone. The proprietor, with polite dignity, cut her short: "If madam does not like the ways of this hotel, he dare not detain her." And he firmly announced that the corpse must leave the hotel that very day, at dawn, that the police had been informed, that an agent would call immediately and attend to all the necessary formalities. . . . "Is it possible to get on Capri at least a plain coffin?" madam asks. . . . Unfortunately not; by no means, and as for making one, there will be no time. It will be necessary to arrange things some other way. . . . For instance, he gets English soda-water in big, oblong boxes. . . . The partitions could be taken out from such a box. . . .

By night, the whole hotel was asleep. A waiter opened the window in Number 43—it faced a corner of the garden where a consumptive banana-tree grew in the shadow of a high stone wall set with broken glass on the top—turned out the electric light, locked the door, and went away. The deceased remained alone in the darkness. Blue stars looked down at him from the black sky, the cricket in the wall started his melancholy, care-free song. In the dimly lighted corridor two chambermaids were sitting on the window-sill, mending something. Then Luigi came in, in slippered feet, with a heap of clothes on his arm.

"*Pronto?*"—he asked in a stage whisper, as if greatly concerned, directing his eyes toward the terrible door, at the end of the corridor. And waving his free hand in that direction, "*Partenza!*" he cried out in a whisper, as if seeing off a train,—and the chambermaids, choking with noiseless laughter, put their heads on each other's shoulders.

Then, stepping softly, he ran to the door, slightly rapped at it, and inclining his ear, asked most obsequiously in a subdued tone of voice:

"*Ha sonata, Signore?*"

And, squeezing his throat and thrusting his lower jaw forward, he answered himself in a drawling, grating, sad voice, as if from behind the door: "Yes, come in. . . ."

At dawn, when the window panes in Number Forty-three grew white, and a damp wind rustled in the leaves of the banana-tree, when the pale-blue morning sky rose and stretched over Capri, and the sun, rising from behind the distant mountains of Italy, touched into gold the pure, clearly outlined summit of Monte Solaro, when the masons, who mended the paths for the tourists on the island, went out to their work—an oblong box was brought to room number forty-three. Soon it grew very heavy and painfully pressed against the knees of the assistant doorman who was conveying it in a one-horse carriage along the white highroad which winded on the slopes, among stone fences and vineyards, all the way down to the seacoast. The driver, a sickly man, with red eyes, in an old short-sleeved coat and in worn-out shoes, had a drunken headache; all night long he had played dice at the eatinghouse —and he kept on flogging his vigorous little horse. According to Sicilian custom, the animal was heavily burdened with decorations: all sorts of bells tinkled on the bridle, which was ornamented with colored woolen fringes; there were bells also on the edge of the high saddle; and a bird's feather, two feet long, stuck in the trimmed crest of the horse, nodded up and down. The driver kept silence: he was depressed by his wrongheadedness and vices, by the fact that last night he had lost in gambling all the copper coins with which his pockets had been full,—neither more nor less than four liras and forty centesimi. But on such a morning, when the air is so fresh, and the sea stretches nearby, and the sky is serene with a morning serenity,—a headache passes rapidly and one becomes carefree again. Besides, the driver was also somewhat cheered by the unexpected earnings which the Gentleman from San Francisco, who bumped his dead head against the walls of the box behind his back, had brought him. The little steamer, shaped like a great bug, which lay far down, on the tender and brilliant blue filling to the brim the Neapolitan bay, was blowing the signal of departure,—and the sounds swiftly resounded all over Capri. Every bend of the island, every ridge and stone was seen as distinctly as if there were no air between heaven and earth. Near the quay the driver was overtaken by the head doorman who conducted in an auto the wife and daughter of the Gentleman from San Francisco. Their faces were pale and their eyes sunken with tears and a sleepless night. And in ten minutes the little steamer was again stirring up the water and picking its way toward Sorrento and Castellamare, carrying the American family away from Capri forever. . . . Meanwhile, peace and rest were restored on the island.

Two thousand years ago there had lived on that island a man who became utterly entangled in his own brutal and filthy actions. For some unknown reason he usurped the rule over millions of men and found himself bewildered by the absurdity of this power, while the fear that someone might kill him unawares, made him commit deeds inhuman beyond all measure. And mankind has forever retained his memory, and those who, taken together, now rule the world, as incomprehensibly and, essentially, as cruelly as he did, —come from all the corners of the earth to look at the remnants of the stone house he inhabited, which stands on one of the steepest cliffs of the island. On that wonderful morning the tourists, who had come to Capri for precisely that purpose, were still asleep in the various hotels, but tiny long-eared asses under red saddles were already being led to the hotel entrances. Americans and Germans, men and women, old and young, after having arisen and breakfasted heartily, were to scramble on them, and the old beggar-women of Capri, with sticks in their sinewy hands, were again to run after them along stony, mountainous paths, all the way up to the summit of Monte Tiberia. The dead old man from San Francisco, who had planned to keep the tourists company but who had, instead, only scared them by reminding them of death, was already shipped to Naples, and soothed by this, the travelers slept soundly, and silence reigned over the island. The stores in the little town were still closed, with the exception of the fish and greens market on the tiny square. Among the plain people who filled it, going about their business, stood idly by, as usual, Lorenzo, a tall old boatman, a carefree reveller and once a handsome man, famous all over Italy, who had many times served as a model for painters. He had brought and already sold—for a song—two big sea-crawfish, which he had caught at night and which were rustling in the apron of Don Cataldo, the cook of the hotel where the family from San Francisco had been lodged,—and now Lorenzo could stand calmly until nightfall, wearing princely airs, showing off his rags, his clay pipe with its long reed mouth-piece, and his red woolen cap, tilted on one ear. Meanwhile, among the precipices of Monte Solare, down the ancient Phoenician road, cut in the rocks in the form of a gigantic staircase, two Abruzzi mountaineers were coming from Anacapri. One carried under his leather mantle a bagpipe, a large goat's skin with two pipes; the other, something in the nature of a wooden flute. They walked, and the entire country, joyous, beautiful, sunny, stretched below them; the rocky shoulders of the island, which lay at their feet, the fabulous blue in which it swam, the shining morning vapors over the sea westward, beneath the dazzling sun, and the wavering masses of Italy's mountains, both near and distant, whose beauty human word is powerless to render. . . . Midway they slowed up. Overshadowing the road stood, in a grotto of the rock wall of Monte Solare, the Holy Virgin, all radiant, bathed in the warmth and the splendor of the sun. The rust of her snow-white plaster-of-Paris vestures and queenly crown was touched into gold, and there were meekness and mercy in her eyes raised toward the heavens, toward the eternal and beatific abode of her thrice-blessed Son. They bared their heads, applied the pipes to their lips, and praises flowed on, candid and humbly-joyous, praises to the sun and the morning, to Her, the Immaculate Intercessor for all who suffer in this evil and beautiful world, and to Him who had been born of her womb in the cavern of Bethlehem, in a hut of lowly shepherds in distant Judea.

As for the body of the dead Gentleman from San Francisco, it was on its way home, to the shores of the New World, where a grave awaited it. Having undergone many humiliations and suffered much human neglect, having wandered about a week from one port warehouse to another, it finally got on that same famous ship which had brought the family, such a short while ago and with such a pomp, to the Old World. But now he was concealed from the living: in a tar-coated coffin he was lowered deep into the black hold of the steamer. And again did the ship set out on its far sea journey. At night it sailed by the island of Capri, and, for those who watched it from the island, its lights slowly disappearing in the dark sea, it seemed infinitely sad. But there, on the vast steamer, in its lighted halls shining with brilliance and marble, a noisy dancing party was going on, as usual.

On the second and the third night there was again a ball—this time in mid-ocean, during the furious storm sweeping over the ocean, which roared like a funeral mass and rolled up mountainous seas fringed with mourning silvery foam. The Devil, who from the rocks of Gibraltar, the stony gateway of two worlds, watched the ship vanish into night and storm, could hardly distinguish from behind the snow the innumerable fiery eyes of the ship. The Devil was as huge as a cliff, but the ship was even bigger, a many-storied, many-stacked giant, created by the arrogance of the New Man with the old heart. The blizzard battered the ship's rigging and its broad-necked stacks, whitened with snow, but it remained firm, majestic—and terrible. On its uppermost deck, amidst a snowy whirlwind there loomed up in loneliness the cozy, dimly lighted cabin, where, only half awake, the vessel's ponderous pilot reigned over its entire mass, bearing the semblance of a pagan idol. He heard the wailing moans and the furious screeching of the siren, choked by the storm, but the nearness of that which was behind the wall and which in the last account was incomprehensible to him, removed his fears. He was reassured by the thought of the large, armored cabin, which now and then was filled with mysterious rumbling sounds and with the dry creaking of blue fires, flaring up and exploding around a man with a metallic headpiece, who was eagerly catching the indistinct voices of the vessels that hailed him, hundreds of miles away. At the very bottom, in the under-water womb of the "Atlantis," the huge masses of tanks and various other machines, their steel parts shining dully, wheezed with steam and oozed hot water and oil; here was the gigantic kitchen, heated by hellish furnaces, where the motion of the vessel was being generated; here seethed those forces terrible in their concentration which were transmitted to the keel of the vessel, and into that endless round tunnel, which was lighted by electricity, and looked like a gigantic cannon barrel, where slowly, with a punctuality and certainty that crushes the human soul, a colossal shaft was revolving in its oily nest, like a living monster stretching in its lair. As for the middle part of the "Atlantis," its warm, luxurious cabins, dining-rooms, and halls, they radiated light and joy, were astir with a chattering smartly-dressed crowd, were filled with the fragrance of fresh flowers, and resounded with a string orchestra. And again did the slender supple pair of hired lovers painfully turn and twist and at times clash convulsively amid the splendor of lights, silks, diamonds, and bare feminine shoulders: she—a sinfully modest pretty girl, with lowered eyelashes and an innocent hair-dressing, he—a tall, young man, with black hair, looking as if it were pasted, pale with powder, in most exquisite patent-leather shoes, in a narrow, long-skirted dresscoat,—a beautiful man resembling a leech. And no one knew that this couple had long since been weary of torturing themselves with a feigned beatific torture under the sounds of shamefully-melancholy music; nor did any one know what lay deep, deep, beneath them, on the very bottom of the hold, in the neighborhood of the gloomy and sultry maw of the ship, that heavily struggled with the ocean, the darkness, and the storm. . . .

John Galsworthy

SALVATION OF A FORSYTE

SWITHIN FORSYTE lay in bed. The corners of his mouth under his white moustache drooped towards his double chin. He panted: "My doctor says I'm in a bad way, James."

His twin-brother placed his hand behind his ear. "I can't hear you. They tell me I ought to take a cure. There's always a cure wanted for something. Emily had a cure."

Swithin replied: "You mumble so. I hear my man, Adolph. I trained him. . . . You ought to have an ear-trumpet. You're getting very shaky, James."

There was silence; then James Forsyte, as if galvanized, remarked: "I s'pose you've made your will. I s'pose you've left your money to the family; you've nobody else to leave it to. There was Danson died the other day, and left his money to a hospital."

The hairs of Swithin's white moustache bristled. "My fool of a doctor told me to make my will," he said; "I hate a fellow who tells you to make your will. My appetite's good; I ate a partridge last night. I'm all the better for eating. He told me to leave off champagne! I eat a good breakfast. I'm not eighty. You're the same age, James. You look very shaky."

James Forsyte said: "You ought to have another opinion. Have Blank; he's the first man now. I had him for Emily; cost me two hundred guineas. He sent her to Homburg; that's the first place now. The prince was there—everybody goes there."

Swithin Forsyte answered: "I don't get any sleep at night, now I can't get out; and I've bought a new carriage—gave a pot of money for it. D'you ever have bronchitis? They tell me champagne's dangerous; it's my belief I couldn't take a better thing."

James Forsyte rose.

"You ought to have another opinion. Emily sent her love; she would have come in, but she had to go to Niagara. Everybody goes there; it's *the* place now. Rachael goes every morning; she overdoes it—she'll be laid up one of these days. There's a fancy ball there to-night; the Duke gives the prizes."

Swithin Forsyte said angrily: "I can't get things properly cooked here; at the club I get spinach decently done." The bed-clothes jerked at the tremor of his legs.

James Forsyte replied: "You must have done well with Tintos; you must have made a lot of money by them. Your ground-rents must be falling in, too. You must have any amount you don't know what to do with." He mouthed at the words, as if his lips were watering.

Swithin Forsyte glared. "Money!" he said; "my doctor's bill's enormous."

James Forsyte stretched out a cold, damp hand. "Good-bye! You ought to have another opinion. I can't keep the horses waiting: they're a new pair—stood me in three hundred. You ought to take care of yourself. I shall speak to Blank about you. You ought to have him—everybody says he's the first man. Good-bye!"

Swithin Forsyte continued to stare at the ceiling. He thought: 'A poor thing, James! a selfish beggar! Must be worth a couple of hundred thousand!' He wheezed, meditating on life. . . .

He was ill and lonely. For many years he had been lonely, and for two years ill; but as he had smoked his first cigar, so he would live his life—stoutly, to its predestined end. Every day he was driven to the club; sitting forward on the spring cushions of a single brougham, his hands on his knees, swaying a little, strangely solemn. He ascended the steps into that marble hall—the folds of his chin wedged into the aperture of his collar—walking squarely with a stick. Later he would dine, eating majestically, and savouring his food, behind a bottle of champagne set in an ice-pail—his waistcoat defended by a napkin, his eyes rolling a little or glued in a stare on the waiter. Never did he suffer his head or back to droop, for it was not distinguished so to do.

Because he was old and deaf, he spoke to no one; and no one spoke to him. The club gossip, an Irishman, said to each newcomer: "Old Forsyte! Look at 'um! Must ha' had something in his life to sour 'um!" But Swithin had had nothing in his life to sour him.

For many days now he had lain in bed in a room exuding silver, crimson, and electric light, and smelling of opopanax and of cigars. The curtains were drawn, the firelight gleamed: on a table by his bed were a jug of barley-water and *The Times*. He had made an attempt to read, failed, and fell again to thinking. His face with its square chin looked like a block of pale leather bedded in the pillow. It was lonely! A woman in the room would have made all the difference! Why had he never married? He breathed hard, staring frog-like at the ceiling; a memory had come into his mind. It was a long time ago—forty odd years—but it seemed like yesterday. . . .

It happened when he was thirty-eight, for the first and only time in his life travelling on the Continent, with his twin-brother James and a man named Traquair. On the way from Germany to Venice, he had found himself at the Hôtel Goldene Alp at Salzburg. It was late August, and weather for the gods: sunshine on the walls and the shadows of the vine-leaves, and at night, the moonlight, and again on the walls the shadows of the vine-leaves. Averse to the suggestions of other people, Swithin had refused to visit the Citadel; he had spent the day alone in the window of his bedroom, smoking a succession of cigars, and disparaging the appearance of the passers-by. After dinner he was driven by boredom into the streets. His chest puffed out like a pigeon's, and with something of a pigeon's cold and inquiring eye, he strutted, annoyed at the frequency of uniforms, which seemed to him both needless and offensive. His spleen rose at this crowd of foreigners who spoke an unintelligible language, wore hair on their faces, and smoked bad tobacco. 'A queer lot!' he thought. The sound of music from a *café* attracted him, he walked in, vaguely moved by a wish for the distinction of adventure, without the trouble which adventure usually brought with it; spurred too, perhaps, by an after-dinner demon. The *café* was the *bier-halle* of the 'Fifties, with a door at either end, and lighted by a large wooden lantern. On a small dais three musicians were fiddling. Solitary men, or groups, sat at some dozen tables, and the waiters hurried about replenishing glasses; the air was thick with smoke. Swithin sat down. "Wine!" he said sternly. The astonished waiter brought him wine. Swithin pointed to a beer-glass on the table. "Here!" he said, with the same ferocity. The waiter poured out the wine. 'Ah!' thought Swithin, 'they can understand if they like.' A group of officers close by were laughing; Swithin stared at them uneasily. A hollow cough sounded almost in his ear. To his left a man sat reading, with his elbows on the corners of a journal, and his gaunt shoulders raised almost to his eyes. He had a thin, long nose, broadening suddenly at the nostrils; a black-brown beard, spread in a savage fan over his chest; what was visible of the face was the colour of old parchment. A strange, wild, haughty-looking creature! Swithin observed his clothes with some displeasure—they were the clothes of a journalist or strolling actor. And yet he was impressed. This was singular. How could he be impressed by a fellow in such clothes! The man reached out a hand, covered with black hairs, and took up a tumbler that contained a dark-coloured fluid: 'Brandy!' thought Swithin. The crash of a falling chair startled him—his neighbour had risen. He was of immense height, and very thin; his great beard seemed to splash away from his mouth; he was glaring at the group of officers, and speaking. Swithin made out two words: *"Hunde! Deutsche*

Hunde!" 'Hounds! Dutch hounds!' he thought: 'Rather strong!' One of the officers had jumped up, and now drew his sword. The tall man swung his chair up, and brought it down with a thud. Everybody round started up and closed on him. The tall man cried out: "To me, Magyars!"

Swithin grinned. The tall man fighting such odds excited his unwilling admiration; he had a momentary impulse to go to his assistance. 'Only get a broken nose!' he thought, and looked for a safe corner. But at that moment a thrown lemon struck him on the jaw. He jumped out of his chair and rushed at the officers. The Hungarian, swinging his chair, threw him a look of gratitude—Swithin glowed with momentary admiration of himself. A sword blade grazed his arm: he felt a sudden dislike of the Hungarian. 'This is too much,' he thought, and, catching up a chair, flung it at the wooden lantern. There was a crash—faces and swords vanished. He struck a match, and by the light of it bolted for the door. A second later he was in the street.

II

A voice said in English, "God bless you, brother!"

Swithin looked round, and saw the tall Hungarian holding out his hand. He took it, thinking, 'What a fool I've been!' There was something in the Hungarian's gesture which said, "You are worthy of me!" It was annoying, but rather impressive. The man seemed even taller than before; there was a cut on his cheek, the blood from which was trickling down his beard. "You English!" he said. "I saw you stone Haynau—I saw you cheer Kossuth. The free blood of your people cries out to us." He looked at Swithin. "You are a big man, you have a big soul—and strong, how you flung them down! Ha!" Swithin had an impulse to take to his heels. "My name," said the Hungarian, "is Boleskey. You are my friend." His English was good.

'Bulsh-kai-ee, Burlsh-kai-ee,' thought Swithin; 'what a devil of a name!' "Mine," he said sulkily, "is Forsyte."

The Hungarian repeated it.

"You've had a nasty jab on the cheek," said Swithin; the sight of the matted beard was making him feel sick. The Hungarian put his fingers to his cheek, brought them away wet, stared at them, then with an indifferent air gathered a wisp of his beard and crammed it against the cut.

"Ugh!" said Swithin. "Here! Take my handkerchief!"

The Hungarian bowed. "Thank you!" he said; "I couldn't think of it! Thank you a thousand times!"

"Take it!" growled Swithin; it seemed to him suddenly of the first importance. He thrust the handkerchief into the Hungarian's hand, and felt a pain in his arm. 'There!' he thought, 'I've strained a muscle.'

The Hungarian kept muttering, regardless of passers-by, "Swine! How you threw them over! Two or three cracked heads, anyway—the cowardly swine!"

"Look here!" said Swithin suddenly; "which is my way to the Goldene Alp?"

The Hungarian replied, "But you are coming with me, for a glass of wine?"

Swithin looked at the ground. 'Not if I know it!' he thought.

"Ah!" said the Hungarian with dignity, "you do not wish for my friendship!"

'Touchy beggar!' thought Swithin. "Of course," he stammered, "if you put it in that way——"

The Hungarian bowed, murmuring, "Forgive me!"

They had not gone a dozen steps before a youth, with a beardless face and hollow cheeks, accosted them. "For the love of Christ, gentlemen," he said, "help me!"

"Are you a German?" asked Boleskey.

"Yes," said the youth.

"Then you may rot!"

"Master, look here!" Tearing open his coat, the youth displayed his skin, and a leather belt drawn tight round it. Again Swithin felt that desire to take to his heels. He was filled with horrid forebodings—a sense of perpending intimacy with things such as no gentleman had dealings with.

The Hungarian crossed himself. "Brother," he said to the youth, "come you in!"

Swithin looked at them askance, and followed. By a dim light they groped their way up some stairs into a large room, into which the moon was shining through a window bulging over the street. A lamp burned low; there was a smell of spirits and tobacco, with a faint, peculiar scent, as of rose leaves. In one corner stood a czymbal, in another a great pile of newspapers. On the wall hung some old-fashioned pistols, and a rosary of yellow beads. Everything was tidily arranged, but dusty. Near an open fireplace was a table with the remains of a meal. The ceiling, floor, and walls were all of dark wood. In spite of the strange disharmony, the room had a sort of refinement.

The Hungarian took a bottle out of a cupboard and, filling some glasses, handed one to Swithin. Swithin put it gingerly to his nose. 'You never know your luck! Come!' he thought, tilting it slowly into his mouth. It was thick, too sweet, but of a fine flavour.

"Brothers!" said the Hungarian, refilling, "your healths!"

The youth tossed off his wine. And Swithin this time did the same; he pitied this poor devil of a youth now. "Come round to-morrow!" he said, "I'll give you a shirt or two." When the youth was gone, however, he remembered with relief that he had not given his address.

'Better so,' he reflected. 'A humbug, no doubt.'

"What was that you said to him?" he asked of the Hungarian.

"I said," answered Boleskey, "'You have eaten and drunk; and now you are my enemy!'"

"Quite right!" said Swithin, "quite right! A beggar is every man's enemy."

"You do not understand," the Hungarian replied politely. "While he was a beggar—I, too, have had to beg" (Swithin thought, 'Good God! this is awful!'), "but now that he is no longer hungry, what is he but a German? No Austrian dog soils my floors!"

His nostrils, as it seemed to Swithin, had distended in an unpleasant fashion; and a wholly unnecessary raucousness invaded his voice. "I am an exile—all of my blood are exiles. Those Godless dogs!" Swithin hurriedly assented.

As he spoke, a face peeped in at the door.

"Rozsi!" said the Hungarian. A young girl came in. She was rather short, with a deliciously round figure and a thick plait of hair. She smiled, and showed her even teeth; her little, bright, wide-set grey eyes glanced from one man to the other. Her face was round, too, high in the cheek-bones, the colour of wild roses, with brows that had a twist-up at the corners. With a gesture of alarm, she put her hand to her cheek, and called, "Margit!" An older girl appeared, taller, with fine shoulders, large eyes, a pretty mouth, and what Swithin described to himself afterwards as a "pudding" nose. Both girls, with little cooing sounds, began attending to their father's face. Swithin turned his back to them. His arm pained him.

'This is what comes of interfering,' he thought sulkily; 'I might have had my neck broken!' Suddenly a soft palm was placed in his, two eyes, half-fascinated, half-shy, looked at him; then a voice called, "Rozsi!" the door was slammed, he was alone again with the Hungarian, harassed by a sense of soft disturbance.

"Your daughter's name is Rosy?" he said; "we have it in England—from rose, a flower."

"Rozsi (Rozgi)," the Hungarian replied; "your English is a hard tongue, harder than French, German, or Czechish, harder than Russian, or Roumanian —I know no more."

"What?" said Swithin, "six languages?" Privately he thought, 'He knows how to lie, anyway.'

"If you lived in a country like mine," muttered the Hungarian, "with all men's hands against you! A free people—dying—but not dead!"

Swithin could not imagine what he was talking of. This man's face, with its linen bandage, gloomy eyes, and great black wisps of beard, his fierce mutterings, and hollow cough, were all most unpleasant. He seemed to be suffering from some kind of mental dog-bite. His emotion indeed appeared so indecent, so uncontrolled and open, that its obvious sincerity produced a sort of awe in Swithin. It was like being forced to look into a furnace. Boleskey stopped roaming up and down. "You think it's over?" he said; "I tell you, in the breast of each one of us Magyars there is a hell. What is sweeter than life? What is more sacred than each breath we draw? Ah! my country!" These words were uttered so slowly, with such intense mournfulness, that Swithin's jaw relaxed; he converted the movement to a yawn.

"Tell me," said Boleskey, "what would you do if the French conquered you?"

Swithin smiled. Then suddenly, as though something had hurt him, he grunted, "The 'Froggies'? Let 'em try!"

"Drink!" said Boleskey—"there is nothing like it"; he filled Swithin's glass. "I will tell you my story."

Swithin rose hurriedly. "It's late," he said. "This is good stuff, though; have you much of it?"

"It is the last bottle."

"What?" said Swithin; "and you gave it to a beggar?"

"My name is Boleskey-Stefan," the Hungarian said, raising his head; "of the Komorn Boleskeys." The simplicity of this phrase—as who shall say: What need of further description?—made an impression on Swithin; he stopped to listen. Boleskey's story went on and on. "There were many abuses." boomed his deep voice, "much wrong done—much cowardice. I could see clouds gathering—rolling over our plains. The Austrian wished to strangle the breath of our mouths—to take from us the shadow of our liberty —the shadow—all we had. Two years ago—the year of '48, when every man and boy answered the great voice—brother, a dog's life!—to use a pen when all of your blood are fighting, but it was decreed for me! My son was killed; my brothers taken—and myself was thrown out like a dog—I had written out my heart, I had written out all the blood that was in my body!" He seemed to tower, a gaunt shadow of a man, with gloomy, flickering eyes staring at the wall.

Swithin rose, and stammered, "Much obliged—very interesting." Boleskey made no effort to detain him, but continued staring at the wall. "Goodnight!" said Swithin, and stamped heavily downstairs.

III

When at last Swithin reached the Goldene Alp, he found his brother and friend standing uneasily at the door. Traquair, a prematurely dried-up man, with whiskers and a Scotch accent, remarked, "Ye're airly, man!" Swithin growled something unintelligible, and swung up to bed. He discovered a slight cut on his arm. He was in a savage temper—the elements had conspired to show him things he did not want to see; yet now and then a memory of Rozsi, of her soft palm in his, a sense of having been stroked and flattered, came over him. During breakfast next morning his brother and Traquair announced their intention of moving on. James Forsyte, indeed, remarked that it was no place for a "collector," since all the "old" shops were in the hands of Jews or very grasping persons—he had discovered this at once. Swithin pushed his cup aside. "*You* may do what you like," he said, "*I'm* staying here."

James Forsyte replied, tumbling over his own words: "Why! what do you want to stay here for? There's nothing for you to do here—there's nothing to see here, unless you go up the Citadel, an' you won't do that."

Swithin growled, "Who says so?" Having gratified his perversity, he felt in a better temper. He had slung his arm in a silk sash, and accounted for it by saying he had slipped. Later he went out and walked on to the bridge. In the brilliant sunshine spires were glistening against the pearly background of the hills; the town had a clean, joyous air. Swithin glanced at the Citadel and thought, "Looks a strong place! Shouldn't wonder if it were impregnable!" And this for some occult reason gave him pleasure. It occurred to him suddenly to go and look for the Hungarian's house.

About noon, after a hunt of two hours, he was gazing about him blankly, pale with heat, but more obstinate than ever, when a voice above him called "Mister!" He looked up and saw Rozsi. She was leaning her round chin on her round hand, gazing down at him with her deep-set, clever eyes. When Swithin removed his hat, she clapped her hands. Again he had the sense of being admired, caressed. With a careless air, that sat grotesquely on his tall square person, he walked up to the door; both girls stood in the passage. Swithin felt a confused desire to speak in some foreign tongue.

"Maam'selles," he began, "er—*bong jour*—er your father—*père, comment?*"

"We also speak English," said the elder girl; "will you come in, please?"

Swithin swallowed a misgiving and entered. The room had a worn appearance by daylight, as if it had always been the nest of tragic or vivid lives. He sat down, and his eyes said: "I am a stranger, but don't try to get the better of me, please—that is impossible." The girls looked at him in silence. Rozsi wore a rather short skirt of black stuff, a white shirt, and across her shoulders an embroidered yoke; her sister was dressed in dark green, with a coral necklace; both girls had their hair in plaits. After a minute Rozsi touched the sleeve of his hurt arm.

"It's nothing!" muttered Swithin.

"Father fought with a chair, but you had no chair," she said in a wondering voice.

He doubled the fist of his sound arm and struck a blow at space. To his amazement she began to laugh. Nettled at this, he put his hand beneath the heavy table and lifted it. Rozsi clapped her hands. "Ah! now I see—how strong you are!" She made him a curtsey and whisked round to the window. He found the quick intelligence of her eyes confusing; sometimes they seemed to look beyond him at something invisible—this, too, confused him. From Margit he learned that they had been two years in England, where their father had made his living by teaching languages; they had now been a year in Salzburg.

"We wait," suddenly with Rozsi; and Margit, with a solemn face, repeated, "We wait."

Swithin's eyes swelled a little with his desire to see what they were waiting for. How queer they were, with their eyes that gazed beyond him! He looked at their figures. "She would pay for dressing," he thought, and he tried to imagine Rozsi in a skirt with proper flounces, a thin waist, and hair drawn back over her ears. She would pay for dressing, with that supple figure, fluffy hair, and little hands! And instantly his own hands, face, and clothes disturbed him. He got up, examined the pistols on the wall, and felt resentment at the faded, dusty room. 'Smells like a pot-house!' he thought. He sat down again close to Rozsi.

"Do you love to dance?" she asked: "to dance is to live. First you hear the music—how your feet itch! It is wonderful! You begin slow, quick—quicker; you fly—you know nothing—your feet are in the air. It is wonderful!"

A slow flush had mounted into Swithin's face.

"Ah!" continued Rozsi, her eyes fixed on him, "when I am dancing—out there I see the plains—your feet go one—two—three—quick, quick, quick, quicker—you fly."

She stretched herself, a shiver seemed to pass all down her. "Margit! dance!" and, to Swithin's consternation, the two girls—their hands on each other's shoulders—began shuffling their feet and swaying to and fro. Their heads were thrown back, their eyes half-closed; suddenly the step quickened, they swung to one side, then to the other, and began whirling round in front of him. The sudden fragrance of rose leaves enveloped him. Round they flew again. While they were still dancing, Boleskey came into the room. He caught Swithin by both hands.

"Brother, welcome! Ah! your arm is hurt! I do not forget." His yellow face and deep-set eyes expressed a dignified gratitude. "Let me introduce to you my friend Baron Kasteliz."

Swithin bowed to a man with a small forehead, who had appeared softly, and stood with his gloved hands touching his waist. Swithin conceived a sudden aversion for this cat-like man. About Boleskey there was that which made contempt impossible—the sense of comradeship begotten in the fight; the man's height; something lofty and savage in his face; and an obscure instinct that it would not pay to show distaste; but this Kasteliz, with his neat jaw, low brow, and velvety, volcanic look, excited his proper English animosity. "Your friends are mine," murmured Kasteliz. He spoke with suavity, and hissed his s's. A long, vibrating twang quavered through the room. Swithin turned and saw Rozsi sitting at the czymbal; the notes rang under the little hammers in her hands, incessant, metallic, rising and falling with that strange melody. Kasteliz had fixed his glowing eyes on her; Boleskey, nodding his head, was staring at the floor; Margit, with a pale face, stood like a statue.

'What can they see in it?' thought Swithin; 'it's not a tune.' He took up his hat. Rozsi saw him and stopped; her lips had parted with a faintly dismayed expression. His sense of personal injury diminished; he even felt a little sorry for her. She jumped up from her seat and twirled round with a pout. An inspiration seized on Swithin. "Come and dine with me," he said to Boleskey, "to-morrow—the Goldene Alp—bring your friend." He felt the eyes of the whole room on him—the Hungarian's fine eyes; Margit's wide glance; the narrow, hot gaze of Kasteliz; and lastly—Rozsi's. A glow of satisfaction ran down his spine. When he emerged into the street he thought gloomily, 'Now, I've done it!' And not for some paces did he look round; then, with a forced smile, turned and removed his hat to the faces at the window.

Notwithstanding this moment of gloom, however, he was in an exalted state all day, and at dinner kept looking at his brother and Traquair enigmatically. 'What do they know of life?' he thought; 'they might be here a year and get no farther.' He made jokes, and pinned the menu to the waiter's coat-tails. "I like this place," he said, "I shall spend three weeks here." James, whose lips were on the point of taking in a plum, looked at him uneasily.

IV

On the day of the dinner Swithin suffered a good deal. He reflected gloomily on Boleskey's clothes. He had fixed an early hour—there would be fewer people to see them. When the time approached he attired himself with a certain neat splendour, and though his arm was still sore, left off the sling....

Nearly three hours afterwards he left the Goldene Alp between his guests. It was sunset, and along the river-bank the houses stood out, unsoftened by the dusk; the streets were full of people hurrying home. Swithin had a hazy vision of empty bottles, of the ground before his feet, and the accessibility of all the world. Dim recollections of the good things he had said, of his brother and Traquair seated in the background eating ordinary meals with inquiring, acid visages, caused perpetual smiles to break out on his face, and he steered himself stubbornly, to prove that he was a better man than either of his guests. He knew, vaguely, that he was going somewhere with an object; Rozsi's face kept dancing before him, like a promise. Once or twice he gave Kasteliz a glassy stare. Towards Boleskey, on the other hand, he felt quite warm, and recalled with admiration the way he had set his glass down empty, time after time. 'I like to see him take his liquor,' he thought; 'the fellow's a gentleman, after all.'

Boleskey strode on, savagely inattentive to everything; and Kasteliz had become more like a cat than ever. It was nearly dark when they reached a narrow street close to the cathedral. They stopped at a door held open by an old woman. The change from the fresh air to a heated corridor, the noise of the door closed behind him, the old woman's anxious glances, sobered Swithin.

"I tell her," said Boleskey, "that I reply for you as for my son."

Swithin was angry. What business had this man to reply for him!

They passed into a large room, crowded with men and women; Swithin noticed that they all looked at him. He stared at them in turn—they seemed of all classes, some in black coats or silk dresses, others in the clothes of work-people; one man, a cobbler, still wore his leather apron, as if he had rushed there straight from his work. Laying his hand on Swithin's arm, Boleskey evidently began explaining who he was; hands were extended, people beyond reach bowed to him. Swithin acknowledged the greetings with a stiff motion of his head; then seeing other people dropping into seats, he, too, sat down. Some one whispered his name—Margit and Rozsi were just behind him.

"Welcome!" said Margit; but Swithin was looking at Rozsi. Her face was so alive and quivering! 'What's the excitement all about?' he thought. 'How pretty she looks!' She blushed, drew in her hands with a quick tense movement, and gazed again beyond him in the room. 'What is it?' thought Swithin; he had a longing to lean back and kiss her lips. He tried angrily to see what she was seeing in those faces turned all one way.

Boleskey rose to speak. No one moved; not a sound could be heard but the tone of his deep voice. On and on he went, fierce and solemn, and with the rise of his voice, all those faces—fair or swarthy—seemed to be glowing with one and the same feeling. Swithin felt the white heat in those faces—it was not decent! In that whole speech he only understood the one word— "Magyar"—which came again and again. He almost dozed off at last. The twang of a czymbal woke him. 'What?' he thought, 'more of that infernal music!' Margit, leaning over him, whispered: "Listen! Racoczy! it is forbidden!" Swithin saw that Rozsi was no longer in her seat; it was she who was striking those forbidden notes. He looked round—everywhere the same unmoving faces, the same entrancement, and fierce stillness. The music sounded muffled, as if it, too, were bursting its heart in silence. Swithin felt within him a touch of panic. Was this a den of tigers? The way these people listened, the ferocity of their stillness, was frightful! . . . He gripped his chair and broke into a perspiration; was there no chance to get away? 'When

it stops,' he thought, 'there'll be a rush!' But there was only a greater silence.
It flashed across him that any hostile person coming in then would be torn
to pieces. A woman sobbed. The whole thing was beyond words unpleasant.
He rose, and edged his way furtively towards the doorway. There was a cry
of "Police!" The whole crowd came pressing after him. Swithin would soon
have been out, but a little behind he caught sight of Rozsi swept off her
feet. Her frightened eyes angered him. 'She doesn't deserve it,' he thought
sulkily; 'letting all this loose!' and forced his way back to her. She clung to
him, and a fever went stealing through his veins; he butted forward at the
crowd, holding her tight. When they were outside he let her go.

"I was afraid," she said.

"Afraid!" muttered Swithin; "I should think so." No longer touching her,
he felt his grievance revive.

"But you are so strong," she murmured.

"This is no place for you," growled Swithin. "I'm going to see you home."

"Oh!" cried Rozsi; "but papa and—Margit!"

"That's their lookout!" and he hurried her away.

She slid her hand under his arm; the soft curves of her form brushed him
gently, each touch only augmented his ill-humour. He burned with a perverse
rage, as if all the passions in him were simmering and ready to boil over;
it was as if a poison were trying to work its way out of him through the
layers of his stolid flesh. He maintained a dogged silence; Rozsi, too, said
nothing, but when they reached the door, she drew her hand away.

"You are angry!" she said.

"Angry," muttered Swithin; "no! How d'you make that out?" He had a
torturing desire to kiss her.

"Yes, you are angry," she repeated; "I wait here for papa and Margit."

Swithin also waited, wedged against the wall. Once or twice, for his sight
was sharp, he saw her steal a look at him, a beseeching look, and hardened
his heart with a kind of pleasure. After five minutes Boleskey, Margit, and
Kasteliz appeared. Seeing Rozsi they broke into exclamations of relief, and
Kasteliz, with a glance at Swithin, put his lips to her hand. Rozsi's look
said, "Wouldn't you like to do that?" Swithin turned short on his heel, and
walked away.

V

All night he hardly slept, suffering from fever, for the first time in his life.
Once he jumped out of bed, lighted a candle, and going to the glass, scruti-
nised himself long and anxiously. After this he fell asleep, but had frightful
dreams. His first thought when he woke was, 'My liver's out of order!'
and, thrusting his head into cold water, he dressed hastily and went out. He
soon left the house behind. Dew covered everything; blackbirds whistled in
the bushes, the air was fresh and sweet. He had not been up so early since
he was a boy. Why was he walking through a damp wood at this hour of the
morning? Something intolerable and unfamiliar must have sent him out.
No fellow in his senses would do such a thing! He came to a dead stop, and
began unsteadily to walk back. Regaining the hotel, he went to bed again, and
dreamed that in some wild country he was living in a room full of insects,

where a housemaid—Rozsi—holding a broom, looked at him with mournful eyes. There seemed an unexplained need for immediate departure; he begged her to forward his things, and shake them out carefully before she put them into the trunk. He understood that the charge for sending would be twenty-two shillings, thought it a great deal, and had the horrors of indecision. "No," he muttered, "pack, and take them myself." The housemaid turned suddenly into a lean creature; and he awoke with a sore feeling in his heart.

His eye fell on his wet boots. The whole thing was scaring, and jumping up, he began to throw his clothes into his trunks. It was twelve o'clock before he went down, and found his brother and Traquair still at the table arranging an itinerary; he surprised them by saying that he too was coming; and without further explanation set to work to eat. James had heard that there were salt-mines in the neighbourhood—his proposal was to start, and halt an hour or so on the road for their inspection: he said: "Everybody'll ask you if you've seen the salt-mines: I shouldn't like to say I hadn't seen the salt-mines. What's the good, they'd say, of your going there if you haven't seen the salt-mines?" He wondered, too, if they need fee the second waiter —an idle chap!

A discussion followed; but Swithin ate on glumly, conscious that his mind was set on larger affairs. Suddenly on the far side of the street Rozsi and her sister passed, with little baskets on their arms. He started up, and at that moment Rozsi looked round—her face was the incarnation of enticement, the chin tilted, the lower lip thrust a little forward, her round neck curving back over her shoulder. Swithin muttered, "Make your own arrangements— leave me out!" and hurried from the room, leaving James beside himself with interest and alarm.

When he reached the street, however, the girls had disappeared. He hailed a carriage. "Drive!" he called to the man, with a flourish of his stick, and as soon as the wheels had begun to clatter on the stones he leaned back, looking sharply to right and left. He soon had to give up thought of finding them, but made the coachman turn round and round again. All day he drove about, far into the country, and kept urging the driver to use greater speed. He was in a strange state of hurry and elation. Finally, he dined at a little country inn; and this gave the measure of his disturbance—the dinner was atrocious.

Returning late in the evening he found a note written by Traquair. "Are you in your senses, man?" it asked; "we have no more time to waste idling about here. If you want to rejoin us, come on to Danielli's Hotel, Venice." Swithin chuckled when he read it, and feeling frightfully tired, went to bed and slept like a log.

VI

Three weeks later he was still in Salzburg, no longer at the Goldene Alp, but in rooms over a shop near the Boleskeys'. He had spent a small fortune in the purchase of flowers. Margit would croon over them, but Rozsi, with a sober "Many tanks!" as if they were her right, would look long at herself in the glass, and pin one into her hair. Swithin ceased to wonder; he ceased to wonder at anything they did. One evening he found Boleskey deep in conversation with a pale, dishevelled-looking person.

"Our friend Mr. Forsyte—Count D——," said Boleskey.

Swithin experienced a faint, unavoidable emotion; but looking at the Count's trousers, he thought: "Doesn't look much like one!" And with an ironic bow to the silent girls, he turned, and took his hat. But when he had reached the bottom of the dark stairs he heard footsteps. Rozsi came running down, looked out at the door, and put her hands up to her breast as if disappointed: suddenly with a quick glance round she saw him. Swithin caught her arm. She slipped away, and her face seemed to bubble with defiance or laughter; she ran up three steps, looked at him across her shoulder, and fled on up the stairs. Swithin went out bewildered and annoyed.

'What was she going to say to me?' he kept thinking. During these three weeks he had asked himself all sorts of questions: whether he were being made a fool of; whether she were in love with him; what he was doing there, and sometimes at night, with all his candles burning as if he wanted light, the breeze blowing on him through the window, his cigar, half-smoked, in his hand, he sat, an hour or more, staring at the wall. 'Enough of this!' he thought every morning. Twice he packed fully—once he ordered his travelling carriage, but countermanded it the following day. What definitely he hoped, intended, resolved, he could not have said. He was always thinking of Rozsi, he could not read the riddle in her face—she held him in a vice, notwithstanding that everything about her threatened the very fetishes of his existence. And Boleskey! Whenever he looked at him he thought, 'If he were only clean?' and mechanically fingered his own well-tied cravate. To talk with the fellow, too, was like being forced to look at things which had no place in the light of day. Freedom, equality, self-sacrifice!

'Why can't he settle down at some business,' he thought, 'instead of all this talk?' Boleskey's sudden diffidences, self-depreciation, fits of despair, irritated him. "Morbid beggar!" he would mutter; "thank God *I* haven't a thin skin." And proud too! Extraordinary! An impecunious fellow like that! One evening, moreover, Boleskey had returned home drunk. Swithin had hustled him away into his bedroom, helped him to undress, and stayed until he was asleep. 'Too much of a good thing!' he thought, 'before his own daughters, too!' It was after this that he ordered his travelling carriage. The other occasion on which he packed was one evening, when not only Boleskey, but Rozsi herself had picked chicken bones with her fingers.

Often in the mornings he would go to the Mirabel Garden to smoke his cigar; there, in stolid contemplation of the statues—rows of half-heroic men carrying off half-distressed females—he would spend an hour pleasantly, his hat tilted to keep the sun off his nose. The day after Rozsi had fled from him on the stairs, he came there as usual. It was a morning of blue sky and sunlight glowing on the old prim garden, on its yew-trees, and serio-comic statues, and walls covered with apricots and plums. When Swithin approached his usual seat, who should be sitting there but Rozsi!

"Good-morning," he stammered; "you knew this was my seat then?"

Rozsi looked at the ground. "Yes," she answered.

Swithin felt bewildered. "Do you know," he said, "you treat me very funnily?"

To his surprise Rozsi put her little soft hand down and touched his; then, without a word, sprang up and rushed away. It took him a minute to recover.

There were people present; he did not like to run, but overtook her on the bridge, and slipped her hand beneath his arm.

"You shouldn't have done that," he said; "you shouldn't have run away from me, you know."

Rozsi laughed. Swithin withdrew his arm; a desire to shake her seized him. He walked some way before he said, "Will you have the goodness to tell me what you came to that seat for?"

Rozsi flashed a look at him. "To-morrow is the *fête*," she answered.

Swithin muttered, "Is that all?"

"If you do not take us, we cannot go."

"Suppose I refuse," he said sullenly, "there are plenty of others."

Rozsi bent her head, scurrying along. "No," she murmured, "if *you* do not go—I do not wish."

Swithin drew her hand back within his arm. How round and soft it was! He tried to see her face. When she was nearly home he said good-bye, not wishing, for some dark reason, to be seen with her. He watched till she had disappeared; then slowly retraced his steps to the Mirabell Garden. When he came to where she had been sitting, he slowly lighted his cigar, and for a long time after it was smoked out remained there in the silent presence of the statues.

VII

A crowd of people wandered round the booths, and Swithin found himself obliged to give the girls his arms. 'Like a little Cockney clerk!' he thought. His indignation passed unnoticed; they talked, they laughed, each sight and sound in all the hurly-burly seemed to go straight into their hearts. He eyed them ironically—their eager voices, and little coos of sympathy seemed to him vulgar. In the thick of the crowd he slipped his arm out of Margit's, but, just as he thought that he was free, the unwelcome hand slid up again. He tried again, but again Margit reappeared, serene, and full of pleasant humour; and his failure this time appeared to him in a comic light. But when Rozsi leaned across him, the glow of her round cheek, her curving lip, the inscrutable grey gleam of her eyes, sent a thrill of longing through him. He was obliged to stand by while they parleyed with a gipsy, whose matted locks and skinny hands inspired him with a not unwarranted disgust. "Folly!" he muttered, as Rozsi held out her palm. The old woman mumbled, and shot a malignant look at him. Rozsi drew back her hand, and crossed herself. 'Folly!' Swithin thought again; and seizing the girls' arms, he hurried them away.

"What did the old hag say?" he asked.

Rozsi shook her head.

"You don't mean that you believe?"

Her eyes were full of tears. "The gipsies are wise," she murmured.

"Come, what did she tell you?"

This time Rozsi looked hurriedly round, and slipped away into the crowd. After a hunt they found her, and Swithin, who was scared, growled: "You shouldn't do such things—it's not respectable."

On higher ground, in the centre of a clear space, a military band was playing. For the privilege of entering this charmed circle Swithin paid three *kronen,* choosing naturally the best seats. He ordered wine, too, watching Rozsi out of the corner of his eye as he poured it out. The protecting tenderness of yesterday was all lost in this medley. It was every man for himself, after all! The colour had deepened again in her cheeks, she laughed, pouting her lips. Suddenly she put her glass aside. "Thank you, very much," she said, "it is enough!"

Margit, whose pretty mouth was all smiles, cried, *"Lieber Gott!* is it not good—life?" It was not a question Swithin could undertake to answer. The band began to play a waltz. "Now they will dance. *Lieber Gott!* and are the lights not wonderful?" Lamps were flickering beneath the trees like a swarm of fireflies. There was a hum as from a gigantic beehive. Passers-by lifted their faces, then vanished into the crowd; Rozsi stood gazing at them spellbound, as if their very going and coming were a delight.

The space was soon full of whirling couples. Rozsi's head began to beat time. "O Margit!" she whispered.

Swithin's face had assumed a solemn, uneasy expression. A man, raising his hat, offered his arm to Margit. She glanced back across her shoulder to reassure Swithin. "It is a friend," she said.

Swithin looked at Rozsi—her eyes were bright, her lips tremulous. He slipped his hand along the table and touched her fingers. Then she flashed a look at him—appeal, reproach, tenderness, all were expressed in it. Was she expecting him to dance? Did she want to mix with the riff-raff there; with *him* to make an exhibition of himself in this hurly-burly? A voice said, "Good-evening!" Before them stood Kasteliz, in a dark coat tightly buttoned at the waist.

"You are not dancing, *Rozsi Kozsanony?"* (Miss Rozsi). "Let me, then, have the pleasure." He held out his arm. Swithin stared in front of him. In the very act of going she gave him a look that said as plain as words: "Will you not?" But for answer he turned his eyes away, and when he looked again she was gone. He paid the score and made his way into the crowd. But as he went she danced by close to him, all flushed and panting. She hung back as if to stop him, and he caught the glistening of tears. Then he lost sight of her again. To be deserted the first minute he was alone with her, and for that jackanapes with the small head and volcanic glances! It was too much! And suddenly it occurred to him that she was alone with Kasteliz—alone at night, and far from home. 'Well,' he thought, 'what do I care?' and shouldered his way on through the crowd. It served him right for mixing with such people here. He left the fair, but the further he went, the more he nursed his rage, the more heinous seemed her offence, the sharper grew his jealousy. 'A beggarly baron!' was his thought.

A figure came alongside—it was Boleskey. One look showed Swithin his condition. Drunk again! This was the last straw!

Unfortunately Boleskey had recognised him. He seemed violently excited. "Where—where are my daughters?" he began.

Swithin brushed past, but Boleskey caught his arm. "Listen—brother!" he said; "news of my country! After to-morrow——"

"Keep it to yourself!" growled Swithin, wrenching his arm free. He went straight to his lodgings, and, lying on the hard sofa of his unlighted sitting-room, gave himself up to bitter thoughts. But in spite of all his anger, Rozsi's supply-moving figure, with its pouting lips, and roguish appealing eyes, still haunted him.

VIII

Next morning there was not a carriage to be had, and Swithin was compelled to put off his departure till the morrow. The day was grey and misty; he wandered about with the strained, inquiring look of a lost dog in his eyes.

Late in the afternoon he went back to his lodgings. In a corner of the sitting-room stood Rozsi. The thrill of triumph, the sense of appeasement, the emotion, that seized on him, crept through to his lips in a faint smile. Rozsi made no sound, her face was hidden by her hands. And this silence of hers weighed on Swithin. She was forcing him to break it. What was behind her hands? His own face was visible! Why didn't she speak? Why was she here? Alone? That was not right surely.

Suddenly Rozsi dropped her hands; her flushed face was quivering—it seemed as though a word, a sign, even, might bring a burst of tears.

He walked over to the window. 'I must give her time!' he thought; then seized by unreasoning terror at this silence, spun round, and caught her by the arms. Rozsi held back from him, swayed forward and buried her face on his breast. . . .

Half an hour later Swithin was pacing up and down his room. The scent of rose leaves had not yet died away. A glove lay on the floor; he picked it up, and for a long time stood weighing it in his hand. All sorts of confused thoughts and feelings haunted him. It was the purest and least selfish moment of his life, this moment after she had yielded. But that pure gratitude at her fiery, simple abnegation did not last; it was followed by a petty sense of triumph, and by uneasiness. He was still weighing the little glove in his hand, when he had another visitor. It was Kasteliz.

"What can I do for you?" Swithin asked ironically.

The Hungarian seemed suffering from excitement. Why had Swithin left his charges the night before? What excuse had he to make? What sort of conduct did he call this?

Swithin, very like a bull-dog at that moment, answered: What business was it of his?

The business of a gentleman! What right had the Englishman to pursue a young girl?

"Pursue?" said Swithin; "you've been spying, then?"

"Spying—I—Kasteliz—Maurus Johann—an insult!"

"Insult!" sneered Swithin; "d'you mean to tell me you weren't in the street just now?"

Kasteliz answered with a hiss, "If you do not leave the city I will make you, with my sword—do you understand?"

"And if you do not leave my room I will throw you out of the window!"

For some minutes Kasteliz spoke in pure Hungarian while Swithin waited, with a forced smile and a fixed look in his eye. He did not understand Hungarian.

"If you are still in the city to-morrow evening," said Kasteliz at last in English, "I will spit you in the street."

Swithin turned to the window and watched his visitor's retiring back with a queer mixture of amusement, stubbornness, and anxiety. 'Well,' he thought, 'I suppose he'll run me through!' The thought was unpleasant; and it kept recurring, but it only served to harden his determination. His head was busy with plans for seeing Rozsi; his blood on fire with the kisses she had given him.

IX

Swithin was long in deciding to go forth next day. He had made up his mind not to go to Rozsi till five o'clock. 'Mustn't make myself too cheap,' he thought. It was a little past that hour when he at last sallied out, and with a beating heart walked towards Boleskey's. He looked up at the window, more than half expecting to see Rozsi there; but she was not, and he noticed with faint surprise that the window was not open; the plants, too, outside, looked singularly arid. He knocked. No one came. He beat a fierce tattoo. At last the door was opened by a man with a reddish beard, and one of those sardonic faces only to be seen on shoemakers of Teutonic origin.

"What do you want, making all this noise?" he asked in German.

Swithin pointed up the stairs. The man grinned, and shook his head.

"I want to go up," said Swithin.

The cobbler shrugged his shoulders, and Swithin rushed upstairs. The rooms were empty. The furniture remained, but all signs of life were gone. One of his own bouquets, faded, stood in a glass; the ashes of a fire were barely cold; little scraps of paper strewed the hearth; already the room smelt musty. He went into the bedrooms, and with a feeling of stupefaction stood staring at the girls' beds, side by side against the wall. A bit of ribbon caught his eye; he picked it up and put it in his pocket—it was a piece of evidence that she had once existed. By the mirror some pins were dropped about; a little powder had been spilled. He looked at his own disquiet face and thought, 'I've been cheated!'

The shoemaker's voice aroused him. *"Tausend Teufel! Eilen Sie, nur! Zeit is Geld! Kann nich' länger warten!"* Slowly he descended.

"Where have they gone?" asked Swithin painfully. "A pound for every English word you speak. A pound!" and he made an O with his fingers.

The corners of the shoemaker's lips curled. *"Geld! Mff! Eilen Sie, nur!"*

But in Swithin a sullen anger had begun to burn. "If you don't tell me," he said, "it'll be the worse for you."

"Sind ein komischer Kerl!" remarked the shoemaker. *"Hier ist meine Frau!"*

A battered-looking woman came hurrying down the passage, calling out in German, "Don't let him go!"

With a snarling sound the shoemaker turned his back, and shambled off.

The woman furtively thrust a letter into Swithin's hand, and furtively waited.

The letter was from Rozsi.

"Forgive me"—it ran—"that I leave you and do not say good-bye. To-day our father had the call from our dear Father-town so long awaited. In two hours we are ready. I pray to the Virgin to keep you ever safe, and that you do not quite forget me.—Your unforgetting good friend

ROZSI."

When Swithin read it his first sensation was that of a man sinking in a bog; then his obstinacy stiffened. 'I won't be done,' he thought. Taking out a sovereign he tried to make the woman comprehend that she could earn it, by telling him where they had gone. He got her finally to write the words out in his pocket-book, gave her the sovereign, and hurried to the Goldene Alp, where there was a waiter who spoke English.

The translation given him was this:

"At three o'clock they start in a carriage on the road to Linz—they have bad horses—the Herr also rides a white horse."

Swithin at once hailed a carriage and started at full gallop on the road to Linz. Outside the Mirabell Garden he caught sight of Kasteliz and grinned at him. 'I've sold *him* anyway,' he thought; 'for all their talk, they're no good, these foreigners!'"

His spirits rose, but soon fell again. What chance had he of catching them? They had three hours' start! Still, the roads were heavy from the rain of the last two nights—they had luggage and bad horses; his own were good, his driver bribed—he might overtake them by ten o'clock! But did he want to? What a fool he had been not to bring his luggage; he would then have had a respectable position. What a brute he would look without a change of shirt, or anything to shave with! He saw himself with horror, all bristly, and in soiled linen. People would think him mad. 'I've given myself away,' flashed across him, 'what the devil can I say to them?' and he stared sullenly at the driver's back. He read Rozsi's letter again; it had a scent of her. And in the growing darkness, jolted by the swinging of the carriage, he suffered tortures from his prudence, tortures from his passion.

It grew colder and dark. He turned the collar of his coat up to his ears. He had visions of Piccadilly. This wild-goose chase appeared suddenly a dangerous, unfathomable business. Lights, fellowship, security! 'Never again!' he brooded; 'why won't they let me alone?' But it was not clear whether by 'they' he meant the conventions, the Boleskeys, his passions, or those haunting memories of Rozsi. If he had only had a bag with him! What was he going to say? What was he going to get by this? He received no answer to these questions. The darkness itself was less obscure than his sensations. From time to time he took out his watch. At each village the driver made inquiries. It was past ten when he stopped the carriage with a jerk. The stars were bright as steel, and by the side of the road a reedy lake showed in the moonlight. Swithin shivered. A man on a horse had halted in the centre of the road. "Drive on!" called Swithin, with a stolid face. It turned out to be Boleskey, who, on a gaunt white horse, looked like some winged creature. He stood where he could bar the progress of the carriage, holding out a pistol.

'Theatrical beggar!' thought Swithin, with a nervous smile. He made no sign of recognition. Slowly Boleskey brought his lean horse up to the carriage. When he saw who was within he showed astonishment and joy.

"You?" he cried, slapping his hand on his attenuated thigh, and leaning over till his beard touched Swithin. "You have come? You followed us?"

"It seems so," Swithin grunted out.

"You throw in your lot with us. Is it possible? You—you are a knight-errant then!"

"Good God!" said Swithin. Boleskey, flogging his dejected steed, cantered forward in the moonlight. He came back, bringing an old cloak, which he insisted on wrapping round Swithin's shoulders. He handed him, too, a capacious flask.

"How cold you look!" he said. "Wonderful! Wonderful! you English!" His grateful eyes never left Swithin for a moment. They had come up to the heels of the other carriage now, but Swithin, hunched in the cloak, did not try to see what was in front of him. To the bottom of his soul he resented the Hungarian's gratitude. He remarked at last, with wasted irony:

"You're in a hurry, it seems!"

"If we had wings," Boleskey answered, "we would use them."

"Wings!" muttered Swithin thickly; "legs are good enough for me."

X

Arrived at the inn where they were to pass the night, Swithin waited, hoping to get into the house without a "scene," but when at last he alighted the girls were in the doorway, and Margit greeted him with an admiring murmur, in which, however, he seemed to detect irony. Rozsi, pale and tremulous, with a half-scared look, gave him her hand, and, quickly withdrawing it, shrank behind her sister. When they had gone up to their room Swithin sought Boleskey. His spirits had risen remarkably. "Tell the landlord to get us supper," he said; "we'll crack a bottle to our luck." He hurried on the landlord's preparations. The window of the room faced a wood, so near that he could almost touch the trees. The scent from the pines blew in on him. He turned away from that scented darkness, and began to draw the corks of wine-bottles. The sound seemed to conjure up Boleskey. He came in, splashed all over, smelling slightly of stables; soon after, Margit appeared, fresh and serene, but Rozsi did not come.

"Where is your sister?" Swithin said. Rozsi, it seemed, was tired. "It will do her good to eat," said Swithin. And Boleskey, murmuring, "She must drink to our country," went out to summon her, Margit followed him, while Swithin cut up a chicken. They came back without her. She had "a megrim of the spirit."

Swithin's face fell. "Look here!" he said, *"I'll* go and try. Don't wait for me."

"Yes," answered Boleskey, sinking mournfully into a chair; "try, brother, try—by all means, try."

Swithin walked down the corridor with an odd, sweet, sinking sensation in his chest; and tapped on Rozsi's door. In a minute, she peeped forth, with her hair loose, and wondering eyes.

"Rozsi," he stammered, "what makes you afraid of me, *now?*"

She stared at him, but did not answer.

"Why won't you come?"

Still she did not speak, but suddenly stretched out to him her bare arm. Swithin pressed his face to it. With a shiver, she whispered above him, "I will come," and gently shut the door.

Swithin stealthily retraced his steps, and paused a minute outside the sitting-room to regain his self-control.

The sight of Boleskey with a bottle in his hand steadied him.

"She is coming," he said. And very soon she did come, her thick hair roughly twisted in a plait.

Swithin sat between the girls; but did not talk, for he was really hungry. Boleskey too was silent, plunged in gloom; Rozsi was dumb; Margit alone chattered.

"You will come to our Father-town? We shall have things to show you. Rozsi, what things we will show him!" Rozsi, with a little appealing movement of her hands, repeated, "What things we will show you!" She seemed suddenly to find her voice, and with glowing cheeks, mouth full, and eyes bright as squirrels, they chattered reminiscences of the "dear Father-town," of "dear friends," of the "dear home."

'A poor place!' Swithin could not help thinking. This enthusiasm seemed to him common; but he was careful to assume a look of interest, feeding on the glances flashed at him from Rozsi's restless eyes.

As the wine waned Boleskey grew more and more gloomy, but now and then a sort of gleaming flicker passed over his face. He rose to his feet at last.

"Let us not forget," he said, "that we go perhaps to ruin, to death; in the face of all this we go, because our country needs—in this there is no credit, neither to me nor to you, my daughters; but for this noble Englishman, what shall we say? Give thanks to God for a great heart. He comes—not for country, not for fame, not for money, but to help the weak and the oppressed. Let us drink, then, to him; let us drink again and again to heroic Forsyte!" In the midst of the dead silence, Swithin caught the look of suppliant mockery in Rozsi's eyes. He glanced at the Hungarian. Was he laughing at him? But Boleskey, after drinking up his wine, had sunk again into his seat; and there suddenly, to the surprise of all, he began to snore. Margit rose and, bending over him like a mother, murmured: "He is tired—it is the ride!" She raised him in her strong arms, and leaning on her shoulder Boleskey staggered from the room. Swithin and Rozsi were left alone. He slid his hand towards her hand that lay so close, on the rough tablecloth. It seemed to await his touch. Something gave way in him, and words came welling up; for the moment he forgot himself, forgot everything but that he was near her. Her head dropped on his shoulder, he breathed the perfume of her hair. "Good-night!" she whispered, and the whisper was like a kiss; yet before he could stop her she was gone. Her footsteps died away in the passage, but Swithin sat gazing intently at a single bright drop of spilt wine quivering on the table's edge. In that moment she, in her helplessness and emotion, was all in all to him—his life nothing; all the real things—his conventions, convictions, training, and himself—all seemed remote, behind a mist of passion and strange chivalry. Carefully with a bit of bread he soaked up the bright drop; and suddenly, he thought: 'This is tremendous!' For a long time he stood there in the window, close to the dark pine-trees.

XI

In the early morning he awoke, full of the discomfort of this strange place and the medley of his dreams. Lying, with his nose peeping over the quilt, he was visited by a horrible suspicion. When he could bear it no longer, he started up in bed. What if it were all a plot to get him to marry her? The thought was treacherous, and inspired in him a faint disgust. Still, *she* might be ignorant of it! But was she so innocent? What innocent girl would have come to his room like that? What innocent girl? Her father, who pretended to be caring only for his country? It was not probable that any man was such a fool; it was all part of the game—a scheming rascal! Kasteliz, too—his threats! They intended him to marry her? And the horrid idea was strengthened by his reverence for marriage. It was the proper, the respectable condition; he was genuinely afraid of this other sort of *liaison*—it was somehow too primitive! And yet the thought of that marriage made his blood run cold. Considering that she had already yielded, it would be all the more monstrous! With the cold, fatal clearness of the morning light he now for the first time saw his position in its full bearings. And, like a fish pulled out of water, he gasped at what was disclosed. Sullen resentment against this attempt to force him settled deep into his soul.

He seated himself on the bed, holding his head in his hands, solemnly thinking out what such marriage meant. In the first place it meant ridicule, in the next place ridicule, in the last place ridicule. She would eat chicken bones with her fingers—those fingers his lips still burned to kiss. She would dance wildly with other men. She would talk of her "dear Father-town," and all the time her eyes would look beyond him, somewhere or other into some d——d place he knew nothing of. He sprang up and paced the room, and for a moment thought he would go mad.

They meant him to marry her! Even she—she meant him to marry her! Her tantalising inscrutability; her sudden little tendernesses; her quick laughter; her swift, burning kisses; even the movements of her hands; her tears—all were evidence against her. Not one of these things that Nature made her do counted on her side, but how they fanned his longing, his desire, and distress. He went to the glass and tried to part his hair with his fingers, but being rather fine, it fell into lank streaks. There was no comfort to be got from it. He drew his muddy boots on. Suddenly he thought: 'If I could see her alone, I could arrive at some arrangement!' Then, with a sense of stupefaction, he made the discovery that no arrangement could possibly be made that would not be dangerous, even desperate. He seized his hat, and, like a rabbit that has been fired at, bolted from the room. He plodded along amongst the damp woods with his head down, and resentment and dismay in his heart. But, as the sun rose, and the air grew sweet with pine scent, he slowly regained a sort of equability. After all, she had already yielded; it was not as if——! And the tramp of his own footsteps lulled him into feeling that it would all come right. 'Look at the thing practically,' he thought. The faster he walked the firmer became his conviction that he could still see it through. He took out his watch—it was past seven—he began to hasten back. In the yard of the inn his driver was harnessing the horses; Swithin went up to him.

"Who told you to put them in?" he asked.

The driver answered, *"Der Herr."*

Swithin turned away. 'In ten minutes,' he thought, 'I shall be in that carriage again, with this going on in my head! Driving away from England, from all I'm used to—driving to—what?' Could he face it? Could he face all that he had been through that morning; face it day after day, night after night? Looking up, he saw Rozsi at her open window gazing down at him; never had she looked sweeter, more roguish. An inexplicable terror seized on him; he ran across the yard and jumped into his carriage. "To Salzburg!" he cried; "drive on!" And rattling out of the yard without a look behind, he flung a sovereign at the hostler. Flying back along the road faster even than he had come, with pale face, and eyes blank and staring like a pug-dog's, Swithin spoke no single word; nor, till he had reached the door of his lodgings, did he suffer the driver to draw rein.

XII

Towards evening, five days later, Swithin, yellow and travel-worn, was ferried in a gondola to Danielli's Hotel. His brother, who was on the steps, looked at him with an apprehensive curiosity.

"Why, it's you!" he mumbled. "So you've got here safe?"

"Safe?" growled Swithin.

James replied, "I thought you wouldn't leave your friends!" Then, with a jerk of suspicion, "You haven't brought your friends?"

"What friends?" growled Swithin.

James changed the subject. "You don't look the thing," he said.

"Really!" muttered Swithin; "what's that to you?"

He appeared at dinner that night, but fell asleep over his coffee. Neither Traquair nor James asked him any further question, nor did they allude to Salzburg; and during the four days which concluded the stay in Venice Swithin went about with his head up, but his eyes half-closed like a dazed man. Only after they had taken ship at Genoa did he show signs of any healthy interest in life, when, finding that a man on board was perpetually strumming, he locked the piano up and pitched the key into the sea.

That winter in London he behaved much as usual, but fits of moroseness would seize on him, during which he was not pleasant to approach.

One evening when he was walking with a friend in Piccadilly, a girl coming from a side-street accosted him in German. Swithin, after staring at her in silence for some seconds, handed her a five-pound note, to the great amazement of his friend; nor could he himself have explained the meaning of this freak of generosity.

Of Rozsi he never heard again. . . .

This, then, was the substance of what he remembered as he lay ill in bed. Stretching out his hand he pressed the bell. His valet appeared, crossing the room like a cat; a Swede, who had been with Swithin many years; a little man with a dried face and fierce moustache, morbidly sharp nerves, and a queer devotion to his master.

Swithin made a feeble gesture. "Adolf," he said, "I'm very bad."

"Yes, sir!"

"Why do you stand there like a cow?" asked Swithin; "can't you see I'm very bad?"

"Yes, sir!" The valet's face twitched as though it masked the dance of obscure emotions.

"I shall feel better after dinner. What time is it?"

"Five o'clock."

"I thought it was more. The afternoons are very long."

"Yes, sir!"

Swithin sighed, as though he had expected the consolation of denial.

"Very likely I shall have a nap. Bring up hot water at half-past six and shave me before dinner."

The valet moved towards the door. Swithin raised himself.

"What did Mr. James say to you!"

"He said you ought to have another doctor; two doctors, he said, better than one. He said, also, he would look in again on his way 'home.'"

Swithin grunted, "Umph! What else did he say?"

"He said you didn't take care of yourself."

Swithin glared.

"Has anybody else been to see me?"

The valet turned away his eyes. "Mrs. Thomas Forsyte came last Monday fortnight."

"How long have I been ill?"

"Five weeks on Saturday."

"Do you think I'm very bad?"

Adolf's face was covered suddenly with crow's-feet. "You have no business to ask me question like that! I am not paid, sir, to answer question like that."

Swithin said faintly: "You're a peppery fool! Open a bottle of champagne!"

Adolf took a bottle of champagne from a cupboard and held nippers to it. He fixed his eyes on Swithin. "The doctor said——"

"Open the bottle!"

"It is not——"

"Open the bottle—or I give you warning."

Adolf removed the cork. He wiped a glass elaborately, filled it, and bore it scrupulously to the bedside. Suddenly twirling his moustaches, he wrung his hands, and burst out: "It is poison."

Swithin grinned faintly. "You foreign fool!" he said. "Get out!"

The valet vanished.

'He forgot himself!' thought Swithin. Slowly he raised the glass, slowly put it back, and sank gasping on his pillows. Almost at once he fell asleep.

He dreamed that he was at his club, sitting after dinner in the crowded smoking-room, with its bright walls and trefoils of light. It was there that he sat every evening, patient, solemn, lonely, and sometimes fell asleep, his square, pale old face nodding to one side. He dreamed that he was gazing at the picture over the fireplace, of an old statesman with a high collar, supremely finished face, and sceptical eyebrows—the picture, smooth, and reticent as sealing-wax, of one who seemed for ever exhaling the narrow wisdom of final judgments. All round him, his fellow-members were chattering. Only he himself, the old sick member, was silent. If fellows only knew what it was like to sit by yourself and feel ill all the time! What they were saying he had heard a hundred times. They were talking of investments, of cigars, horses, actresses, machinery. What was that? A foreign patent for cleaning boilers? There was no such thing; boilers couldn't be cleaned, any fool knew that! If an Englishman couldn't clean a boiler, no foreigner could clean one. He appealed to the old statesman's eyes. But for once those eyes seemed hesitating, blurred, wanting in finality. They vanished. In their place were Rozsi's little deep-set eyes, with their wide and far-off look; and as he gazed they seemed to grow bright as steel, and to speak to him. Slowly the whole face grew to be there, floating on the dark background of the picture; it was pink, aloof, unfathomable, enticing, with its fluffy hair and quick lips, just as he had last seen it. "Are you looking for something?" she seemed to say: "I could show you."

"I have everything safe enough," answered Swithin, and in his sleep he groaned.

He felt the touch of fingers on his forehead. 'I'm dreaming,' he thought in his dream.

She had vanished; and far away, from behind the picture, came a sound of footsteps.

Aloud, in his sleep, Swithin muttered: "I've missed it."

Again he heard the rustling of those light footsteps, and close in his ear a sound, like a sob. He awoke; the sob was his own. Greats drops of perspiration stood on his forehead. 'What is it?' he thought; 'what have I lost?' Slowly his mind travelled over his investments; he could not think of any single one that was unsafe. What was it, then, that he had lost? Struggling on his pillows, he clutched the wine-glass. His lips touched the wine. 'This isn't the "Heidseck"!' he thought angrily, and before the reality of that displeasure all the dim vision passed away. But as he bent to drink, something snapped, and, with a sigh, Swithin Forsyte died above the bubbles. . . .

When James Forsyte came in again on his way home, the valet, trembling, took his hat and stick.

"How's your master?"

"My master is dead, sir!"

"Dead! He can't be! I left him safe an hour ago!"

On the bed Swithin's body was doubled like a sack; his hand still grasped the glass.

James Forsyte paused. "Swithin!" he said, and with his hand to his ear he waited for an answer; but none came, and slowly in the glass a last bubble rose and burst.

December, 1900.

Erik Axel Karlfeldt

DREAMS AND LIFE

I WOULD that I were a mighty man,
  Who ruled my kingdom and had men dig
  Around my castle a moat so big
No long-legged mischief the space could span.
  I would I could spread a noble feast
  Where each hungry fellow should be my guest,
With all of the lads who were bold and gay.
  And there it should always be said outright
  That black was black and that white was white,
And life should be praised to the very last day.

I would that I were a valiant man.
  Give me a steed and a saddle, O Fate,
  A warrior's sword, a just debate,
And a foeman to conquer if I can!
  And if I'm not named on the triumph day,
  When the troops come back from the finished fray,
Among those who fell where the fight raged hot—
  'Tis all the same, if I fought without fear.
  A man may advance though he be in the rear,
And slumber full soundly, although forgot.

But I'm not a man in these dreams remote.
  No other lances than words I wield,
  In poesy's tourney I bear a shield,
But the rest of the time wear an every-day coat.
  I would I might sing on the sun-kissed heights,
  Yet I dwell at home with the lesser lights,
Where Memory sings like a nightingale.
  The neighbors no less may hear me rejoice;
  When there's air in the lungs and a ring in the voice,
A song may ascend though it sounds from the dale.

MY FOREFATHERS

ON HISTORY'S PAGE their names do not shine,
  For humble and peaceful were they,
    And yet I can see their long, long line
Stretching back through the ages gray.
Yes, here in the ancient iron-rich land
They tilled their fields by the river-strand
And smelted the ore in their day.
Neither thralldom nor pomp could they understand,
But, dwelling each like a king in his house,
They quaffed at their festal carouse.
They kissed their sweethearts in springtime's pride,
As husbands their faith they revered,
The kind they honored, and God they feared,
And calmly they died, satisfied.

My fathers! — in grief, in temptation's hour
I'm strengthened by thoughts of you.
As you could cherish your lowly dower,
I will smile, though my goods be few.
When Pleasure beckoned with vine-wreathed head,
I thought of your fight for your scanty bread:
Should I covet more than my due?
You revived my soul like a river-bath
When I wearied of battling with lust,
And taught that my flesh I should rather distrust
Than the world and the Evil One's wrath.

I see you in dreams, ye sires of my race,
And my soul becomes faint and afraid;
Like a plant I've been torn from my sprouting-place
And I feel that your cause I've betrayed.
I'll tell now of summer and harvest-time
With a merry turn in the play of the rhyme;
'Tis the task of a poet to sing.
And should any poem of mine recall
The surge of the storm, the cataract's fall,
Some thought with a manly ring,
A lark's note, the glow of the heath, somehow,
Or the sigh of the woodland vast,—
You sang in silence through ages past
That song by your cart and your plough.

SNAKE SONG

WHEN I go off the beaten track, I want my flask along,
Since naught's as good for snake bit as a drop o' summat strong.

But now I think of snakes, I mind another class of beast
That's twice as false and slippery and dangerous at least.

They say the snake will crouch among the bushes, and its eye
Can glitter so it fascinates a bird that comes too nigh.

The girl, though, can go anywhere and shoot her winking glance
Wherever she takes notice of a passing pair of pants.

The crawling snake eats only dust, a-many folk declare;
The girl must nibble sugarplums and dine off silverware.

They teach the snake to dance a bit, and fools come up to see;
The girl-child dances in the womb—no need to learn has she.

One single time in all the year the snake will cast its slough;
The girl will change eight times a week and scarce think that's enough.

The poison of the snake may harm your body past control,
But woman's guile can sting to death a young man's very soul.

My song is done, I'll tell no more of hurtful beasts today;
I'm hasting to my sweetheart's nest across the woods away.

SUMMER DANCING

I DANCED one livelong summer.
Ah! such a lovely summer.
There never was such dancing seen
In all this region round.

We'd two and two be roaming
Together in the gloaming,
However far 'twould be to where
We heard the fiddle sound.

In street or glade we'd gather,
It made no difference whether
'Twas in or out, I'd never miss
When there was dancing on.

And always 'twas my pride there
How light I was to guide there,
I never had to wait my turn
Or go before 'twas done.

Oh, we had many a gay night;
On holidays from May night
To Michaelmas, the season through
I'd never see my bed.

For every golden morning
And every gloomy morning
I'd go straight from the dancing to
The fields and milking shed.

But foul the day or fine then
I'd never stop to pine them,
I'd pitch right in with all my heart
And work the whole week through.

I danced the livelong summer.
It was my only summer.
For when 'twas finished I was old,
My fun was finished, too.

EDEN

CALM delight o'er Eden resting,
    Sheen of dawn on leaf and blade.
    Note yon pair of starlings nesting
By the marten undismayed.
And while softly stirs the zephyr,
On her fleet
Sturdy feet
Braving tigers' tails, the heifer;
Baby doves in fearless flight
On the broad wings of the kite.

Nakes through her garden passes
Now the woman, white as snow;
Peas bloom in the wilding grasses,
Beans amid the poppies glow.
And the sty pig, slowly rousing,
Stretches out,
Peers about
Through the sage that tempts to browsing,
While he sniffs with pallid nose
At a red and dewy rose.

Adam loiters, happy-idle,
In the shade the plum boughs yield.
There's the colt has felt no bridle
Scampering through the self-sown field.
Eve is beckoning with an apple—
Where she goes
Springtime blows—
Delicate tints her bosom dapple.
Morn unending leaves it all;
This is Eden ere the fall.

II

Eve stands ashamed in the sun's red glare,
Fingering her fig leaf apron there.
Adam, in trousers green, is grinning
With pain of the gripes and regret for his sinning.
Curled round a branch above, the while,
The serpent squirms with joy of his guile,
And the angel, with tights of blazing
Buff, a huge axe is raising.

Peace is broken and the bliss is o'er,
The paddock dangles at Eden's door
Adam's brow shall be streaming;
Eve shall bear children, screaming.
Flails will thump upon floors of grain;
Out in the wood grows a club for Cain.
Seeking the distant goal assigned him,
Man forgets the home behind him.

Hot is the day, whose warning is done.
Coolness comes not till set of sun.

Sinclair Lewis

TRAVEL IS SO BROADENING

Well, I want to tell you, Mrs. Babbitt, and I know Mrs. Schmaltz heartily agrees with me, that we've never enjoyed a dinner more—that was some of the finest fried chicken I ever tasted in my life —and it certainly is a mighty great pleasure to be able to just have this quiet evening with you and George. Personally, I'm just as glad the Reverend and his wife couldn't come. I yield to no one in my admiration for Reverend Hickenlooper—as you say, there's probably no greater influence for Christian manhood in Zenith—but it's mighty nice to be able to have a quiet chin with you and George.

Now, George, about this trip to the Yellowstone you were talking about. I don't know as I can help an old, trained, long-distance motorist like you, with your wealth of experience, though I never did agree with you about not going into low gear in descending steep hills, but I guess you've got me beat on long-distance motoring, and I've often said to Mrs. Schmaltz—haven't I, Mame!—that there sure is one thing I envy George F. Babbitt for, and that's the time he drove three hundred and sixteen miles in one day, between dawn and midnight. But I don't pretend to have that magnificent physical make-up of yours, George, and I've never been able to stand more'n two hundred and ninety-eight miles in one day's tour, and, you might say, really enjoy it and feel I was relaxing.

But same time, any helpful information that I can give you may be of help to you on your trip, if you decide to make it next summer, I'm certainly mighty glad to give you, if you find it helpful.

Now I myself, I didn't quite get to Yellowstone Park. You know, it's a funny thing how many folks in this man's town think I drove clear from Zenith to Yellowstone Park. I've never claimed anything of the kind.

It's true that when I gave my little talk before the West Side Bridge Club about my trip, they billed it—and in a brief way the West Side Tidings column of the *Evening Advocate* spoke of it—as an account of a trip clear to Yellowstone Park.

But it wasn't a trip clear to Yellowstone Park. The fact is, and I've always been the first to acknowledge it, I didn't get clear to Yellowstone Park but only to the Black Hills, in North Dakota.

The fact is, not only did I want to see the scenic and agricultural wonders of Minnesota and Wisconsin and Dakota and all like that, but Mame has a brother-in-law—I'm sure Mrs. Schmaltz will excuse me for speaking of family matters, in the presence of old friends like you two—and she has this brother-in-law that had met with misfortune, and one of the objects of our trip was to stop and see if we couldn't help him straighten out his affairs—why say, the poor devil was in such stresses and difficult straits that he'd actually had to borrow money to help him carry on his business, he's in the drug and stationery business. Why say—

And a mighty fine gentleman he is, and his wife is a mighty bright cultured little woman; she subscribes to the *Ladies' Home Journal* and reads it right through every month. And poor old Lafayette—that's Mrs. Schmaltz's brother-in-law's name—he was very well educated; he not only went through a pharmacy college and got his degree, but he also studied cost-accountancy by mail. But somehow he just couldn't make a go of it. I guess he was kind of a dreamer. When he started his first drug-store, he also took an agency for the Florida Transplanted Palm and Orange Tree Company, and in Dakota he couldn't hardly sell any palms at all—those Swede farmers may be all right as farmers, but they ain't up to the cultural point of palms yet. And then later in another town he went into partnership with a gentleman that had found oil there, and also wanted to start a radiator factory—

And say, that wasn't such a bad idea as it sounded. Of course this was in town where there wasn't any iron or coal anywheres around, and the railroad connections wasn't very good, but still, it was cold as hell—excuse me, Mrs. Babbitt—it was awful' cold in the winter, and where do you need radiators as much as where it's cold? But still, things didn't work out quite right. Come to find out, there wasn't any oil in the oil field, and somehow the radiator factory couldn't seem to compete with the trust, and so poor old Lafayette lost money almost as fast as he made it.

So when we drove out to see him—

You know how bad luck besets the just with the unjust, and say, by this time, poor old Lafe and his wife were so hard up against it that they didn't even have an automobile!

And their radio was so old and so cheap that they couldn't hardly get Minneapolis on it!

Well, that'll give you an idea about how miserably poor and pursued by ill fortune they were—they lived in Tomahawk City, North Dakota.

Well, so, to make a long story short, Mame and I went to see them, and I gave him what advice I could, and then we ran on and gave the Black Hills the once-over, but we didn't have the time to make Yellowstone Park, but still, that was only four, or maybe it might have been six or eight hundred miles farther on, so I can give you practically a detailed description of the road and stopping-places and so on for the whole distance.

And say, I certainly do recommend your making the trip. They can say what they want to. Some people claim that reading books is the greatest cultural influence, and still others maintain that you can get the most in the quickest split-second time by listening to lectures, but what I always say is, "There's nothing more broadening than travel."

Well, now you just take this, just for an example: When I crossed Minnesota, I found—in fact I saw it myself, firsthand—that there were as many Swedes as Germans there. And funny names—say, they certainly had the funniest names! Swanson and Kettleson and Shipstead, and all like that—simply screams. I says to Mame, "Well, Mrs. Schmaltz," I says—I often call her that when we're funning around—"Well, Mrs. Schmaltz," I says, "you wanted to get a kick out of this trip, and here you got it," I says, "in all these funny names."

And all like that.

We get to thinking, here in Zenith, that everybody, I mean every *normal* fellow, lives just like we do, but out there in Minnesota I found a lot of the folks never even heard of our mayor here in Zenith—they just talk about Minneapolis and Saint Paul politics! I tell you, travel like that gives a fellow a whole new set of insights into human character and how big the world is, after all, and as our pastor, Dr. Edwards, often says, the capacity of the Lord for producing new sets of psychological set-ups is practically, you might say, absolutely unlimited.

Well, so I'll give you the main, broad outlines of the trip. Considering that it must be about two thousand miles from here to Yellowstone Park, naturally I can't go into details, but just suggest the big towns that you want to make for, and general cautions about long-distance touring if you're going to do it scientifically.

Yes, thanks, I'll have a cigar, but I'm not drinking anything. Well, make it very mild. Fine, that's fine. After all, as I often tell my boy, Robby, since prohibition *is* a law of the land, we ought to drink nothing at all or only very little. That'll be fine. Whoa-up! Well, since you've poured it, can't waste it, eh? Just a little siphon. Fine! Attaboy!

Well, as I say, I'll make it short. We started out for Dakota, just Mame here and me—the children was busy with their schools and study—

I don't know if I've told you, but Delmerine has found she had more kind of talent for painting than for music, though to me she's got one of the nicest voices I ever heard in so young a girl, but she was informed by some of the best authorities that she'd do even better at art than at music, so she switched to the Art Institute, and Robby had to sort of make up some extra courses this last summer—

But not to go into that, the point is that Mame and I started off just by ourselves.

Now I hope Mame will excuse me—she knows how I like to kid her now and then—but what I mean is, just about when we were ready to start, she got an idea it'd be a good idea to take along her old Aunt Sarah, that lives out here in Rosedale.

"Let's take Aunt Sarah along, and give her a good time," she says.

"Let's take who along and do what?" I says.

"Why, let's take Aunt Sarah. She hasn't ever been anywhere," she says.

"Fine!" I says. "Say, that'll be just elegant. Let's also and at the same time take along the St. Agatha Orphan Asylum, the Salvation Army, and the convalescents of the Zenith General Hospital," I says, "so we can have a really chummy time."

Well, with Mame here, I can't very well tell you all the remarks we passed, but anyway, we shoved Aunt Sarah into the discard—say, that old girl whistles through her teeth, and the only time she ever was kissed was when Brigham Young passed through here ninety-two years ago—but by golly, I got to admit it, Mame got back at me.

I'd had a kind of a sneaking idea I might work in Jackie, our dog—and a mighty fine useful dog he is, too—but I had to swap Jackie for Aunt Sarah, and so we started off with nobody aboard except Mrs. Schmaltz and me.

Now I know that the first question you'll want to ask me is what kind of an outfit you ought to take along on a trip like this. I don't pretend to be any Ammunsun, and if I've ever found any South Poles, the newspapers forgot to tell me about it. But I'll give you my own experience for what it's worth.

Now about clothes—

There's those that maintain a fellow on as long and you might call it adventurous trip like this had ought to just wear an old suit of regular clothes. And there's those that maintain you ought to wear corduroy. Say, many and many's the hour I've sat in on debates between these two schools. But as for me, say, give me a nice suit of khaki coat and pants, every time. It may get dirtier than hell, but it never shows it's dirty, so what difference does it make?

And Mame the same way. She had specially made up for her a nice khaki jacket and breeches, and while sometimes she used to worry, and ask me if it didn't make her look the least lee-tle bit broad in the hips, I used to say to her, "Hell—" Excuse me, Mrs. Babbitt. "Rats," I said to her, "if you're comfy in 'em and if you find 'em convenient for crawling through barb-wire fences and all like that, whose business is it," I asked her, "whether some folks think it makes you look broad amidships or not!"

Now, Mamie, don't you go giving me those dirty looks, because remember we're right in the bosom of the family, you might say.

And now here's one thing I found mighty important.

Aside from the regular shoes that you wear when driving—and they ought to be a good stout pair of shoes, because who knows when you may want to sneak into an orchard and steal some apples, or even go up on a hill to see a view, or something like that—you ought to take along a pair of easy shoes for the evening—also more elegant; show 'em when you arrive in one of these hick hotels that you may be dressed comfortable for the auto trip, but back home you can dress just as good as the next fellow, and maybe better.

Personally, I was awful' fortunate. I had an old pair of pumps, and I had 'em blacked up and they looked almost practically as good as new.

Funny, I'll never forget buying those pumps.

Here's the way it happened:

I was in Chicago, on a business trip, you understand, and I happened to be wandering along South State Street, in the poorer section, and I come on a bargain sale of shoes and footwear, and I spotted these pumps, and they looked pretty good to me. And the fellow that owned the store, but he was a Kike, you understand, he come out, and he says—of course he spoke practically illiterate—and he says to me, "Hey, mister, I vill sell you dem shoes cheap"—you know how those fellows talk.

Well, I just looked at him in a kind of amused way, and of course I could see that he could see I wasn't the kind of ignorant bird he was accustomed to deal with, and I says to him, "Ah, so, my friend," I says, "so you'll sell them to me cheap, will you!"

"Sure," he says, "you bet; I'll let you have dem at a rock-bottoms price."

"Well, friend," I says to him, "I'm sure that's awful nice of you, but what makes you think—" And I just kind of laughed. "What makes you think," I said, "that I require any such articles of footwear?"

"Vell, I can tell dat you're a gentlemans that puts on a dress-suit frequent, and dese is real dress-suit shoes," he says. "Dey come from the bankrupt sale from the real bonton élite store from Chicago," he says, "in fact from Waffle-heim and Spoor, and they're too good for my class of custom," he says.

Well sir, just out of idle curiosity, I looked 'em over, and upon my word, if I didn't think he was telling the truth, for once. Say, them pumps, if they was what they looked like they was, wasn't worth one cent less than fifteen bucks, or anyway twelve-fifty. Well, of course I got kind of all excited inside. I knew then just how this Doctor—well, whatever his name is that writes for the *Saturday Evening Post,* I knew just how he feels when he finds a first edition of Harold Bell Wright for a dollar and a quarter and later maybe he's able to sell it for a couple thousand.

Well, I tried not to look excited, and I said, casual, I said to him, "Well, brother, they look like they were about my size, and I'll give you two bucks for 'em."

Well sir, you'd laughed if you could 've seen him go up in the air. Say, he just clawed the air. He hollers and shouts and he claims they're worth five-fifty. You know how these doggone foreigners carry on—and say, if you're a student of philosophy you'll realize that their actions also indicate an inner spiritual something, you might say, that indicates why they can't ever compete with the clear, sure, short-cut mentality of the Nordics. He waves his hands and—

Oh, you know.

But say, I'm afraid I'm drifting away from my subject a little. Fact is, I jewed him down, and I got 'em for three and a half, and say, they fitted like a glove, and I wore 'em at some of them finest parties and soirées in Zenith for five years, and then when we started on the Western tour, they were just the thing to take along to rest your feet in the evening. And be sure and take something like that—stylish but restful.

Now as to your auto equipment, George.

You want to have a Pull-U-Out or some other device for getting you out of a mud-hole if you get stuck in it. It's perfectly true that wherever you go now, motor-touring in the United States, you find perfect cement roads. But some-times—You know how it is. Here and there's gaps in the perfect cement high-way, and you will get stuck in the mud.

And of course you want chains along, and extra tires. And what I recom-mend especially is one of these stoves with solid alcohol. When you're tour-ing, you get a little tired of restaurants where you can't get anything but a small steak and beef stew, but fact is that sometimes you'd like a little *food,* and if you happen to feel inclined that way, of course the only thing you can do is to cook it for yourself.

In 'most all these small towns you go into a place—well, outside it's got a big fine illuminated electric sign with "Eats" or something like that on it, so you think it's going to be a snappy up-to-date joint, but you get in and you find it's run by some retired farmer and his daughter and the old woman. Pop's principal job is leaning on the cash register and annoying a toothpick. He's too busy thinking about what a civilized city guy he's become to do any work except play cashier—with six customers an hour!—or maybe he's admiring all the art treasures in the place—the snappy picture of two pears and a lobster, and the signs like "Watch Your Hat and Coat," and "No Trust, No Bust," and "Ham and Eggs Country Style, 20c"—country style meaning they throw in a piece of Certain-teed asphalt-treated toast with the relics.

Then out in the kitchen is Ma, doing what she thinks is cooking. The only thing she don't burn is the drinking-water. And Daughter has the idea she's waiting on table. But Daughter ain't interested in anybody but traveling salesmen that she thinks are unmarried—which no traveling salesman is since God made little apples. And all over the place there's a nice pleasing odor of burnt steak and onions.

So you sit up on a nice high stool, that's cleaned regular once a day by wiping it off with the rag that they use to grease the griddle, and you say to Daughter, "Say, could you bring us some cornbeef hash?" And she looks at you like an evangelist looks at a guy that he thinks has put a lead quarter in the plate, and she says, "The hash is out."

And then you think—and you find out you ain't much of a thinker—you'll have a pork chop, or maybe a T-bone steak, or some roast beef, and then finally you says, kind of irritated, "Well what can we get?"

"Say," she says, "don't get fresh! You can have a small steak or you can have ham and eggs—only I think the eggs is all out."

God! I've always held and maintained that America is the one and only nation that knows how to provide elegant chow, but even a patriot like me, sometimes I feel that we got this said elegant chow every place in the country except three: cities, towns, and farmhouses.

So you carry along a little stove.

And then you ought to have a windshield spot-light, and a spade, and—

(Here, by request of the publishers, are omitted thirty-seven other articles recommended by Mr. Schmaltz.—EDITOR.)

Well, the first day, what with one thing and another and packing, we didn't get off till noon, having had a light lunch before starting, and say, I could've killed that Pole hired girl we had at that time—She cooked up some scrambled eggs and never let us know they was ready, and they was all cold, and for a fellow that likes really nice tasty grub, a cold scrambled egg isn't hardly worth eating.

But anyway, we got away at exactly three minutes after twelve—I kind of kept a schedule of our timing on this trip, and mileage, and daily consumption of oil and gas, and say, if I had my figures here, I could show you that we got more mileage on Dainty Daisy gas than on Samson, with all the Samson claims for power-plus, and as I say, we got started kind of late, and so we didn't plan to make much of a run that day, but only to Mittewoc, a hundred and seventy-five miles.

I never like to run more than two hundred and fifty miles a day. I know you don't agree with me, George, but I feel that when you run three hundred or three hundred and fifty, you don't really see all the scenery as thoroughly and study the agriculture and other features of the country as closely as you might if you just jogged along at a nice steady forty-five or fifty miles an hour instead of speeding. But be that as it may. We planned to take it easy and not get in before seven-thirty.

Say, that day was a revelation of progress.

When I first drove that road, it was just a plain dirt road running through a lot of unkempt farms, and now every mile or so you'd find a dandy up-to-date hot-dog stand—some like log-cabins and some like Chinese pagodas or Indian wigwams or little small imitations of Mount Vernon about ten feet high, and all like that, and stocking every known refreshment for the inner man—hot dogs and apple pie and chewing-gum and cigars and so on and so forth—and of course up-to-date billboards all along the road to diversify it, and garages maybe every five miles, and in every town a dandy free auto camp providing free water and wood for the tourists. And so many of the farmers quitting their old toilsome routine and selling apples and cider to the motorists—I asked one of 'em, by the way, how he could keep his supply up, and come to find out, he didn't have an apple tree on the place—he got 'em all from a grocery store in the next town. Oh, motoring certainly has made a great and wonderful change in the country!

We didn't have any special experiences that first day—just one or two little incidents. I remember there was a fellow, he looked like a hobo, he waved his hand and stopped us.

"Well, my friend, what do you want?" I says—he was a shabby-looking cuss.

"Could you give me a lift?" he says.

"A lift?" I says.

"Yuh, I'd like a lift," he says.

"You've got two good feet to walk on, haven't you?" I says.

"Yuh," he says, "but I'm going a long ways."

"Oh you are, are you!" I says. "Look here, my friend, let me give you a piece of advice."

"I ain't asking for advice," he says. "I'm asking for a lift."

Then of course I got a little sore, him sassing me in that uncalled-for fashion, and I says, "Well, I might 've given you a lift," I says, "if you hadn't got so fresh, but now—Well, all I can say is, if you'd buckle down to business and tend to business and earn some money," I says, "you'd maybe have an auto of your own, and you wouldn't have to ask people for a lift. Good *day!*" I says, and I drove on. I guess maybe that taught him a lesson. "You buckle down to work and not waste time asking for a lift," I told him, "and maybe you'll have an auto of your own!"

Then we stopped in a little burg—awful little hick hamlet it was, called, if I remember rightly, New Paris, and we stopped for an ice-cream soda, and when I was parking, I bumped just the least little bit into the car ahead of me. Didn't hurt him one little bit, and just bent my bumper a little, but my God, to hear the other fellow squeal about it, you'd thought I'd smashed his car to pieces and killed his Aunt Jenny. Great big rube he was—fellow with no dignity.

Even though I was born and brought up a city man, I admire the farmer and honor his efforts. What, after all, would we do without wheat and corn and flax and barley and radishes and so on? But same time, a lot of those hicks have no manners or dignity. Like this fellow.

He rushed right across the sidewalk from where he'd been putting in the afternoon holding up the front of the Red Ball Grocery Store, I remember it was—and say, that's one of the best chains of grocery stores in the country— and he bawls:

"Hey, you hit my car!"

"I'm quite aware of the fact," I says, coldly—the big bum!—if he thought he could frighten *me!* And so I got out, and looked things over, and I'd just bumped his spare tire, on the back, the least little bit.

"Well, what are you going to do about it?" he says.

"What am I going to do about it?" I says.

"Yes, what're you going to do about it?"

"Well, inasmuch and considering as I haven't perpetrated the least dam- age," I informed him, "it strikes me that probably I'm not going to do any- thing about it."

"We'll see about that!" he says.

"We certainly will!" I says. "You can call the officers of the law," I says, "and we'll see how they'll adjust matters. And I might just call to your atten- tion the fact that you're not parked at the requisite and regulation angle," I says, "and we'll see what the authorities have to say about *that!*"

Well, of course I was pulling an awful bluff. I didn't know what the park- ing regulations were, at all. But then I figured that probably he didn't, either! And of course I knew that if he did call the constabule, by heck, he'd do a lot of lying and falsifying and all those kind of things that make you so sick when you're dealing with a roughneck. But then, I was all prepared for him —I figured that I'd tell the cop I was a big city lawyer and knew more about motor law than anybody since God was a boy, and bluff him out.

And say, it worked like a charm!

This fellow positively got white.

"Well, you ought to be careful," he grumbles—you'd 'ev died to see him trying to crawl out of it—and say, that ended the whole matter.

And what I didn't tell him, and what I didn't feel called on to tell him, if he couldn't see it himself, was that the way I'd hit his spare tire—something stuck out and I'd smashed hell out of his valve stem, so when Mr. Farmer come to put it on, he'd have one fine awful time, and served him right for the way he'd talked to me—say, many's the time I've laughed when I thought about that poor hick, 'way off seventeen miles from Nowhere, with a punc- ture, starting to put on this bum tire!

So Mame and I went into the drug-store and I had a strawberry ice-cream soda, and she, if I remember rightly—correct me, Mame, if I'm wrong—she had a lemon phosphate, and then we drove to the nearest garage, and I had my bumper straightened.

That was a nice garage, too, for such a tiny little burg.

I drove up and tooted my horn, and out come a young fellow in overalls, and I said, "Say, Cap'n, I hit a mosquito up the road a piece, and I wonder if you could straighten my bumper."

"Sure," he says.

"Could you do it right away?" I says. "I've got a date up the road to meet Gertrude Ederle and swim across the Channel with her."

"Sure," he says. You could see (my God, think of what it must mean to live in a hog-wallow like that and not hardly ever meet any educated people except when they stopped like I did!)—you could see he appreciated a little real Kiwanis Club kidding.

And so he got busy, and say, with a jack he had that bumper straightened in about ten seconds, and so we drove on.

And those were about all the interesting incidents, and considering I want to get on and outline the whole itinerary for you—

Oh, there was one little thing.

We stopped at a farmhouse for a drink of water—not water for the radiator, you understand; isn't it one of the wonders of modern science the way the radiator of a really fine car don't hardly need refilling at all?—I mean just for some water to drink. Well, I went up to the front door, and some old hag of a farm-wife came to the door, and I took off my hat, just as polite as if she was an important customer in my store, and I says to her, "Madam, I wonder if my wife and I can trouble you for a drink of water."

Well, she stands there and looks at me—by golly, I got kind of irritated, discourtesy like that to a wayfarer—and she looks at me and she says, "You're the sixteenth autoist today that's stopped and asked for a drink of water. And every time I've gone 'way down by the barn, to the pump, and brought it. And the last person, and she called herself a lady, kicked like all get out because she didn't think the glass I brought her was clean enough. And all I have to do is to cook and bake and sweep and mend and do for four men, and tend the chickens, and hoe the garden, and help milk the cows. And I'm getting tired of being a free waitress for city autoists on top of that!"

Well, there may have been a certain modicum of reason to what she said.

I tell you, George, I'm always the first to open his heart and purse-strings to the call of the poor and needy. Why say, here just a couple of months ago, we took up a collection at the Kiwanis Club to buy a newsboy a suit of clothes. But same *time*—

Why do these hicks insist on giving themselves away? Why can't they try to learn nice manners, like you and I do?

What I'd 've liked to do was to give her one quick wallop on the jaw, but I just raised my hat again, like I was the Beau of Brummell, and I says, "I am very sorry to have bothered you, madam! Good *afternoon!*"

And I marched off and never looked back once! I'll bet she felt ashamed, and I hope to God she did!

Along about five we stopped to get some hot dogs and sauerkraut and coffee at a mighty nice little burg, right up to date, all brick pavement and snappy little bungalows and a lovely movie palace and a new brick armory and one of the highest water-towers we saw on the whole trip and a dandy cigar-store called "The Hang-out," and important industrially, too—big cheese factory and a rubber factory—place I'd always wanted to see and had heard a lot about—it was called Carcassonne.

And then we hiked on, and we got to Mittewoc at 7:13 on the dot.

And then, if I can just get Mame to admit it, we had the father and mother of a row about where we were going to stay that night.

There was a nice hotel there—the Ishpeming Arms—nice big clean lobby with elegant deep leather rocking-chairs, and the brass spittoons shined up like they were table ware—and Mame thought we ought to go there.

But I says to her, "It isn't a question of money," I says. "I guess I can afford the best hotels about as well as the next fellow. But it never *hurts* to save a little money; and besides," I says, "it's half the fun, as well as information, of a trip like this to get right down among the common, ordinary folks that ride in flivvers," I said, "and I've heard they've got a dandy tourist auto camp here, camping and parking space free, and with cottages with bedclothes at a dollar a night," I says, "and I vote we try it once, and brush up against the common people, and if we don't like it tonight," I says, "we don't need to try it again."

Well, we argued a lot, but Mame is a mighty good little sport, if she'll let me say so in her presence, and make a long story short, we drove over to the tourist park.

Well sir, it was as pretty a place and fixed up as swell as you'd want to see anywhere. It was right on the bank of the Appleseed River, and there was several nice willow trees scattered through the grounds, and even, if I remember rightly—correct me if I'm wrong, Mame—there was a nice big oak tree. Of course the grounds were just the least little bit dirty, but what could you expect, with forty to sixty people camping there every night?

They had a dandy little store, painted in an art yellow with a mighty artistic sign, "Ye Old Autoists' General Store," that, say, that place had every want and necessity for a touring party, even with kids along. They carried tires and canvas water buckets and gas and canned goods and diapers and lolly pops and cotton gloves and maps and magazines and near-beer and everything you could think of.

Then there was a lot of marked-out spaces for cars and for tents, for those that had tents, and a nice line of outdoor ovens with plenty of wood provided free, and dandy shower baths in tents, and finally about half a dozen cottages for them that didn't carry tents, and we got one. And for a dollar, say, it wasn't so bad—it had a double bed with nice clean linen, and a chair.

So we settled down, and I says to Mame, "Let's make out like we're just tourists, without a bean to our names," and she entered right into the spirit of the thing, and we bought a frying-pan and a stew-pan at the store, and some canned stuff, and we had a dandy little supper, cooked by Mame's own fair hands—canned vegetable soup, and canned wienies (say, did you ever know that wienies are named after Ween, a German city?) and fried potatoes, and to top it off, some chocolate-almond bars.

Well, some of the folks had started a big camp-fire and we all sat around it, just like one big family, and we sang a lot of old-time songs—and what I always say is, these modern songs haven't got the melody and sentiment like those old ancient songs have—we sang "After the Ball," and "Daisy, Daisy, Gimme Your Answer True," and "Onward, Christian Soldiers," and "Toy Land," and "Two Little Girls in Blue," and all like that.

And I got to talking with a lot of different folks, and say, hardly more'n 40 per cent. were up to the Chevrolet class, and yet they were as fine a bunch of

set with silver roses and St. Olav's image on the buckle; his dagger bore gilt mounts on hilt and sheath.

Olav went up into the balcony and struck three light blows upon the door. Then he stood waiting.

A bird began trilling and piping—it burst forth like a fountain above the sleepy twittering from the thickets round about. Olav saw the bird as a dot against the sky—it sat on a fir twig against the yellowing northern heaven. He could see how it drew itself in and swelled itself out, like a little heart beating. The hosts of cloud high up began to flush, a flush spread over the hill-side with a rosy reflection in the water.—Olav knocked at the door again, much harder—it rang out in the morning stillness so that the boy held his breath and listened for a movement in any of the houses.

Soon after, the door was opened ajar—the girl slipped out. Her hair hung about her, ruffled and lustreless; it was yellow-brown and very curly. She was in her bare smock; the neck, which was of white linen, was worked with green and blue flowers, but below, it was of coarse grey stuff, and it was too long for her and trailed about her narrow pink feet. She carried her clothes over her arm and had a wallet in her hand. This she gave to Olav, threw down her bundle of clothes, and shook her hair from her face, which was still flushed with sleep—one cheek redder than the other. She took a waist-band and girt up her smock with it.

She was tall and thin, with slight limbs, a long, slender throat, and a small head. Her face was a triangle, her forehead low and broad, but it was snow-white and finely arched at the temples under the thick folds of hair; the thin cheeks were too much drawn in, making the chin too long and pointed; the straight little nose was too low and short. But for all that her little face had a restless charm of its own: the eyes were very large and dark grey, but the whites were as blue as a little child's, and they lay in deep shadow beneath the straight black lines of her brows and her full, white eyelids; the mouth was narrow, but the lips were red as berries—and with her bright pink and white complexion Ingunn Steinfinnsdatter was fair now in her young girl-hood.

"Make haste," said Olav, as she sat on the stair winding her linen hose tightly around her legs; and she took good time about it. "You were best carry hose and shoes till the grass be dry."

"I will not go barefoot on the wet ground in this cold—" the girl shivered a little.

"You will be warmer when once you have made an end of putting on your clothes—you must not be so long about it—'tis rosy morning already, cannot you see?"

Ingunn made no answer, but took off her hose-band and began again to wind it about her leg. Olav hung her clothes over the rail of the balcony.

"You must have a cloak with you—do you not see we shall have showers today?"

"My cloak is down with mother—I forgot to take it with me last night. It looks now like fine weather—but if there comes a shower, we shall find some place to creep under."

"What if it rains while we are in the boat? You cannot walk in the town without a cloak either. But I see well enough you will borrow my cloak, as is your way—"

Ingunn looked up at him over her shoulder. "Why are you so cross today, Olav?"—and she began to be busy with her footgear again.

Olav was ready with an answer; but as she bent down to her shoe, the smock slipped from her shoulders, baring her bosom and upper arm. And instantly a wave of new feelings swept over the boy—he stood still, bashful and confused, and could not take his eyes off this glimpse of her naked body. It was as though he had never seen it before; a new light was thrown on what he knew of old—as with a sudden landslip within him, his feelings for his foster-sister came to rest in a new order. With a burst of fervour he felt a tenderness which had in it both pity and a touch of pride; her shoulders sank so weakly in a slant to the faint rounding of the shoulder-joint; the thin, white upper arms looked soft, as though she had no muscles under the silky skin— the boy's senses were tricked with a vision of corn that is as yet but milky, before it has fully ripened. He had a mind to stoop down and pat her consolingly—such was his sudden sense of the difference between her feeble softness and his own wiry, muscular body. Oft had he looked at her before, in the bath house, and at himself, his hard, tough, well-rounded chest, his muscles firmly braced over the stomach, and swelling into a knot as he bent his arm. With childish pride he had rejoiced that he was a boy.

Now this self-glorious sense of being strong and well made became strangely shot through with tenderness, because she was so weak—he would know how to protect her. He would gladly have put his arm around that slender back, clasped her little girlish breasts beneath his hand. He called to mind that day last spring when he himself had fallen on his chest over a log—it was where Gunleik's new house was building—he had torn both his clothes and his flesh. With a shudder in which were mingled horror and sweetness he thought that never more would he let Ingunn climb up on the roof with them at Gunleik's farm.

He blushed as she looked at him.

"You are staring?—Mother will never know I have borrowed her smock; she never wears it herself."

"Do you not feel the cold?" he asked; and Ingunn's surprise was yet greater, for he spoke as low and shyly as though she had really come to some hurt in their game.

"Oh, not enough to make my nails go blue," she said laughing.

"No, but can you not get your clothes on quickly?" he said anxiously. "You have goose-flesh on your arms."

"If I could but get my smock together—" The edges at the throat were stiff with sewing; she struggled, but could not get the stuff through the tiny ring of her brooch.

Olav laid down the whole load that he had just taken on his back. "I will lend you mine—it has a bigger ring." He took the gold brooch from his bosom and handed it to her. Ingunn looked at him, amazed. She had pestered him to lend her this trinket before now, but that he himself should offer to let her wear it was something new, for it was a costly jewel, of pure gold and fairly big. Along the outer edge were inscribed the Angel's Greeting and *Amor vincit omnia*. Her kinsman Arnvid Finnsson said that in the Norse tongue this meant "Love conquers all things," since the Lady Sancta Maria conquers all the malice of the fiend by her loving supplication.

Ingunn had put on her red holy-day garments and bound her silken girdle about her waist—she combed her tangled hair with her fingers.

"You must even lend me your comb, Olav!"

Although he had but just collected all his things again, he laid them down once more, searched out a comb from his pouch, and gave it to her without impatience.

But as they plodded along the road between the fences down in the village, Olav's dizzy exaltation forsook him little by little. The weather had cleared and the sun was broiling hot—and as time went on, it *was* a load: wallet, axe, cloak, and boots. True, Ingunn had once offered to carry some of it; but that was when they were passing through the forest and it was cool beneath the firs, with a grateful fresh scent of pine-needles and hair-moss and young leaves. The sun barely gilded the tree-tops, and the birds sang with full throat—and then the boy was still swayed by his new-born emotion. She bade him stop, she had to plait her hair anew, for she had forgotten her hair-band—ay, 'twas like her. But her tawny mane waved so finely over her fore-head as she loosed the braids, making shady hollows at the temples, where the first short hairs lay close and curly; it softened his heart to look at it. So when she spoke of carrying, he only shook his head; and afterwards he heard no more of it.

Down here on the fiord it was full summer. The children climbed a fence and made straight across an enclosure; the meadow was a slope of flowers, pink clouds of caraway and golden globe-flowers. Where there was a thin patch of soil among the rocks, the violets grew thick as a carpet, and within the shade of the alder-brake red catch-flies blazed amid the luxuriant green. Ingunn stopped again and again to pluck flowers, and Olav grew more and more impatient; he longed to get down to the boat and be rid of his burden. He was hungry too—as yet neither of them had tasted food. But when she said that they could sit down and eat here in the shade by the brook, he replied shortly that it would be as he said. When they had got hold of a boat, they could make a meal before rowing away, but not till then.

"You will always have your way," said Ingunn querulously.

"Ay, if I let you have yours we might reach the town tomorrow morning. But if you will listen to me, we shall be back at Frettastein by that time."

Then she laughed, flung away her flowers, and ran after him.

All the way down, the children had followed the brook which ran north of the houses at Frettastein. On nearing the village it became a little river—on the flat, before it fell into the fiord, it spread out and ran broad and shallow over a bed of large smooth stones. The lake here formed a great round bay, with a beach strewed with sharp grey rocks which had fallen from the mountain-side. A line of old alder-trees grew along the bank of the stream right out to the lake.

At high-water mark, where beach and greensward met, the path led by a cairn. The boy and girl stopped, hurried through a Paternoster and an Ave, and then each threw a stone upon the cairn as a sign that they had done their

Christian duty by the dead. It was said to be one who had slain himself, but it was so long ago that Olav and Ingunn at any rate had never heard who the poor wretch might be.

They had to cross the stream in order to reach the point where Olav had thought he could borrow a boat. This was easy enough for him, who walked barefoot, but Ingunn had not gone many steps before she began to whimper —the round pebbles slipped under her feet and the water was so cold and she was spoiling her best shoes.

"Do but stand where you are and I will come and fetch you," said Olav, and waded back to her.

But when he had taken her up in his arms, he could not see where he put his feet, and in the middle of the river he fell with her.

The icy water took away his breath for a moment—the whole world seemed to slew over. As long as he lived, this picture remained burnt into him—all that he saw as he lay in the stream with Ingunn in his arms: light and shade dropping in patches through the alder-leaves upon the running water, the long, grey curve of the beach beyond, and the blue lake glittering in the sunshine.

Then he got to his feet, dripping wet and ashamed, strangely ashamed with his empty arms—and they waded ashore. Ingunn took it ill, as she swept the water from her sleeves and wrung out first her hair-pleats and then the edge of her dress.

"Oh, hold your mouth now," Olav begged in a low and cheerless voice. "Must you always be whining over great things and small—?"

The sky was now blue and cloudless, and the fiord quite smooth, with small patches of glittering white sunshine. Its bright surface reflected the land on the other shore, with tufts of light-green foliage amid the dark pine forest and farms and fields mounting the hill-side. It had become very warm —the sweet breath of the summer day was heavy about the two young people. In their wet clothes it felt cold merely to enter the airy shade of the birches on the point.

The fisher widow's cot was no more than a turf hovel boarded at one end, in which was a door. There was no other house in the place but a byre of stones and turf, with an open shed outside to keep the stacks of hay and dried leaves from the worst of the winter weather. Outside the cabin lay heaps of fish refuse. It stank horribly and swarms of blue flies buzzed up as the children came near. These heaps of offal were alive and crawling with maggots—so as soon as Olav had made known his errand and the widow had answered that they might have the boat and welcome, he took the wallet and went off under the trees. It was an odd thing about Olav that ever since he was a little boy it had given him a quite absurd feeling of disgust to see maggots moving in anything.

But Ingunn had brought with her a piece of bacon for the widow, Aud. She came of the folk of Steinfinn's thralls and now she was eager for news of the manor, so Ingunn was delayed awhile.

The boy had found a dry and sunny spot down by the water; there they could sit and dry themselves as they ate. Soon Ingunn came, carrying in her hands a bowl of fresh milk. And with the prospect of food, and now that it was settled about the boat, Olav was suddenly glad at heart—it was grand after all to be out on his own errand and to be going to Hamar. At heart he was well pleased too that Ingunn was with him; he was used to her following him everywhere, and if at times she was a little troublesome, he was used to that too.

He grew rather sleepy after eating—Steinfinn's house-carls were not used to early rising. So he stretched himself on the ground with his head buried in his arms, letting the sun bake his wet back, and he made no more ado about the need of haste. All at once Ingunn asked if they should bathe in the fiord.

Olav woke and sat up. "The water is too cold—" and all at once he turned red in the face and blushed more and more. He turned his head aside and stared at the ground.

"I am freezing in my wet clothes," said Ingunn. "We shall be so fine and warm after it—" she bound her plaits in a ring about her head, sprang up, and loosened her belt.

"I will not," muttered Olav in a hesitating voice. His cheeks and brows pricked with heat. Suddenly he jumped up and, without saying more to her, turned and walked up the point into the grove of firs.

Ingunn looked after him a moment. She was used to his being vexed when she would not do as he said. He would be cross for a while, till he grew kind again of himself. Calmly and caring nothing, she undressed and tottered out over the sharp grey stones, which cut her feet, till she reached a little bank of sand.

Olav walked quickly over the grey moss, which crunched under his feet. It was bone-dry already on these crags that jutted into the lake—the firs stifled it with their vapour. It was not much more than a bowshot to the other side of the point.

A great bare rock ran out into the water. Olav leapt on to it and lay down with his face in his hands.

Then the thought came to him—she could never drown? Perhaps he ought not to have left her. But he *could* not go back—

Down in the water it was as though a golden net quivered above stones and mud—the reflection of sunlight on the surface. He grew giddy from looking down—felt as if he were afloat. The rock he lay on seemed to be moving through the water.

And all the time he could not help thinking of Ingunn and being tormented by the thought. He felt plunged into guilt and shame, and it grieved him. They had been used to bathe from his canoe in the tarn above, swimming side by side in the brown water, into which a yellow dust was shed from the flowering spruces around. But now they could not be together as before—

It was just as when he lay in the stream and saw the familiar world turned upside-down in an instant. He felt as if he had had another fall; humbled and ashamed and terrified, he saw the things he had seen every day from another angle, as he lay on the ground.

It had been so simple and straightforward a thing that he should marry Ingunn when they were grown up. And he had always looked to Steinfinn to decide when it should be. The lad might feel a tingling when Steinfinn's house-carls told tales of their commerce with women. But to him it had been clear that they did these things because they were men without ties, while he, being born to an estate, must keep himself otherwise. It had never disturbed his rest to think that he and Ingunn would live together and have children to take the inheritance after them.

Now he felt he had been the victim of a betrayal—he was changed from what he had been, and Ingunn was changed in his eyes. They were wellnigh grown up, though none had told them this was coming; and these things that Steinfinn's serving-men and their womenfolk had to do with—ah, they tempted him too, for all she was his betrothed and he had an estate and she a dowry in her coffer.

He saw her as she lay there face down on the short, dry grass. She rested on one arm beneath her breast, so that her dress was drawn tight over the gentle rounding of her bosom; her tawny plaits wound snake-like in the heather. When she had said that about bathing, an ugly thought had come over him—together with a meaningless fear, strong as the fear of death; for it seemed to him that they were as two trees, torn up by the spring flood and adrift on a stream—and he was afraid the stream would part them asunder. At that fiery moment he seemed to have full knowledge of what it meant to possess her and what to lose her.

But what was the sense of thinking of such things, when all who had power and authority over them had ordained that they should be joined together? There was no man and no thing to part them. None the less, with a tremor of anxiety he felt his childish security shrivel up and vanish, the certainty that all the future days of his life were threaded for him like beads upon a string. He could not banish the thought that *if* Ingunn were taken from him, he knew nothing of the future. Somewhere deep down within him murmured the voice of a tempter: he must secure her, as the rude and simple serving-men secured the coarse womenfolk they had a mind to—and if anyone stretched out a hand towards her that was his, he would be wild, like the he-wolf showing his teeth as he stands over his prey; like the stallion rearing and snorting with rage to receive the bear and fight to the death for his mares, while they stand in a ring about the scared and quivering foals.

The boy lay motionless, staring himself dizzy and hot at the play of light in the gliding water, while he strove with these new thoughts—both what he knew and what he dimly guessed. When Ingunn gave a call just behind him, he started up as though waked from sleep.

"You were foolish not to care for a swim," she said.

"Come now!" Olav jumped down to the beach and walked quickly before her. "We have stayed here far too long."

After rowing awhile he grew calmer. It felt good to swing his body in steady strokes. The beat of the oars in the rowlocks, the wash of the water under the boat, lulled his agitation.

It was broiling hot now and the light from the sky and lake dazzled and hurt the eyes—the shores were bathed in heat haze. And when Olav had rowed for wellnigh two hours, it began to tell on him severely. The boat was heavy; and he had not thought how unpractised he was at rowing. This was not the same as poling and splashing about the tarn at home. He had to keep far out, for the shore wound in bays and inlets; at times he was afraid he might be clean out of his course. The town might lie hidden behind one of these head-lands, invisible from the boat—perhaps he had already passed it. Olav saw now that he was in strange country; he remembered nothing from his last journey in these parts.

The sun burned his back; the palms of his hands were sore; and his legs were asleep, so long had he sat with his feet against the stretcher. But the back of his neck ached worst of all. The lake gleamed far around the tiny boat—it was a long way to land on every side. Now and again he felt he was rowing against a current. And there was scarce a craft to be seen that day, whether far out or close under the shore. Olav toiled at the oars, glum and morose, fearing he would never reach the town.

Ingunn sat in the stern of the boat facing the sun, so that her red kirtle was ablaze; her face under the shade of her velvet hood was flushed with the reflection. She had thrown Olav's cloak about her, for the air on the water was chill to her sitting still, she said; and then she had drawn the hood down to shade her eyes. It was a fine cloak of grey-green Flanders cloth with a cowl of black velvet—one of the things Olav had had from Hestviken. Ingunn had a well-dressed look in all the ample folds of her garments. She held one hand in the water—and Olav felt an envy of the senses; how good and cool it must be! The girl looked fresh and unweary; she sat and took her ease.

Then he pulled harder—all the harder for the pain he felt in hands and shoulders and in the small of his back; he clenched his teeth and rowed furi-ously a short space. It was a great deed he had undertaken for her sake, this rowing; and he knew, with pride and a melancholy sense of injury, that he would never have thanks for it: there she sits playing with her hand over the side and never has a thought of *my* toiling. The sweat poured off him, and his outgrown kirtle chafed worse and worse at the arm-holes. He had forgotten that it was *his* business that brought them; once more he pursed his lips, swept his arm across his red and sweaty face, and took a few more mighty pulls.

"Now I see the towers over the woods," said Ingunn at last.

Olav turned and looked over his shoulder—it hurt his stiff neck past believ-ing. Across the perfectly hopeless expanse of a fiord he saw the light stone towers of Christ Church above the trees on a point of land. Now he was so tired that he could have given up altogether.

He rounded the point, where the convent of preaching friars lay far out on raised foundations; it was a group of dark timber houses about a stave-church, with roofs of tarred shingles, one above the other, dragon heads on the gables and gilt weathercocks above the ridge-turret, in which the mass bell hung.

Olav put in to the monks' pier. He washed the worst of the sweat from him before he climbed up, stiff and spent. Ingunn was already at the convent gate talking with the lay brother who had charge of some labourers; they were bearing bales of goods down to a little trading craft. Brother Vegard was at home, she told Olav as he came up—now they must ask leave to speak with him; he could best advise them in this business.

Olav thought they could ill trouble the monk with such a trifle. Brother Vegard was wont to come twice a year to Frettastein and he was the children's confessor. He was a wise and kindly man and always used the opportunity to give them such counsel and exhortation as the young people of that house lacked all too often. But Olav had never spoken a word to Brother Vegard unbidden, and to put him to the pains of coming to the parlour for their sake seemed to him far too bold. They could well inquire the way to the smith of the brother porter.

But Ingunn would not give in. As Olav himself had hinted, it was perhaps a hazardous thing to hand over such an heirloom to a smith of whom they knew nothing. But maybe Brother Vegard would send a man from the convent with them—ay, it was not impossible he might offer to go with them himself. That Olav did not believe. But he let Ingunn have her way.

She had a motive for it, which she kept to herself. Once, long ago, she had visited the convent with her father, and then they had been given wine, which the monks made from apples and berries in their garden. So good and sweet a drink she had never tasted before or since—and she secretly hoped that Brother Vegard might offer them a cup of it.

The parlour was but a closet in the guest-house; the convent was a poor one, but the children had never seen another and they thought it a brave and fine room, with the great crucifix over the door. In a little while Brother Vegard came in; he was a middle-aged man of great stature, weather-beaten, with a wreath of grizzled hair.

He received the children's greeting in friendly fashion, but seemed pressed for time. With awkward concern Olav came out with his errand. Brother Vegard told them the way shortly and plainly: past Christ Church eastward through Green Street, past the church of Holy Cross, and down to the left along the fence of Karl Kjette's garden, down to the field where was a pond; the smith's house was the biggest of the three that stood on the other side of the little mere. Then he took leave of the children and was going: "You will sleep in the guest-house tonight, I ween?"

Olav said they must set out for home after vespers.

"But milk you must have—and you will be here for vespers?"

They had to say yes to this. But Ingunn looked a little disappointed. She had expected to be offered other than milk and she had looked forward to hearing vespers in the minster; the boys of the school sang so sweetly. But now they durst not go elsewhere than to St. Olav's.

The monk was already at the door, when he turned sharply, as something came into his mind: "So that is how it is—Steinfinn has sent for Jon smith today? Are you charged to bid the armourer come to Frettastein, Olav?" he asked, with a trace of anxiety.

"No, father. I am but come on my own errand." Olav told him what it was and showed the axe.

The monk took it and balanced it in both hands.

"A goodly weapon you have there, my Olav," he said, but more coolly than Olav had ever thought a man could speak of *his* axe. Brother Vegard looked at the gold inlay on the cheeks. "It is old, this—they do not make such things nowadays. This is an heirloom, I trow?"

"Yes, father. I had it of my father."

"I have heard of a horned axe like this which they say was at Dyfrin in old days—when the old barons' kin held the manor. That must be near a hundred years ago. There was much lore about that axe; it had a name and was called Wrathful Iron."

"Ay, my kindred came from thence—Olav and Torgils are yet family names with us. But this axe is called Kin-fetch—and I know not how it came into my father's possession."

"It must be another then—such horned axes were much used in old days," said the monk; he passed his hand along the finely curved blade. "And maybe that is lucky for you, my son—if I mind me rightly, bad luck followed that axe I spoke of."

He repeated his directions, took a kindly leave of the children, and went out.

Then they went off to find the smith. Ingunn strode in front; she looked like a grown maid in her long, trailing dress. Olav tramped behind, tired and downcast. He had looked forward so much to the journey to town—scarce knowing what he looked for in it. Whenever he had been here before, it was in the company of grown men, and it had been a fair-day in the town; to his serious and inquiring eyes all had been excitement and festivity: the bargaining of the men, the booths, the houses, the churches they had been in; they had been offered drink in the houses, and the street had been full of horses and folk. Now he was only a raw youth wandering about with a young girl, and there was no place where he could turn in; he knew no one, had no money; and they had not time to enter the churches. In an hour or two they must set out for home. And he had an unspeakable dread of the endless rowing and then the walk up through the fields—God alone knew what time of night they would reach home! And then they might look for a chiding for having run away!

They found the way to the smith. He looked at the axe well and long, turned it this way and that, and said it would be a hard matter to mend it. These horned axes had gone well-nigh out of use; 'twas not easy to fit an edge on them that would not spring loose with a heavy blow, on a helm, to wit, or even on a tough skull. This came from the shape of the blade, a great half-moon with barbs at either end, Ay, he would do his best, but he could not promise that the gold inlay should come to no harm by his welding and hammering. Olav considered a moment, but could see naught else to be done—he gave the axe to the smith and bargained with him as to the price of the work.

But when Olav told where he came from, the smith looked up and scanned his face: "Then you would have it back in all haste, I trow? So that is the way of it—are they making ready their axes at Frettastein these days?"

Olav said he knew naught of *that*.

"Nay, nay. Has Steinfinn any plan, he is not like to tell his boys of it—"

Olav looked at the smith as though he would say something, but checked himself. He took his leave and departed.

They had passed the pond, and Ingunn wished to turn into a road between fences which led up to Green Street. But Olav took her by the arm: "We can go here."

The houses in Green Street were built on a ridge of high ground. Below them ran a brook of dirty water at the edge of the fields behind the townsmen's outhouses and kaleyards. By the side of the brook was a trodden path.

Ashes, apple-trees, and great rose-bushes in the gardens shaded the path, so the air felt cool and moist. Blue flies darted like sparks in the green shadows, where nettles and all kinds of coarse weeds grew luxuriantly, for folk threw out their refuse on this side, making great muck-heaps behind the outhouses. The path was slippery with grease that sweated out of the rotting heaps, and the air was charged with smells—fumes of manure, stench of carrion, and the faint odour of angelica which bordered the stream with clouds of greenish-white flowers.

But beyond the brook the fields lay in full afternoon sunshine; the little groves of trees threw long shadows over the grass. The fields stretched right down to the small houses along Strand Street, and beyond them lay the lake, blue with a golden glitter, and the low shore of Holy Isle in the afternoon haze.

The children walked in silence; Olav was now a few paces in front. It was very still here in the shade behind the gardens—nothing but the buzzing of the flies. A cowbell tinkled above on the common. Once the cuckoo called—spectrally clear and far away on a wooded ridge.

Then a woman's scream rang out from one of the houses, followed by the laughter of a man and a woman. In the garden a man had caught a girl from behind; she dropped her pail, full of fishes' heads and offal, and it rolled down to the fence; the couple followed, stumbling and nearly falling. When they caught sight of the two children, the man let go the girl; they stopped laughing, whispered, and followed them with their eyes.

Instinctively Olav had halted for a moment, so that Ingunn came up beside him and he placed himself between her and the fence. A blush crept slowly over his fair features and he looked down at the path as he led Ingunn past. These houses in the town that Steinfinn's house-carls had talked so much about—for the first time it made him hot and gripped his heart to think of them, and he wondered whether this was one of those houses.

The path turned and Olav and Ingunn saw the huge grey mass and pale leaden roof of Christ Church and the stone walls of the Bishop's palace above the trees a little way in front of them. Olav stopped and turned to the girl.

"Tell me, Ingunn—did you hear what Brother Vegard said—and the smith?"

"What mean you?"

"Brother Vegard asked if Steinfinn had sent for the armourer to Frettastein," said Olav slowly. "And Jon smith asked if we made ready our axes now."

"What meant they? Olav—you look so strangely!"

"Nay, I know not. Unless there is news at the Thing—folk are breaking up from the Thing these days, the first of them—"

"What mean you—?"

"Nay, I know not. Unless Steinfinn has made some proclamation—"

The girl raised both hands abruptly and laid them on Olav's breast. He laid both his palms upon them and pressed her hands against his bosom. And as they stood thus, there welled up again in Olav more powerfully than before that new feeling that they were adrift—that something which had been was now gone for ever; they were drifting toward the new and unknown. But as he gazed into her tense dark eyes, he saw that she felt the same. And he knew in his whole body and his whole soul that she had turned to him and clutched at him because it was the same with her as with him—she scented the change that was coming over them and their destiny, and so she clung to him instinctively, because they had so grown together throughout their forlorn, neglected childhood that now they were nearer to each other than any beside.

And this knowledge was unutterably sweet. And while they stood motionless looking into each other's face, they seemed to become one flesh, simply through the warm pressure of their hands. The raw chill of the pathway that went through their wet shoes, the sunshine that poured warmly over them, the strong blended smell that they breathed in, the little sounds of the afternoon—they seemed to be aware of them all with the senses of one body.

The pealing of the church bells broke in upon their mute and tranquil rapture—the mighty brazen tones from the minster tower, the busy little bell from Holy Cross Church—and there was a sound of ringing from St. Olav's on the point.

Olav dropped the girl's hands. "We must make haste."

Both felt as though the peal of bells had proclaimed the consummation of a mystery. Instinctively they took hands, as though after a consecration, and they went on hand in hand until they reached the main street.

The monks were in the choir and had already begun to chant vespers as Olav and Ingunn entered the dark little church. No light was burning but the lamp before the tabernacle and the little candles on the monks' desks. Pictures and metal ornaments showed but faintly in the brown dusk which gathered into gloom under the crossed beams of the roof. There was a strong smell of tar, of which the church had recently received its yearly coat, and a faint, sharp trace of incense left behind from the day's mass.

In their strangely agitated mood they remained on their knees inside the door, side by side, and bowed their heads much lower than usual as they whispered their prayers with unwonted devotion. Then they rose to their feet and stole away to one side and the other.

There were but few people in church. On the men's side sat some old men, and one or two younger knelt in the narrow aisle—they seemed to be the convent's labourers. On the women's side he saw none but Ingunn; she stood leaning against the farthest pillar, trying to make out the pictures painted on the baldachin over the side altar.

Olav took a seat on the bench—now he felt again how fearfully stiff and tired he was all over. The palms of his hands were blistered.

The boy knew nothing of what the monks sang. Of the Psalms of David he had learnt no more than the Miserere and De profundis, and those but fairly well. But he knew the chant—saw it inwardly as a long, low wave that broke with a short, sharp turn and trickled back over the pebbles; and at first, whenever they came to the end of a psalm and sang *Gloria Patri, et Filio, et Spiritu Sancto,* he whispered the response: *Sicut erat in principio et nunc et semper et in sæcula sæculorum. Amen.* The monk who led the singing had a fine deep, dark voice. In drowsy well-being Olav listened to the great male voice which rose alone and to the choir joining in, verse after verse throughout the psalms. After all the varied emotions of the day peace and security fell upon his soul, as he sat in the dark church looking at the white-clad singers and the little flames of the candles behind the choir-screen. He would do the right and shun the wrong, he thought—then God's might and compassion would surely aid him and save him in all his difficulties.

Pictures began to swarm before his inner vision: the boat, Ingunn with the velvet hood over her fair face, the glitter on the water behind her, the floor-boards covered with shining fish-scales—the dark, damp path among nettles and angelica—the fence they had climbed and the flowery meadow through which they had run—the golden net over the bottom of the lake—all these scenes succeeded one another behind his closed and burning eyelids.

He awoke as Ingunn took him by the shoulder. "You have been asleep," she said reprovingly.

The church was empty, and just beside him the south door stood open to the green cloister garth in the evening sun. Olav yawned and stretched his stiff limbs. He dreaded the journey home terribly; this made him speak to her a little more masterfully than usual: " 'Twill soon be time to set out, Ingunn."

"Yes." She sighed deeply. "Would we might sleep here tonight!"

"You know we cannot do that."

"Then we could have heard mass in Christ Church in the morning. We never see strange folk, we who must ever bide at home—it makes the time seem long."

"You know that one day it will be otherwise with us."

"But you have been in Oslo too, you have, Olav."

"Ay, but I remember nothing of it."

"When we come to Hestviken, you must promise me this, that you will take me thither some time, to a fair or a gathering."

"That I may well promise you, methinks."

Olav was so hungry his entrails cried out for food. So it was good to get warm groats and whey in the guest-room of the convent. But he could not help thinking all the time of the row home. And then he was uneasy about his axe.

But now they fell into talk with two men who also sat at meat in the guest-house. They came from a small farm that lay by the shore a little to the north of the point where Olav and Ingunn were to land, and they asked to be taken in their boat. But they would fain stay till after complin.

Again Olav sat in the dark church listening to the deep male voices which chanted the great king's song to the King of kings. And again the images of that long, eventful day flickered behind his weary eyelids—he was on the point of falling asleep.

He was awakened by the voices changing to another tune; through the dark little church resounded the hymn:

Te lucis ante terminum
Rerum Creator poscimus
Ut pro tua clementia
Sis præsul et custodia.

Procul recedant somnia
Et noctium phantasmata;
Hostemque nostrum comprime,
Ne polluantur corpora.

Præsta, Pater piissime,
Patrique compar Unice,
Cum Spiritu Paraclito
*Regnans per omne sæculum.**

He knew this; Arnvid Finnsson had often sung it to them in the evening, and he knew pretty well what the words meant in Norse. He let himself sink stiffly on his knees at the bench, and with his face hidden in his hands he said his evening prayers.

It had clouded over when they went down to the boat; the sky was flecked with grey high up and the fiord was leaden with dark stripes. The wooded slopes on both sides seemed plunged in darkness.

The strangers offered to row, and so Olav sat in the stern with Ingunn. They shot forward at a different pace now, under the long, steady strokes of the two young peasants; but Olav's boyish pride suffered no great injury nevertheless—it was so good to sit and be rowed.

After a while a few drops of rain fell. Ingunn spread out the folds of the heavy cloak and bade him come closer.

So they both sat wrapped in it and he had to put an arm around her waist. She was so slender and warm and supple, good to hold clasped. The boat flew lightly through the water in the blue dusk of the summer night. Lighter shreds of mist with scuds of rain drifted over the lake and the hills around, but they were spared the rain. Soon the two young heads sank against one another, cheek to cheek. The men laughed and bade them lie down upon their empty sacks in the bottom of the boat.

Ingunn nestled close to him and fell asleep at once. Olav sat half up, with his neck against the stern seat; now and again he opened his eyes and looked up at the cloudy sky. Then his weariness seemed to flow over him, strangely sweet and good. He started up as the boat grounded on the sand outside Aud's cabin.

The men laughed. No, why should they have waked him?—'twas nothing of a row.

It was midnight. Olav guessed that they had rowed it in less than half the time he had taken. He helped the men to shove the boat up on the beach; then they said good-night and went. First they became two queerly black spots losing themselves in the dark rocky shore of the bay, and soon they had wholly disappeared into the murky summer night.

Olav's back was wet with bilge-water and he was stiff from his cramped position, but Ingunn was so tired that she whimpered—she would have it

*1. Ere daylight be gone, we pray Thee, Creator of the world, that of Thy mercy Thou wilt be our Guide and Guardian.

2. May the visions and spectres of the night be far from us; hold back our enemy, lest our bodies be defiled.

3. Hear our prayer, O Father most holy, and Thou, only-begotten Son, equal to the Father, who with the Holy Ghost, the Comforter, reignest for ever and ever.

(Ambrosian hymn, seventh century)

they must rest before setting out to walk home. Olav himself would best have liked to go at once—he felt it would have suppled his limbs so pleasantly to walk in the fresh, cool night, and he was afraid of what Steinfinn would say, if he had come home. But Ingunn was too tired, he saw—and they both dreaded to pass the cairn or to be out at all in the dead of night.

So they shared the last of the food in their wallet and crept into the cabin. Just inside the door was a little hearth, from which some warmth still came. A narrow passage led in, which divided the earthen floor into two raised halves. On one side they heard Aud snoring; they felt their way among utensils and gear to the couch which they knew was on the other.

But Olav could not fall asleep. The air was thick with smoke even down to the floor and it hurt his chest—and the smell of raw fish and smoked fish and rotten fish was not to be borne. And his worn limbs twinged and tingled.

Ingunn lay uneasily, turning and twisting in the darkness. "I have no room for my head—surely there is an earthen pot just behind me—"

Olav felt for it and tried to push it away. But there was so much gear stowed behind, it felt as if it would all clatter down on them if he moved anything. Ingunn crawled farther down, doubled herself up, and lay with head and arms on his chest. "Do I crush you?" In a moment she was fast asleep.

After a while he slipped from under the warm body, heavy with sleep. Then he got his feet down on the passage, stood up, and stole out.

It was already growing light. A faint, cold air, like a shudder, breathed through the long, limber boughs of the birches and shook down a few icy drops; a pale gust blew over the steel-grey mirror of the lake.

Olav looked inland. It was so inconceivably still—there was as yet no life in the village; the farms were asleep and fields and meadows and groves were asleep, pale in the grey dawn. Scattered over the screes behind the nearest houses stood a few spruce-firs as though lifeless, so still and straight were they. The sky was almost white, with a faint yellow tinge in the north above the black tree-tops. Only high up floated a few dark shreds of the night's clouds.

It was so lonely to be standing here, the only one awake, driven out by this new feeling which chased him incessantly farther and farther away from the easy self-confidence of childhood. It was about this hour yesterday that he had risen—it seemed years ago.

He stood, shy and oppressed at heart, listening to the stillness. Now and again there was the clatter of a wooden bell; the widow's cow was moving in the grove. Then the cuckoo called, unearthly clear and far away somewhere in the dark forests, and some little birds began to wake. Each of the little sounds seemed only to intensify the immense hush of space.

Olav went to the byre and peeped in, but drew his head back at once before the sharp scent of lye that met him. But the ground was good and dry under the lean-to roof; brown and bare, with some wisps from the winter's stacks of hay and leaves. He lay down, rolled up like an animal, and went to sleep in a moment.

He was awakened by Ingunn shaking him. She was on her knees beside him. "Have you lain out here?"

" 'Twas so thick with smoke in the cabin." Olav rose to his knees and shook the wisps and twigs from his clothes.

The sun came out above the ridge, and the tops of the firs seemed to take fire as it rose higher. And now there was a full-throated song of birds all through the woods. Shadows still lay over the land and far out on the deep blue lake, but on the other side of the water the sunshine flooded the forest and the green hamlets on the upper slopes.

Olav and Ingunn remained on their knees, facing one another, as though in wonder. And without either's saying anything they laid their arms on each other's shoulders and leaned forward.

They let go at the same time and looked at each other with a faint smile of surprise. Then Olav raised his hand and touched the girl's temples. He pushed back the tawny, dishevelled hair. As she let him do it, he put his other arm about her, drew her toward him, and kissed her long and tenderly on the sweet, tempting pit under the roots of the hair.

He looked into her face when he had done it and a warm tingling ran through him—she liked him to do that. Then they kissed each other on the lips, and at last he took courage to kiss her on the white arch of her throat.

But not a word did they say. When they stood up, he took the empty wallet and his cloak and set out. And so they walked in silence, he before and she behind, along the road through the village, while the morning sun shed its light farther and farther down the slopes.

On the higher ground folk were already astir on all the farms. As they went through the last of the woods, it was full daylight. But when they came to the staked gate where the home fields of Frettastein began, they saw no one about. Perhaps they might come well out of their adventure after all.

Behind the bushes by the gate they halted for a moment and looked at each other—the dazed, blissful surprise broke out in their eyes once more. Quickly he touched her hand, then turned to the gate again, and pulled up the stakes.

When they entered the courtyard, the door of the byre stood open, but no one was to be seen. Ingunn made for the loft-room where she had slept the night before.

All at once she turned and came running back to Olav. "Your brooch—" she had taken it off and held it out to him.

"You may have it—I will give it you," he said quickly. He took off her little one, which he had worn instead, and put it in her hand which held the gold brooch. "No, you are not to give me yours in exchange. I have brooches enough, I have—"

He turned abruptly, blushing, ran from her grasp, and strode off rapidly toward the hall.

He drew a deep breath, much relieved after all to find that the rooms beyond were empty. One of the dogs got up and came to meet him, wagging its tail; Olav patted it and spoke a friendly word or two.

He stretched himself and yawned with relief on getting off his tight clothes. The coat had chafed him horribly under the arms—he could not possibly wear it again, unless it was altered. Ingunn could do that.

As he was about to fling himself into his sleeping-place, he saw that there was already a man lying there. "Are you all come home now?" asked the other drowsily. Olav knew by the voice it was Arnvid Finnsson.

"No, it is but I. I had an errand in the town," he said, as calmly as if there were nothing strange in his going to Hamar on business of his own. Arnvid grunted something. In a moment they were both snoring.

Henri Bergson

WHY DO WE LAUGH?

WHAT does laughter mean? What is the basal element in the laughable? What common ground can we find between the grimace of a merry-andrew, a play upon words, an equivocal situation in a burlesque and a scene of high comedy? What method of distillation will yield us invariably the same essence from which so many different products borrow either their obtrusive odour or their delicate perfume? The greatest of thinkers, from Aristotle downwards, have tackled this little problem, which has a knack of baffling every effort, of slipping away and escaping only to bob up again, a pert challenge flung at philosophic speculation.

Our excuse for attacking the problem in our turn must lie in the fact that we shall not aim at imprisoning the comic spirit within a definition. We regard it, above all, as a living thing. However trivial it may be, we shall treat it with the respect due to life. We shall confine ourselves to watching it grow and expand. Passing by imperceptible gradations from one form to another, it will be seen to achieve the strangest metamorphoses. We shall disdain nothing we have seen. Maybe we may gain from this prolonged contact, for the matter of that, something more flexible than an abstract definition,—a practical, intimate acquaintance, such as springs from a long companionship. And maybe we may also find that, unintentionally, we have made an acquaintance that is useful. For the comic spirit has a logic of its own, even in its wildest eccentricities. It has a method in its madness. It dreams, I admit, but it conjures up in its dreams visions that are at once accepted and understood by the whole of a social group. Can it then fail to throw light for us on the way that human imagination works, and more particularly social, collective, and popular imagination? Begotten of real life and akin to art, should it not also have something of its own to tell us about art and life?

At the outset we shall put forward three observations which we look upon as fundamental. They have less bearing on the actually comic than on the field within which it must be sought.

The first point to which attention should be called is that the comic does not exist outside the pale of what is strictly *human*. A landscape may be beautiful, charming and sublime, or insignificant and ugly; it will never be laughable. You may laugh at an animal, but only because you have detected in it some human attitude or expression. You may laugh at a hat, but what you are making fun of, in this case, is not the piece of felt or straw, but the shape that men have given it,—the human caprice whose mould it has assumed. It is strange that so important a fact, and such a simple one too, has not attracted to a greater degree the attention of philosophers. Several have defined man as "an animal which laughs." They might equally well have defined him as an animal which is laughed at; for if any other animal, or some lifeless object, produces the same effect, it is always because of some resemblance to man, of the stamp he gives it or the use he puts it to.

Here I would point out, as a symptom equally worthy of notice, the *absence of feeling* which usually accompanies laughter. It seems as though the comic could not produce its disturbing effect unless it fell, so to say, on the surface of a soul that is thoroughly calm and unruffled. Indifference is its natural environment, for laughter has no greater foe than emotion. I do not mean that we could not laugh at a person who inspires us with pity, for instance, or even with affection, but in such a case we must, for the moment, put our affection out of court and impose silence upon our pity. In a society composed of pure intelligences there would probably be no more tears, though perhaps there would still be laughter; whereas highly emotional souls, in tune and unison with life, in whom every event would be sentimentally prolonged and re-echoed, would neither know nor understand laughter. Try, for a moment, to become interested in everything that is being said and done; act, in imagination, with those who act, and feel with those who feel; in a word, give your sympathy its widest expansion: as though at the touch of a fairy wand you will see the flimsiest of objects assume importance, and a gloomy hue spread over everything. Now step aside, look upon life as a disinterested spectator: many a drama will turn into a comedy. It is enough for us to stop our ears to the sound of music in a room, where dancing is going on, for the dancers at once to appear ridiculous. How many human actions would stand a similar test? Should we not see many of them suddenly pass from grave to gay, on isolating them from the accompanying music of sentiment? To produce the whole of its effect, then, the comic demands something like a momentary anesthesia of the heart. Its appeal is to intelligence, pure and simple.

This intelligence, however, must always remain in touch with other intelligences. And here is the third fact to which attention should be drawn. You would hardly appreciate the comic if you felt yourself isolated from others. Laughter appears to stand in need of an echo. Listen to it carefully: it is not an articulate, clear, well-defined sound; it is something which would fain be prolonged by reverberating from one to another, something beginning with a crash, to continue in successive rumblings, like thunder in a mountain. Still, this reverberation cannot go on for ever. It can travel within as wide a circle as you please: the circle remains, none the less, a closed one. Our laughter is always the laughter of a group. It may, perchance, have happened to you, when seated in a railway carriage or at *table d'hôte,* to hear travellers relating to one another stories which must have been comic to them, for they laughed heartily. Had you been one of their company, you would have laughed like them, but, as you were not, you had no desire whatever to do so. A man who was once asked why he did not weep at a sermon when everybody else was shedding tears replied: "I don't belong to the parish!" What that man thought of tears would be still more true of laughter. However spontaneous it seems, laughter always implies a kind of secret freemasonry, or even complicity, with other laughers, real or imaginary. How often has it been said that the fuller the theatre, the more uncontrolled the laughter of the audience! On the other hand, how often has the remark been made that many comic effects are incapable of translation from one language to another, because they refer to the customs and ideas of a particular social group! It is through not understanding the importance of this double fact that the comic has been looked upon as a mere curiosity in which the mind finds amusement, and laughter itself as a strange, isolated phenomenon, without any bearing on the rest of human activity. Hence those definitions which tend to make the comic into an abstract relation between ideas: "an intellectual contrast," "a patent absurdity," etc., definitions which, even were they really suitable to every form of the comic, would not in the least explain why the comic makes us laugh. How, indeed, should it come about that this particular logical relation, as soon as it is perceived, contracts, expands and shakes our limbs, whilst all other relations leave the body unaffected? It is not from this point of view that we shall approach the problem. To understand laughter, we must put it back into its natural environment, which is society, and above all must we determine the utility of its function, which is a social one. Such, let us say at once, will be the leading idea of all our investigations. Laughter must answer to certain requirements of life in common. It must have a *social* signification.

Let us clearly mark the point towards which our three preliminary observations are converging. The comic will come into being, it appears, whenever a group of men concentrate their attention on one of their number, imposing silence on their emotions and calling into play nothing but their intelligence. What, now, is the particular point on which their attention will have to be concentrated, and what will here be the function of intelligence? To reply to these questions will be at once to come to closer grips with the problem. But here a few examples have become indispensable.

II

A man, running along the street, stumbles and falls; the passers-by burst out laughing. They would not laugh at him, I imagine, could they suppose that the whim had suddenly seized him to sit down on the ground. They laugh because his sitting down is involuntary. Consequently, it is not his sudden change of attitude that raises a laugh, but rather the involuntary element in this change,—his clumsiness, in fact. Perhaps there was a stone on the road. He should have altered his pace or avoided the obstacle. Instead of that, through lack of elasticity, through absentmindedness and a kind of physical obstinacy, *as a result, in fact, of rigidity or of momentum,* the muscles continued to perform the same movement when the circumstances of the case called for something else. That is the reason of the man's fall, and also of the people's laughter.

Now, take the case of a person who attends to the petty occupations of his everyday life with mathematical precision. The objects around him, however, have all been tampered with by a mischievous wag, the result being that when he dips his pen into the inkstand he draws it out all covered with mud, when he fancies he is sitting down on a solid chair he finds himself sprawling on the floor, in a word his actions are all topsy-turvy or mere beating the air, while in every case the effect is invariably one of momentum. Habit has given the impulse: what was wanted was to check the movement or deflect it. He did nothing of the sort, but continued like a machine in the same straight line. The victim, then, of a practical joke is in a position similar to that of a runner who falls,—he is comic for the same reason. The laughable element in both cases consists of a certain *mechanical inelasticity,* just where one would expect to find the wideawake adaptability and the living pliableness of a human being. The only difference in the two cases is that the former happened of itself, whilst the latter was obtained artificially. In the first instance, the passer-by does nothing but look on, but in the second the mischievous wag intervenes.

All the same, in both cases the result has been brought about by an external circumstance. The comic is therefore accidental: it remains, so to speak, in superficial contact with the person. How is it to penetrate within? The necessary conditions will be fulfilled when mechanical rigidity no longer requires for its manifestation a stumbling-block which either the hazard of circumstance or human knavery has set in its way, but extracts by natural processes, from its own store, an inexhaustible series of opportunities for externally revealing its presence. Suppose, then, we imagine a mind always thinking of what it has just done and never of what it is doing, like a song which lags behind its accompaniment. Let us try to picture to ourselves a certain inborn lack of elasticity of both senses and intelligence, which brings it to pass that we continue to see what is no longer visible, to hear what is no longer audible, to say what is no longer to the point: in short, to adapt ourselves to a past and therefore imaginary situation, when we ought to be shaping our conduct in accordance with the reality which is present. This time the comic will take up its abode in the person himself; it is the person who will supply it with everything—matter and form, cause and opportunity. Is it then surprising that the absent-minded individual—for this is the character we have just been describing—has usually fired the imagination of comic authors? When La Bruyère came across this particular type, he realised, on analysing it, that he had got hold of a recipe for the wholesale manufacture of comic effects. As a matter of fact he overdid it, and gave us far too lengthy and detailed a description of *Ménalque,* coming back to his subject, dwelling and expatiating on it beyond all bounds. The very facility of the subject fascinated him. Absentmindedness, indeed, is not perhaps the actual fountain-head of the comic, but surely it is contiguous to a certain stream of facts and fancies which flows straight from the fountain-head. It is situated, so to say, on one of the great natural watersheds of laughter.

Now, the effect of absentmindedness may gather strength in its turn. There is a general law, the first example of which we have just encountered, and which we will formulate in the following terms: when a certain comic effect has its origin in a certain cause, the more natural we regard the cause to be, the more comic shall we find the effect. Even now we laugh at absentmindedness when presented to us as a simple fact. Still more laughable will be the absentmindedness we have seen springing up and growing before our very eyes, with whose origin we are acquainted and whose life-history we can reconstruct. To choose a definite example: suppose a man has taken to reading nothing but romances of love and chivalry. Attracted and fascinated by his heroes, his thoughts and intentions gradually turn more and more towards them, till one fine day we find him walking among us like a somnambulist. His actions are distractions. But then his distractions can be traced back to a definite, positive cause. They are no longer cases of *absence* of mind, pure and simple; they find their explanation in the *presence* of the individual in quite definite, though imaginary, surroundings. Doubtless a fall is always a fall, but it is one thing to tumble into a well because you were looking anywhere but in front of you, it is quite another thing to fall into it because you were intent upon a star. It was certainly a star at which Don Quixote was gazing. How profound is the comic element in the overromantic, Utopian bent of mind! And yet, if you reintroduce the idea of absentmindedness, which acts as a go-between, you will see this profound comic element uniting with the most superficial type. Yes, indeed, these whimsical wild enthusiasts, these madmen who are yet so strangely reasonable, excite us to laughter by playing on the same chords within ourselves, by setting in motion the same inner mechanism, as does the victim of a practical joke or the passer-by who slips down in the street. They, too, are runners who fall and simple souls who are being hoaxed—runners after the ideal who stumble over realities, childlike dreamers for whom life delights to lie in wait. But, above all, they are past-masters in absentmindedness, with this superiority over their fellows that their absentmindedness is systematic and organised around one central idea, and that their mishaps are also quite coherent, thanks to the inexorable logic which reality applies to the correction of dreams, so that they kindle in those around them, by a series of cumulative effects, a hilarity capable of unlimited expansion.

Now, let us go a little further. Might not certain vices have the same relation to character that the rigidity of a fixed idea has to intellect? Whether as a moral kink or a crooked twist given to the will, vice has often the appearance of a curvature of the soul. Doubtless there are vices into which the soul plunges deeply with all its pregnant potency, which it rejuvenates and drags along with it into a moving circle of reincarnations. Those are tragic vices. But the vice capable of making us comic is, on the contrary, that which is brought from without, like a ready-made frame into which we are to step. It lends us its own rigidity instead of borrowing from us our flexibility. We do not render it more complicated; on the contrary, it simplifies us. Here, as we shall see later on in the concluding section of this study, lies the essential difference between comedy and drama. A drama, even when portraying passions or vices that bear a name, so completely incorporates them in the person that their names are forgotten, their general characteristics effaced, and we no longer think of them at all, but rather of the person in whom they are assimilated; hence, the title of a drama can seldom be anything else than a proper noun. On the other hand, many comedies have a common noun as their title: *l'Avare, le Joueur,* etc. Were you asked to think of a play capable of being called *le Jaloux,* for instance, you would find that *Sganarelle* or *George Dandin* would occur to your mind, but not *Othello: le Jaloux* could only be the title of a comedy. The reason is that, however intimately vice, when comic, is associated with persons, it none the less retains its simple, independent existence, it remains the central character, present though invisible, to which the characters in flesh and blood on the stage are attached. At times it delights in dragging them down with its own weight and making them share in its tumbles. More frequently, however, it plays on them as on an instrument or pulls the strings as though they were puppets. Look closely: you will find that the art of the comic poet consists in making us so well acquainted with the particular vice, in introducing us, the spectators, to such a degree of intimacy with it, that in the end we get hold of some of the strings of the marionette with which he is playing, and actually work them ourselves; this it is that explains part of the pleasure we feel. Here, too, it is really a kind of automatism that makes us laugh—an automatism, as we have already remarked, closely akin to mere absentmindedness. To realise this more fully, it need only be noted that a comic character is generally comic in proportion to his ignorance of himself. The comic person is unconscious. As though wearing the ring of Gyges with reverse effect, he becomes invisible to himself while remaining visible to all the world. A character in a tragedy will make no change in his conduct because he will know how it is judged by us; he may continue therein even though fully conscious of what he is and feeling keenly the horror he inspires in us. But a defect that is ridiculous, as soon as it feels itself to be so, endeavours to modify itself or at least to appear as though it did. Were Harpagon to see us laugh at his miserliness, I do not say that he would get rid of it, but he would either show it less or show it differently. Indeed, it is in this sense only that laughter "corrects men's manners." It makes us at once endeavour to appear what we ought to be, what some day we shall perhaps end in being.

It is unnecessary to carry this analysis any further. From the runner who falls to the simpleton who is hoaxed, from a state of being hoaxed to one of absentmindedness, from absentmindedness to wild enthusiasm, from wild enthusiasm to various distortions of character and will, we have followed the line of progress along which the comic becomes more and more deeply imbedded in the person, yet without ceasing, in its subtler manifestations, to recall to us some trace of what we noticed in its grosser forms, an effect of automatism and of inelasticity. Now we can obtain a first glimpse—a distant one, it is true, and still hazy and confused—of the laughable side of human nature and of the ordinary function of laughter.

What life and society require of each of us is a constantly alert attention that discerns the outlines of the present situation, together with a certain elasticity of mind and body to enable us to adapt ourselves in consequence. *Tension* and *elasticity* are two forces, mutually complementary, which life brings into play. If these two forces are lacking in the body to any considerable extent, we have sickness and infirmity and accidents of every kind. If they are lacking in the mind, we find every degree of mental deficiency, every variety of insanity. Finally, if they are lacking in the character, we have cases of the gravest inadaptability to social life, which are the sources of misery and at times the causes of crime. Once these elements of inferiority that affect the serious side of existence are removed—and they tend to eliminate themselves in what has been called the struggle for life—the person can live, and that in common with other persons. But society asks for something more; it is not satisfied with simply living, it insists on living well. What it now has to dread is that each one of us, content with paying attention to what affects the essentials of life, will, so far as the rest is concerned, give way to the easy automatism of acquired habits. Another thing it must fear is that the members of whom it is made up, instead of aiming after an increasingly delicate adjustment of wills which will fit more and more perfectly into one another, will confine themselves to respecting simply the fundamental conditions of this adjustment: a cut-and-dried agreement among the persons will not satisfy it, it insists on a constant striving after reciprocal adaptation. Society will therefore be suspicious of all *inelasticity* of character, of mind and even of body, because it is the possible sign of a slumbering activity as well as of an activity with separatist tendencies, that inclines to swerve from the common centre round which society gravitates: in short, because it is the sign of an eccentricity. And yet, society cannot intervene at this stage by material repression, since it is not affected in a material fashion. It is confronted with something that makes it uneasy, but only as a symptom—scarcely a threat, at the very most a gesture. A gesture, therefore, will be its reply. Laughter must be something of this kind, a sort of *social gesture*. By the fear which it inspires, it restrains eccentricity, keeps constantly awake and in mutual contact certain activities of a secondary order which might retire into their shell and go to sleep, and in short, softens down whatever the surface of the social body may retain of mechanical inelasticity. Laughter, then, does not belong to the province of esthetics alone, since unconsciously (and even immorally in many particular instances) it pursues a utilitarian aim of general improvement. And yet there is something esthetic about it, since the comic comes into being just when society and the individual, freed from the worry of self-preservation, begin to regard themselves as works of art. In a word, if a circle be drawn round those actions and dispositions—implied in individual or social life— to which their natural consequences bring their own penalties, there remains outside this sphere of emotion and struggle—and within a neutral zone in which man simply exposes himself to man's curiosity—a certain rigidity of body, mind and character that society would still like to get rid of in order to obtain from its members the greatest possible degree of elasticity and sociability. This rigidity is the comic, and laughter is its corrective.

Still, we must not accept this formula as a definition of the comic. It is suitable only for cases that are elementary, theoretical and perfect, in which the comic is free from all adulteration. Nor do we offer it, either, as an explanation. We prefer to make it, if you will, the *leitmotiv* which is to accompany all our explanations. We must ever keep it in mind, though without dwelling on it too much, somewhat as a skilful fencer must think of the discontinuous movements of the lesson whilst his body is given up to the continuity of the fencing-match. We will now endeavour to reconstruct the sequence of comic forms, taking up again the thread that leads from the horseplay of a clown up to the most refined effects of comedy, following this thread in its often unforeseen windings, halting at intervals to look around, and finally getting back, if possible, to the point at which the thread is dangling and where we shall perhaps find—since the comic oscillates between life and art—the general relation that art bears to life.

III

Let us begin at the simplest point. What is a comic physiognomy? Where does a ridiculous expression of the face come from? And what is, in this case, the distinction between the comic and the ugly? Thus stated, the question could scarcely be answered in any other than an arbitrary fashion. Simple though it may appear, it is, even now, too subtle to allow of a direct attack. We should have to begin with a definition of ugliness, and then discover what addition the comic makes to it; now, ugliness is not much easier to analyse than is beauty. However, we will employ an artifice which will often stand us in good stead. We will exaggerate the problem, so to speak, by magnifying the effect to the point of making the cause visible. Suppose, then, we intensify ugliness to the point of deformity, and study the transition from the deformed to the ridiculous.

Now, certain deformities undoubtedly possess over others the sorry privilege of causing some persons to laugh; some hunchbacks, for instance, will excite laughter. Without at this point entering into useless details, we will simply ask the reader to think of a number of deformities, and then to divide them into two groups: on the one hand, those which nature has directed towards the ridiculous; and on the other, those which absolutely diverge from it. No doubt he will hit upon the following law: *A deformity that may become comic is a deformity that a normally built person could successfully imitate.*

Is it not, then, the case that the hunchback suggests the appearance of a person who holds himself badly? His back seems to have contracted an ugly stoop. By a kind of physical obstinacy, by *rigidity,* in a word, it persists in the habit it has contracted. Try to see with your eyes alone. Avoid reflection, and above all, do not reason. Abandon all your prepossessions; seek to recapture a fresh, direct and primitive impression. The vision you will reacquire will be one of this kind. You will have before you a man bent on cultivating a certain rigid attitude whose body, if one may use the expression, is one vast grin.

Now, let us go back to the point we wished to clear up. By toning down a deformity that is laughable, we ought to obtain an ugliness that is comic. A laughable expression of the face, then, is one that will make us think of something rigid and, so to speak, coagulated, in the wonted mobility of the face. What we shall see will be an ingrained twitching or a fixed grimace. It may be objected that every habitual expression of the face, even when graceful and beautiful, gives us this same impression of something stereotyped? Here an important distinction must be drawn. When we speak of expressive beauty or even expressive ugliness, when we say that a face possesses expression, we mean expression that may be stable, but which we conjecture to be mobile. It maintains, in the midst of its fixity, a certain indecision in which are obscurely portrayed all possible shades of the state of mind it expresses, just as the sunny promise of a warm day manifests itself in the haze of a spring morning. But a comic expression of the face is one that promises nothing more than it gives. It is a unique and permanent grimace. One would say that the person's whole moral life has crystallised into this particular cast of features. This is the reason why a face is all the more comic, the more nearly it suggests to us the idea of some simple mechanical action in which its personality would for ever be absorbed. Some faces seem to be always engaged in weeping, others in laughing or whistling, others, again, in eternally blowing an imaginary trumpet, and these are the most comic faces of all. Here again is exemplified the law according to which the more natural the explanation of the cause, the more comic is the effect. Automatism, *inelasticity,* habit that has been contracted and maintained, are clearly the causes why a face makes us laugh. But this effect gains in intensity when we are able to connect these characteristics with some deep-seated cause, a certain *fundamental absentmindedness,* as though the soul had allowed itself to be fascinated and hypnotised by the materiality of a simple action.

We shall now understand the comic element in caricature. However regular we may imagine a face to be, however harmonious its lines and supple its movements, their adjustment is never altogether perfect: there will always be discoverable the signs of some impending bias, the vague suggestion of a possible grimace, in short, some favourite distortion towards which nature seems to be particularly inclined. The art of the caricaturist consists in detecting this, at times, imperceptible tendency, and in rendering it visible to all eyes by magnifying it. He makes his models grimace, as they would do themselves if they went to the end of their tether. Beneath the skin-deep harmony of form, he divines the deep-seated recalcitrance of matter. He realises disproportions and deformations which must have existed in nature as mere inclinations, but which have not succeeded in coming to a head, being held in check by a higher force. His art, which has a touch of the diabolical, raises up the demon who had been overthrown by the angel. Certainly, it is an art that exaggerates, and yet the definition would be very far from complete were exaggeration alone alleged to be its aim and object, for there exist caricatures that are more lifelike than portraits, caricatures in which the exaggeration is scarcely noticeable, whilst, inversely, it is quite possible to exaggerate to excess without obtaining a real caricature. For exaggeration to be comic, it must not appear as an aim, but rather as a means that the artist is using in order to make manifest to our eyes the distortions which he sees in embryo. It is this process of distortion that is of moment and interest. And that is precisely why we shall look for it even in those elements of the face that are incapable of movement, in the curve of a nose or the shape of an ear. For, in our eyes, form is always the outline of a movement. The caricaturist who alters the size of a nose, but respects its ground plan, lengthening it, for instance, in the very direction in which it was being lengthened by nature, is really making the nose indulge in a grin. Henceforth we shall always look upon the original as having determined to lengthen itself and start grinning. In this sense, one might say that Nature herself often meets with the successes of a caricaturist. In the movement through which she has slit that mouth, curtailed that chin and bulged out that cheek, she would appear to have succeeded in completing the intended grimace, thus outwitting the restraining supervision of a more reasonable force. In that case, the face we laugh at is, so to speak, its own caricature.

To sum up, whatever be the doctrine to which our reason assents, our imagination has a very clear-cut philosophy of its own: in every human form it sees the effort of a soul which is shaping matter, a soul which is infinitely supple and perpetually in motion, subject to no law of gravitation, for it is not the earth that attracts it. This soul imparts a portion of its winged lightness to the body it animates: the immateriality which thus passes into matter is what is called gracefulness. Matter, however, is obstinate and resists. It draws to itself the ever-alert activity of this higher principle, would fain convert it to its own inertia and cause it to revert to mere automatism. It would fain immobilise the intelligently varied movements of the body in stupidly contracted grooves, stereotype in permanent grimaces the fleeting expressions of the face, in short imprint on the whole person such an attitude as to make it appear immersed and absorbed in the materiality of some mechanical occupation instead of ceaselessly renewing its vitality by keeping in touch with a living ideal. Where matter thus succeeds in dulling the outward life of the soul, in petrifying its movements and thwarting its gracefulness, it achieves, at the expense of the body, an effect that is comic. If, then, at this point we wish to define the comic by comparing it with its contrary, we should have to contrast it with gracefulness even more than with beauty. It partakes rather of the unsprightly than of the unsightly, of *rigidness* rather than of *ugliness*.

IV

We will now pass from the comic element in *forms* to that in *gestures* and *movements*. Let us at once state the law which seems to govern all the phenomena of this kind. It may indeed be deduced without any difficulty from the considerations stated above.

The attitudes, gestures and movements of the human body are laughable in exact proportion as that body reminds us of a mere machine.

There is no need to follow this law through the details of its immediate applications, which are innumerable. To verify it directly, it would be sufficient to study closely the work of comic artists, eliminating entirely the element of caricature, and omitting that portion of the comic which is not inherent in the drawing itself. For, obviously, the comic element in a drawing is often a borrowed one, for which the text supplies all the stock-in-trade. I mean that the artist may be his own understudy in the shape of a satirist, or even a playwright, and that then we laugh far less at the drawings themselves than at the satire or comic incident they represent. But if we devote our whole attention to the drawing with the firm resolve to think of nothing else, we shall probably find that it is generally comic in proportion to the clearness, as well as the subtleness, with which it enables us to see a man as a jointed puppet. The suggestion must be a clear one, for inside the person we must distinctly perceive, as though through a glass, a set-up mechanism. But the suggestion must also be a subtle one, for the general appearance of the person, whose every limb has been made rigid as a machine, must continue to give us the impression of a living being. The more exactly these two images, that of a person and that of a machine, fit into each other, the more striking is the comic effect, and the more consummate the art of the draughtsman. The originality of a comic artist is thus expressed in the special kind of life he imparts to a mere puppet.

We will, however, leave on one side the immediate application of the principle, and at this point insist only on the more remote consequences. The illusion of a machine working in the inside of the person is a thing that only crops up amid a host of amusing effects; but for the most part it is a fleeting glimpse, that is immediately lost in the laughter it provokes. To render it permanent, analysis and reflection must be called into play.

In a public speaker, for instance, we find that gesture vies with speech. Jealous of the latter, gesture closely dogs the speaker's thought, demanding also to act as interpreter. Well and good; but then it must pledge itself to follow thought through all the phases of its development. An idea is something that grows, buds, blossoms and ripens from the beginning to the end of a speech. It never halts, never repeats itself. It must be changing every moment, for to cease to change would be to cease to live. Then let gesture display a like animation! Let it accept the fundamental law of life, which is the complete negation of repetition! But I find that a certain movement of head or arm, a movement always the same, seems to return at regular intervals. If I notice it and it succeeds in diverting my attention, if I wait for it to occur and it occurs when I expect it, then involuntarily I laugh. Why? Because I now have before me a machine that works automatically. This is no longer life, it is automatism established in life and imitating it. It belongs to the comic.

This is also the reason why gestures, at which we never dreamt of laughing, become laughable when imitated by another individual. The most elaborate explanations have been offered for this extremely simple fact. A little reflection, however, will show that our mental state is ever changing, and that if our gestures faithfully followed these inner movements, if they were as fully alive as we, they would never repeat themselves, and so would keep imitation at bay. We begin, then, to become imitable only when we cease to be ourselves. I mean our gestures can only be imitated in their mechanical uniformity, and therefore exactly in what is alien to our living personality. To imitate any one is to bring out the element of automatism he has allowed to creep into his person. And as this is the very essence of the ludicrous, it is no wonder that imitation gives rise to laughter.

Still, if the imitation of gestures is intrinsically laughable, it will become even more so when it busies itself in deflecting them, though without altering their form, towards some mechanical occupation, such as sawing wood, striking on an anvil, or tugging away at an imaginary bell-rope. Not that vulgarity is the essence of the comic,—although certainly it is to some extent an ingredient,—but rather that the incriminated gesture seems more frankly mechanical when it can be connected with a simple operation, as though it were intentionally mechanical. To suggest this mechanical interpretation ought to be one of the favourite devices of parody. We have reached this result through deduction, but I imagine clowns have long had an intuition of the fact.

This seems to me the solution of the little riddle propounded by Pascal in one passage of his *Thoughts:* "Two faces that are alike, although neither of them excites laughter by itself, make us laugh when together, on account of their likeness." It might just as well be said: "The gestures of a public speaker, no one of which is laughable by itself, excite laughter by their repetition." The truth is that a really living life should never repeat itself. Wherever there is repetition or complete similarity, we always suspect some mechanism at work behind the living. Analyse the impression you get from two faces that are too much alike, and you will find that you are thinking of two copies cast in the same mould, or two impressions of the same seal, or two reproductions of the same negative,—in a word, of some manufacturing process or other. This deflection of life towards the mechanical is here the real cause of laughter.

And laughter will be more pronounced still, if we find on the stage not merely two characters, as in the example from Pascal, but several, nay, as great a number as possible, the image of one another, who come and go, dance and gesticulate together, simultaneously striking the same attitudes and tossing their arms about in the same manner. This time, we distinctly think of marionettes. Invisible threads seem to us to be joining arms to arms, legs to legs, each muscle in one face to its fellow-muscle in the other: by reason of the absolute uniformity which prevails, the very litheness of the bodies seems to stiffen as we gaze, and the actors themselves seem transformed into lifeless automata. Such, at least, appears to be the artifice underlying this somewhat obvious form of amusement. I daresay the performers have never read Pascal, but what they do is merely to realise to the full the suggestions contained in Pascal's words. If, as is undoubtedly the case, laughter is caused in the second instance by the hallucination of a mechanical effect, it must already have been so, though in more subtle fashion, in the first.

Continuing along this path, we dimly perceive the increasingly important and far-reaching consequences of the law we have just stated. We faintly catch still more fugitive glimpses of mechanical effects, glimpses suggested by man's complex actions, no longer merely by his gestures. We instinctively feel that the usual devices of comedy, the periodical repetition of a word or a scene, the systematic inversion of the parts, the geometrical development of a farcical misunderstanding and many other stage contrivances must derive their comic force from the same source,—the art of the playwright probably consisting in setting before us an obvious clockwork arrangement of human events, while carefully preserving an outward aspect of probability and thereby retaining something of the suppleness of life.

Grazia Deledda

THE SHOES

IT OFTEN happened now that Elia Carái had nothing to do; for times were bad, folk hesitated about going to law, and even people like famous barristers and emeritus professors and retired government officials had to work as simple attorneys. But even when he had no cases, Elia used to go to the Law Courts all the same, settle down in the waiting-room, and there, leaning his note-book on his knee or on the wall, he would write poems in dialect to his wife. The storm raged around him. The crowd surged hither and thither; poor women, who had come about a matter of a few pence, shouted abuse at each other, as solemn and tragic as if they had the whole world to divide; swindlers, perfectly ready to swear they owed nothing to their own creditors, went by with their heads in the air and their chests thrust forward proudly; the solicitors, poorer than their own clients, went round from one to the other wondering how they could manage to get hold of a sheet of stamped paper. Elia took it all very calmly. He wrote, in his old-fashioned verse, which he dedicated to his wife:

> *Su mundu lu connosco e donzi cosa*
> *Chi succedit succedere deviat.*

"I know what the world is like, and I know that everything that happens was destined to happen. I am a poet and a philosopher; nothing ever surprises me in this world. Life is a see-saw, one day up and the next day down, and the next day up again. Do not despair, my golden lily. Perhaps Uncle Agostino, who has driven his wife out of the house and disinherited her, will remember us one day. Then we will go to the seaside together, we will watch the boats in the distance, and hold hands like a honeymoon couple. And, after all, we too are happy now; peace and love reign in our dwellings, and thou, Cedar of Lebanon, *Venus hermosa,* art my riches and my queen. . . ."

One winter morning, a carter slapped Elia heavily on the shoulder with a hand that felt like stone.

"Run, man! I've just been to Terranova with a load of rubbish, and I saw the carrier, your Uncle Agostino. He's dangerously ill. . . ."

Elia stood up calmly and smoothed his grey hair with his hand as a sign of grief.

"I will go and tell my wife the sad news at once."

His wife did not seem much disturbed by the sad news; she did not even get up from the doorstep where she was sitting, trying to get warm in the sun. She was respectably dressed, wore shoes, and had her hair done in the latest fashion; but her worn, frayed frock, her old shoes, and thin hair framing her dead-white, anæmic face like a halo, only served to show off her poverty more clearly. Her great eyes, which had once seemed so dark, were now a kind of golden hazel-colour, and indifferent and staring, like the eyes of a hare.

From inside the house, where the two occupied one little ground-floor room giving on to the yard, came a noise like the noise of the Law Courts. It was the owners of the house quarrelling, while in the public-house that belonged to them, men were playing *morra* and laughing.

Elia's wife behaved like her husband in the Law Courts—inert, and indifferent to what went on around her. He loved her and wanted her just like that.

"Do you know what I'm going to do?" he asked, stroking her hair and looking up at the sky. "I'm going."

"Where?"

"Where? But haven't you been listening? To Uncle Agostino's, of course. It's fine to-day," he added, without saying all that he was thinking; but his wife must have guessed because she looked down at his shoes, which were worn and full of holes, and asked:

"What about money for the journey?"

"I've got enough. Never you mind about me, don't worry. In this world everything is bound to go all right in the end, if only you take things calmly and sensibly; the only thing that really matters is being fond of people and treating them kindly. I was just thinking about that sort of thing this morning; here . . . would you like to read it?"

He tore the sheet off his pad, and blushed as he shyly let it drop into her lap. It was all he left her in the way of provisions while he was away.

He set off on foot. He had only three lire in the world, and he was much too wise to lose time by trying to borrow money for the journey.

He was, however, used to this sort of thing; he never expected anything to help him apart from his philosophic calm and his Uncle Agostino's will. He was an excellent walker, and thought far more about his shoes than about his feet; if matters went as well as he expected, then everything would be mended in due course.

Matters went well as far as Orosei. The road was downhill all the way, smooth and straight, accompanied, preceded, and followed by the most beautiful scenery; the very sight of it made one forget all earthly cares and troubles. It was like travelling in an enchanted land; the sun, like a great diamond, shed its cold, pure lustre around; the rocks and the grass were glistening. Then, as he went farther down, Elia felt the sun grow warmer and more golden, and at last, on the marble background of hills towards the sea, he saw, as in spring, pink almond-blossom in flower.

But the sun went down with cruel suddenness; after a short spell of twilight, the cold night fell, and Elia felt his feet were getting wet. His shoes had given way. This was obviously one of the things that were destined to happen, but all the same he did not accept it with his usual philosophical calm. He could not possibly mend them or get someone to lend him a pair now. It was very uncomfortable walking with holes in one's shoes, and dreadfully lacking in dignity, moreover, to appear at one's uncle's house looking like a beggar. For the sake of the future, for his wife's health and well-being, he must get hold of a pair of shoes at all costs. The question was, how? Elia had not the slightest idea. And, meanwhile, he reached the village.

The streets were dark and swept by sea-wind; not a soul was astir. Only, on the piazza, a tiny inn shed a hospitable light. Elia went in and asked for a night's lodging; he paid in advance and was given a bed in a dirty-looking room where two other wayfarers were asleep. One of them was snoring like Pluto. Elia lay down with his clothes on, but he could not get to sleep; he saw endless rows of shoes along all the streets in the world, among houses, and out in the fields; whenever there was a man, there was a pair of shoes. A great many pairs were hidden away in drawers and cupboards and all sorts of odd corners; others stood at the end of their master's bed, watching over his sleep; others were waiting outside doors, and there were still others, like his own, that shared the poverty and despair of their wearers. . . .

The roaring of the wind outside, and the snoring of the man beside him, made an accompaniment to his obsession. The hours went by; a star rose in the heavens, delicately blue as if steeped in the waters of the sea, and stopped outside the rattling window-panes. Elia thought of his wife, and the poems he wrote for her, and the easy life they would both lead if only Uncle Agostino left them all his belongings. . . .

He got up and bent over, trembling, to take the snoring man's shoes. They were heavy; their worn nails felt cold against his hot fingers. He put them down, and groped about on the floor to find the other man's shoes, but he found nothing.

Then he heard a vague noise in the corridor, like the steps of unshod feet. He stopped there motionless, crouching down with his hands on the floor, and trembling like a frightened animal. He realized to the full the extent of his degradation; an instinctive sadness, like the sorrow of a heart in danger, weighed heavily upon him. But as soon as the noise had stopped, he went out to the door to see there was no one there; and by the light of a tiny lamp at the end of the passage he saw a cat rubbing itself against the wall with its tail in the air, and a pair of elastic-sided shoes by the door beside it, throwing a shadow on the floor like two great hooks.

He took them, hid them under his cloak, and went downstairs. A man was sleeping on a mat in the yard so as to watch over people's horses; the big gates were just closed with a latch. Elia managed to get away quietly, and found himself on the sea front, by the grey sea under the twinkling stars that seemed to wish to fall down from the sky, lower and lower. . . .

"It's odd, how everything in man and nature has a tendency to fall," mused Elia, walking quickly with the wind across the dark, hollow land, the dark mountains, and the grey sea.

After walking half an hour or so, he decided it was the moment to put on the stolen shoes. He sat down on a milestone, put on the shoes, and felt them critically. He was delighted; they were soft and roomy; but as he bent down over them he felt the sense of degradation suddenly overwhelm him again. . . .

"What if they follow me? A pretty figure I'll cut then. . . . Whatever will my wife say! 'While you're about it, Elia Carái, you might just as· well steal a million lire as a pair of shoes!' "

Then: "A million lire! The question is where to find them, then I'd take them at once," he added, laughing at himself, stretching out his feet, and wriggling his toes about inside his shoes. It was an odd thing; but his feet burned and throbbed, and seemed to have a violent objection to being inside those shoes.

When he started walking back, with his own shoes under his arm so that he could put them on quickly and throw away the other pair if by any chance he was being followed, he found he could not walk anything like as quickly as before. His legs shook, and he stopped every now and then, seeming to hear steps coming up behind him.

Dawn rose from the pale sea behind a veil of mist, and terrified him, like a ghost. Now the people he had met on the road to Crosei could see him quite well, and when they reached the village and heard the story of the stolen shoes, they would be able to say: "Yes, I met a man who looked rather a suspicious character; he had a sort of parcel thing under his cloak."

As a matter of fact he did meet a peasant, walking quiet and dark through the dawn, with a knapsack and a stick; and Elia imagined he turned round to look at him and smiled.

Day was breaking, sad and grey; the clouds, like great, black, tangled skeins, ran from mountain to sea, from sea to mountain, clinging to cliffs and rocks that unravelled them a little. And the crows cawed as they passed over the windswept moorlands.

The quiet landscape of the day before seemed to have disappeared; now everything looked tortured and diabolical, and Elia thought he could hear voices in the distance, the voices of people following and mocking him.

At last he put on his old shoes again and left the others by the roadside; but still he found no peace. Fantastic happenings went on in his mind; one of the two poor travellers he had slept with was on the same road and picked up the shoes; then this man was followed and found out and pronounced guilty and let in for goodness knows how many awful punishments. . . . Or else the people he imagined were after him found the stolen shoes and went on tormenting him and tormenting him until finally in great shame he confessed what he had done. What would his wife say? The idea grew in his childish mind, excited by exhaustion, cold, and hunger, and spread like the great clouds in the stormy winter sky. He wished he had never set out at all, and had not forsaken his usual peace and quiet merely to run after a shadow. His uncle's legacy would probably involve endless worries and complications; and meanwhile, he had completely disgraced himself.

He turned back, found the shoes where he had left them, and stood a long while looking at them sheepishly. He wondered what he had better do. If he hid them or buried them, it did not alter the fact that they had been stolen. He had stolen them; and the thought of that moment when he was on all-fours on the floor, trembling like a frightened animal, would cast its shadow over his whole existence.

He hid the stolen shoes under his cloak again and went back to the village, lingering on the way so as not to get there before evening. He had eaten nothing for twenty-four hours, and felt so weak that the wind made him sway like a blade of grass. He arrived at the inn in a dream, ready to confess what he had done; but everything was quiet, no one mentioned the theft or bothered about him or his cloak in the least. He had supper and asked for a bed; he was given the same one as on the previous night. He put back the shoes where he had found them and then went to sleep. His sleep was heavy as death; he had to be woken up and told it was twelve o'clock. He bought a loaf of bread with the penny he had left, and went on his way again.

The weather was fine again now, and the moors, shut in between the dark mountains and the blue sea, had all the sorrowful enchantment of a primitive landscape; everything was green and strong, but, just as you see in certain human lives, it seemed as if no flowers could ever bloom there.

Elia was walking well, in spite of his old shoes; and because of them, he enjoyed the privilege of being treated everywhere as a tramp, and given milk and bread to eat.

When he arrived, he found his uncle had died a few hours previously. The maid looked at Elia rather suspiciously, and asked:

"Are you really his nephew? Then why didn't you come sooner?"

Elia did not answer.

"The master was expecting you. He sent a wire to you three days ago. He always used to say you were his only relative, but that you'd forgotten all about him. So this morning, when he saw you hadn't come, he decided to leave everything to the sailors' orphans."

Elia went home and found his wife sitting there in the sun, pale and indifferent to everything.

"Why on earth didn't you say I'd already gone, when the telegram came, my good woman?"

"But surely you'd have got there anyhow, wouldn't you? Why did you take such a long time?"

Elia did not answer.

Ladislas Reymont

DEATH

FATHER, eh, father, get up, do you hear?—Eh, get a move on!'
'Oh God, or Blessed Virgin! Aoh!' groaned the old man, who was being violently shaken. His face peeped out from under his sheepskin, a sunken, battered, and deeply-lined face, of the same colour as the earth he had tilled for so many years; with a shock of hair, grey as the furrows of ploughed fields in autumn. His eyes were closed; breathing heavily he dropped his tongue from his half-open bluish mouth with cracked lips.

'Get up! hi!' shouted his daughter.

'Grandad!' whimpered a little girl who stood in her chemise and a cotton apron tied across her chest, and raised herself on tiptoe to look at the old man's face.

'Grandad!' There were tears in her blue eyes and sorrow in her grimy little face. 'Grandad!' she called out once more, and plucked at the pillow.

'Shut up!' screamed her mother, took her by the nape of the neck and thrust her against the stove.

'Out with you, damned dog!' she roared, when she stumbled over the old half-blind bitch who was sniffing the bed. 'Out you go! will you . . . you carrion!' and she kicked the animal so violently with her clog that it tumbled over, and, whining, crept towards the closed door. The little girl stood sobbing near the stove, and rubbed her nose and eyes with her small fists.

'Father, get up while I am still in a good humour!'

The sick man was silent, his head had fallen on one side, his breathing became more and more laboured. He had not much longer to live.

'Get up. What's the idea? Do you think you are going to do your dying here? Not if I know it! Go to Julina, you old dog! You've given the property to Julina, let her look after you . . . come now . . . while I'm yet asking you!'

'Oh blessed Child Jesus! oh Mary . . .'

A sudden spasm contracted his face, wet with anxiety and sweat. With a jerk his daughter tore away the feather-bed, and, taking the old man round the middle, she pulled him furiously half out of the bed, so that only his head and shoulders were resting on it; he lay motionless like a piece of wood, and, like a piece of wood, stiff and dried up.

'Priest . . . His Reverence . . .' he murmured under his heavy breathing.

'I'll give you your priest! You shall kick your bucket in the pigsty, you sinner . . . like a dog!' She seized him under the armpits, but dropped him again directly, and covered him entirely with the feather-bed, for she had noticed a shadow flitting past the window. Some one was coming up to the house.

She scarcely had time to push the old man's feet back into the bed. Blue in the face, she furiously banged the feather-bed and pushed the bedding about.

The wife of the peasant Dyziak came into the room.

'Christ be praised.'

'In Eternity . . .' growled the other, and glanced suspiciously at her out of the corners of her eyes.

'How do you do? Are you well?'

'Thank God . . . so so . . .'

'How's the old man? Well?'

She was stamping the snow off her clogs near the door.

'Eh . . . how should he be well? He can hardly fetch his breath any more.'

'Neighbour . . . you don't say so . . . neighbour . . .' She was bending down over the old man.

'Priest,' he sighed.

'Dear me . . . just fancy . . . dear me, he doesn't know me! The poor man wants the priest. He's dying, that's certain, he's all but dead already . . . dear me! Well, and did you send for his Reverence?'

'Have I got any one to send?'

'But you don't mean to let a Christian soul die without the sacrament?'

'I can't run off and leave him alone, and perhaps . . . he may recover.'

'Don't you believe it . . . hoho . . . just listen to his breathing. That means that his inside is withering up. It's just as it was with my Walek last year when he was so ill.'

'Well, dear, you'd better go for the priest, make haste . . . look!'

'All right, all right. Poor thing! He looks as if he couldn't last much longer. I must make haste . . . I'm off . . .' and she tied her apron more firmly over her head.

'Good-bye, Antkowa.'

'Go with God.'

Dyziakowa went out, while the other woman began to put the room in order; she scraped the dirt off the floor, swept it up, strewed wood-ashes, scrubbed her pots and pans and put them in a row. From time to time she turned a look of hatred on to the bed, spat, clenched her fists, and held her head in helpless despair.

'Fifteen acres of land, the pigs, three cows, furniture, clothes—half of it, I'm sure, would come to six thousand . . . good God!'

And as though the thought of so large a sum was giving her fresh vigour, she scrubbed her saucepans with a fury that made the walls ring, and banged them down on the board.

'May you . . . may you!' She continued to count up: 'Fowls, geese, calves, all the farm implements. And all left to that trull! May misery eat you up . . . may the worms devour you in the ditch for the wrong you have done me, and for leaving me no better off than an orphan!'

She sprang towards the bed in a towering rage and shouted:

'Get up!' And when the old man did not move, she threatened him with her fists and screamed into his face:

'That's what you've come here for, to do your dying here, and I am to pay for your funeral and buy you a hooded cloak . . . that's what he thinks. I don't think! You won't live to see me do it! If your Julina is so sweet, you'd better make haste and go to her. Was it I who was supposed to look after you in your dotage? She is the pet, and if you think . . .'

She did not finish, for she heard the tinkling of the bell, and the priest entered with the sacrament.

Antkowa bowed down to his feet, wiping tears of rage from her eyes, and after she had poured the holy water into a chipped basin and put the asperges-brush beside it, she went out into the passage, where a few people who had come with the priest were waiting already.

'Christ be praised.'

'In Eternity.'

'What is it?'

'Oh nothing! Only that he's come here to give up . . . with us, whom he has wronged. And now he won't give up. Oh dear me . . . poor me!'

She began to cry.

'That's true! He will have to rot, and you will have to live,' they all answered in unison and nodded their heads.

'One's own father,' she began again. '. . . Have we, Antek and I, not taken care of him, worked for him, sweated for him, just as much as they? Not a single egg would I sell, not half a pound of butter, but put it all down his throat; the little drop of milk I have taken away from the baby and given it to him, because he was an old man and my father . . . and now he goes and gives it all to Tomek. Fifteen acres of land, the cottage, the cows, the pigs, the calf, and the farm-carts and all the furniture . . . is that nothing? Oh, pity me! There's no justice in this world, none . . . Oh, oh!'

She leant against the wall, sobbing loudly.

'Don't cry, neighbour, don't cry. God is full of mercy, but not always towards the poor. He will reward you some day.'

'Idiot, what's the good of talking like that?' interrupted the speaker's husband. 'What's wrong is wrong. The old man will go, and poverty will stay.'

'It's hard to make an ox move when he won't lift up his feet,' another man said thoughtfully.

'Eh . . . You can get used to everything in time, even to hell,' murmured a third, and spat from between his teeth.

The little group relapsed into silence. The wind rattled the door and blew snow through the crevices on to the floor. The peasants stood thoughtfully, with bared heads, and stamped their feet to get warm. The women, with their hands under their cotton aprons, and huddled together, looked with patient resigned faces towards the door of the living-room.

At last the bell summoned them into the room; they entered one by one, pushing each other aside. The dying man was lying on his back, his head deeply buried in the pillows; his yellow chest, covered with white hair, showed under the open shirt. The priest bent over him and laid the wafer upon his outstretched tongue. All knelt down and, with their eyes raised to the ceiling, violently smote their chests, while they sighed and sniffled audibly. The women bent down to the ground and babbled: 'Lamb of God that takest away the sins of the world.'

The dog, worried by the frequent tinkling of the bell, growled ill-temperedly in the corner.

The priest had finished the last unction, and beckoned to the dying man's daughter.

'Where's yours, Antkowa?'

'Where should he be, your Reverence, if not at his daily job?'

For a moment the priest stood, hesitating, looked at the assembly, pulled his expensive fur tighter round his shoulders; but he could not think of anything suitable to say; so he only nodded to them and went out, giving them his white, aristocratic hand to kiss, while they bent towards his knees.

When he had gone they immediately dispersed. The short December day was drawing to its close. The wind had gone down, but the snow was now falling in large, thick flakes. The evening twilight crept into the room. Antkowa was sitting in front of the fire; she broke off twig after twig of the dry firewood, and carelessly threw them upon the fire.

She seemed to be purposing something, for she glanced again and again at the window, and then at the bed. The sick man had been lying quite still for a considerable time. She got very impatient, jumped up from her stool and stood still, eagerly listening and looking about; then she sat down again.

Night was falling fast. It was almost quite dark in the room. The little girl was dozing, curled up near the stove. The fire was flickering feebly with a reddish light which lighted up the woman's knees and a bit of the floor.

The dog started whining and scratched at the door. The chickens on the ladder cackled low and long.

Now a deep silence reigned in the room. A damp chill rose from the wet floor.

Antkowa suddenly got up to peer through the window at the village street; it was empty. The snow was falling thickly, blotting out everything at a few steps' distance. Undecided, she paused in front of the bed, but only for a moment; then she suddenly pulled away the feather-bed roughly and determinedly, and threw it on to the other bedstead. She took the dying man under the armpits and lifted him high up.

'Magda! Open the door.'

Magda jumped up, frightened, and opened the door.

'Come here . . . take hold of his feet.'

Magda clutched at her grandfather's feet with her small hands and looked up in expectation.

'Well, get on . . . help me to carry him! Don't stare about . . . carry him, that's what you've got to do!' she commanded again, severely.

The old man was heavy, perfectly helpless, and apparently unconscious; he did not seem to realize what was being done to him. She held him tight and carried, or rather dragged him along, for the little girl had stumbled over the threshold and dropped his feet, which were drawing two deep furrows in the snow.

The penetrating cold had restored the dying man to consciousness, for in the yard he began to moan and utter broken words:

'Julisha . . . oh God . . . Ju . . .'

'That's right, you scream . . . scream as much as you like, nobody will hear you, even if you shout your mouth off!'

She dragged him across the yard, opened the door of the pigsty with her foot, pulled him in, and dropped him close to the wall.

The sow came forward, grunting, followed by her piglets.

'Malusha! malu, malu, malu!'

The pigs came out of the sty and she banged the door, but returned almost immediately, tore the shirt open on the old man's chest, tore off his chaplet, and took it with her.

'Now die, you leper!'

She kicked his naked leg, which was lying across the opening, with her clog, and went out.

The pigs were running about in the yard; she looked back at them from the passage.

'Malusha! malu, malu, malu!'

The pigs came running up to her, squeaking; she brought out a bowlfull of potatoes and emptied it. The mother-pig began to eat greedily, and the piglets poked their pink noses into her and pulled at her until nothing but their loud smacking could be heard.

Antkowa lighted a small lamp above the fireplace and tore open the chaplet, with her back turned towards the window. A sudden gleam came into her eyes, when a number of banknotes and two silver roubles fell out.

'It wasn't just talk then, his saying that he'd put by the money for the funeral.' She wrapped the money up in a rag and put it into the chest.

'You Judas! May eternal blindness strike you!'

She put the pots and pans straight and tried to cheer the fire which was going out.

'Drat it! That plague of a boy has left me without a drop of water.'

She stepped outside and called 'Ignatz! Hi! Ignatz!'

A good half-hour passed, then the snow creaked under stealthy footsteps and a shadow stole past the window. Antkowa seized a piece of wood and stood by the door which was flung wide open; a small boy of about nine entered the room.

'You stinking idler! Running about the village, are you? And not a drop of water in the house!'

Clutching him with one hand she beat the screaming child with the other.

'Mummy! I won't do it again. . . . Mummy, leave off. . . . Mumm . . .'

She beat him long and hard, giving vent to all her pent-up rage.

'Mother! Ow! All ye Saints! She's killing me!'

'You dog! You're loafing about, and not a drop of water do you fetch me, and there's no wood . . . am I to feed you for nothing, and you worrying me into the bargain?' She hit harder.

At last he tore himself away, jumped out by the window, and shouted back at her with a tear-choked voice:

'May your paws rot off to the elbows, you dog of a mother! May you be stricken down, you sow! . . . You may wait till you're manure before I fetch you any water!'

And he ran back to the village.

The room suddenly seemed strangely empty. The lamp above the fireplace trembled feebly. The little girl was sobbing to herself.

'What are you snivelling about?'

'Mummy . . . oh . . . oh . . . grandad . . .'

She leant, weeping, against her mother's knee.

'Leave off, idiot!'

She took the child on her lap, and, pressing her close, she began to clean her head. The little thing babbled incoherently, she looked feverish; she rubbed her eyes with her small fists and presently went to sleep, still sobbing convulsively from time to time.

Soon afterwards the husband returned home. He was a huge fellow in a sheepskin, and wore a muffler round his cap. His face was blue with cold; his moustache, covered with hoar-frost, looked like a brush. He knocked the snow off his boots, took muffler and cap off together, dusted the snow off his fur, clapped his stiff hands against his arms, pushed the bench towards the fire, and sat down heavily.

Antkowa took a saucepan full of cabbage off the fire and put it in front of her husband, cut a piece of bread and gave it him, together with the spoon. The peasant ate in silence, but when he had finished he undid his fur, stretched his legs, and said: 'Is there any more?'

She gave him the remains of their midday porridge; he spooned it up after he had cut himself another piece of bread; then he took out his pouch, rolled a cigarette and lighted it, threw some sticks on the fire and drew closer to it. A good while later he looked round the room. 'Where's the old man?'

'Where should he be? In the pigsty.'

He looked questioningly at her.

'I should think so! What should he loll in the bed for, and dirty the bedclothes? If he's got to give up, he will give up all the quicker in there. . . . Has he given me a single thing? What should he come to me for? Am I to pay for his funeral and give him his food? If he doesn't give up now—and I tell you, he is a tough one—then he'll eat us out of house and home. If Julina is to have everything let her look after him—that's nothing to do with me.'

'Isn't my father . . . and cheated us . . . he has. I don't care. . . . The old speculator!'

Antek swallowed the smoke of his cigarette and spat into the middle of the room.

'If he hadn't cheated us we should now have . . . wait a minute . . . we've got five . . . and seven and a half . . . makes . . . five and . . . seven . . .'

'Twelve and a half. I had counted that up long ago; we could have kept a horse and three cows . . . bah! . . . the carrion!'

Again he spat furiously.

The woman got up, laid the child down on the bed, took the little rag bundle from the chest and put it into her husband's hand.

'What's that?'

'Look at it.'

He opened the linen rag. An expression of greed came into his face, he bent forward towards the fire with his whole frame, so as to hide the money, and counted it over twice.

'How much is it?'

She did not know the money values.

'Fifty-four roubles.'

'Lord! So much?'

Her eyes shone; she stretched out her hand and fondled the money.

'How did you come by it?'

'Ah bah . . . how? Don't you remember the old man telling us last year that he had put by enough to pay for his funeral?'

'That's right, he did say that.'

'He had stitched it into his chaplet and I took it from him; holy things shouldn't knock about in a pigsty, that would be sinful; then I felt the silver through the linen, so I tore that off and took the money. That is ours; hasn't he wronged us enough?'

'That's God's truth. It's ours; that little bit at least is coming back to us. Put it by with the other money, we can just do with it. Only yesterday Smoletz told me he wanted to borrow a thousand roubles from me; he will give his five acres of ploughed fields near the forest as security.'

'Have you got enough?'

'I think I have.'

'And will you begin to sow the fields yourself in the spring?'

'Rather . . . if I shouldn't have quite enough now, I will sell the sow; even if I should have to sell the little ones as well I must lend him the money. For he won't be able to redeem it,' he added, 'I know what I know. We shall go to the lawyer and make a proper contract that the ground will be mine unless he repays the money within five years.'

'Can you do that?'

'Of course I can. How did Dumin get hold of Dyziak's fields? . . . Put it away; you may keep the silver, buy what you like with it. Where's Ignatz?'

'He's run off somewhere. Ha! no water, it's all gone. . . .'

The peasant got up without a word, looked after the cattle, went in and out, fetched water and wood.

The supper was boiling in the saucepan. Ignatz cautiously crept into the room; no one spoke to him. They were all silent and strangely ill at ease. The old man was not mentioned; it was as if he had never been.

Antek thought of his five acres; he looked upon them as a certainty. Momentarily the old man came into his mind, and then again the sow he had meant to kill when she had finished with the sucking-pigs. Again and again he spat when his eyes fell on the empty bedstead, as if he wanted to get rid of an unpleasant thought. He was worried, did not finish his supper, and went to bed immediately after. He turned over from side to side; the potatoes and cabbage, groats and bread gave him indigestion, but he got over it and went to sleep.

When all was silent, Antkowa gently opened the door into the next room where the bundles of flax lay. From underneath these she fetched a packet of banknotes wrapped up in a linen rag, and added the money. She smoothed the notes many times over, opened them out, folded them up again, until she had gazed her fill; then she put out the light and went to bed beside her husband.

Meanwhile the old man had died. The pigsty, a miserable lean-to run up of planks and thatched with branches, gave no protection against wind and weather. No one heard the helpless old man entreating for mercy in a voice trembling with despair. No one saw him creep to the closed door and raise himself with a superhuman effort to try and open it. He felt death gaining upon him; from his heels it crept upwards to his chest, holding it as in a vise, and shaking him in terrible spasms; his jaws closed upon each other, tighter and tighter, until he was no longer able to open them and scream. His veins were hardening till they felt like wires. He reared up feebly, till at last he broke down on the threshold, with foam on his lips, and a look of horror at being left to die of cold, in his broken eyes; his face was distorted by an expression of anguish which was like a frozen cry. There he lay.

The next morning before dawn Antek and his wife got up. His first thought was to see what had happened to the old man.

He went to look, but could not get the door of the pigsty to open, the corpse was barring it from the inside like a beam. At last, after a great effort, he was able to open it far enough to slip in, but he came out again at once, terror-stricken. He could hardly get fast enough across the yard and into the house; he was almost senseless with fear. He could not understand what was happening to him; his whole frame shook as in a fever, and he stood by the door panting and unable to utter a word.

Antkowa was at that moment teaching little Magda her prayer. She turned her head towards her husband with questioning eyes.

'Thy will be done . . .' she babbled thoughtlessly.

'Thy will . . .'

'. . . be done . . .'

'. . . be done . . .' the kneeling child repeated like an echo.

'Well, is he dead?' she jerked out, '. . . on earth . . .'

'. . . on earth . . .'

'To be sure, he's lying across the door,' he answered under his breath.

'. . . as it is in Heaven . . .'

'. . . is in Heaven . . .'

'But we can't leave him there; people might say we took him there to get rid of him—we can't have that . . .'

'What do you want me to do with him?'

'How do I know? You must do something.'

'Perhaps we can get him across here?' suggested Antek.

'Look at that now . . . let him rot! Bring him in here? Not if . . .'

'Idiot, he will have to be buried.'

'Are we to pay for his funeral? . . . but deliver us from evil . . . what are you blinking your silly eyes for? . . . go on praying.'

'. . . deliver . . . us . . . from . . . evil . . .'

'I shouldn't think of paying for that, that's Tomek's business by law and right.'

'. . . Amen . . .'

'Amen.'

She made the sign of the cross over the child, wiped its nose with her fingers and went up to her husband.

He whispered: 'We must get him across.'

'Into the house . . . here?'

'Where else?'

'Into the cowshed; we can lead the calf out and lay him down on the bench, let him lie in state there, if he likes . . such a one as he has been!'

'Monika!'

'Eh?'

'We ought to get him out there.'

'Well, fetch him out then.'

'All right . . . but . . .'

'You're afraid, what?'

'Idiot . . . damned . . .'

'What else?'

'It's dark . . .'

'If you wait till it's day, people will see you.'

'Let's go together.'

'You go if you are so keen.'

'Are you coming, you carrion, or are you not?' he shouted at her; 'he's your father, not mine.' And he flung out of the room in a rage.

The woman followed him without a word.

When they entered the pigsty, a breath of horror struck them, like the exhalation from a corpse. The old man was lying there, cold as ice; one half of his body had frozen on to the floor; they had to tear him off forcibly before they could drag him across the threshold and into the yard.

Antkowa began to tremble violently at the sight of him; he looked terrifying in the light of the grey dawn, on the white coverlet of snow, with his anguished face, wide-open eyes, and drooping tongue on which the teeth had closed firmly. There were blue patches on his skin, and he was covered with filth from head to foot.

'Take hold,' whispered the man, bending over him. 'How horribly cold he is!'

The icy wind which rises just before the sun, blew into their faces, and shook the snow off the swinging twigs with a dry crackle.

Here and there a star was still visible against the leaden background of the sky. From the village came the creaking noise of the hauling of water, and the cocks crew as if the weather were going to change.

Antkowa shut her eyes and covered her hands with her apron, before she took hold of the old man's feet; they could hardly lift him, he was so heavy. They had barely put him down on a bench when she fled back into the house, throwing out a linen-rag to her husband to cover the corpse.

The children were busy scraping potatoes; she waited impatiently at the door.

'Have done . . . come in! . . . Lord, how long you are!'

'We must get some one to come and wash him,' she said, laying the breakfast, when he had come in.

'I will fetch the deaf-mute.'

'Don't go to work to-day.'

'Go . . . no, not I . . .'

They did not speak again, and ate their breakfast without appetite, although as a rule they finished their four quarts of soup between them.

When they went out into the yard they walked quickly, and did not turn their heads towards the other side. They were worried, but did not know why; they felt no remorse; it was perhaps more a vague fear of the corpse, or fear of death, that shook them and made them silent.

When it was broad day, Antek fetched the village deaf-mute, who washed and dressed the old man, laid him out, and put a consecrated candle at his head.

Antek then went to give notice to the priest and to the Soltys of his father-in-law's death and his own inability to pay for the funeral.

'Let Tomek bury him; he has got all the money.'

The news of the old man's death spread rapidly throughout the village. People soon began to assemble in little groups to look at the corpse. They murmured a prayer, shook their heads, and went off to talk it over.

It was not till towards evening that Tomek, the other son-in-law, under pressure of public opinion, declared himself willing to pay for the funeral.

On the third day, shortly before this was to take place, Tomek's wife made her appearance at Antek's cottage.

In the passage she almost came nose to nose with her sister, who was just taking a pail of dishwater out to the cowshed.

'Blessed be Jesus Christ,' she murmured, and kept her hand on the door-handle.

'Now: look at that . . . soul of a Judas!' Antkowa put the pail down hard. 'She's come to spy about here. Got rid of the old one somehow, didn't you? Hasn't he given everything to you . . . and you dare show yourself here, you trull! Have you come for the rest of the rags he left here, what?'

'I bought him a new sukmana at Whitsuntide, he can keep that on, of course, but I must have the sheepskin back, because it has been bought with money I have earned in the sweat of my brow,' Tomekowa replied calmly.

'Have it back, you mangy dog, have it back?' screamed Antkowa. 'I'll give it you, you'll see what you will have . . .' and she looked round for an object that would serve her purpose. 'Take it away? You dare! You have crawled to him and lickspittled till he became the idiot he was and made everything over to you and wronged me, and then . . .'

'Everybody knows that we bought the land from him, there are witnesses . . .'

'Bought it? Look at her! You mean to say you're not afraid to lie like that under God's living eyes? Bought it! Cheats, that's what you are, thieves, dogs! You stole the money from him first, and then. . . . Didn't you make him eat out of the pig-pail? Adam is a witness that he had to pick the potatoes out of the pig-pail, ha! You've let him sleep in the cowshed, because, you said, he stank so that you couldn't eat. Fifteen acres of land and a dower-life like that . . . for so much property! And you've beaten him too, you swine, you monkey!'

'Hold your snout, or I'll shut it for you and make you remember, you sow, you trull!'

'Come on then, come on, you destitute creature!'

'I . . . destitute?'

'Yes, you! You would have rotted in a ditch, the vermin would have eaten you up, if Tomek hadn't married you.'

'I, destitute? Oh you carrion!'

They sprang at each other, clutching at each other's hair; they fought in the narrow passage, screaming themselves hoarse all the time.

'You street-walker, you loafer . . . there! that's one for you! There's one for my fifteen acres, and for all the wrong you have done me, you dirty dog!'

'For the love of God, you women, leave off, leave off! It's a sin and a shame!' cried the neighbours.

'Let me go, you leper, will you let go?'

'I'll beat you to death, I will tear you to pieces, you filth!'

They fell down, hitting each other indiscriminately, knocked over the pail, and rolled about in the pigwash. At last, speechless with rage and only breathing hard, they still banged away at each other. The men were hardly able to separate them. Purple in the face, scratched all over, and covered with filth, they looked like witches. Their fury was boundless; they sprang at each other again, and had to be separated a second time.

At last Antkowa began to sob hysterically with rage and exhaustion, tore her own hair and wailed: 'Oh Jesus! Oh little child Jesus! Oh Mary! Look at this pestiferous woman . . . curse those heathen . . . oh! oh! . . .' she was only able to roar, leaning against the wall.

Tomekowa, meanwhile, was cursing and shouting outside the house, and banging her heels against the door.

The spectators stood in little groups, taking counsel with each other, and stamping their feet in the snow. The women looked like red spots dabbed on to the wall; they pressed their knees together, for the wind was penetratingly cold. They murmured remarks to each other from time to time, while they watched the road leading to the church, the spires of which stood out clearly behind the branches of the bare trees. Every minute some one or other wanted to have another look at the corpse; it was a perpetual coming and going. The small yellow flames of the candles could be seen through the half-open door, flaring in the draught, and momentarily revealing a glimpse of the dead man's sharp profile as he lay in the coffin. The smell of burning juniper floated through the air, together with the murmurings of prayers and the grunts of the deaf-mute.

At last the priest arrived with the organist. The white pine coffin was carried out and put into the cart. The women began to sing the usual lamentations, while the procession started down the long village street towards the cemetery.

The priest intoned the first words of the Service for the Dead, walking at the head of the procession with his black biretta on his head; he had thrown a thick fur cloak over his surplice; the wind made the ends of his stole flutter; the words of the Latin hymn fell from his lips at intervals, dully, as though they had been frozen; he looked bored and impatient, and let his eyes wander into the distance. The wind tugged at the black banner, and the pictures of heaven and hell on it wobbled and fluttered to and fro, as though anxious to display themselves to the rows of cottages on either side, where women with shawls over their heads and bare-headed men were standing huddled together.

They bowed reverently, made the sign of the cross, and beat their breasts.

The dogs were barking furiously from behind the hedges, some jumped on to the stone walls and broke into long-drawn howls.

Eager little children peeped out from behind the closed windows, beside toothless used-up old people's faces, furrowed as fields in autumn.

A small crowd of boys in linen trousers and blue jackets with brass buttons, their bare feet stuck into wooden sandals, ran behind the priest, staring at the pictures of heaven and hell, and intoning the intervals of the chant with thin, shivering voices: a! o! . . . They kept it up as long as the organist did not change the chant.

Ignatz proudly walked in front, holding the banner with one hand and singing the loudest of all. He was flushed with exertion and cold, but he never relaxed, as though eager to show that he alone had a right to sing, because it was his grandfather who was being carried to the grave.

They left the village behind. The wind threw itself upon Antek, whose huge form towered above all the others, and ruffled his hair; but he did not notice the wind, he was entirely taken up with the horses and with steadying the coffin, which was tilting dangerously at every hole in the road.

The two sisters were walking close behind the coffin, murmuring prayers and eyeing each other with furious glances.

'Tsutsu! Go home! . . . Go home at once, you carrion!' One of the mourners pretended to pick up a stone. The dog, who had been following the cart, whined, put her tail between her legs, and fled behind a heap of stones by the roadside; when the procession had moved on a good bit, she ran after it in a semi-circle, and anxiously kept close to the horses, lest she should be prevented again from following.

The Latin chant had come to an end. The women, with shrill voices, began to sing the old hymn: 'He who dwelleth under the protection of the Lord.'

It sounded thin. The blizzard, which was getting up, did not allow the singing to come to much. Twilight was falling.

The wind drove clouds of snow across from the endless, steppe-like plains, dotted here and there with skeleton trees, and lashed the little crowd of human beings as with a whip.

'. . . and loves and keeps with faithful heart His word . . .,' they insisted through the whistling of the tempest and the frequent shouts of Antek, who was getting breathless with cold: 'Woa! woa, my lads!'

Snowdrifts were beginning to form across the road like huge wedges, starting from behind trees and heaps of stones.

Again and again the singing was interrupted when the people looked round anxiously into the white void: it seemed to be moving when the wind struck it with dull thuds; now it towered in huge walls, now it dissolved like breakers, turned over, and furiously darted sprays of a thousand sharp needles into the faces of the mourners. Many of them returned half-way, fearing an increase of the blizzard, the others hurried on to the cemetery in the greatest haste, almost at a run. They got through the ceremony as fast as they could; the grave was ready, they quickly sang a little more, the priest sprinkled holy water on the coffin; frozen clods of earth and snow rolled down, and the people fled home.

Tomek invited everybody to his house, because 'the reverend Father had said to him, that otherwise the ceremony would doubtless end in an ungodly way at the public-house.'

Antek's answer to the invitation was a curse. The four of them, including Ignatz and the peasant Smoletz, turned into the inn.

They drank four quarts of spirits mixed with fat, ate three pounds of sausages, and talked about the money transaction.

The heat of the room and the spirits soon made Antek very drunk. He stumbled so on the way home that his wife took him firmly under the arm.

Smoletz remained at the inn to drink an extra glass in prospect of the loan, but Ignatz ran home ahead as fast as he could, for he was horribly cold.

'Look here, mother . . .,' said Antek, 'the five acres are mine! aha! mine, do you hear? In the autumn I shall sow wheat and barley, and in the spring we will plant potatoes . . . mine . . . they are mine! . . . God is my comfort, sayest thou . . .,' he suddenly began to sing.

The storm was raging and howling.

'Shut up! You'll fall down, and that will be the end of it.'

'. . . His angel keepeth watch . . .,' he stopped abruptly. The darkness was impenetrable, nothing could be seen at a distance of two feet. The blizzard had reached the highest degree of fury; whistling and howling on a gigantic scale filled the air, and mountains of snow hurled themselves upon them.

From Tomek's cottage came the sound of funeral chants and loud talking when they passed by.

'These heathen! These thieves! You wait, I'll show you my five acres! Then I shall have ten. You won't lord it over me! Dogs'-breed . . . aha! I'll work, I'll slave, but I shall get it, eh, mother? we will get it, what?' he hammered his chest with his fist, and rolled his drunken eyes.

He went on like this for a while, but as soon as they reached their home, the woman dragged him into bed, where he fell down like a dead man. But he did not go to sleep yet, for after a time he shouted: 'Ignatz!'

The boy approached, but with caution, for fear of contact with the paternal foot.

'Ignatz, you dead dog! Ignatz, you shall be a first-class peasant, not a beggarly professional man,' he bawled, and brought his fist down on the bedstead.

'The five acres are mine, mine! Foxy Germans,[1] you . . . da . . .' He went to sleep.

William Butler Yeats

THE LAND OF HEART'S DESIRE

CHARACTERS

MAURTEEN BRUIN	MARY BRUIN
BRIDGET BRUIN	FATHER HART
SHAWN BRUIN	A FAERY CHILD

The Scene is laid in the Barony of Kilmacowen, in the County of Sligo, and at a remote time.

SCENE—*A room with a hearth on the floor in the middle of a deep alcove to the Right. There are benches in the alcove and a table; and a crucifix on the wall. The alcove is full of a glow of light from the fire. There is an open door facing the audience to the Left, and to the left of this a bench. Through the door one can see the forest. It is night, but the moon or a late sunset glimmers through the trees and carries the eye far off into a vague, mysterious world.* MAURTEEN BRUIN, SHAWN BRUIN, *and* BRIDGET BRUIN *sit in the alcove at the table or about the fire. They are dressed in the costume of some remote time, and near them sits an old priest,*

[1] The term 'German' is used for 'foreigner' generally, whom the Polish peasant despises.

FATHER HART. *He may be dressed as a friar. There is food and drink upon the table.* MARY BRUIN *stands by the door reading a book. If she looks up she can see through the door into the wood.*

B<small>RIDGET</small>. Because I bid her clean
      the pots for supper
    She took that old book down
      out of the thatch;
She has been doubled over it ever
    since.
We should be deafened by her groans
    and moans
Had she to work as some do, Father
    Hart;
Get up at dawn like me and mend
    and scour
Or ride abroad in the boisterous
    night like you,
The pyx and blessed bread under
    your arm.
SHAWN. Mother, you are too cross.
BRIDGET. You've married her,
And fear to vex her and so take her
    part.
MAURTEEN (*to* FATHER HART). It is
    but right that youth should side
    with youth;
She quarrels with my wife a bit at
    times,
And is too deep just now in the old
    book!
But do not blame her greatly; she
    will grow
As quiet as a puff-ball in a tree
When but the moons of marriage
    dawn and die
For half a score of times.
FATHER HART. Their hearts are wild,
As be the hearts of birds, till children
    come.
BRIDGET. She would not mind the
    kettle, milk the cow,
Or even lay the knives and spread
    the cloth.
SHAWN. Mother, if only——
MAURTEEN. Shawn, this is half empty;

Go, bring up the best bottle that we
    have.
FATHER HART. I never saw her read a
    book before,
What can it be?
MAURTEEN (*to* SHAWN). What are you
    waiting for?
You must not shake it when you
    draw the cork;
It's precious wine, so take your time
    about it.
(*To Priest.*)   (SHAWN *goes.*)
There was a Spaniard wrecked at
    Ocris Head,
When I was young, and I have still
    some bottles.
He cannot bear to hear her blamed;
    the book
Has lain up in the thatch these fifty
    years;
My father told me my grandfather
    wrote it,
And killed a heifer for the binding
    of it—
But supper's spread, and we can talk
    and eat
It was little good he got out of the
    book,
Because it filled his house with ram-
    bling fiddlers,
And rambling ballad-makers and the
    like.
The griddle-bread is there in front
    of you.
Colleen, what is the wonder in that
    book,
That you must leave the bread to
    cool? Had I
Or had my father read or written
    books
There were no stocking stuffed with
    yellow guineas
To come when I am dead to Shawn
    and you.
FATHER HART. You should not fill your
    head with foolish dreams.
What are you reading?
MARY. How a Princess Edane,

William Butler Yeats

279

A daughter of a King of Ireland,
    heard
A voice singing on a May Eve like
    this,
And followed half awake and half
    asleep,
Until she came into the Land of
    Faery,
Where nobody gets old and godly
    and grave,
Where nobody gets old and crafty
    and wise,
Where nobody gets old and bitter
    of tongue.
And she is still there, busied with
    a dance
Deep in the dewy shadow of a wood,
Or where stars walk upon a moun-
    tain-top.
MAURTEEN. Persuade the colleen to
    put down the book;
My grandfather would mutter just
    such things,
And he was no judge of a dog or
    a horse,
And any idle boy could blarney him;
Just speak your mind.
FATHER HART. Put it away, my col-
    leen;
God spreads the heavens above us
    like great wings
And gives a little round of deeds and
    days,
And then come the wrecked angels
    and set snares,
And bait them with light hopes and
    heavy dreams,
Until the heart is puffed with pride
    and goes
Half shuddering and half joyous
    from God's peace;
And it was some wrecked angel,
    blind with tears,
Who flattered Edane's heart with
    merry words.
My colleen, I have seen some other
    girls
Restless and ill at ease, but years
    went by

And they grew like their neighbours
    and were glad
In minding children, working at the
    churn,
And gossiping of weddings and of
    wakes;
For life moves out of a red flare of
    dreams
Into a common light of common
    hours,
Until old age bring the red flare
    again.
MAURTEEN. That's true—but she's too
    young to know it's true.
BRIDGET. She's old enough to know
    that it is wrong
To mope and idle.
MAURTEEN. I've little blame for her;
She's dull when my big son is in the
    fields,
And that and maybe this good
    woman's tongue
Have driven her to hide among her
    dreams
Like children from the dark under
    the bed-clothes.
BRIDGET. She'd never do a turn if I
    were silent.
MAURTEEN. And maybe it is natural
    upon May Eve
To dream of the good people. But
    tell me, girl,
If you've the branch of blessed
    quicken wood
That women hang upon the post of
    the door
That they may send good luck into
    the house?
Remember they may steal new-mar-
    ried brides
After the fall of twilight on May Eve,
Or what old women mutter at the fire
Is but a pack of lies.
FATHER HART. It may be truth.
We do not know the limit of those
    powers
God has permitted to the evil spirits
For some mysterious end. You have
    done right (*to* MARY);

It's well to keep old innocent customs up.

(MARY BRUIN *has taken a bough of quicken wood from a seat and hung it on a nail in the doorpost. A girl child strangely dressed, perhaps in faery green, comes out of the wood and takes it away.*)

MARY. I had no sooner hung it on the nail
Before a child ran up out of the wind;
She has caught it in her hand and fondled it;
Her face is pale as water before dawn.

FATHER HART. Whose child can this be?

MAURTEEN. No one's child at all.
She often dreams that some one has gone by,
When there was nothing but a puff of wind.

MARY. They have taken away the blessed quicken wood,
They will not bring good luck into the house;
Yet I am glad that I was courteous to them,
For are not they, likewise, children of God?

FATHER HART. Colleen, they are the children of the fiend,
And they have power until the end of Time,
When God shall fight with them a great pitched battle
And hack them into pieces.

MARY. He will smile,
Father, perhaps, and open His great door.

FATHER HART. Did but the lawless angels see that door
They would fall, slain by everlasting peace;
And when such angels knock upon our doors,

Who goes with them must drive through the same storm.

(*A thin old arm comes round the door-post and knocks and beckons. It is clearly seen in the silvery light.* MARY BRUIN *goes to door and stands in it for a moment.* MAURTEEN BRUIN *is busy filling* FATHER HART'S *plate.* BRIDGET BRUIN *stirs the fire.*)

MARY (*coming to table*). There's somebody out there that beckoned me
And raised her hand as though it held a cup,
And she was drinking from it, so it may be
That she is thirsty.

(*She takes milk from the table and carries it to the door.*)

FATHER HART. That will be the child
That you would have it was no child at all.

BRIDGET. And maybe, Father, what he said was true;
For there is not another night in the year
So wicked as to-night.

MAURTEEN. Nothing can harm us
While the good Father's underneath our roof.

MARY. A little queer old woman dressed in green.

BRIDGET. The good people beg for milk and fire
Upon May Eve—woe to the house that gives,
For they have power upon it for a year.

MAURTEEN. Hush, woman, hush!

BRIDGET. She's given milk away.
I knew she would bring evil on the house.

MAURTEEN. Who was it?

MARY. Both the tongue and face were strange.

MAURTEEN. Some strangers came last week to Clover Hill;

She must be one of them.

BRIDGET. I am afraid.

FATHER HART. The Cross will keep all evil from the house
While it hangs there.

MAURTEEN. Come, sit beside me, colleen,
And put away your dreams of discontent,
For I would have you light up my last days,
Like the good glow of the turf; and when I die
You'll be the wealthiest hereabout, for, colleen,
I have a stocking full of yellow guineas
Hidden away where nobody can find it.

BRIDGET. You are the fool of every pretty face,
And I must spare and pinch that my son's wife
May have all kinds of ribbons for her head.

MAURTEEN. Do not be cross; she is a right good girl!
The butter is by your elbow, Father Hart.
My colleen, have not Fate and Time and Change
Done well for me and for old Bridget there?
We have a hundred acres of good land,
And sit beside each other at the fire.
I have this reverend Father for my friend,
I look upon your face and my son's face—
We've put his plate by yours—and here he comes,
And brings with him the only thing we have lacked,
Abundance of good wine. (SHAWN *comes in.*) Stir up the fire,
And put new turf upon it till it blaze;

To watch the turf-smoke coiling from the fire,
And feel content and wisdom in your heart,
This is the best of life; when we are young
We long to tread a way none trod before,
But find the excellent old way through love,
And through the care of children, to the hour
For bidding Fate and Time and Change goodbye.

(MARY *takes a sod of turf from the fire and goes out through the door.* SHAWN *follows her and meets her coming in.*)

SHAWN. What is it draws you to the chill o' the wood?
There is a light among the stems of the trees
That makes one shiver.

MARY. A little queer old man
Made me a sign to show he wanted fire
To light his pipe.

BRIDGET. You've given milk and fire
Upon the unluckiest night of the year and brought,
For all you know, evil upon the house.
Before you married you were idle and fine
And went about with ribbons on your head;
And now—no, Father, I will speak my mind—
She is not a fitting wife for any man——

SHAWN. Be quiet, Mother!

MAURTEEN. You are much too cross.

MARY. What do I care if I have given this house,
Where I must hear all day a bitter tongue,
Into the power of faeries!

BRIDGET. You know well

How calling the good people by that
　　name,
Or talking of them over much at all,
May bring all kinds of evil on the
　　house.

MARY. Come, faeries, take me out of
　　this dull house!
Let me have all the freedom I have
　　lost;
Work when I will and idle when I
　　will!
Faeries, come take me out of this
　　dull world,
For I would ride with you upon the
　　wind.
Run on the top of the dishevelled
　　tide,
And dance upon the mountains like
　　a flame.

FATHER HART. You cannot know the
　　meaning of your words.

MARY. Father, I am right weary of
　　four tongues:
A tongue that is too crafty and too
　　wise,
A tongue that is too godly and too
　　grave,
A tongue that is more bitter than
　　the tide,
And a kind tongue too full of drowsy
　　love,
Of drowsy love and my captivity.
　　(SHAWN BRUIN *leads her to a seat
　　at the left of the door.*)

SHAWN. Do not blame me; I often lie
　　awake
Thinking that all things trouble your
　　bright head.
How beautiful it is—your broad pale
　　forehead
Under a cloudy blossoming of hair!
Sit down beside me here—these are
　　too old,
And have forgotten they were ever
　　young.

MARY. O, you are the great door-post
　　of this house,
And I the branch of blessed quicken
　　wood,

And if I could I'd hang upon the
　　post,
Till I had brought good luck into
　　the house.
　　(*She would put her arms about
　　him, but looks shyly at the
　　priest and lets her arms fall.*)

FATHER HART. My daughter, take his
　　hand—by love alone
God binds us to Himself and to the
　　hearth,
That shuts us from the waste beyond
　　His peace,
From maddening freedom and be-
　　wildering light.

SHAWN. Would that the world were
　　mine to give it you,
And not its quiet hearths alone, but
　　even
All that bewilderment of light and
　　freedom,
If you would have it.

MARY. I would take the world
And break it into pieces in my hands
To see you smile watching it crum-
　　ble away.

SHAWN. Then I would mould a world
　　of fire and dew,
With no one bitter, grave or over
　　wise,
And nothing marred or old to do
　　you wrong,
And crowd the enraptured quiet of
　　the sky
With candles burning to your lonely
　　face.

MARY. Your looks are all the candles
　　that I need.

SHAWN. Once a fly dancing in a beam
　　of the sun,
Or the light wind blowing out of
　　the dawn,
Could fill your heart with dreams
　　none other knew,
But now the indissoluble sacrament
Has mixed your heart that was most
　　proud and cold
With my warm heart for ever; the
　　sun and moon

Must fade and heaven be rolled up
   like a scroll;
But your white spirit still walk by
   my spirit.
     (*A Voice singing in the wood.*)
MAURTEEN. There's some one singing.
   Why, it's but a child.
It sang, "The lonely of heart is
   withered away."
A strange song for a child, but she
   sings sweetly.
Listen, listen!
     (*Goes to door.*)
MARY. O, cling close to me,
Because I have said wicked things
   to-night.
THE VOICE. The wind blows out of the
   gates of the day,
The wind blows over the lonely of
   heart,
And the lonely of heart is withered
   away.
While the faeries dance in a place
   apart,
Shaking their milk-white feet in a
   ring,
Tossing their milk-white arms in the
   air;
For they hear the wind laugh and
   murmur and sing
Of a land where even the old are
   fair,
And even the wise are merry of
   tongue;
But I heard a reed of Coolaney say,
"When the wind has laughed and
   murmured and sung
The lonely of heart is withered
   away!"
MAURTEEN. Being happy, I would
   have all others happy,
So I will bring her in out of the cold.
     (*He brings in the faery child.*)
THE CHILD. I tire of winds and waters
   and pale lights.
MAURTEEN. And that's no wonder,
   for when night has fallen
The wood's a cold and a bewildering
   place,

But you are welcome here.
THE CHILD. I am welcome here.
For when I tire of this warm little
   house
There is one here that must away,
   away.
MAURTEEN. O, listen to her dreamy
   and strange talk.
Are you not cold?
THE CHILD. I will crouch down beside
   you,
For I have run a long, long way this
   night.
BRIDGET. You have a comely shape.
MAURTEEN. Your hair is wet.
BRIDGET. I'll warm your chilly feet.
MAURTEEN. You have come indeed
A long, long way—for I have never
   seen
Your pretty face—and must be tired
   and hungry,
Here is some bread and wine.
THE CHILD. The wine is bitter.
Old mother, have you no sweet food
   for me?
BRIDGET. I have some honey.
     (*She goes into the next room.*)
MAURTEEN. You have coaxing ways,
The mother was quite cross before
   you came.
     (BRIDGET *returns with the honey
     and fills a porringer with
     milk.*)
BRIDGET. She is the child of gentle
   people; look
At her white hands and at her pretty
   dress.
I've brought you some new milk, but
   wait a while
And I will put it to the fire to warm,
For things well fitted for poor folk
   like us
Would never please a high-born
   child like you.
THE CHILD. From dawn, when you
   must blow the fire ablaze,
You work your fingers to the bone,
   old mother.

The young may lie in bed and dream
and hope,
But you must work your fingers to
the bone
Because your heart is old.
BRIDGET. The young are idle.
THE CHILD. Your memories have made
you wise, old father;
The young must sigh through many
a dream and hope,
But you are wise because your heart
is old.
(BRIDGET *gives her more bread
and honey.*)
MAURTEEN. O, who would think to
find so young a girl
Loving old age and wisdom?
THE CHILD. No more, mother.
MAURTEEN. What a small bite! The
milk is ready now. (*Hands it
to her.*) What a small sip!
THE CHILD. Put on my shoes, old
mother.
Now I would like to dance now I
have eaten,
The reeds are dancing by Coolaney
lake,
And I would like to dance until the
reeds
And the white waves have danced
themselves asleep.
(BRIDGET *puts on the shoes, and
the* CHILD *is about to dance,
but suddenly sees the cruci-
fix and shrieks and covers
her eyes.*)
What is that ugly thing on the black
cross?
FATHER HART. You cannot know how
naughty your words are!
That is our Blessed Lord.
THE CHILD. Hide it away!
BRIDGET. I have begun to be afraid
again.
THE CHILD. Hide it away!
MAURTEEN. That would be wicked-
ness!
BRIDGET. That would be sacrilege!
THE CHILD. The tortured thing!

Hide it away!
MAURTEEN. Her parents are to blame.
FATHER HART. That is the image of
the Son of God.
THE CHILD (*caressing him*)
Hide it away, hide it away!
MAURTEEN. No, no.
FATHER HART. Because you are so
young and like a bird,
That must take fright at every stir
of the leaves,
I will go take it down.
THE CHILD. Hide it away!
And cover it out of sight and out
of mind!
(FATHER HART *takes crucifix from
wall and carries it towards
inner room.*)
FATHER HART. Since you have come
into this barony,
I will instruct you in our blessed
faith;
And being so keen witted you'll soon
learn.
(*To the others.*)
We must be tender to all budding
things,
Our Maker let no thought of Calvary
Trouble the morning stars in their
first song.
(*Puts crucifix in inner room.*)
THE CHILD. Here is level ground for
dancing; I will dance.
(*Sings.*)
"The wind blows out of the gates of
the day,
The wind blows over the lonely of
heart,
And the lonely of heart is withered
away."
(*She dances.*)
MARY (*to* SHAWN). Just now when she
came near I thought I heard
Other small steps beating upon the
floor,
And a faint music blowing in the
wind,
Invisible pipes giving her feet the
tune.

SHAWN. I heard no steps but hers.

MARY. I hear them now,
The unholy powers are dancing in
the house.

MAURTEEN. Come over here, and if
you promise me
Not to talk wickedly of holy things
I will give you something.

THE CHILD. Bring it me, old father.

MAURTEEN. Here are some ribbons
that I bought in the town
For my son's wife—but she will let
me give them
To tie up that wild hair the winds
have tumbled.

THE CHILD. Come, tell me, do you
love me?

MAURTEEN. Yes, I love you.

THE CHILD. Ah, but you love this fireside. Do you love me?

FATHER HART. When the Almighty
puts so great a share
Of His own ageless youth into a
creature,
To look is but to love.

THE CHILD. But you love Him?

BRIDGET. She is blaspheming.

THE CHILD. And do you love me too?

MARY. I do not know.

THE CHILD. You love that young man
there,
Yet I could make you ride upon the
winds,
Run on the top of the dishevelled
tide,
And dance upon the mountains like
a flame.

MARY. Queen of Angels and kind
saints defend us!
Some dreadful thing will happen.
A while ago
She took away the blessed quicken
wood.

FATHER HART. You fear because of her
unmeasured prattle;
She knows no better. Child, how old
are you?

THE CHILD. When winter sleep is
abroad my hair grows thin,
My feet unsteady. When the leaves
awaken
My mother carries me in her golden
arms;
I'll soon put on my womanhood and
marry
The spirits of wood and water, but
who can tell
When I was born for the first time?
I think
I am much older than the eagle cock
That blinks and blinks on Ballygaw-
ley Hill,
And he is the oldest thing under the
moon.

FATHER HART. O she is of the faery
people.

THE CHILD. One called,
I sent my messengers for milk and
fire,
She called again and after that I
came.
(*All except* SHAWN *and* MARY
BRUIN *gather behind the
priest for protection.*)

SHAWN (*rising*). Though you have
made all these obedient,
You have not charmed my sight and
won from me
A wish or gift to make you powerful;
I'll turn you from the house.

FATHER HART. No, I will face her.

THE CHILD. Because you took away the
crucifix
I am so mighty that there's none
can pass,
Unless I will it, where my feet have
danced
Or where I've whirled my finger-
tops.
(SHAWN *tries to approach her
and cannot.*)

MAURTEEN. Look, look!
There something stops him—look
how he moves his hands
As though he rubbed them on a wall
of glass!

FATHER HART. I will confront this mighty spirit alone;
Be not afraid, the Father is with us,
The Holy Martyrs and the Innocents,
The adoring Magi in their coats of mail,
And He who died and rose on the third day,
And all the nine angelic hierarchies.
(*The* CHILD *kneels upon the settle beside* MARY *and puts her arms about her.*)
Cry, daughter, to the Angels and the Saints.

THE CHILD. You shall go with me, newly-married bride,
And gaze upon a merrier multitude.
White-armed Nuala, Aengus of the Birds,
Feacra of the hurtling foam, and him
Who is the ruler of the Western Host,
Finvarra, and their Land of Heart's Desire,
Where beauty has no ebb, decay no flood,
But joy is wisdom, Time an endless song.
I kiss you and the world begins to fade.

SHAWN. Awake out of that trance—and cover up
Your eyes and ears.

FATHER HART. She must both look and listen,
For only the soul's choice can save her now.
Come over to me, daughter; stand beside me;
Think of this house and of your duties in it.

THE CHILD. Stay and come with me, newly-married bride,
For if you hear him you grow like the rest;
Bear children, cook, and bend above the churn,
And wrangle over butter, fowl, and eggs,
Until at last, grown old and bitter of tongue,
You're crouching there and shivering at the grave.

FATHER HART. Daughter, I point you out the way to Heaven.

THE CHILD. But I can lead you, newly-married bride,
Where nobody gets old and crafty and wise,
Where nobody gets old and godly and grave,
Where nobody gets old and bitter of tongue,
And where kind tongues bring no captivity;
For we are but obedient to the thoughts
That drift into the mind at a wink of the eye.

FATHER HART. By the dear Name of the One crucified,
I bid you, Mary Bruin, come to me.

THE CHILD. I keep you in the name of your own heart.

FATHER HART. It is because I put away the crucifix
That I am nothing, and my power is nothing.
I'll bring it here again.

MAURTEEN (*clinging to him*). No.

BRIDGET. Do not leave us.

FATHER HART. O, let me go before it is too late;
It is my sin alone that brought it all.
(*Singing outside.*)

THE CHILD. I hear them sing, "Come, newly-married bride,
Come, to the woods and waters and pale lights."

MARY. I will go with you.

FATHER HART. She is lost, alas!

THE CHILD (*standing by the door*). But clinging mortal hope must fall from you,
For we who ride the winds, run on the waves,

And dance upon the mountains are more light
Than dewdrops on the banner of the dawn.

MARY. O, take me with you.

SHAWN. Beloved, I will keep you.
I've more than words, I have these arms to hold you,
Nor all the faery host, do what they please,
Shall ever make me loosen you from these arms.

MARY. Dear face! Dear voice!

THE CHILD. Come, newly-married bride.

MARY. I always loved her world—and yet—and yet——

THE CHILD. White bird, white bird, come with me, little bird.

MARY. She calls me!

THE CHILD. Come with me, little bird.
(*Distant dancing figures appear in the wood.*)

MARY. I can hear songs and dancing.

SHAWN. Stay with me.

MARY. I think that I would stay—and yet—and yet——

THE CHILD. Come, little bird, with crest of gold.

MARY (*very softly*). And yet——

THE CHILD. Come, little bird with silver feet!
(MARY BRUIN *dies, and the* CHILD *goes.*)

SHAWN. She is dead!

BRIDGET. Come from that image; body and soul are gone.
You have thrown your arms about a drift of leaves,

Or bole of an ash-tree changed into her image.

FATHER HART. Thus do the spirits of evil snatch their prey,
Almost out of the very hand of God;
And day by day their power is more and more,
And men and women leave old paths, for pride
Comes knocking with thin knuckles on the heart.
(*Outside there are dancing figures, and it may be a white bird, and many voices singing:*)
"The wind blows out of the gates of the day,
The wind blows over the lonely of heart,
And the lonely of heart is withered away;
While the faeries dance in a place apart,
Shaking their milk-white feet in a ring,
Tossing their milk-white arms in the air;
For they hear the wind laugh and murmur and sing
Of a land where even the old are fair,
And even the wise are merry of tongue;
But I heard a reed of Coolaney say—
'When the wind has laughed and murmured and sung,
The lonely of heart is withered away.'"

THE WISDOM OF THE KING

THE high-queen of Ireland had died in childbirth, and her child was put to nurse with a woman who lived in a little house, within the border of the wood. One night the woman sat rocking the cradle, and meditating upon the beauty of the child, and praying that the gods might grant him wisdom equal to his beauty. There came a knock at the door, and she got up wondering, for the nearest neighbours were in the High-King's house a mile away and the night was now late. "Who is knocking?" she cried, and a thin voice answered, "Open! for I am a crone of the grey hawk, and I come from the darkness of the great wood." In terror she drew back the bolt, and a grey-clad woman, of a great age, and of a height more than human, came in and stood by the head of the cradle. The nurse shrank back against the wall, unable to take her eyes from the woman, for she saw by the gleaming of the firelight that the feathers of the grey hawk were upon her head instead of hair. "Open!" cried another voice, "for I am a crone of the grey hawk, and I watch over his nest in the darkness of the great wood." The nurse opened the door again, though her fingers could scarce hold the bolts for trembling, and another grey woman, not less old than the other, and with like feathers instead of hair, came in and stood by the first. In a little, came a third grey woman, and after her a fourth, and then another and another and another, until the hut was full of their immense bodies. They stood silent for a long time, but at last one muttered in a low thin voice: "Sisters, I knew him far away by the redness of his heart under his silver skin"; and then another spoke: "Sisters, I knew him because his heart fluttered like a bird under a net of silver cords"; and then another took up the word: "Sisters, I knew him because his heart sang like a bird that is happy in a silver cage." And after that they sang together, those who were nearest rocking the cradle with long wrinkled fingers; and their voices were now tender and caressing, now like the wind blowing in the great wood, and this was their song:

> Out of sight is out of mind:
> Long have man and woman-kind,
> Heavy of will and light of mood,
> Taken away our wheaten food,
>
> Taken away our Altar stone;
> Hail and rain and thunder alone,
> And red hearts we turn to grey,
> Are true till Time gutter away.

When the song had died out, the crone who had first spoken said: "We have nothing more to do but to mix a drop of our blood into his blood." And she scratched her arm with the sharp point of a spindle, which she had made the nurse bring to her, and let a drop of blood, grey as the mist, fall upon the lips of the child; and passed out into the darkness.

When the crones were gone, the nurse came to her courage again, and hurried to the High-King's house, and cried out in the midst of the assembly hall that the Sidhe had bent over the child that night; and the king and his poets and men of law went with her to the hut and gathered about the cradle, and were as noisy as magpies, and the child sat up and looked at them.

Two years passed over, and the king died; and the poets and the men of law ruled in the name of the child, but looked to see him become the master himself before long, for no one had seen so wise a child, and everything had been well but for a miracle that began to trouble all men; and all women, who, indeed, talked of it without ceasing. The feathers of the grey hawk had begun to grow in the child's hair, and though his nurse cut them continually, in but a little while they would be more numerous than ever. This had not been a matter of great importance, for miracles were a little thing in those days, but for an ancient law of Ireland that none who had any blemish of body could sit upon the throne; and as a grey hawk is a brute thing of the air, it was not possible to think of one in whose hair its feathers grew as other than marred and blasted; nor could the people separate from their admiration of the wisdom that grew in him a horror as at one of unhuman blood. Yet all were resolved that he should reign, for they had suffered much from foolish kings and their own disorders; and no one had any other fear but that his great wisdom might bid him obey the law, and call some other to reign in his stead.

When the child was seven years old the poets and the men of law were called together by the chief poet, and all these matters weighed and considered. The child had already seen that those about him had hair only, and, though they had told him that they too had had feathers but had lost them because of a sin committed by their forefathers, they knew that he would learn the truth when he began to wander into the country round about. After much consideration they made a new law commanding every one upon pain of death to mingle artificially the feathers of the grey hawk into his hair; and they sent men with nets and slings and bows into the countries round about to gather a sufficiency of feathers. They decreed also that any who told the truth to the child should be put to death.

The years passed, and the child grew from childhood into boyhood and from boyhood into manhood, and became busy with strange and subtle thought, distinctions between things long held the same, resemblance of things long held different. Multitudes came from other lands to see him and to question him, but there were guards set at the frontiers, who compelled all to wear the feathers of the grey hawk in their hair. While they listened to him his words seemed to make all darkness light and filled their hearts like music; but when they returned to their own lands his words seemed far off, and what they could remember too strange and subtle to help them in their lives. A number indeed did live differently afterwards, but their new life was less excellent than the old: some among them had long served a good cause, but when they heard him praise it, they returned to their own lands to find what they had loved less lovable, for he had taught them how little divides the false and true; others, again, who had served no cause, but had sought in peace the welfare of their own households, found their bones softer and less ready for toil, for he had shown them greater purposes; and numbers of the young, when they had heard him upon all these things, remembered certain strange words that made ordinary joys nothing, and sought impossible joys and grew unhappy.

Among those who came to look at him and to listen to him was the daughter of a little king who lived a great way off; and when he saw her he loved, for she was beautiful, with a beauty unlike that of other women; but her heart was like that of other women, and when she thought of the mystery of the hawk feathers she was afraid. Overwhelmed with his greatness, she half accepted, and yet half refused his love, and day by day the king gave her gifts the merchants had carried from India or maybe from China itself; and still she was ever between a smile and a frown; between yielding and withholding. He laid all his wisdom at her feet, and told a multitude of things that even the Sidhe have forgotten, and he thought she understood because her beauty was like wisdom.

There was a tall young man in the house who had yellow hair, and was skilled in wrestling; and one day the king heard his voice among the salley bushes. "My dear," it said, "I hate them for making you weave these dingy feathers into your beautiful hair, and all that the bird of prey upon the throne may sleep easy o' nights"; and then the low, musical voice he loved answered: "My hair is not beautiful like yours; and now that I have plucked the feathers out of your hair I will put my hands through it, thus, and thus, and thus; for it does not make me afraid." Then the king remembered many things that he had forgotten without understanding them, chance words of his poets and his men of law, doubts that he had reasoned away; and he called to the lovers in a trembling voice. They came from among the salley bushes and threw themselves at his feet and prayed for pardon. He stooped down and plucked the feathers out of the hair of the woman and turned away without a word. He went to the hall of assembly, and having gathered his poets and his men of law about him, stood upon the daïs and spoke in a loud, clear voice: "Men of law, why did you make me sin against the laws? Men of verse, why did you make me sin against the secrecy of wisdom? for law was made by man for the welfare of man, but wisdom the gods have made, and no man shall live by its light, for it and the hail and the rain and the thunder follow a way that is deadly to mortal things. Men of law and men of verse, live according to your kind, and call Eocha of the Hasty Mind to reign over you, for I set out to find my kindred." He then came down among them, and drew out of the hair of first one and then another the feathers of the grey hawk, and, having scattered them over the rushes upon the floor, passed out, and none dared to follow him, for his eyes gleamed like the eyes of the birds of prey; and no man saw him again or heard his voice.

DOWN BY THE SALLEY GARDENS

Down by the salley gardens my love and I did meet;
 She pass'd the salley gardens with little snow-white feet.
 She bid me take love easy, as the leaves grow on the tree;
But I, being young and foolish, with her would not agree.

In a field by the river my love and I did stand,
And on my leaning shoulder she laid her snow-white hand.
She bid me take life easy, as the grass grows on the weirs;
But I was young and foolish, and now am full of tears.

THE LAKE ISLE OF INNISFREE

I will arise and go now, and go to Innisfree,
 And a small cabin build there, of clay and wattles made;
 Nine bean rows will I have there, a hive for the honey bee,
 And live alone in the bee-loud glade.

And I shall have some peace there, for peace comes dropping slow,
Dropping from the veils of the morning to where the cricket sings;
There midnight's all a-glimmer, and noon a purple glow,
 And evening full of the linnet's wings.

I will arise and go now, for always night and day
I hear lake water lapping with low sounds by the shore;
While I stand on the roadway, or on the pavements gray,
 I hear it in the deep heart's core.

Jacinto Benavente

HIS WIDOW'S HUSBAND

CHARACTERS

CAROLINA	CASALONGA
EUDOSIA	ZURITA
PAQUITA	VALDIVIESO
FLORENCIO	

The scene is laid in a provincial capital

CAROLINA *is seated as* ZURITA *enters.*

ZURITA. My friend!

CAROLINA. My good Zurita, it is so thoughtful of you to come so promptly! I shall never be able to repay all your kindness.

ZURITA. I am always delighted to be of service to a friend.

CAROLINA. I asked them to look for you everywhere. Pardon the inconvenience, but the emergency was extreme. I am in a terrible position; all the tact in the world can never extricate me from one of those embarrassing predicaments—unless you assist me by your advice.

ZURITA. Count upon my advice; count upon me in anything. However, I cannot believe that you are really in an embarrassing predicament.

CAROLINA. But I am, my friend; and you are the only one who can advise me. You are a person of taste; your articles and society column are the standard of good form with us. Everybody accepts and respects your decisions.

ZURITA. Not invariably, I am sorry to say—especially now that I have taken up the suppression of the hips, which are fatal to the success of any *toilette*. Society was formerly very select in this city, but it is no longer the same, as you no doubt have occasion to know. Too many fortunes have been improvised, too many aristocratic families have descended in the scale. There has been a great change in society. The *parvenus* dominate—and money is so insolent! People who have it imagine that other things can be improvised—as education, for example, manners, good taste. Surely you must realize that such things cannot be improvised. Distinction is a hothouse plant. We grow too few gardenias nowadays—like you, my friend. On the other hand, we have an abundance of sow-thistles. Not that I am referring to the Nuñez family. . . . How do you suppose those ladies enliven their Wednesday evenings? With a gramophone, my friend, with a gramophone—just like any vulgar café; although I must confess that it is an improvement upon the days when the youngest sang, the middle one recited, and all played together.

Nevertheless it is horrible. You can imagine my distress.

CAROLINA. You know, of course, that I never take part in their Wednesdays. I never call unless I am sure they are not at home.

ZURITA. But that is no longer a protection; they leave the gramophone. And the maid invites you to wait and entertain yourself with the *Mochuelo*. What is a man to do? It is impossible to resent the records upon the maid. But we are wandering from the subject. You excite my curiosity.

CAROLINA. You know that to-morrow is the day of the unveiling of the statue of my husband, of my previous husband—

ZURITA. A fitting honor to the memory of that great, that illustrious man. This province owes him much, and so does all Spain. We who enjoyed the privilege of calling ourselves his friends, should be delighted to see justice done to his deserts at last, here where political jealousies and intrigue have always belittled the achievements of our eminent men. But Don Patricio Molinete could have no enemies. Tomorrow will atone for much of the pettiness of the past.

CAROLINA. No doubt. I feel I ought to be proud and happy, although you understand the delicacy of my position. Now that I have married again, my name is not the same. Yet it is impossible to ignore the fact that once it was mine, especially as everybody knows that we were a model couple. I might perhaps have avoided the situation by leaving town for a few days on account of my health, but then that might have been misinterpreted. People might have thought that I was displeased, or that I declined to participate.

ZURITA. Assuredly. Although your name is no longer the same, owing to circumstances, the force of which we appreciate, that is no reason why you should be deprived of the honor of having borne it worthily at the time. Your present husband has no right to take offense.

CAROLINA. No, poor Florencio! In fact, he was the first to realize that I ought to take a leading part in the rejoicing. Poor Florencio was always poor Patricio's greatest admirer. Their political ideas were the same; they agreed in everything.

ZURITA. Apparently.

CAROLINA. As I have reason to know. Poor Patricio loved me dearly; perhaps that was what led poor Florencio to imagine that there was something in me to justify the affection of that great-hearted and intelligent man. It was enough for me to know that Florencio was Patricio's most intimate friend in order to form my opinion of him. Of course, I recognize that Florencio's gifts will never enable him to shine so brilliantly, but that is not to say that he is wanting in ability. He lacks ambition, that is all. All his desires are satisfied at home with me, at his own fireside. And I am as well pleased to have it so. I am not ambitious myself. The seasons which I spent with my husband in Madrid were a source of great uneasiness to me. I passed the week during which he was Minister of Agriculture in one continual state of anxiety. Twice he nearly had a duel—over some political question. I did not know which way to turn. If he had ever become Prime Minister, as was actually predicted by a newspaper which he controlled, I should have been obliged to take to my bed for the week.

ZURITA. You are not like our senator's wife, Señora Espinosa, nor the wife of our present mayor. They will never rest, nor allow others to do so, until they see their husbands erected in marble.

CAROLINA. Do you think that either Espinosa or the mayor are of a caliber to deserve statues?

ZURITA. Not publicly, perhaps. In a private chapel, in the class of martyrs and husbands, it might not be inappropriate. But I am growing impatient.

CAROLINA. As you say, friend Zurita, it might seem marked for me to leave the city. Yet if I remain I must attend the unveiling of the monument to my poor Patricio; I must be present at the memorial exercises to-night in his honor; I must receive the delegations from Madrid and the other cities, as well as the committees from the rest of the province. But what attitude ought I to assume? If I seem too sad, nobody will believe that my feeling is sincere. On the other hand, it would not be proper to appear altogether reconciled. Then people would think that I had forgotten too quickly. In fact, they think so already.

ZURITA. Oh, no! You were very young when you became a widow. Life was just beginning for you.

CAROLINA. It is a delicate matter, however, to explain to my sisters-in-law. Tell me, what ought I to wear? Anything severe, an attempt at mourning, would be ridiculous, since I am going with my husband; on the other hand, I should not like to suggest a festive spirit. What do you think, friend Zurita? Give me your advice. What would you wear?

ZURITA. It is hard to say; the problem is difficult. Something rich and black, perhaps, relieved by a note of violet. The unveiling of a monument to perpetuate the memory of a great man is not an occasion for mourning. Your husband is partaking already of the joys of immortality, in which, no doubt, he anticipates you.

CAROLINA. Thank you so much.

ZURITA. Do not thank me. You have done enough. You have been faithful to his memory. You have married again, but you have married a man who was your husband's most intimate friend. You have not acted like other widows of my acquaintance—Señora Benítez, for example. She has been living for two years with the deadliest enemy her husband had in the province, without any pretense at getting married— which in her case would have been preposterous.

CAROLINA. There is no comparison.

ZURITA. No, my friend; everybody sympathizes with your position, as they ought.

CAROLINA. The only ones who worry me are my sisters-in-law. They insist that my position is ridiculous, and that of my husband still more so. They do not see how we can have the effrontery to present ourselves before the statue.

ZURITA. Señora, I should not hesitate though it were that of the Commander. Your sisters-in-law exaggerate. Your present husband is the only one you have to consider.

CAROLINA. I have no misgivings upon that score. I know that both will appreciate that my feelings are sincere, one in this world, and the other from the next. As for the rest, the rest——

ZURITA. The rest are your friends and your second husband's friends, as we were of the first. We shall all take your part. The others you can afford to neglect.

CAROLINA. Thanks for those words of comfort. I knew that you were a good friend of ours, as you were also of his.

ZURITA. A friend to both, to all

three; *sí, señora,* to all three. But here is your husband.

(DON FLORENCIO *enters.*)

ZURITA. Don Florencio! My friend!

FLORENCIO. My dear Zurita! I am delighted to see you! I wish to thank you for that charming article in memory of our never-to-be-forgotten friend. It was good of you, and I appreciate it. You have certainly proved yourself an excellent friend of his. Thanks, my dear Zurita, thanks! Carolina and I are both indebted to you for your charming article. It brought tears to our eyes. Am I right, Carolina?

CAROLINA. We were tremendously affected by it.

FLORENCIO. Friend Zurita, I am deeply gratified. For the first time in the history of the province, all parties have united to do honor to this region's most eminent son. But have you seen the monument? It is a work of art. The statue is a perfect likeness —it is the man, the man himself! The allegorical features are wonderfully artistic—Commerce, Industry, and Truth taken together in the nude. Nothing finer could be wished. You can imagine the trouble, however, we had with the nudes. The conservative element opposed the nudes, but the sculptor declined to proceed if the nudes were suppressed. In the end we won a decisive victory for Art.

CAROLINA. Do you know, I think it would have been just as well not to have had any nudes? What was the use of offending anybody? Several of our friends are going to remain away from the ceremonies upon that account.

FLORENCIO. How ridiculous! That only shows how far we are behind the times. You certainly have no feeling of that sort after having been the companion of that great, that liberal man. I remember the trip we took to Italy together—you surely recollect it, Carolina. I never saw a man so struck with admiration at those marvellous monuments of pagan and Renaissance art. Oh, what a man! What a wonderful man! He was an artist. Ah! Before I forget it, Carolina, Gutiérrez asked me for any pictures you have for the special edition of his paper, and I should like to have him publish the verses which he wrote you when you were first engaged. Did you ever see those verses? That man might have been a poet—he might have been anything else for that matter. Talk about letters! I wish you could see his letters. Carolina, let us see some of those letters he wrote you when you were engaged.

CAROLINA. Not now. This is hardly the time. . . .

FLORENCIO. Naturally. In spite of the satisfaction which we feel, these are trying days for us. We are united by our memories. I fear I shall never be able to control myself at the unveiling of the statue.

CAROLINA. Florencio, for heaven's sake, you must! You must control yourself.

ZURITA. Yes, do control yourself. You must.

FLORENCIO. I am controlling myself.

ZURITA. If there is nothing further that I can do. . . .

CAROLINA. No, thank you, Zurita. I am awfully obliged to you. Now that I know what I am to wear, the situation does not seem half so embarrassing.

ZURITA. I understand. A woman's position is never so embarrassing as when she is hesitating as to what to put on.

CAROLINA. Until to-morrow then?

ZURITA. Don Florencio!

FLORENCIO. Thank you again for your charming article. It was admirable! Admirable!

(ZURITA *retires.*)

FLORENCIO. I see that you feel it deeply; you are touched. So am I. It is foolish to attempt to conceal it.

CAROLINA. I don't know how to express it, but—I am upset.

FLORENCIO. Don't forget the pictures, however, especially the one where the three of us were taken together on the second platform of the Eiffel tower. It was particularly good.

CAROLINA. Yes, something out of the ordinary. Don't you think, perhaps, that our private affairs, our family life. . . . How do we know whether at this time, in our situation. . . .

FLORENCIO. What are you afraid of? That is the woman of it. How narrow-minded! You ought to be above such pettiness after having been the wife of such an intelligent man. Every detail of the private life of the great has its interest for history. Those of us who knew him, who in a certain sense were his colaborers—you will not accuse me of immodesty—his colaborers in the great work of his life, owe it to history to see that the truth be known.

CAROLINA. Nevertheless I hardly think I would print those letters—much less the verses. Do you remember what they said?

FLORENCIO. Of course I remember:

"Like a moth on a pin I preserve all
    your kisses! . . ."

Everybody makes allowances for poetry. Nobody is going to take seriously what he reads in a poem. He married you anyway. Why should any one object?

CAROLINA. Stop, Florencio! What are you talking about? We are making ourselves ridiculous.

FLORENCIO. Why should we make ourselves ridiculous? Although I shall certainly stand by you, whatever you decide, if for no other reason than that I am your husband, his widow's husband. Otherwise people might think that I wanted you to forget, that I was jealous of his memory; and you know that is not the case. You know how I admired him, how I loved him—just as he did me. Nobody could get along with him as well as I could; he was not easy to get along with, I do not need to tell you that. He had his peculiarities—they were the peculiarities of a great man—but they were great peculiarities. Like all great men, he had an exaggerated opinion of himself. He was horribly stubborn, like all strong characters. Whenever he got on one of his hobbies no power on earth could pry him off of it. It is only out of respect that I do not say he was pigheaded. I was the only one who had the tact and the patience to do anything with him; you know that well enough. How often you said to me: "Oh, Florencio! I can't stand it any longer!" And then I would reason with you and talk to him, and every time that you had a quarrel I was the one who consoled you afterward.

CAROLINA. Florencio, you are perfectly disgusting! You have no right to talk like this.

FLORENCIO. Very well then, my dear. I understand how you feel. This is a time when everybody is dwelling on his virtues, his good qualities, but I want you to remember that that great man had also his faults.

CAROLINA. You don't know what you are talking about.

FLORENCIO. Compare me with him——

CAROLINA. Florencio! You know that in my mind there has never been any comparison. Comparisons are odious.

FLORENCIO. Not necessarily. But of course you have not! You have never regretted giving up his distinguished name, have you, Carolina, for this humble one of mine? Only I want you to understand that if I had desired to shine, if I had been ambitious. . . . I have talent myself. Now admit it!

CAROLINA. Of course I do, my dear, of course! But what is the use of talking nonsense?

FLORENCIO. What is the matter with you, anyway? You are nervous to-day. It is impossible to conduct a sensible conversation.—Hello! Your sisters-in-law! I am not at home.

CAROLINA. Don't excite yourself. They never ask for you.

FLORENCIO. I am delighted! . . . . Well, I wish you a short session and escape.

CAROLINA. I am in a fine humor for this sort of thing myself.

(FLORENCIO *goes out.*

EUDOSIA *and* PAQUITA *enter.*)

EUDOSIA. I trust that we do not intrude?

CAROLINA. How can you ask? Come right in.

EUDOSIA. It seems we find you at home for once.

CAROLINA. So it seems.

PAQUITA. Strange to say, whenever we call you always appear to be out.

CAROLINA. A coincidence.

EUDOSIA. The coincidence is to find you at home. [*A pause*] We passed your husband on the street.

CAROLINA. Are you sure that you would recognize him?

PAQUITA. Oh! He was not alone.

CAROLINA. Is that so?

EUDOSIA. Paquita saw him with Somolino's wife, at Sanchez the confectioner's.

CAROLINA. Very possibly.

PAQUITA. I should not make light of it, if I were you. You know what Somolino's wife is, to say nothing of Sanchez the confectioner.

CAROLINA. I didn't know about the confectioner.

EUDOSIA. No respectable woman, no woman who even pretends to be respectable, would set foot in his shop since he married that French girl.

CAROLINA. I didn't know about the French girl.

EUDOSIA. Yes, he married her—I say married her to avoid using another term. He married her in Bayonne—if you call such a thing marriage—civilly, which is the way French people marry. It is a land of perdition.

CAROLINA. I am very sorry to hear it because I am awfully fond of sweetmeats. I adore *bonbons* and *marrons glacés,* and nobody here has as good ones as Sanchez, nor anywhere else for that matter.

PAQUITA. In that case you had as well deny yourself, unless you are prepared to invite criticism. Somolino's wife is the only woman who enters the shop and faces the French girl, who gave her a recipe for dyeing her hair on the spot. You must have noticed how she is doing it now.

CAROLINA. I hadn't noticed.

EUDOSIA. It is not jet-black any more; it is baby-pink—so she is having the Frenchwoman manicure her nails twice a week. Have you noticed the condition of her nails? They are the talk of the town.

(*A pause.*

PAQUITA. Well, I trust he is satisfied.

CAROLINA. Who is he?

PAQUITA. I do not call him your husband. Oh, our poor, dear brother!

CAROLINA. I have not the slightest idea what you are talking about.

EUDOSIA. So he has had his way at last and desecrated the statue of our poor brother with the figures of those naked women?

PAQUITA. As large as life.

CAROLINA. But Florencio is not responsible. It was the sculptor and the committee. I cannot see anything objectionable in them myself. There are such figures on all monuments. They are allegorical.

EUDOSIA. I could understand, perhaps, why the statue of Truth should be unclothed. Something of the sort was always expected of Truth. But I must say that Commerce and Industry might have had a tunic at least. Commerce, in my opinion, is particularly indecent.

PAQUITA. We have declined the seats which were reserved for us. They were directly in front and you could see everything.

EUDOSIA. I suppose you still intend to be present? What a pity that there is nobody to give you proper advice!

CAROLINA. As I have been invited, I judge that I shall be welcome as I am.

PAQUITA. Possibly—if it were good form for you to appear at all. But when you exhibit yourself with that man—who was his best friend—after only three short years!

CAROLINA. Three long years.

EUDOSIA. No doubt they seemed long to you. Three years, did I say? They were like days to us who still keep his memory green!

PAQUITA. Who still bear his name, because no other name sounds so noble in our ears.

EUDOSIA. Rather than change it, we have declined very flattering proposals.

CAROLINA. I am afraid that you have made a mistake. You remember that your brother was very anxious to see you married.

PAQUITA. He imagined that all men were like him, and deserved wives like us, our poor, dear brother! Who would ever have dreamed he could have been forgotten so soon? Fancy his emotions as he looks down on you from the skies.

CAROLINA. I do not believe for one moment that he has any regrets. If he had, then what would be the use of being in paradise? Don't you worry about me. The best thing that a young widow can do is marry at once. I was a very young widow.

EUDOSIA. You were twenty-nine.

CAROLINA. Twenty-six.

EUDOSIA. We concede you twenty-six. At all events, you were not a child—not to speak of the fact that no widow can be said to be a child.

CAROLINA. No more than a single woman can be said to be old. However, I fail to see that there would be any impropriety in my being present at the unveiling of the statue.

EUDOSIA. Do you realize that the premature death of your husband will be the subject of all the speakers? They will dwell on the bereavement which we have suffered through the loss of such an eminent man. How do you propose to take it? When people see you standing there, complacent and satisfied, alongside of that man, do you suppose they will ever believe that you are not reconciled?

PAQUITA. What will your husband do while they are extolling the genius of our brother, and he knows that he never had any?

CAROLINA. That was not your

brother's opinion. He thought very highly of Florencio.

EUDOSIA. Very highly. Our poor, dear brother! Among his other abilities he certainly had an extraordinary aptitude for allowing himself to be deceived.

CAROLINA. That assumption is offensive to me; it is unfair to all of us.

EUDOSIA. I hope you brought it with you, Paquita?

PAQUITA. Yes; here it is.
(*Taking out a book.*)

EUDOSIA. Just look through this book if you have a moment. It arrived to-day from Madrid and is on sale at Valdivieso's. Just glance through it.

CAROLINA. What is the book? (*Reading the title upon the cover*) "Don Patricio Molinete, the Man and His Work. A Biography. Together with His Correspondence and an Estimate of His Life." Why, thanks——

PAQUITA. No, do not thank us. Read, read what our poor brother has written to the author of this book, who was one of his intimate friends.

CAROLINA. Recaredo Casalonga. Ah! I remember—a rascal we were obliged to turn out of the house. Do you mean to say that scamp Casalonga has any letters? Merely to hear the name makes me nervous.

EUDOSIA. But go on! Page two hundred and fourteen. Is that the page, Paquita?

PAQUITA. It begins on page two hundred and fourteen, but before it amounts to anything you turn the page.

CAROLINA. Quick, quick! Let me see. What does he say? What are these letters? What is this? He says that I. . . . But there is not a word of truth in it. My husband could never have written this.

EUDOSIA. But there it is in cold type. You don't suppose they would dare to print——

CAROLINA. But this is outrageous; this book is a libel. It invades the private life—the most private part of it! It must be stopped.

EUDOSIA. It cannot be stopped. You will soon see whether or not it can be stopped.

PAQUITA. Probably the edition is exhausted by this time.

CAROLINA. Is that so? We shall see! We shall see!—Florencio! Florencio! Come quickly! Florencio!

EUDOSIA. Perhaps he has not yet returned.

PAQUITA. He seemed to be enjoying himself.

CAROLINA. Nonsense! He was never out of the house. You are two old busybodies!

EUDOSIA. Carolina! You said that without thinking.

PAQUITA. I cannot believe my ears. Did you say busybodies?

CAROLINA. That is exactly what I said. Now leave me alone. I can't stand it. It is all your fault. You are insupportable!

EUDOSIA AND PAQUITA. Carolina!

CAROLINA. Florencio! Florencio!

(FLORENCIO *enters.*)

FLORENCIO. What is it, my dear? What is the matter? Ah! You? I am delighted. . . .

EUDOSIA. Yes, we! And we are leaving this house, where we have been insulted—forever!

PAQUITA. Where we have been called busybodies!

EUDOSIA. Where we have been told that we were insupportable!

PAQUITA. And when people say such things you can imagine what they think!

FLORENCIO. But Eudosia, Paquita. . . . I do not understand. As far as I am concerned. . . .

EUDOSIA. The person who is now your wife will make her explanations to you.

PAQUITA. I never expected to be driven out of our brother's house like this!

EUDOSIA. Our poor, dear brother!

FLORENCIO. But Carolina——

CAROLINA. Let them go! Let them go! They are impossible.

PAQUITA. Did you hear that, Eudosia? We are impossible!

EUDOSIA. I heard it, Paquita. There is nothing left for us to hear in this house.

CAROLINA. Yes there is! You are as impossible as all old maids.

EUDOSIA. There was something for us to hear after all! Come, Paquita.

PAQUITA. Come, Eudosia.

(*They go out.*)

FLORENCIO. What is this trouble between you and your sisters-in-law?

CAROLINA. There isn't any trouble. We were arguing, that was all. There is nothing those women like so much as gossip, or making themselves disagreeable in any way they can. Do you remember Casalonga?

FLORENCIO. Recaredo Casalonga? I should say I did remember him! That man was a character, and strange to say, a profound philosopher with it all. He was quite a humorist.

CAROLINA. Yes, he was. Well, this philosopher, this humorist, has conceived the terribly humorous idea of publishing this book.

FLORENCIO. Let me see. "Don Patricio Molinete, the Man and His Work. A Biography. Together with His Correspondence and an Estimate of His Life." A capital idea! They were great friends, you know, although I don't suppose that there can be anything particular in the book. What could Casalonga tell us anyway?

CAROLINA. Us? Nothing. But go on, go on.

FLORENCIO. You don't say! Letters of Patricio's. Addressed to whom?

CAROLINA. To the author of the book, so it seems. Personal letters, they are confidential. Go on, go on.

FLORENCIO. "Dear Friend: Life is sad. Perhaps you ask the cause of my disillusionment. How is it that I have lost my faith in the future, in the future of our unfortunate land?" I remember that time. He was already ill. This letter was written after he had liver complaint and took a dark view of everything. Ah! What a pity that great men should be subject to such infirmities! Think of the intellect being made the slave of the liver! We are but dust. "The future of this unfortunate land. . . ."

CAROLINA. No, that doesn't amount to anything. Lower down, lower down. Go on.

FLORENCIO. "Life is sad!"

CAROLINA. Are you beginning all over again?

FLORENCIO. No, he repeats himself. What is this? "I never loved but once in my life; I never loved but one woman—my wife." He means you.

CAROLINA. Yes. Go on, go on.

FLORENCIO. "I never trusted but one friend, my friend Florencio." He means me.

CAROLINA. Yes, yes; he means you. But go on, go on.

FLORENCIO. I wonder what he can be driving at. Ah! What does he say? That you, that I. . . .

CAROLINA. Go on, go on.

FLORENCIO. "This woman and this man, the two greatest, the two pure, the two unselfish passions of my life, in whom my very being was consumed—how can I bring myself to confess it? I hardly dare admit it to myself! They are in love—they love each other madly—in secret—perhaps without even suspecting themselves."

CAROLINA. What do you think of that?

FLORENCIO. Suspecting themselves. . . . "They are struggling to overcome their guilty passion, but how long will they continue to struggle? Yet I am sorry for them both. What ought I to do? I cannot sleep."

CAROLINA. What do you say?

FLORENCIO. Impossible! He never wrote such letters. Besides, if he did, they ought never to have been published.

CAROLINA. But true or false, they have been published, and here they are. Ah! But this is nothing! You ought to see what he says farther on. He goes on communicating his observations, and there are some, to be perfectly frank, which nobody could have made but himself.

FLORENCIO. You don't mean to tell me that you think these letters are genuine?

CAROLINA. They might be for all we know. He gives dates and details.

FLORENCIO. And all the time we thought he suspected nothing!

CAROLINA. You do jump so at conclusions, Florencio. How could he suspect? You know how careful we were about everything, no matter what happened, so as not to hurt his feelings.

FLORENCIO. This only goes to show all the good that it did us.

CAROLINA. He could only suspect —that it was the truth; that we were loving in silence.

FLORENCIO. Then perhaps you can explain to me what was the use of all this silence? Don't you see that what he has done now is to go and blurt the whole thing out to this rascal Casalonga?—an unscrupulous knave whose only interest in the matter is to turn these confidences to his own advantage! It is useless to attempt to defend it. Such foolishness was unpardonable. I should never have believed it of my friend. If he had any doubts about me— about us—why didn't he say so? Then we could have been more careful, and have done something to ease his mind. But this notion of running and telling the first person who happens along. . . . What a position does it leave me in? In what light do we appear at this time? Now, when everybody is paying respect to his memory, and I have put myself to all this trouble in order to raise money for this monument—what are people going to think when they read these things?

CAROLINA. I always said that we would have trouble with that monument.

FLORENCIO. How shall I have the face to present myself to-morrow before the monument?

CAROLINA. My sisters-in-law were right. We are going to be conspicuous.

FLORENCIO. Ah! But this must be stopped. I shall run at once to the offices of the papers, to the judicial authorities, to the governor, to all the booksellers. As for this Casalonga— Ah! I will settle with him! Either he will retract and confess that these letters are forgeries from beginning to end, or I will kill him! I will fight with him in earnest!

CAROLINA. Florencio! Don't forget yourself! You are going too far. You don't mean a duel? To expose your life?

FLORENCIO. Don't you see that it is impossible to submit to such an indignity? Where is this thing going to stop? Is nobody's private life to be secure? And this goes deeper than the private life—it impugns the sanctity of our intentions.

CAROLINA. No, Florencio!

FLORENCIO. Let me go!

CAROLINA. Florencio! Anything but a duel! No, no!

FLORENCIO. Ah! Either he will retract and withdraw the edition of this libel or, should he refuse. . . .

CAROLINA. Zurita!

FLORENCIO. My friend. . . . You are just in time!

(ZURITA *enters.*)

ZURITA. Don Florencio. . . . Carolina. . . . Don't say a word! I know how you feel.

FLORENCIO. Did you see it? Did you hear it? Is this a civilized country in which we live?

CAROLINA. But surely he has not heard it already?

ZURITA. Yes, at the Club. Some one had the book; they were passing it around. . . .

FLORENCIO. At the Club?

ZURITA. Don't be alarmed. Everybody thinks it is blackmail—a case of *chantage*. Don Patricio could never have written such letters.

FLORENCIO. Ah! So they think that?

ZURITA. Even if he had, they deal with private matters, which ought never to have been made public.

FLORENCIO. Exactly my idea—with private matters; they are confidential.

ZURITA. I lost no time, as you may be sure, in hurrying to Valdivieso's shop, where the books are on sale. I found him amazed; he was entirely innocent. He bought the copies supposing that the subject was of timely importance; that it was of a serious nature. He hurried at once to withdraw the copies from the window, and ran in search of the author.

FLORENCIO. Of the author? Is the author in town?

ZURITA. Yes, he came with the books; he arrived with them this morning.

FLORENCIO. Ah! So this scamp Casalonga is here, is he? Tell me where I can find him!

ZURITA. At the Hotel de Europa.

CAROLINA. Florencio! Don't you go! Hold him back! He means to challenge him.

ZURITA. Never! It is not worth the trouble. Besides, you ought to hold yourself above such things. Your wife is above them.

FLORENCIO. But what will people say, friend Zurita? What will people say?

ZURITA. Everybody thinks it is a huge joke.

FLORENCIO. A joke? Then our position is ridiculous.

ZURITA. I did not say that. What I do say. . . .

FLORENCIO. No, no, friend Zurita; you are a man of honor, you know that it is necessary for me to kill this man.

CAROLINA. But suppose he is the one who kills you? No, Florencio, not a duel! What is the use of the courts?

FLORENCIO. No, I prefer to fight. My dear Zurita, run in search of another friend and stop at the Hotel de Europa as my representatives. Seek out this man, exact reparation upon the spot—a reparation which shall be resounding, complete. Either he declares over his own signature that those letters are impudent forgeries or, should he refuse. . . .

CAROLINA. Florencio!

FLORENCIO. Stop at nothing! Do not haggle over terms. Let it be pistols with real bullets, as we pace forward each to each!

ZURITA. But Don Florencio!

CAROLINA. Don't go, I beg of you! Don't leave the house!

FLORENCIO. You are my friend—go at once!

CAROLINA. No, he will never go!

ZURITA. But Don Florencio! Consider. . . . The situation is serious.

FLORENCIO. When a man is made ridiculous the situation ceases to be serious! How shall I have the face to show myself before the monument? I—his most intimate friend! She, my wife, his widow! And everybody thinking all the while of those letters, imagining that I, that she. . . . No, no! Run! Bring me that retraction at once.

ZURITA. Not so fast! I hear the voice of Valdivieso.

FLORENCIO. Eh? And Casalonga's! Has that man the audacity to present himself in my house?

ZURITA. Be calm! Since he is here, perhaps he comes to explain. Let me see—— (*He goes out.*

CAROLINA. Florencio! Don't you receive him! Don't you have anything to do with that man!

FLORENCIO. I am in my own house. Never fear! I shall not forget to conduct myself as a gentleman. Now we shall see how he explains the matter; we shall see. But you had better retire first. Questions of honor are not for women.

CAROLINA. You know best; only I think I might remain within earshot. I am nervous. My dear!—Where are your arms?

FLORENCIO. What do I need of arms?

CAROLINA. Be careful just the same. Keep cool! Think of me.

FLORENCIO. I am in my own house. Have no fear.

CAROLINA. It upsets me dreadfully to see you in such a state.

FLORENCIO. What are you doing now?

CAROLINA. Removing these vases in case you should throw things. I

should hate awfully to lose them; they were a present.

FLORENCIO. Hurry, dear!

CAROLINA. I am horribly nervous. Keep cool, for heavens' sake! Control yourself. (*Goes out.*

(ZURITA *re-enters.*)

ZURITA. Are you calmer now?

FLORENCIO. Absolutely. Is that man here?

ZURITA. Yes, Valdivieso brought him. He desires to explain.

FLORENCIO. Who? Valdivieso? Naturally. But that other fellow, that Casalonga—what does he want?

ZURITA. To have a few words with you; to offer a thousand explanations.

FLORENCIO. No more than one explanation is possible.

ZURITA. Consider a moment. In my opinion it will be wiser to receive him. He appears to be innocent.

FLORENCIO. Of the first instincts of a gentleman.

ZURITA. Exactly. I did not venture to put it so plainly. He attaches no importance to the affair whatever.

FLORENCIO. Of course not! It is nothing to him.

ZURITA. Nothing. However, you will find him disposed to go to any length—retract, make a denial, withdraw the book from circulation. You had best have a few words with him. But first promise me to control yourself. Shall I ask them to come in?

FLORENCIO. Yes. . . . yes! Ask them to come in.

ZURITA. Poor Valdivieso is awfully put out. He always had such a high opinion of you. You are one of the two or three persons in this town who buy books. It would be a tremendous relief to him if you would only tell him that you knew he was incapable. . . .

FLORENCIO. Thoroughly! Poor Valdivieso! Ask him to come in; ask them both to come in.

(ZURITA *retires and returns presently with* VALDIVIESO *and* CASALONGA.)

VALDIVIESO. Señor Don Florencio! I hardly know what to say. I am sure that you will not question my good faith in the matter. I had no idea. . . . in fact I never suspected. . . .

FLORENCIO. I always knew you were innocent; but this person. . . .

CASALONGA. Come, come now! Don't blame it on me. How the devil was I to know that you were here—and married to his widow! Sport for the gods!

FLORENCIO. Do you hear what he says?

ZURITA. I told you that he appeared to be innocent.

FLORENCIO. And I told you that he was devoid of the first instincts of a gentleman; although I failed to realize to what an extent. Sir——

CASALONGA. Don't be absurd! Stop making faces at me.

FLORENCIO. In the first place, I don't recall that we were ever so intimate.

CASALONGA. Of course we were! Of course! Anyhow, what difference does it make? We were together for a whole season; we were inseparable. Hard times those for us both! But what did we care? When one of us was out of money, all he had to do was to ask the other, and be satisfied.

FLORENCIO. Yes; I seem to recall that the other was always I.

CASALONGA. Ha, ha, ha! That might be. Stranger things have happened. But you are not angry with me, are you? The thing is not worth all this fuss.

FLORENCIO. Do you hear what he says?

VALDIVIESO. You may be sure that if I had had the slightest idea. . . .

I bought the books so as to take advantage of the timeliness of the monument. If I had ever suspected. . . .

CASALONGA. Identically my position —to take advantage of the monument. Life is hard. While the conservatives are in power, I am reduced to extremities. I am at my wit's end to earn an honest penny.

FLORENCIO. I admire your colossal impudence. What are you going to do with a man like this?

ZURITA. Exactly the question that occurred to me. What are you going to do?

CASALONGA. For a time I was reduced to writing plays—like everybody else—although mine were better. That was the reason they did not succeed. Then I married my last landlady; I was obliged to settle with her somehow. A little difference arose between us, so we agreed to separate amicably after smashing all the furniture. However, that will be of no interest to you.

FLORENCIO. No, no, it is of no interest to me.

CASALONGA. A novel, my boy! A veritable work of romance! I wandered all over the country explaining views for the cinematograph. You know what a gift I have for talk? Wherever I appeared the picture houses were crowded—even to the exits. Then my voice gave out. I was obliged to find some other outlet for my activities. I thought of my friends. You know what friends are; as soon as a man needs them he hasn't any friends. Which way was I to turn? I happened to hear that you were unveiling a monument to the memory of friend Patricio. Poor Patricio! That man was a friend! He could always be relied upon. It occurred to me that I might write out a few pages of reminiscences—preferably something personal—and publish any letters of his which I had chanced to preserve.

FLORENCIO. What luck!

CASALONGA. Pshaw! Bread and butter—bread and butter, man! A mere pittance. It occurred to me that they would sell better here than anywhere else—this is where he lived. So I came this morning third class—think of that, third class!—and hurried at once to this fellow's shop. I placed two thousand copies with him, which he took from me at a horrible discount. You know what these booksellers are. . . .

VALDIVIESO. I call you to witness—what was customary under the circumstances. He was selling for cash.

CASALONGA. Am I the man to deny it? You can divide mankind into two classes—knaves and fools.

VALDIVIESO. Listen to this—

CASALONGA. You are not one of the fools.

VALDIVIESO. I protest! How am I to profit by the transaction? Do you suppose that I shall sell a single copy of this libel now that I know that it is offensive to my particular, my excellent friend, Don Florencio, and to his respected wife?

FLORENCIO. Thanks, friend Valdivieso, thanks for that.

VALDIVIESO. I shall burn the edition, although you can imagine what that will cost.

FLORENCIO. The loss will be mine. It will be at my expense.

CASALONGA. What did I tell you? Florencio will pay. What are you complaining about?—If I were in your place, though, I'd be hanged if I would give the man one penny.

VALDIVIESO. What? When you have collected spot cash?

CASALONGA. You don't call that collecting? Not at that discount. The paper was worth more.

FLORENCIO. The impudence of the thing was worth more than the paper.

CASALONGA. Ha, ha, ha! Really, I cannot find it in my heart to be angry with you. You are too clever! But what was I to do? I had to find some outlet for my activities. Are you going to kill me?

FLORENCIO. I have made my arrangements. Do you suppose that I will submit meekly to such an indignity? If you refuse to fight, I will hale you before the courts.

CASALONGA. Drop that tragic tone. A duel? Between us? Over what? Because the wife of a friend—who at the same time happens to be your wife—has been intimate with you? Suppose it had been with some one else!

FLORENCIO. That supposition is improper.

CASALONGA. You are the first man I ever heard of who was offended because it was said that he had been intimate with his wife. The thing is preposterous. How are we ever going to fight over it?

ZURITA. I can see his point of view.

FLORENCIO. Patricio could never have written those letters, much less to you.

CASALONGA. Talk as much as you like, the letters are genuine. Although it may have been foolish of Patricio to have written them—that is a debatable question. I published them so as to enliven the book. A little harmless suggestion—people look for it; it adds spice. Aside from that, what motive could I have had for dragging you into it?

FLORENCIO. I admire your frankness at least.

ZURITA. What do you propose to do with this man?

FLORENCIO. What do you propose?

CASALONGA. You know I was always

fond of you. You are a man of ability.

FLORENCIO. Thanks.

CASALONGA. You have more ability than Patricio had. He was a worthy soul, no doubt, but between us, who were in the secret, an utter blockhead.

FLORENCIO. Hardly that.

CASALONGA. I need not tell you what reputations amount to in this country. If he had had your brains, your transcendent ability. . . .

FLORENCIO. How can I stop this man from talking?

CASALONGA. You have always been too modest in my opinion; you have remained in the background in order to give him a chance to shine, to attract attention. Everybody knows that his best speeches were written by you.

FLORENCIO. You have no right to betray my confidence.

CASALONGA. Yes, gentlemen, it is only just that you should know. The real brains belonged to this man, he is the one who should have had the statue. As a friend he is wonderful, unique!

FLORENCIO. How am I going to fight with this man?

CASALONGA. I will give out a statement at once—for public consumption—declaring that the letters are forgeries—or whatever you think best; as it appeals to you. Fix it up for yourself. It is of no consequence anyhow. I am above this sort of thing. I should be sorry, however, to see this fellow receive more than his due, which is two *reals* a copy, or what he paid me.

VALDIVIESO. I cannot permit you to meddle in my affairs. You are a rogue and a cheat.

CASALONGA. A rogue and a cheat? In that case you are the one I will fight with. You are no friend of mine. You are an exploiter of other men's brains.

VALDIVIESO. You are willing to fight with me, are you—a respectable man, the father of a family? After swindling me out of my money!

CASALONGA. Swindling? That is no language to use in this house.

VALDIVIESO. I use it where I like.

FLORENCIO. Gentlemen, gentlemen! This is my house, this is the house of my wife!

ZURITA. Valdivieso!

CASALONGA. (*To* FLORENCIO). I choose you for my second. And you too, my friend—what is your name?

VALDIVIESO. But will you listen to him? Do you suppose that I will fight with this rascal, with the first knave who happens along? I, the father of a family?

CASALONGA. I cannot accept your explanation. My friends will confer with yours and apprise us as to the details. Have everything ready for this afternoon.

VALDIVIESO. Do you stand here and sanction this nonsense? You cannot believe one word that he says. No doubt it would be convenient for you to retire and use me as a Turk's head to receive all the blows, when you are the one who ought to fight!

FLORENCIO. Friend Valdivieso, I cannot permit reflections upon my conduct from you. After all, you need not have purchased the book, which you did for money, knowing that it was improper, since it contained matter which was offensive to me.

VALDIVIESO. Are you speaking in earnest?

FLORENCIO. I was never more in earnest in my life.

CASALONGA. Yes, sir, and it is high time for us all to realize that it is in earnest. It was all your fault. Nobody buys without sampling the wares. It was your business to have pointed out to me the indiscretion I was about to commit. (*To* FLORENCIO) I am perfectly willing to withdraw if you wish to fight him, to yield my place as the aggrieved party to you. I should be delighted to act as one of your seconds, with our good friend here—what is your name?

ZURITA. Zurita.

CASALONGA. My good friend Zurita.

VALDIVIESO. Am I losing my mind? This is a trap which you have set for me, a despicable trap!

FLORENCIO. Friend Valdivieso, I cannot tolerate these reflections. I am incapable of setting a trap.

ZURITA. Ah! And so am I! When you entered this house you were familiar with its reputation.

CASALONGA. You have forgotten with whom you are speaking.

VALDIVIESO. Nonsense! This is too much. I wash my hands of the whole business. Is this the spirit in which my advances are received? What I will do now is sell the book—and if I can't sell it, I will give it away! Everybody can read it then—and they can talk as much as they want to. This is the end! I am through.

FLORENCIO. Wait? What was that? I warn you not to sell so much as one copy!

ZURITA. I should be sorry if you did. Take care not to drag me into it.

CASALONGA. Nor me either.

VALDIVIESO. Enough! Do as you see fit—and I shall do the same. This is the end—the absolute end! It is the finish! (*Rushes out.*

FLORENCIO. Stop him!

CASALONGA. It won't be necessary. I shall go to the shop and take back the edition. Whatever you intended to pay him you can hand directly to me. I am your friend; besides I need the money. This man shall not get

the best of me. Oh! By the way, what are you doing to-night? Have dinner with me. I shall expect you at the hotel. Don't forget! If you don't show up, I may drop in myself and have dinner with you.

FLORENCIO. No! What would my wife say? She has trouble enough.

CASALONGA. Nonsense! She knows me, and we should have a good laugh. Is she as charming, as good-looking, as striking as ever? I am keen for her. I don't need to ask whether she is happy. Poor Patricio was a character! What a sight he was! What a figure! And age doubled him for good measure. I'll look in on you later. It has been a rare pleasure this time. There are few friends like you. Come, shake hands! I am touched; you know how it is. See you later! If I don't come back, I have killed my man and am in jail for it. Tell your wife. If I can help out in any way. . . . Good-by, my friend—ah, yes! Zurita. I have a terrible head to-day. See you later! (*Goes out.*

FLORENCIO. Did you ever see anything equal to it? I never did, and I knew him of old. But he has made progress.

ZURITA. His assurance is fairly epic.

FLORENCIO. What are you going to do with a man who takes it like this? You cannot kill him in cold blood——

(CAROLINA *re-enters.*)

FLORENCIO. Ah! Carolina! Were you listening? You heard everything.

CAROLINA. Yes, and in spite of it I think he is fascinating.

FLORENCIO. Since Carolina feels that way it simplifies the situation.

ZURITA. Why not? She heard the compliments. The man is irresistible.

FLORENCIO. Carolina, it comes simply to this: nobody attaches any importance to the matter. Only two or three copies have been sold.

CAROLINA. Yes, but one of them was to my sisters-in-law, which is the same as if they had sold forty thousand. They will tell everybody.

FLORENCIO. They were doing it anyhow; there is no further cause for worry.

CAROLINA. At all events, I shall not attend the unveiling to-morrow, and you ought not to go either.

FLORENCIO. But wife!

ZURITA. Ah! The unveiling. . . . I had forgotten to mention it.

CAROLINA. To mention what?

ZURITA. It has been postponed.

FLORENCIO. How?

ZURITA. The committee became nervous at the last moment over the protests against the nudes. After seeing the photographs many ladies declined to participate. At last the sculptor was convinced, and he has consented to withdraw the statue of Truth altogether, and to put a tunic upon Industry, while Commerce is to have a bathing-suit.

CAROLINA. That will be splendid!

ZURITA. All this, however, will require several days, and by that time everything will have been forgotten.

(CASALONGA *re-enters with the books. He is completely out of breath and drops them suddenly upon the floor, where they raise a tremendous cloud of dust.*)

CAROLINA. *Ay!*

CASALONGA. I had you scared! At your service. . . . Here is the entire edition. I returned him his thousand pesetas—I declined to make it another penny. I told you that would be all that was necessary. I am a man of my word. Now it is up to you. No more could be asked! I am your friend and have said enough. I shall have to find some other outlet for my activities. That will be all for to-day.

FLORENCIO. I will give you two

thousand pesetas. But beware of a second edition!

CASALONGA. Don't begin to worry so soon. With this money I shall have enough to be decent at least—at least for two months. You know me, señora. I am Florencio's most intimate friend, as I was Patricio's most intimate friend, which is to say one of the most intimate friends you ever had.

CAROLINA. Yes, I remember.

CASALONGA. But I have changed since that time.

FLORENCIO. Not a bit of it! He is just the same.

CASALONGA. Yes, the change is in you. You are the same, only you have improved. (*To* CAROLINA) I am amazed at the opulence of your beauty, which a fortunate marriage has greatly enhanced. Have you any children?

CAROLINA. No. . . .

CASALONGA. You are going to have some.

FLORENCIO. Flatterer!

CASALONGA. But I must leave before night: there is nothing for me to do here.

FLORENCIO. No, you have attended to everything. I shall send it after you to the hotel.

CASALONGA. Add a little while you are about it to cover expenses—by way of a finishing touch.

FLORENCIO. Oh, very well!

CASALONGA. That will be all. Señora, if I can be of service. . . . My good Zurita! Friend Florencio! Before I die I hope to see you again.

FLORENCIO. Yes! Unless I die first.

CASALONGA. I know how you feel. You take the worst end for yourself.

FLORENCIO. Allow me that consolation.

CASALONGA. God be with you, my friend. Adios! Rest in peace. How different are our fates! Life to you is sweet. You have everything—love, riches, satisfaction. While I—I laugh through my tears! (*Goes out.*

CAROLINA. That cost you money.

FLORENCIO. What else did you expect? I gave up to avoid a scandal upon your account. I could see that you were nervous. I would have fought if I could have had my way; I would have carried matters to the last extreme. Zurita will tell you so.

CAROLINA. I always said that monument would cost us dear.

FLORENCIO. Obviously! Two thousand pesetas now, besides the twenty-five thousand which I subscribed for the monument, to say nothing of my uniform as Chief of Staff which I had ordered for the unveiling. Then there are the banquets to the delegates. . . .

ZURITA. Glory is always more expensive than it is worth.

FLORENCIO. It is not safe to be famous even at second hand.

CAROLINA. But you are not sorry?

FLORENCIO. No, my Carolina, the glory of being your husband far outweighs in my eyes the disadvantages of being the husband of his widow.

CURTAIN

Anatole France

LUCIFER

E si compiacque tanto Spinello di farlo orribile e contrafatto, che si dice (tanto può alcuna fiata l'immaginazione) che la detta figura da lui dipinta gli apparve in sogno, domandandolo dove egli l' avesse veduta si brutta.[1]

(*Vite de' piu eccellenti pittori,* da Messer Giorgio Vasari.—"Vita di Spinello.")

ANDREA TAFI, painter and worker-in-mosaic of Florence, had a wholesome terror of the Devils of Hell, particularly in the watches of the night, when it is given to the powers of Darkness to prevail. And the worthy man's fears were not unreasonable, for in those days the Demons had good cause to hate the Painters, who robbed them of more souls with a single picture than a good little Preaching Friar could do in thirty sermons. No doubt the Monk, to instil a soul-saving horror in the hearts of the faithful, would describe to the utmost of his powers "that day of wrath, that day

[1] "And so successful was Spinello with his horrible and portentous Production that it was commonly reported—so great is alway the force of fancy—that the said figure (of Lucifer trodden underfoot by St. Michael in the Altar-piece of the Church of St. Agnolo at Arezzo) painted by him had appeared to the artist in a dream, and asked him in what place he had beheld him under so brutish a form."

Lives of the most Excellent Painters, by Giorgio Vasari.—"Life of Spinello."

of mourning," which is to reduce the universe to ashes, *teste David et Sibylla,* borrowing his deepest voice and bellowing through his hands to imitate the Archangel's last trump. But there! it was "all sound and fury, signifying nothing," whereas a painting displayed on a Chapel wall or in the Cloister, showing Jesus Christ sitting on the Great White Throne to judge the living and the dead, spoke unceasingly to the eyes of sinners, and through the eyes chastened such as had sinned by the eyes or otherwise.

It was in the days when cunning masters were depicting at Santa-Croce in Florence and the Campo Santo of Pisa the mysteries of Divine Justice. These works were drawn according to the account in verse which Dante Alighieri, a man very learned in Theology and in Canon Law, wrote in days gone by of his journey to Hell and Purgatory and Paradise, whither by the singular great merits of his lady, he was able to make his way alive. So everything in these paintings was instructive and true, and we may say surely less profit is to be had of reading the most full and ample Chronicle than from contemplating such representative works of art. Moreover, the Florentine masters took heed to paint, under the shade of orange groves, on the flower-starred turf, fair ladies and gallant knights, with Death lying in wait for them with his scythe, while they were discoursing of love to the sound of lutes and viols. Nothing was better fitted to convert carnal-minded sinners who quaff forgetfulness of God on the lips of women. To rebuke the covetous, the painter would show to the life the Devils pouring molten gold down the throat of Bishop or Abbess, who had commissioned some work from him and then scamped his pay.

This is why the Demons in those days were bitter enemies of the painters, and above all of the Florentine painters, who surpassed all the rest in subtlety of wit. Chiefly they reproached them with representing them under a hideous guise, with the heads of bird and fish, serpents' bodies and bats' wings. This sore resentment which they felt will come out plainly in the history of Spinello of Arezzo.

Spinello Spinelli was sprung of a noble family of Florentine exiles, and his graciousness of mind matched his gentle birth; for he was the most skilful painter of his time. He wrought many and great works at Florence; and the Pisans begged him to complete Giotto's wall-paintings in their Campo Santo, where the dead rest beneath roses in holy earth shipped from Jerusalem. At last, after working long years in divers cities and getting much gold, he longed to see once more the good city of Arezzo, his mother. The men of Arezzo had not forgotten how Spinello, in his younger days, being enrolled in the Confraternity of Santa Maria della Misericordia, had visited the sick and buried the dead in the plague of 1383. They were grateful to him beside for having by his works spread the fame of their city over all Tuscany. For all these reasons they welcomed him with high honours on his return.

Still full of vigour in his old age, he undertook important tasks in his native town. His wife would tell him:

"You are rich, Spinello. Do you rest, and leave younger men to paint instead of you. It is meet a man should end his days in a gentle, religious quiet. It is tempting God to be for ever raising new and wordly monuments, mere heathen towers of Babel. Quit your colours and your varnishes, Spinello, or they will destroy your peace of mind."

So the good dame would preach, but he refused to listen, for his one thought was to increase his fortune and renown. Far from resting on his laurels, he arranged a price with the Wardens of Sant' Agnolo for a history of St. Michael, that was to cover all the Choir of the Church and contain an infinity of figures. Into this enterprise he threw himself with extraordinary ardour. Rereading the parts of Scripture that were to be his inspiration, he set himself to study deeply every line and every word of these passages. Not content with drawing all day long in his workshop, he persisted in working both at bed and board; while at dusk, walking below the hill on whose brow Arezzo proudly lifts her walls and towers, he was still lost in thought. And we may say the story of the Archangel was already limned in his brain when he started to sketch out the incidents in red chalk on the plaster of the wall. He was soon done tracing these outlines; then he fell to painting above the high altar the scene that was to outshine all the others in brilliancy. For it was his intent therein to glorify the leader of the hosts of Heaven for the victory he won before the beginning of time. Accordingly Spinello represented St. Michael fighting in the air against the serpent with seven heads and ten horns, and he figured with delight, in the bottom part of the picture, the Prince of the Devils, Lucifer, under the semblance of an appalling monster. The figures seemed to grow to life of themselves under his hand. His success was beyond his fondest hopes; so hideous was the countenance of Lucifer, none could escape the nightmare of its foulness. The face haunted the painter in the streets and even went home with him to his lodging.

Presently when night was come, Spinello lay down in his bed beside his wife and fell asleep. In his slumbers he saw an Angel as comely as St. Michael, but black; and the Angel said to him:

"Spinello, I am Lucifer. Tell me, where had you seen me, that you should paint me as you have, under so ignominious a likeness?"

The old painter answered trembling, that he had never seen him with his eyes, never having gone down alive into Hell, like Messer Dante Alighieri; but that, in depicting him as he had done, he was for expressing in visible lines and colours the hideousness of sin.

Lucifer shrugged his shoulders, and the hill of San Gemignano seemed of a sudden to heave and stagger.

"Spinello," he went on, "will you do me the pleasure to reason awhile with me? I am no mean Logician; He you pray to knows that."

Receiving no reply, Lucifer proceeded in these terms:

"Spinello, you have read the books that tell of me. You know of my enterprise, and how I forsook Heaven to become the Prince of this World. A tremendous adventure,—and a unique one, had not the Giants in like fashion assailed the god Jupiter, as yourself have seen, Spinello, recorded on an ancient tomb where this Titanic war is carved in marble."

"It is true," said Spinello, "I have seen the tomb, shaped like a great tun, in the Church of Santa Reparata at Florence. 'Tis a fine work of the Romans."

"Still," returned Luicifer, smiling, "the Giants are not pictured on it in the shape of frogs or chameleons or the like hideous and horrid creatures."

"True," replied the painter, "but then they had not attacked the true God, but only a false idol of the Pagans. 'Tis a mighty difference. The fact is clear, Lucifer, you raised the standard of revolt against the true and veritable King of Earth and Heaven."

"I will not deny it," said Lucifer. "And how many sorts of sins do you charge me with for that?"

"Seven, it is like enough," the painter answered, "and deadly sins one and all."

"Seven!" exclaimed the Angel of Darkness; "well! the number is canonical. Everything goes by sevens in my history, which is close bound up with God's. Spinello, you deem me proud, angry and envious. I enter no protest, provided you allow that glory was my only aim. Do you deem me covetous? Granted again; Covetousness is a virtue for Princes. For Gluttony and Lust, if you hold me guilty, I will not complain. Remains *Indolence*."

As he pronounced the word, Lucifer crossed his arms across his breast, and shaking his gloomy head, tossed his flaming locks:

"Tell me, Spinello, do you really think I am indolent? Do you take me for a coward? Do you hold that in my revolt I showed a lack of courage? Nay! you cannot. Then it was but just to paint me in the guise of a hero, with a proud countenance. You should wrong no one, not even the Devil. Cannot you see that you insult Him you make prayer to, when you give Him for adversary a vile, monstrous toad? Spinello, you are very ignorant for a man of your age. I have a great mind to pull your ears, as they do to an ill-conditioned schoolboy."

At this threat, and seeing the arm of Lucifer already stretched out towards him, Spinello clapped his hand to his head and began to howl with terror.

His good wife, waking up with a start, asked him what ailed him. He told her with chattering teeth, how he had just seen Lucifer and had been in terror for his ears.

"I told you so," retorted the worthy dame; "I knew all those figures you will go on painting on the walls would end by driving you mad."

"I am not mad," protested the painter. "I saw him with my own eyes; and he is beautiful to look on, albeit proud and sad. First thing tomorrow I will blot out the horrid figure I have drawn and set in its place the shape I beheld in my dream. For we must not wrong even the Devil himself."

"You had best go to sleep again," scolded his wife. "You are talking stark nonsense, and unchristian to boot."

Spinello tried to rise, but his strength failed him and he fell back unconscious on his pillow. He lingered on a few days in a high fever, and then died.

SYLVESTRE BONNARD FINDS JEANNE

I

Lusance, August 8, 1874.

WHEN I stepped from the train at the Melun station, night had already spread its peace over the silent country. The earth, heated all day by a heavy sun, by a "fat sun" as the harvesters of the Val de Vire say, exhaled a strong, hot smell. Along the surface of the land the dense perfume of grass trailed. I brushed away the dust of the railroad car, and joyfully inhaled the pure air.

My travelling-bag—filled by my housekeeper with linen and various small toilet articles, *munditis,* seemed so light in my hand that I swung it about just as a schoolboy swings his strapped package of elementary books when the class is let out.

Would to Heaven that I were again a little urchin at school! But it is fully sixty years since my good dead mother made me some *tartines* of bread and preserves, and placed them in a basket of which she slipped the handle over my arm, and then led me, thus prepared, to the school kept by Monsieur Douloir, at a corner of the Passage du Commerce well known to the sparrows, between a court and a garden. The enormous Monsieur Douloir smiled upon us genially and patted my cheek to show, no doubt, the affectionate interest with which I immediately inspired him. But when my mother had passed out of the court, startling the sparrows as she went, Monsieur Douloir ceased to smile—he showed no more affectionate interest; he appeared, on the contrary, to consider me as a very troublesome little being. I discovered, later on, that he entertained the same feelings towards all his pupils. He distributed whacks with his rod with an agility unexpected in so corpulent a person. But his first tender interest invariably reappeared when he spoke to any of our mothers in our presence; and always at such times, while warmly praising our remarkable aptitudes, he would bestow on us an affectionate look. Still, those were happy days which I passed on the benches of Monsieur Douloir with my little playfellows, who, like myself, cried and laughed by turns with all their might, from morning till evening.

After more than half a century these souvenirs float up again, fresh and bright as ever, to the surface of memory, under this starry sky, that has not changed since then, and whose serene and immutable lights will doubtless see many other schoolboys such as I was slowly turn into hoary savants, afflicted with catarrh.

Stars, who have shown down upon each wise or foolish head among all my forgotten ancestors, it is under your soft light that I now feel stir within me a certain poignant regret! I would that I could have a son who might be able to see you when I shall see you no more. I would now be a father and a grandfather if you had been willing, Clémentine; you whose cheeks used to look so fresh under your pink hood. But you married Monsieur Achille Allier, a rich country gentleman.

I have not seen you since your marriage, Clémentine, and I can imagine your life flowed sweetly and beautifully in your rustic manor house. By chance one day, I learned from one of your friends that you had died, leaving a daughter who looked like you. On hearing this news which twenty years earlier would have upset all the strength of my soul, there grew within me a great silence. The feeling that filled me completely was not that of a sharp pain, but the profound and quiet sadness of a soul that has learned the great lessons of nature. I understood that what I had loved was only a shadow. But the memory of you is still the charm of my life. Your gentle form after slowly fading has disappeared beneath the thick grass. Your daughter's youth is already passed. Her beauty is laid aside. And yet I see you always, Clémentine, with your yellow curls and your pink hood.

Beautiful Night! She rules, with such noble repose, over men and animals alike, kindly loosed by her from the yoke of daily toil; and even I feel her benign influence, although my habits of sixty years have so changed me that I can feel most things only through the signs which represent them. My world is wholly formed of words—so much of a philologist I have become! Each one dreams the dream of life in his own way. I have dreamed it in my library; and when the hour shall come in which I must leave this world, may it please God to take me from my ladder—from before my shelves of books! . . .

"Well, well! it is really he! How are you, Monsieur Sylvestre Bonnard? And where were you going over the countryside while I was waiting for you at the station with my cabriolet? You escaped me when the train came in, and I was driving back, disappointed, to Lusance. Give me your valise, and get up here beside me in the carriage. Why, do you know it is fully seven kilometres from here to the château?"

Who addresses me thus, at the top of his lungs, from the height of his cabriolet? Monsieur Paul de Gabry, nephew and heir of Monsieur Honoré de Gabry, peer of France in 1842, who recently died at Monaco. And it was precisely to Monsieur Paul de Gabry's house that I was going with that valise of mine, so carefully strapped by my housekeeper. This excellent young man has just inherited, conjointly with his two brothers-in-law, the property of his uncle, who, belonging to a very ancient family of distinguished lawyers, had accumulated in his château at Lusance a library rich in MSS., some dating back to the thirteenth century. It was for the purpose of making an inventory and a catalogue of these MSS. that I had come to Lusance at the urgent request of Monsieur Paul de Gabry, whose father, a perfect gentleman and distinguished bibliophile, had maintained the most pleasant relations with me during his lifetime. To tell the truth, the son has not inherited the fine tastes of his father. Monsieur Paul devotes himself to sport; he is a great authority on horses and dogs; and I much fear that of all the sciences capable of satisfying or of duping the inexhaustible curiosity of mankind, those of the stable and the kennel are the only ones thoroughly mastered by him.

I cannot say I was surprised to meet him, since we had made a rendezvous; but I acknowledge that I had become so preoccupied with my own thoughts that I had forgotten all about the Château de Lusance and its inhabitants, and that the voice of the gentleman calling out to me as I started to follow the country road winding away before me—"*un bon ruban de queue,*" as they say—had given me quite a start.

I fear my face must have betrayed my incongruous distraction by a certain stupid expression which it is apt to assume in most of my social transactions. My valise was pulled up into the carriage, and I followed my valise. My host pleased me by his straightforward simplicity.

"I don't know anything myself about your old parchments," he said; "but I think you will find some folks to talk to at the house. Besides the curé, who writes books himself, and the doctor, who is a very good fellow—although a liberal—you will meet somebody able to keep you company. I mean my wife. She is not a very learned woman, but there are few things which she can't divine pretty well. Then I count upon being able to keep you with us long enough to make you acquainted with Mademoiselle Jeanne, who has the fingers of a magician and the soul of an angel."

"And is this delightfully gifted young lady one of your family?" I asked.

"Oh, no," replied Monsieur Paul, keeping his eyes fixed upon the ears of his horse, whose hoofs rang loudly over the road blue-tinted by the moon-shine. "She is my wife's friend, an orphan. Her father managed to get us into some very serious trouble; and we did not get off with a fright either!"

Then he shook his head, and changed the subject. He gave me due warning of the ruinous condition in which I would find the château and the park; they had been absolutely deserted for thirty-two years.

I learned from him that Monsieur Honoré de Gabry, his uncle, had been on very bad terms with some poachers, whom he used to shoot at like rabbits. One of them, a vindictive peasant, who had received a whole charge of shot in his face, lay in wait for the Seigneur one evening behind the trees of the mall, and very nearly succeeded in killing him, for the ball took off the tip of his ear.

"My uncle," Monsieur Paul continued, "tried to discover who had fired the shot; but he could not see any one, and he walked back slowly to the house. The day after he called his steward, and ordered him to close up the manor and the park, and allow no living soul to enter. He expressly forbade that anything should be touched, or looked after, or any reparations made on the estate during his absence. He added, between his teeth, that he would return at Easter, or Trinity Sunday, as they say in the song; and just as the song has it, Trinity Sunday passed without a sign of him. He died last year at Monaco; my brother-in-law and myself were the first to enter the château after it had been abandoned for thirty-two years. We found a chestnut tree growing in the middle of the parlor. As for the park, it was useless trying to visit it, because there were no more paths, no alleys."

My companion ceased to speak; and only the regular hoof-beat of the trot-ting horse, and the chirping of insects in the grass, broke the silence. On either hand, the sheaves standing in the fields took, in the vague moonlight, the appearance of tall white women kneeling down; and I abandoned myself awhile to those wonderful childish fancies which the charm of night always suggests. After driving under the heavy shadows of the mall, we turned to the right and rolled up a lordly avenue, at the end of which the château suddenly rose into view—a black mass, with turrets like pepper pots. We followed a sort of causeway, which gave access to the court-of-honor, and which, passing over a moat full of running water, doubtless replaced a long-vanished drawbridge. The loss of that drawbridge must have been, I think, the first of various humiliations to which the warlike manor had been subjected ere being reduced to that pacific aspect with which it received me. The stars reflected themselves with marvellous clearness in the dark water. Monsieur Paul, like a courteous host, escorted me to my chamber in the very top of the building, at the end of a long corridor; and then, excusing himself for not presenting me at once to his wife by reason of the lateness of the hour, bade me good-night.

My apartment, painted in white, and hung with chintz, seemed to keep some traces of the elegant gallantry of the eighteenth century. A heap of still-glowing ashes—which testified to the pains taken to dispel humidity—filled the fireplace, whose marble mantelpiece supported a bust of Marie Antoinette in *biscuit*. Attached to the frame of the tarnished and discolored mirror, two brass hooks, that had once doubtless served the ladies of old-fashioned days to hang their *chatelaines* on, seemed to offer a very opportune means of suspending my watch, which I took care to wind up beforehand; for, contrary to the opinion of the Thelemites, I hold that man is only master of time, which is Life itself, when he has divided it into hours, minutes, and seconds —that is to say, into parts proportioned to the brevity of human existence.

And I thought to myself that life really seems short to us only because we measure it irrationally by our own mad hopes. We have all of us, like the old man in the fable, a new wing to add to our building. I want, for example, before I die, to finish my "History of the Abbots of Saint-Germain-des-Prés." The time God allots to each one of us is like a precious tissue which we embroider as we best know how. I had begun my woof with all sorts of philological illustrations. . . . So my thoughts wandered on; and at last, as I bound my *foulard* about my head, the notion of Time led me back to the past; and for the second time within the same round of the dial I thought of you, Clémentine—to bless you again in your posterity, if you have any, before blowing out my candle and falling asleep to the song of the frogs.

II

Lusance, August 9.

During luncheon I had many opportunities to appreciate the good taste, tact, and intelligence of Madame de Gabry, who told me that the château had its ghosts, and was especially haunted by the "Lady-with-three-wrinkles-in-her-back," a poisoner during her lifetime, and thereafter a Soul-in-pain. I could never describe how much wit and animation she gave to this old nurse's tale. We took our coffee on the terrace, whose balusters, clasped and forcibly torn away from their stone coping by a vigorous growth of ivy, remained suspended in the grasp of the amorous plant like bewildered Athenian women in the arms of ravishing Centaurs.

The château, shaped something like a four-wheeled wagon, with a turret at each of the four angles, had lost all original character by reason of repeated remodellings. It was merely a fine spacious building, nothing more. It did not appear to me to have suffered much damage during its abandonment of thirty-two years. But when Madame de Gabry conducted me into the great salon of the ground-floor, I saw that the planking was bulged in and out, the plinths rotten, the wainscotings split apart, the paintings of the piers turned black and hanging more than half out of their settings. A chestnut-tree, after forcing up the planks of the floor, had grown tall under the ceiling, and was reaching out its large-leaved branches towards the glassless windows.

I could not look at this spectacle without anxiety, as I remembered that the rich library of Monsieur Honoré de Gabry, in an adjoining apartment, must have been exposed for the same length of time to the same forces of decay. Yet, as I looked at the young chestnut-tree in the salon, I could not but admire the magnificent vigor of Nature, and that resistless power which forces every germ to develop into life. On the other hand I felt saddened to think that, whatever effort we scholars may make to preserve dead things from passing away, we are laboring painfully in vain. Whatever has lived becomes the necessary food of new existences. And the Arab who builds himself a hut out of the marble fragments of a Palymra temple is really more of a philosopher than all the guardians of museums at London, Munich, or Paris.

Lusance, August 11.

God be praised! The library on the east side has not been irretrievably spoiled. The books are intact inside their closed shelves.

All day long I have been classifying MSS. . . . The sun came in through the lofty uncurtained windows; and, during my reading, often very interesting, I could hear the languid bumble-bees bump heavily against the windows, and the flies, intoxicated with light and heat, making their wings hum in circles round my head. So loud became their humming about three o'clock that I looked up from the document I was reading—a document containing very precious materials for the history of Melun in the thirteenth century—to watch the concentric movements of those tiny creatures. *"Bestions,"* Lafontaine calls them. I was compelled to confess that the effect of heat upon the wings of a fly is totally different from that it exerts upon the brain of a paleographical archivist; for I found it very difficult to think, and a rather pleasant languor weighing upon me, from which I could rouse myself only by a very determined effort. The dinner-bell then startled me in the midst of my labors; and I had barely time to put on my new dress-coat, so as to make a respectable appearance before Madame de Gabry.

The repast, generously served, seemed to prolong itself for my benefit. I am more than a fair judge of wine; and my host, who discovered my knowledge in this regard, was friendly enough to open a certain bottle of Château-Margaux in my honor. With deep respect I drank of this famous and knightly old wine, which comes from the slopes of Bordeaux, and of which the flavor and exhilarating power are beyond all praise. The ardor of it spread gently through my veins, and filled me with an almost juvenile animation. Seated beside Madame de Gabry on the terrace, in the gloaming which bathed in mystery the huge shapes of the trees, I took pleasure in communicating my impressions of the scenes to my hostess. I discoursed with a vivacity quite remarkable on the part of a man so devoid of imagination as I am. I described to her spontaneously, without quoting from my old texts, the caressing melancholy of the evening, and the beauty of that natal earth which feeds us, not only with bread and wine, but also with ideas, sentiments, beliefs, and which will at last take us all back to her maternal breast again, like so many tired little children at the close of a long day.

"Monsieur," said the kind lady, "you see these old towers, those trees, that sky; is it not quite natural that the personages of the popular tales and folk-songs should have been evoked by such scenes? Why, over there is the very path which Little Red Ridinghood followed when she went to the woods to pick nuts. Across this changeful and always vapory sky the fairy chariots used to roll; and the north tower might have sheltered under its pointed roof that same old spinning woman whose distaff pricked the Sleeping Beauty in the Wood."

I continued to muse upon her pretty fancies, while Monsieur Paul related to me, as he puffed a very strong cigar, the history of some suit he had brought against the commune about a water-right. Madame de Gabry, feeling the chill night-air, began to shiver under the shawl her husband had wrapped about her, and left us to go to her room. I then decided, instead of going to my own, to return to the library and continue my examination of the manuscripts. In spite of the protests of Monsieur Paul, I entered what I may call, in old-fashioned phrase, "the book-room," and started to work by the light of a lamp.

After having read fifteen pages, evidently written by some ignorant and careless scribe, for I could scarcely discern their meaning, I plunged my hand into the pocket of my coat to get my snuff-box; but this movement, usually so natural and almost instinctive, this time cost me some effort and even fatigue. Nevertheless, I got out the silver box, and took from it a pinch of the odorous powder, which, somehow or other, I managed to spill all over my shirt-bosom under my baffled nose. I am sure my nose must have expressed its disappointment, for it is a very expressive nose. More than once it betrayed my secret thoughts, and especially upon a certain occasion at the public library of Coutances, where I discovered, right in front of my colleague Brioux, the "Cartulary of Notre-Dame-des-Anges."

What a delight! My little eyes remained as dull and expressionless as ever behind my spectacles. But at the mere sight of my thick pug-nose, which quivered with joy and pride, Brioux knew that I had found something. He noted the volume I was looking at, observed the place where I put it back, pounced upon it as soon as I turned my back, copied it secretly, and published it in haste, for the sake of playing me a trick. But his edition swarms with errors, and I had the satisfaction of afterwards criticizing some of the gross blunders he made.

But to come back to the point at which I left off: I began to suspect that I was getting very sleepy indeed. I was looking at a chart of which the interest may be divined from the fact that it contained mention of a hutch sold to Jehan d'Estonville, priest, in 1212. But although, even then, I could recognize the importance of the document, I did not give it that attention it so strongly invited. My eyes would keep turning, against my will, towards a certain corner of the table where there was nothing whatever interesting to a learned mind. There was only a big German book there, bound in pigskin, with brass studs on the sides, and very thick cording upon the back. It was a fine copy of a compilation which has little to recommend it except the wood engravings it contains, and which is well known as the "Nuremberg Chronicle." This volume, with its covers slightly open, was placed on its edge, with the back upwards.

I could not say for how long I had been staring causelessly at this old folio, when my eyes were captivated by a sight so extraordinary that even a person as devoid of imagination as I could not but have been greatly astonished by it.

I perceived, all of a sudden, without having noticed her coming into the room, a little creature seated on the back of the book, with one knee bent and one leg hanging down—somewhat in the attitude of the amazons of Hyde Park or the Bois de Boulogne on horseback. She was so small that her swinging foot did not reach the table, over which the trail of her dress extended in a serpentine line. But her face and figure were those of an adult. The fulness of her corsage and the roundness of her waist could leave no doubt of that, even for an old *savant* like myself. I will venture to add that she was very handsome, with a proud mien; for my iconographic studies have long accustomed me to recognize at once the perfection of a type and the character of a physiognomy. The countenance of this lady who had seated herself inopportunely on the back of a "Nuremberg Chronicle" expressed a mingling of haughtiness and mischievousness. She had the air of a queen, but a capricious queen; and I judged, from the mere expression of her eyes, that she was accustomed to wield great authority somewhere, in a very whimsical manner. Her mouth was imperious and mocking, and those blue eyes of hers seemed to laugh in a disquieting way under her finely arched black eyebrows. I have always heard that black eyebrows are very becoming to blondes; and this lady was very blonde. On the whole, the impression she gave me was one of greatness.

It may seem odd to say that a person who was no taller than a wine-bottle, and who might have been hidden in my coat pocket—but that it would have been very disrespectful to put her in it—gave me precisely an idea of greatness. But in the fine proportions of the lady seated upon the "Nuremberg Chronicle" there was such a proud elegance, such a harmonious majesty, and she maintained an attitude at once so easy and so noble, that she really seemed to me a very great person. Although my ink-bottle, which she examined with an expression of such mockery as appeared to indicate that she knew in advance every word that could ever come out of it at the end of my pen, was for her a deep basin in which she would have blackened her gold-clocked pink stockings up to the garter, I can assure you that she was great, and imposing even in her sprightliness.

Her costume, worthy of her face, was extremely magnificent; it consisted of a dress of gold-and-silver brocade, and a mantle of nacarat velvet, lined with vair. Her head-dress was a sort of *hennin,* with two high points; and pearls of splendid lustre made it bright and luminous as a crescent moon. Her little white hand held a wand. That wand drew my attention very strongly, because my archæological studies had taught me to recognize with certainty every sign by which the notable personages of legend and of history are distinguished. This knowledge came to my aid on this occasion. I examined the wand, and saw that it appeared to have been cut from a branch of hazel.

"Then it is a fairy's wand," I said to myself;—"consequently the lady who carries it is a fairy."

Happy at thus discovering what sort of a person was before me, I tried to collect my mind sufficiently to make her a graceful compliment. It would have given me much satisfaction, I confess, if I could have talked to her about the part taken by her people, not less in the life of the Saxon and Germanic races, than in that of the Latin Occident. Such a dissertation, it appeared to me, would have been an ingenious method of thanking the lady for having thus appeared to an old scholar, contrary to the invariable custom of her kindred, who never show themselves but to innocent children or ignorant village-folk.

Because one happens to be a fairy, one is none the less a woman, I said to myself; and since Madame Récamier, according to what I heard J. J. Ampère say, was concerned about the impression her beauty made on little chimney sweeps, surely the supernatural lady seated upon the Nuremberg Chronicle might feel flattered to hear an erudite man discourse learnedly about her, as about a medal, a seal, a fibula, or a token. But such an undertaking, which would have cost my timidity a great deal, became totally out of the question when I observed the Lady of the Chronicle suddenly take from an alms-purse hanging at her girdle the very smallest nuts I had ever seen, crack the shells between her teeth, and throw them at my nose, while she nibbled the kernels with the gravity of a sucking child.

At this conjuncture, I did what the dignity of science demanded of me—I remained silent. But the nutshells caused such a painful tickling that I put up my hand to my nose, and found, to my great surprise, that my spectacles were straddling the very end of it—so that I was actually looking at the lady, not through my spectacles, but over them. This was incomprehensible, because my eyes, worn out over old texts, cannot ordinarily distinguish anything without glasses—could not tell a melon from a decanter, though the two were placed close up to my nose.

That nose of mine, remarkable for its size, its shape, and its coloration, legitimately attracted the attention of the fairy; for she seized my goose-quill pen, which was sticking up from the ink-bottle like a plume, and she began to pass the feather-end of that pen over my nose. I had had more than once, in company, occasion to suffer cheerfully from the innocent mischief of young ladies, who made me join their games, and would offer me their cheeks to kiss through the back of a chair, or invite me to blow out a candle which they would lift suddenly above the range of my breath. But until that moment no person of the fair sex had ever subjected me to such a whimsical piece of familiarity as that of tickling my nose with my own feather pen. Happily I remembered the maxim of my late grandfather, who was accustomed to say that everything was permissible on the part of ladies, and that whatever they do to us is to be regarded as a grace and a favor. Therefore, as a grace and a favor I received the nutshells and the titillations with my own pen, and I tried to smile. Much more!—I even found speech.

"Madame," I said, with dignified politeness, "you accord the honor of a visit not to a silly child, nor to a boor, but to a bibliophile who is very happy to make your acquaintance, and who knows that long ago you used to make elf-knots in the manes of mares at the crib, drink the milk from the skimming-pails, slip *graines-à gratter* down the backs of our great-grandmothers, make the hearth sputter in the faces of the old folks, and, in short, fill the house with disorder and gayety. You can also boast of giving the nicest frights in the world to lovers who stayed out in the woods too late af evenings. But I thought you had vanished out of existence at least three centuries ago. Can it really be, Madame, that you are still to be seen in this age of railroads and telegraphs? My concierge, who used to be a nurse in her young days, does not know your story; and my little neighbor, whose nose is still wiped for him by his nurse, declares that you do not exist."

"What do you yourself think about it?" she cried, in an argentine voice, straightening up her royal little figure in a very haughty fashion, and whipping the back of the Nuremberg Chronicle as though it were a hippogriffe.

"I don't really know," I answered, rubbing my eyes.

This reply, indicating a deeply scientific scepticism, had the most deplorable effect upon my questioner.

"Monsieur Sylvestre Bonnard," she said to me, "you are nothing but an old pedant. I always suspected as much. The smallest little ragamuffin who goes along the road with his shirt-tail sticking out through a hole in his trousers knows more about me than all the old spectacled folks in your Institutes and your Academies. To know is nothing at all; to imagine is everything. Nothing exists except that which is imagined. I am imaginary. That is to exist, I should certainly think! I am dreamed of, and I appear. Everything is only dream; and as nobody ever dreams about you, Sylvestre Bonnard, it is *you* who do not exist. I charm the world; I am everywhere—on a moonbeam, in the trembling of a hidden spring, in the moving of leaves that murmur, in the white vapors that rise each morning from the hollow meadow, in the thickets of pink brier—everywhere! . . . I am seen; I am loved. There are sighs uttered, weird thrills of pleasure felt by those who follow the light print of my feet, as I make the dead leaves whisper. I make the little children smile; I give wit to the dullest-minded nurses. Leaning above the cradles, I play, I comfort, I lull to sleep—and you doubt whether I exist! Sylvestre Bonnard, your warm coat covers the hide of an ass!"

She ceased speaking: her delicate nostrils swelled with indignation; and while I admired, despite my vexation, the heroic anger of this little person, she pushed my pen about in the ink-bottle, backward and forward, like an oar, and then suddenly threw it at my nose, point first.

I rubbed my face, and felt it all covered with ink. She had disappeared. My lamp was extinguished. A ray of moonlight streamed down through a window and descended upon the Nuremberg Chronicle. A strong cool wind, which had risen very suddenly without my knowledge, was blowing my papers about. My table was all stained with ink. I had left my window open during the storm. What an imprudence!

III

Lusance, August 12.

I wrote to my housekeeper, as I promised, that I was safe and sound. But I took good care not to tell her that I had caught cold from going to sleep in the library at night with the window open; for the good woman would have been as unsparing in her remonstrances to me as parliaments to kings. "At your age, Monsieur," she would have been sure to say, "one ought to have more sense." She is simple enough to believe that sense grows with age. I seem to her an exception to this rule.

Not having any similar motive for concealing my experiences from Madame de Gabry, I told her about my vision.

I don't know the art of fiction. It may be, however, that in telling the story and in writing it I invented here and there happenings and words which were not there in the first place, not for the purpose of changing the truth, but rather from a secret desire to clarify and complete that which remained obscure and confused.

Madame de Gabry listened to me, and seemed to enjoy what I told her.

"Why, that was a charming dream of yours," she said; "and one must have real genius to dream such a dream."

"Then I am a real genius when I am asleep," I answered.

"When you dream," she replied; "and you are always dreaming."

I know that Madame de Gabry, in making this remark, only wished to please me; but that intention alone deserves my utmost gratitude, and it is therefore in a spirit of thankfulness and kindliest remembrance that I write down her words, which I will read over and over again until my dying day, and which will never be read by any one save myself.

I passed the next few days in completing the inventory of the manuscripts in the Lusance library. Certain confidential observations dropped by Monsieur Paul de Gabry, however, caused me some painful surprise, and made me decide to pursue the work after a different manner from that in which I had begun it. From those few words I learned that the fortune of Monsieur Honoré de Gabry, which had been badly managed for many years, and subsequently swept away to a large extent through the failure of a banker whose name I do not know, had been transmitted to the heirs of the old French nobleman only under the form of mortgaged real estate and irrecoverable assets.

Monsieur Paul, by agreement with his joint heirs, had decided to sell the library, and I was intrusted with the task of making arrangements to have the sale effected upon advantageous terms. But, totally ignorant as I was of all business methods and trade-customs, I thought it best to get the advice of a publisher who was one of my private friends. I wrote him at once to come and join me at Lusance; and while waiting for his arrival I took my hat and cane and made visits to the different churches of the diocese, in several of which I knew there were certain mortuary inscriptions to be found which had never been correctly copied.

So I left my hosts and departed on my pilgrimage. Exploring the churches and the cemeteries every day, visiting the parish priests and the village notaries, supping at the public inns with peddlers and cattle-dealers, sleeping at nights between sheets scented with lavender, I passed one whole week in the quiet but profound enjoyment of observing the living engaged in their various daily occupations even while I was thinking of the dead. As for the purpose of my researches, I made only a few mediocre discoveries, which caused me only a mediocre joy, and one therefore salubrious and not at all fatiguing. I copied a few interesting epitaphs; and I added to this little collection a few recipes for cooking country dishes, which a certain good priest kindly gave me.

With these riches, I returned to Lusance: and I crossed the court-of-honor with such secret satisfaction as a *bourgeois* feels on entering his own home. This was the effect of the kindness of my hosts; and the impression I received on crossing their threshold proves, better than any reasoning, the excellence of their hospitality.

I entered the great parlor without meeting a soul and the young chestnut-tree there spreading out its broad leaves seemed to me like an old friend. But the next thing which I saw—on the console—caused me such a shock of surprise that I readjusted my glasses upon my nose with both hands at once, and then felt myself over so as to get at least some superficial proof of my own existence. In less than one second there thronged into my mind twenty different conjectures—the most rational of which was that I had suddenly become crazy. It seemed to me absolutely impossible that what I was looking at could exist; yet it was equally impossible for me not to see it as a thing actually existing. What caused my surprise was resting on the console, above which rose a great dull speckled mirror.

I saw myself in that mirror; and I can say that I saw for once in my life the perfect image of stupefaction. But I made proper allowance for myself; I approved myself for being so stupefied by a really stupefying thing.

The object I was thus examining with a degree of astonishment that all my reasoning power failed to lessen, obtruded itself on my attention though quite motionless. The persistence and fixity of the phenomenon excluded any idea of hallucination. I am totally exempt from all nervous disorders capable of influencing the sense of sight. The cause of such visual disturbance is, I think, generally due to stomach trouble; and, thank God! I have an excellent stomach. Moreover, visual illusions are accompanied with special abnormal conditions which impress the victims of hallucination themselves, and inspire them with a sort of terror. Now, I felt nothing of this kind; the object which I saw, although seemingly impossible in itself, appeared to me under all the natural conditions of reality. I observed that it had three dimensions, and colors, and that it cast a shadow. Ah! how I stared at it! Tears came into my eyes so that I had to wipe the glasses of my spectacles.

Finally I found myself obliged to yield to the evidence, and to affirm that I had really before my eyes the Fairy, the very same Fairy I had been dreaming of in the library a few evenings before. It was she, it was she, I tell you! She had the same air of child-queen, the same proud supple poise; she held the same hazel wand in her hand; she still wore her double-peaked head-dress, and the trail of her long brocade robe undulated about her little feet. Same face, same figure. It was she indeed; and to prevent any possible doubt of it, she was seated on the back of a huge old-fashioned book strongly resembling the "Nuremberg Chronicle." Her immobility but half reassured me; I was really afraid that she was going to take some more nuts out of her alms-purse and throw the shells at my face.

I was standing there, waving my hands and gaping, when the musical and laughing voice of Madame de Gabry suddenly rang in my ears.

"So you are examining your fairy, Monsieur Bonnard!" said my goddess. "Well, do you think the resemblance good?"

It was very quickly said; but even while hearing it I had time to perceive that my fairy was a statuette in colored wax, modelled with much taste and spirit by some novice hand. But the phenomenon, even thus reduced by a rational explanation, did not cease to excite my surprise. How, and by whom, had the Lady of the Chronicle been enabled to assume plastic existence? That was what remained for me to learn.

Turning towards Madame Gabry, I perceived that she was not alone. A young girl dressed in black was standing beside her. She had large intelligent eyes, of a gray as sweet as that of the sky of the Isle of France, and at once artless and characteristic in their expression. At the extremities of her rather thin arms were fidgeting uneasily two slender hands, supple, but slightly red, as it becomes the hands of young girls to be. Sheathed in her closely fitting merino robe, she had the slim grace of a young tree; and her large mouth bespoke frankness. I could not describe how much the child pleased me at first sight! She was not beautiful; but the three dimples of her cheeks and chin seemed to laugh, and her whole person, which revealed the awkwardness of innocence, had something in it indescribably good and sincere.

My gaze alternated from the statuette to the young girl; and I saw her blush—so frankly and fully!—the crimson passing over her face as by waves.

"Well," said my hostess, who had become sufficiently accustomed to my distracted moods to put the same question to me twice, "is that the very same lady who came in to see you through the window that you left open? She was very bold, but then you were quite imprudent! Anyhow, do you recognize her?"

"It is her very self," I replied; "I see her now on that console precisely as I saw her on the table in the library."

"Then, if that be so," replied Madame de Gabry, "you have to blame for it, in the first place, yourself, as a man who, although devoid of all imagination, to use your own words, knew how to depict your dream in such vivid colors; in the second place, me, who was able to remember and repeat faithfully all your dream; and, lastly, Mademoiselle Jeanne, whom I now introduce to you, for she herself modelled that wax-figure precisely according to my instructions."

Madame de Gabry had taken the young girl's hand as she spoke; but the latter had suddenly broken away from her, and was already running through the park.

Madame de Gabry cried after her. "How can one be so shy? Come back here to be scolded."

But it was all of no avail; the frightened child disappeared among the shrubbery. Madame de Gabry seated herself in the only chair remaining in the dilapidated parlor.

"I should be much surprised," she said, "if my husband had not already spoken to you of Jeanne. She is a sweet child, and we both love her very much. Tell me the truth; what do you think of her statuette?"

I replied that the work was full of good taste and spirit, but that it showed some want of study and practice on the author's part; otherwise I had been extremely touched to think that those young fingers should have thus embroidered an old man's rough sketch of fancy, and figured so brilliantly the dreams of a dotard like myself.

"The reason I ask your opinion," replied Madame de Gabry, seriously, "is that Jeanne is a poor orphan. Do you think she could earn her living by modelling statuettes like this one?"

"As for that, no!" I replied; "and I think there is no reason to regret the fact. You say the girl is affectionate and sensitive; I can well believe you; I could believe it from her face alone. There are excitements in artist-life which impel generous hearts to act out of all rule and measure. This young creature is modelled out of a loving clay. Let her marry."

"But she has no dowry!" replied Madame de Gabry.

Then, lowering her voice, she said:

"You are our friend; I can tell you everything. The father of this child was a well-known banker. He had an adventurous spirit. He was not a dishonest man; he deceived himself before he ever deceived others. We had frequent dealings with him. He bewitched us all, my husband, my uncle, my cousins. His ruin was sudden. In the disaster my uncle's fortune, as Paul told you, was three-quarters lost. We were not so badly hit, and since we have no children . . . He died shortly after this time, leaving absolutely nothing: which makes me say he was honest. You must know his name; it was in all the papers, Noël Alexandre. His wife was very charming; I think she had once been beautiful. She liked social life perhaps too much but she showed great courage and dignity at the time of her husband's ruin. She died a year after his death leaving Jeanne alone in the world. She had not been able to save any of her own fortune, which was considerable. Madame Noël Alexandre was an Allier, the daughter of Achille Allier of Nevers."

"Clémentine's daughter!" I cried. "Clémentine is dead and her daughter is dead! Humanity is almost entirely made up of the dead. There are so few living compared with the multitude who have died. What is this life, briefer than the briefest memory of man?"

And I made this silent prayer:

"From wheresoever you are at this moment, Clémentine, look down upon his heart now cooled by age, yet whose blood once boiled for your sake, and say whether it is not reanimated by the mere thought of being able to love what remains of you on earth. Everything passes away since you have passed away; but life is immortal; it is life we must love in its forms eternally renewed. With all my books, I was like a child playing with marbles. My life, these last few days, takes on meaning, interest. I am a grandfather. Clémentine's granddaughter is poor. No one but I shall provide her dowry."

Seeing that I wept, Madame de Gabry walked slowly away.

Knut Hamsun

THE CALL OF LIFE

D OWN near the inner harbor in Copenhagen there is a street called Vestervold, a relatively new, yet desolate, boulevard. There are few houses to be seen on it, few gas lamps, and almost no people whatever. Even now, in summer, it is rare that one sees people promenading there.

Well, last evening I had something of a surprise in that street.

I had taken a few turns up and down the sidewalk when a lady came towards me from the opposite direction. There were no other people in sight. The gas lamps were lighted, but it was nevertheless dark—so dark that I could not distinguish the lady's face. One of the usual creatures of the night, I thought to myself, and passed her by.

At the end of the boulevard I turned about and walked back. The lady had also turned about, and I met her again. She is waiting for some one, I thought, and I was curious to see whom she could be waiting for. And again I passed her by.

When I met her the third time I tipped my hat and spoke to her.

"Good evening! Are you waiting for some one?"

She was startled. No—that is, yes—she was waiting for some one.

Did she object to my keeping her company till the person she was expecting arrived?

No—she did not object in the least, and she thanked me. For that matter, she explained, she was not expecting any one. She was merely taking the air —it was so still here.

We strolled about side by side. We began talking about various things of no great consequence. I offered my arm.

"Thank you, no," she said, and shook her head.

There was no great fun promenading in this way; I could not see her in the dark. I struck a match to see what time it was. I held the match up and looked at her too.

"Nine-thirty," I said.

She shivered as if she were freezing. I seized the opportunity.

"You are freezing?" I asked. "Shan't we drop in some place and get something to drink? At Tivoli? At the National?"

"But, don't you see, I can't go anywhere now," she answered.

And I noticed then for the first time that she wore a very long black veil.

I begged her pardon, and blamed the darkness for my mistake. And the way in which she took my apology at once convinced me that she was not one of the usual night wanderers.

"Won't you take my arm?" I suggested again. "It may warm you a bit."

She took my arm.

We paced up and down a few turns. She asked me to look at the time again.

"It is ten," I said. "Where do you live?"

"On Gamle Kongevei."

I stopped her.

"And may I see you to your door?" I asked.

"Not very well," she answered. "No, I can't let you . . . You live on Bredgade, don't you?"

"How do you know that?" I asked surprised.

"Oh, I know who you are," she answered.

A pause. We walked arm in arm down the lighted streets. She walked rapidly, her long veil streaming behind.

"We have better hurry," she said.

At her door in Gamle Kongevei she turned toward me as if to thank me for my kindness in escorting her. I opened the door for her, and she entered slowly. I thrust my shoulder gently against the door and followed her in. Once inside she seized my hand. Neither of us said anything.

We mounted two flights of stairs and stopped on the third floor. She herself unlocked the door to her apartment, then opened a second door, and took me by the hand and led me in. It was presumably a drawing-room; I could hear a clock ticking on the wall. Once inside the door the lady paused a moment, threw her arms about me suddenly, and kissed me tremblingly, passionately, on the mouth. Right on the mouth.

"Won't you be seated," she suggested. "Here is a sofa. Meanwhile I'll get a light."

And she lit a lamp.

I looked about me, amazed, yet curious. I found myself in a spacious and extremely well furnished drawing-room with other, half-open doors leading into several rooms on the side. I could not for the life of me make out what sort of person it was I had come across.

"What a beautiful room!" I exclaimed. "Do you live here?"

"Yes, this is my home," she answered.

"Is this your home? You live with your parents then?"

"Oh, no," she laughed. "I am an old woman, as you'll see!"

And she removed her veil and her wraps.

"There—see! What did I tell you!" she said, and threw her arms about me once again, abruptly, driven by some uncontrollable urge.

She might have been twenty-two or three, wore a ring on her right hand, and might for that matter really have been a married woman. Beautiful? No, she was freckled, and had scarcely any eyebrows. But there was an effervescent life about her, and her mouth was strangely beautiful.

I wanted to ask her who she was, where her husband was, if she had any, and whose house this was I was in, but she threw herself about me every time I opened my mouth and forbade me to be inquisitive.

"My name is Ellen," she explained. "Would you care for something to drink? It really won't disturb anyone if I ring. Perhaps you'd step in here, in the bed-room, meanwhile."

I went into the bed-room. The light from the drawing-room illumined it partially. I saw two beds. Ellen rang and ordered wine, and I heard a maid bring in the wine and go out again. A little later Ellen came into the bedroom after me, but she stopped short in the door. I took a step towards her. She uttered a little cry and at the same time came towards me.

This was last evening.

What further happened? Ah, patience! There is much more!

It was beginning to grow light this morning when I awoke. The daylight crept into the room on either side of the curtain. Ellen was also awake and smiled toward me. Her arms were white and velvety, her breast unusually high. I whispered something to her, and she closed my mouth with hers, mute with tenderness. The day grew lighter and lighter.

Two hours later I was on my feet. Ellen was also up, busy dressing herself —she had got her shoes on. Then it was I experienced something which even now strikes me as a gruesome dream. I was at the wash stand. Ellen had some errand or other in the adjoining room, and as she opened the door I turned around and glanced in. A cold draft from the open windows in the room rushed in upon me, and in the center of the room I could just make out a corpse stretched out on a table. A corpse, in a coffin, dressed in white, with a gray beard, the corpse of a man. His bony knees protruded like madly clenched fists underneath the sheet and his face was sallow and ghastly in the extreme. I could see everything in full daylight. I turned away and said not a word.

When Ellen returned I was dressed and ready to go out. I could scarcely bring myself to respond to her embraces. She put on some additional clothes; she wanted to accompany me down as far as the street door, and I let her come, still saying nothing. At the door she pressed close to the wall so as not to be seen.

"Well, good-bye," she whispered.

"Till tomorrow?" I asked, in part to test her.

"No, not tomorrow."

"Why not tomorrow?"

"Not so many questions, dear. I am going to a funeral tomorrow, a relation of mine is dead. Now there—you know it."

"But the day after tomorrow?"

"Yes, the day after tomorrow, at the door here. I'll meet you. Good-bye!"

I went.

Who was she? And the corpse? With its fists clenched and the corners of its mouth drooping—how ghastly comic! The day after tomorrow she would be expecting me. Ought I to see her again?

I went straight down to the Bernina Café and asked for a directory. I looked up the number so and so Gamle Kongevei, and—there—there was the name. I waited some little time till the morning papers were out. Then I turned quickly to the announcements of deaths. And—sure enough—there I found hers too, the very first in the list, in bold type: "My husband, fifty-three years old, died today after a long illness." The announcement was dated the day before.

I sat for a long time and pondered.

A man marries. His wife is thirty years younger than he. He contracts a lingering illness. One fair day he dies.

And the young widow breathes a sigh of relief.

ISAK AND INGER

THE long, long road over the moors and up into the forest—who trod it into being first of all? Man, a human being, the first that came here. There was no path before he came. Afterward, some beast or other, following the faint tracks over marsh and moorland, wearing them deeper; after these again some Lapp gained scent of the path, and took that way from field to field, looking to his reindeer. Thus was made the road through the great Almenning—the common tracts without an owner; no-man's-land.

The man comes, walking toward the north. He bears a sack, the first sack, carrying food and some few implements. A strong, coarse fellow, with a red iron beard, and little scars on face and hands; sites of old wounds—were they gained in toil or fight? Maybe the man has been in prison, and is looking for a place to hide; or a philosopher, maybe, in search of peace. This or that, he comes; the figure of a man in this great solitude. He trudges on; bird and beast are silent all about him; now and again he utters a word or two; speaking to himself. "Eyah—well, well . . ."—so he speaks to himself. Here and there, where the moors give place to a kindlier spot, an open space in the midst of the forest, he lays down the sack and goes exploring; after a while he returns, heaves the sack to his shoulder again, and trudges on. So through the day, noting time by the sun; night falls, and he throws himself down on the heather, resting on one arm.

A few hours' rest, and he is on the move again: "Eyah, well . . ."—moving northward again, noting time by the sun; a meal of barley cakes and goats' milk cheese, a drink of water from the stream, and on again. This day too he journeys, for there are many kindly spots in the woods to be explored. What is he seeking? A place, a patch of ground? An emigrant, maybe, from the homestead tracts; he keeps his eyes alert, looking out; now and again he climbs to the top of a hill, looking out. The sun goes down once more.

He moves along the western side of a valley; wooded ground, with leafy trees among the spruce and pine, and grass beneath. Hours of this, and twilight is falling, but his ear catches the faint purl of running water, and it heartens him like the voice of a living thing. He climbs the slope, and sees the valley half in darkness below; beyond, the sky to the south. He lies down to rest.

The morning shows him a range of pasture and woodland. He moves down, and there is a green hillside; far below, a glimpse of the stream, and a hare bounding across. The man nods his head, as it were approvingly—the stream is not so broad but that a hare may cross it at a bound. A white grouse sitting close upon its nest starts up at his feet with an angry hiss, and he nods again: feathered game and fur—a good spot this. Heather, bilberry, and cloudberry cover the ground; there are tiny ferns, and the seven-pointed star flowers of the wintergreen. Here and there he stops to dig with an iron tool, and finds good mould, or peaty soil, manured with the rotted wood and fallen leaves of a thousand years. He nods, to say that he has found himself a place to stay and live: ay, he will stay here and live. Two days he goes exploring the country round, returning each evening to the hillside. He sleeps at night on a bed of stacked pine; already he feels at home here, with a bed of pine beneath an overhanging rock.

The worst of his task had been to find the place; this no-man's place, but his. Now, there was work to fill his days. He started at once, stripping birch bark in the woods farther off, while the sap was still in the trees. The bark he pressed and dried, and when he had gathered a heavy load, carried it all the miles back to the village, to be sold for building. Then back to the hill-side, with new sacks of food and implements; flour and pork, a cooking-pot, a spade—out and back along the way he had come, carrying loads all the time. A born carrier of loads, a lumbering barge of a man in the forest—oh, as if he loved his calling, tramping long roads and carrying heavy burdens; as if life without a load upon one's shoulders were a miserable thing, no life for him.

One day he came up with more than the load he bore; came leading three goats in a leash. He was proud of his goats as if they had been horned cat-tle, and tended them kindly. Then came the first stranger passing, a nomad Lapp; at sight of the goats, he knew that this was a man who had come to stay, and spoke to him.

"You going to live here for good?"

"Ay," said the man.

"What's your name?"

"Isak. You don't know of a woman body anywhere'd come and help?"

"No. But I'll say a word of it to all I meet."

"Ay, do that. Say I've creatures here, and none to look to them."

The Lapp went on his way. Isak—ay, he would say a word of that. The man on the hillside was no runaway; he had told his name. A runaway? He would have been found. Only a worker, and a hardy one. He set about cut-ting winter fodder for his goats, clearing the ground, digging a field, shifting stones, making a wall of stones. By the autumn he had built a house for himself, a hut of turf, sound and strong and warm; storms could not shake it, and nothing could burn it down. Here was a home; he could go inside and shut the door, and stay there; could stand outside on the door-slab, the owner of that house, if any should pass by. There were two rooms in the hut; for himself at the one end, and for his beasts at the other. Farthest in, against the wall of rock, was the hayloft. Everything was there.

Two more Lapps come by, father and son. They stand resting with both hands on their long staves, taking stock of the hut and the clearing, noting the sound of the goat-bells up on the hillside.

"*Goddag*," say the Lapps. "And here's fine folk come to live." Lapps talk that way, with flattering words.

"You don't know of any woman hereabouts to help?" says Isak, thinking always of but one thing.

"Woman to help? No. But we'll say a word of it."

"Ay, if you'd be so good. That I've a house and a bit of ground here, and goats, but no woman to help. Say that."

Oh, he had sought about for a woman to help each time he had been down to the village with his loads of bark, but there was none to be found. They would look at him, a widow or an old unmarried one or so, but all afraid to offer, whatever might be in their minds. Isak couldn't tell why. Couldn't tell why? Who would go as help to live with a man in the wilds, ever so many miles away—a whole day's journey to the nearest neighbour? And the man himself was no way charming or pleasant by his looks, far from it; and when he spoke it was no tenor with eyes to heaven, but a coarse voice, something like a beast's.

Well, he would have to manage alone.

In winter, he made great wooden troughs, and sold them in the village, carrying sacks of food and tools back through the snow; hard days when he was tied to a load. There were the goats, and none to look to them; he could not be away for long. And what did he do? Need made him wise; his brain was strong and little used; he trained it up to ever more and more. His first way was to let the goats loose before starting off himself, so that they could get a full feed among the undergrowth in the woods. But he found another plan. He took a bucket, a great vessel, and hung it up by the river so that a single drop fell in at a time, taking fourteen hours to fill it. When it was full to the brim, the weight was right; the bucket sank, and in doing so, pulled a line connected with the hayloft; a trap-door opened, and three bundles of fodder came through—the goats were fed.

That was his way.

A bright idea; an inspiration, maybe, sent from God. The man had none to help him but himself. It served his need until late in the autumn; then came the first snow, then rain, then snow again, snowing all the time. And his machine went wrong; the bucket was filled from above, opening the trap too soon. He fixed a cover over, and all went well again for a time; then came winter, the drop of water froze to an icicle, and stopped the machine for good.

The goats must do as their master—learn to do without.

Hard times—the man had need of help, and there was none, yet still he found a way. He worked and worked at his home; he made a window in the hut with two panes of real glass, and that was a bright and wonderful day in his life. No need of lighting fires to see; he could sit indoors and work at his wooden troughs by daylight. Better days, brighter days . . . eyah!

He read no books, but his thoughts were often with God; it was natural, coming of simplicity and awe. The stars in the sky, the wind in the trees, the solitude and the wide-spreading snow, the might of earth and over earth filled him many times a day with a deep earnestness. He was a sinner and feared God; on Sundays he washed himself out of reverence for the holy day, but worked none the less as through the week.

Spring came; he worked on his patch of ground, and planted potatoes. His live stock multiplied; the two she-goats had each had twins, making seven in all about the place. He made a bigger shed for them, ready for further increase, and put a couple of glass panes in there too. Ay, 'twas lighter and brighter now in every way.

And then at last came help; the woman he needed. She tacked about for a long time, this way and that across the hillside, before venturing near; it was evening before she could bring herself to come down. And then she came—a big, brown-eyed girl, full-built and coarse, with good, heavy hands, and rough hide brogues on her feet as if she had been a Lapp, and a calfskin bag slung from her shoulders. Not altogether young; speaking politely; somewhere nearing thirty.

There was nothing to fear; but she gave him greeting and said hastily: "I was going cross the hills, and took this way, that was all."

"Ho," said the man. He could barely take her meaning, for she spoke in a slovenly way; also, she kept her face turned aside.

"Ay," said she, " 'tis a long way to come."

"Ay, it's that," says the man. "Cross the hills, you said?"

"Yes."

"And what for?"

"I've my people there."

"Eh, so you've your people there? And what's your name?"

"Inger. And what's yours?"

"Isak."

"Isak? H'm. D'you live here yourself, maybe?"

"Ay, here, such as it is."

"Why, 'tis none so bad," said she to please him.

Now he had grown something clever to think out the way of things, and it struck him then she'd come for that very business and no other; had started out two days back just to come here. Maybe she had heard of his wanting a woman to help.

"Go inside a bit and rest your feet," said he.

They went into the hut and took a bit of the food she had brought, and some of his goats' milk to drink; then they made coffee, that she had brought with her in a bladder. Settled down comfortably over their coffee until bedtime. And in the night, he lay wanting her, and she was willing.

She did not go away next morning; all that day she did not go, but helped about the place; milked the goats, and scoured pots and things with fine sand, and got them clean. She did not go away at all. Inger was her name. And Isak was his name.

And now it was another life for the solitary man. True, this wife of his had a curious slovenly way of speech, and always turning her face aside, by reason of a hare-lip that she had, but that was no matter. Save that her mouth was disfigured, she would hardly have come to him at all; he might well be grateful for that she was marked with a hare-lip. And as to that, he himself was no beauty. Isak with the iron beard and rugged body, a grim and surly figure of a man; ay, as a man seen through a flaw in the window-pane. His look was not a gentle one; as if Barabbas might break loose at any minute. It was a wonder Inger herself did not run away.

She did not run away. When he had been out, and came home again, there was Inger at the hut; the two were one, the woman and the hut.

It was another mouth for him to feed, but no loss in that; he had more freedom now, and could go and stay as he needed. And there were matters to be looked to away from home. There was the river; pleasant to look at, and deep and swift besides; a river not to be despised; it must come from some big water up in the hills. He got himself some fishing gear and went exploring;

in the evening he came back with a basket of trout and char. This was a great thing to Inger, and a marvel; she was overwhelmed, being no way used to fine dishes. She clapped her hands and cried out: "Why! wherever . . ." And she was not slow to see how he was pleased at her surprise, and proud of it, for she said more in the same strain—oh, she had never seen the like, and how had he ever managed to find such things!

Inger was a blessing, too, in other ways. No clever head nor great in wit, maybe—but she had two lambing ewes with some of her kinsfolk, and brought them down. It was the best they could have wished for at the hut; sheep with wool and lambs, four new head to their stock about the place; it was growing, getting bigger; a wonder and a marvel how their stock was grown. And Inger brought more; clothes, and little trifles of her own, a looking-glass, and a string of pretty glass beads, a spinning-wheel, and carding-combs. Why, if she went on that gait, the hut would soon be filled from floor to roof, and no room for more! Isak was astonished in his turn at all this wealth of goods, but being a silent man, and slow to speak, he said nothing, only shambled out to the door-slab and looked at the weather, and shambled in again. Ay, he had been lucky indeed; he felt himself more and more in love, or drawn towards her, or whatever it might be.

"You've no call to fetch along all such stuff," said he. " 'Tis more than's needed."

"I've more if I like to fetch it. And there's Uncle Sivert besides—you've heard of him?"

"No."

"Why, he's a rich man, and district treasurer besides."

Love makes a fool of the wise. Isak felt he must do something grand himself, and overdid it. "What I was going to say; you've no need to bother with hoeing potatoes. I'll do it myself the evening, when I come home."

And he took his ax and went off to the woods.

She heard him felling in the woods, not so far off; she could hear from the crash that he was felling big timber. She listened for a while, and then went out to the potato field and set to work hoeing. Love makes fools wise.

Isak came home in the evening, hauling a huge trunk by a rope. Oh, that simple and innocent Isak, he made all the noise he could with his tree-trunk, and coughed and hemmed, all for her to come out and wonder at him. And sure enough:

"Why, you're out of your senses," said Inger when she came out. "Is that work for a man single-handed?" He made no answer; wouldn't have said a word for anything. To do a little more than was work for a man single-handed was nothing to speak of—nothing at all. A stick of timber—huh! "And what are you going to do with it?" she asked.

"Oh, we'll see," he answered carelessly, as if scarcely heeding she was there. But when he saw that she had hoed the potatoes after all he was not pleased. It was as if she had done almost as much as he; and that was not to his liking. He slipped the rope from the tree-trunk and went off with it once more.

"What, haven't you done yet?"

"No," said he gruffly.

And he came back with another stick like the last, only with no noise nor sign of being out of breath; hauled it up to the hut like an ox, and left it there.

That summer he felled a mass of timber, and brought it to the hut.

Inger packed up some food one day in her calfskin bag. "I'd thought of going across to see my people, just how they're faring."

"Ay," said Isak.

"I must have a bit of talk with them about things."

Isak did not go out at once to see her off, but waited quite a while. And when at last he shambled out, looking never the least bit anxious, never the least bit miserable and full of fear, Inger was all but vanished already through the fringe of the forest.

"Hem!" He cleared his throat, and called, "Will you be coming back maybe?" He had not meant to ask her that, but . . .

"Coming back? Why, what's in your mind? Of course I'll be coming back." "H'm."

So he was left alone again—eyah, well . . . ! With his strength, and the love of work that was in him, he could not idle in and out about the hut doing nothing; he set to, clearing timber, felling straight, good sticks, and cutting them flat on two sides. He worked at this all through the day, then he milked the goats and went to bed.

Sadly bare and empty now in the hut; a heavy silence clung about the peat walls and the earthen floor; a deep and solemn loneliness. Spinning-wheel and carding-combs were in their place; the beads, too, were safe as they had been, stowed away in a bag under the roof. Inger had taken nothing of her belongings. But Isak, unthinkably simple as he was, grew afraid of the dark in the light summer nights, and saw Shapes and Things stealing past the window. He got up before dawn, about two o'clock by the light, and ate his breakfast, a mighty dish of porridge to last the day, and save the waste of time in cooking more. In the evening he turned up new ground, to make a bigger field for the potatoes.

Three days he worked with spade and ax by turns; Inger should be coming on the next. 'Twould be but reasonable to have a platter of fish for her when she came—but the straight road to the water lay by the way she would come, and it might seem . . . So he went a longer way; a new way, over the hills where he had never been before. Grey rock and brown, and strewed about with bits of heavy stone, heavy as copper or lead. There might be many things in those heavy stones; gold or silver, like as not—he had no knowledge of such things, and did not care. He came to the water; the fly was up, and the fish were biting well that night. He brought home a basket of fish that Inger would open her eyes to see! Going back in the morning by the way he had come, he picked up a couple of the heavy little stones among the hills; they were brown, with specks of dark blue here and there, and wondrous heavy in the hand.

Inger had not come, and did not come. This was the fourth day. He milked the goats as he had used to do when he lived alone with them and had no other to help; then he went up to a quarry near by and carried down stones; great piles of carefully chosen blocks and flakes, to build a wall. He was busy with no end of things.

On the fifth evening, he turned in to rest with a little fear at his heart—but there were the carding-combs and spinning-wheel, and the string of beads. Sadly empty and bare in the hut, and never a sound; the hours were long, and when at last he did hear something like a sound of footsteps outside, he told himself that it was fancy, nothing more. "Eyah, *Herregud!*"[1] he murmured, desolate in spirit. And Isak was not one to use words lightly. There was the tramping of feet again outside, and a moment after something gliding past the window; something with horns, something alive. He sprang up, over to the door, and lo, a vision! "God or the devil," muttered Isak, who did not use words lightly. He saw a cow; Inger and a cow, vanishing into the shed.

If he had not stood there himself and heard it—Inger talking softly to the cow in the shed—he would not have believed. But there he stood. And all at once a black misgiving came into his mind: a clever wife, ay, a manager of wonders—but, after all . . . No, it was too much, and that was the only word for it. A spinning-wheel and carding-combs at a pinch; even the beads per-haps, though they were over fine to be come by in any way proper and natu-ral. But a cow, picked up straying on the road, maybe, or in a field—it would be missed in no time, and have to be found.

Inger stepped out of the shed, and said with a proud little laugh:

"It's only me. I've brought my cow along."

"H'm," said Isak.

"It was that made me so long—I couldn't go but softly with her over the hills."

"And so you've brought a cow?" said he.

"Yes," said she, all ready to burst with greatness and riches on earth. "Don't you believe me, perhaps?"

Isak feared the worst, but made no sign, and only said:

"Come inside and get something to eat."

"Did you see her? Isn't she a pretty cow?"

"Ay, a fine cow," said Isak. And speaking as carelessly as he could, he asked, "Where d'you get her?"

"Her name's Goldenhorns. What's that wall to be for you've been building up here? You'll work yourself to death, you will. Oh, come and look at the cow, now, won't you?"

They went out to look, and Isak was in his underclothes, but that was no matter. They looked and looked the cow all over carefully, in every part, and noted all the markings, head and shoulders, buttocks and thighs, where it was red and white, and how it stood.

"How old d'you think she might be?" asked Isak cautiously.

"Think? Why, she's just exactly a tiny way on in her fourth year. I brought her up myself, and they all said it was the sweetest calf they'd ever seen. But will there be feed enough here, d'you think?"

Isak began to believe, as he was only too willing to do, that all was well. "As for the feed, why, there'll be feed enough, never fear."

Then they went indoors to eat and drink and make an evening together. They lay awake talking of Cow; of the great event. "And isn't she a dear cow,

[1] Literally, "Lord God." The word is frequently used, as here, in a sense of resignation, as it were a sigh.

too? Her second's on the way. And her name's Goldenhorns. Are you asleep, Isak?"

"No."

"And what do you think, she knew me again; knew me at once, and followed me like a lamb. We lay up in the hills a bit last night."

"Ho?"

"But she'll have to be tied up through the summer, all the same, or she'll be running off. A cow's a cow."

"Where's she been before?" asked Isak at last.

"Why, with my people, where she belonged. And they were quite sorry to lose her, I can tell you; and the little ones cried when I took her away."

Could she be making it all up, and coming out with it so pat? No, it wasn't thinkable. It must be true, the cow was hers. Ho, they were getting well-to-do, with this hut of theirs, this farm of theirs; why, 'twas good enough for any one. Ay, they'd as good as all they could wish for already. Oh, that Inger; he loved her and she loved him again; they were frugal folk; they lived in primitive wise, and lacked for nothing. "Let's go to sleep!" And they went to sleep. And wakened in the morning to another day, with things to look at, matters to see to, once again; ay, toil and pleasure, ups and downs, the way of life.

As, for instance, with those timber baulks—should he try to fit them up together? Isak had kept his eyes about him down in the village, with that very thing in mind, and seen how it was done; he could build with timber himself, why not? Moreover, it was a call upon him; it must be done. Hadn't they a farm with sheep, a farm with a cow already, goats that were many already and would be more?—their live stock alone was crowding them out of the turf hut; something must be done. And best get on with it at once, while the potatoes were still in flower, and before the haytime began. Inger would have to lend a hand here and there.

Isak wakes in the night and gets up, Inger sleeping fine and sound after her long tramp, and out he goes to the cowshed. Now it must not be thought that he talked to Cow in any obsequious and disgustful flattery; no, he patted her decently, and looked her over once more in every part, to see if there should, by chance, be any sign, any mark of her belonging to strange owners. No mark, no sign, and Isak steals away relieved.

There lies the timber. He falls to, rolling the baulks, then lifting them, setting them up against the wall in a framework; one big frame for a parlour, and a smaller one—there must be a room to sleep in. It was heavy work, hard-breathing work, and his mind being set on it, he forgot the time. There comes a smoke from the roof-hole of the hut, and Inger steps out and calls to breakfast.

"And what are you busy with now?" asked Inger.

"You're early about," says Isak, and that was all.

Ho, that Isak with his secrets and his lordly ways! But it pleased him, maybe, to have her asking and wondering, and curious about his doings. He ate a bit, and sat for a while in the hut before going out again. What could he be waiting for?

"H'm," says he at last, getting up. "This won't do. Can't sit here idling today. Work to be done."

"Seems like you're building," says Inger. "What?"

And he answered condescendingly, this great man who went about building with timber all by himself, he answered: "Why, you can see as much, I take it." .

"Yes. . . . Yes, of course."

"Building—why, there's no help for it as I can see. Here's you come bringing a whole cow to the farm—that means a cowshed, I suppose?"

Poor Inger, not so eternally wise as he, as Isak, that lord of creation. And this was before she learned to know him, and reckon with his way of putting things. Says Inger:

"Why, it's never a cowshed you're building, surely?"

"Ho," says he.

"But you don't mean it? I—I thought you'd be building a house first."

"Think so?" says Isak, putting up a face as if he'd never in life have thought of that himself.

"Why, yes. And put the beasts in the hut."

Isak thought for a bit. "Ay, maybe 'twould be best so."

"There," says Inger, all glad and triumphant. "You see I'm some good after all."

"Ay, that's true. And what'd you say to a house with two rooms in?"

"*Two* rooms? Oh . . . ! Why, 'twould be just like other folks. Do you think we could?"

They did. Isak he went about building, notching his baulks and fitting up his framework; also he managed a hearth and fireplace of picked stones, though this last was troublesome, and Isak himself was not always pleased with his work. Haytime came, and he was forced to climb down from his building and go about the hillsides far and near, cutting grass and bearing home the hay in mighty loads. Then one rainy day he must go down to the village.

"What you want in the village?"

"Well, I can't say exactly as yet. . . ."

He set off, and stayed away two days, and came back with a cooking-stove —a barge of a man surging up through the forest with a whole iron stove on his back. " 'Tis more than a man can do," said Inger. "You'll kill yourself that gait." But Isak pulled down the stone hearth, that didn't look so well in the new house, and set up the cooking-stove in its place. " 'Tisn't every one has a cooking-stove," said Inger. "Of all the wonders, how we're getting on! . . ."

Haymaking still; Isak bringing in loads and masses of hay, for woodland grass is not the same as meadow grass, more's the pity, but poorer by far. It was only on rainy days now that he could spare time for his building; 'twas a lengthy business, and even by August, when all the hay was in, safely stored under the shelter of the rock, the new house was still but half-way done. Then by September: "This won't do," said Isak. "You'd better run down to the village and get a man to help." Inger had been something poorly of late, and didn't run much now, but all the same she got herself ready to go.

But Isak had changed his mind again; had put on his lordly manner again, and said he would manage by himself. "No call to bother with other folk," says he; "I can manage it alone."

" 'Tis more than one man's work," says Inger. "You'll wear yourself out."

"Just help me to hoist these up," says Isak, and that was all.

October came, and Inger had to give up. This was a hard blow, for the roof-beams must be got up at any cost, and the place covered in before the autumn rains; there was not a day to be lost. What could be wrong with Inger? Not going to be ill? She would make cheese now and then from the goats' milk, but beyond that she did little save shifting Goldenhorns a dozen times a day where she grazed.

"Bring up a good-sized basket, or a box," she had said, "next time you're down to the village."

"What d'you want that for?" asked Isak.

"I'll just be wanting it," said Inger.

Isak hauled up the roof-beams on a rope, Inger guiding them with one hand; it seemed a help just to have her about. Bit by bit the work went on; there was no great height to the roof, but the timber was huge and heavy for a little house.

The weather kept fine, more or less. Inger got the potatoes in by herself, and Isak had the roofing done before the rain came on in earnest. The goats were brought in of a night into the hut and all slept there together; they managed somehow, they managed everyway, and did not grumble.

Isak was getting ready for another journey down to the village. Said Inger very humbly:

"Do you think perhaps you could bring up a good-sized basket, or a box?"

"I've ordered some glass windows," said Isak. "And a couple of painted doors. I'll have to fetch them up," said he in his lordly way.

"Ay well, then. It's no great matter about the basket."

"What did you want with a basket? What's it for?"

"What's it for? . . . Oh, haven't you eyes in your head!"

Isak went off deep in thought. Two days later he came back, with a window and a door for the parlour, and a door for the bedroom; also he had hung round his neck in front a good-sized packing-case, and full of provisions to boot.

"You'll carry yourself to death one day," said Inger.

"Ho, indeed!" Isak was very far indeed from being dead; he took out a bottle of medicine from his pocket—naphtha it was—and gave it to Inger with orders to take it regularly and get well again. And there were the windows and the painted doors that he could fairly boast of; he set to work at once fitting them in. Oh, such little doors, and second-hand at that, but painted up all neat and fine again in red and white; 'twas almost as good as having pictures on the walls.

And now they moved into the new building, and the animals had the turf hut to themselves, only a lambing ewe was left with Cow, lest she should feel lonely.

They had done well, these builders in the waste; ay, 'twas a wonder and a marvel to themselves.

Isak worked on the land until the frost set in; there were stones and roots to be dug up and cleared away, and the meadow to be levelled ready for next year. When the ground hardened, he left his field work and became a woodman, felling and cutting up great quantities of logs.

"What do you want with all these logs?" Inger would say.

"Oh, they'll be useful some way," said Isak off-handedly, as though he had no plan. But Isak had a plan, never fear. Here was virgin forest, a dense growth, right close up to the house, a barrier hedging in his fields where he wanted room. Moreover, there must be some way of getting the logs down to the village that winter; there were folk enough who would be glad of wood for firing. It was sound enough, and Isak was in no doubt; he stuck to his work in the forest, felling trees and cutting them up into logs.

Inger came out often, to watch him at work. He took no notice, but made as if her coming were no matter, and not at all a thing he wished for her to do; but she understood all the same that it pleased him to have her there. They had a strange way, too, of speaking to each other at times.

"Couldn't you find things to do but come out here and get stark frozen?" says Isak.

"I'm well enough for me," says Inger. "But I can't see there's any living sense in you working yourself to death like you do."

"Ho! You just pick up that coat of mine there and put it on you."

"Put on your coat? Likely, indeed. I've no time to sit here now, with Goldenhorns ready to calve and all."

"H'm. Calving, you say?"

"As if you didn't know! But what do you think now about that same calf. Let it stay and be weaned, maybe?"

"Do as you think; 'tis none of my business with calves and things."

"Well, 'twould be a pity to eat up calf, seems to me. And leave us with but one cow on the place."

"Don't seem to me like you'd do that anyway," says Isak.

That was their way. Lonely folk, ugly to look at and overfull of growth, but a blessing for each other, for the beasts, and for the earth.

And Goldenhorns calved. A great day in the wilderness, a joy and a delight. They gave her flour-wash, and Isak himself saw to it there was no stint of flour, though he had carried it all the way himself, on his back. And there lay a pretty calf, a beauty, red-flanked like her mother, and comically bewildered at the miracle of coming into the world. In a couple of years she would be having calves of her own.

" 'Twill be a grand fine cow when she grows up," said Inger. "And what are we to call her, now? I can't think."

Inger was childish in her ways, and no clever wit for anything.

"Call her?" said Isak. "Why, Silverhorns, of course; what else?"

The first snow came. As soon as there was a passable road, Isak set out for the village, full of concealment and mystery as ever, when Inger asked his errand. And sure enough, he came back this time with a new and unthinkable surprise. A horse and sledge, nothing less.

"Here's foolishness," says Inger. "And you've not stolen it, I suppose?"

"Stolen it?"

"Well, found it, then?"

Now if only he could have said: " 'Tis my horse—our horse. . . ." But to tell the truth, he had only hired it, after all. Hired horse and sledge to cart his logs.

Isak drove down with his loads of firewood, and brought back food, herrings and flour. And one day he came up with a young bull on the sledge; bought it for next to nothing, by reason they were getting short of fodder down in the village. Shaggy and thin, no ways a beauty, but decently built for all that, and wanted no more than proper feed to set it right. And with a cow they had already . . . "What'll you be bringing up next?" said Inger.

Isak brought up a host of things. Brought up planks and a saw he had got in exchange for timber; a grindstone, a wafer iron, tools—all in exchange for his logs. Inger was bursting with riches, and said each time: "What, more things! When we've cattle and all a body could think of!"

They had enough to meet their needs for no little time to come, and were well-to-do folk. What was Isak to start on again next spring? He had thought it all out, tramping down beside his loads of wood that winter; he would clear more ground over the hillside and level it off, cut up more logs to dry through the summer, and take down double loads when the snow came fit for sledging. It worked out beautifully.

But there was another matter Isak had thought of times out of number: that Goldenhorns, where had she come from, whose had she been? There was never a wife on earth like Inger. Ho! a wild thing she was, that let him do as he pleased with her, and was glad of it. But—suppose one day they were to come for the cow, and take it away—and worse, maybe, to come after? What was it Inger herself had said about the horse: "You haven't stolen it, I suppose, or found it?" That was her first thought, yes. That was what she had said; who could say if she were to be trusted—what should he do? He had thought of it all many a time. And here he had brought up a mate himself for the cow—for a stolen cow, maybe!

And there was the horse he would have to return again. A pity—for 'twas a little friendly beast, and grown fond of them already.

"Never mind," said Inger comfortingly. "Why, you've done wonders already."

"Ay, but just now with the spring coming on—and I've need of a horse. . . ."

Next morning he drove off quietly with the last load, and was away two days. Coming back on foot the third day, he stopped as he neared the house, and stood listening. There was a curious noise inside. . . . A child crying—Eyah, *Herregud!* . . . Well, there it was; but a terrible strange thing. And Inger had never said a word.

He stepped inside, and there first thing of all was the packing-case—the famous packing-case that he had carried home slung round his neck in front; there it was, hung up by a string at each end from the ceiling, a cradle and a bedplace for the child. Inger was up, pottering about half-dressed—she had milked the cow and the goats, as it might have been just an ordinary day.

The child stopped crying. "You're through with it already?" said Isak.

"Ay, I'm through with it now."

"H'm."

"It came the first evening you were gone."

"H'm."

"I'd only to get my things off and hang up the cradle there, but it was too much for me, like, and I had to lie down."

"Why didn't you tell me before?"

"Why, I couldn't say to a minute when it'd be. 'Tis a boy."

"Ho, a boy."

"And I can't for the life of me think what we're to call him," said Inger.

Isak peeped at the little red face; well shaped it was, and no hare-lip, and a growth of hair all thick on the head. A fine little fellow for his rank and station in a packing-case; Isak felt himself curiously weak. The rugged man stood there with a miracle before him; a thing created first of all in a sacred mist, showing forth now in life with a little face like an allegory. Days and years, and the miracle would be a human being.

"Come and have your food," said Inger. . . .

Isak is a woodman, felling trees and sawing logs. He is better off now than before, having a saw. He works away, and mighty piles of wood grow up; he makes a street of them, a town, built up of stacks and piles of wood. Inger is more about the house now, and does not come out as before to watch him at his work; Isak must find a pretext now and then to slip off home for a moment instead. Queer to have a little fellow like that about the place! Isak, of course, would never dream of taking any notice—'twas but a bit of a thing in a packing-case. And as for being fond of it . . . But when it cried, well, it was only human nature to feel just a little something for a cry like that; a little tiny cry like that.

"Don't touch him!" says Inger. "With your hands all messed up with resin and all!"

"Resin, indeed!" says Isak. "Why, I haven't had resin on my hands since I built this house. Give me the boy, let me take him—there, he's as right as can be!"

Early in May came a visitor. A woman came over the hills to that lonely place where none ever came; she was of Inger's kinsfolk, though not near, and they made her welcome.

"I thought I'd just look in," she says, "and see how Goldenhorns gets on since she left us."

Inger looks at the child, and talks to it in a little pitying voice: "Ah, there's none asks how he's getting on, that's but a little tiny thing."

"Why, as for that, any one can see how he's getting on. A fine little lad and all. And who'd have thought it a year gone, Inger, to find you here with house and husband and child and all manner of things."

" 'Tis no doing of mine to praise. But there's one sitting there that took me as I was and no more."

"And wedded?—Not wedded yet, no, I see."

"We'll see about it, the time this little man's to be christened," says Inger. "We'd have been wedded before, but couldn't come by it, getting down to a church and all. What do you say, Isak?"

"Wedded?" says Isak. "Why, yes, of course."

"But if as you'd help us, Oline," says Inger. "Just to come up for a few days in the off time once, and look to the creatures here while we're away?"

Ay, Oline would do that.

"We'll see it's no loss to you after."

Why, as to that, she'd leave it to them. . . . "And you're building again, I see. Now what'll that be for? Isn't there built enough?"

Inger sees her chance and puts in here: "Why, you must ask him about that. I'm not to know."

"Building?" says Isak. "Oh, 'tis nothing to speak of. A bit of a shed, maybe, if we should need it. What's that you were saying about Goldenhorns? You'd like to see her?"

They go across to the cowshed, and there's cow and calf to show, and an ox to boot. The visitor nods her head, looking at the beasts, and at the shed; all fine as could be, and clean as couldn't be cleaner. "Trust Inger for looking after creatures every way," says Oline.

Isak puts a question: "Goldenhorns was at your place before?"

"Ay, from a calf. Not my place, though; at my son's. But 'tis all the same. And we've her mother still."

Isak had not heard better news a long while; it was a burden lighter. Goldenhorns was his and Inger's by honest right. To tell the truth, he had half thought of getting rid of his trouble in a sorry way; to kill off the cow that autumn, scrape the hide, bury the horns, and thus make away with all trace of Cow Goldenhorns in this life. No need for that now. And he grew mightily proud of Inger all at once.

"Ay, Inger," says he. "She's one to manage things, that's true. There's not her like nor equal to be found. 'Twas a poor place here till I got a woman of my own, as you might say."

"Why, 'tis but natural so," says Oline.

And so this woman from across the hills, a soft-spoken creature with her wits about her, and by name Oline, she stayed with them a couple of days, and had the little room to sleep in. And, when she set out for home, she had a bundle of wool that Inger had given her, from the sheep. There was no call to hide that bundle of wool, but Oline took care that Isak should not see it.

Then the child and Isak and his wife again; the same world again, and the work of the day, with many little joys and big. Goldenhorns was yielding well, the goats had dropped their kids and were yielding well; Inger had a row of red and white cheeses already, stored away to get ripe. It was her plan to save up cheeses till there were enough to buy a loom. Oh, that Inger; she knew how to weave.

And Isak built a shed—he too had a plan of his own, no doubt. He set up a new wing built out from the side of the turf hut, with double panelling boards, made a doorway in it, and a neat little window with four panes; laid on a roof of outer boards, and made do with that till the ground thawed and he could get turf. All that was useful and necessary; no flooring, no smooth-planed walls, but Isak had fixed up a box partition, as for a horse, and a manger.

It was nearing the end of May. The sun had thawed the high ground; Isak roofed in his shed with turf and it was finished. Then one morning he ate a meal to last for the day, took some more food with him, shouldered pick and spade, and went down to the village.

"Bring up three yards of cotton print, if you can," Inger called after him.

"What do you want with that?" said Isak.

Isak was long away; it almost seemed as if he had gone for good. Inger looked at the weather every day, noting the way of the wind, as if she were expecting a sailing-ship; she went out at nighttime to listen; even thought of taking the child on her arm and going after him. Then at last he came back, with a horse and cart. *"Ptro!"* shouted Isak as he drew up; shouted so as to be heard. And the horse was well behaved, and stood as quiet as could be, nodding at the turf hut as if it knew the place again. Nevertheless, Isak must call out, "Hi, come and hold the horse a bit, can't you?"

Out goes Inger. "Where is it now? Oh, Isak, have you hired him again? Where have you been all this time? 'Tis six days gone."

"Where d'you think I'd be? Had to go all sorts of ways round to find a road for this cart of mine. Hold the horse a bit, can't you?"

"Cart of yours! You don't mean to say you've bought that cart?"

Isak dumb; Isak swelling with things unspoken. He lifts out a plough and a harrow he has brought; nails, provisions, a grindstone, a sack of corn. "And how's the child?" he asks.

"Child's all right. Have you bought that cart, that's what I want to know? For here have I been longing and longing for a loom," says she jestingly, in her gladness at having him back again.

Isak dumb once more, for a long space, busied with his own affairs, pondering, looking round for a place to put all his goods and implements; it was hard to find room for them all. But when Inger gave up asking, and began talking to the horse instead, he came out of his lofty silence at last.

"Ever see a farm *without* a horse and cart, and plough and harrows, and all the rest of it? And since you want to know, why, I've bought that horse and cart, and all that's in it," says he.

And Inger could only shake her head and murmur: "Well, I never did see such a man!"

Isak was no longer littleness and humility; he had paid, as it were, like a gentleman, for Goldenhorns. "Here you are," he could say. "I've brought along a horse; we can call it quits."

He stood there, upright and agile, against his wont; shifted the plough once more, picked it up and carried it with one hand and stood it up against the wall. Oh, he could manage an estate! He took up the other things: the harrow, the grindstone, a new fork he had bought, all the costly agricultural implements, treasures of the new home, a grand array. All requisite appliances—nothing was lacking.

"H'm. As for that loom, why, we'll manage that too, I dare say, as long as I've my health. And there's your cotton print; they'd none but blue, so I took that."

There was no end to the things he brought. A bottomless well, rich in all manner of things, like a city store.

Says Inger: "I wish Oline could have seen all this when she was here."

Just like a woman! Sheer senseless vanity—as if that mattered! Isak sniffed contemptuously. Though perhaps he himself would not have been displeased if Oline had been there to see.

The child was crying.

"Go in and look after the boy," said Isak. "I'll look to the horse."

He takes out the horse and leads it into the stable: ay, here is Isak putting his horse into the stable! Feeds it and strokes it and treats it tenderly. And how much was owing now, on that horse and cart?—Everything, the whole sum, a mighty debt; but it should all be paid that summer, never fear. He had stacks of cordwood to pay with, and some building bark from last year's cut, not to speak of heavy timber. There was time enough. But later on, when the pride and glory had cooled off a little, there were bitter hours of fear and anxiety; all depended on the summer and the crops; how the year turned out.

The days now were occupied in field work and more field work; he cleared new bits of ground, getting out roots and stones; ploughing, manuring, harrowing, working with pick and spade, breaking lumps of soil and crumbling them with hand and heel; a tiller of the ground always, laying out fields like velvet carpets. He waited a couple of days longer—there was a look of rain about—and then he sowed his corn.

For generations back, into forgotten time, his fathers before him had sowed corn; solemnly, on a still, calm evening, best with a gentle fall of warm and misty rain, soon after the grey goose flight. Potatoes were a new thing, nothing mystic, nothing religious; women and children could plant them—earth-apples that came from foreign parts, like coffee; fine rich food, but much like swedes and mangolds. Corn was nothing less than bread; corn or no corn meant life or death.

Isak walked bareheaded, in Jesu name, a sower. Like a tree-stump with hands to look at, but in his heart like a child. Every cast was made with care, in a spirit of kindly resignation. Look! the tiny grains that are to take life and grow, shoot up into ears, and give more corn again; so it is throughout all the earth where corn is sown. Palestine, America, the valleys of Norway itself—a great wide world, and here is Isak, a tiny speck in the midst of it all, a sower. Little showers of corn flung out fanwise from his hand; a kindly clouded sky, with a promise of the faintest little misty rain.

Carl Spitteler

ANNIVERSARY CELEBRATIONS

I AM not the only one who cannot altogether respond to the jubilation felt by a nation when one of its great men attains the age of sixty, or seventy, or eighty years. On the contrary, I find myself in most excellent company— *viz.* the company of those whose anniversaries are thus celebrated. For of all the people who take part in a jubilee, the jubilarian himself is the least disposed to feel jubilant. His mood is one apart, full of melancholy and bitterness. The patient endure it in silence, the defiant save themselves from the threatened operation by taking to the woods, if, indeed, they do not, like Grillparzer, call down fire and brimstone from heaven.

"But it really, at bottom, pleases them, in spite of a little sadness." Certainly, a little gentle sadness is pleasant, like every tempered suffering. And your voluminous protestations of affection, gratitude, and admiration may soften them, may move them, may move them perhaps even to tears. Many an unconscious grudge may vanish, all sorts of evil tensions may be relaxed. "After all, it did my heart good." Excellent, if that is all you want. But this "doing good after all" unfortunately reminds me of another case, which has little of the jubilee about it—*viz.* a death in the family. One probably does good "after all" to those concerned when one's sympathy moves them to tears. On this principle your jubilees become jubilees of condolence. In fine, in the mouth of the man whose jubilee is being celebrated—and, after all, he counts a little in the matter—the jubilee tastes like a bitter-sweet pastry, soaked in a saline infusion.

You approach the gentleman with congratulations? Congratulations on what, if I may venture to ask? One generally felicitates a man when he has attained something that he wanted—*e.g.* when he has been elected Mayor, or has become a Privy Councillor, or has won the chief prize in a sweepstake, or has married a charming bride, or has become the father of a healthy and vigorous boy-baby (mother and child doing as well as could be expected). But in the case of a jubilee, what has the poor victim attained? His seventieth year. An accursed prize! It amounts to a permit for cancer in the stomach or softening of the brain.

Yes, indeed, it is a fine idea to have a national festival of admiration for a single living individual—if only it came in good time and sprang spontaneously from a naïve overflow of enthusiasm. On the other hand an admiration which is born of the calendar; which waits pedantically for a date and as late a date as possible at that, in order not to be too early, *i.e.* in good time; which follows the beat of the conductor's baton, so as to come in at the proper moment—an admiration, in short, which is organised like a corner in copper, a gracious, condescending admiration, where the great age of the man celebrated is allowed to count as an extenuating circumstance—that is a truly rancid national fête. Do you imagine for one minute that the hero of the occasion does not see the strings by which this precious jubilee is worked? Do you think he cannot measure and weigh the impresarios who have contracted for the national enthusiasm; the grave-diggers, who squeeze his hand, while his obituary, ready for the press, sticks out of their pockets? It is an elevated lot, that of a king. But a king by grace of the king-makers? And what sort of king-makers! Let us out with it boldly. Your so-called poet jubilees are bookseller jubilees. In the second line they are biographic and monographic jubilees. At the age of seventy a poet will soon be a testator. That's where the honey comes in.

Would you like to know for whom these anniversaries were originally intended? Who is really refreshed by them? Who is he for whom they are really good, not merely good "on the whole"? The answer is easy. He who has no other merit than his advanced age; he who, his whole life long, has had nothing else to celebrate but his birthdays. A humble bookkeeper, a subordinate official, an obscure schoolmaster in an obscure town, who has done his duty honestly and modestly for twenty-five or fifty years, deserves a celebration of his age or (rather) of his period of service; and he doubtless feels his soul uplifted on the occasion. Now, for the first time in their life, they feel that they are in the limelight; for once at least they feel their petty ambition gratified; henceforth they can lay on the sick-bed beside them the sweet illusion that they have really done something, have had some value, have attained some end. Those, therefore, who celebrate the seventieth birthday of a great poet elevate him to the dizzy height of the bookkeeper of Brandt's celebrated Swiss Pills.

One thing is certain. Before his seventieth birthday the victim had a sixtieth birthday, before that a fiftieth, and so on. Why were no cheers uttered, no speeches made, no paragraphs printed, and no toasts drained on these occasions? I understand perfectly that jubilees have no overtures, only tattoos. All the same, a silence of thirty years before the first chord is rather excessive, and a sudden fortissimo of the whole orchestra after the muted passage seems rather abrupt. True fame does not orchestrate in this way; it prefers *sempre crescendo*. But, naturally, one cannot expect measure from a jubilee of which the tempo is wrong.

Jesting apart, the contrast between a silence of many years and the sudden *tutti con timpani* at the end of one's life is so startling a phenomenon, that it gives us pause and demands an explanation. I have often asked myself whether green-eyed jealousy does not, after all, have a finger in the pie. I have asked myself the question and I have answered "yes"; and I still give the same answer.

The chief reason, however, occurred to me by chance when Germany was perpetrating the jubilee of Paul Heyse. [One perpetrates a jubilee just as one perpetrates a solecism.] One of the leading German journals published a brief, in which it was seriously argued that it ought not to establish a precedent for celebrating an author at such a ridiculously early age as his sixtieth birthday. There it stands, in cold print, frankly and honestly. Let us grasp the idea, hold it fast, and see that it never more escapes us. A poet of sixty is too young to have a jubilee. Consequently, it is agreed that it is the robustness, the full vigour of creative power (and nothing else) that vitiates this hushed pause in honour of genius. A poet must not be publicly honoured until he has at least one foot in the grave. As already said, such a golden axiom as this must not be allowed to perish from the earth; it must be a never-dying possession of posterity, like the sayings of the Seven Sages.

However, it is not really envy that speaks in this manner. For envy does not declare itself so frankly; it whispers. No, it is rather the delectable postulate that the importance of a poet does not begin until he is "a complete and rounded whole", until we can "survey at a glance" his "full activity", until we can "outline a lifesize portrait" of him. In other words, when we can discuss, explain, edit, comment upon, and emend him; when, in fact, we can grind him in the literary mortar.

This is the real "open sesame". Not his works—God forbid, those are quite secondary; what is really important is his image and superscription as a poet, the place and number assigned to the man in the history of literature. If we never knew it before, we should know it now. Modern Germany, in spite of all its fuss and gabble about Goethe and poetry, is concerned with literary history, not with literature. The aim is to lecture on the poet, not to enjoy him.

I shall probably have a long time to wait before the advent of the jubilee which I should really enjoy and in which I should gladly play a part. I mean the jubilee in honour of a great work immediately after its first appearance.

HYLAS AND KALEIDUSA
OVER HILL AND VALE

(From "Olympian Spring")

The night had fled, pursued by Chanticleer;
The busy day officiously drew near,
While yet the air, though waked by whispering beams,
Stretched in the half-light, drowsy still with dreams.
Behold! there creeps the dew-wet vines among,
Parting with careful hand the tendrils long,
Hylas, fleet Hermes' brother. Through the rows,
Stirred by the morning-breezes, down he goes,
Rallied by blackbirds, by grasshoppers rated;
But now on level ground he lands elated,
When—curse!—a blinding ray, as diamond bright,
The East, the South, are red with vivid light,
All heaven seems to break in fiery brands,
And on the car of flame Apollo stands!
"O brother Hylas, whither now away
Stealing while yet the valley-lands are grey?
Whom to avoid or meet?" Caught in the act,
Hylas blinks upward: "Brother dear, in fact
We think alike, that walking, sleeping, wooing,
By two alone are really worth the doing.
The difference is this—a cloud for thee,
But earthly woods are good enough for me."

So spake he, hurrying on. And soon he could
Plunge in the shelter of a friendly wood;
There he stood still, and feigned a cuckoo-cry—
A turtle-dove cooed softly in reply,
And fresh as morning, for the road arrayed,
Stepped the nymph Kaleidusa from the shade.
A kiss, a laughing word—then through the chace
They run with linkèd arms and equal pace;
Bravely they march, and in their hearts anew

The coloured day, the magic air, the blue,
The enchanted blossoms—freshly born are all,
And eyes look love, though maiden-lashes fall.
For everything that is, or far or near,
To their untroubled gaze gives answer clear—
The whispering grass, the clouds that sail on high,
Can keep no secrets from a lover's eye.
"Hark to the humming bees in shade o'erhead,
Telling the limes about us, love!"—He said:
"O Kaleidusa, I can see and hear
A world of beauty, yet for me more dear
The sound of your fond footsteps on the grass,
The sighs that o'er your bosom gently pass—
For all the organ-tones that ever were
I would not change that little song, I swear!"
And thus they wandered on with sturdy day,
Till rapturous noon upon the thickets lay;
Then tempted by the breath of waters cool
They bathed in dancing brook or shadowed pool,
And, limbs relaxed in dappled hazel-bowers,
Lay side by side, supine, for hours and hours.
But freshening breezes promised fresh delight,
So, stretching arms and legs, they sprang upright,
Leaped, clapped their hands for joy—and soon the two
Ran singing all the glades and clearings through.
No matter where. The way they scorned to learn.

Now evening says to afternoon: "My turn!"
So saying, spreads her pair of dusky wings
And broad on sunlit banks their shadow flings;
Lets fall her purple cloak, whence darkness creeps,
Lured from the shimmering borders where it sleeps.
Then on a bench near by behold her sit,
Open earth's picture-book, and paint in it.
"May I?" asked Kaleidusa. "Would you mind?"
And standing on her tiptoes watched behind.
Mysterious in soft clear tints there grew
Between the o'erarching branches, maidens two,
Morpho and Pantaphila, Pan's girl-brood,
Gleefully changing forms in childish mood—
To birds and beasts their slender selves distorting,
Now as a heron on the breezes sporting,
Now as a roe-deer leaping in the air—
A wish, and once again they both stood fair
And slim, Pan's gentle girls, no more, no less . . .
The village yonder rings with happiness;
Children are playing soldiers: "One, two, three!"
But "Three" is hardly said ere ends their glee,
And at the house-door, thoughtful men, sit they,

And next the passing-bell tolls each away.
"What does it matter?" murmurs the mill-stream;
"Morpho and man and change—it's all a dream.
They call it Nature, I am told. Let be!
It is Ananke's gay-grim fantasy!"

Thus for a while on evening's brink delaying,
The lovers, hand in hand, went fondly straying,
Till softly, dimly, in the vale below,
Red-capped, the twilight-shepherds come and go,
Gathering their herds of dreams to fold and sleep;
And from the brook, aroused from slumber deep,
Sly Pan phantasmal darts on bat-like wings,
Round grove and glade to weave his wizard rings;
While Day with subtle fingers, now set free,
Charms pregnant scents from every bush and tree.
Homeward the lovers turn beneath the moon,
Radiant with memories, ardent friendship's boon,
And when that lurker at cross-roads, Farewell,
Parts them relentlessly, they scarce rebel—
No wish is unfulfilled, no thought can sorrow,
And kisses murmur happily: "To-morrow!"

But envy on such bliss too well can fare,
And all things now conspired against the pair.
Good sport to break such union, anyway—
And Hylas, going home the selfsame day,
Was ambushed by hedge-nymphs: "Hylas, look here!
Does she use hooks-and-eyes, or does she smear
Lime on your feet, that Kaleidusa-thing?
For to her skirts like any burr you cling,
Or like a carthorse meekly after trot!
Thank God, there still are nymphs, and quite a lot
Fairer than Kaleidusa! Take your pick!
You're charming—it's a shame! Come with us quick—
One moment? You'll be glad. We'll be so kind!"
Hylas rejoined: "I'd better speak my mind.
On Kaleidusa's toe—the little one—
She wears a bead, and this will catch the sun;
And when it does, the path seems all ablaze
With colours which to my enchanted gaze
Are lovelier far than sunlight. I should grieve
To part with hues like those, you may believe.
Moreover, 'twixt her tongue and teeth, you see,
She has a music-box, and sings to me,
And then the whole world sings and my heart sings—
These are her lime, or glue, or such-like things.
If e'er the colours fade, the music cease,
I'll part with her, and take you, if you please."

On homeward path, where ditch and bank are wide,
Bold satyrs tempted her that eventide.
"Peculiar taste at best, I'm bound to say,
O'er stones and stubble trudging every day,
With Hylas, like two mill-wheels on the grind!
What can you see in him? You must be blind.
Are there not satyrs plenty and to spare,
But you must basely with Olympian pair?
I know where money is, if that's your pleasure,
And if you only knew, such hidden treasure!"
Said Kaleidusa: "I will speak my mind.
Ten thousand valleys in the world we find;
A berry grows in each, and there alone,
And every one has flavours all its own.
That's why I wander—I have set my heart
On tasting every one in every part.
And none can tell like Hylas where they grow—
Come, let me pass! The reason now you know."
"All right. You'll soon be sick of this, my friend!"
"On the last day, when all the world shall end."

Thus from seducers' cunning broken free,
They march together towards eternity.

But at the noon-hour on a sultry day,
When in the hazel-grove the lovers lay:
"Look there!" cried Kaleidusa. "On that tree
The writing—what it says I'll have to see!"
Jumped up and read. Thus the inscription clear:
"Caution! Who recklessly lies dreaming here
Shall know in sleep what future he shall find.
Keep off! The future never yet was kind."
"I'm satisfied," said she, "those words to heed.
Fair is the present. That is all I need."
And saying this, returned and with a smile
Sat down, embraced her love, and slept awhile.
And so till seven days had passed and gone;
But the dark word upon the eighth would run
Through Kaleidusa's head. While Hylas slept
Under that tree to dream alone she crept,
A little dazed she was. Scarce closed her eyes,
Ere in her dream she moaned with anguished cries,
And Hylas waked. "Can I believe my ears!"
He rubbed his eyes. "Oh love! Were those your tears?
Your eyes are wet—they hardly seem to see!"
"No, they are dry; they have not wept," said she.
Then, as again they wandered on their way:
"How languid are your feet," he cried, "to-day!
How sorrowful and heavy droops your head!"
"I am not weary; it is you," she said.

But late that evening, in the chill moonlight,
When to Olympus he had taken flight
As ever, and about her caves austere
Yawned, and the world seemed solitary, drear,
She sank upon the ground, and rent the vale
With deep-drawn sobs, like to the nightingale;
Music was in them, music of the heart,
Love and despair and longing—all took part.
Then from the grove there came the sister-pair,
Each took her hand, and pitying stroked her hair:
"Say, sister, what thy sorrow? Can it be
Some word from Hylas thus afflicting thee,
Wounding thy heart? He never meant it so!
Why wilt thou weep the tears of lightless woe?"
"Alas!" she moaned. "Sweet sisters—nay, not he,
Not Hylas, but myself hath wounded me.
I slept beneath the awful tree of fate,
Where they that dream shall know the things that wait.
I saw my love forsake me, pass me by,
No look vouchsafing me, and no reply."
"What's done is done. Thou canst not backward turn."
"Then will I die—yes, die, such doom to learn."
"Wild words—for well thou knowest, sister fair,
Immortal is the wood-nymph's soul of air;
We reckon not with death as mortals use,
At best we change to morning-scents or dews."
She cried: "And such the change I gladly choose!
I will not stay, till he shall thus forget,
I'll have him miss me sorely, pine and fret."
And she stood firm. No tears, no pleading tender
Could wring from her one moment of surrender.

And so the sisters, chanting a sad song,
Were lost the winding forest-paths among,
While she—she wondered, through the night of storm,
What shape her soul could choose, what airy form,
To glide within his heart and there to stay,
Stirring remembrance in him every day.
"This—this?" Her burdened spirit sorely wrought,
But could not find the answer that she sought,
So sick her will, so feverish her brain—
And tears were all the fruit of all her pain.
At last across the sky swept morning's blue,
And lit sad earth with many a laughing hue,
And "Ah?" she sighed, "the piteous hour is near
When through the trees to find me comes my dear!
Not knowing, from Olympus now, maybe,
All glad and sure he wings—ah, woe is me!
My petty pride, my purpose, what are they

If once I hear his voice—up, up, away!"
Swift from the clearing to the wood ran she.
"Courage!" she said. "For so it has to be."
Yet though she thus might urge her fainting heart,
How sweet was life—and she with life must part.

Then in the sea incarnadine o'erhead
Rose the great firebird Phœnix from his bed,
And lighting on a fir-tree preened his wings
Of shimmering flame, and glanced at earthly things;
Then closed his eyes, opened his beak, and sang
His matin-song—like some bronze bell it rang,
Ornate with images, and thus they soared,
The pregnant words that golden voice outpoured:
"What soul, you ask, is this that from the dew
With radiant eyes looks earnestly at you?
Hear! These are tidings from the Son of Light,
Written on vale and field throughout the night
When he, a captive far in desert lands,
Through prison-bars will stretch his longing hands—
Thus daily to dark earth in secret giving
Assurance that he still is loving, living.
Aurosa, whom he loves yet ne'er may meet,
Scans the brave letter, sad and yet so sweet;
At peep of day the forest-gloom she leaves,
From silvered lawns the dewy message weaves
With careful fingers, till she understands
The love-words traced by those beloved hands.
Secret the cipher, to none other known;
The hallowed script is clear to her alone,
Gem of her diadem, Horizon named—
Soon as the first of morning-beams has flamed
She reads the rune: 'In this we meet at last!'
And reason answers love, her heart beats fast.
Then will she hide herself and letter too;
The world is naught to her, so he is true."

Thus from his eyrie sang the great firebird;
The clearing and the flame-red forest heard—
But hark! the voice of Hylas from the hill
On "Kaleidusa!" calling, calling still . . .
Loudly it rang. Or breathless she or frightened,
Or by some sudden hopeful thought enlightened—
Ceasing to run, against a sapling leant
And through her hollowed hands a summons sent:
"O Father Pan! The wood-nymph calls on thee,
Now from her sore distress to set her free!"
Pan stood before her: "Whence this anguished cry?"
Faltering she said: "I long to change, to die."

"Once dead, no wish, no might, can thee restore."
"O Father Pan, I know, and long the more."
"To what, then, wilt thou change thy spirit fair?"
"To some bright ray that comes from everywhere
And seems to Hylas as myself, and so
Will make his yearning and his love to grow."
"Then, Kaleidusa, come—embrace me here."
"Father, kind Father Pan, I shrink, I fear!"
"Was never death but wrestled first with life,
Nor changing form but knows that awful strife."

Sore was the struggle, fierce was Pan's embrace,
Ere the fond soul was torn from out its place,
And Kaleidusa's spirit, breaking free,
Could soar unhindered to infinity.
Not here she was, not there, but everywhere,
Informing all the azure distance fair;
And then she'd have him see her starry crown:
"Hylas, I'm here!" and flashed her glances down.
And Hylas, crying out in sore amaze,
Wept his lost love on whom he might not gaze.
Now from the thicket, sent by Father Pan,
Morpho and Pantaphila to him ran:
"O Hylas, trust our magic! Do not move,
And we will show thee how to see thy love."
So speaking, Morpho with her fingers light
Draws both his hands behind and holds them tight.
"Shut your two eyes," next Pantaphila bids
And softly breathes her kisses on his lids.
"Look up!" And lo! in one heart-warming ray
He knows his Kaleidusa—and away
With longing arms he rushes . . . Hapless wight!
Never shall Hylas touch the radiant sprite;
Though oft he thinks to grasp her, she will still
Elude him, running swift o'er vale and hill.

And so at every hour of every day
His darling torment leads him far astray;
O'er vale and hill he hunts her through the land—
Ever the tricksome gleam escapes his hand,
Though ever flashing: "Come! I wait you here!"
And roguish Kaleidusa laughs: "More dear—
O joy!—more close by far shall be the tie
Than when through woods we wandered, he and I."

Henrik Pontoppidan

A FISHER NEST

Far out by the open sea there was a poor little fisher-hamlet—ten small, black, wooden huts. Half buried in the sand, the string of low houses crept like a caterpillar behind the high, naked sand-down over which the breakers scattered their foam.

On calm summer days, while the sun was melting the tar out of the timber walls and heating the sand till it glowed and burned under the feet, the little hamlet would sometimes expand in its solitude with a beauty as ephemeral as that of a butterfly bursting its chrysalis and hovering on bright wings above the desolation of its usual dreary existence. On the downs wet fishing nets sagged from row upon row of high poles. On the beach below, crowds of half naked, noisy children played, and here and there sun-burned women in scarlet skirts squatted around a fire in the sand, boiling pitch.

But at the first equinoctial storm, when the clouds came low down over the desolate, sand-swept hills, when the big white sea-gulls huddled together in the rolling surf, and the wind-chafed dunes foamed like driven snow, then the little hamlet would again hide behind the down. Loopholes and hatches were closed, and the doors barred; even the smoke would not rise from the openings in the black-burned buildings, but hung timidly over the roofs. Day after day the little fisher-colony seemed plunged in a heavy sleep, while great flakes of white foam were carried past it on the wind.

But sometimes on dark nights it happened that, through the roar of the sea breaking against the shore, another sound could be heard—a door was opened against the wind, but instantly forced back and closed by the storm. A man crawled up the slope of the down, and holding one hand behind his ear, lay flat on the ground to listen. After a while another man came and lay down beside him. A few drowsy words, punctured by hours of silence, passed between them.

Then, suddenly, they both rose and, running quickly toward the houses, knocked at a door in one place, at a shutter in another, and everywhere they called out the same word.

In a moment, square-shouldered men with bearded faces emerged from the darkness. Clad in heavy, stiff cloaks, they moved about without speaking, busying themselves with ropes, ladders, and boat-hooks. At last they gathered around a little horn lantern and marched in a troop toward the east, behind the downs.

Here and there in an open door appeared the head and bust of a half naked woman with her hair hanging in disorder around her shoulders; but as soon as the men disappeared, the doors were closed—and again nothing was heard but the never ceasing, hollow roar of the sea.

A moment later a flame rose against the black sky, high up in the sand-hills to the east. It was a lighted pitch torch from which dark, red sparks were flying over the country.

An hour or two passed.

Suddenly a shriek of many voices is heard from the sea. In the same moment the torch is extinguished. All is darkness.

But out there in the breakers it is as if the gale had gathered all its force and risen in its wildest strength. It sounds like the flapping wings of a giant bird in distress. Near the shore a ship's cables are broken, there is a commotion on deck, and the sound of a loud, commanding voice is drowned in a confused shouting from many men mingled with the piercing, agonized cry of a woman.

Under the dune by the sea the stocky little men are sitting in a circle, gathered around the lantern which throws a ruddy glow over the sand and the bearded faces. They sit in quiet expectation, folding their hands around their raised knees or resting their heads on their hands, as if asleep.

No one speaks. Now and then, when the woman's cry of anguish and the monotonous howling of the sailors fighting in the rigging becomes heart-rending, they look stealthily at each other and try to smile. An old fellow, the last in the line, steals away and mutters something over a rosary which he has managed to pull out of his jacket.

Then there comes a moment when the sea seems to rise and, trembling, gathers all its strength. A series of rolling, thundering sounds like reports of distant cannon is heard on land. Then all is silent. Not a cry.

But soon the seething waters between the dunes and the sea are filled with broken wreckage tossed about and whirled around as in a boiling caldron. Something is washed ashore; other things are carried away again by the waves or crushed on the spot. A big piece of the mast with a rope attached to it is thrown on land, and a cry is heard from a shipwrecked man who is clinging to it.

He is saved.

But in the same moment he is stabbed with a knife in his side, and falls backward. The men surround him, and the lantern is put close to his face, as he sinks feebly on the sand with a last startled gaze.

"It's wine!" mutters the man who holds the lantern, after looking at the dark hair and olive skin of the dying sailor.

The others nod approvingly. A bandy-legged little fellow bends down and fumbles at the clothes of the stranger and examines the glittering ear-rings in his ears. To make sure that he will not revive, he stabs him again, and leaving him with the deep, oozing wound in his side, he waddles toward the sea.

Here his comrades are busy saving wreckage out of the surf with hooks and ropes. When the morning slowly dawns over the sea in a cold, gray mist, barrels of wine and broken planks are pulled ashore. As fast as the waves carry them toward the beach, the dead bodies are hauled on land and plundered. Boxes and cases with colored silk goods are broken open and examined.

While this is going on, the women from the fisher-huts bring hot beer in big, wooden pitchers which they circulate among the men. Trembling in the morning cold, they crowd together on the edge of the down, and with a greedy flash in their eyes, they glance at the wealth heaped together there.

Toward noon, when there is nothing more to save, and when the naked corpses have been buried carefully under the sand, the barrels are rolled into the huts with great merriment, and the big, wooden pitchers are placed on the tables. The men and women, the latter clad in silk dresses, sit down on benches around them, and day after day the little fisher-hamlet abandons itself to a wild intoxication, singing and rioting through the long, dark nights, while sand and white foam-flakes are whirling past.

But all this belongs to a very remote age, far, far back in time. The saga of the fisher-hamlet is almost forgotten to-day, up there in the desolate solitude, where year after year sea and sand have effaced and levelled, smoothed and buried everything.

It may happen, however, on fine summer evenings when the sun is setting in blood-red clouds, throwing a fiery glow over the sea, that a respectable head of a family, who is taking a pleasure trip through this beautiful part of the country, will stop before a wreck on the beach half washed away by the sea, and lost in admiration at the sight, will repeat the tales of the bloody scenes and nightly terrors of that remote age while his children listen attentively.

As he explains this, he shows them the solidly built life-boat station on the dune, or he points to the east, toward the narrow, flat peninsula, where the high lighthouse proudly rises toward the sky as a last stronghold of the land.

In time the downs, too, have been influenced by civilization, and long, straight lines of lymegrass and sea reed have been planted as a protection against the flying sand. Stretches of light brown heather and peaceful moors are now seen among the dunes, where the fox abides on silent summer nights.

The fisher-hamlet itself, which has kept its strange, caterpillar shape, is now a thriving village, with a church and a clergyman, with merchants and an inn, with many small houses, whose tile-covered roofs appear more intensely red among the greenish white sand-hills.

On quiet summer days, when the sun melts the tar in the few remaining old wooden huts, and heats the sand till it burns under the feet, the village again unfolds itself in its solitude, as it did in bygone days. It spreads over the dunes, with black poles and nets and drying fish, with noisy crowds of bare-legged children on the beach, and sunburned women in scarlet skirts who crouch in the sand around a steaming kettle, pealing potatoes.

Along the shore painters are sitting—one behind the other—under large yellow umbrellas like frogs under mushrooms. Poets with long hair and notebooks are seen everywhere, while in the village crowds of tourists eagerly observe this unfamiliar scene and the interesting primitive life of its inhabitants.

Toward noon the heat grows oppressive. There is no air stirring. From the stifling heat a white haze rises and hangs over the village.

Outside the houses, ducks, pigs, and children are asleep on the glaring sand. Heavy and sleepy looking women with bare legs and half-fastened dresses are passing in and out, glancing sullenly toward a small door in one of the tiny houses where a young tourist with a mosquito veil around his hat is joking with a group of lively fisher girls. The laughter of these young girls is soon the only sound heard in the village.

Even the bare-legged little maids who have been running around the whole morning, their skirts tucked up, splashing in the surf, are tired out and sit down in the shade, under some boats that have been hauled on land. Here they rest with hands folded in their laps and let their eyes follow the little chattering sea-birds that skim over the surface of the water and dive down to catch fish.

An elderly gentleman with a high, gray hat pushed to the back of his head, a gray dust-coat, and an immense spy-glass hanging down on his stomach, comes out on the hotel steps and with a satisfied grimace breathes the polluted air, heavy with the odor of dung and of fish rotting on the strand.

High up on the downs the fishermen are sitting, with small pipes in their mouths, mending their nets. A few among them have fallen asleep, chin on chest, but most of them are chattering, now and then looking toward the sea with a dull glance—this large, empty, milky-blue sea, lying there, quiet and shining, so hopelessly desolate that all life would have seemed extinct save for the heaving and sinking of the waves down below the beach.

Suddenly one day, a big steamer hove in sight in the northeast. It was the Two Brothers, an English freighter headed toward the Kattegat, bound evidently for one of the Baltic ports. Behind it trailed for miles a streak of dense, woolly smoke, as the boat pressed on with full steam ahead.

On deck all was quiet. Soundings had just been taken with no report of shoals.

The sailors were lying in the shade on the lower deck—a mixed crew of Germans, Swedes, and Irishmen, in red-checked woolen shirts. They were sleeping face downward on the deck. The captain himself was keeping watch. He sat in his cosy little cabin on the bridge, whence he might comfortably observe the course of the ship and examine the sunny coast they were passing.

He was a little, short-necked Englishman, stuffed with beef and porter, with a face red and shining like a copper kettle. The motionless, milky eyes expressed deadly dullness. Not a line in his face moved while he was sitting there, quietly smoking a sweet-smelling shag after lunch.

But he was not alone. Sitting close to him, almost on his lap, was a young, slender woman, twisting his coarse beard with her white, quick fingers. Neither spoke. Sometimes, when the strong smoke which he was blowing unceremoniously down over her made her cough, she would mischievously pull his shaggy beard. But at the slightest impatient grumbling from this lump of flesh she would let the beard go and nestle close to him with a droll expression like a frightened kitten.

This was Little Mary. That is what she called herself. Captain Charles—if ever he deigned to speak to her at all—called her simply Mary.

The crew—who rarely saw her—the cook, and the steward, addressed her as "Miss." And when she went for her daily walk in the afternoon, up and down the deck, quiet, erect, with English correctness, her hands in the pockets of her tightly buttoned jacket, the first mate and the sailors politely made way for her, and nothing in their manner showed that they knew all about her.

She had come on board more than two months ago at Liverpool, and Captain Charles had several times brought his fist down on the table before her, swearing that he would put her on shore in the first English port they entered and send her back to the den of misery where she belonged. But the mild summer winds and several lucky trips had made him soft. There was always an imploring glance in her eyes which he could not resist, and she had put her little hand around his neck so gently that he regularly withdrew his order, and he even felt something like a heart move beneath the fat under his vest. Mary was only seventeen.

He now rested, satiated and motionless after his lunch, and abandoned himself to daydreams. Strange fancies had come. Why should he not keep her for the rest of the summer—and perhaps for the winter, too? He might even marry the girl. He had got into the habit of having her about, and he did not like to think of being without her. Of course he would be the laughing-stock of his comrades if he really married her. And there would be a great commotion home in Grangemouth. But why not let them laugh? As long as he was at sea he would not know. And then—Mary was only seventeen. As for her past, there was an excuse in the home she had come from. Her father was a worthless fellow who had more than once in a fit of drunkenness ill-treated and half killed her, and her mother, a dissolute old woman, had herself taught the girl her profession. Besides, Mary was only a child and hardly knew what sort of life she had been drawn into. While he was lost in this revery, and Mary amused herself by letting her head rest on his chest, rocked up and down by his breathing, they suddenly felt a few light shocks through the ship, and a moment later, it stopped, while the stamping of the machinery increased to a furious speed.

Captain Charles's heavy body was alert in a moment. Throwing Mary off, he rushed out of the door with an oath, made the machine stop, and bent over the railing of the bridge. Yes— to be sure! The ship had stopped. Through the clear, glassy green water pebbles and shells were shining down on the sandy shoal which they had struck quite softly.

His face, which for a moment had been colorless, turned purple, but after having looked along the ship's side, and after having, as he thought, made sure that no harm was done, he turned to the crew, who had come running from all parts of the ship, looked over the railing, and reassured them with a calm "All right."

"Half speed!—back—half speed!" he called out to the engineers.

And when the machine again began to work he walked up and down the bridge several times, puffing violently at his shag-pipe, to get over his fright.

But the ship did not move. Not even at his command "Full speed back!" did it move. However much the machine puffed and heaved, however black and angry the smoke gushed out of the smoke-stack, the heavy ship did not stir. It only groaned a little at the exertion with a clattering noise of iron.

Meanwhile the catastrophe had been noticed on shore by a painter and some fishermen who posed for him, standing in the shallow water dressed in heavy sea-boots and pulling their nets. A hurried message was sent to the slumbering city to wake the people from their siesta.

And now there was a stir. At first one by one, then crowds, the men came sauntering across the dunes with laughter gurgling in their stomachs, while the women and children invaded the highest part of the down behind the village and from this vantage point, shading their eyes with their hands, looked steadily toward the north. Everywhere people were hurrying over the sand, shouting and beckoning to each other from a distance. The stranding commissioner and the police officer were passing in an open carriage, and all the tourists had left the lunch table of the inn in haste to rush toward the stranding place. The man in the high, gray hat was ahead of the others, using his long legs like stilts. A napkin, which in the confusion he had pushed into his pocket, was hanging out behind.

The whole town stirred with feverish commotion. People paused before the front doors to ask questions or explain. But it was not till it became known as an incontestable fact that the ship was stuck, solidly stuck, in the sand, that the enxiety gave way to a stormy mirth, which extended even to the children and made them run up and down the streets, shouting "Hurrah." The merchant jumped up on the office chair, and with a smile he ordered the big cask of whisky to be brought up from the cellar. Neighbors and friends called on each other, and everywhere there was a smell of coffee. Even old folks and cripples who could scarcely walk hobbled on till they reached the top of the nearest dune, where they revelled in the sight of the big, smoking sea-monster lying out there, groaning and struggling to free itself.

In front of the place where the steamer had run ashore, the beach was black with people, and around the steamer—it was stuck several hundred yards from land, on the third reef—there was a gathering of boats from the salvage corporation, shouting to the captain whenever he showed himself on the bridge.

Captain Charles, however, pretended not to see or hear anything of this. Through the first mate he had forbidden all strangers to board his ship and obstinately refused all offers of help. He ordered his own big boat to be lowered and had some men row two anchors away from the ship, tugging with strong chains at the rear bar. The engineers had been given orders to increase the steam, and even to go as far as the red line; for off they must.

While this was going on, he walked up and down the bridge, his hands in the pockets of his jacket, or he sat in the cabin on the bridge, drinking straight whisky out of a big beer glass. Mary's round cat's eyes followed his every movement and watched anxiously the expression of his red face. A few times she had ventured to approach him, but with a snarl he had pushed her away violently.

At last the two anchors were cast. Again the machine began to work, the steam whirled, and the chains tightened, but the ship did not move an inch; it only sank deeper into the sand after each vain attempt.

The group on the shore grew larger, and the number of boats on the water kept increasing. Fishermen from the remotest part of the peninsula and from a neighboring village toward the south were dragging their boats along the shore. At last a whole fleet of small vessels gathered around the stranded steamer, pushing each other, and paddling along with shouts and laughter. They were especially interested in guessing at the kind of cargo the ship might carry. Cotton or iron would make the biggest salvage money, and that was what they hoped for. It could hardly be coal, as no apparatus for unloading could be seen.

At some distance from the others lay a six-oar boat carrying the stranding commissioner. He was a portly, thick-set man, who tried to look at the whole scene with an air of sublime indifference. In reality no one could be more interested in the value of cargo and ship than he, as he had—through his mere presence—a legal claim to one half percent of the salvage sum.

The customs officer, a fat man with gold-rimmed glasses, approached in another boat and saluted him.

"What do you think of this, consul?" he said, and laughed in his fiery red beard which seemed to be ablaze in the sun. "To run ashore in the middle of the day and in this kind of weather. If that is not a present!" The stranding commissioner shrugged his shoulders, a movement that might be interpreted in any way.

"I suppose it is iron," the officer continued. "Anyhow, that is what people say."

"Heaven knows!" the other answered with an almost priestly solemnity, and looked into the air. "She looks like a coal steamer—English, of course."

The customs officer laughed again.

"English, yes. And as tough and tenacious as English beef. Can you understand, consul, how it is possible that he still hopes to get off?"

"Well now,—he may still succeed," the commissioner answered with a delusive expression of Christian sympathy. Only in the corners of his mouth the play of muscles betrayed the anxiety of his soul.

"Pardon me, gentlemen, is it true, what they say that the salvage-steamer has been telegraphed for?" It was the man with the gray silk hat. He had hired a boat with four seasoned old fishermen and, trembling with excitement, he was sitting in the stern with the spyglass in his hand. "Can it really be so?" he continued, as no one answered. "I was told that, according to a reliable report, the boat was expected here."

"Yes, she may be here in a moment," said the consul, looking toward the east.

And there, coming from the south, around the peninsula, appeared a small steamer. The consul gave a signal to his sailors, and the oars dipped into the water. A few minutes later the boat was at the side of the stranded ship.

He made himself known to the first mate and asked if help was wanted. Captain Charles, who from his cabin on the bridge had seen the little steamer stop and anchor at some distance, answered "No." "No," he repeated with clenched teeth, bringing his fist down on the table. The mate hesitated before taking this answer. A whisky bottle was standing before the captain, and he had emptied the third glass.

The consul left and rowed away at once toward land.

Some hours passed. The crowd kept increasing, as the women came and brought food for their husbands. They camped on the sand. The whisky bottles were circulating. All were hilarious, as if celebrating a national festival.

Toward sunset the surface of the sea suddenly ruffled, and the boats still lying around the ship began to rock. As yet there were no clouds to be seen, but there was a strange, dim look about the sun, and the sea seemed to rise out there against the horizon.

A quarter of an hour passed, and the sea grew so rough that the boats had to seek land. The men pushed them on shore by stemming their shoulders against the sides, and the women began to seek shelter under the large prows.

Now the sky was hidden by clouds, and the winds increased in strength, so that the position of the ship became critical. It was lying in the breakers with its broad-side turned toward the sea, which already began to pound against it. From the shore one could see how one white-crested wave after the other splashed over the gunwale.

Those of the spectators on the seashore who were provided with telescopes suddenly noticed that there was a great activity on board. The sailors were running to and fro on deck. A boat was lowered, and the clattering of an anchor chair was heard. It was clear that a last decisive attempt would be made. Huge masses of smoke with showers of sparks rolled out against the dark sky, and then the crew began to work.

It looked quite ghastly seen from the shore. Some of the women began to wail. But for this, it was very quiet on land now. Toward the northwest a blood-red sun was setting behind large masses of dark clouds.

Then the machine suddenly stopped again. After a long delay, they saw through the growing darkness how the flag of distress was slowly hoisted. At the same time, a feeble, long-winded and hoarse signal was heard from the steam whistle.

"She's crying now," they said, and they laughed.

The eight-oar boat of the district had been brought and was pushed into the sea, with the stranding commissioner and the attorney who had to accredit the salvage conditions with the seal of the law. There was still a third person seated in the boat, a thin little man in a grey cloak, holding his hat with his black-gloved left hand. It was the agent of the salvage company, who had been landed by the small steamer, directly after its arrival, and who, since then, had been on the shore.

The gale had almost blown up a storm, yet the skilled crew led the boat through the waves, with steady strokes of the oars, and twenty minutes later the three officials were put on board. The first mate received them and led them below deck into the officers' mess. Here Captain Charles was sitting, much intoxicated, behind a table over which a lamp was hanging. The light, thrown back from the inside of a white painted tin shade, was falling on the mahogany table-top, the rest of the room was left in a greenish twilight.

He received the strangers without any greeting and asked shortly how much it would cost.

The agent of the salvage company asked permission to look over the shipping-papers. When they were brought and he had learned the value of the cargo, the age of the ship, the amount of the insurance, etc., he answered: "Six thousand pounds."

A convulsive shock passed through the frame of Captain Charles. It was as if his intoxication suddenly left him, and he became sober again. Then a strange, proud smile of despair played around his bluish-white lips.

"I see," he said half to himself.

There was silence for a few minutes. The sea was knocking against the side of the ship, right at the Captain's back, and in there in the narrow room, the chafing of the waves had a strange, hollow, and ghostly sound. The young attorney, who was not yet accustomed to these scenes, grew paler and paler and looked toward the door. Over their heads on deck heavy boots were tramping.

"Four thousand pounds," the captain said at last.

The agent shrugged his shoulders regretfully. "Impossible."

The stranding commissioner, whose duty it was to assist the captain and to look after the interests of the ship, then made an effort to mediate. But as he knew that the salvage company made it a rule never to change an estimate, and it was to his own interest to keep the salvage sum as high as possible, he quickly turned against the captain with many sympathetic words, and in passable English tried to make him understand that on account of the increasing danger of the position in which the ship was placed, there was no other way; he would have to accept.

The agent, who quite agreed with this statement, added that, if his conditions were not accepted before an hour had elapsed, the salvage-steamer would have to return, as he, under the present circumstances, did not dare to let it remain here during the night. Besides he begged to say that only for ten minutes longer would he feel bound to the very favorable offer he had made.

Captain Charles still remained silent. He put his short, fat arms on the table and was looking from one to the other of the men with slow, understanding nods. After the last words of the agent his pale lips quivered for a moment. Then he turned to the first mate, who had been present during the negotiations as his witness, and asked him for writing materials.

A few hours later the Two Brothers was tugged loose and found seaworthy. In the dark stormy night, when the lights were shining from every hut in the small village in the downs, when the people had already begun to feast on the third part of the salvage-money, when the tables of the inn and the bars of the tavern were crowded with people, the foreign steamer passed on toward the east, around the neck of land, continuing its solitary trip out across the sea.

The first mate kept the watch. Captain Charles had shut himself up in his quarters with a bottle of whisky, but without Mary. The poor child was sitting in the corner of her narrow berth in her own small cabin, looking into the darkness with her round cat's eyes. She had read her fate in the furious glance of her master when he had pushed her away in the afternoon. Her hour of freedom had passed. In the first port the ship entered he would carry out his order and send her back to the old den of misery, hunger, and dirt, to the blows of her father and the curses of her mother.

Or?

The sea is deep. The sea is merciful . . .

The next morning, when the Two Brothers sailed into the Sound, Mary was no longer on board.

As it flashed upon my vision I uttered an involuntary cry of admiration, for there, at a bend of the broad Gunga, lay, great and splendid in its beauty, the city of Kosambi. With its walls and towers, its piled-up masses of houses, its terraces, its quays and ghâts lit up by the setting sun, it really looked like a city of red gold—a city such as Benares was until the sins of its inhabitants changed it to stone and mortar—while the cupolas that were of real gold shone like so many suns. Columns of smoke, dark red brown from the temple courts above, light blue from the funeral pyres on the banks below, rose straight into the air; and borne aloft on these, as if it were a canopy, there hung over the whole a veil woven of the tenderest tints of mother-of-pearl, while in the background, flung forth in the wildest profusion, flashed and burned every hue of heaven. On the sacred stream which imaged all this glory and multiplied it a thousandfold in the shimmer of its waters, rocked countless boats, gay with many-coloured sails and streamers; and, distant though they were, we could yet see the broad stairs of the ghâts[2] swarming with people, and numerous bathers already plashing in the sparkling waves beneath. A sound of joyous movement, floating out upon the air like the busy hum of innumerable bees, was borne up to us from time to time.

As thou canst imagine, I felt I was looking upon a city of the thirty-three gods, rather than one of human beings; indeed, the whole valley of the Gunga with its luxuriant richness looked to us, men of the hills, like Paradise. And of a truth, this very place, of all others on earth, was to be Paradise Revealed to me.

That same night I slept under the hospitable roof of Panada, my father's old friend.

Early on the following day, I hurried to the nearest ghât, and descended, with feelings which I cannot attempt to describe, into the sacred waters which should not only cleanse me from the dust of my journey but from my sins as well. These were, owing to my youth, of no great gravity; but I filled a large bottle from the river to take to my father. Alas! it never came into his possession, as thou wilt later learn.

The good Panada, a grey-haired old gentleman of venerable appearance, now conducted me to the markets of the City, and, with his friendly assistance, I was able, in the course of the next few days, to sell my wares at a good profit, and to lay in an abundance of those products of the northern plain which are so highly prized among our people.

My business was thus brought to a happy conclusion long before the embassy had begun to think of getting ready to start on its return journey; and I was in no way sorry, for I had now full liberty to see the town and to enjoy its pleasures, which I did to the full, in the company of Somadatta, the son of my host.

II

One delightful afternoon we betook ourselves to a public garden outside of the town—a really magnificent park it was, lying close to the high banks

[2]Landing-stage with magnificent flights of steps for bathers—ordinarily varied by projections and kiosks and crowned by a monumental arch or gateway.

of the Gunga, with shady groups of trees, large lotus ponds, marble summer-houses, and jasmine arbours, in which at this hour of the day life and bustle reigned supreme. Here we were gently rocked in a golden swing by the attendants, while with ravished hearts we listened to the lovesick notes of the kokila and the sweet chatter of the green parrots. All at once there rose on the air the merry tinkling of anklets, and instantly my friend sprang out of the swing and called to me—

"Look, Kamanita! The fairest maidens in Kosambi are just approaching, virgins specially chosen from the richest and most noble houses, come to do honour to the goddess who dwells on the Vindhayas by engaging in ball games. Thou canst count thyself fortunate, my friend, for at this game we may see them without restraint. Come, let us not miss the chance."

Naturally, I waited for no second bidding, but made haste to follow.

On a spacious stage decorated with precious stones, the maidens appeared at once, ready for the game. And, if it must be acknowledged that it was a rare sight to behold this galaxy of fair young creatures in all their glory of shimmering silk, airy muslin veils, of pearls, sparkling jewels and gold bangles, what must be said of the game itself that gave to all these gracious limbs such varied opportunities of displaying their wealth of subtle beauty in the most charming of positions and movements? And yet that was, as it were, but a prologue. For when these gazelle-eyed worshippers had entertained us for a considerable time with games of the most varied description, they all stepped back, save one, who remained alone in the centre of the jewelled stage: in the centre of the stage, and—in the centre of my heart.

Ah! my friend, what shall I say? To talk of her beauty would be audacity! I should need to be a poet like Bharata himself to conjure up to your fancy even a faint reflection of it. Let it suffice that this maiden, with the gentle radiance of the moon in her face, was of faultless form and glowed in every limb with the freshness of youth; that I felt her to be the incarnate goddess of Fortune and Beauty; and that every smallest hair on my body quivered with delight as I beheld her.

Presently she began, in honour of the goddess whom she so fitly represented, a performance worthy of a great artist. Dropping the ball easily on the stage, as it slowly rose she gave it, with flower-like hand, thumb slightly bent, and tender fingers outstretched, a sharp downward blow, then struck it, as it rebounded, with the back of her hand and caught it again in mid-air as it fell. She tossed it in slow, in moderate, in quick time, now inciting it to rapid motion, anon gently quieting it. Then striking it alternately with the right hand and with the left, she drove it towards every point of the compass and caught it as it returned. If thou art really acquainted with the mysteries of ball-play—as it seemeth to me from the intelligence of thine expression thou art—I need only tell thee that thou hast probably never seen the Curnapada and the Gitamarga so perfectly mastered.

Then she did something that I had never seen, and of which I had not even heard. She took, I must tell thee, two golden balls, and while her feet moved in the dance to the tinkling of the jewels she wore, she made the balls spring so rapidly in lightning-like lines, that one saw but, as it were, the golden bars of a cage in which a wondrous bird hopped daintily to and fro. It was at this point that our eyes suddenly met.

And to this day, O stranger, I do not understand how it was that I did not instantly drop dead, to be reborn in a heaven of bliss. It may well be, however, that my deeds done in a former life, the fruits of which I have to enjoy in this, were not yet exhausted. Indeed, this balance from my wanderings in the past has, in very truth, carried me safely through various mortal dangers down to the present day, and will, I trust and expect, suffice for a long time to come.

But to return. At this instant one of the balls, which had hitherto been so obedient to her, escaped and flew in a mighty curve down from the stage. Many young folks rushed to seize it. I reached it at the same moment as another youthful, richly dressed man, and we flew at one another, because neither was willing to yield it. Owing to my absolute familiarity with the tricks of the wrestler, I succeeded in tripping him up; but he, in order to hold me back, caught at the crystal chain which I wore round my neck, and to which an amulet was attached. The chain snapped, he went crashing to the earth, and I secured the ball. In a fury, he sprang up and hurled the chain at my feet. The amulet was a tiger-eye, no very specially precious stone, yet it was an infallible safeguard against the evil eye; and now, just as his lighted upon me, I must needs be without it. But what mattered that to me? Did I not hold in my hand the ball which a moment before her lily-hand had touched? And at once, as a highly skilled player should, I succeeded in pitching it with so accurate an aim that it came down just in front of one corner of the stage, and, rising again with a gentle movement, landed, as if tamed, within reach of the fair player, who had not for a moment ceased to keep the other in motion, and who now wove herself again into her golden cage, amid the wild jubilation of the numerous spectators. With that the ball-play in honour of the goddess Lakshmi came to an end, the maidens disappeared from the stage, and we turned our steps homeward.

On the way, my friend remarked it was fortunate that I had no purpose to serve at court; for the young man from whom I had captured the ball was no less a personage than the son of the Minister of State, and every one had noticed from his looks that he had sworn undying hatred to me. That did not move me in the least; how much rather had I learned who my goddess was. I fought shy of asking, however; in fact, when Somadatta wanted to tease me about the fair one, I even made as if I were perfectly indifferent, praised with the language of a connoisseur the finish of her play, but added, at the same time, that we had in my native town lady-players at least as skilful—while in my heart of hearts I begged the incomparable one to pardon this my falsehood.

I need hardly say that night brought no sleep to my eyes, which I only closed in order to be possessed anew by the blissful vision I had seen. The following day I spent in a corner of my host's garden, far removed from all the noise of day, where the sandy soil under a mango-tree ministered cooling to my love-tortured body, my only companion the seven-stringed vina, to which I confided my longing. As soon, however, as the lessening heat permitted my going out, I persuaded Somadatta to drive with me to the public gardens although he would have greatly preferred to be present at a quail fight. In vain, however, did I wander through the whole park. Many maidens were there, everywhere engaged in games as though bent on luring me with false hopes from one spot to another, but that peerless one—Lakshmi's very image—was not among them.

Bitterly disappointed I now made as though I were possessed by an irresistible longing again to enjoy the strangely fascinating life of the Gunga. We visited all the ghâts, and finally got into a boat in order to make one of the light-hearted flotilla which, evening by evening, rocked to and fro on the waves of the sacred stream, and I lingered till the play of light and the golden glow of evening were extinguished and the blaze of torches and the glimmer of lanterns danced and whirled on its glassy surface.

Then at last I was obliged to give up my silent but none the less passionate hope and bid my boatman steer for the nearest ghât.

After a sleepless night, I remained in my room, and in order to occupy and relieve my mind, which was utterly possessed by her image, till I should again be able to hasten to the public gardens, I sought with the aid of brush and colour to transfer to the tablet on my wall, her fair lineaments as I last beheld them, when, dancing, she struck the golden ball. I was unable to eat a morsel; for even as the Çakora with its exquisitely tender song lives only upon the rays of the moon, so did I live solely upon the rays that emanated from her whose face was as the moon in its fairness, though these came to me but through the mists of memory; yet I hoped, and that confidently, they would this evening in the pleasure gardens refresh and vivify me with all their glow and radiance. Alas! I was again doomed to disappointment.

Afterwards Somadatta wished to take me to the gaming-tables, for he was as passionately addicted to dice as Nala, after the demon Kali had entered into him. I feigned tiredness.

Instead, however, of going home, I betook myself again to the ghâts and out on the river; but, to my unspeakable grief, with no better result than on the preceding evening.

III

As I knew that for me sleep was not to be thought of, I did not undress at all that evening, but sat down at the head of my bed on the grass mat intended for devotional exercises, and spent the night there in pious and fitting fashion, filled with fervent love thoughts, and absorbed in prayer to the lotus-bearing Lakshmi, *her* celestial prototype; but the early morning sun found me again at work with brush and colour.

Several hours had flown away as if on wings while I was thus occupied, when Somadatta entered the room. I had but just time, when I heard him coming, to thrust the panel and painting materials under the bed. I did it quite involuntarily.

Somadatta took a low chair, sat down beside me, and looked at me with a smile on his face.

"I perceive of a truth," he said, "that our house is to have the honour of being the spiritual birthplace of a holy man. Thou fastest as do only the most strenuous ascetics, and dost refrain from the luxurious bed. For neither on thy pillows nor on thy mattress is there to be seen the faintest impress of thy body and the white sheet is without a crease. Nevertheless, although as the result of thy fasting thou art already grown quite slim, thy body is not yet entirely devoid of weight, as the curious may see from this grass matting on which thou hast obviously spent the night in prayer and meditation. But I find that, for so holy a tenant, this room looks somewhat too worldly. Here on thy toilet table the salve jar—untouched, it is true; the box of sandal powder; the flagon of scented water and the dish with bark of the citron tree and betel! There on the wall, the wreath of yellow amaranths, and the lute, but—where is the panel which usually hangs on that hook?"

In my embarrassment I was unable to frame any answer to this question, and he meanwhile discovered the missing board, and drew it forth from under the bed.

"Why! why! what wicked and crafty wizard!" he cried, "has caused the fascinating picture of a maiden playing ball to appear by magic on the board which I myself hung quite empty on yonder hook?—plainly, with evil intent, to assail the embryo ascetic and tempt him at the very beginning of his career, and thus to confound sense and thought in him. Or, after all, can it be that this is the work of a god?—for we know, as a fact, that the gods fear the omnipotence of the great ascetics; and, commencing as thou hast done, the Vindhya Mountains might well begin to belch smoke at the fervency of thy penitence; yea, owing to the accumulation of thy merit, the kingdom of the heavenly deities might almost begin to totter. And now I also know which deity it is! It is certainly he whom we name the Invisible, the god with the flower darts, who bears a fish in his banner— Kama, the god of love, from whom thou hast thy name, as I now remember. And—heavens, what do I see?—this is Vasitthi, the daughter of the rich goldsmith!"

As I thus, for the first time, heard the name of my beloved, my heart began to beat violently and my face grew pale from agitation.

"I see, my dear friend," this incorrigible jester went on, "that the idea of the magic of Kama hath given thee a great fright, and, truly, we shall be obliged to do something in order to avert his anger. In such a case, however, I feel that woman's counsel is not to be despised. I shall show this picture to my beloved Medini, who was also of those at the dance and who is, further-more, the foster-sister of the fair Vasitthi."

With that, he was about to go away, taking the panel with him. Perceiving, however, what the rogue had in mind, I bade him wait, as the picture still lacked an inscription. I mixed some beautiful red of a brilliant hue and in a few minutes had written, in the daintiest of script, a verse of four lines which related in simple language the incident of the golden ball. The verse, when read backwards, stated that the ball with which she had played, was my heart, which I myself sent back to her even at the risk of her rejecting it. It was possible, however, to read the verse perpendicularly through the lines, and when so read, from top to bottom, it voiced in saddest words the despair into which my separation from her had plunged me; did one read it in the opposite direction, then the reader learned that nevertheless I dared to hope.

But of all that I conveyed to her in such surreptitious fashion, I said noth-ing, so that Somadatta was by no means enchanted with this specimen of my poetic skill. It seemed to him much too simple, and he informed me that I ought certainly to mention how the god Kama, alarmed at my asceticism, had by his magic skill created this picture with which to tempt me and that by it I had been wholly vanquished—Somadatta, like so many others, being most of all taken with his own wit.

After he had carried off the picture, I felt myself in a particularly exalted and energetic frame of mind, for a step had now been taken which, in its consequences, might lead to the longed-for goal of all my happiness. I was now able to eat and drink, and, after a light meal, I took down the vina from the wall and drew from its chords melodies that were sometimes no more than tuneful sighs, but anon grew exulting and joyous, while I repeated the heavenly name of Vasitthi in a thousand endearing accents.

So Somadatta found me when a few hours later he came in with the picture in his hand. "The ball-playing destroyer of thy peace has also betaken herself to verse," said he, "but I cannot say that I am able to find great store of matter in what she has written, although the handwriting may be considered unusually pretty."

And it was indeed pretty. I saw before me—with what joy of heart, how shall I say?—a second verse of four lines written in characters like sprays of tender blossoms swayed by summer zephyrs, and looking as if they had been breathed upon the picture. Somadatta had, of course, been unable to find any meaning in them, for they referred solely to that which he had not perceived, and showed me that my fair one had correctly read my strophe in every direction—backwards, upwards, and downwards. It gave me an exalted idea of her education and knowledge, no less than did the revelation of her rare spirit in the graciously humorous turn she gave to my fiery declaration, which she chose to accept as a piece of gallantry or an effusion to which too much importance should not be attached.

I now attempted, I confess, to read her verse in the criss-cross fashion which had been possible with mine, in the hope that I might find in it a covert confession or other secret message, perhaps even the invitation to a rendezvous, but in vain. And I told myself at once that this was in truth but a convincing proof of the highest and most refined feminine virtue; my darling showed me that she was perfectly capable of understanding the subtlety and daring ways of the masculine mind but could not be induced to imitate them.

Besides which I found immediate comfort for my disappointed expectations in Somadatta's next words.

"But this fair one with the beautiful brows, if she be no great poetess, has really a good heart. She knows that for a long time I have not seen her foster-sister, my beloved Medini, save at large social gatherings, where only the eyes may speak and even these but by stealth. And so she has arranged a meeting for to-morrow night, on the terrace of her father's palace. To-night, it is, I regret to say, not possible, as her father gives a banquet; so till to-morrow we must have patience. Perhaps thou wouldst like to accompany me on this adventure?"

As he said this, he laughed with much slyness and I laughed with him, and assured him that he should have my company. In the best of humours we took the chessboard which was leaning against the wall and were about to beguile the time by engaging in this animating game when a man-servant came in and announced that a stranger wished to speak with me.

In the entrance hall I found the ambassador's servant, who informed me that I must prepare for departure and come to the courtyard of the palace that very night, bringing my wagons, in order to be able to start with the first glimmer of daylight on the morrow.

My despair knew no bounds. I imagined I must in some mysterious way have offended one of the deities. As soon as I was able to collect my thoughts I dashed away to the ambassador and filled his ears with lies about some business that I had not yet arranged, and that could not possibly be brought to a satisfactory conclusion in so short a time. With hot tears I besought him to put off the journey for but a single day.

"But thou saidst eight days ago that thou wert ready," he replied.

I assured him that afterwards, and quite unexpectedly, the opportunity of gaining a valuable prize had presented itself. And that was indeed no false-hood, for what gain could mean more to me than the conquest of this incom-parable maiden?

So I finally succeeded in wiling this one day from him.

The hours of the next day wore quickly away, filled as they were with the preparations necessary for our journey, so that the time, in spite of my long-ing, did not drag. When evening came, our carts stood loaded in the court-yard. Everything was prepared for yoking in the oxen, so that, as soon as I should appear—that is, before daybreak—we might be able to start.

IV

Now that night and darkness had come, we betook ourselves, Somadatta and I, clad in dark apparel which we had gathered well up about us, our loins firmly belted, and with swords in our hands, to the western side of the pala-tial house of the goldsmith, where, crowning the steep and rocky side of a deep ravine, lay the terrace we sought. With the help of a bamboo pole which we had brought with us, and by a dexterous use of the few existing projec-tions, we climbed the face of the rock at a spot veiled in deep shadow, got over the wall with ease, and found ourselves on a spacious terrace decorated with palms, asoka trees, and magnificent flowering plants of every descrip-tion, which, now bathed in the silver light of the moon, lay spread out be-fore us.

Not far away, beside a young girl on a garden bench, and looking like a visitant from the spheres in her wonderful likeness to Lakshmi, sat the great-eyed maiden who played ball with my heart; and, at the sight, I began to tremble so violently that I was obliged to lean against the parapet, the touch of whose marble cooled and quieted my fevered and drooping senses.

Meanwhile Somadatta hastened to his beloved, who had sprung up with a low cry.

Seeing which, I also pulled myself together so far as to be able to approach the incomparable one. She, to all appearance surprised at the arrival of a stranger, had risen and seemed undecided as to whether she should go or stay, the while her eyes, like those of a startled young antelope, shot sidelong glances at me, and her body quivered like a tendril swaying in a gentle breeze. As for me, I stood in steadily increasing confusion, with disordered locks, and tell-tale eyes, and was barely able to stammer the few words in which I told her how much I appreciated the unhoped-for happiness of meeting her here. But she, when she noticed my great shyness, seemed herself to become calmer. She sat down on the bench again, and invited me with a gentle movement of her lotus-hand to take a seat beside her; and then, in a voice full of tremulous sweetness, assured me that she was very glad to be able to thank me for having flung the ball back to her with such skill that the game suffered no interruption; for, had that happened, the whole merit of her performance would have been lost and the goddess so clumsily honoured would have visited her anger upon her, or would at least have sent her no happiness. To which I replied that she owed me no thanks as I had at the very most but made good my own default, and, as she did not seem to understand what I meant by that, I ventured to remind her of the meeting of our eyes and of the ensuing confusion which caused her to fail in her stroke so that the ball flew away. But she reddened violently and absolutely refused to acknowledge such a thing,—what should have confused her in that?

"I imagine," I answered, "that from my eyes, which must have rivalled flowers in full blossom then, such a sweet odour of admiration streamed forth that for a moment thou wast stupefied and so thy hand went beside the ball."

"Eh! eh! What talk is that of thine about admiration?" she retorted, "thou art accustomed at home to see much more skilful players."

From which remark I gathered with satisfaction that I had been talked of and that the words I had used to Somadatta had been accurately repeated. But I grew hot and then cold at the thought that I had spoken almost slightingly, and I hastened to assure her that there was not one word of truth in my statement, and that I had only spoken so in order not to betray my precious secret to my friend. But she wouldn't believe that, or made as if she didn't, and, in speaking of it, I happily forgot my bashfulness, grew passionately eager to convince her, and told her how, at sight of her, the Love God had rained his flower darts upon me. "I was convinced," I said, "that in a former existence she had been my wife—whence otherwise such a sudden and irresistible love have arisen? But if that were so, then she must not less have recognised in me her former husband, and a like love must have sprung up in her breast also."

With such audacious words did I impetuously besiege her, till at length she hid her burning and tearful cheek on my breast, and acknowledged in words that were scarce audible that it had been with her as with me, and that she would surely have died had not her foster-sister most opportunely brought her the picture.

Then we kissed and fondled one another countless times, and felt as if we should expire for joy until suddenly the thought of my impending departure fell like a dark shadow athwart my happiness and forced a deep sigh from me.

Dismayed, Vasitthi asked why I sighed—but when I told her of the cause, she sank back on the bench in a fainting condition, and broke into a perfect tempest of tears and heart-rending sobs. Vain were all my attempts to comfort my heart's dearest. In vain did I assure her that so soon as the rainy season was over, I would return and never again leave her, even if I had to take service as a day labourer in Kosambi. Spoken to the winds were all my assurances that my despair at the separation was not less than her own, and that only stern, inexorable necessity tore me away from her so soon. She was scarcely able between her sobs to utter the few words needed to ask why it was so imperative to go away as early as to-morrow, just as we had found one another. But when I then explained it all to her very exactly and with every detail, she seemed neither to hear nor to comprehend a syllable. "Oh, she saw perfectly that I was longing to get back to my native town where there were many more beautiful maidens than she, who were also far more skilful ball-players, as I had myself acknowledged."

I might affirm, protest, and swear what I chose—she adhered to her assertion, and ever more copiously flowed her tears. Can any one wonder that I shortly thereafter lay at her feet, covering the hand that hung limply down with kisses and tears; and that I promised not to leave her? And who was then more blissful than I, when Vasitthi flung her soft arms around me, and kissed me again and again, laughing and crying for joy? It is true she now instantly said, "There, thou seest, it was not at all so necessary for thee to travel away, for then thou wouldst unquestionably have had to go." But when I set myself once more to explain everything clearly to her, she closed my mouth with a kiss and said that she knew I loved her and that she did not really mean what she had said of the girls in my native town. Filled with tender caresses and sweet confidences, the hours flew by as in a dream, and there would have been no end to all our bliss had not Somadatta and Medini suddenly appeared to tell us that it was high time to think of returning home.

In the courtyard at Somadatta's we found everything ready for my setting out. I called the overseer of the ox-wagons to me, and—bidding him use the utmost dispatch—sent him to the ambassador, with the information that my business was, I was sorry to say, not yet entirely settled and that I must, as a consequence, relinquish the idea of making the journey under the escort of the embassy. My one request was that he would be so good as give my love to my parents, and therewith I commended myself to his favour.

Scarcely had I stretched myself on my bed, in order—if possible—to enjoy a few hours' sleep—when the ambassador himself entered. Thoroughly dismayed, I bowed deeply before him, while he, in a somewhat surly voice, asked what this unheard-of behaviour meant,—I was to come with him at once.

In reply, I was about to speak of my still unfinished business, but he stopped me peremptorily.

"What nonsense! Business! Enough of such lies. Dost thou suppose I should not know what kind of business is on hand when a young puppy suddenly declares himself unable to leave a town, even if I had not seen that thy wagons already stand fully loaded, and with the oxen put to, in the courtyard?"

Of course I now stood scarlet with shame, and trembling, completely taken in my lie. But when he ordered me to come with him at once, as already too many of the precious, cool, morning hours had been lost, he encountered an opposition for which he was plainly not prepared. From a tone of command he passed to a threatening one, and finally had recourse to pleading. He reminded me that my parents had only decided to send me on such a distant journey because they knew that I could perform it in his company and under his protection.

But he could have advanced no argument less suited to his purpose. For I at once said to myself that then I should have to wait till another embassy went to Kosambi before I could return to my Vasitthi. No, I would show my father that I was well able to conduct a caravan, alone, through all the hardships and dangers of the road.

It is true the ambassador now painted all of these dangers in sufficiently gloomy colours, but all he said was spoken to the winds. Finally, in a great rage, he left me; "he was not to blame, and I must smart for my own folly."

To me it seemed as if I were relieved from an insufferable burden; I had now surrendered myself so completely to my love. In this sweet consciousness I fell asleep, and did not wake until it was time for us to betake ourselves to the terrace where our loved ones awaited us.

Night after night we came together there, and on each occasion Vasitthi and I discovered new treasures in our mutual affection and bore away with us an increased longing for our next meeting. The moonlight seemed to me to be more silvery, the marble cooler, the scent of the double-jasmines more intoxicating, the call of the kokila more languishing, the rustling of the palms more dreamy, and the restless whispering of the asokas more full of mysterious promise, than they could possibly be elsewhere in all the world.

Oh! how distinctly I can yet recall the splendid asoka trees which stood along the whole length of the terrace and underneath which we so often wandered, holding each other in close embrace. "The Terrace of the Sorrowless" it was called, from those trees which the poets name the "Sorrowless Tree," and sometimes "Heartsease." I have never elsewhere seen such magnificently grown specimens. The spear-shaped sleepless leaves gleamed in the rays of the moon and whispered in the gentle night-wind, and in between them glowed the golden, orange, and scarlet flowers, although we were as yet only at the beginning of the Vasanta season. But then, O brother, how should these trees not have stood in all their glory, seeing that, as thou knowest, the asoka at once opens his blossoms if his roots be but touched by the foot of a beautiful maiden.

One wonderful night, when the moon was at its full—to me it seems as if it were but yesterday—I stood beneath them with the dear cause of their early bloom, my sweet Vasitthi. Beyond the deep shadow of the ravine, we gazed far out into the land. We saw before us the two rivers wind like silver ribbons away over the vast plain and unite at that most sacred spot, which people call the "Triple-lock," because they believe that the "Heavenly Gunga" joins them there as third—for by this beautiful name, they, in that land, call the wonderful heavenly glow which we in the South know as the Milky Way —and Vasitthi, raising her hand, pointed to where it shone far above the tree-tops.

Then we spoke of the mighty Himavat[3] in the North, whence the beloved Gunga flows down; the Himavat, whose snow-covered peaks are the habita-

[3]Ancient name of the Himalayas.

tions of the gods and whose immense forests and deep chasms have afforded shelter to the great ascetics. But with even greater pleasure did I follow to where it takes its rise, the course of the Jumna.

"Oh," I called out, "had I but a fairy bark of mother-of-pearl, with my wishes for sails, and steered by my will, that it might bear us on the bosom of that silver stream upward to its source. Then should Hastinapura rise again from its ruins and the towering palaces ring with the banqueting of the revellers and the strife of the dice-players. Then the sands of Kurukshetra should yield up their dead. There the hoary Bhishma in silver armour, over which hang his white locks, should tower above the field on his lofty chariot and rain his polished arrows upon the foe; the valiant Phagadatta should come dashing on, mounted on his battle-inflamed, trunk-brandishing bull elephant; the agile Krishna should sweep with the four white battle steeds of Arjuna into the fiercest tumult of the fight. Oh! how I envied the ambassador his belonging to the warrior caste, when he told me that his ancestors also had taken part in that never-to-be-forgotten encounter. But that was foolish. For not by descent only do we possess ancestors. We are our own ancestors. Where was I then? Probably even there, among the combatants. For, although I am a merchant's son, the practice of arms has always been my greatest delight; and it is not too much to say that, sword in hand, I am a match for any man."

Vasitthi embraced me rapturously and called me her hero; I must quite certainly be one of those heroes who yet live in song! which of them, we could not, of course, know, as the perfume of the coral tree would scarcely penetrate to us through the sweet aroma of the "sorrowless" trees.

I asked her to tell me something of the nature of that perfume of which, to say truth, I had never heard. Indeed I found that romance, like all things else, blossomed far more luxuriously here in the valley of the Gunga than with us among the mountains.

So she related to me how once, on his progress through Indra's world, Krishna had, at the martial games, won the celestial coral tree and had planted it in his garden, a tree whose deep red blossoms shed their fragrance far around. And, she said, he who, by any chance, inhaled this perfume, remembered in his heart the long, long past, times long since vanished, out of his former lives.

"But only the saints are able to inhale this perfume here on earth," she said, and added almost roguishly, "and we two shall, I fear me, hardly become such. But what does that matter? Even if we were not Nala and Damayanti, I am sure we loved each other quite as much—whatever our names may have been. And perhaps, after all, Love and Faith are the only realities, merely changing their names and forms. They are the melodies, and we, the lutes on which they are played. The lute is shattered and another is strung, but the melody remains the same. It sounds, it is true, fuller and nobler on the one instrument than on the other, just as my new vina sounds far more beautiful than my old one. We, however, are two splendid lutes for the gods to play upon,—from which to draw the sweetest of all music."

I pressed her silently to my breast, deeply moved, as well as astonished at these strange thoughts.

But she added—and smiled gently, probably guessing what was in my mind—"Oh! I know, I really ought not to have such thoughts; our old family Brahman became quite angry on one occasion when I hinted at something of the kind; I was to pray to Krishna and leave thinking to the Brahmans. So, as I may not think, but may surely believe, I will believe that we were, really and truly, Nala and Damayanti."

And raising her hands in prayer to the asoka before us, in all its glory of shimmering blossom and flimmering leaf, she spoke to it in the words which Damayanti, wandering heart-broken in the woods, uses to the asoka; but on her lips, the flexible Çloka verses of the poet seemed to grow without effort and to blossom ever more richly, like a young shoot transplanted to hallowed soil—

"Thou Sorrowless One! the heart-rending cry of the stricken maiden hear!
Thou that so fittingly 'Heartsease' art named, give peace of thy peace to me!
Eyes of the gods are thine all-seeing blossoms; their lips, thy whispering leaves.
Tell me, oh! tell, where my heart's hero wanders, where my loved Nala waits."

Then she looked on me with love-filled eyes, in whose tears the moonlight was clearly mirrored, and spoke with lips that were drawn and quivering—

"When thou art far away, and dost recall to mind this scene of our bliss, then imagine to thyself that I stand here and speak thus to this noble tree. Only then I shall not say 'Nala,' but 'Kamanita.'"

I locked her in my arms, and our lips met in a kiss full of unutterable feeling.

Suddenly there was a rustling in the summit of the tree above us. A large, luminous red flower floated downward and settled on our tear-bedewed cheeks. Vasitthi took it in her hand, smiled, hallowed it with a kiss, and gave it to me. I hid it in my breast.

Several flowers had fallen to the ground in the avenue of trees. Medini, who sat beside Somadatta, on a bench not far from us, sprang to her feet, and, holding up several yellow asoka blossoms, came towards us, calling out—

"Look, sister! The flowers are beginning to fall already. Soon there will be enough of them for your bath."

"You don't mean those yellow things! Vasitthi may not, on any account, put them into her bath-water," exclaimed my mischievous friend—"that is, if her flower-like body is to blossom in harmony with her love. I assure you, only such scarlet flowers as that one which friend Kamanita has just concealed in his robe, should be used. For it is written in the golden Book of Love: 'Saffron yellow affection it is called, when it attracts attention, indeed, but, notwithstanding, later fades away; scarlet, however, when it does not later fade but becomes only too apparent.'"

At the same time he and Medini laughed in their merry, confidential way.

Vasitthi, however answered gravely, though with her sweet smile, and gently but firmly pressed my hand—

"Thou dost mistake, dear Somadatta! My love has the colour of no flower. For I have heard it said that the colour of the truest love is not red but black —black as Çiva's throat became when the god swallowed the poison which would otherwise have destroyed all created beings. And so it must ever be. True love must be able to withstand the poison of life, and must be willing to taste the bitterest, in order that the loved one may be spared. And from that bitterest it will assuredly prefer to choose its colour, rather than from any pleasures, however dazzling."

In such wise spoke my beloved Vasitthi, that night under the sorrowless trees.

Verner von Heidenstam

A CLEAN WHITE SHIRT

P RIVATE BENGT GETING had got a Cossack's pike through his breast, and his comrades laid him on a heap of twigs in a copse, where Pastor Rabenius gave him the Holy Communion. This was on the icy ground before the walls of Veperik, and a whistling norther tore the dry leafage from the bushes.

"The Lord be with thee!" whispered Rabenius softly and paternally. "Are you prepared now to depart hence after a good day's work?"

Bengt Geting lay with his hands knotted, bleeding to death. The hard eyes stood wide open, and the obstinate and scraggy face was so tanned by sun and frost that the bluish pallor of death shone out only over his lips.

"No," he said.

"That is the first time I have heard a word from your mouth, Bengt Geting."

The dying man knotted his hands all the harder, and chewed with his lips, which opened themselves for the words against his will.

"For once," he said slowly, "even the meanest and raggedest of soldiers may speak out."

He raised himself painfully on his elbow, and ejaculated such a piercing cry of anguish that Rabenius did not know whether it came from torment of soul or of body.

He set down the chalice on the ground, and spread a handkerchief over it, so that the leaves that were tumbling about should not fall into the brandy.

"And this," he stammered, pressing his hands to his forehead, "this I, who am a servant of Christ, shall be constrained to witness, morning after morning, evening after evening."

Soldiers crowded forward from all sides between the bushes to see and hear the fallen man, but their captain came in a wrathful mood with sword drawn.

"Tie a cloth over the fellow's mouth!" he shouted. "He has always been the most obstinate man in the battalion. I am no more inhuman than another, but I must do my duty, and I have a mass of new and untrained folk that have come with Lewenhaupt. These have been scared by his wailing, and refuse to go forward. Why don't you obey? I command here."

Rabenius took a step forward. On his curled white peruke he had a whole garland of yellow leaves.

"Captain," he said, "beside the dying the servant of God alone commands, but in glad humility he delivers his authority to the dying man himself. For three years I have seen Bengt Geting march in the line, but never yet have I seen him speak with any one. Now on the threshold of God's judgment-seat may no one further impose silence on him."

"With whom should I have spoken?" asked the bleeding trooper bitterly. "My tongue is as if tied and lame. Weeks would go by without my saying a word. No one has ever asked me about anything. It was only the ear that had to be on guard so that I did not fail to obey. 'Go,' they have said, 'go through marsh and snow.' To that there was nothing to answer."

Rabenius knelt and softly took his hands in his.

"But now you shall speak, Bengt Geting. Speak, speak, now that all are gathered about to hear you. You are now the only one of us all who has the right to speak. Is there a wife or perhaps an aged mother at home to whom you want me to send a message?"

"My mother starved me and sent me to the troops, and never since then has a woman had anything else to say to me than the same, 'Get away, Bengt Geting, go, go! What do you want with us?'"

"Have you anything to repent?"

"I repent that as a child I did not jump into the mill-race, and that, when you stood before the regiment on Sunday and admonished us to go patiently on and on, I didn't step forward and strike you down with my musket.—But do you want to know what causes me to dread? Have you never heard the wagon-drivers and outposts tell how in the moonlight they have seen their comrades that were shot limp in crowds after the army and hop about on their mangled legs and cry, 'Greetings to mother!'—They call them the Black Battalion. It's into the Black Battalion that I'm to go now. But the worst is that I shall be buried in my ragged coat and my bloody shirt. That's the one thing I can't get out of my mind. A plain trooper doesn't want to be taken home like the dead General Liewen, but I'm thinking of the fallen comrades at Dorfsniki, where the king had a coffin of a couple of boards and a clean white shirt given to each man. Why should they be treated so much better than I? Now in this year of misfortune a man is laid out as he falls. I'm so deeply sunk in misery that the only thing in the world I can be envious of is their clean white shirts."

"My poor friend," answered Rabenius quietly, "in the Black Battalion—if you believe in it now—you will have great company. Gyldenstolpe and Sperling and Lieutenant-Colonel Mörner already lie shot on the field. And do you recall the thousand others? Do you remember the friendly Lieutenant-Colonel Wattrang, who came riding to our regiment and gave an apple to every soldier, and who now lies among the Royal Dragoons, and all our comrades under the meadow at Holofzin? And do you remember my predecessor, Nicholas Uppendich, a mighty proclaimer of the Word, who fell at Kalisch in his priestly array? Grass has grown and snow fallen over his mould, and no one can point out with his foot the sod where he sleeps."

Rabenius bowed yet deeper, and felt the man's forehead and hands.

"In ten or at most fifteen minutes you will have ceased to live. Perhaps these minutes might replace the past years, if you sanctify them rightly. You are no longer one of us. Don't you see that your spiritual guide is lying on his knees by you with head uncovered? Speak now and tell me your last wish; no, your last command. Consider but one thing. The regiment is disorganized on your account, and meanwhile the others go forward with glory, or stand already on the storming ladders. You have frightened the younger fellows with your death-wound and your wailing, and you alone can make it good again. Now they listen only to you, and you alone have it in your power to make them go against the enemy. Consider that your last words will be last forgotten, and perhaps sometime will be repeated for those at home, who sit and roast their potatoes behind the oven."

Bengt Geting lay motionless, and a shadow of perplexity passed over his glance. Then he gently raised his arms as if for an invocation and whispered, "Lord, help me to do even so!"

He gave a sign that now he was able only to whisper, and Rabenius laid his face to his so as to be able to hear his words. Then Rabenius motioned to the soldiers, but his voice trembled so that he could hardly make himself heard. "Now Bengt Geting has spoken," he said. "This is his last wish, that you should take him between you on your muskets and carry him with you in his old place on the line, where he has stubbornly marched day after day and year after year."

The drums now struck up, the music began, and with his cheek on the shoulder of one of the soldiers Bengt Geting was carried forward step by step over the field toward the foe. Around him followed the whole regiment, and ever with bared head Rabenius went behind him, and did not notice that he was already dead.

"I shall see to it," he whispered, "that you get a clean white shirt. You know that the king does not regard himself as more than the humblest soldier, and it is so that he himself wishes sometime to lie."

INVOCATION AND PROMISE

I F THE neighbor-lands three should cry: "Forget
Our greatness of bygone ages!"
I'd answer: "Arise, O North, who yet
May'st be what my dream presages!"
The vision of greatness may bring again
New deeds like those of our betters.
Come, open the graves—nay, give us men
For Science and Art and Letters!

Ay, close to a cliff, let our people stand,
Where a fool his poor neck may shatter.
There are other things, men, to hold in your hand
Than a brim-full Egyptian platter.

It were better the plate should be split in two
Than that hearts should rot when still living.
That no race may be more great than you,—
That's the goal, why count we the striving?

It were better to feel the avenger's might
Than that years unto naught should have hasted,
It were better our people should perish quite
And our fields and cities be wasted.
It is braver the chance of the dice to take
Than to mope till our fire is expended;
It is finer to hear the bow-string break
Than never the bow to have bended.

I wake in the night, but I hear no sound
Save the waters seeting and churning.
Like a soldier of Judah, prone on the ground,
I could pray with passionate yearning.
I ask not a year of sunshine bright,
Nor for golden crops I importune.
Kind Fate, let the blazing thunderbolt smite
My people with years of misfortune!

Yea, smite us and lash us into one,
And the bluest of springs will follow.
Ye smile, my folk, but with face as of stone,
Ye sing, but your joy is hollow.
Ye rather would dance in silk attire
Than solve your own riddle clearly.
To youthful deeds ye might yet aspire
If again ye could weep sincerely.

Then on, fair daughter, in hardship bred,
Let shyness and sloth forsake thee!
We love thee so that, if thou wert dead,
Our love to life could awake thee.
Though our bed be hard, though the midnight lowers,
We'll be true while the tempest rages,
Thou people, thou land, thou speech that is ours,
Thou voice of our souls to the ages!

Romain Rolland

LIGHTNING STRIKES CHRISTOPHE

THUNDER falls when it will, and where it will. But there are peaks which attract it. Certain places—certain souls—breed storms: they create them, or draw them from all points of the horizon: and certain ages of life, like certain months of the year, are so saturated with electricity, that thunderstorms are produced in them,—if not at will—at any rate when they are expected.

The whole being of a man is taut for it. Often the storm lies brooding for days and days. The pale sky is hung with burning, fleecy clouds. No wind stirs. The still air ferments, and seems to boil. The earth lies in a stupor: no sound comes from it. The brain hums feverishly: all nature awaits the explosion of the gathering forces, the thud of the hammer which is slowly rising to fall back suddenly on the anvil of the clouds. Dark, warm shadows pass: a fiery wind rises through the body, the nerves quiver like leaves. . . . Then silence falls again. The sky goes on gathering thunder.

In such expectancy there is voluptuous anguish. In spite of the discomfort that weighs so heavily upon you, you feel in your veins the fire which is consuming the universe. The soul surfeited boils in the furnace, like wine in a vat. Thousands of germs of life and death are in labor in it. What will issue from it? The soul knows not. Like a woman with child, it is silent: it gazes in upon itself: it listens anxiously for the stirring in its womb, and thinks: "What will be born of me?" . . .

Sometimes such waiting is in vain. The storm passes without breaking: but you wake heavy, cheated, enervated, disheartened. But it is only postponed: the storm will break: if not to-day, then to-morrow: the longer it is delayed, the more violent will it be. . . .

Now it comes! . . . The clouds have come up from all corners of the soul. Thick masses, blue and black, torn by the frantic darting of the lightning: they advance heavily, drunkenly, darkening the soul's horizon, blotting out light. An hour of madness! . . . The exasperated Elements, let loose from the cage in which they are held bound by the Laws which hold the balance between the mind and the existence of things, reign, formless and colossal, in the night of consciousness. The soul is in agony. There is no longer the will to live. There is only longing for the end, for the deliverance of death. . . .

And suddenly there is lightning!
Christophe shouted for joy.

Joy, furious joy, the sun that lights up all that is and will be, the godlike joy of creation! There is no joy but in creation. There are no living beings but those who create. All the rest are shadows, hovering over the earth, strangers to life. All the joys of life are the joys of creation: love, genius, action,—quickened by flames issuing from one and the same fire. Even those who cannot find a place by the great fireside: the ambitious, the egoists, the sterile sensualists,—try to gain warmth in the pale reflections of its light.

To create in the region of the body, or in the region of the mind, is to issue from the prison of the body: it is to ride upon the storm of life: it is to be He who Is. To create is to triumph over death.

Wretched is the sterile creature, that man or that woman who remains alone and lost upon the earth, scanning their withered bodies, and the sight of themselves from which no flame of life will ever leap! Wretched is the soul that does not feel its own fruitfulness, and know itself to be big with life and love, as a tree with blossom in the spring! The world may heap honors and benefits upon such a soul: it does but crown a corpse.

When Christophe was struck by the flash of lightning, an electric fluid coursed through his body: he trembled under the shock. It was as though on the high seas, in the dark night, he had suddenly sighted land. Or it was as though in a crowd he had gazed into two eyes saluting him. Often it would happen to him after hours of prostration when his mind was leaping desperately through the void. But more often still it came in moments when he was thinking of something else, talking to his mother, or walking through the streets. If he were in the street a certain human respect kept him from too loudly demonstrating his joy. But if he were at home nothing could keep him back. He would stamp. He would sound a blare of triumph: his mother knew that well, and she had come to know what it meant. She used to tell Christophe that he was like a hen that has laid an egg.

He was permeated with his musical imagination. Sometimes it took shape in an isolated phrase complete in itself: more often it would appear as a nebula enveloping a whole work: the structure of the work, its general lines, could be perceived through a veil, torn asunder here and there by dazzling phrases which stood out from the darkness with the clarity of sculpture. It was only a flash: sometimes others would come in quick succession: each lit up other corners of the night. But usually, the capricious force having once shown itself unexpectedly, would disappear again for several days into its mysterious retreats, leaving behind it a luminous ray.

This delight in inspiration was so vivid that Christophe was disgusted by everything else. The experienced artist knows that inspiration is rare and that intelligence is left to complete the work of intuition: he puts his ideas under the press and squeezes out of them the last drop of the divine juices that are in them—(and if need be sometimes he does not shrink from diluting them with clear water).—Christophe was too young and too sure of himself not to despise such contemptible practices. He dreamed impossibly of producing nothing that was not absolutely spontaneous. If he had not been deliberately blind he would certainly have seen the absurdity of his aims. No doubt he was at that time in a period of inward abundance in which there was no gap, no chink, through which boredom or emptiness could creep. Everything served as an excuse to his inexhaustible fecundity: everything that his eyes saw or his ears heard, everything with which he came in contact in his daily life: every look, every word, brought forth a crop of dreams. In the boundless heaven of his thoughts he saw circling millions of milky stars, rivers of living light.—And yet, even then, there were moments when everything was suddenly blotted out. And although the night could not endure, although he had hardly time to suffer from these long silences of his soul, he did not escape a secret terror of that unknown power which came upon him, left him, came again, and disappeared. . . . How long, this time? Would it ever come again?—His pride rejected that thought and said: "This force is myself. When it ceases to be, I shall cease to be: I shall kill myself."—He never ceased to tremble: but it was only another delight.

But, if, for the moment, there was no danger of the spring running dry, Christophe was able already to perceive that it was never enough to fertilize a complete work. Ideas almost always appeared rawly: he had painfully to dig them out of the ore. And always they appeared without any sort of sequence, and by fits and starts: to unite them he had to bring to bear on them an element of reflection and deliberation and cold will, which fashioned them into new form. Christophe was too much of an artist not to do so: but he would not accept it: he forced himself to believe that he did no more than transcribe what was within himself, while he was always compelled more or less to transform it so as to make it intelligible.—More than that: sometimes he would absolutely forge a meaning for it. However violently the musical idea might come upon him it would often have been impossible for him to say what it meant. It would come surging up from the depths of life, from far beyond the limits of consciousness: and in that absolutely pure Force, which eluded common rhythms, consciousness could never recognize in it any of the motives which stirred in it, none of the human feelings which it defines and classifies: joys, sorrows, they were all merged in one single passion which was unintelligible, because it was above the intelligence. And yet, whether it understood or no, the intelligence needed to give a name to this form, to bind it down to one or other of the structures of logic, which man is forever building indefatigably in the hive of his brain.

So Christophe convinced himself—he wished to do so—that the obscure power that moved him had an exact meaning, and that its meaning was in accordance with his will. His free instinct, risen from the unconscious depths, was willy-nilly forced to plod on under the yoke of reason with perfectly clear ideas which had nothing at all in common with it. And work so produced was no more than a lying juxtaposition of one of those great subjects that Christophe's mind had marked out for itself, and those wild forces which had an altogether different meaning unknown to himself.

He groped his way, head down, borne on by the contradictory forces warring in him, and hurling into his incoherent works a fiery and strong quality of life which he could not express, though he was joyously and proudly conscious of it.

The consciousness of his new vigor made him able for the first time to envisage squarely everything about him, everything that he had been taught to honor, everything that he had respected without question: and he judged it all with insolent freedom. The veil was rent: he saw the German lie.

Every race, every art has its hypocrisy. The world is fed with a little truth and many lies. The human mind is feeble: pure truth agrees with it but ill: its religion, its morality, its states, its poets, its artists, must all be presented to it swathed in lies. These lies are adapted to the mind of each race: they vary from one to the other: it is they that make it so difficult for nations to understand each other, and so easy for them to despise each other. Truth is the same for all of us: but every nation has its own lie, which it calls its idealism: every creature therein breathes it from birth to death: it has become a condition of life: there are only a few men of genius who can break free from it through heroic moments of crisis, when they are alone in the free world of their thoughts.

It was a trivial thing which suddenly revealed to Christophe the lie of German art. It was not because it had not always been visible that he had not seen it: he was not near it, he had not recoiled from it. Now the mountain appeared to his gaze because he had moved away from it.

He was at a concert of the *Städtische Townhalle*. The concert was given in a large hall occupied by ten or twelve rows of little tables—about two or three hundred of them. At the end of the room was a stage where the orchestra was sitting. All round Christophe were officers dressed up in their long, dark coats,—with broad, shaven faces, red, serious, and commonplace: women talking and laughing noisily, ostentatiously at their ease: jolly little girls smiling and showing all their teeth: and large men hidden behind their beards and spectacles, looking like kindly spiders with round eyes. They got up with every fresh glass to drink a toast: they did this almost religiously: their faces, their voices changed: it was as though they were saying Mass: they offered each other the libations, they drank of the chalice with a mixture of solemnity and buffoonery. The music was drowned under the conversation and the clinking of glasses. And yet everybody was trying to talk and eat quietly. The *Herr Konzertmeister,* a tall, bent old man, with a white beard hanging like a tail from his chin, and a long aquiline nose, with spectacles, looked like a philologist.—All these types were familiar to Christophe. But on that day he had an inclination—he did not know why—to see them as caricatures. There are days like that when, for no apparent reason, the grotesque in people and things which in ordinary life passes unnoticed, suddenly leaps into view.

The programme of the music included the *Egmont* overture, a valse of Waldteufel, *Tannhäuser's Pilgrimage to Rome,* the overture to the *Merry Wives* of Nicolai, the religious march of *Athalie,* and a fantasy on the *North Star.* The orchestra played the Beethoven overture correctly, and the valse deliciously. During the *Pilgrimage of Tannhäuser,* the uncorking of bottles was heard. A big man sitting at the table next to Christophe beat time to the *Merry Wives* by imitating Falstaff. A stout old lady, in a pale blue dress, with a white belt, golden pince-nez on her flat nose, red arms, and an enormous waist, sang in a loud voice *Lieder* of Schumann and Brahms. She raised her eyebrows, made eyes at the wings, smiled with a smile that seemed to curdle on her moon-face, made exaggerated gestures which must certainly have called to mind the *café-concert* but for the majestic honesty which shone in her: this mother of a family played the part of the giddy girl, youth, passion: and Schumann's poetry had a faint smack of the nursery. The audience was in ecstasies.—But they grew solemn and attentive when there appeared the Choral Society of the Germans of the South (*Süddeutschen Männer Liedertafel*), who alternately cooed and roared part songs full of feeling. There were forty, and they sang four parts: it seemed as though they had set themselves to free their execution of every trace of style that could properly be called choral: hotch-potch of little melodious effects, little timid puling shades of sound, dying *pianissimos,* with sudden swelling, roaring *crescendos,* like some one beating on an empty box: no breadth or balance, a mawkish style: it was like Bottom:

"Let me play the lion. I will roar you as gently as any sucking dove. I will roar you as it were a nightingale."

Christophe listened from the beginning with growing amazement. There was nothing new in it all to him. He knew these concerts, the orchestra, the audience. But suddenly it all seemed to him false. All of it: even to what he most loved, the *Egmont* overture, in which the pompous disorder and correct agitation hurt him in that hour like a want of frankness. No doubt it was not Beethoven or Schumann that he heard, but their absurd interpreters, their cud-chewing audience whose crass stupidity was spread about their works like a heavy mist.—No matter, there was in the works, even the most beautiful of them, a disturbing quality which Christophe had never before felt.— What was it? He dared not analyze it, deeming it a sacrilege to question his beloved masters. But in vain did he shut his eyes to it: he had seen it. And, in spite of himself, he went on seeing it: like the *Vergognosa* at Pisa he looked between his fingers.

He saw German art stripped. All of them—the great and the idiots—laid bare their souls with a complacent tenderness. Emotion overflowed, moral nobility trickled down, their hearts melted in distracted effusions: the sluice gates were opened to the fearful German tender-heartedness: it weakened the energy of the stronger, it drowned the weaker under its grayish waters: it was a flood: in the depths of it slept German thought. And what thoughts were those of a Mendelssohn, a Brahms, a Schumann, and, following them, the whole legion of little writers of affected and tearful *Lieder!* Built on sand. Never rock. Wet and shapeless clay.—It was all so foolish, so childish often, that Christophe could not believe that it never occurred to the audience. He looked about him: but he saw only gaping faces, convinced in advance of the beauties they were hearing and the pleasure that they ought to find in it. How could they admit their own right to judge for themselves? They were filled with respect for these hallowed names. What did they not respect? They were respectful before their programmes, before their glasses, before themselves. It was clear that mentally they dubbed everything excellent that remotely or nearly concerned them.

Christophe passed in review the audience and the music alternately: the music reflected the audience, the audience reflected the music. Christophe felt laughter overcoming him and he made faces. However, he controlled himself. But when the Germans of the South came and solemnly sang the *Confession* that reminded him of the blushes of a girl in love, Christophe could not contain himself. He shouted with laughter. Indignant cries of "Ssh!" were raised. His neighbors looked at him, scared: their honest, scandalized faces filled him with joy: he laughed louder than ever, he laughed, he laughed until he cried. Suddenly the audience grew angry. They cried: "Put him out!" He got up, and went, shrugging his shoulders, shaking with suppressed laughter. His departure caused a scandal. It was the beginning of hostilities between Christophe and his birthplace.

After that experience Christophe shut himself up and set himself to read once more the works of the "hallowed" musicians. He was appalled to find that certain of the masters whom he loved most had *lied*. He tried hard to doubt it at first, to believe that he was mistaken.—But no, there was no way out of it. He was staggered by the conglomeration of mediocrity and untruth which constitutes the artistic treasure of a great people. How many pages could bear examination!

From that time on he could begin to read other works, other masters, who were dear to him, only with a fluttering heart. . . . Alas! There was some spell cast upon him: always there was the same discomfiture. With some of them his heart was rent: it was as though he had lost a dear friend, as if he had suddenly seen that a friend in whom he had reposed entire confidence had been deceiving him for years. He wept for it. He did not sleep at night: he could not escape his torment. He blamed himself: perhaps he had lost his judgment? Perhaps he had become altogether an idiot?—No, no. More than ever he saw the radiant beauty of the day and with more freshness and love than ever he felt the generous abundance of life: his heart was not deceiving him. . . .

But for a long time he dared not approach those who were the best for him, the purest, the Holy of Holies. He trembled at the thought of bringing his faith in them to the test. But how resist the pitiless instinct of a brave and truthful soul, which will go on to the end, and see things as they are, whatever suffering may be got in doing so?—So he opened the sacred works, he called upon the last reserve, the imperial guard. . . . At the first glance he saw that they were no more immaculate than the others. He had not the courage to go on. Every now and then he stopped and closed the book: like the son of Noah, he threw his cloak about his father's nakedness. . . .

Then he was prostrate in the midst of all these ruins. He would rather have lost an arm, than have tampered with his blessed illusions. In his heart he mourned. But there was so much sap in him, so much reserve of life, that his confidence in art was not shaken. With a young man's naïve presumption he began life again as though no one had ever lived it before him. Intoxicated by his new strength, he felt—not without reason, perhaps—that with a very few exceptions there is almost no relation between living passion and the expression which art has striven to give to it. But he was mistaken in thinking himself more happy or more true when he expressed it. As he was filled with passion it was easy for him to discover it at the back of what he had written: but no one else would have recognized it through the imperfect vocabulary with which he designated its variations. Many artists whom he condemned were in the same case. They had had, and had translated profound emotions: but the secret of their language had died with them.

Christophe was no psychologist: he was not bothered with all these arguments: what was dead for him had always been so. He revised his judgment of the past with all the confident and fierce injustice of youth. He stripped the noblest souls, and had no pity for their foibles. There were the rich melancholy, the distinguished fantasy, the kindly thinking emptiness of Mendelssohn. There were the bead-stringing and the affectation of Weber, his dryness of heart, his cerebral emotion. There was Liszt, the noble priest, the circus rider, neo-classical and vagabond, a mixture in equal doses of real and false nobility, of serene idealism and disgusting virtuosity. Schubert, swallowed up by his sentimentality, drowned at the bottom of leagues of stale, transparent water. The men of the heroic ages, the demi-gods, the Prophets, the Fathers of the Church, were not spared. Even the great Sebastian, the man of ages, who bore in himself the past and the future,—Bach,—was not free of untruth, of fashionable folly, of school-chattering. The man who had seen God, the man who lived in God, seemed sometimes to Christophe to have had an insipid and sugared religion, a Jesuitical style, rococo. In his cantatas there were languorous and devout airs—(dialogues of the Soul coquetting with Jesus)—which sickened Christophe: then he seemed to see chubby cherubims with round limbs and flying draperies. And also he had a feeling that the genial *Cantor* always wrote in a closed room: his work smacked of stuffiness: there was not in his music that brave outdoor air that was breathed in others, not such great musicians, perhaps, but greater men—more human— than he. Like Beethoven or Händel. What hurt him in all of them, especially in the classics, was their lack of freedom: almost all their works were "constructed." Sometimes an emotion was filled out with all the commonplaces of musical rhetoric, sometimes with a simple rhythm, an ornamental design, repeated, turned upside down, combined in every conceivable way in a mechanical fashion. These symmetrical and twaddling constructions—classical and neo-classical sonatas and symphonies—exasperated Christophe, who, at that time, was not very sensible of the beauty of order, and vast and well-conceived plans. That seemed to him to be rather masons' work than musicians'.

But he was no less severe with the romantics. It was a strange thing, and he was more surprised by it than anybody,—but no musicians irritated him more than those who had pretended to be—and had actually been—the most free, the most spontaneous, the least constructive,—those, who, like Schumann, had poured drop by drop, minute by minute, into their innumerable little works, their whole life. He was the more indignantly in revolt against them as he recognized in them his adolescent soul and all the follies that he had vowed to pluck out of it. In truth, the candid Schumann could not be taxed with falsity: he hardly ever said anything that he had not felt. But that was just it: his example made Christophe understand that the worst falsity in German art came into it not when the artists tried to express something which they had not felt, but rather when they tried to express the feelings which they did in fact feel—*feelings which were false*. Music is an implacable mirror of the soul. The more a German musician is naïve and in good faith, the more he displays the weaknesses of the German soul, its uncertain depths, its soft tenderness, its want of frankness, its rather sly idealism, its incapacity for seeing itself, for daring to come face to face with itself. That false idealism is the secret sore even of the greatest—of Wagner. As he read his works Christophe ground his teeth. *Lohengrin* seemed to him a blatant lie. He loathed the huxtering chivalry, the hypocritical mummery, the hero without fear and without a heart, the incarnation of cold and selfish virtue admiring itself and most patently self-satisfied. He knew it too well, he had seen it in reality, the type of German Pharisee, foppish, impeccable, and hard, bowing down before its own image, the divinity to which it has no scruple about sacrificing others. *The Flying Dutchman* overwhelmed him with its massive sentimentality and its gloomy boredom. The loves of the barbarous decadents of the *Tetralogy* were of a sickening staleness. Siegmund carrying off his sister sang a tenor drawing-room song. Siegfried and Brünnhilde, like respectable German married people, in the *Götterdämmerung* laid bare before each other, especially for the benefit of the audience, their pompous and voluble conjugal passion. Every sort of lie had arranged to meet in that work: false idealism, false Christianity, false Gothicism, false legend, false gods, false humans. Never did more monstrous convention appear than in that theater which was to upset all the conventions. Neither eyes, nor mind, nor heart could be deceived by it for a moment: if they were, then they must wish to be so.—They did wish to be so. Germany was delighted with that doting, childish art, an art of brutes let loose, and mystic, namby-pamby little girls.

And Christophe could do nothing: as soon as he heard the music he was caught up like the others, more than the others, by the flood, and the diabolical will of the man who had let it loose. He laughed, and he trembled, and his cheeks burned, and he felt galloping armies rushing through him! And he thought that those who bore such storms within themselves might have all allowances made for them. What cries of joy he uttered when in the hallowed works which he could not read without trembling he felt once more his old emotion, ardent still, with nothing to tarnish the purity of what he loved! These were glorious relics that he saved from the wreck. What happiness they gave him! It seemed to him that he had saved a part of himself. And was it not himself? These great Germans, against whom he revolted, were they not his blood, his flesh, his most precious life? He was only severe with them because he was severe with himself. Who loved them better than he? Who felt more than he the goodness of Schubert, the innocence of Haydn, the tenderness of Mozart, the great heroic heart of Beethoven? Who more often than he took refuge in the murmuring of the forests of Weber, and the cool shade of the cathedrals of John Sebastian, raising against the gray sky of the North, above the plains of Germany, their pile of stone, and their gigantic towers with their sun-tipped spires?—But he suffered from their lies, and he could not forget them. He attributed them to the race, their greatness to themselves. He was wrong. Greatness and weaknesses belong equally to the race whose great, shifting thought flows like the greatest river of music and poetry at which Europe comes to drink.—And in what other people would he have found the simple purity which now made it possible for him to condemn it so harshly?

He had no notion of that. With the ingratitude of a spoiled child he turned against his mother the weapons which he had received from her. Later, later, he was to feel all that he owed to her, and how dear she was to him. . . .

But he was in a phase of blind reaction against all the idols of his childhood. He was angry with himself and with them because he had believed in them absolutely and passionately—and it was well that it was so. There is an age in life when we must dare to be unjust, when we must make a clean sweep of all admiration and respect got at second-hand, and deny everything —truth and untruth—everything which we have not of ourselves known for truth. Through education, and through everything that he sees and hears about him, a child absorbs so many lies and blind follies mixed with the essential verities of life, that the first duty of the adolescent who wishes to grow into a healthy man is to sacrifice everything.

Christophe was passing through that crisis of healthy disgust. His instinct was impelling him to eliminate from his life all the undigested elements which encumbered it.

First of all to go was that sickening sweet tenderness which sucked away the soul of Germany like a damp and moldy river-bed. Light! Light! A rough, dry wind which should sweep away the miasmas of the swamp, the misty staleness of the *Lieder, Liedchen, Liedlein,* as numerous as drops of rain in which inexhaustibly the Germanic *Gemüt* is poured forth: the countless things like *Sehnsucht* (Desire), *Heimweh* (Homesickness), *Aufschwung* (Soaring), *Trage* (A question), *Warum?* (Why?), *an den Mond* (To the Moon), *an die Sterne* (To the Stars), *an die Nachtigall* (To the Nightingale), *an den Frühling* (To Spring), *an den Sonnenschein* (To Sunshine): like *Frühlingslied* (Spring Song), *Frühlingslust* (Delights of Spring), *Frühlings-gruss* (Hail to the Spring), *Frühlingsfahrt* (A Spring Journey), *Frühlings-nacht* (A Spring Night), *Frühlingsbotschaft* (The Message of Spring): like *Stimme der Liebe* (The Voice of Love), *Sprache der Liebe* (The Language of Love), *Trauer der Liebe* (Love's Sorrow), *Geist der Liebe* (The Spirit of Love), *Fülle der Liebe* (The Fullness of Love): like *Blumenlied* (The Song of the Flowers), *Blumenbrief* (The Letter of the Flowers), *Blumengruss* (Flowers' Greeting): like *Herzeleid* (Heart Pangs), *Mein Herz ist schwer* (My Heart is Heavy), *Mein Herz ist betrübt* (My Heart is Troubled), *Mein Aug' ist trüb* (My Eye is Heavy): like the candid and silly dialogues with the *Röselein* (The Little Rose), with the brook, with the turtle dove, with the lark: like those idiotic questions: *"If the briar could have no thorns?"*—*"Is an old husband like a lark who has built a nest?"*—*"Is she newly plighted?"*: the whole deluge of stale tenderness, stale emotion, stale melancholy, stale poetry. . . . How many lovely things profaned, rare things, used in season or out! For the worst of it was that it was all useless: a habit of undressing their hearts in public, a fond and foolish propensity of the honest people of Germany for plunging loudly into confidences. With nothing to say they were always talking! Would their chatter never cease?—As well bid frogs in a pond be silent.

It was in the expression of love that Christophe was most rawly conscious of untruth: for he was in a position to compare it with the reality. The conventional love songs, lacrymose and proper, contained nothing like the desires of man or the heart of woman. And yet the people who had written them must have loved at least once in their lives! Was it possible that they could have loved like that? No, no, they had lied, as they always did, they had lied to themselves: they had tried to idealize themselves. . . . Idealism! That meant that they were afraid of looking at life squarely, were incapable of seeing things like a man, as they are.—Everywhere the same timidity, the same lack of manly frankness. Everywhere the same chilly enthusiasm, the same pompous lying solemnity, in their patriotism, in their drinking, in their religion. The *Trinklieder* (Drinking Songs) were prosopopeia to wine and the bowl: *"Du, herrlich Glas . . ."* ("Thou, noble glass . . ."). Faith—the one thing in the world which should be spontaneous, springing from the soul like an unexpected sudden stream—was a manufactured article, a commodity of trade. Their patriotic songs were made for docile flocks of sheep basking in unison. . . . Shout, then!—What! Must you go on lying—*"idealizing"*— till you are surfeited, till it brings you to slaughter and madness! . . .

Christophe ended by hating all idealism. He preferred frank brutality to such lying. But at heart he was more of an idealist than the rest, and he had not—he could not have—any more real enemies than the brutal realists whom he thought he preferred.

He was blinded by passion. He was frozen by the mist, the anæmic lying, "the sunless phantom Ideas." With his whole being he reached upwards to the sun. In his youthful contempt for the hypocrisy with which he was surrounded, or for what he took to be hypocrisy, he did not see the high, practical wisdom of the race which little by little had built up for itself its grandiose idealism in order to suppress its savage instincts, or to turn them to account. Not arbitrary reasons, not moral and religious codes, not legislators and statesmen, priests and philosophers, transform the souls of peoples and often impose upon them a new nature: but centuries of misfortune and experience, which forge the life of peoples who have the will to live.

And yet Christophe went on composing: and his compositions were not examples of the faults which he found in others. In him creation was an irresistible necessity which would not submit to the rules which his intelligence laid down for it. No man creates from reason, but from necessity.—It is not enough to have recognized the untruth and affectation inherent in the majority of the feelings to avoid falling into them: long and painful endeavor is necessary: nothing is more difficult than to be absolutely true in modern society with its crushing heritage of indolent habits handed down through generations. It is especially difficult for those people, those nations who are possessed by an indiscreet mania for letting their hearts speak—for making them speak—unceasingly, when most generally it had much better have been silent.

Christophe's heart was very German in that: it had not yet learned the virtue of silence: and that virtue did not belong to his age. He had inherited from his father a need for talking, and talking loudly. He knew it and struggled against it: but the conflict paralyzed part of his forces.—And he had another gift of heredity, no less burdensome, which had come to him from his grandfather: an extraordinary difficulty—in expressing himself exactly.—He was the son of a *virtuoso*. He was conscious of the dangerous attraction of virtuosity: a physical pleasure, the pleasure of skill, of agility, of satisfied muscular activity, the pleasure of conquering, of dazzling, of enthralling in his own person the many-headed audience: an excusable pleasure, in a young man almost an innocent pleasure, though none the less destructive of art and soul: Christophe knew it: it was in his blood: he despised it, but all the same he yielded to it.

And so, torn between the instincts of his race and those of his genius, weighed down by the burden of a parasitical past, which covered him with a crust that he could not break through, he floundered along, and was much nearer than he thought to all that he shunned and banned. All his compositions were a mixture of truth and turgidness, of lucid strength and faltering

His village home lay there at the end of the waste land, beyond the sugar-cane field, hidden among the shadows of the banana and the slender areca palm, the coconut and the dark green jack-fruit trees.

I stopped for a moment in my lonely way under the starlight, and saw spread before me the darkened earth surrounding with her arms countless homes furnished with cradles and beds, mothers' hearts and evening lamps, and young lives glad with a gladness that knows nothing of its value for the world.

ON THE SEASHORE

On the seashore of endless worlds children meet.
The infinite sky is motionless overhead and the restless water is boisterous. On the seashore of endless worlds the children meet with shouts and dances.

They build their houses with sand, and they play with empty shells. With withered leaves they weave their boats and smilingly float them on the vast deep. Children have their play on the seashore of worlds.

They know not how to swim, they know not how to cast nets. Pearl-fishers dive for pearls, merchants sail in their ships, while children gather pebbles and scatter them again. They seek not for hidden treasures, they know not how to cast nets.

The sea surges up with laughter, and pale gleams the smile of the sea-beach. Death-dealing waves sing meaningless ballads to the children, even like a mother while rocking her baby's cradle. The sea plays with children, and pale gleams the smile of the sea-beach.

On the seashore of endless worlds children meet. Tempest roams in the pathless sky, ships are wrecked in the trackless water, death is abroad and children play. On the seashore of endless worlds is the great meeting of children.

THE SOURCE

The sleep that flits on baby's eyes—does anybody know from where it comes? Yes, there is a rumour that it has its dwelling where, in the fairy village among shadows of the forest dimly lit with glow-worms, there hang two shy buds of enchantment. From there it comes to kiss baby's eyes.

The smile that flickers on baby's lips when he sleeps—does anybody know where it was born? Yes, there is a rumour that a young pale beam of a crescent moon touched the edge of a vanishing autumn cloud, and there the smile was first born in the dream of a dew-washed morning—the smile that flickers on baby's lips when he sleeps.

The sweet, soft freshness that blooms on baby's limbs—does anybody know where it was hidden so long? Yes, when the mother was a young girl it lay pervading her heart in tender and silent mystery of love—the sweet, soft freshness that has bloomed on baby's limbs.

BABY'S WAY

If baby only wanted to, he could fly up to heaven this moment.

It is not for nothing that he does not leave us.

He loves to rest his head on mother's bosom, and cannot ever bear to lose sight of her.

Baby knows all manner of wise words, though few on earth can understand their meaning.

It is not for nothing that he never wants to speak.

The one thing he wants is to learn mother's words from mother's lips. That is why he looks so innocent.

Baby had a heap of gold and pearls, yet he came like a beggar on to this earth.

It is not for nothing he came in such a disguise.

This dear little naked mendicant pretends to be utterly helpless, so that he may beg for mother's wealth of love.

Baby was so free from every tie in the land of the tiny crescent moon.

It was not for nothing he gave up his freedom.

He knows that there is room for endless joy in mother's little corner of a heart, and it is sweeter far than liberty to be caught and pressed in her dear arms.

Baby never knew how to cry. He dwelt in the land of perfect bliss.

It is not for nothing he has chosen to shed tears.

Though with the smile of his dear face he draws mother's yearning heart to him, yet his little cries over tiny troubles weave the double bond of pity and love.

THE UNHEEDED PAGEANT

Ah, who was it coloured that little frock, my child, and covered your sweet limbs with that little red tunic?

You have come out in the morning to play in the courtyard, tottering and tumbling as you run.

But who was it coloured that little frock, my child?

What is it makes you laugh, my little life-bud?

Mother smiles at you standing on the threshold.

She claps her hands and her bracelets jingle, and you dance with your bamboo stick in your hand like a tiny little shepherd.

But what is it makes you laugh, my little life-bud?

O beggar, what do you beg for, clinging to your mother's neck with both your hands?

O greedy heart, shall I pluck the world like a fruit from the sky to place it
on your little rosy palm?
O beggar, what are you begging for?

The wind carries away in glee the tinkling of your anklet bells.
The sun smiles and watches your toilet.
The sky watches over you when you sleep in your mother's arms, and the
morning comes tiptoe to your bed and kisses your eyes.
The wind carries away in glee the tinkling of your anklet bells.

The fairy mistress of dreams is coming towards you, flying through the
twilight sky.
The world-mother keeps her seat by you in your mother's heart.
He who plays his music to the stars is standing at your window with his
flute.
And the fairy mistress of dreams is coming towards you, flying through
the twilight sky.

SLEEP-STEALER

Who stole sleep from baby's eyes? I must know.
Clasping her pitcher to her waist mother went to fetch water from the
village near by.
It was noon. The children's playtime was over; the ducks in the pond were
silent.
The shepherd boy lay asleep under the shadow of the banyan tree.
The crane stood grave and still in the swamp near the mango grove.
In the meanwhile the Sleep-stealer came and, snatching sleep from baby's
eyes, flew away.
When mother came back she found baby travelling the room over on all
fours.

Who stole sleep from our baby's eyes? I must know. I must find her and
chain her up.
I must look into that dark cave, where, through boulders and scowling
stones, trickles a tiny stream.
I must search in the drowsy shade of the *bakula* grove, where pigeons coo
in their corner, and fairies' anklets tinkle in the stillness of starry nights.
In the evening I will peep into the whispering silence of the bamboo forest,
where fireflies squander their light, and will ask every creature I meet, "Can
anybody tell me where the Sleep-stealer lives?"

Who stole sleep from baby's eyes? I must know.
Shouldn't I give her a good lesson if I could only catch her!
I would raid her nest and see where she hoards all her stolen sleep.
I would plunder it all, and carry it home.
I would bind her two wings securely, set her on the bank of the river, and
then let her play at fishing with a reed among the rushes and water-lilies.

When the marketing is over in the evening, and the village children sit in their mothers' laps, then the night birds will mockingly din her ears with: "Whose sleep will you steal now?"

THE BEGINNING

"Where have I come from, where did you pick me up?" the baby asked its mother.

She answered, half crying, half laughing, and clasping the baby to her breast,—

"You were hidden in my heart as its desire, my darling.

You were in the dolls of my childhood's games; and when with clay I made the image of my god every morning, I made and unmade you then.

You were enshrined with our household deity, in his worship I worshipped you.

In all my hopes and my loves, in my life, in the life of my mother you have lived.

In the lap of the deathless Spirit who rules our home you have been nursed for ages.

When in girlhood my heart was opening its petals, you hovered as a fragrance about it.

Your tender softness bloomed in my youthful limbs, like a glow in the sky before the sunrise.

Heaven's first darling, twin-born with the morning light, you have floated down the stream of the world's life, and at last you have stranded on my heart.

As I gaze on your face, mystery overwhelms me; you who belong to all have become mine.

For fear of losing you I hold you tight to my breast. What magic has snared the world's treasure in these slender arms of mine?"

WHEN AND WHY

When I bring you coloured toys, my child, I understand why there is such a play of colours on clouds, on water, and why flowers are painted in tints— when I give coloured toys to you, my child.

When I sing to make you dance, I truly know why there is music in leaves, and why waves send their chorus of voices to the heart of the listening earth —when I sing to make you dance.

When I bring sweet things to your greedy hands, I know why there is honey in the cup of the flower, and why fruits are secretly filled with sweet juice—when I bring sweet things to your greedy hands.

When I kiss your face to make you smile, my darling, I surely understand what pleasure streams from the sky in morning light, and what delight the summer breeze brings to my body—when I kiss you to make you smile.

DEFAMATION

Why are those tears in your eyes, my child?
How horrid of them to be always scolding you for nothing!
You have stained your fingers and face with ink while writing—is that why they call you dirty?
O, fie! Would they dare to call the full moon dirty because it has smudged its face with ink?

For every little trifle they blame you, my child. They are ready to find fault for nothing.
You tore your clothes while playing—is that why they call you untidy?
O, fie! What would they call an autumn morning that smiles through its ragged clouds?

Take no heed of what they say to you, my child.
They make a long list of your misdeeds.
Everybody knows how you love sweet things—is that why they call you greedy?
O, fie! What then would they call us who love you?

PLAYTHINGS

Child, how happy you are sitting in the dust, playing with a broken twig all the morning!
I smile at your play with that little bit of a broken twig.
I am busy with my accounts, adding up figures by the hour.
Perhaps you glance at me and think, "What a stupid game to spoil your morning with!"
Child, I have forgotten the art of being absorbed in sticks and mud-pies.
I seek out costly playthings, and gather lumps of gold and silver.
With whatever you find you create your glad games. I spend both my time and my strength over things I can never obtain.
In my frail canoe I struggle to cross the sea of desire, and forget that I too am playing a game.

THE FURTHER BANK

I long to go over there to the further bank of the river,
Where those boats are tied to the bamboo poles in a line;
Where men cross over in their boats in the morning with ploughs on their shoulders to till their far-away fields;
Where the cowherds make their lowing cattle swim across to the riverside pasture;
Whence they all come back home in the evening, leaving the jackals to howl in the island overgrown with weeds.

Mother, if you don't mind, I should like to become the boatman of the ferry when I am grown up.

They say there are strange pools hidden behind that high bank,

Where flocks of wild ducks come when the rains are over, and thick reeds grow round the margins where water-birds lay their eggs;

Where snipes with their dancing tails stamp their tiny footprints upon the clean soft mud;

Where in the evening the tall grasses crested with white flowers invite the moonbeam to float upon their waves.

Mother, if you don't mind, I should like to become the boatman of the ferryboat when I am grown up.

I shall cross and cross back from bank to bank, and all the boys and girls of the village will wonder at me while they are bathing.

When the sun climbs the mid sky and morning wears on to noon, I shall come running to you, saying, "Mother, I am hungry!"

When the day is done and the shadows cower under the trees, I shall come back in the dusk.

I shall never go away from you into the town to work like father.

Mother, if you don't mind, I should like to become the boatman of the ferryboat when I am grown up.

Gerhart Hauptmann

THE SUNKEN BELL

ACT ONE

SCENE: *A fir-clad glade in the mountains. R. up stage, beneath an overhanging rock, a hut, with practicable door and windows. L. C. an old well.*

RAUTENDELEIN *is seated on the edge of the well, combing her thick golden locks and addressing a bee which she is trying to drive away. In one hand she has a mirror.*

RAUTENDELEIN. Thou buzzing, golden, wight—whence com'st thou here?
Thou sipper of sweets, thou little wax-maker!
Nay! Tease me not, thou sun-born good-for-naught!
Dost hear? . . . Begone! . . . 'Tis time I combed my hair
With Granny's golden comb. Should I delay,
She'll scold me when she comes. Begone, I say!

What? . . . Loit'ring still? . . . Away—away with thee!
Am I a rose bush? . . . Are my lips a rose?
Off to the wood with thee, beyond the brook!
There, there, my pretty bee, bloom cowslips fair,
And crocuses, and violets—thou canst suck
Thy fill of them. Dost think I jest? No. No.
Quick! Get thee home. Thou'rt not in favor here.
Thou knowest Granny's cast a spell on thee
For furnishing the Church with altar-lights.
Come! Must I speak again? Go not too far!
Hey! . . . Chimney! Puff some smoke across the glade,
To drive away this naughty, wilful, bee.
Ho! Gander! Hither! Hither! . . . Hurry! Hurry!
Away! Away! (*Bee flies off.*) . . . At last! . . .
    (RAUTENDELEIN *combs her hair quietly for a moment or two. Then, leaning over the well, she calls down.*)

                                      Hey! Nickelmann!
(*Pauses.*)
He does not hear me. Well—I'll sing to myself.

    Where do I come from? . . . Whither go?
    Tell me—I long to know!
    Did I grow as the birds of the woodland gay?
    Am I a fay?
    Who asks the sweet flower
    That blooms in the dell,
    And brightens the bower,
    Its tale to tell?
    Yet, oft, as I sit by my well, alone,
    I sigh for the mother I ne'er have known.
    But my weird I must dree—
    And I'm fair to see—
    A golden-haired maid of the forest free!
(*Pause. She calls.*)
Hey! Nickelmann! Come up! 'Tis lonely here.
Granny's gone gathering fir-apples. I'm dull! . .
Wilt keep me company and tell me tales?
Why then, to-night, perhaps, as a reward . . .
I'll creep into some farmer's yard and steal
A big, black, cock for thee! . . . Ah, here he come
The silver bubbles to the surface mount!
If he should bob up now, the glass he'd break,
That such bright answer to my nod doth make.
    (*Admiring her reflection in the well.*)
Godden' to thee, my sweet maid o' the well!
Thy name? . . . Rautendelein? . . . Indeed! I see—
Thou'rt jealous of my beauty. Look at me.
For I, not thou, Rautendelein should be.
What didst thou answer? Didst thou dare to point

Thy finger at thy soft twin-breasts? . . . Nay, nay—
I'm fairer; fair as Freya. Not for naught
My hair was spun out of the sunbeams red,
To shine, in golden glory, even as the sun
Shines up at us, at noon, from out a lake.
Aha! Thou spread'st thy tresses, like a net,
All fiery-scarlet, set to catch the fishes!
Thou poor, vain, foolish, trull . . . There! Catch this stone.
  (*Throwing pebble down the well and disturbing the reflection.*)
Thy hour is ended. Now—I'm fair alone!
  (*Calling.*)
Ho! Nickelmann! Come—help me pass the time!
  (THE NICKELMANN, *a water-spirit, half emerges from the well, and flops over
the edge. He is streaming with water. Weeds cling to his head. He snorts
like a seal, and his eyes blink as if the daylight hurt them.*)
He's here! . . . Ha! Ha! Ha! Ha! How dreadfully plain
He is! . . . Didst thou not hear me call! Dear, dear—
It makes one's flesh creep but to know him near!
THE NICKELMANN (*croaking*). Brekekekex!
RAUTENDELEIN (*mocking*).   Brekekekex! Ay, ay—
It smells of springtide. Well, is that so strange?
Why—every lizard, mole, and worm, and mouse—
The veriest water-rat—had scented that.
The quail, the hare, the trout, the fly, the weeds,
Had told thee Spring was here.
THE NICKELMANN (*touchily*).   Brekekekex!
Be not too nosey-wise. Dost understand?
Thou ape, thou midge, thou tomtit, irk me not!
I say, beware! . . . So, Quorax! Quack! Quack! Quack!
      RAUTENDELEIN. If Master Uncle's cross to-day,
      I'll leave him all alone to play.
      And I'll go dance a ring-a-round.
      Partners a-plenty, I'll be bound,
      For pretty maidens may be found.
  (*Calling.*)
Heigh-a-aye!
Voice of WOOD-SPRITE (*heard without*). Heigh-a-o!
RAUTENDELEIN. My merry faun, come—dance with me, I pray!
  (*Enter the* WOOD-SPRITE, *skipping comically across the glade.*)
THE WOOD-SPRITE. Nay, I'm no dancer; but I know a leap
Would make the mountain-goat with envy weep.
If that won't do for thee, I know a game
Will please thee more, my nixey. Fly with me;
I'll show thee in the woods a willow tree
All hollowed out with age, where never came
The sound of babbling brook, nor crow of cock.
There, in the shadow of some friendly rock,
I'll cut for thee, my own, the wond'rous pipe
All maids must dance to.

RAUTENDELEIN (*eluding him*).   Thanks, I'm not yet ripe
For such as thou! An thou must play thy pranks,
Go—woo thy wood-wench. She may like thy shanks!
Or—go to thy dear partner, who—they say—
Another baby bears thee every day;
Except on Sundays, when, at early morn,
Three dirty little brats to thee are born!
Ha! Ha! Ha!
   (*She runs off into the hut, laughing. The* WOOD-SPRITE *vainly pursues her and returns disconsolate.*)
THE NICKELMANN. Brekekekex! How mad the baggage seems!
The lightning blast thee!
THE WOOD-SPRITE (*sitting*). Ay! . . . I'd love to tame her.
   (*He produces a short pipe and lights it by striking a match on his hoof.*)
THE NICKELMANN. And how go things at home?
THE WOOD-SPRITE.   So so. So so.
It's warmer here than on the hills. You're snug.
Up yonder the wind shrieks and howls all day;
The swollen clouds drift damp about the peaks,
And burst at last, like sponges, when they're squeezed.
A foul time we have of it!
THE NICKELMANN.   And is that all?
THE WOOD-SPRITE. No . . . Yesterday I cut
My first spring salad. It grew near my hut.
This morning, early, I went out,
And, roaming carelessly about,
Through brush and brier,
Then climbing higher,
At last I reached the topmost wood.
There I espied a hateful brood
Of mortals, who did sweat and stew,
And dig the earth, and marble hew.
A curse upon their church and creed—
Their chapels, and their clanging bells*—
THE NICKELMANN. Their bread they mix with cummin-seed!†
THE WOOD-SPRITE. They plague us in our woods and wells.
But vain is all our wrath and woe.
Beside the deep abyss 'twill grow
With tower and spire, and, overhead,
The cross that you and I do dread.
Ay! . . . The noisy monster was all but hung
In the lofty steeple, and soon had rung.
But I was alert! We shall never hear
That bell! It is drowned in the mere!
   (*Changing tone.*)
By cock and pie!

*The sprites and dwarfs hated bells, especially church bells, as disturbers of their ancient privacy.
†Cummin-seed was obnoxious to the sprites.

A devil of a joke! . . . I stood on the brink
Of the cliff, chewing sorrel, to help me think,
As I rested against a stump of birch,
'Mid the mountain grasses, I watched the church.
When, all of a sudden, I saw the wing
Of a blood-red butterfly, trying to cling
To a stone. And I marked how it dipped, and tipped,
As if from a blossom the sweet it sipped.
I called. It fluttered, to left and to right,
Until on my hand I felt it light.
I knew the elf. It was faint with fright.
We babbled o' this,
And we babbled o' that,
Of the frogs that had spawned
Ere the day had dawned,—
We babbled and gabbled, a-much. I wis:
Then it broke
Into tears! . . .
I calmed its fears.
And again it spoke.
"O, they're cracking their whips,
"And they gee! and they whoa!
"As they drag it aloft
"From the dale below.
" 'Tis some terrible tub, that has lost its lid,
"All of iron! Will nobody rid
"Our woods of the horrible thing? 'Twould make
"The bravest moss-mannikin shudder and quake.
"They swear they will hang it, these foolish people,
"High up in the heart of the new church steeple,
"And they'll hammer, and bang, at its sides all day
"To frighten good spirits of earth away!"

I hummed, and I hawed, and I said, ho ho!
As the butterfly fell to the earth: while I
Stole off in pursuit of a herd near by.
I guzzled my fill of good milk, I trow!
Three udders ran dry. They will seek in vain
So much as a drop of it more to drain.
Then, making my way to a swirling stream,
I hid in the brush, as a sturdy team
Came snorting, and panting, along the road—
Eight nags, tugging hard at their heavy load.
We will bide our time, quoth I—and lay
Quite still in the grass, till the mighty dray
Rumbled by:—when, stealing from hedge to hedge,
And hopping and skipping from rock to rock,
I followed the fools. They had reached the edge
Of the cliff when there came—a block!

With flanks all a-quiver, and hocks a-thrill,
They hauled and they lugged at the dray until,
Worn out by the struggle to move the bell,
They had to lie down for a moment. Well—
Quoth I to myself, the Faun will play
Them a trick that will spare them more work to-day.
One clutch at the wheel—I had loosened a spoke—
A wrench, and a blow, and the wood-work broke.
A wobble, a crack, and the hateful bell
Rolled over—and into the gulf it fell!
And oh, how it sounded,
And clanged, as it bounded,
From crag to crag, on its downward way:
Till at last in the welcoming splash and the spray
Of the lake it was lost—for aye!

(*During the* WOOD-SPRITE's *speech night has drawn near. It is now dusk. Several times, towards the end of the narrative, faint cries for help have been heard, coming from the wood. Enter from back,* HEINRICH. *As he approaches the hut, the* WOOD-SPRITE *vanishes in the wood and the* NICKELMANN *disappears in the well.* HEINRICH *is about 30 years of age. His face is pale and careworn.*)

HEINRICH. Good people—open! Quick! I've lost my way!
Help! Help! I've fallen! . . . I am weak . . . I faint!
Will no one answer? . . . Help! Kind people! Help!

(*He sinks on the ground, unconscious, near the hut. The sun has set—dark purple clouds hang over the hills. The wind rises. Enter from the wood, carrying a basket on her back,* OLD WITTIKIN.)

WITTIKIN. Rautendel'! Come and help me with my load!
I've too much on my shoulders. Come, I say!
I'm scant o' breath! . . . Where can the girl be dawdling?

(*A bat flies across the glade.*)

Ho! Stop thy gadding, flitter-mouse, and list!
Thou'lt fill thy greedy craw quite soon enough.
Come hither. Fly through yonder hole and see
If she's within. Then send her quick to me!

(*Faint lightning.* WITTIKIN *shakes her fist at the sky.*)

Ay, ay, I see thee, Father Thor! . . . 'Twill storm!
But give thy noisy goats not too much rope,
And see thy great red beard gleams not too bright.
Rautendel'! Hey! Rautendel' . . . Dost not hear?

(*A squirrel skips across the path.*)

Hey! Squirrel! Thou hast fleet and nimble feet.
Hop thou into the hut, and, shouldst thou meet
Rautendel', send her hither. As a treat,
I'll give thee, for thy pains, a nut to eat!

(WITTIKIN *sees* HEINRICH *and touches him contemptuously with her foot.*)

What's this? A stranger? Well, well, I declare!
And pray, what brings you here, my man, so late?
Rautendel'! . . . Hey! Rautendel'! (*To* HEINRICH). Are you dead?
Plague take you! As if I'd not more'n enough

To worry me—what wi' the Bailiff and the Priest
Hunting me down like a mad dog. And now
I find a dead man at my door—Rautendel'!
A rare time I'd have of it, I'll be bound,
If they should find this fellow lying here.
They'd burn my house about my ears. (*To* HEINRICH.) Art dumb?
Ay. Ay.

(RAUTENDELEIN *enters from hut, and looks out inquiringly.*)
                    Oho! Thou'rt come at last. Look there!
We have a visitor. And what a one!
He's still enough. Go! Fetch a truss of hay,
And make a litter.

RAUTENDELEIN. In the hut?

WITTIKIN (*grumbling*).   What next?
Nay, nay. We've no room in the hut for him.

(*Exit into hut.* RAUTENDELEIN *follows her. She reappears a moment later, with an armful of hay, and is about to kneel beside* HEINRICH, *when he recovers consciousness.*)

HEINRICH. Where am I? Maiden—wilt thou answer me?

RAUTENDELEIN. Why, in the mountains.

HEINRICH.   In the mountains? Ay—
But how . . . and why? What brought me here to-night?

RAUTENDELEIN. Nay, gentle stranger, naught know I of that.
Why fret thyself about such trifles? See—
Here I have brought thee hay. So lay thy head
Down and take all the rest thou need'st.

HEINRICH.   Yes! Yes!
'Tis rest I need. Indeed—indeed—thou'rt right.
But rest will come to me no more, my child!
(*Uneasily.*)
Now . . . tell me . . . what has happened?

RAUTENDELEIN.   Nay, if I knew . . .

HEINRICH. Meseems . . . methinks . . . and . . . then . . . all ends in dreams.
Ay, surely, I am dreaming.

RAUTENDELEIN.   Here is milk.
Thou must drink some of it, for thou art weak.

HEINRICH (*eagerly*). Thanks, maiden. I will drink. Give me the milk.
(*He drinks from a bowl which she offers him.*)

RAUTENDELEIN (*While he drinks.*) Thou art not used to mountain ways. Thy home
Lies in the vale below, where mortals dwell.
And, like a hunter who once fell from the cliff
While giving chase to some wild mountain fowl,
Thou hast climbed far too high. And yet . . . that man
Was not quite fashioned as the man thou art.

HEINRICH (*After drinking and looking ecstatically and fixedly at* RAUTENDELEIN.)
Speak on! Speak on! Thy drink was very sweet.
But sweeter still thy voice . . .

(*Again becoming anxious.*)

                        She said—a man
Not fashioned like myself. A better man—
And yet he fell! . . . Speak on, my child.

RAUTENDELEIN.   Why speak?
What can my words avail? I'll rather go
And fetch thee water from the brook, to wash
The blood and dust from off thy brow . . .

HEINRICH (*Pleading and grasping her by the wrist.* RAUTENDELEIN *stands undecided.*)   Ah, stay!
And look into mine eyes with thy strange eyes.
For lo, the world, within thine eyes renewed,
So sweetly bedded, draws me back to life!
Stay, child. O stay!

RAUTENDELEIN (*uneasy*). Then . . . as thou wilt. And yet . . . .

HEINRICH (*fevered and imploring*). Ah, stay with me! Thou wilt not leave
    me so?
Thou dost not dream how dear to me thou art.
O, wake me not, my child. I'll tell thee all.
I fell . . . Yet—no. Speak thou; for thy dear voice
Has Heaven's own music. God did give it thee.
And I will listen. Speak! . . . Wilt thou not speak?
Wilt thou not sing to me? Why then . . . I must . . .
I fell. I know not how—I've told thee that—
Whether the path gave way beneath my feet;
Whether 'twas willingly I fell, or no—
God wot. Enough. I fell into the gulf.
    (*More fevered.*)
And then I clutched at a wild cherry tree
That grew between the rocks. It broke—and I,
Still clasping a bough tightly, felt a shower
Of pale pink blossoms riot round my head;
Then swift was hurled to the abyss—and died!
And even now I'm dead. It must be so.
Let no one wake me!

RAUTENDELEIN (*uncertainly*). Yet thou seem'st alive!

HEINRICH. I know—I know—what once I did not know:
That Life is Death, and only Death is Life.
    (*Collapsing again.*)
I fell. I lived—and fell. The bell fell, too!
We two—the bell and I. Was I the first—
To slip, and next—the bell? Or—the reverse?
Who seeks to know? And who could prove the truth?
And even were it proven, what care I?
Then I was living. Now—ah, now . . . I'm dead.
    (*Tenderly.*)
Ah, go not yet!
    (*Looks at his hand*)
                    My hand! . . . 'Tis white as milk!

My hand! . . . It hangs so heavy! . . . It seems dead.
I cannot lift it! . . . Yet— How sweet thou art!
The mere touch of thy soft hair doth bring relief,
As water of Bethesda! . . . Nay, do not fear!
My hand shall never harm thee—thou art holy!
Where have we met? . . . I surely know thy face.
Somewhere, but where, or when, I cannot tell,
I wrought for thee, and strove—in one grand Bell,
To wed the silver music of thy voice
With the warm gold of a Sun-holiday.
It should have been a master-work! . . . I failed.
Then wept I tears of blood.

RAUTENDELEIN.   Wept tears of blood?
I cannot follow thee. What be these tears?

HEINRICH (*trying to raise his head*). Thou lovely picture! . . . Help me to
     sit up.
     (RAUTENDELEIN *stoops and supports his head.*)
Dost thou bend down to me? Then, with love's arms,
Do thou release me from this cruel Earth,
Whereunto the hour nails me, as to a cross.
Release me! For thou canst. I know thou canst!
And, with thy tender hands, pluck off the thorns
That crown my head. No crown! Love—only Love!
     (*His head is slightly raised. He seems exhausted.*)
                                   Thanks! Thanks!
     (*Gently and in a lost kind of way as he looks at the landscape.*)
Here all is beautiful! The rustling boughs
Have such a strange, full sound. The darkling arms
Of the great firs move so mysteriously.
How solemnly their heads sway to and fro!
The very soul of fairy fantasy
Sighs through the wood. It murmurs low, and then,
Still gently whisp'ring, stirs the tiny leaves.
Now it goes singing through the green wood-grass.
And now, veiled all in misty white, it nears—
It stretches out its long white hand and points
At me! . . . Now closer, it draws! It touches my ear . . .
My tongue . . . my eyes! . . . 'Tis gone! Yet thou art here!
Thou art my fantasy! . . Kiss me, sweet fantasy!
     (*He faints.*)

RAUTENDELEIN (*half to herself*). Thy speech is strange. I know not what to
     make of 't.
     (*She suddenly resolves to go.*)
Lie thou, and sleep.

HEINRICH (*dreaming*). Kiss me, sweet fantasy!
     (RAUTENDELEIN *stops, and gazes at* HEINRICH. *The darkness deepens.* RAU-
TENDELEIN *suddenly grows frightened and calls.*)

RAUTENDELEIN. O grandmother!

WITTIKIN (*from within the hut*). Well, girl?

RAUTENDELEIN. Come here! Come here!

WITTIKIN (*as above*). Nay, come thou here, and help me make the fire!

RAUTENDELEIN. O Granny!

WITTIKIN. Hark'ee, wench. Dost hear me? Come.
'Tis time we fed the goat. And then to milk it!

RAUTENDELEIN. Grandmother! Help him! Help him! He is dying!

(*Enter from hut,* WITTIKIN. *She stands on the threshold, holding a milk pail in her left hand, and calls to her cat.*)

WITTIKIN. Here! Puss, Puss, Puss!

(*She looks carelessly at* HEINRICH.)

He hasn't budged, I see.
Well—mortals all must die. No help for it.
What matter? Let him be. He's better so.
Come—pussy! pussy! . . . Here is milk for thee—
Why, where is pussy?

(*Calling.*)

Hurry, hurry, wood-folk, when I call!
Here, I've milk a-plenty for ye all!
Hurry, hurry, hurry, trold and sprite!

(*Enter ten droll little* TROLDS, *male and female. They bustle about the milk pail.*)

Here is bread—for every one a bite!
Here's enough to drink, and here's to eat:
Food that dukes and earls 'ud count a treat.

(*To one of the* TROLDS.)

Thou, go!
Thou art full, I trow.

(*To the other* TROLDS.)

For thee a sop—
And for thee a drop—
Now enough ye've guzzled,
And off ye hop!

(*They riot and shout.*)

I'll have ye muzzled,
Unless ye stop!
Nay, this won't do—
Ye riotous crew!
Enough for to-day!
Away! Away!

(*The* TROLDS *vanish into the wood. Moonlight. The* WOOD-SPRITE *appears, seated on the rocks beyond the hut. Putting his horny hands to his mouth, he imitates the echo of a cry for help.*)

THE WOOD-SPRITE. Help! Help!

WITTIKIN. Why, what's amiss?

DISTANT VOICES (*from the wood*). Heinrich! Heinrich!

THE WOOD-SPRITE (*as above*). Help! Help!

WITTIKIN (*threateningly to the* WOOD-SPRITE). Fool, thy knavish antics cease!
Leave our mountain-folk in peace!
Ay, ay. It pleases thee to vent thy spite

On the poor glass-workers! . . . Thou lov'st to bite
Stray dogs—to lead lost travelers into fogs,
And see them floundering in the moorland bogs.
THE WOOD-SPRITE. Granny, never heed my jests.
Soon thou shalt have noble guests!
Who rides on the goose's down?
The barber, light as lather.
Who rides on the goose's crown?
The parson, reverend father—
The teacher, with his cue—
Three screech-owls—all for you!
THE VOICES (*nearer*). Heinrich!
THE WOOD-SPRITE (*as before*).   Help!
WITTIKIN.   Now may the lightning strike thee!
Wouldst hang a schoolmaster about my neck,
And eke a parson?
    (*Shaking her fist at the* WOOD-SPRITE.)
                    Thou shalt smart for this.
I'll send thee swarming gnats, and stinging flies,
To plague thee till thou shalt be so distraught
Thou'lt long to hide thyself.
THE WOOD-SPRITE (*with malignant glee*). They're coming, Granny!
    (*He disappears.*)
WITTIKIN. Well, and what then? They're no concern o' mine.
    (*To* RAUTENDELEIN, *who is gazing fixedly at* HEINRICH.)
Into the hut! Blow out the light! To bed!
Quick, wench!
RAUTENDELEIN (*sullen and defiant*). I won't!
WITTIKIN.   What? Disobey me?
RAUTENDELEIN.   Yes!
WITTIKIN. And why?
RAUTENDELEIN.   They'll take him from me.
WITTIKIN.   Well? What of 't?
RAUTENDELEIN. They must not take him, Granny!
WITTIKIN.   Girl, ha' done!
And let them deal wi' him as they may list.
Dust will to dust, and some day he must die.
So let him die. He'll be the better for 't.
See how life irks him, how it rends his heart,
Wi' pain and agony.
HEINRICH (*Dreaming*). The Sun sets fast!
WITTIKIN. He never saw the Sun, girl! Let him be.
Come. Follow me. Be warned, or thou wilt rue!
    (*Exit into hut. Cries of "Heinrich! Heinrich!"* RAUTENDELEIN *listens for a moment. Then she suddenly breaks a flowery twig from a bough, and draws a circle with it round* HEINRICH *as she speaks the following lines.*)
    RAUTENDELEIN. With the first fresh buds of Spring,
        Lo, I draw the magic ring!
        Safe from every harm and ill,

Thus thou art. It is my will!
Thou art thine, and thine, and mine.
None may cross the mystic line!
Be thou youth, or man, or maid,
Here thou surely must be stayed!
(*She hides behind the trees in shadow.*)
(*Enter one after the other, from the wood, the* VICAR, *the* BARBER, *and the*
SCHOOLMASTER.)
THE VICAR. I see a light.
THE SCHOOLMASTER.   And I!
THE VICAR.   Where are we now?
THE BARBER. God only knows. Again I hear that cry
Of "Help! Help! Help!"
THE VICAR.   It is the Master's voice!
THE SCHOOLMASTER. I heard no cry.
THE BARBER.   It came from yonder height.
THE SCHOOLMASTER. If one fell up to Heaven, that might be,
But, as a general rule, one tumbles—down:
From cliff to vale, and not from vale to cliff.
The Master lies—I'd stake my soul upon 't—
Full fifty fathoms deeper: not up here.
THE BARBER. Ods bodikins! Did you not hear him then?
If that was not the voice of Master Heinrich,
May I be set to shave old Rübezahl!
As I'm a living barber, I will swear
I heard a cry.
THE SCHOOLMASTER. Where from?
THE VICAR.   What place is this?
Ere we continue, tell me that, my friends.
My face is bleeding; I can hardly drag
One foot after another. How they do ache!
I'll go no further.
A VOICE.   Help!
THE VICAR.   Again that voice!
THE BARBER. And this time it was close to where we stand!
THE VICAR (*sitting wearily*). I'm racked with pain. Indeed, my worthy friends,
I can no more. So leave me, in God's name.
In truth, though you should beat me black and blue,
You could not make me budge another step.
I am worn out. Alack, that this glad day
Should end so sadly! Who had ever thought
Such things could happen! And the mighty bell—
The noblest of the Master's master-works——!
Thy ways, O Lord, indeed pass finding out
And are most wonderful!
THE BARBER.   Ay, Father, ay.
And do you wish to know what place this be?
Well, I will tell you. If you'll be advised,
You'll get from hence—and that without delay.

'Twere better far we spent the livelong night
Bare-backed, and in a hornet's nest, than here.
For, by the Lord, we're on the Silver Hill!
Within a hundred steps should stand the house
Of that accursèd witch. So—let's away!

THE VICAR. I cannot budge.

THE SCHOOLMASTER.   Nay, come, I pray you, come.
Worse things than witches are encountered here.
If they were all, I should not turn a hair.
Ah, there's no wilder spot for leagues around—
A paradise of smugglers, thieves, and rogues—
A trysting-place for cut-throat murderers—
So infamous that Peter,—he who longed
To know what fear and trembling meant—might learn
Both easily—if he but came this way.

THE BARBER. Yes. One and one make two—we all know that.
But that is not the only thing worth knowing.
I hope, my master, you may never learn
What witchcraft means! . . The hellish sluts who lurk,
Like toads in a hole, hatching their evil plots,
May send you illnesses, and plague your ox,
Make blood flow from the udders of your cows
Instead of milk, and rot your sheep with worms—
Or curse your children with unwholesome wens,
And horrible ulcers. All this they can do.

THE SCHOOLMASTER. You're wandering, Sirs. The night has turned your heads.
While you go babbling here of witches' games,
Your ears grow dull. Heard you not moans? By Heaven!
I see the very man we seek!

THE VICAR.   See whom?

THE SCHOOLMASTER. Why, Master Heinrich.

THE BARBER.   Oh, he's lost his wits!

THE VICAR. 'Twas witchcraft.

THE SCHOOLMASTER.   Nay, then two and two's not four,
But five. And that's impossible. Prate not
Of witches. For, as I do hope for Heaven,
There lies the master bell-founder himself!
Look! Now the clouds have ceased to hide the moon.
Look, gentlemen! Now! Now! Well—was I right?

THE VICAR. Indeed you were, my master.

THE BARBER.   'Tis the bell-founder!

(*All three hurry towards* HEINRICH, *but recoil on reaching the edge of the magic ring.*)

THE VICAR. Oh!

THE BARBER.   Oh!

THE SCHOOLMASTER.   Oh! Oh!

RAUTENDELEIN (*Becoming visible for a moment among the trees.*)
       Ha! Ha! Ha! Ha! Ha! Ha!

(*She vanishes amid peals of mocking laughter. A pause.*)

THE SCHOOLMASTER (*bewildered*). What was it?

THE BARBER.   Ay. What was 't?

THE VICAR.   I heard a laugh!

THE SCHOOLMASTER. The bright light dazzled me. I do believe
It's made a hole in my head as big as my fist.

THE VICAR. You heard the laughter?

THE BARBER.   Ay, and something cracked.

THE VICAR. The laughter seemed to come from every pine
That rustles round us in the growing gloom.
There! Yonder! Where the horn-owl hoots and flies!

THE BARBER. Didn't I tell you of these devilish folk?
O Lord, O Lord! I warned you of their spells.
D'ye think we're safe here? As for me, I quake—
My flesh creeps. Curses on the hag, say I!

THE VICAR (*Raising the crucifix which hangs round his neck, and moving
    steadfastly towards the hut*). You may be right. Yet, though the Devil
    himself
Dwelt here, I'd still say: Courage! On!
Against him we will pit God's Holy Word!
Ah! never yet was Satan's craft more clear
Than when he hurled the Master and the bell
To death—God's servant and his instrument—
The bell that, from the edge of the abyss
Had sung the hymn of everlasting Love,
And Peace, and Mercy, through the firmament!
Here stand we as true soldiers of the Lord!
I'll knock!

THE BARBER. D—d—don't risk it!

THE VICAR.   Yes! I say, I'll knock!
  (*He knocks at the door of the hut.*)

WITTIKIN (*from within the hut*). Who's there?

THE VICAR.   A Christian!

WITTIKIN.   Christian or no Christian,
What d'you want?

THE VICAR.   Open!

WITTIKIN. (*Appearing in the doorway carrying a lighted lantern.*)
                 Well? What's your will?

THE VICAR. In God's name, woman, whom thou dost not know——

WITTIKIN. Oho! A pious opening, I declare!

THE SCHOOLMASTER. Thou carrion-crow, how durst thou wag thy tongue?
The measure's full—thy time is meted out.
Thy evil life and thy accursèd deeds
Have made thee hated through the countryside.
So—an thou do not now as thou art bid—
Ere dawn the red cock* from thy roof shall crow—
Thy den of thieves shall flame and smoke to Heaven!

THE BARBER (*Crossing himself repeatedly*). Thou wicked cat! I'm not afraid
    of thee!

*In Germany "der rothe Hahn" is a symbol of incendiarism.

Ay—scowl, and glare, and glower, as thou wilt!
Though thy red eyes should like upon my corpse,
They'll find the Cross before them. Do as thou'rt bid!
THE VICAR. I charge thee, woman, in God's holy name,
Have done with all thy devilish juggleries,
And help this man! Here lies a child of God,
A Master, gifted with a wondrous art
That him doth honor, while it puts to shame
The damnèd companies of air and Hell.
WITTIKIN (*Who has been prowling round* HEINRICH *with her lantern.*)
And, what's all that to do wi' me? Enough!
You're welcome to the creature. Take him hence.
What harm did I to him? For aught I care,
He may live on, till he has spent his breath.
I'll wager that won't be so very long!
Ye name him "Master," and ye love the sound
O' the big iron bells the creature makes.
Ye all are hard o' hearin', or ye'd know
There's no good in his bells. He knows it, too.
Ah, I could tell ye, an' I would, what's wrong.
The best and worst o' them ring false. They're cracked.
There! Take the litter. Bear the man away—
The "Master," as ye call him! Master Milksop!
    (*To* HEINRICH.)
Get up! Go home and help the parson preach!
Go—help the schoolmaster to birch his boys—
Go—mix the lather in the barber's shop!
    (*The* BARBER *and the* SCHOOLMASTER *lift* HEINRICH *on to the litter.*)
THE VICAR. Thou wicked, scolding hag! Restrain thy tongue!
Thy way shall lead thee straight to Hell. Begone!
WITTIKEN. O, spare your sermons. I ha' heard ye preach.
I know, I know. 'Tis sinful to ha' senses.
The earth's a coffin, and the Heavens above
Are but a coffin-lid. The stars are holes;
The sun's a bigger hole in the blue sky.
The world 'ud come to grief wi'out the priests,
And God himself ye'd make a bug-a-boo!
The Lord should take a rod to ye—poor fools!
Ay, fools are ye—all, all! and nothing more!
    (*She bangs open her door and goes into hut.*)
THE VICAR. Thou beldame!

THE BARBER.   For Heaven's sake—don't vex her more!
If you should goad her further, we are lost.
    (*Exeunt the* VICAR, *the* SCHOOLMASTER, *and the* BARBER *into the wood, bearing away* HEINRICH *on the litter. The moon shines out, and lights up the peaceful landscape.* FIRST, SECOND, *and* THIRD ELVES *steal out of the wood one after the other and join hands in a dance.*)
FIRST ELF (*whispering*). Sister!

SECOND ELF (*as above*).   Sister!

FIRST ELF (*as above*).
                                White and chill
Shines the moon across the hill.
Over bank, and over brae,
Queen she is, and Queen shall stay.

SECOND ELF. Whence com'st thou?

FIRST ELF.
                                From where the light
In the waterfall gleams bright,
Where the glowing flood doth leap,
Roaring, down into the deep.
Then, from out the mirk and mist,
Where the foaming torrent hissed,
Past the dripping rocks and spray,
Up I swiftly made my way.

THIRD ELF (*joining them*). Sisters, is it here ye dance?

FIRST ELF. Wouldst thou join us? Quick—advance!

SECOND ELF. And whence com'st thou?

THIRD ELF.
                                Hark and hist!
Dance, and dance, as ye may list!
'Mid the rocky peaks forlorn
Lies the lake where I was born.
Starry gems are mirrored clear
On the face of that dark mere.
Ere the fickle moon could wane,
Up I swept my silver train.
Where the mountain breezes sigh,
Over clove and crag came I!

FOURTH ELF (*entering*). Sisters!

FIRST ELF.
                                Sister! Join the round!

ALL (*together*). Ring-a-ring-a-ring-around!

FOURTH ELF. From Dame Holle's flowery brae,
Secretly I stole away.

FIRST ELF. Wind and wander, in and out!

ALL (*together*). Ring-a-ring-a-round-about!

(*Lightning and distant thunder.*)

(*Enter suddenly, from the hut,* RAUTENDELEIN. *Clasping her hands behind her head, she watches the dance from the doorway. The moonlight falls full on her.*)

RAUTENDELEIN. Ho, my fairies!

FIRST ELF. Hark! A cry!

SECOND ELF. Owch! My dress is all awry!

RAUTENDELEIN. Ho, ye fairies!

THIRD ELF.
                                O, my gown!
Flit and flutter, up and down.

RAUTENDELEIN (*joining in the dance*). Let me join the merry round.
Ring-a-ring-a-ring-around!
Silver nixey, sweetest maid,
See how richly I'm arrayed.
All of silver, white and rare,

Granny wove my dress so fair.
Thou, my fairy brown, I vow,
Browner far am I than thou.
And, my golden sister fair,
I can match thee with my hair,
Now I toss it high—behold,
Thou hast surely no such gold.
Now it tumbles o'er my face:
Who can rival me in grace?
ALL (*together*). Wind and wander, in and out,
Ring-a-ring-a-round-about!
RAUTENDELEIN. Into the gulf there fell a bell.
Where is it lying? Will ye tell?
ALL (*together*). Wind and wander, in and out,
Ring-a-ring-a-round-about!
Daisy and forget-me-not,
Fairy footsteps injure not.

(*Enter the* WOOD-SPRITE, *skipping. Thunder—this time louder. During the following speech, a storm rages—thunder and hail.*)

THE WOOD-SPRITE. Daisy and forget-me-not
Crush I in the earth to rot.
If the moorland's all a-drip
'Tis because I leap, and skip!
Now the bull doth seek his mate,
Bellows at the stable gate.
And the heifer, sleeping by,
Lifts her head and lows reply.
On the stallion's warm brown hide
Every fly doth seek his bride,
While the midges dance above,
Fill the air with life and love.
See! The ostler woos the maid!
Buss her, fool! Dost fear the jade?
With the rotting straw for bed,
Soft and tender, lo they wed!
Hul'lo! Hul'lo! Heigh-o-hey!
Whisp'ring's over for to-day.
Done the dancing, hushed and chill,
Lusty life is master still!
Be it early, be it late,
Mews the tom-cat, mews its mate.
Nightingale, and thrush, and stork,
Hart, and hare, and hen, and hawk,
Snipe, and quail, and swan, and duck,
Crane, and pheasant, doe and buck,
Beetle, moth, and mole, and louse,
Toad, and frog, and bat, and mouse,
Bee, and gnat, and moth, and fly—
All must love, and all must die!

(*The* WOOD-SPRITE *snatches up one of the* ELVES *and carries her off into the wood. The three other* ELVES *vanish in different directions.* RAUTENDELEIN *remains standing alone and sad, in the middle of the glade. The storm gradually dies away.*)

(THE NICKELMANN *rises from the well, as before.*)

THE NICKELMANN. Brekekekex!—Brekekekex! Hey! Ho!
Why dost thou stand there?

RAUTENDELEIN.   Thou dear water-sprite—
Alas, I am so sad. So sad am I!

THE NICKELMANN (*mockingly*). Brekekekex! And which eye hurts thee, dear?

RAUTENDELEIN (*gaily*). The left eye. But, perhaps, thou think'st I jest?

THE NICKELMANN. Ay, surely, surely.

RAUTENDELEIN (*pointing to a tear in her eye.*) Look—what can it be?

THE NICKELMANN. What dost thou mean?

RAUTENDELEIN.   Why—see what's in my eye!

THE NICKELMANN. What's in thine eye? Come—let me see it close.

RAUTENDELEIN. A warm, wet, drop has fallen on my lid.

THE NICKELMANN. The deuce it has! Come nearer—let me see.

RAUTENDELEIN (*holding out the tear to him*). A tiny, pure, warm, glitt'ring,
    drop of dew.
There, only see!

THE NICKELMANN. By Heaven! 'Tis beautiful.
How would it please thee an I took the thing
And set it in a fine, pink shell for thee?

RAUTENDELEIN. Why, as thou wilt. I'll lay it on the edge
Of the well. What can it be?

THE NICKELMANN.   A wondrous gem!
Within that little globe lies all the pain,
And all the joy, the world can ever know.
'Tis called—a tear!

RAUTENDELEIN.   A tear! . . . I must have wept.
So now at last I've learned what these tears be . . .
O, tell me something!

THE NICKELMANN.   Come to me, dear child!

RAUTENDELEIN. Not I, forsooth. What good were that to me?
The edge of thine old well is wet and rough;
'Tis overrun with spiders, worms and—worse.
They irk me—all of them. And so dost thou.

THE NICKELMANN. Brekekekex! I grieve to hear it, dear.

RAUTENDELEIN. Another of those drops! How strange!

THE NICKELMANN.   More rain!
Behold! Now Father Thor is all ablaze.
The lightnings from his beard fall soft, and blink
Like babies' eyes, setting the misty train
Of rolling clouds aglow with purple flame.
And yonder, near the grey, mark how a flight
Of ravens rushes madly through the night
To keep him company. With every flash
Their wings gleam wetter in the whirling rain.

Hark, child, how thirstily our Mother Earth
Drinks every drop! And how the trees and grass,
The flies and worms, grow glad in the quick light!
  (*Lightning.*)
Quorax! Now in the valley! Master! Hail!
Old Thor is kindling a rare Easter fire.
His hammer flares—twelve thousand miles it sweeps!
The church-tower totters—now the belfry cracks!
The smoke pours out! . . .

RAUTENDELEIN.   Enough! Enough! No more!
Come, tell me something else. I'm tired of Thor.

THE NICKELMANN. Thou saucy sparrow, thou——. Brekekekex!
What ails the creature? When it's stroked—it pecks.
A pretty way to thank one! When you're done,
You're no bit further than ere you'd begun!
Am I not right? . . . Still pouting, eh? . . . Well, well.
What wouldst thou know?

RAUTENDELEIN.   O, nothing. Do but go!

THE NICKELMANN. Naught thou wouldst know?

RAUTENDELEIN.   Naught!

THE NICKELMANN (*imploringly*).   Then, speak thou, I pray.

RAUTENDELEIN. I long to leave you all and go away!
  (*Her eyes fill with tears and she stares into the distance.*)

THE NICKELMANN (*with anguish*). What have I done to thee? Where wouldst
  thou go?
Is it the world of men that thou wouldst know?
I warn thee, maiden. Man's a curious thing,
Who naught but woe to such as thou could bring.
Although, perchance, with ours his fate's entwined,
He is, yet is not quite, of our own kind.
His world is ours—and yet, I say, beware!
Half here, he lives—half, no one could tell where!
Half he's our brother; yet, this many a day,
A foe he's been, and lost to us for aye.
Woe, woe to all who our free mountains flee
To join these mortals, hoping bliss to see!
Man's feet are in the Earth. In toil and pain
He lives his fleeting life. And yet—he's vain.
He's like a plant that in a cellar shoots,
And needs must pluck and pluck at its own roots.
So, languishing for light, he rots away,
Nor ever knows the joy of one sun-ray.
The breath of Spring that kisses the green leaf,
To sickly boughs brings death, and not relief.
Pry thou no further, but let Man alone:
Lest thou should hang about thy neck—a stone.
Man will but sadden thee with his grey skies,
And turn thy happy laugh to tears and sighs.
Thou shalt be chained unto an ancient Book.

Accurst—no more upon the Sun thou'lt look!

RAUTENDELEIN. Grandmother says thou art a learned seer.
Yet, an thou wilt but in thy waters peer,
Thou'lt see that never yet a rill did flow
But longed into the world of men to go.

THE NICKELMANN (*angrily*). Quorax! Brekekekex! Be not so bold.
Hear now the words of one ten centuries old!
Let slavish streams pursue their fated way,
Work, wash, for men, and grind their corn each day,
Water their cabbages and garden stuff,
And swallow—Heav'n knows what! And now . . . enough!
  (*Warmly and earnestly.*)
But, O, my dear Princess Rautendelein,
For thee a King's chamber were none too fine.
I know a rare crown, all of crystal so green,
In a great golden hall, thou shalt wear it, my queen.
The floor and the roof are of clear blue stone,
Red coral the coffers and the chests I own. . .

RAUTENDELEIN. And what though thy coffers of coral be wrought?
Life lived with the fishes were good for naught.
And though thy King's crown of pure sapphire should be,
Thy daughters should prink it alone with thee.
My own golden tresses are far more dear;
Their touch a caress is; my crown is—here!
  (*She turns to go.*)

THE NICKELMANN. Where art thou going?

RAUTENDELEIN (*airily and indifferently*).   What is that to thee?

THE NICKELMANN (*sorrowfully*). Much. Much. Brekekekex!

RAUTENDELEIN.   Oh, whither I will
Go I.

THE NICKELMANN. And whither wouldst go?

RAUTENDELEIN.   Away and away!

THE NICKELMANN. Away and away?

RAUTENDELEIN (*flinging her arms aloft*). To the world—of men!
  (*She vanishes in the wood.*)

THE NICKELMANN (*terrified*). Quorax!
  (*Whimpering.*)
                            Quorax!
  (*Softly.*)
                                        Quorax!
  (*Shaking his head sadly.*)
                                        Brekekekex!

CURTAIN

ACT TWO

An old-fashioned room in the house of HEINRICH *the bell-founder. A deep recess occupies half the back wall. In the recess is a large open fireplace, with a chimney above it. A copper kettle is suspended above the unlighted fire. The other half of the back wall, set at an angle, is lighted by a large old-fashioned window, with bottle-glass panes. Below this window, a bed. Doors R. and L. That on the R. leads to the workshop, while that on the L. leads to the courtyard. L. C. a table and chairs placed. On the table: a full jug of milk, mugs, and a loaf of bread. Near the table, a tub. The room is decorated with works by Adam Kraft, Peter Fischer, etc., conspicuous among them a painted wooden image of Christ on the Cross.*

DISCOVERED: *Seated at the farther side of the table, and, in their Sunday best, the two* CHILDREN (*boys*) *of* HEINRICH (*aged respectively five and nine*), *with their mugs of milk before them.* MAGDA, *their mother, also in her Sunday best, enters L., with a bunch of cowslips in her hand.*

Early morning. The light grows brighter as the action progresses.

MAGDA. See, children, what I've brought you from the fields!
Beyond the garden—a whole patch grew wild.
Now we can make ourselves look fine and gay,
In honor of your father's birthday feast.
FIRST CHILD. O, give me some!
SECOND CHILD.   And me!
MAGDA.   There! Five for each!
And every single one they say's a key*
That opens Heaven. Now drink your milk, my dears,
And eat your bread. 'Tis almost time to start.
The road to church, you know, is long and steep.
NEIGHBOR (*a woman*).
   (*Looking in at the window.*)
What! Up already, neighbor?
MAGDA (*at the window.*)   Yes, indeed.
I hardly closed my eyes the livelong night.
But, 'twas not care that kept me wide-awake.
So now I'm just as fresh as if I'd slept
Sound as a dormouse. Why, how bright it is!
NEIGHBOR. Ay. Ay. You're right.
MAGDA.   You'll come with us, I hope?
Now don't say no. You'll find it easy walking
On the road . . . These tiny feet
Shall lead the way, and gently mark our steps.
If you must have the truth, I long for wings:
I'm wild to-day with joy and eagerness!
NEIGHBOR. And has your good-man not been home all night?
MAGDA. What are you dreaming of? I'll be content

*In German the cowslip is called "Himmelschlüssel," *i. e.,* "the key of Heaven."

If only the big bell is safely hung
In time to ring the people in to mass!
You see—the time was short. They'd none to waste.
And as for sleeping—if the Master snatched
So much as one short wink in the wood-grass—
Why, Heaven be praised! But, oh, what does it matter?
The work was hard: but great is the reward.
You cannot think how pure, and clear, and true,
The new bell sounds. Just wait until you hear
Its voice ring out to-day from the church tower.
'Tis like a prayer, a hymn, a song of praise—
Filling the heart with comfort and with gladness.
NEIGHBOR. No doubt, ma'am. Yet one thing amazes me.
From my front door, as doubtless you're aware,
The church upon the hill is plainly seen.
Now—I had heard that when the bell was hung
A white flag would be hoisted from the tower.
I've seen no sign of that white flag. Have you?
MAGDA. O, look again. It must be there by now.
NEIGHBOR. No, no. It's not.
MAGDA.   Well, even were you right,
It would not frighten me. Did you but know
The fret and toil and pain, by night and day,
It costs the Master to complete his work,
You would not wonder if the final stroke
Should be delayed a bit. I understand.
By this time, I'll be bound, the flag is there.
Why, yes, I'm sure it is, could we but see 't.
NEIGHBOR. I can't believe it. In the village streets
They do say something dreadful has occurred.
Dark omens, boding evil, fill the air.
But now, a farmer saw a naked witch,
Perched on a boar's back, riding through his corn.
Lifting a stone, he cast it at the hag—
Straightway his hand dropped—palsied to the knuckles!
'Tis said that all the mischievous mountain sprites
Are leagued and up in arms against the bell.
How strange you have not heard all this before!
Well—now the Bailiff's gone into the hills,
With half the village at his heels, to see . . .
MAGDA. The Bailiff? Merciful God! What can be wrong?
NEIGHBOR. Why, nothing's certain. All may yet be well.
There—don't take on so, neighbor. Come—be calm!
It's not so bad as that. Now don't 'ee fret.
It seems the wagon and the bell broke down . . .
That's all we've heard.
MAGDA.   Pray Heav'n that be the worst!
What matters one bell more or less! . . . If he,
The Master, be but safe—these flowers may stay.

Yet—till we know what's happened . . . Here, prithee,
Take the two children . . .

(*She lifts the two* CHILDREN *through the window.*)
Will you?

NEIGHBOR. Why, to be sure.

MAGDA. Thanks. Take them home with you. And, as for me,
Ah, I must go, as fast as go I can.
To see what may be done—to help. For I
Must be with my dear Master—or, I die!

(*Exit hurriedly.*)

(*The* NEIGHBOR *retires with the* CHILDREN. *Confused noise of voices without. Then a piercing cry from* MAGDA.)

(*Enter quickly the* VICAR, *sighing, and wiping the tears from his eyes. He looks round the room hastily, and turns down the coverlet of the bed. Then, hurrying to the door, he meets the* SCHOOLMASTER *and the* BARBER, *carrying* HEINRICH *in on the litter seen in Act One.* HEINRICH *reclines on a rude bed of green branches.* MAGDA, *half beside herself with anguish, follows, supported by a* MAN *and a* WOMAN. *Crowd of* VILLAGERS *presses in behind* MAGDA. HEINRICH *is laid on his own bed.*)

THE VICAR (*to* MAGDA). Bear up, my mistress! Put your trust in God!
We laid him on our litter as one dead;
Yet, on the way, he came to life again,
And, as the doctor told us, only now,
Hope's not yet lost.

MAGDA (*moaning*). Dear God, who speaks of hope?
A moment since, I was so happy! . . . Now—
What's come to me? What's happened? Won't you speak?
Where are the children?

THE VICAR. Put your trust in God.
Do but have patience, mistress. Patience and faith!
Often—remember—in our direst need
God's help is nearest. And, forget not this:
Should He, of His all-wisdom, have resolved,
In His own time, to call the Master hence,
Still there shall be this comfort for your soul—
Your husband goes from Earth to endless bliss.

MAGDA. Why do you speak of comfort, reverend Sir?
Do I need comfort? Nay—he will get well.
He must get well.

THE VICAR. So all of us do hope.
But . . . should he not . . . God's holy will be done.
Come now what may, the Master's fight is won.
To serve the Lord, he fashioned his great bell.
To serve the Lord, he scaled the mountain-heights—
Where the malignant powers of Darkness dwell,
And the Abyss defies the God of Hosts.
Serving the Lord, at last he was laid low—
Braving the hellish spirits in his path.
They feared the gospel that his bell had rung:

So leagued themselves against him, one and all,
In devilish brotherhood. God punish them!
THE BARBER. A wonder-working woman lives hard by,
Who heals, as the Disciples healed of old,
By prayer and faith.
THE VICAR.   Let some one search for her
And when she's found, return with her at once.
MAGDA. What's come to him? Why do you stand and gape?
Off with you all! You shall not stare at him
With your unfeeling eyes. D'you hear? Begone!
Cover him—so—with linen, lest your looks
Should shame the Master. Now—away with you!
Get to the juggler's, if you needs must gape.
Ah, God! What's happened? . . . Are ye all struck dumb?
THE SCHOOLMASTER. Truly, 'tis hard to tell just what took place.
Whether he tried to stop the bell—or what . . .
This much is certain: if you could but see
How deep he fell, you would go down on your knees
And thank the Lord. For, if your husband lives,
'Tis nothing short of the miraculous!
HEINRICH (*feebly*). Give me a little water!
MAGDA (*driving out the* VILLAGERS *quickly*). Out you go!
THE VICAR. Go, my good people. He has need of rest.
   (VILLAGERS *withdraw.*)
If I can serve you, Mistress, why, you know
Where you may find me.
THE BARBER.   Yes, and me.
THE SCHOOLMASTER.   And m
No. On reflection, I'll stay here.
MAGDA   You'll go!
HEINRICH. Give me some water!
   (*The* VICAR, SCHOOLMASTER, *and* BARBER *withdraw slowly, talking low, shaking their heads, and shrugging their shoulders.*)
MAGDA (*hastening to* HEINRICH *with water*). Heinrich, are you awake?
HEINRICH. I'm parched. Give me some water. Can't you hear?
MAGDA (*unable to control herself*). Nay, patience.
HEINRICH.   Magda, all too soon I'll learn
What patience means. Bear with me yet a while.
It will not be for long.
   (*He drinks.*)
                    Thanks, Magda. Thanks.
MAGDA. Don't speak to me so strangely, Heinrich. Don't!
I . . . I'm afraid.
HEINRICH (*fevered and angry*). Thou must not be afraid.
When I am gone, thou'lt have to live alone.
MAGDA. I cannot . . . no, I will not . . . live without thee!
HEINRICH. Thy pain is childish. Torture me no more!
It is unworthy,—for thou art a mother.
Bethink thee what that word means, and be brave!

MAGDA. Ah, do not be so stern and harsh with me!

HEINRICH (*painfully*). The plain truth harsh and stern? Again I say—
Thy place is by the bedside of thy boys.
There lies thy joy, thy peace, thy work, thy life.
All—all is tucked up in their fair, white sheets.
Could it be otherwise, 'twere infamous!

MAGDA (*falling on his neck*). So help me Heav'n, I love thee far, far, more
Than our dear children, and myself, and all!

HEINRICH. Then woe unto ye all, too soon bereaved!
And thrice-unhappy I, untimely doomed
To snatch the milk and bread from your poor lips!
Yet, on my tongue, I feel them turn to poison.
That, too, is just! . . . Farewell. Thee I commend
To one from whom none living may escape.
Many a man has found Death's deepest shadow
Prove but a welcome light. God grant it be!
  (*Tenderly.*)
Give me thy hand. I've done thee many a wrong
By word and deed. Often I've grieved thy heart,
Far, far, too often. But thou wilt forgive me!
I would have spared thee, had I but been free.
I know not what compelled me; yet I know
I could not choose but stab thee—and myself.
Forgive me, Magda!

MAGDA.   I forgive thee? What?
If thou dost love me, Heinrich, be less sad:
Or thou wilt bring the tears back. Rather—scold.
Thou knowest well how dear——

HEINRICH (*painfully*).   I do not know!

MAGDA. Nay, who, but thou, did wake my woman's soul?
Till thou didst come, I was a poor, dull, clod,
Pining away beneath a cheerless sky.
Thou—thou—didst rescue me and make me live,
Fill me with joy, and set my heart in the sun.
And never did I feel thy love more sure
Then when, with thy strong hand, thou'dst draw my face
Out of the dark, and turn it towards the light.
And thou wouldst have me pardon thee! For what?
Do I not owe thee all I love in life?

HEINRICH. Strangely entangled seems the web of souls.

MAGDA (*stroking his hair tenderly*). If I have ever been a help to thee—
If I have sometimes cheered thy working hours—
If favor in thine eyes I ever found . . .
Bethink thee, Heinrich: I, who would have given
Thee everything—my life—the world itself—
I had but that to pay thee for thy love!

HEINRICH (*uneasily*). I'm dying. That is best. God means it well.
Should I live on . . . Come nearer, wife, and hear me.
'Tis better for us both that I should die.

Thou think'st, because we blossomed out together,
I was the sun that caused thy heart to bloom.
But that the eternal Wonder-Worker wrought,
Who, on the wings of His chill winter-storms,
Rides through a million million woodland flowers,
Slaying them, as He passes, in their Spring!
'Tis better for us both that I should die.
See: I was cracked and ageing—all misshaped.
If the great Bell-Founder who moulded me
Tosses aside His work, I shall not mourn.
When He did hurl me down to the abyss,
After my own poor, faulty, handiwork,
I did not murmur: for my work was bad!
Good-wife—the bell that sank into the mere
Was not made for the heights—it was not fit
To wake the answering echoes of the peaks!
MAGDA. I cannot read the meaning of thy words.
A work—so highly-prized, so free from flaw,
So clear and true that, when it first rang out
Between the mighty trees from which it hung,
All marveled and exclaimed, as with one voice,
"The Master's bell sings as the Angels sing!"
HEINRICH (*fevered*). 'Twas for the valley, not the mountain-top!
MAGDA. That is not true! Hadst thou but heard, as I,
The Vicar tell the Clerk, in tones that shook,
"How gloriously 'twill sound upon the heights!" . . .
HEINRICH. 'Twas for the valley—not the mountain-top!
I only know 't. The Vicar does not know.
So I must die—I wish to die, my child.
For, look now: should I heal—as men would call 't—
Thanks to the art of our good village leech,
I'd be at best a botch, a crippled wretch;
And so the warm and generous draught of life—
Ofttimes I've found it bitter, ofttimes sweet,
But ever it was strong, as I did drink 't—
Would turn to a stale, flat, unsavory brew,
Thin and grown cold and sour. I'll none of it!
Let him who fancies it enjoy the draught.
Me it would only sicken and repel.
Hush! Hear me out. Though thou shouldst haply find
A doctor of such skill that he could cure me,
Giving me back my joy—nerving my hand.
Till it could turn to the old, daily task—
Even then, Magda, I were still undone.
MAGDA. For God's sake, husband, tell me what to think!
What has come over thee—a man so strong,
So blessed, so weighted down with Heaven's best gifts;
Respected, loved, of all—of all admired,
A master of thy craft! . . . A hundred bells

Hast thou set ringing, in a hundred towers.
They sing thy praise, with restless industry;
Pouring the deep, glad, beauty of thy soul
As from a hundred wine-cups, through the land.
At eve, the purple-red—at dawn, God's gold—
Know thee. Of both thou art become a part.
And thou—rich, rich, beyond thy greatest need—
Thou, voicing God—able to give, and give,
Rolling in happiness, where others go
Begging their daily dole of joy or bread—
Thou look'st unthankfully upon thy work!
Then, Heinrich, why must I still bear the life
That thou dost hate so? . . . What is life to me?
What could that be to me which thou dost scorn—
Casting it from thee, like a worthless thing!
HEINRICH. Mistake me not. Now thou thyself hast sounded
Deeper and clearer than my loudest bells.
And many a one I've made! . . . I thank thee, Magda.
Yet thou shalt understand my thought. Thou must.
Listen! . . . The latest of my works had failed.
With anguished heart I followed where they climbed,
Shouting and cursing loudly, as the bell
Was dragged towards the peak. And then—it fell.
It fell a hundred fathoms deep, ay more,
Into the mere. There, in the mere, now lies
The last and noblest work my art could mould!
Not all my life, as I have lived it, Magda,
Had fashioned, or could fashion, aught so good.
Now I have thrown it after my bad work.
While I lie drinking the poor dregs of life,
Deep in the waters of the lake it's drowned.
I mourn not for what's lost. And then—I mourn:
Knowing this only—neither bell, nor life,
Shall evermore come back. Alas! woe's me!
My heart's desire was bound up in the tones—
The buried tones—I never more shall hear.
And now the life to which I clung so tight
Is turned to bitterness, and grief, and rue,
Madness, and gloom, confusion, pain, and gall!

Well, let life go! The service of the valleys
Charms me no longer, and no more their peace
Calms my wild blood. Since on the peak I stood,
All that I am has longed to rise, and rise,
Cleaving the mists, until it touched the skies!
I would work wonders with the power on high:
And, since I may not work them, being so weak;
Since, even could I, with much straining, rise,
I should but fall again—I choose to die!

Youth—a new youth—I'd need, if I should live:
Out of some rare and magic mountain flower
Marvelous juices I should need to press—
Heart-health, and strength, and the mad lust of triumph,
Stealing my hand to work none yet have dreamed of!
MAGDA. O Heinrich, Heinrich, did I but know the spot
Where that thou pantest for, the Spring of Youth,
Lies hid, how gladly would these feet of mine
Wear themselves out to find it for thee! Yea,
Even though the waters which restored thy life
Should bring me death!
HEINRICH (*tormented, collapsing and delirious*). Thou dearest, truest! . . .
    No, I will not drink!
Keep it! . . . The Spring is full of blood! . . . blood! . . . blood!
I will not! . . . No! . . . Leave me . . . and . . . let me . . . die!
    (*He becomes unconscious.*)
    (*Enter the* VICAR.)
THE VICAR. How goes it with the patient, mistress?
MAGDA.   Ill!
Terribly ill! He's sick in every part.
Some strange, mysterious pain's consuming him.
I know not what to fear, and what to hope.
    (*Hurriedly throwing a scarf over her shoulders.*)
Did you not speak of a woman who works miracles?
THE VICAR. I did. Indeed, 'tis that has brought me back.
She lives . . . at most a mile away from here . . .
Her name . . . I can't recall it. But she lives,
If I mistake not, in the pinewood . . . Ay . . .
Her name . . .
MAGDA.   Not Wittikin?
THE VICAR.   How can you ask!
Why, she's a wicked witch, the Devil's dam,
And she must die. By now they're up in arms,
Eager for battle with the pestilent fiend.
With cudgels, torches, stones, they're hurrying fast
To make an end of her. For you must know
She's charged with all the evil that afflicts us.
No. I was thinking of . . . Frau Findeklee . . . .
A shepherd's widow . . . and a worthy soul . . . .
Her husband left her an old recipe
Which, as I am assured by many here,
Has wondrous virtues. Will you go for her?
MAGDA. Yes, yes, most reverend Sir!
THE VICAR.   You'll go at once?
    (*Enter* RAUTENDELEIN, *disguised as a peasant girl, and carrying a basket of berries in her hand.*)
MAGDA (*to* RAUTENDELEIN). What wouldst thou, child? . . . Who art thou? . . .
THE VICAR.   Why—'tis Anna.
Anna—the maiden from the wayside inn.

Nay, 'twould be vain to question her. Alas,
She's dumb. A good girl. Ah, she's brought some berries.
MAGDA. Come here, my child . . . What was't I wished to say . . .
Ah, yes! This man lies sick. When he awakes
Be near to help him. Dost thou understand me?
Frau Findeklee . . . That was the name, you said? . . .
But, no; I cannot go. It is too far.
If you'll stay here a moment, I am sure,
My neighbor will go for me . . . I'll come back.
And don't forget . . . O God, my heart will break!
  (*Exit.*)
THE VICAR (*to* RAUTENDELEIN). Stand here, my child; or, if thou wilt, sit down,
Be good and do the very best thou canst.
Make thyself helpful, while they need thy help.
God will reward thee for the work thou doest.
Thou art greatly changed, dear child, since last I saw thee.
But keep thou honest—be a good, true maid—
For the dear Lord has blessed thee with much beauty.
In truth, my dear, now that I look at thee,
Thou art, yet art not, Anna. As a princess,
Stepped from the pages of some fairy book,
Thou seem'st. So quickly changed! Who would have thought
It possible! Well, well! . . . Thou'lt keep him cool?
He's burning! (*To* HEINRICH) May God bring thee back to health!
  (*Exit.*)
  (RAUTENDELEIN, *who till now has seemed shy and meek, changes suddenly
and bustles about the hearth.*)
    RAUTENDELEIN. Flickering spark in the ash of death,
    Glow with life of living breath!
    Red, red wind, thy loudest blow!
    I, as thou, did lawless grow!
        Simmer, sing, and simmer!
  (*The flame leaps up on the hearth.*)

      .   .   .   .   .

    Kettle swaying left and right—
    Copper-lid, thou'rt none too light!
    Bubble, bubble, broth and brew,
    Turning all things old to new!
        Simmer, sing, and simmer!

      .   .   .   .   .

    Green and tender herbs of Spring,
    In the healing draught I fling.
    Drink it sweet, and drink it hot—
    Life and youth are in the pot!
        Simmer, sing, and simmer!

      .   .   .   .   .

And now to scrape the roots and fetch the water.
The cask is empty . . . But we need more light!

(*She throws the window wide open.*)
A glorious day! But there'll be wind anon.
A mighty cloud, in shape like some huge fish,
Lies on the hills. To-morrow it will burst;
And roystering spirits will ride madly down,
Sweeping athwart the pines, to reach the vale.
Cuckoo! Cuckoo! . . . Here, too, the cuckoo calls,
And the swift swallow darts across the sky . . .
 (HEINRICH *has opened his eyes, and lies staring at* RAUTENDELEIN.)
But now to scrape my roots, and fetch the water. . . .
I've much to do since I turned waiting-maid.
Thou, thou, dear flame, shalt cheer me at my work.
HEINRICH (*amazed*). Tell me . . . who art thou?
RAUTENDELEIN (*quickly and unconcernedly*).   I? Rautendelein.
HEINRICH. Rautendelein? I never heard that name.
Yet somewhere I have seen thee once before.
Where was it?
RAUTENDELEIN.   Why, 'twas on the mountain-side.
HEINRICH. True. True. 'Twas there—what time I fevered lay.
I dreamt I saw thee there . . . Again I dream.
At times we dream strange dreams! See. Here's my house.
There burns the fire upon the well-known hearth.
Here lie I, in my bed, sick unto death.
I push the window back. There flies a swallow.
Yonder the nightingales are all at play.
Sweet scents float in—of jasmine . . . elder-blossom . . .
I see . . . I feel . . . I know . . . the smallest thing—
Even to the pattern of this coverlet . . .
Each thread . . . each tiny knot . . . I could describe—
And yet I'm dreaming.
RAUTENDELEIN.   Thou art dreaming? Why?
HEINRICH (*in anguish*). Because . . . I must be dreaming.
RAUTENDELEIN.   Art thou so sure?
HEINRICH. Yes. No. Yes. No. I'm wandering. Let me dream on!
Thou askest if I am so sure. I know not.
Ah, be it what it will: or dream, or life—
It is. I feel it, see it—thou dost live!
Real or unreal, within me or without,
Child of my brain, or whatsoe'er thou art,
Still I do love thee, for thou art thyself.
So stay with me, sweet spirit. Only stay!
RAUTENDELEIN. So long as thou shalt choose.
HEINRICH.   Then . . . I do dream.
RAUTENDELEIN (*familiarly*). Take care. Dost see me lift this little foot
With the rosy heel? Thou dost? Why, that is well.
Now—here's a hazel nut. I take it—so—
Between my finger and my dainty thumb—
I set my heel on it. Crack! Now, 'tis broken.
Was that a dream?

HEINRICH.   That only God can tell.

RAUTENDELEIN. Now watch me. See. I'll come quite close to thee,
And sit upon thy bed. So. Here I am! . . .
Feasting away as merrily as thou wilt . . .
Hast thou not room enough?

HEINRICH.   I've all I need.
But tell me whence thou'rt sprung and who has sent thee!
What would'st thou of a broken, suffering, man,
A bundle of sorrow, drawing near the end
Of his brief pilgrimage . . . ?

RAUTENDELEIN.   I like thee.
Whence I did spring I know not—nor could tell
Whither I go. But Granny said one day
She found me lying in the moss and weeds.
A hind did give me suck. My home's the wood,
The mountain-side, the crag, the storm-swept moor—
Where the wind moans and rages, shrieks and groans,
Or purrs and mews, like some wild tiger-cat!
There thou wilt find me, whirling through the air;
There I laugh loud and shout for sheer mad joy;
Till faun and nixey, gnome and water-sprite,
Echo my joy and split their sides with laughter.
I'm spiteful when I'm vexed, and scratch and bite:
And who should anger me had best beware.
Yet—'tis no better when I'm left alone:
For good and bad in me's all mood and impulse.
I'm thus, or thus, and change with each new whim.
But thee I am fond of . . . Thee I would not scratch.
And, if thou wilt, I'll stay. Yet were it best
Thou camest with me to my mountain home.
Then thou should'st see how faithfully I'd serve thee.
I'd show thee diamonds, and rubies rare,
Hid at the bottom of unfathomed deeps.
Emeralds, and topazes, and amethysts—
I'd bring thee all—I'd hang upon thy lids!
Froward, unruly, lazy, I may be;
Spiteful, rebellious, wayward, what thou wilt!
Yet thou shouldst only need to blink thine eye,
And ere thou'dst time to speak, I'd nod thee—yes.
And Granny tells me . . .

HEINRICH.   Ah, thou dear, dear child.
Tell me, who is thy Granny?

RAUTENDELEIN.   Dost thou not know?

HEINRICH. No.

RAUTENDELEIN. Not know Granny?

HEINRICH.   No, I am a man,
And blind.

RAUTENDELEIN. Soon thou shalt see! To me is given
The power to open every eye I kiss

To the most hidden mysteries of earth
And air.
HEINRICH. Then . . . kiss me!
RAUTENDELEIN.   Thou'lt keep still?
HEINRICH.   Nay, try me!
RAUTENDELEIN (*kissing his eyes*). Ye eyes, be opened!
HEINRICH.   Ah, thou lovely child,
Sent to enchant me in my dying hour—
Thou fragrant blossom, plucked by God's own hand
In the forgotten dawn of some dead Spring—
Thou free, fair, bud—ah, were I but that man
Who, in the morn of life, fared forth so glad—
How I would press thee to this leaping heart!
Mine eyes were blinded. Now, they're filled with light,
And, as by instinct, I divine thy world.
Ay, more and more, as I do drink thee in,
Thou dear enigma, I am sure I see.
RAUTENDELEIN. Why—look at me, then, till thine eyes are tired.
HEINRICH. How golden gleams thy hair! How dazzling bright! . . .
With thee for company, thou dearest dream,
Old Charon's boat becomes a bark for kings,
That spreads its purple sails to catch the sun
Lighting it eastward on its stately way.
Feel'st thou the Western breeze that creeps behind us,
Flecking with foam from tiny waterfalls
The swelling bosom of the blue South seas,
And showering diamonds on us? Dost thou not feel it?
And we, reclining here on cloth of gold,
In blissful certitude of what must be,
Do scan the distance that divides us twain . . .
Thou knowest well from what! . . . For thou hast seen
The fair green island, where the birch bends down,
Bathing its branches in the azure flood—
Thou hearest the glad song of all Spring's choirs,
Waiting to welcome us . . .
RAUTENDELEIN.   Yes! Yes! I hear it!
HEINRICH (*collapsing*). So be it. I am ready. When I awake,
A voice shall say to me—Come thou with me.
Then fades the light! . . . Here now the air grows chill.
The seer dies, as the blind man had died.
But I have seen thee . . . seen . . . thee . . . !
    RAUTENDELEIN (*with incantations*). Master, sleep is thine!
    When thou wakest, thou art mine.
    Happy dreams shall dull thy pain,
    Help to make thee whole again.
  (*She bustles about by the hearth.*)
    Hidden treasures, now grow bright!
    In the depths ye give no light.

Glowing hounds in vain do bark,
Whine and whimper in the dark!
We, who serve him, glad will be:
For the Master sets us free!
(*Addressing* HEINRICH, *and with gestures.*)
One, two, three. A new man be!
For the future thou art free!

HEINRICH (*awaking*). What's happened to me? . . . From what wondrous sleep
Am I aroused? . . . What is this glorious sun
That, streaming through the window, gilds my hand?
O, breath of morning! Heaven, if 'tis thy will—
If 'tis thy strength that rushes through my veins—
If, as a token of thy power, I feel
This strange, new, beating heart within my breast?
Then, should I rise again—again I'd long
To wander out into the world of life:
And wish, and strive, and hope, and dare, and do . . .
And do . . . and do . . . !

(RAUTENDELEIN *has meanwhile moved to L. and stands, leaning against the wall, gazing fixedly at* HEINRICH. *A dazzling light falls on her face. Enter* MAGDA.)

Ah, Magda. Is it thou?

MAGDA. Is he awake?
HEINRICH.   Yes, Magda. Is it thou?
MAGDA (*delightedly*). How is it with thee?
HEINRICH (*overcome with emotion*).   Well. Ah, well! I'll live!
I feel it. I shall live . . . Yes! I shall . . . live!

(*As he speaks, he gazes fixedly, not at* MAGDA, *but at* RAUTENDELEIN, *who stands in an elfin attitude, looking toward him, with an unnatural light on her face.*)

MAGDA. (*Overjoyed and embracing* HEINRICH, *who seems unconscious of her presence.*) He lives! He lives! O dearest Heinrich! Dearest!

CURTAIN

ACT THREE

A deserted glass-works in the mountains, near the snow fields. L., an earthenware pipe, through which water from the natural rock runs into a natural stone trough. R., a "practicable" smith's forge, with chimney and bellows. Through the open entrance to the glass-works at back, R., is seen a mountain landscape, with peaks, moors, and dense fir-woods. Close to the entrance is a precipitous descending slope. In the roof is an outlet for the smoke. L., the rock forms a rude, pointed vault.

DISCOVERED: THE WOOD-SPRITE. *After throwing a stump on a heap of pine-wood outside, he enters, reluctantly, and looks round.* THE NICKELMANN *rises from the water-trough, remaining immersed up to his breast.*

THE NICKELMANN. Brekekekex! Come in!

THE WOOD-SPRITE.   Ah, there thou art!

THE NICKELMANN. Ay. Plague upon this nasty smoke and soot!

THE WOOD-SPRITE. Have they gone out?

THE NICKELMANN.   Have who gone out?

THE WOOD-SPRITE.   Why—they.

THE NICKELMANN. Yes. I suppose so. Else they would be here.

THE WOOD-SPRITE. I've seen old Horny.

THE NICKELMANN.   Ugh!

THE WOOD-SPRITE.   . . . With saw and axe.

THE NICKELMANN. What did he say?

THE WOOD-SPRITE.   He said . . . thou croakedst much.

THE NICKELMANN. Then let the booby keep his ears closed tight.

THE WOOD-SPRITE. And then he said . . . thou quackedst dismally.

THE NICKELMANN. I'll wring his neck for him.

THE WOOD-SPRITE.   And serve him right!

THE NICKELMANN. More necks than one I'd wring—

THE WOOD-SPRITE (*laughing*).   Accursèd wight!

He crowds us from our hills. He hacks and hews,
Digs up our metals, sweats, and smelts, and brews.
The earth-man and the water-sprite he takes
To drag his burdens, and, to harness, breaks.
Our fairest elf's his sweetheart. As for us,
We must stand by, and watch them—as they buss.
She steals my cherished flowers, my red-brown ores,
My gold, my precious stones, my resinous stores.
She serves him like a slave, by night and day.
'Tis he she kisses—us she keeps at bay.
Naught stands against him. Ancient trees he fells.
The earth quakes at his tread, and all the dells
Ring with the echo of his thunderous blows.
His crimson smithy furnace glows and shines
Into the depths of my most secret mines.
What he is up to, only Satan knows!

THE NICKELMANN. Brekekekex! Hadst thou the creature slain,
A-rotting in the mere long since he had lain—
The maker of the bell, beside the bell.
And so when next I had wished to throw the stones,
The bell had been my box—the dice, his bones!

THE WOOD-SPRITE. By cock and pie! That, truly, had been well.

THE NICKELMANN. But, as it is, he's hale and strong, and works.
Each hammer-stroke my marrow thrills and irks.
   (*Whimpering.*)
He makes her rings, and chains, and bracelets rare—
Kisses her neck, her breast, her golden hair.

THE WOOD-SPRITE. Now, by my goaty face, thou must be crazed.
An old chap whine and whimper? I'm amazed.
He has a fancy for the child? What then?
'Tis plain she does not love you water-men.

Cheer up! Although she shall not be thy bride,
The sea is deep: the earth is long and wide.
Catch some fair nixey, and your passion slake.
Live like a pacha: riot—be a rake!
Soon thou'lt be cured: and when they hie to bed,
Thou wilt not even turn to wag thy head.
THE NICKELMANN. I'll have his blood, I say! . . .
THE WOOD-SPRITE.   She dotes on him.
Thou'rt powerless.
THE NICKELMANN.   I'll tear him limb from limb!
THE WOOD-SPRITE. She will not have thee, and thy rage is vain.
While Granny stands his friend, thy cries of pain
Will all be wasted. Ay, this loving pair
Is closely guarded. Patience! and beware!
THE NICKELMANN. Patience? I hate the word!
THE WOOD-SPRITE.   Time runs on fast:
And men are men. Their passion is soon past.
    RAUTENDELEIN (*heard singing without*). A beetle sat in a tree!
    Zum! Zum!
    A coat all black and white had he!
    Zum! Zum!
  (*She enters.*)
Oho! We've company. Godden, Godden to you.
Hast washed that gold for me, good Nickelmann?
Hast brought the pine-stumps, as I ordered thee,
Dear Goat's-Foot? . . . See: I bend beneath the weight
Of the rare treasures I have found to-day.
Oh, I'm no laggard when I set to work!
Here I have diamonds: here, crystals clear.
This little bag is filled with gold-dust. Look!
And here is honeycomb . . . How warm it grows!
THE NICKELMANN. Warm days are followed by still warmer nights.
RAUTENDELEIN. Maybe. Cold water is thine element:
So get thee whence thou cam'st, and cool thyself.
  (*The* WOOD-SPRITE *laughs.*)
  (*The* NICKELMANN *sinks silently down into his trough and disappears.*)
He will not stop until he's angered me.
THE WOOD-SPRITE (*still laughing*). Ods bobs!
RAUTENDELEIN   My garter's twisted at the knee!
It cuts me. Oh!
THE WOOD-SPRITE. Shall I untwist it, dear?
RAUTENDELEIN. A pretty page thou'dst make! . . . No. Go away.
Thou bring'st ill smells with thee . . . and oh, the gnats!
Why, they are swarming round thee now, in clouds.
THE WOOD-SPRITE. I love them better than the butterflies
That flap their dusty wings about thy face,
Now hanging on thy lips—now on thy hair,
Or clinging to thy hip and breast at night.
RAUTENDELEIN (*laughing*). There! That will do. Enough!

THE WOOD-SPRITE. A happy thought!
Give me this cart-wheel. How did it come here?
RAUTENDELEIN. That thou couldst answer best, thou mischievous rogue.
THE WOOD-SPRITE. Had I not broken down the dray, I trow,
Thy falcon were not now meshed in thy net.
So give me thanks—and let me take the thing.
I'll have it tied with ropes, and smeared with pitch,
And when it's lighted, I will roll it down
The steepest hillside. Ah! That were a joke!
RAUTENDELEIN. Not for the village-folk. Their huts would flame.
THE WOOD-SPRITE. The flame of sacrifice! The red, red wind!
RAUTENDELEIN. But I'll not hear of it. So—get thee gone!
THE WOOD-SPRITE. Thou'rt in a hurry? . . . Must I really go?
Then tell me first—what is the Master doing?
RAUTENDELEIN. He's working a great work!
THE WOOD-SPRITE. Ah, yes, no doubt!
We know how bells are cast: by day
Ye work—at night, ye kiss and play.
Hill pines for dale, dale pines for hill,
Then, quick, the Master works his will:
A bastard thing, half brute, half God—
The pride of Earth—to Heaven a clod.
Come to the hazelwoods with me!
What he could be to thee, I'll be.
To honor thee shall be my pleasure—
Ape not the Virgin pure, my treasure!
RAUTENDELEIN. Thou beast! Thou rogue! I'll blind thy thankless eyes,
Should'st thou not cease that Master to despise
Whose hammer, clanging through the dark, long night,
Strikes to redeem thee! . . . For, without his might,
Thou, I, and all of our unhappy race,
Are curst, and kept beyond the pale of grace.
Yet, stay! . . . Be what thou wilt, thy strength is vain.
Here he, the Master, and his will, must reign!
THE WOOD-SPRITE. What's that to me? . . . My greeting to thy love.
Some day, thou'lt see, I'll be thy turtle-dove.
 (*Exit laughing. Short pause.*)
RAUTENDELEIN. What ails me? . . . Here the air seems close and warm.
I'll hie to some cool grot beside the snow.
The dripping water, green and cold as ice,
Will soon refresh me . . . To-day I trod on a snake,
As it lay sunning itself on a green stone.
It bit at me—up yonder by the falls.
Heigho! How close it is! . . . Steps! . . . Hark! Who comes?
 (*Enter the* VICAR, *in mountain costume. He pants for breath as he stands outside the door.*)
THE VICAR. Ho! Master Barber! Follow me. This way!
The road was rough. But here I stand, at last.
Well, well. I've come to do God's own good work.

My pains will be repaid a hundred-fold
If, like the Blessèd Shepherd, I should find
One poor, lost sheep, and bring him safely home.
So, courage! Courage! (*He enters.*) Is there no one here?
  (*He sees* RAUTENDELEIN.)
Ah, there thou art. I might have known as much!
RAUTENDELEIN (*pale and angry*). What do you seek?
THE VICAR.   That thou shalt quickly learn.
Ay, soon enough, as God shall be my witness.
Give me but time to get my breath again
And dry my face a bit. And now, my child—
I pray thee, tell me—art thou here alone?
RAUTENDELEIN. Thou hast no right to question me!
THE VICAR.   Oho!
A pretty answer, truly. But thou art frank—
Thou showest me thy very self at once.
So much the better. Now my course is plain.
Thou creature! . . .
RAUTENDELEIN.   Man, beware!
THE VICAR. (*Folding his hands and approaching her.*) I fear thee not!
My heart is pure and true. Thou canst not harm me.
He who did give my poor old limbs the strength
To brave thee in thy hidden mountain home
Will not forsake me now. Thou devilish thing,
Think not to daunt me with thy scornful glance—
Waste thy infernal witchcraft not on me!
Thou—thou hast lured him hither—to thy hills!
RAUTENDELEIN. Whom?
THE VICAR.   Whom? Why, Master Heinrich. Canst thou ask?
With magic spells, and sweet unhallowed draughts,
Thou hast witched him, till he obeys thee like a dog.
A man so upright, pious to the core;
A father and a husband! Thou great God!
This mountain trull had but to raise her hand
And, in a trice, she had tied him to her skirts,
Dragged him away with her, where'er she pleased,
Shaming the honor of all Christendom.
RAUTENDELEIN. If I'm a robber, 'twas not thou I robbed!
THE VICAR. What! 'Tis not I thou hast robbed? Thou insolent jade,
Not me alone, not only his wife and boys—
No—all mankind thou hast cheated of this man!
RAUTENDELEIN (*suddenly transformed and in triumph*). Ah, look before thee!
  See who comes this way!
Dost thou not hear the free and even sound
Of his firm footsteps? Shall thy sland'rous flouts
Not even now be turned to joyous shouts?
Dost thou not feel my Balder's conqu'ring glance
Dart through thy soul, and stir thee, as the dance?
The grass his foot treads down is proud and glad.

A King draws nigh! Thou, beggarly wretch, art sad?
Hail! Hail! O Master, Master! Thee I greet!
(*She runs to meet* HEINRICH, *and throws herself into his arms as he enters.*)
(HEINRICH *is attired in a picturesque working costume. In his hand he holds a hammer. He enters hand in hand with* RAUTENDELEIN, *and recognizes the* VICAR.)

HEINRICH. Welcome! Thrice welcome, friend!

THE VICAR.   Now God be praised!
Belovèd Master: is it yourself I see?
You, who but lately came so near to death,
Now stand before me, beaming with rude strength,
Straight as a stout young beech, and hale and well—
You, who did seem a sickly, tottering man,
Hopeless, and ageing? What has wrought this change?
How, in a moment, has the grace of God,
With but a puff of His all-quickening breath,
Helped you to spring from your sick-bed to life,
Ready to dance, as David danced, and sing,
Praising the Lord, your Saviour and your King!

HEINRICH. 'Tis even as you say.

THE VICAR.   You are a marvel!

HEINRICH. That also is true. In all my frame I feel
Wonders are being worked.

  (*To Rautendelein.*)

                          Go thou, my dear.
The Vicar must be thirsty. Bring some wine.

THE VICAR. I thank you. But—I will not drink to-day.

HEINRICH. Go. Bring the wine. I'll vouch for it. 'Tis good.
Well—as you please. I pray you, do not stand.
This is my first encounter with a friend
Since I released myself from the distress
And shame that sickness brings. I had not hoped
To welcome you, before all others, here—
Within the narrow sphere that bounds my work.
Now am I doubly glad: for now 'tis clear
You have learned what strength, and love, and duty mean.
I see you breaking, with one resolute blow,
The murderous chains of worldly interest—
Fleeing mankind, to seek the one true God.

THE VICAR. Now, God be thanked! You are the old, true, Heinrich
They lied, who, in the valley, had proclaimed
You were no more the man that once we knew.

HEINRICH. That man am I, and yet . . . another man.
Open the windows—Light and God stream in!

THE VICAR. A goodly saying.

HEINRICH.   Ay. The best I know.

THE VICAR. I know some better. Yet your saying's good.

HEINRICH. Then, if you are ready, give me your right hand.
I swear, by Cock and Swan and Head of Horse,

With all my soul to serve you as your friend.
I'll open to you wide the gates of Spring—
The Spring that fills my heart.

THE VICAR.   Do as you say.
'Twill not be the first time. You know me well.

HEINRICH. I know you. Yes. And though I knew you not,
Yea, though a vulgar soul your face should hide,
So boundless is my craving to do good,
That I——. Enough. Gold always will be gold.
And even on the souls of sycophants
Good seed's not wasted.

THE VICAR.   Master, tell me this:
What was the meaning of your curious oath?

HEINRICH. By Cock and Swan?

THE VICAR.   Ay; and by Head of Horse?

HEINRICH. I know not how the words came to my lips . . .
Methinks . . . the weathercock on your church steeple—
The horse's head upon your neighbor's roof—
The swan that soared into the bright blue sky—
Or . . . something else—was in my mind just then.
What does it matter? . . . Ah, here comes the wine.
Now, in the deepest sense of every word,
I drink to our good health . . . yours . . . thine . . . and mine.

THE VICAR. I thank you: and once more I wish good health
To him who has so wondrously been healed.

HEINRICH (*pacing to and fro*). Yes. I am healed—indeed. I feel it here—
Here, in my breast, that swells as I draw in
Strength and new rapture with each living breath.
It is as though the very youth of May
Gladdened my heart and streamed into my being.
I feel it in my arm—'tis hard as steel;
And in my hand, that, as the eagle's claw,
Clutches at empty air, and shuts again,
Wild with impatience to achieve great deeds.
Saw you the sanctuary in my garden?

THE VICAR. What do you mean?

HEINRICH.   There! . . . 'Tis another marvel.
Look!

THE VICAR. I see nothing.

HEINRICH.   I mean yonder tree,
That seems so like a glowing evening-cloud.
For the god Freyr once rested in its boughs.
From its green branches, and from round its stem,
Comes the voluptuous hum of countless bees—
Hark how they buzz and swarm about the flowers
Eager to sip sweet draughts from every bud!
I feel that I am like that wondrous tree . . .
Even as he came down into those boughs,
So did the god descend into my soul,

And, in an instant, it was all a-bloom.
If any bees go thirsting, let them suck!
THE VICAR. Go on, go on, my friend. I love to listen.
You and your blossoming tree indeed may boast.
Whether your fruit shall ripen, rests with God!
HEINRICH. Surely, dear friend. Does He not order all?
He hurled me down the precipice. 'Twas He
Who raised me up and caused my life to bloom.
He made the fruit, and flowers, and all that grows.
Yet—pray that He may bless my new-born Summer!
What's germed within me's worthy of the blessing—
Worthy of ripening: really and indeed.
It is a work like none I had yet conceived;
A chime, of all the noblest metals wrought,
That, of itself, shall ring and, ringing, live.
If I but put my hand up to my ear,
Straightway I hear it sing. I close my eyes—
Form after form at once grows palpable.
Behold. What now is freely given to me,
Of old—when ye were wont to acclaim me "Master"—
In nameless agony, I vainly sought.
I was no Master then, nor was I happy.
Now am I both; I am happy and a Master!
THE VICAR. I love to hear men call you by that name.
Yet it seems strange that you yourself should do so.
For what church are you making your great work?
HEINRICH. For no church.
THE VICAR.   Then—who ordered it, my friend?
HEINRICH. He who commanded yonder pine to rise
In strength and majesty beside the abyss! . . .
But—seriously: the little church you had built
Lies half in ruins—half it has been burned.
So I must find a new place on the heights:
A new place, for a new, a nobler, temple!
THE VICAR. O, Master, Master! . . . But, I will not argue.
Perchance we have misunderstood each other.
To put things plainly, what I mean is this:
As your new work must cost so very dear . . .
HEINRICH. Yes. It is costly.
THE VICAR.   Such a chime as yours . . .
HEINRICH. Oh, call it what you will.
THE VICAR.   You said—a chime?
HEINRICH. A name I gave to that which none may name,
Nor can, nor shall baptize, except itself.
THE VICAR. And tell me, pray—who pays you for your work?
HEINRICH. Who pays me for my work? Oh, Father! Father!
Would you give joy to joy—add gold to gold? . . .
If I so named it, and the name you love—
Call my great work—a chime! . . . But 'tis a chime

Such as no minster in the world has seen.
Loud and majestic is its mighty voice.
Even as the thunder of a storm it sounds,
Rolling and crashing o'er the meads in Spring.
Ay, in the tumult of its trumpet-tones,
All the church-bells on earth it shall strike dumb.
All shall be hushed, as through the sky it rings
The glad new Gospel of the new-born light!

.   .   .   .   .

Eternal Sun!* Thy children, and my children,
Know thee for Father, and proclaim thy power.
Thou, aided by the kind and gentle rain,
Didst raise them from the dust and give them health!
So now—their joy triumphant they shall send
Singing along thy clear, bright, path to Heaven!
And now, at last, like the grey wilderness
That thou hast warmed, and mantled with thy green,
Me thou hast kindled into sacrifice!
I offer thee myself, and all I am! . . .
O Day of Light—when, from the marble halls
Of my fair Temple, the first waking peal
Shall shake the skies—when, from the sombre clouds
That weighed upon us through the winter night,
Rivers of jewels shall go rushing down
Into a million hands outstretched to clutch!
Then all who drooped, with sudden power inflamed,
Shall bear their treasure homeward to their huts,
There to unfurl, at last, the silken banners,
Waiting—so long, so long—to be upraised,
And, pilgrims of the Sun, draw near the Feast!

.   .   .   .   .

O, Father, that great Day! . . . You know the tale
Of the lost Prodigal? . . . It is the Sun
That bids his poor, lost, children to my Feast.
With rustling banners, see the swelling host
Draw nearer, and still nearer to my Temple.
And now the wondrous chime again rings out,
Filling the air with such sweet, passionate sound
As makes each breast to sob with rapturous pain.
It sings a song, long lost and long forgotten,
A song of home—a childlike song of Love,
Born in the waters of some fairy well—
Known to all mortals, and yet heard of none!
And as it rises, softly first, and low,
The nightingale and dove seem singing, too;
And all the ice in every human breast

*In the German the Sun is feminine. The original passage has consequently been modified.

Is melted, and the hate, and pain, and woe,
Stream out in tears.

. . . . .

Then shall we all draw nearer to the Cross,
And, still in tears, rejoice, until at last
The dead Redeemer, by the Sun set free,
His prisoned limbs shall stir from their long sleep,
And, radiant with the joy of endless youth,
Come down, Himself a youth, into the May!

(HEINRICH's *enthusiasm has swelled as he has spoken the foregoing speech, till at last it has become ecstatic. He walks to and fro.* RAUTENDELEIN, *who has been silently watching him all this time, showing her love and adoration by the changing expression of her face, now approaches* HEINRICH, *with tears in her eyes, kneels beside him, and kisses his hand. The* VICAR *has listened to* HEINRICH *with growing pain and horror. Towards the end of* HEINRICH's *speech he has contained himself with difficulty. After a brief pause he answers. At first he speaks with enforced calm. Gradually, however, his feeling carries him away.*)

THE VICAR. And now, dear Master, I have heard you out:
Now every syllable those worthy men
Had told me of your state, alas, is proved.
Yea, even to the story of this chime of bells.
I cannot tell you all the pain I feel! . . .
A truce to empty words! If here I stand,
'Tis not because I thirsted for your marvels.
No! 'Tis to help you in your hour of need!
HEINRICH. My need? . . . And so you think I am in need?
THE VICAR. Man! Man! Bestir yourself. Awake! You dream!
A dreadful dream, from which you'll surely wake
To everlasting sorrow. Should I fail
To rouse you, with God's wise and holy words,
You are lost, ay, lost for ever, Master Heinrich!
HEINRICH. I do not think so.
THE VICAR.   What saith the Good Book?*
"Those whom He would destroy, He first doth blind."
HEINRICH. If God so willed it—you'd resist in vain.
Yet, should I own to blindness,
Filled as I feel myself with pure, new life,
Bedded upon a glorious morning cloud,
Whence with new eyes I drink in all the heavens;
Why, then, indeed, I should deserve God's curse,
And endless Darkness.
THE VICAR.   Master Heinrich—friend,
I am too humble to keep pace with you.
A simple man am I—a child of Earth:
The superhuman lies beyond my grasp.
But one thing I do know, though you forget,

*So it stands in the original.

That wrong is never right, nor evil, good.
HEINRICH. And Adam did not know so much in Eden!
THE VICAR. Fine phrases, sounding well, but meaningless.
They will not serve to cloak your deadly sin.
It grieves me sore—I would have spared you this.
You have a wife, and children . . .
HEINRICH.   Well—what more?
THE VICAR. You shun the church, take refuge in the mountains;
This many a month you have not seen the home
Where your poor wife sits sighing, while, each day,
Your children drink their lonely mother's tears!
   (*A long pause.*)
HEINRICH (*with emotion*). Could I but wipe away those sorrowful tears,
How gladly would I do it! . . . But I cannot.
In my dark hours, I've digged into my soul,
Only to feel, I have no power to dry them.
I, who am now all love, in love renewed,
Out of the overflowing wealth I own,
May not fill up their cup! For, lo, my wine
Would be to them but bitter gall and venom!
Should he whose hand is as the eagle's claw
Stroke a sick child's wet cheek? . . . Here none but God
Could help!
THE VICAR.   For this there is no name but madness,
And wicked madness. Yes. I speak the truth.
Here stand I, Master, overcome with horror
At the relentless cruelty of your heart.
Now Satan, aping God, hath dealt a blow—
Yes, I must speak my mind—a blow so dread
That even he must marvel at his triumph.
That work, Almighty God, whereof he prates—
Do I not know 't? . . . 'Tis the most awful crime
Ever was hatched within a heathen brain!
Far rather would I see the dreadful plagues
Wherewith the Lord once scourged rebellious Egypt
Threaten our Christendom, then watch your Temple
Rise to the glory of Beelzebub.
Awake! Arise! Come back, my son, to Christ!
It is not yet too late! Cast out this witch!
Renounce this wanton hag—ay, cast her out!
This elf, this sorceress, this cursèd sprite!
Then in a trice, the evil spell shall fade
And vanish into air. You shall be saved!
HEINRICH. What time I fevered lay, a prey to death,
She came, and raised me up, and made me well.
THE VICAR. 'Twere better you had died—than live like this!
HEINRICH. Why, as to that, think even as you will.
But, as for me—I took life's burden up.
I live anew, and, till death comes, must thank

Her who did give me life.

THE VICAR. Now—I have done!
Too deep, yea to the neck, you are sunk in sin!
Your Hell, decked out in beauty as high Heaven,
Shall hold you fast. I will not waste more words.
Yet mark this, Master: witches make good fuel,
Even as heretics, for funeral-pyres.
Vox populi, vox Dei! Your ill deeds,
Heathen, and secret once, are now laid bare.
Horror they wake, and soon there shall come hate.
So it may happen that the storm, long-curbed,
All bounds shall overleap, and that the people
Whom you have outraged in their holiest faith,
Shall rise against you in their own defence,
And crush you ruthlessly!
  (*Pause.*)

HEINRICH (*calmly*). And now hear me . . .
I fear you not! . . . Should they who panting lie
Dash from my hand the cup of cooling wine
I bore to them: if they would rather thirst—
Why, then, it is their will—perhaps their fate—
And none may justly charge me with their act.
I am no longer thirsty. I have drunk.
If it is fitting that, of all men, you—
Who have closed your eyes against the truth—should be
That man who now assails so hatefully
The blameless cup-bearer, and flings the mud
Of Darkness 'gainst his soul, where all is light:
Yet I am I! . . . What I would work, I know.
And if, ere now, full many a faulty bell
My stroke has shattered, once again will I
Swing my great hammer, for a mightier blow,
Dealt at another bell the mob has made—
Fashioned of malice, gall, and all ill things,
Last but not least among them ignorance.

THE VICAR. Then, go your way! Farewell. My task is done.
The hemlock of your sin no man may hope
To rid your soul of. May God pity you!
But this remember! There's a word named rue!
And some day, some day, as your dreams you dream,
A sudden arrow, shot from out the blue,
Shall pierce your breast! And yet you shall not die,
Nor shall you live. In that dread day you'll curse
All you now cherish—God, the world, your work,
Your wretched self you'll curse. Then . . . think of me!

HEINRICH. Had I a fancy to paint phantoms, Vicar,
I'd be more skilful in the art than you.
The things you rave of never shall come true,
And I am guarded well against your arrow.

No more it frets me, nor my heart can shake,
Than that old bell, which in the water rolled—
Where it lies buried now, and hushed—forever!
THE VICAR. That bell shall toll again! Then think of me!

ACT FOUR

SCENE: *The glass-works as in Act Three. A rude door has been hewn out of the rocky wall, L. Through this, access is obtained to a mountain-cave. R., the open forge, with bellows and chimney. The fire is lighted. Near the forge stands an anvil.*

DISCOVERED: HEINRICH, *at the anvil, on which he is laying a bar of red-hot iron which he holds tight with his tongs. Near him stand six little* DWARFS *attired as mountaineers. The* FIRST DWARF *holds the tongs with* HEINRICH; *the* SECOND DWARF *lifts the great forge hammer and brings it down with a ringing blow on the iron. The* THIRD DWARF *works the bellows. The* FOURTH DWARF *stands motionless, intently watching the progress of the work. The* FIFTH DWARF *stands by, waiting. In his hand he holds a club, ready to strike. The* SIXTH DWARF *sits perched on the stump of a tree. On his head he wears a glittering crown. Here and there lie fragments of forged iron and castings, models and plans.*

HEINRICH (*to* SECOND DWARF). Strike hard! Strike harder! Till thy arm hangs limp.
Thy whimpering does not move me, thou poor sluggard—
Shouldst thou relax before the time I set,
I'll singe thy beard for thee in these red flames.
    (SECOND DWARF *throws his hammer down.*)
Oho! 'Tis as I thought. Well, wait, thou imp!
And thou shalt see I mean what I have threaten'd!
    (SECOND DWARF *struggles and screams as* HEINRICH *holds him over the fire.* THIRD DWARF *goes to work more busily than ever at the bellows.*)
FIRST DWARF (*with the tongs*). I can't hold on. My hand is stiff, great Master!
HEINRICH. I'm coming.
    (*He turns to* SECOND DWARF). Well, dost thou feel stronger now?
    (SECOND DWARF *nods reassuringly, and hammers away for dear life.*)
HEINRICH. By Cock and Swan! I'll have no mercy on you!
    (*He clutches the tongs again.*)
No blacksmith living could a horseshoe shape
An he should stand on trifles with such rogues.
No sooner have they struck the first good stroke
When off they'd go, and leave the rest to chance.
And as for counting on them for the zeal
That spurs an honest workman to attempt
Ten thousand miracles—why, 'twould be mad.
To work! To work! Hot iron bends—not cold! (*To* FIRST DWARF.)

What art thou at?

FIRST DWARF. (*Busily trying to mould the red-hot iron with his hand.*)
             I'm moulding it with my hand.

HEINRICH. Thou reckless fool. What? Hast thou lost thy wits?
Wouldst thou reduce thy clumsy paw to ashes?
Thou wretched dwarf, if thou shouldst fail me now,
What power had I? . . . Without thy helping art,
How could I hope to see my cherished work
Rise from the summit of my temple towers
Into the free and sunlit air of heaven?

FIRST DWARF. The iron is well forged. The hand is whole—
Deadened and numbed a little: that is all.

HEINRICH. Off to the well with thee! The Nickelmann
Will cool thy fingers with his water-weeds.
    (*To the* SECOND DWARF.)
Now take the rest thou'st earned, thou lazy imp,
And make the most of it. I'll comfort seek
In the reward that comes of honest effort.
    (*He picks up the newly forged iron, sits, and examines it.*)
Ah, here's rare work for you! The kindly powers
Have crowned our labor with this good result.
I am content. Methinks I have cause to be,
Since, out of shapelessness, a shape has grown.
And, out of chaos, this rare masterpiece:
Nicely proportioned—here . . . above . . . below . . .
Just what was needed to complete the work.
    (*The* FOURTH DWARF *clambers on to a stool and whispers in* HEINRICH's *ear.*)
What art thou muttering, imp? Disturb me not,
Lest I should tie thy hands and feet together,
And clap a gag into thy chattering throat!
    (DWARF *retreats in alarm.*)
What's out of joint in the great scheme? What's wrong?
What irks thee? Speak when thou art questioned, dwarf!
Never as now was I so filled with joy;
Never were heart and hand more surely one.
What art thou grumbling at? Am I not Master?
Wouldst thou, poor hireling, dare to vie with me?
Well—out with it! Thy meaning—Speak! Be plain!
    (DWARF *returns and whispers.* HEINRICH *turns pale, sighs, rises, and angrily lays the iron on the anvil.*)
Then may the Devil end this work himself!
I'll grow potatoes, and plant cabbages.
I'll eat and drink and sleep, and then—I'll die!
    (FIFTH DWARF *approaches the anvil.*)
Thou, fellow, do not dare to lay thy hand on 't!
Ay, burst with fury, an thou wilt. I care not.
And let thy hair stand straight on end—thy glance
Dart death. Thou rogue! Who yields but once to thee,
Or fails to hold thee tightly in his clutch,

Might just as well bow down and be thy slave,
And wait till, with thy club, thou end his pain!

(FIFTH DWARF *angrily shatters the iron on the anvil;* HEINRICH *grinds his teeth with rage.*)

Well, well! Run riot! No more work to-night.
A truce to duty. Get ye hence, ye dwarfs!
Should morning, as I hope, put fresh, new life
Into this frame of mine—I'll call ye back.
Go!—Work unbidden would avail me naught.

(*To* THIRD DWARF.)

Come—drop thy bellows, dwarf. With all thy might,
Thou'dst hardly heat me a new iron to-night.

Away! Away!

(*All the* DWARFS, *with the exception of the one with the crown, vanish through the door L.*)

And thou, crowned King, who only once shalt speak—
Why dost thou linger? Get thee gone, I say.
Thou wilt not speak to-day, nor yet to-morrow:
Heaven only knows if thou wilt ever speak!
My work! . . . My work! When will it end! . . . I'm tired!
I love thee not, sad twilight hour, that liest
Pressed 'twixt the dying day and growing night.
Thou wringest from my nerveless hand the hammer,
Yet bring'st me not the sleep, the dreamless sleep,
That gives men rest. A heart athirst for work
Knows it must wait, and wait in idleness:
And so—in pain—it waits . . . for the new day.
The sun, wrapped round in purple, slowly sinks
Into the depths . . . and leaves us here alone.
While we, who are used to light, look helpless on,
And, stripped of everything, must yield to night.
Rags are the coverlets that cloak our sleep.
At noon we're kings . . . at dusk we're only beggars.

(*He throws himself on a couch and lies dreaming, with wide-open eyes. A white mist comes in through the open door. When it disappears, the* NICKELMANN *is discovered leaning over the edge of the water-trough.*)

THE NICKELMANN. Quorax! . . . Brekekekex! . . . So there he lies—
This Master Earth-Worm—in his mossgrown house.
He's deaf and blind, while crookback imps do creep
Like the grey mists upon the mountain-side.
Now they uplift their shadowy hands, and threaten!
Now they go wringing them, as though in pain!
He sleeps! He does not heed the moaning pines;
The low, malignant piping of the elves
That makes the oldest fir-trees quake and thrill,
And, like a hen that flaps her foolish wings,
Beat their own boughs against their quivering flanks . . . !
Now, he grows chiller, as the winter-grey
Searches the marrow in his bones. And still,

Even in sleep, he toils!
Give over, fool! Thou canst not fight with God!
'Twas God that raised thee up, to prove thy strength;
And now, since thou art weak, He casts thee down!
(HEINRICH *tosses about and moans in his sleep.*)
Vain is thy sacrifice. For Sin is Sin.
Thou hast not wrung from God the right to change
Evil to good—or wages give to guilt.
Thou'rt foul with stains. Thy garments reek with blood.
Now, call thou ne'er so loud, the gentle hand
That might have washed thee clean, thou'lt never see!
Black spirits gather in the hills and dales.
Soon in thine anguished ear the sound shall ring
Of the wild huntsmen and the baying hounds!
They know what game they hunt! . . . And now, behold!
The giant builders of the air upraise
Castles of cloud, with monstrous walls and towers.
Frowning and grim, they move against thy heights,
Eager to crush thy work, and thee, and all!
HEINRICH. Help! Help! Rautendelein! An alp! I choke!
THE NICKELMANN. She hears thee—and she comes—but brings **no help!**
Though she were Freya, and though thou wert Balder—
Though sun-tipped shafts did fill thy radiant quiver,
And ev'ry shaft that thou shouldst point went home—
Thou must be vanquished. Hear me!

> A sunken bell in the deep mere lies,
> Under the rocks and the rolling:
> And it longs to rise—
> In the sunlight again to be tolling!
> The fishes swim in, and the fishes swim out,
> As the old bell tosses, and rolls about.
> It shudders and sways as they come and go,
> And weeping is heard, and the sound of woe.
> A muffled moan, and a throb of pain,
> Answer the swirling flood—
> For the mouth of the bell is choked with blood!
> Woe, woe, to thee, man, when it tolls again!
>   Bim! . . . Boom!
> The Lord save thee from thy doom!
>   Bim! . . . Boom!
> Hark to the knell!
> Death is the burden of that lost bell!
>   Bim! . . . Boom!
> The Lord save thee from thy doom!

(*The* NICKELMANN *sinks into the well.*)
HEINRICH. Help! Help! A nightmare chokes me! Help! Help! Help!
(*He awakes.*)
Where am I? . . . Am I living?

(He rubs his eyes and looks round him.)
                                         No one here?
RAUTENDELEIN *(entering)*. I'm here! Did'st call?
HEINRICH.   Yes! Come! Come here to me.
Lay thy dear hand upon my forehead—so,
And let me stroke thy hair . . . and feel thy heart.
Come. Nearer. In thy train thou bring'st the scent
Of the fresh woods and rosemary. Ah, kiss me!
Kiss me!
RAUTENDELEIN. What ails thee, dearest?
HEINRICH.   Nothing, nothing!
Give me a coverlet . . . I lay here chilled . . .
Too tired to work . . . My heart grew faint . . . and then
Dark powers of evil seemed to enter in . . .
Laid hold of me, possessed me, plagued me sore,
And tried to throttle me . . . But now I'm well.
Have thou no fear, child. I'm myself again!
Now let them come!
RAUTENDELEIN.   Who?
HEINRICH.   Why, my foes.
RAUTENDELEIN.   What foes?
HEINRICH. My nameless enemies—ay, one and all!
I stand upon my feet, as once I stood.
Ready to brave them, though they filled my sleep
With crawling, creeping, cowardly terrors!
RAUTENDELEIN. Thou'rt fevered, Heinrich!
HEINRICH.   Ay, 'tis chill to-night.
No matter. Put thy arms around me. So.
RAUTENDELEIN. Thou, dearest, dearest!
HEINRICH.   Tell me this, my child.
Dost trust in me?
RAUTENDELEIN.   Thou Balder! Hero! God!
I press my lips against the fair white brow
That overhangs the clear blue of thine eyes.
    (Pause.)
HEINRICH. So—I am all thou say'st? . . . I am thy Balder?
Make me believe it—make me know it, child!
Give my faint soul the rapturous joy it needs,
To nerve it to its task. For, as the hand,
Toiling with tong and hammer, on and on,
To hew the marble and to guide the chisel,
Now bungles here, now there, yet may not halt,
And nothing, small or great, dare leave to chance,
So do we ofttimes lose our passionate faith,
Feel the heart tighten, and the eyes grow dim,
Till, in the daily round of drudging work,
The clear projection of the soul doth vanish.
For, to preserve that Heaven-sent gift is hard.
No clamp have we, no chain, to hold it fast.

'Tis as the aura that surrounds a sun,
Impalpable. That lost, all's lost.
Defrauded now we stand, and tempted sore
To shirk the anguish that foreruns fruition.
What, in conception, seemed all ecstacy,
Now turns to sorrow. But—enough of this.
Still straight and steady doth the smoke ascend
From my poor human sacrifice to Heaven.
Should now a Hand on high reject my gift,
Why, it may do so. Then the priestly robe
Falls from my shoulder—by no act of mine;
While I, who erst upon the heights was set,
Must look my last on Horeb, and be dumb!
But now bring torches! Lights! And show thine art!
Enchantress! Fill the winecup! We will drink!
Ay, like the common herd of mortal men,
With resolute hands our fleeting joy we'll grip!
Our unsought leisure we will fill with life,
Not waste it, as the herd, in indolence.
We will have music!

RAUTENDELEIN.   O'er the hills I flew:
Now, as a cobweb, on the breezes drifting,
Now frolicing as a bee, or butterfly,
And darting hungrily from flower to flower.
From each and all, from every shrub and plant,
Each catch-fly, harebell, and forget-me-not,
I dragged the promise, and I forced the oath,
That bound them never to do harm to thee.
And so—the blackest elf, most bitter foe
To thee, so good and white, should vainly seek
To cut thy death-arrow!*

HEINRICH.   What is this arrow?
I know the spirit! . . . Yes, I know 't! . . . There came
A spirit to me once, in priestly garb,
Who, threat'ning, raised his hand, the while he raved
Of some such arrow that should pierce my heart.
Who'll speed the arrow from his bow, I say?
Who—who will dare?

RAUTENDELEIN.   Why, no one, dearest. No one.
Thou'rt proof against all ill, I say—thou'rt proof.
And now, blink but thine eye, or only nod,
And gentle strains shall upward float, as mist,
Hem thee about, and, with a wall of music,
Guard thee from call of man, and toll of bell:
Yea, mock at even Loki's mischievous arts.
Make the most trifling gesture with thy hand,
These rocks shall turn to vaulted palace-halls,
Earth-men unnumbered shall buzz round, and stand

*It was an old belief that dangerous arrows were shot down from the air by elves.

Ready to deck the floor, the walls, the board!
Yet—since by dark, fierce foes we are beset,
Wilt thou not flee into the earth with me?
There we need fear no icy giant's breath—
There the vast halls shall shine with dazzling light——
HEINRICH. Peace, child. No more. What were thy feast to me
So long as solemn, mute, and incomplete,
My work the hour awaits, wherein its voice
Shall loudly usher in the Feast of Feasts! . . .
I'll have one more good look at the great structure.
So shall new fetters bind me to it fast.
Take thou a torch, and light me on my way.
Haste! Haste! . . . Since now I feel my nameless foes
Busy at work to do me injury—
Since now the fabric's menaced at the base—
'Tis meet the Master, too, should toil—not revel.
For, should success his weary labor crown,
The secret wonder stand at last revealed,
In gems and gold expressed, and ivory,
Even to the faintest, feeblest, of its tones—
His work should live, triumphant, through the ages!
'Tis imperfection that draws down the curse,
Which, could we brave it here, we'd make a mock of.
Ay, we will make a mock of 't!
   (*He moves to the door and halts.*)
                                     Well, child? . . .
Why dost thou linger! . . . Have I grieved thee?
                                                    No!
RAUTENDELEIN.
No! No!
HEINRICH. What ails thee?
RAUTENDELEIN.   Nothing!
HEINRICH.   Thou poor soul!
I know what grieves thee.—Children, such as thou,
Run lightly after the bright butterflies,
And often, laughing, kill what most they love.
But I am not a butterfly. I am more.
RAUTENDELEIN. And I? Am I a child? . . . No more than that?
HEINRICH. Ay, truly, thou art more! . . . That to forget
Were to forget the brightness of my life.
The dew that glistened in thy shining eyes
Filled me with pain. And then I pained thee, too.
Come! 'Twas my tongue, not I, that hurt thee so.
My heart of hearts knows naught, save only love.
Nay—do not weep so. See—now I am armed;
Thou hast equipped me for the game anew.
Lo, thou hast filled my empty hands with gold;
Given me courage for one more last throw!
Now I can play with Heaven! . . . Ah, and I feel
So blessed, so wrapped in thy strange loveliness—

Yet, when I, wond'ring, seek to grasp it all,
I am baffled. For thy charm's unsearchable.
And then I feel how near joy's kin to pain—
Lead on! And light my path!

THE WOOD-SPRITE (*without*).   Holdrio!
Up! Up! Bestir yourselves! Plague o' the dawdlers!
The heathen temple must be laid in ashes!
Haste, reverend Sir! Haste, Master Barber, haste!
Here there is straw and pitch a-plenty. See!
The Master's cuddling his fair elfin bride—
And while he toys with her, naught else he heeds.

HEINRICH. The deadly nightshade must have made him mad.
What art thou yelling in the night, thou rogue?
Beware!

THE WOOD-SPRITE (*defiantly*). Of thee?

HEINRICH.   Ay, fool. Beware of me!
I know the way to manage such as thou,
I'll grab thee by thy beard, thou misshaped oaf;
Thou shalt be shorn and stripped, and when thou'rt tamed,
When thou hast learned to know who's master here,
I'll make thee work and slave for me—thou goat-shank!
What? . . . Neighing, eh? . . . Dost see this anvil, beast?
And, here, this hammer? It is hard enough
To beat thee to a jelly.

THE WOOD-SPRITE. (*Turning his back on* HEINRICH *insolently*.)
                      Bah! Hammer away!
Many and many a zealot's flashing sword
Has tickled me, ere it was turned to splinters.
The iron on thy anvil's naught but clay,
And, like a cow's dug, at the touch it bursts.

HEINRICH. We'll see, thou windbag, thou hobgoblin damned!
Wert thou as ancient as the Wester wood,
Or did thy power but match thy braggart tongue—
I'll have thee chained, and make thee fetch and carry,
Sweep, drudge, draw water, roll huge stones and rocks,
And shouldst thou loiter, beast, I'll have thee flayed!

RAUTENDELEIN. Heinrich! He warns thee!

THE WOOD-SPRITE.   Ay! Go to! Go to!
'Twill be a mad game when they drag thee hence
And roast thee, like an ox! And I'll be by!
But now to find the brimstone, oil, and pitch,
Wherewith to make a bonfire that shall smoke
Till daylight shall be blotted out in darkness.
    (*Exit.*)
    (*Cries and murmurs of many voices heard from below, without.*)

RAUTENDELEIN. Dost thou not hear them, Heinrich? Men are coming!
Hark to their boding cries! . . . They are for thee!
    (*A stone flung from without strikes* RAUTENDELEIN.)
Help, grandmother!

HEINRICH.   So that is what was meant!
I dreamt a pack of hounds did hunt me down
The hounds I hear. The hunt has not begun!
Their yelping, truly, could not come more pat.
For, though an angel had hung down from Heaven,
All lily-laden, and, with gentle sighs,
Entreated me to steadfastness,
He had convinced me less than those fierce cries
Of the great weight and purport of my mission.
Come one, come all! What's yours I guard for you!
I'll shield you from your selves! . . . That be my watchword!
    (*Exit with hammer.*)
RAUTENDELEIN. (*Alone and in excitement.*) Help, help, Bush-Grandmother!
    Help, Nickelmann!
    (*The* NICKELMANN *rises from the well.*)
Ah, my dear Nickelmann, I beg of you—
Bid water, quick, come streaming from the rocks,
Wave upon wave, and drive them all away!
Do! Do!
THE NICKELMANN. Brekekekex! What shall I do?
RAUTENDELEIN. Let thy wild waters sweep them to the abyss!
THE NICKELMANN. I cannot.
RAUTENDELEIN.   But thou canst, good Nickelmann!
THE NICKELMANN. And if I should—what good were that to me?
I have no cause to wish well to the Master.
He'd love to lord it over God and men.
'Twould suit me if the fools should strike him down!
RAUTENDELEIN. Oh, help him—help! Or it will be too late!
THE NICKELMANN. What wilt thou give me, dear?
RAUTENDELEIN.   I give thee?
THE NICKELMANN.   Yes.
RAUTENDELEIN. Ah, what thou wilt!
THE NICKELMANN.   Oho! Brekekekex!
Then strip thy pretty gown from thy brown limbs,
Take off thy crimson shoon, thy dainty cap.
Be what thou art! Come down into my well—
I'll spirit thee a thousand leagues away.
RAUTENDELEIN. Forsooth! How artfully he'd made his plans!
But now I tell thee once, and once for all;
Thou'dst better clear thy pate of all thy schemes.
For, shouldst thou live to thrice thy hoary age—
Shouldst thou grow old as Granny—shouldst thou forever
Prison me close in thine own oyster shells,
I would not look at thee!
THE NICKELMANN.   Then . . . he must die.
RAUTENDELEIN. Thou liest! . . . I'm sure of 't. Thou liest! Hark!
Ah, well thou knowest his clear-sounding voice!
Dost think I do not see thee shrink in fear?
    (*The* NICKELMANN *disappears in the well.*)

(*Enter* HEINRICH *in triumph, and flushed with the excitement of the strife.
He laughs.*)

HEINRICH. They came at me like hounds, and, even as hounds,
I drove them from me with the flaming brands!
Great boulders then I rolled upon their heads:
Some perished—others fled! Come—give me drink!
War cools the breast—'tis steeled by victory.
The warm blood rushes through my veins. Once more
My pulse throbs joyously. War does not tire.
War gives a man the strength of twenty men,
And hate and love makes new!

RAUTENDELEIN.   Here, Heinrich. Drink!

HEINRICH. Yes, give it me, my child. I am athirst
For wine, and light, and love, and joy, and thee!
    (*He drinks.*)
I drink to thee, thou airy elfin sprite!
And, with this drink, again I thee do wed.
Without thee, my invention would be clogged,
I were a prey to gloom—world-weariness.
My child, I entreat thee, do not fail me now.
Thou art the very pinion of my soul.
Fail not my soul!

RAUTENDELEIN.   Ah, do not thou fail me!

HEINRICH. That God forbid! . . . Ho! Music!

RAUTENDELEIN.   Hither! Hither!
Come hither, little people! Elves and gnomes!
Come! Help us to make merry! Leave your homes!
Tune all your tiny pipes, and harps, and flutes,
    (*Faint elfin music heard without.*)
And watch me dance responsive to your lutes!
With glowworms, gleaming emerald, lo, I deck
My waving tresses and my dainty neck.
So jeweled, and adorned with fairy light,
I'll make e'en Freya's necklace seem less bright!

HEINRICH (*interrupting*). Be still! . . . Methought . . .

RAUTENDELEIN.   What?

HEINRICH.   Didst not hear it then?

RAUTENDELEIN. Hear what?

HEINRICH.   Why—nothing.

RAUTENDELEIN.   Dearest, what is wrong?

HEINRICH. I know not . . . But, commingling with thy music . . .
Methought I heard . . . a strain . . . a sound . . .

RAUTENDELEIN.   What sound?

HEINRICH. A plaint . . . a tone . . . a long, long, buried tone . . .
No matter. It was nothing! Sit thou here!
Give me thy rose-red lips. From this fair cup
I'll drink forgetfulness!

    (*They kiss. Long and ecstatic pause. Then* HEINRICH *and* RAUTENDELEIN
move, locked in each other's arms, through the doorway.)

See! Deep and cool and monstrous yawns the gulf
That parts us from the world where mortals dwell.
I am a man. Canst understand me, child? . . .
Yonder I am at home . . . and yet a stranger—
Here I am strange . . . and yet I seem at home.
Canst understand?

RAUTENDELEIN.   Yes!

HEINRICH.   Yet thou eyest me
So wildly. Why?

RAUTENDELEIN.   I'm filled with dread—with horror!

HEINRICH. With dread? Of what?

RAUTENDELEIN.   Of what? I cannot tell.

HEINRICH. 'Tis nothing. Let us rest.

(HEINRICH *leads* RAUTENDELEIN *towards the doorway in the rocks, L. He stops suddenly, and turns towards the open country.*)

Yet may the moon,
That hangs so chalky-white in yonder heavens,
Not shed the still light of her staring eyes
On what's below . . . may she not flood with brightness
The valley whence I rose to these lone heights!
For what lies hid beneath that pall of grey
I dare not gaze on! . . . Hark! Child! Didst hear nothing?

RAUTENDELEIN. Nothing! And what thou saidst was dark to me!

HEINRICH. What! Dost thou still not hear 't?

RAUTENDELEIN.   What should I hear?—
The night wind playing on the heath, I hear—
I hear the cawing of the carrion-kite—
I hear thee, strangely uttering strange, wild, words,
In tones that seem as though they were not thine!

HEINRICH. There! There! Below . . . where shines the wicked moon
Look! Yonder!—Where the light gleams on the waters!

RAUTENDELEIN. Nothing I see! Nothing!

HEINRICH.   With thy gerfalcon eyes
Thou seest naught? Art blind? What drags its way
Slowly and painfully along . . . There . . . See!

RAUTENDELEIN. Thy fancy cheats thee!

HEINRICH.   No! . . . It was no cheat,
As God shall pardon me! . . . Peace! Peace! I say!
Now it climbs over the great boulder, yonder—
Down by the footpath . . .

RAUTENDELEIN.   Heinrich! Do not look!
I'll close the doors and rescue thee by force!

HEINRICH. No! Let me be! . . . I must look down! I will!

RAUTENDELEIN. See—how the fleecy clouds whirl round and round,
As in a giant cauldron, 'mid the rocks!
Weak as thou art, beware! Go not too near!

HEINRICH. I am not weak! . . . 'Twas fancy. Now 'tis gone!

RAUTENDELEIN. That's well! Now be once more our Lord and Master!
Shall wretched visions so undo thy strength?

No! Take thy hammer! Swing it wide and high! . . .

HEINRICH. Dost thou not see them, where they climb and climb? . . .

RAUTENDELEIN. Where?

HEINRICH. There! . . . Now they have reached the rocky path.
Clad only in their little shirts they come!

RAUTENDELEIN. Who come?

HEINRICH. Two little lads, with bare, white feet.
They hold an urn between them . . . 'Tis so heavy!
Now one, and now the other, bends his knee . . .
His little, baby knee, to raise it up . . .

RAUTENDELEIN. O, help him, mother—help him in his need!

HEINRICH. A halo shines about their tiny heads . . .

RAUTENDELEIN. Some will-o'-the-wisp!

HEINRICH. No! . . . Kneel, and clasp thy hands!
Now . . . see . . . they are coming. Now . . . they are here!

(*He kneels, as the phantom forms of two* CHILDREN, *barefooted and clad only in their nightgowns, ascend from below and advance painfully towards him. Between them they carry a two-handled pitcher.*)

FIRST CHILD (*faintly*). Father!

HEINRICH. My child!

FIRST CHILD. Our mother sends thee greeting.

HEINRICH. Thanks, thanks, my dear, dear lad! All's well with her?

FIRST CHILD (*slowly and sadly*). All's very well! . . .

(*The first faint tones of the sunken bell are heard from the depths.*)

HEINRICH. What have you brought with you?

SECOND CHILD. A pitcher.

HEINRICH. Is't for me?

SECOND CHILD. Yes, father dear.

HEINRICH. What is there in the pitcher, my dear boy?

SECOND CHILD. 'Tis something salt! . . .

FIRST CHILD. . . . And bitter!

SECOND CHILD. Mother's tears!

HEINRICH. Merciful God!

RAUTENDELEIN. What art thou staring at?

HEINRICH. At them . . . at them . .

RAUTENDELEIN. At whom?

HEINRICH. Hast thou not eyes?
At them!
(*To the* CHILDREN.)
Where is your mother? Speak, oh, speak!

FIRST CHILD. Our mother?

HEINRICH. Yes! Where is she!

SECOND CHILD. With . . . the . . . lilies . . .
The water-lilies . . .

(*The bell tolls loudly.*)

HEINRICH. Ah! The bell!

RAUTENDELEIN. What bell?

HEINRICH. The old, old, buried bell! . . . It rings! It tolls!
Who dealt this blow at me? . . . I will not listen!

Help! Help me! . . . Help! . . .
RAUTENDELEIN.   Come to your senses, Heinrich!
HEINRICH. It tolls! . . . God help me! . . . Who has dealt this blow?
Hark, how it peals! Hark, how the buried tones
Swell louder, louder, till they sound as thunder,
Flooding the world! . . .
     (*Turning to* RAUTENDELEIN.)
                                   I hate thee! I abhor thee!
Back! Lest I strike thee! Hence! Thou witch! Thou trull!
Accursèd spirit! Curst be thou and I!
Curst be my work! . . . And all! . . . Here! Here am I! . . .
I come! . . . I come! . . . Now may God pity me! . . .
     (*He makes an effort, rises, stumbles, rises again, and tears himself away.*)
     (*The* CHILDREN *have vanished.*)
RAUTENDELEIN. Stay! Heinrich! Stay! . . . Woe's me! Lost! . . . Lost for aye!

CURTAIN

ACT FIVE

The fir-clad glade seen in Act One.
TIME: *Between midnight and dawn.*
DISCOVERED: *Three* ELVES, *resting near the well.*

FIRST ELF. The flame glows bright!
SECOND ELF.   The wind of sacrifice—
The red, red wind—blows in the vale!
THIRD ELF   And lo,
The dark smoke from the pine-clad peak streams down
Into the gulf!
FIRST ELF.   And, in the gulf, white clouds
Lie thickly gathered! From the misty sea
The wond'ring herds lift up their drowsy heads,
Lowing, impatient, for their sheltered stalls!
SECOND ELF. A nightingale within the beechwood sang:
It sang and sobbed into the waning night—
Till, all a-quiver with responsive woe,
I sank upon the dewy grass and wept.
THIRD ELF. 'Tis strange! I lay upon a spider's web.
Between the blades of meadow-grass it hung,
All woven out of marvelous purple threads,
And softer than a royal shift it clung.
I lay, and rested, while the glistening dew
Flashed up at me from the green mead below:
And so, my heavy lids did gently droop,
Until at last I slept. When I awoke,
The light had faded in the distant west:
My bed had turned to grey. But, in the east,

Thick clouds went up, and up, that hid the moon,
While all the rocky ridge was covered o'er
With molten metal, glowing in the night.
And, in the bloody glare that downward streamed,
Methought—'twas strange—the fields did stir with life,
And whisp'rings, sighs, and voices low I heard
That filled the very air with wretchedness.
Ah, it was pitiful! . . . Then, quick, I hailed
A fire-fly, who his soft, green lamp had trimmed.
But on he flew. And so alone I lay,
Trembling with fear, and lost in wonderment.
Till, winged and gleaming as the dragon-fly,
The dearest, loveliest, of all the elves,
Who from afar his coming had proclaimed,
Rustled and fell into my waiting arms.
And, as we prattled in our cosy bed,
Warm tears were mingled with our kisses sweet,
And then he sighed, and sobbed, and pressed me tight,
Mourning for Balder . . . Balder, who was dead!

FIRST ELF (*rising*). The flame grows bright!

SECOND ELF (*rising*).   'Tis Balder's funeral pyre!

THIRD ELF. (*Who meanwhile has moved slowly to the edge of the wood.*)
Balder is dead! . . . I'm chill!
  (*She vanishes.*)

FIRST ELF.   A curse doth fall
Upon the land—as Balder's funeral pall!
  (*Fog drifts across the glade. When it clears away the* ELVES *have vanished.*)
  (*Enter* RAUTENDELEIN, *slowly and wearily descending from the hillside. She drags herself towards the well, halting to rest, sitting and rising again with an effort, on her way. When she speaks, her voice is faint and strange.*)

RAUTENDELEIN. Whither? . . . Ah, whither? . . . I sat till late,
While the gnomes ran wild in my hall of state.
They brought me a red, red cup to drain—
And I drank it down, in pain.
    For the wine I drank was blood!

      .   .   .   .   .

And, when I had drained the last red drop,
My heart in my bosom seemed to stop:
For a hand of iron had gripped the strings—
And still with a burning pain it wrings
    The heart that I long to cool!

      .   .   .   .   .

Then a crown on my wedding-board they laid—
All of rose-red coral and silver made.
As I set it upon my brow I sighed.
Woe's me! Now the Water-man's won his bride!
    And I'll cool my burning heart!

      .   .   .   .   .

Three apples fell into my lap last night,
Rose-red, and gold, and white—
Wedding-gifts from my water-sprite.
I ate the white apple, and white I grew:
I ate the gold apple, and rich I grew—
    And the red one last I ate!

      .   .   .   .   .

Pale, white, and rosy-red,
A maiden sat—and she was dead.
Now, Water-man, unbar thy gate—
I bring thee home thy dead, dead, mate.
Deep down in the cold, damp, darkness, see—
With the silver fishes I come to thee . . .
    Ah, my poor, burnt, aching, heart!
(*She descends slowly into the well.*)
(THE WOOD-SPRITE *enters from the wood, crosses to the well, and calls down.*)
THE WOOD-SPRITE. Hey! Holdrio! Old frog-king! Up with thee!
Hey! Holdrio! Thou web-foot wight bewitched!
Dost thou not hear me, monster? Art asleep?
I say, come up!—and though beside thee lay
Thy fairest water-maid, and plucked thy beard,
I'd still say, leave thy reedy bed and come!
Thou'lt not repent it: for, by cock and pie,
What I've to tell thee is worth many a night
Spent in the arms of thy most lovesick sprite.
THE NICKELMANN (*from below*). Brekekekex!
THE WOOD-SPRITE.   Up! Leave thy weedy pool!
THE NICKELMANN (*from below*). I have no time. Begone, thou chattering fool!
THE WOOD-SPRITE. What? What? Thou toad-i'-the-hole, thou hast no time
To spare from wallowing in thy mud and slime?
I say, I bring thee news. Didst thou not hear?
What I foretold's come true. I played the seer!
He's left her! . . . Now, an thou wilt but be spry,
Thou'lt haply catch thy wondrous butterfly!
A trifle jaded—ay, and something worn:
But, Lord, what care the Nickelmann and Faun?
Rare sport thou'lt find her, comrade, even now—
Ay, more than thou hadst bargained for, I'll vow.
THE NICKELMANN. (*Rising from the well and blinking slyly*). Forsooth! . . .
    He's tired of her, the minx! And so
Thou'dst have me hang upon her skirts? . . . No, no!
THE WOOD-SPRITE. What? . . . Hast thou wearied of this beauty, too?
Why, then—I would her whereabouts I knew!
THE NICKELMANN. Go hunt for her!
THE WOOD-SPRITE.   I've sought her, like a dog:
Above—below, through mirk, and mist, and fog.
I've climbed where never mountain-goat had been,
And every marmot far and near I've seen.

Each falcon, glede, and finch, and rat, and snake,
I've asked for news. But none could answer make.
Woodmen I passed—around a fire they slept—
From them I stole a brand, and upward crept:
Till, grasping in my hand the burning wood,
At last before the lonely forge I stood.
And now the smoke of sacrifice ascends!
Loud roar the flames—each rafter cracks and bends!
The power the Master boasted once is fled:
For ever and for aye, 'tis past and dead!
THE NICKELMANN. I know. I know. Thy news is old and stale.
Hast thou disturbed me with this idle tale?
Much more I'd tell thee—ay, who tolled the bell!
And how the clapper swung that rang the knell!
Hadst thou but seen, last night, as I did see,
What ne'er before had been, nor more shall be,
The hand of a dead woman, stark and cold,
Go groping for the bell that tossed and rolled.
And hadst thou heard the bell then make reply,
Peal upon peal send thundering to the sky—
Till, like the lioness that seeks her mate,
It thrilled the Master, even as the Voice of Fate!
I saw the woman—drowned. Her long, brown hair
Floated about her face: 'twas wan with care.
And alway, when her hand the bell had found,
The awful knell did loud, and louder, sound!
I'm old, and used to many a gruesome sight:
Yet horror seized me, and—I took to flight!
Hadst thou but seen, last night, what I have seen,
Thou wouldst not fret about thine elfin quean.
So, let her flit at will, from flower to flower:
I care not, I! Her charm has lost its power.
THE WOOD-SPRITE. Ods bodikins! I care, though, for the maid.
So—each to his own taste. I want the jade.
And once I hold her panting in these arms,
'Tis little I shall reck of dead alarms!
THE NICKELMANN. Quorax! Brekekekex! Oho! I see.
So that is still the flea that's biting thee?
Well—kill it, then. Go hunt her till thou'rt spent.
Yet, though a-hunting twice ten years thou went,
Thou shouldst not have her. 'Tis for me she sighs!
She has no liking for thy goaty eyes.
A hen-pecked Water-man, alack, I'm tied
By every whim and humor of my bride.
Now fare thee well. Thou'rt free, to come, or go:
But, as for me—'tis time I went below!
   (*He disappears in the well.*)
THE WOOD-SPRITE (*calling down the well*). So sure as all the stars in heaven
   do shine—

So sure as these stout shanks and horns are mine—
So sure as fishes swim and birds do fly—
A man-child in thy cradle soon shall lie!
Good-night. Sleep well! And now, be off to bed!
On! On! Through brush and brier! . . . The flea is dead!
  (THE WOOD-SPRITE *skips off.*)
  (OLD WITTIKIN *issues from the hut and takes down her shutters.*)
WITTIKIN. 'Twas time I rose. I sniff the morning air.
A pretty hurly there has been to-night.
  (*A cock crows.*)
Oho! I thought so. Kikereekikee!
No need to give thyself such pains for me—
Thou noisy rogue—as if we did not know
What's coming, ere such cocks as thou did crow.
Thy hen another golden egg has laid?
And soon the sun shall warm the mirky glade?
Ay. Crow thy loudest, gossip! Sing and sing!
The dawn draws near. So strut thy fill and sing.
Another day's at hand. But—here 'tis dark . . .
Will no mad jack-o'-lantern give me a spark? . . .
I'll need more light to do my work, I wis . . .
And, as I live, my carbuncle I miss.
  (*She fumbles in her pocket and produces a carbuncle.*)
Ah, here it is.
HEINRICH (*heard without*). Rautendelein!
WITTIKIN.   Ay, call her!
She'll answer thee, I wager, thou poor brawler!
HEINRICH (*without*). Rautendelein! I come. Dost thou not hear?
WITTIKIN. Thou'lt need to call her louder, man, I fear.
  (HEINRICH, *worn and weary, appears on the rocks above the hut. He is pale and in tatters. In his right hand he holds a heavy stone, ready to hurl it back into the depths.*)
HEINRICH. Come, if you dare! Be it priest, or be it barber,
Sexton, or schoolmaster—I care not who!
The first who dares another step to take,
Shall fall and headlong plunge into the gulf!
'Twas ye who drove my wife to death, not I!
Vile rabble, witless wretches, beggars, rogues—
Who weeks together mumble idle prayers
For a lost penny! Yet, so base are ye,
That, where ye can, God's everlasting love
Ye cheat of ducats! . . . Liars! Hypocrites!
Like rocks ye are heaped about your nether-land,
Ringing it round, as with a dam of stone,
Lest haply God's own waters, rushing in,
Should flood your arid Hell with Paradise.
When shall the great destroyer wreck your dam?
I am not he . . . Alas! I am not the man!
  (*He drops the stone and begins to ascend.*)

WITTIKIN. That way is barred. So halt! And climb no more.

HEINRICH. Woman, what burns up yonder?

WITTIKIN. Nay, I know not.
Some man there was, I've heard, who built a thing,
Half church, half royal castle. Now—he's gone!
And, since he's left it, up it goes in flame.
  (HEINRICH *makes a feeble effort to press upward.*)
Did I not tell thee, man, the road was barred?
He who would pass that way had need o' wings.
And thy wings have been broken.

HEINRICH. Ah, broken or no,
I tell thee, woman, I must reach the peak!
What flames up yonder is my work—all mine!
Dost understand me? . . . I am he who built it.
And all I was, and all I grew to be,
Was spent on it . . . I can . . . I can . . . no more!

WITTIKIN. (*Pause.*) Halt here a while. The roads are still pitch-dark.
There is a bench. Sit down and rest.

HEINRICH. I? . . . Rest? . . .
Though thou shouldst bid me sleep on silk and down,
That heap of ruins still would draw me on.
The kiss my mother—long she's joined the dust—
Did press years since upon my fevered brow,
Would bring no blessing to me now, no peace:
'Twould sting me like a wasp.

WITTIKIN. Ay, so it would!
Wait here a bit, man. I will bring thee wine.
I've still a sup or two.

HEINRICH. I must not wait.
Water! I thirst! I thirst!

WITTIKIN. Go, draw, and drink!
  (HEINRICH *moves to the well, draws, sits on the edge of the well, and drinks.
  A faint, sweet voice is heard from below, singing mournfully.*)

THE VOICE (*from below*). Heinrich, my sweetheart, I loved thee true.
  Now thou art come to my well to woo.
  Wilt thou not go?
  Love is all woe—
  Adieu! Adieu!

HEINRICH. Woman, what voice was that? Speak—answer me!
What called and sang to me in such sad tones?
It murmured, "Heinrich!" . . . from the depths it came . . .
And then it softly sighed, "Adieu! Adieu!"
Who art thou, woman? And what place is this?
Am I awaking from some dream? . . . These rocks,
Thy hut, thyself, I seem to know ye all!
Yet all are strange. Can that which me befell
Have no more substance than a peal that sounds,
And, having sounded, dies away in silence?
Woman, who art thou?

WITTIKIN. I? . . . And who art thou?

HEINRICH. Dost ask me that? . . . Yes! Who am I? God wot!
How often have I prayed to Heaven to tell me! . . .
Who am I, God! . . . But Heaven itself is mute.
Yet this I do know: whatsoe'er I be,
Hero or weakling, demi-god or beast—
I am the outcast child of the bright Sun—
That longs for home: all helpless now, and maimed,
A bundle of sorrow, weeping for the Light
That stretches out its radiant arms in vain,
And yearns for me! . . . What dost thou there?

WITTIKIN. Thou'lt learn that soon enough.

HEINRICH (*rising*). Nay, I'll begone!
Now, with thy bloody lamplight, show me a way
Will lead me onward, upward, to the heights!
Once I am there, where erst I Master stood.
Lonely I'll live—thenceforth a hermit be—
Who neither rules, nor serves.

WITTIKIN. I doubt it much!
What thou would'st seek up yonder is not that.

HEINRICH. How canst thou know?

WITTIKIN. We know what we do know.
They'd almost run thee down, my friend? . . . Ay, ay!
When life shines bright, like wolves ye men do act,
Rend and torture it. But, when death comes,
No bolder are ye than a flock of sheep,
That trembles at the wolf. Ay, ay, 'tis true!
The herds that lead ye are but sorry carles
Who with the hounds do hunt and loudly yelp:
They do not set their hounds to hunt the wolf:
Nay, nay: their sheep they drive into its jaws! . . .
Thou'rt not much better than the other herds.
Thy bright life thou has torn and spurned away.
And when death fronted thee, thou wast not bold.

HEINRICH. Ah, woman, list! . . . I know not how it came
That I did spurn and kill my clear bright life:
And, being a Master, did my task forsake,
Like a mere 'prentice, quaking at the sound
Of my own handiwork, the bell which I
Had blessed with speech. And yet 'tis true! Its voice
Rang out so loud from its great iron throat,
Waking the echoes of the topmost peaks,
That, as the threatening peal did rise and swell,
It shook my soul! . . . Yet I was still the Master!
Ere it had shattered me who moulded it,
With this same hand, that gave it form and life,
I should have crushed and ground it into atoms.

WITTIKIN. What's past, is past: what's done, is done, for aye.
Thou'lt never win up to thy heights, I trow.

This much I'll grant: thou wast a sturdy shoot,
And mighty—yet too weak. Though thou wast called,
Thou'st not been chosen! . . . Come. Sit down beside me.
HEINRICH. Woman! Farewell!
WITTIKIN. Come here, and sit thee down.
Strong—yet not strong enow!
Who lives, shall life pursue. But be thou sure,
Up yonder thou shalt find it nevermore.
HEINRICH. Then let me perish here, where now I stand!
WITTIKIN. Ay, so thou shalt. He who has flown so high,
Into the very Light, as thou hast flown,
Must perish, if he once fall back to Earth!
HEINRICH. I know it. I have reached my journey's end.
So be it.
WITTIKIN. Yes! Thou hast reached the end!
HEINRICH. Then tell me—
Thou who dost seem to me so strangely wise—
Am I to die and never more set eyes
On what, with bleeding feet, I still must seek?
Thou dost not answer me? . . . Must I go hence—
Leave my deep night, and pass to deepest darkness—
Missing the afterglow of that lost light?
Shall I not see her once . . . ?
WITTIKIN. Whom wouldst thou see?
HEINRICH. I would see her. Whom else? . . . Dost not know that?
WITTIKIN. Thou hast one wish! . . . It is thy last! . . . So—wish.
HEINRICH (quickly). I have wished!
WITTIKIN. Then thou shalt see her once again.
HEINRICH (rising and ecstatically). Ah, mother! . . . Why I name thee thus,
    I know not . . .
Art thou so mighty? . . . Canst thou do so much? . . .
Once I was ready for the end, as now:
Half hoping, as each feeble breath I drew,
That it might be the last. But then she came—
And healing, like the breeze in early Spring,
Rushed through my sickly frame: and I grew well . . .
All of a sudden, now I feel so light,
That I could soar up to the heights again.
WITTIKIN. Too late!
    (HEINRICH recoils in terror.)
Thy heavy burdens weigh thee down:
Thy dead ones are too mighty for thee. See!
I place three goblets on the table. So.
The first I fill with white wine. In the next,
Red wine I pour: the last I fill with yellow.
Now, shouldst thou drain the first, thy vanished power
Shall be restored to thee. Shouldst drink the second,
Once more thou shalt behold the spirit bright
Whom thou hast lost. But an thou dost drink both,

Thou must drain down the last.

(*She turns to enter the hut. On the threshold she halts and utters the next words with solemn emphasis.*)

I say thou must!

(*She goes into the hut.*)

(HEINRICH *has listened to the preceding speech like a man dazed. As* OLD WITTIKIN *leaves him, he rouses himself and sinks on a bench.*)

HEINRICH. Too late! . . . She said, "Too late!" . . . Now all is done!
O heart, that knowest all, as ne'er before:
Why dost thou question? . . . Messenger of Fate!
Thy fiat, as the axe, doth sharply fall,
Cutting the strand of life! . . . It is the end!
What's left is respite! . . . But I'll profit by 't.
Chill blows the wind from the abyss. The day
That yonder gleam so faintly doth forerun,
Piercing the sullen clouds with pale white shafts,
I shall not see. So many days I have lived:
Yet this one day I shall not live to see!

(*He raises the first goblet.*)

Come then, thou goblet, ere the horror come!
A dark drop glistens at the bottom. One!
A last one . . . Why, thou crone, hadst thou no more?
So be it! (*He drinks.*) And now to thee, thou second cup!

(*He raises the second goblet.*)

It was for thee that I did drain the first.
And, wert thou missing, thou delicious draught,
Whose fragrance tempts to madness, the carouse
Whereunto God has bid us in this world
Were all too poor, meseems—unworthy quite,
Of thee, who dost the festal board so honor.
Now I do thank thee—thus!

(*He drinks.*)

The drink is good.

(*A murmur as of æolian harps floats on the air while he drinks.*)

(RAUTENDELEIN *rises slowly from the well. She looks weary and sad. She sits on the edge of the well, combing her long flowing locks. Moonlight.* RAUTENDELEIN *is pale. She sings into vacancy. Her voice is faint.*)

RAUTENDELEIN. All, all alone, in the pale moon-shine,
  I comb my golden hair,
    Fair, fairest Rautendelein!
  The mists are rising, the birds take flight,
  The fires burn low in the weary night . . .

THE NICKELMANN (*from below*). Rautendelein!

RAUTENDELEIN.   I'm coming!

THE NICKELMANN (*from below*).   Come at once!

RAUTENDELEIN. Woe, woe, is me!
  So tight I am clad,
  A maid o' the well, bewitched and so sad!

THE NICKELMANN (*from below*). Rautendelein!

RAUTENDELEIN.   I'm coming!
THE NICKELMANN (*from below*).   Come thou now!
RAUTENDELEIN. I comb my hair in the moonlight clear,
And think of the sweetheart who loved me dear.
The blue-bells all are ringing.
Ring they of joy? Ring they of pain?
Blessing and bane—
Answers the song they are singing!
Now down I go, to my weedy well—
No more I may wait:
I must join my mate—
Farewell! Farewell!
(*She prepares to descend.*)
Who calls so softly?
HEINRICH.   I.
RAUTENDELEIN.   Who'rt thou?
HEINRICH.   Why—I.
Do but come nearer—ah, why wouldst thou fly?
RAUTENDELEIN. I dare not come! . . . I know thee not. Away!
For him who speaks to me, I am doomed to slay.
HEINRICH. Why torture me? Come. Lay thy hand in mine,
And thou shalt know me.
RAUTENDELEIN.   I have never known thee.
HEINRICH. Thou know'st me not?
RAUTENDELEIN.   No!
HEINRICH.   Thou hast never seen me?
RAUTENDELEIN. I cannot tell.
HEINRICH.   Then may God cast me off!
I never kissed thee till thy lips complained?
RAUTENDELEIN. Never.
HEINRICH.   Thou'st never pressed thy lips to mine?
THE NICKELMANN (*from below*). Rautendelein!
RAUTENDELEIN.   I'm coming!
THE NICKELMANN.   Come. I wait!
HEINRICH. Who called to thee?
RAUTENDELEIN.   The Water-man—my mate!
HEINRICH. Thou seest my agony—the pain and strife
That rend my soul, and eat away my life!
Ah, torture me no longer. Set me free!
RAUTENDELEIN. Then, as thou wilt. But how?
HEINRICH.   Come close to me!
RAUTENDELEIN. I cannot come.
HEINRICH.   Thou canst not?
RAUTENDELEIN.   No. I am bound.
HEINRICH. By what?
RAUTENDELEIN (*retreating*). I must begone to join the round,
A merry dance—and though my foot be sore,
Soon, as I dancing go, it burns no more.
Farewell! Farewell!

HEINRICH.   Where art thou? Stay, ah stay!

RAUTENDELEIN (*disappearing behind the well*). Lost, lost, for ever!

HEINRICH.   The goblet—quick, I say!

There . . there . . the goblet! . . . Magda? Thou? . . So pale! . . .

Give me the cup. Who brings it, I will hail

My truest friend.

RAUTENDELEIN (*reappearing*). I bring it.

HEINRICH.   Be thou blessed.

RAUTENDELEIN. Yes. I will do it. Leave the dead to rest!

   (*She gives* HEINRICH *the goblet.*)

HEINRICH. I feel thee near me, thou dear heart of mine!

RAUTENDELEIN (*retreating*). Farewell! Farewell! I never can be thine!

Once I was thy true love—in May, in May—

Now all is past, for aye! . . .

HEINRICH.   For aye!

RAUTENDELEIN.   For aye!

Who sang thee soft to sleep with lullabies?

Who woke thee with enchanting melodies?

HEINRICH. Who, who—but thou?

RAUTENDELEIN.   Who am I?

HEINRICH.   Rautendelein!

RAUTENDELEIN. Who poured herself into thy veins, as wine?

Whom didst thou drive into the well to pine?

HEINRICH. Thee, surely thee!

RAUTENDELEIN.   Who am I?

HEINRICH.   Rautendelein!

RAUTENDELEIN. Farewell! Farewell!

   (*He drinks.*)

HEINRICH.   Nay: lead me gently down.

Now comes the night—the night that all would flee.

   (RAUTENDELEIN *hastens to him, and clasps him about the knees.*)

RAUTENDELEIN (*exultingly*). The Sun is coming!

HEINRICH.   The Sun!

RAUTENDELEIN (*half sobbing, half rejoicing*).   Ah, Heinrich!

HEINRICH.   Thanks!

RAUTENDELEIN. (*Embracing* HEINRICH, *she presses her lips to his, and then
   gently lays him down as he dies.*) Heinrich!

HEINRICH (*ecstatically*).   I hear them! 'Tis the Sun-bells' song!

The Sun . . the Sun . . draws near! . . The Night is . . . long!

   (*Dawn breaks. He dies.*)

Maurice Maeterlinck

INTERIOR

CHARACTERS

In the Garden—

THE OLD MAN

THE STRANGER

MARTHA } Granddaughters of
MARY   } the Old Man

A PEASANT

THE CROWD

In the House—

THE FATHER

THE MOTHER

THE TWO DAUGHTERS } Silent
                   } personages
THE CHILD

The interval that elapses between the occurrence of a disaster and the breaking of the news to the bereaved is one full of tragedy; and here the pathetic ignorance of the drowned girl's family and the painful knowledge of the reluctant bearers of the evil tidings provide material for a touching little play—slight material to all appearance, but in the hands of M. Maeterlinck sufficient for the display of a wealth of kindly wisdom and sympathetic knowledge of human nature.

An old garden planted with willows. At the back, a house, with three of the ground-floor windows lighted up. Through them a family is pretty distinctly visible, gathered for the evening round the lamp. The FATHER is seated at the chimney corner. The MOTHER, resting one elbow on the table, is gazing into vacancy. Two young girls, dressed in white, sit at their embroidery, dreaming and smiling in the tranquillity of the room. A child is asleep, his head resting on his mother's left arm. When one of them rises, walks, or makes a gesture, the movements appear grave, slow, apart, and as though spiritualized by the distance, the light, and the transparent film of the windowpanes.

THE OLD MAN and THE STRANGER enter the garden cautiously.

THE OLD MAN. Here we are in the part of the garden that lies behind the house. They never come here. The doors are on the other side. They are closed and the shutters shut. But there are no shutters on this side of the house, and I saw the light . . . Yes, they are still sitting up in the lamplight. It is well that they have not heard us; the mother or the girls would perhaps have come out, and then what should we have done?

THE STRANGER. What are we going to do?

THE OLD MAN. I want first to see if they are all in the room. Yes, I see the father seated at the chimney corner. He is doing nothing, his hands resting on his knees. The mother is leaning her elbow on the table . . .

THE STRANGER. She is looking at us.

THE OLD MAN. No, she is looking at nothing; her eyes are fixed. She cannot see us; we are in the shadow of the great trees. But do not go any nearer . . . There, too, are the dead girl's two sisters; they are embroidering slowly. And the little child has fallen asleep. It is nine on the clock in the corner . . . They divine no evil, and they do not speak.

THE STRANGER. If we were to attract the father's attention, and make some sign to him? He has turned his head this way. Shall I knock at one of the windows? One of them will have to hear of it before the others . . .

THE OLD MAN. I do not know which to choose . . . We must be very careful. The father is old and ailing —the mother too—and the sisters are too young . . . And they all loved her as they will never love again. I have never seen a happier household . . . No, no! do not go up to the window; that would be the worst thing we could do. It is better that we should tell them of it as simply as we can, as though it were a commonplace occurrence; and we must not appear too sad, else they will feel that their sorrow must exceed ours, and they will not know what to do . . . Let us go round to the other side of the garden. We will knock at the door, and go in as if nothing had happened. I will go in first: they will not be surprised to see me; I sometimes look in of an evening, to bring them some flowers or fruit, and to pass an hour or two with them.

THE STRANGER. Why do you want me to go with you? Go alone; I will wait until you call me. They have never seen me—I am only a passerby, a stranger . . .

THE OLD MAN. It is better that I should not be alone. A misfortune announced by a single voice seems more definite and crushing. I thought of that as I came along . . . If I go in alone, I shall have to speak at the very first moment; they will know all in a few words; I shall have nothing more to say; and I dread the silence which follows the last words that tell of a misfortune. It is then that the heart is torn. If we enter together, I shall go roundabout to work; I shall tell them, for example: "They found her thus, or thus . . . She was floating on the stream, and her hands were clasped . . ."

THE STRANGER. Her hands were not clasped; her arms were floating at her sides.

THE OLD MAN. You see, in spite of ourselves we begin to talk—and the misfortune is shrouded in its details. Otherwise, if I go in alone, I know them well enough to be sure that the very first words would produce a terrible effect, and God knows what would happen. But if we speak to them in turns, they will listen to us, and will forget to look the evil tidings in the face. Do not forget that the mother will be there, and that her life hangs by a thread . . . It is well that the first wave of sorrow should waste its strength in unnecessary words. It is wisest to let people gather round the unfortunate and talk as they will. Even the most indifferent carry off, without knowing it, some portion of the sorrow. It is dispersed without effort and without noise, like air or light . . .

THE STRANGER. Your clothes are

soaked and are dripping on the flag-stones.

THE OLD MAN. It is only the skirt of my mantle that has trailed a little in the water. You seem to be cold. Your coat is all muddy . . . I did not notice it on the way, it was so dark.

THE STRANGER. I went into the water up to my waist.

THE OLD MAN. Had you found her long when I came up?

THE STRANGER. Only a few moments. I was going towards the village; it was already late, and the dusk was falling on the river bank. I was walking along with my eyes fixed on the river, because it was lighter than the road, when I saw something strange close by a tuft of reeds . . . I drew nearer, and I saw her hair, which had floated up almost into a circle round her head, and was swaying hither and thither with the current . . . (*In the room the two young girls turn their heads towards the window.*)

THE OLD MAN. Did you see her two sisters' hair trembling on their shoulders?

THE STRANGER. They turned their heads in our direction—they simply turned their heads. Perhaps I was speaking too loudly. (*The two girls resume their former position.*) They have turned away again already . . . I went into the water up to my waist, and then I managed to grasp her hand and easily drew her to the bank. She was as beautiful as her sisters . . .

THE OLD MAN. I think she was more beautiful . . . I do not know why I have lost all my courage . . .

THE STRANGER. What courage do you mean? We did all that man could do. She had been dead for more than an hour.

THE OLD MAN. She was living this morning! I met her coming out of church. She told me that she was going away; she was going to see her grandmother on the other side of the river in which you found her. She did not know when I should see her again . . . She seemed to be on the point of asking me something; then I suppose she did not dare, and she left me abruptly. But now that I think of it—and I noticed nothing at the time!—she smiled as people smile who want to be silent, or who fear that they will not be understood . . . Even hope seemed like a pain to her; her eyes were veiled, and she scarcely looked at me.

THE STRANGER. Some peasants told me that they saw her wandering all the afternoon on the bank. They thought she was looking for flowers . . . It is possible that her death . . .

THE OLD MAN. No one can tell . . . What can any one know? She was perhaps one of those who shrink from speech, and everyone bears in his breast more than one reason for ceasing to live. You cannot see into the soul as you see into that room. They are all like that—they say nothing but trivial things, and no one dreams that there is aught amiss. You live for months by the side of one who is no longer of this world, and whose soul cannot stoop to it; you answer her unthinkingly; and you see what happens. They look like lifeless puppets, and all the time so many things are passing in their souls. They do not themselves know what they are. She might have lived as the others live. She might have said to the day of her death: "Sir, or Madam, it will rain this morning," or, "We are going to lunch; we shall be thirteen at table," or "The fruit is not yet ripe." They speak smilingly of the flowers that have fallen, and they weep in the darkness. An angel from heaven would not see what ought to be seen; and men understand nothing until after all is over . . . Yesterday evening she was there, sitting in the lamplight like her sisters; and you would not see them now as they ought to be seen if this had not happened . . . I seem to see her for the first time . . . Something new must come into our ordinary life before we can understand it. They are at your side day and night; and you do not really see them until the moment when they depart forever. And yet, what a strange little soul she must have had —what a poor little, artless, unfathomable soul she must have had—to have said what she must have said, and done what she must have done!

THE STRANGER. See, they are smiling in the silence of the room . . .

THE OLD MAN. They are not at all anxious—they did not expect her this evening.

THE STRANGER. They sit motionless and smiling. But see, the father puts his fingers to his lips . . .

THE OLD MAN. He points to the child asleep on its mother's breast . . .

THE STRANGER. She dares not raise her head for fear of disturbing it . . .

THE OLD MAN. They are not sewing any more. There is a dead silence . . .

THE STRANGER. They have let fall their skein of white silk . . .

THE OLD MAN. They are looking at the child . . .

THE STRANGER. They do not know that others are looking at them . . .

THE OLD MAN. We, too, are watched . . .

THE STRANGER. They have raised their eyes . . .

THE OLD MAN. And yet they can see nothing . . .

THE STRANGER. They seem to be happy, and yet there is something— I cannot tell what . . .

THE OLD MAN. They think themselves beyond the reach of danger. They have closed the doors, and the windows are barred with iron. They have strengthened the walls of the old house; they have shot the bolts of the three oaken doors. They have foreseen everything that can be foreseen . . .

THE STRANGER. Sooner or later we must tell them. Some one might come in and blurt it out abruptly. There was a crowd of peasants in the meadow where we left the dead girl —if one of them were to come and knock at the door . . .

THE OLD MAN. Martha and Mary are watching the little body. The peasants were going to make a litter of branches, and I told my eldest granddaughter to hurry on and let us know the moment they made a start. Let us wait till she comes; she will go with me. . . . I wish we had not been able to watch them in this way. I thought there was nothing to do but to knock at the door, to enter quite simply, and to tell all in a few phrases. . . . But I have watched them too long, living in the lamplight. . . . (*Enter* MARY.)

MARY. They are coming, grandfather.

THE OLD MAN. Is that you? Where are they?

MARY. They are at the foot of the last slope.

THE OLD MAN. They are coming silently.

MARY. I told them to pray in a low voice. Martha is with them.

THE OLD MAN. Are there many of them?

MARY. The whole village is around the bier. They had brought lanterns; I bade them put them out.

THE OLD MAN. What way are they coming?

MARY. They are coming by the little path. They are moving slowly.

THE OLD MAN. It is time . . .

MARY. Have you told them, grandfather?

THE OLD MAN. You can see that we have told them nothing. There they are, still sitting in the lamplight. Look, my child, look: you will see what life is . . .

MARY. Oh! how peaceful they seem! I feel as though I were seeing them in a dream.

THE STRANGER. Look there—I saw the two sisters give a start.

THE OLD MAN. They are rising . . .

THE STRANGER. I believe they are coming to the windows.

(*At this moment one of the two sisters comes up to the first window, the other to the third; and resting their hands against the panes they stand gazing into the darkness.*)

THE OLD MAN. No one comes to the middle window.

MARY. They are looking out; they are listening . . .

THE OLD MAN. The elder is smiling at what she does not see.

THE STRANGER. The eyes of the second are full of fear.

THE OLD MAN. Take care: who knows how far the soul may extend around the body. . . . (*A long silence.* MARY *nestles close to* THE OLD MAN's *breast and kisses him.*)

MARY. Grandfather!

THE OLD MAN. Do not weep, my child; our turn will come. (*A pause.*)

THE STRANGER. They are looking long. . . .

THE OLD MAN. Poor things, they would see nothing though they looked for a hundred thousand years—the night is too dark. They are looking this way; and it is from the other side that misfortune is coming.

THE STRANGER. It is well that they are looking this way. Something, I do not know what, is approaching by way of the meadows.

MARY. I think it is the crowd; they are too far off for us to see clearly.

THE STRANGER. They are following the windings of the path—there they come in sight again on that moonlit slope.

MARY. Oh! how many they seem to be. Even when I left, people were coming up from the outskirts of the town. They are taking a very roundabout way. . . .

THE OLD MAN. They will arrive at last, none the less. I see them, too—they are crossing the meadows—they look so small that one can scarcely distinguish them among the herbage. You might think them children playing in the moonlight; if the girls saw them, they would not understand. Turn their backs to it as they may, misfortune is approaching step by step, and has been looming larger for more than two hours past. They cannot bid it stay; and those who are bringing it are powerless to stop it. It has mastered them, too, and they must needs serve it. It knows its goal, and it takes its course. It is unwearying, and it has but one idea. They have to lend it their strength. They are sad, but they draw nearer. Their hearts are full of pity, but they must advance. . . .

MARY. The elder has ceased to smile, grandfather.

THE STRANGER. They are leaving the windows. . . .

MARY. They are kissing their mother. . . .

THE STRANGER. The elder is stroking the child's curls without wakening it.

MARY. Ah! the father wants them to kiss him, too. . . .

THE STRANGER. Now there is silence. . . .

MARY. They have returned to their mother's side.

THE STRANGER. And the father keeps his eyes fixed on the great pendulum of the clock . . .

MARY. They seem to be praying without knowing what they do. . . .

THE STRANGER. They seem to be listening to their own souls. . . . (*A pause.*)

MARY. Grandfather, do not tell them this evening!

THE OLD MAN. You see, you are losing courage, too. I knew you ought not to look at them. I am nearly eighty-three years old, and this is the first time that the reality of life has come home to me. I do not know why all they do appears to me so strange and solemn. There they sit awaiting the night, simply, under their lamp, as we should under our own; and yet I seem to see them from the altitude of another world, because I know a little fact which as yet they do not know . . . Is it so, my children? Tell me, why are you, too, pale? Perhaps there is something else that we cannot put in words, and that makes us weep? I did not know that there was anything so sad in life, or that it could strike such terror to those who look on at it. And even if nothing had happened, it would frighten me to see them sit there so peacefully. They have too much confidence in this world. There they sit, separated from the enemy by only a few poor panes of glass. They think that nothing will happen because they have closed their doors, and they do not know that it is in the soul that things always happen, and that the world does not end at their house-door. They are so secure of their little life, and do not dream that so many others know more of it than they, and that I, poor old man, at two steps from

their door, hold all their little happiness, like a wounded bird, in the hollow of my old hands, and dare not open them . . .

MARY. Have pity on them, grandfather. . . .

THE OLD MAN. We have pity on them, my child, but no one has pity on us.

MARY. Tell them to-morrow, grandfather; tell them when it is light, then they will not be so sad.

THE OLD MAN. Perhaps you are right, my child. . . . It would be better to leave all this in the night. And the daylight is sweet to sorrow. . . . But what would they say to us to-morrow? Misfortune makes people jealous; those upon whom it has fallen want to know of it before strangers—they do not like to leave it in unknown hands. We should seem to have robbed them of something.

THE STRANGER. Besides, it is too late now; already I can hear the murmur of prayers.

MARY. They are here—they are passing behind the hedges. (*Enter* MARTHA.)

MARTHA. Here I am. I have guided them hither—I told them to wait in the road. (*Cries of children are heard.*) Ah! the children are still crying. I forbade them to come, but they want to see, too, and the mothers would not obey me. I will go and tell them—no, they have stopped crying. Is everything ready? I have brought the little ring that was found upon her. I have some fruit, too, for the child. I laid her to rest myself upon the bier. She looks as though she were sleeping. I had a great deal of trouble with her hair—I could not arrange it properly. I made them gather marguerites—it is a pity there were no other flowers. What are you doing here? Why are you not with them? (*She looks in at the windows.*) They are not weeping! They—you have not told them!

THE OLD MAN. Martha, Martha, there is too much life in your soul; you cannot understand. . . .

MARTHA. Why should I not understand? (*After a silence, and in a tone of grave reproach.*) You really ought not to have done that, grandfather. . . .

THE OLD MAN. Martha, you do not know. . . .

MARTHA. I will go and tell them.

THE OLD MAN. Remain here, my child, and look for a moment.

MARTHA. Oh, how I pity them! They must wait no longer. . . .

THE OLD MAN. Why not?

MARTHA. I do not know, but it is not possible!

THE OLD MAN. Come here, my child. . . .

MARTHA. How patient they are!

THE OLD MAN. Come here, my child. . . .

MARTHA (*turning*). Where are you, grandfather? I am so unhappy, I cannot see you any more. I do not myself know now what to do. . . .

THE OLD MAN. Do not look any more; until they know all. . . .

MARTHA. I want to go with you. . . .

THE OLD MAN. No, Martha, stay here. Sit beside your sister on this old stone bench against the wall of the house, and do not look. You are too young, you would never be able to forget it. You cannot know what a face looks like at the moment when Death is passing into its eyes. Perhaps they will cry out, too . . . Do not turn round. Perhaps there will be no sound at all. Above all things, if there is no sound, be sure you do not turn and look. One can never foresee the course that sorrow will take. A few little sobs wrung from

the depths, and generally that is all. I do not know myself what I shall do when I hear them—they do not belong to this life. Kiss me, my child, before I go. (*The murmur of prayers has gradually drawn nearer. A portion of the crowd forces its way into the garden. There is a sound of deadened footfalls and of whispering.*)

THE STRANGER (*to the crowd*). Stop here—do not go near the window. Where is she?

A PEASANT. Who?

THE STRANGER. The others—the bearers.

A PEASANT. They are coming by the avenue that leads up to the door. (THE OLD MAN *goes out.* MARTHA *and* MARY *have seated themselves on the bench, their backs to the windows. Low murmurings are heard among the crowd.*)

THE STRANGER. Hush! Do not speak. (*In the room the taller of the two sisters rises, goes to the door, and shoots the bolts.*)

MARTHA. She is opening the door!

THE STRANGER. On the contrary, she is fastening it. (*A pause.*)

MARTHA. Grandfather has not come in?

THE STRANGER. No. She takes her seat again at her mother's side. The others do not move, and the child is still sleeping. (*A pause.*)

MARTHA. My little sister, give me your hands.

MARY. Martha! (*They embrace and kiss each other.*)

THE STRANGER. He must have knocked—they have all raised their heads at the same time—they are looking at each other.

MARTHA. Oh! oh! my poor little sister! I can scarcely help crying out, too. (*She smothers her sobs on her sister's shoulder.*)

THE STRANGER. He must have

knocked again. The father is looking at the clock. He rises. . . .

MARTHA. Sister, sister, I must go in too—they cannot be left alone.

MARY. Martha, Martha! (*She holds her back.*)

THE STRANGER. The father is at the door—he is drawing the bolts—he is opening it cautiously.

MARTHA. Oh!—you do not see the . . .

THE STRANGER. What?

MARTHA. The bearers . . .

THE STRANGER. He has only opened it a very little. I see nothing but a corner of the lawn and the fountain. He keeps his hand on the door—he takes a step back—he seems to be saying, "Ah, it is you!" He raises his arms. He carefully closes the door again. Your grandfather has entered the room . . . (*The crowd has come up to the window.* MARTHA *and* MARY *half rise from their seat, then rise altogether and follow the rest towards the windows, pressing close to each other.* THE OLD MAN *is seen advancing into the room. The two* SISTERS *rise; the* MOTHER *also rises, and carefully settles the* CHILD *in the armchair which she has left, so that from outside the little one can be seen sleeping, his head a little bent forward, in the middle of the room. The* MOTHER *advances to meet* THE OLD MAN, *and holds out her hand to him, but draws it back again before he has had time to take it. One of the girls wants to take off the visitor's mantle, and the other pushes forward an armchair for him. But* THE OLD MAN *makes a little gesture of refusal. The* FATHER *smiles with an air of astonishment.* THE OLD MAN *looks toward the windows.*)

THE STRANGER. He dares not tell them. He is looking towards us. (*Murmurs in the crowd.*)

THE STRANGER. Hush! (THE OLD MAN, *seeing faces at the windows, quickly averts his eyes. As one of the girls is still offering him the armchair, he at last sits down and passes his right hand several times over his forehead.*)

THE STRANGER. He is sitting down. . . . (*The others who are in the room also sit down, while the* FATHER *seems to be speaking volubly. At last* THE OLD MAN *opens his mouth, and the sound of his voice seems to arouse their attention. But the* FATHER *interrupts him.* THE OLD MAN *begins to speak again, and little by little the others grow tense with apprehension. All of a sudden the* MOTHER *starts and rises.*)

MARTHA. Oh! the mother begins to understand! (*She turns away and hides her face in her hands. Renewed murmurs among the crowd. They elbow each other. Children cry to be lifted up, so that they may see too. Most of the mothers do as they wish.*)

THE STRANGER. Hush! he has not told them yet. . . . (*The* MOTHER *is seen to be questioning* THE OLD MAN *with anxiety. He says a few more words; then, suddenly, all the others rise, too, and seem to question him. Then he slowly makes an affirmative movement of his head.*)

THE STRANGER. He has told them—he has told them all at once!

VOICES IN THE CROWD. He has told them! he has told them!

THE STRANGER. I can hear nothing. . . . (THE OLD MAN *also rises, and, without turning, makes a gesture indicating the door, which is behind him. The* MOTHER, *the* FATHER, *and the two* DAUGHTERS *rush to this door, which the* FATHER *has difficulty in opening.* THE OLD MAN *tries to prevent the* MOTHER *from going out.*)

VOICES IN THE CROWD. They are going out! they are going out! (*Con-*

fusion among the crowd in the gar-
den. All hurry to the other side of
the house and disappear, except THE
STRANGER, *who remains at the win-*
dows. In the room, the folding door
is at last thrown wide open; all go
out at the same time. Beyond can be
seen the starry sky, the lawn and the

fountain in the moonlight; while, left
alone in the middle of the room, the
CHILD *continues to sleep peacefully*
in the armchair. A pause.)

THE STRANGER. The child has not
wakened! (*He also goes out.*)

CURTAIN

Paul Heyse

L'ARRABIATA

THE DAY had scarcely dawned. Over Vesuvius hung one broad gray stripe
of mist, stretching across as far as Naples, and darkening all the small
towns along the coast. The sea lay calm. Along the shore of the narrow
creek that lies beneath the Sorrento cliffs, fishermen and their wives were
at work already, some with giant cables drawing their boats to land, with
the nets that had been cast the night before, while others were rigging their
craft, trimming the sails, or fetching out oars and masts from the great grated
vaults that have been built deep into the rocks for shelter to the tackle overnight. Nowhere an idle hand; even the very aged, who had long given up
going to sea, fell into the long chain of those who were hauling in the nets.
Here and there, on some flat housetop, an old woman stood and spun, or
busied herself about her grandchildren, whom their mother had left to help
her husband.

"Do you see, Rachela? yonder is our padre curato," said one to a little
thing of ten, who brandished a small spindle by her side; "Antonio is to
row him over to Capri Madre Santissima! but the reverend signore's eyes
are dull with sleep!" and she waved her hand to a benevolent-looking little
priest, who was settling himself in the boat, and spreading out upon the
bench his carefully tucked-up skirts.

The men upon the quay had dropped their work to see their pastor off,
who bowed and nodded kindly, right and left.

"What for must he go to Capri, granny?" asked the child. "Have the
people there no priest of their own, that they must borrow ours?"

"Silly thing!" returned the granny. "Priests they have in plenty—and the
most beautiful of churches, and a hermit too, which is more than we have.
But there lives a great signora, who once lived here; she was so very ill!
Many's the time our padre had to go and take the Most Holy to her, when

they thought she could not live the night. But with the Blessed Virgin's help she got strong and well, and was able to bathe every day in the sea. When she went away, she left a fine heap of ducats behind her for our church, and for the poor; and she would not go, they say, until our padre promised to go and see her over there, that she might confess to him as before. It is quite wonderful, the store she lays by him! Indeed, and we have cause to bless ourselves for having a curato who has gifts enough for an archbishop, and is in such request with all the great folks. The Madonna be with him!" she cried, and waved her hand again, as the boat was about to put from shore.

"Are we to have fair weather, my son?" inquired the little priest, with an anxious look toward Naples.

"The sun is not yet up," the young man answered; "when he comes, he will easily do for that small trifle of mist."

"Off with you, then! that we may arrive before the heat."

Antonio was just reaching for his long oar to shove away the boat, when suddenly he paused, and fixed his eyes upon the summit of the steep path that leads down from Sorrento to the water. A tall and slender girlish figure had become visible upon the heights, and was now hastily stepping down the stones, waving her handkerchief. She had a small bundle under her arm, and her dress was mean and poor. Yet she had a distinguished if somewhat savage way of throwing back her head, and the dark tress wreathed around it was like a diadem.

"What have we to wait for?" inquired the curato.

"There is someone coming who wants to go to Capri—with your permission, padre. We shall not go a whit the slower. It is a slight young thing, but just eighteen."

At that moment the young girl appeared from behind the wall that bounds the winding path.

"Laurella!" cried the priest. "And what has she to do in Capri?"

Antonio shrugged his shoulders. She came up with hasty steps, her eyes fixed straight before her.

"Ha! l'Arrabiata! good-morning!" shouted one or two of the young boatmen. But for the curato's presence, they might have added more; the look of mute defiance with which the young girl received their welcome appeared to tempt the more mischievous among them.

"Good-day, Laurella!" now said the priest. "How are you? Are you coming with us to Capri?"

"If I may, padre."

"Ask Antonio there; the boat is his. Every man is master of his own, I say, as God is master of us all."

"There is half a carlino, if I may go for that?" said Laurella, without looking at the young boatman.

"You need it more than I," he muttered, and pushed aside some orange-baskets to make room: he was to sell the oranges in Capri, which little isle of rocks has never been able to grow enough for all its visitors.

"I do not choose to go for nothing," said the girl, with a slight frown of her dark eyebrows.

"Come, child," said the priest; "he is a good lad, and had rather not enrich himself with that little morsel of your poverty. Come now, and step in," and he stretched out his hand to help her, "and sit you down by me. See, now, he has spread his jacket for you, that you may sit the softer. Young folks are all alike; for one little maiden of eighteen they will do more than for ten of us reverend fathers. Nay, no excuse, Tonino. It is the Lord's own doing, that like and like should hold together."

Meantime Laurella had stepped in, and seated herself beside the padre, first putting away Antonio's jacket without a word. The young fellow let it lie, and, muttering between his teeth, he gave one vigorous push against the pier, and the little boat flew out into the open bay.

"What are you carrying there in that little bundle?" inquired the padre, as they were floating on over a calm sea, now just beginning to be lighted up with the earliest rays of the rising sun.

"Silk, thread, and a loaf, padre. The silk is to be sold at Anacapri, to a woman who makes ribbons, and the thread to another."

"Spun by yourself?"

"Yes, sir."

"You once learned to weave ribbons yourself, if I remember right?"

"I did, sir; but mother has been much worse, and I cannot stay so long from home; and a loom to ourselves we are not rich enough to buy."

"Worse, is she? Ah! dear, dear! when I was with´you last, at Easter, she was up."

"The spring is always her worst time. Ever since those last great storms, and the earthquakes she has been forced to keep her bed from pain."

"Pray, my child. Never slacken your prayers and petitions that the Blessed Virgin may intercede for you; and be industrious and good, that your prayers may find a hearing."

After a pause: "When you were coming toward the shore, I heard them calling after you. 'Good-morning, l'Arrabiata!' they said. What made them call you so? It is not a nice name for a young Christian maiden, who should be meek and mild."

The young girl's brown face glowed all over, while her eyes flashed fire.

"They always mock me so, because I do not dance and sing, and stand about to chatter, as other girls do. I might be left in peace, I think; I do *them* no harm."

"Nay, but you might be civil. Let others dance and sing, on whom this life sits lighter; but a kind word now and then is seemly even from the most afflicted."

Her dark eyes fell, and she drew her eyebrows closer over them, as if she would have hidden them.

They went on a while in silence. The sun now stood resplendent above the mountain chain; only the tip of Mount Vesuvius towered beyond the group of clouds that had gathered about its base; and on the Sorrento plains the houses were gleaming white from the dark green of their orange-gardens.

"Have you heard no more of that painter, Laurella?" asked the curato— "that Neapolitan, who wished so much to marry you?" She shook her head. "He came to make a picture of you. Why would you not let him?"

"What did he want it for? There are handsomer girls than I. Who knows what he would have done with it? He might have bewitched me with it, or hurt my soul, or even killed me, mother says."

"Never believe such sinful things!" said the little curato very earnestly. "Are not you ever in God's keeping, without whose will not one hair of your head can fall? and is one poor mortal with an image in his hand to prevail against the Lord? Besides, you might have seen that he was fond of you; else why should he want to marry you?"

She said nothing.

"And wherefore did you refuse him? He was an honest man, they say, and comely; and he would have kept you and your mother far better than you ever can yourself, for all your spinning and silk-winding."

"We are so poor!" she said passionately; "and mother has been ill so long, we should have become a burden to him. And then I never should have done for a signora. When his friends came to see him, he would only have been ashamed of me."

"How can you say so? I tell you the man was good and kind; he would even have been willing to settle in Sorrento. It will not be so easy to find another, sent straight from heaven to be the saving of you, as this man, indeed, appeared to be."

"I want no husband—I never shall," she said, very stubbornly, half to herself.

"Is this a vow? or do you mean to be a nun?"

She shook her head.

"The people are not so wrong who call you wilful, although the name they give you is not kind. Have you ever considered that you stand alone in the world, and that your perverseness must make your sick mother's illness worse to bear, her life more bitter? And what sound reason can you have to give for rejecting an honest hand, stretched out to help you and your mother? Answer me, Laurella."

"I have a reason," she said reluctantly, and speaking low; "but it is one I cannot give."

"Not give! not give to me? not to your confessor, whom you surely know to be your friend—or is he not?"

Laurella nodded.

"Then, child, unburden your heart. If your reason be a good one, I shall be the very first to uphold you in it. Only you are young, and know so little of the world. A time may come when you will find cause to regret a chance of happiness thrown away for some foolish fancy now."

Shyly she threw a furtive glance over to the other end of the boat, where the young boatman sat, rowing fast. His woolen cap was pulled deep down over his eyes; he was gazing far across the water, with averted head, sunk, as it appeared, in his own meditations.

The priest observed her look, and bent his ear down closer.

"You did not know my father?" she whispered, while a dark look gathered in her eyes.

"Your father, child! Why, your father died when you were ten years old. What can your father (Heaven rest his soul in paradise!) have to do with this present perversity of yours?"

"You did not know him, padre; you did not know that mother's illness was caused by him alone."

"And how?"

"By his ill-treatment of her; he beat her and trampled upon her. I well remember the nights when he came home in his fits of frenzy. She never said a word, and did everything he bade her. Yet he would beat her so, my heart felt ready to break. I used to cover up my head and pretend to be asleep, but I cried all night. And then, when he saw her lying on the floor, quite suddenly he would change, and lift her up and kiss her till she screamed and said he smothered her. Mother forbade me ever to say a word of this; but it wore her out. And in all these long years since father died, she has never been able to get well again. And if she should soon die—which God forbid!—I know who it was that killed her."

The little curato's head wagged slowly to and fro; he seemed uncertain how far to acquiesce in the young girl's reasons. At length he said: "Forgive him, as your mother has forgiven! And turn your thoughts from such distressing pictures, Laurella; there may be better days in store for you, which will make you forget the past."

"Never shall I forget that!" she said, and shuddered. "And you must know, padre, it is the reason why I have resolved to remain unmarried. I never will be subject to a man, who may beat and then caress me. Were a man now to want to beat or kiss me, I could defend myself; but mother could not—neither from his blows nor kisses—because she loved him. Now, I will never so love a man as to be made ill and wretched by him."

"You are but a child, and you talk like one who knows nothing at all of life. Are all men like that poor father of yours? Do all ill-treat their wives, and give vent to every whim and gust of passion? Have you never seen a good man yet? or known good wives, who live in peace and harmony with their husbands?"

"But nobody ever knew how father was to mother; she would have died sooner than complain or tell of him, and all because she loved him. If this be love—if love can close our lips when they should cry out for help—if it is to make us suffer without resistance, worse than even our worst enemy could make us suffer—then, I say, I never will be fond of mortal man."

"I tell you you are childish; you know not what you are saying. When your time comes, you are not likely to be consulted whether you choose to fall in love or not." After a pause, he added, "And that painter: did you think he could have been cruel?"

"He made those eyes I have seen my father make, when he begged my mother's pardon and took her in his arms to make it up. I know those eyes. A man may make such eyes, and yet find it in his heart to beat a wife who never did a thing to vex him! It made my flesh creep to see those eyes again."

After this she would not say another word. The curato also remained silent. He bethought himself of more than one wise saying, wherewith the maiden might have been admonished; but he refrained, in consideration of the young boatman, who had been growing rather restless toward the close of this confession.

When, after two hours' rowing, they reached the little bay of Capri,

Antonio took the padre in his arms, and carried him through the last few ripples of shallow water, to set him reverently down upon his legs on dry land. But Laurella did not wait for him to wade back and fetch her. Gathering up her little petticoat, holding in one hand her wooden shoes and in the other her little bundle, with one splashing step or two she had reached the shore. "I have some time to stay at Capri," said the priest. "You need not wait—I may not perhaps return before to-morrow. When you get home, Laurella, remember me to your mother; I will come and see her within the week. You mean to go back before it gets dark?"

"If I find an opportunity," answered the girl, turning all her attention to her skirts.

"I must return, you know," said Antonio, in a tone which he believed to be one of great indifference. "I shall wait here till the Ave Maria. If you should not come, it is the same to me."

"You must come," interposed the little priest; "you never can leave your mother all alone at night. Is it far you have to go?"

"To a vineyard by Anacapri."

"And I to Capri. So now God bless you, child—and you, my son."

Laurella kissed his hand, and let one farewell drop, for the padre and Antonio to divide between them. Antonio, however, appropriated no part of it to himself; he pulled off his cap exclusively to the padre, without even looking at Laurella. But after they had turned their backs, he let his eyes travel but a short way with the padre, as he went toiling over the deep bed of small, loose stones; he soon sent them after the maiden, who, turning to the right, had begun to climb the heights, holding one hand above her eyes to protect them from the scorching sun. Just before the path disappeared behind high walls, she stopped, as if to gather breath, and looked behind her. At her feet lay the marina; the rugged rocks rose high around her; the sea was shining in the rarest of its deep-blue splendor. The scene was surely worth a moment's pause. But, as chance would have it, her eyes, in glancing past Antonio's boat, met Antonio's own, which had been following her as she climbed.

Each made a slight movement, as persons do who would excuse themselves for some mistake; and then, with her darkest look, the maiden went her way.

Hardly one hour had passed since noon, and yet for the last two Antonio had been sitting waiting on the bench before the fishers' tavern. He must have been very much preoccupied with something, for he jumped up every moment to step out into the sunshine, and look carefully up and down the roads, which, parting right and left, lead to the only two little towns upon the island. He did not altogether trust the weather, he then said to the hostess of the osteria; to be sure, it was clear enough, but he did not quite like that tint of sea and sky. Just so it had looked, he said, before the last awful storm, when the English family had been so nearly lost; surely she must remember it?

No, indeed, she said, she didn't.

Well, if the weather should happen to change before night, she was to think of him, he said.

"Have you many fine folk over there?" she asked him, after a while.

"They are only just beginning; as yet, the season has been bad enough; those who came to bathe, came late."

"The spring came late. Have you not been earning more than we at Capri?"

"Not enough to give me macaroni twice a week, if I had had nothing but the boat—only a letter now and then to take to Naples, or a gentleman to row out into the open sea, that he might fish. But you know I have an uncle who is rich; he owns more than one fine orange-garden; and, 'Tonino,' says he to me, 'while I live you shall not suffer want; and when I am gone you will find that I have taken care of you.' And so, with God's help, I got through the winter."

"Has he children, this uncle who is rich?"

"No, he never married; he was long in foreign parts, and many a good piastre he has laid together. He is going to set up a great fishing business, and set me over it, to see the rights of it."

"Why, then you are a made man, Tonino!"

The young boatman shrugged his shoulders. "Every man has his own burden," said he, starting up again to have another look at the weather, turning his eyes right and left, although he must have known that there can be no weather side but one.

"Let me fetch you another bottle," said the hostess; "your uncle can well afford to pay for it."

"Not more than one glass; it is a fiery wine you have in Capri, and my head is hot already."

"It does not heat the blood; you may drink as much of it as you like. And here is my husband coming; so you must sit a while, and talk to him."

And in fact, with his nets over his shoulder, and his red cap upon his curly head, down came the comely padrone of the osteria. He had been taking a dish of fish to that great lady, to set before the little curato. As soon as he caught sight of the young boatman, he began waving him a most cordial welcome; and he came to sit beside him on the bench, chattering and asking questions. Just as his wife was bringing her second bottle of pure unadulterated Capri, they heard the crisp sand crunch, and Laurella was seen approaching from the left-hand road to Anacapri. She nodded slightly in salutation; then stopped, and hesitated.

Antonio sprang from his seat. "I must go," he said. "It is a young Sorrento girl, who came over with the signor curato in the morning. She has to get back to her sick mother before night."

"Well, well, time enough yet before night," observed the fisherman; "time enough to take a glass of wine. Wife, I say, another glass!"

"I thank you; I had rather not"; and Laurella kept her distance.

"Fill the glasses, wife; fill them both, I say; she only wants a little pressing."

"Don't," interposed the lad. "It is a wilful head of her own she has; a saint could not persuade her to do what she does not choose." And, taking a hasty leave, he ran down to the boat, loosened the rope, and stood waiting for Laurella. Again she bent her head to the hostess, and slowly approached the water, with lingering steps. She looked around on every side, as if in hopes of seeing some other passenger. But the marina was deserted. The

fishermen were asleep, or rowing about the coast with rods or nets; a few
women and children sat before their doors, spinning or sleeping; such
strangers as had come over in the morning were waiting for the cool of
the evening to return. She had not time to look about her long; before she
could prevent him, Antonio had seized her in his arms and carried her to
the boat, as if she had been an infant. He leaped in after her, and with a
stroke or two of his oar they were in deep water.

She had seated herself at the end of the boat, half turning her back to
him, so that he could only see her profile. She wore a sterner look than ever;
the low, straight brow was shaded by her hair; the rounded lips were firmly
closed; only the delicate nostril occasionally gave a wilful quiver. After they
had gone on a while in silence, she began to feel the scorching of the sun;
and, unloosening her bundle, she threw the handkerchief over her head, and
began to make her dinner of the bread; for in Capri she had eaten nothing.

Antonio did not stand this long; he fetched out a couple of the oranges
with which the baskets had been filled in the morning. "Here is something
to eat to your bread, Laurella," he said. "Don't think I kept them for you;
they had rolled out of the basket, and I only found them when I brought the
baskets back to the boat."

"Eat them yourself; bread is enough for me."

"They are refreshing in this heat, and you have had to walk so far."

"They gave me a drink of water, and that refreshed me."

"As you please," he said, and let them drop into the basket.

Silence again. The sea was smooth as glass. Not a ripple was heard
against the prow. Even the white sea-birds that roost among the caves
of Capri pursued their prey with soundless flight.

"You might take the oranges to your mother," again commenced Tonino.

"We have oranges at home; and when they are gone, I can go and buy
some more."

"Nay, take these to her, and give them to her with my compliments."

"She does not know you."

"You could tell her who I am."

"I do not know you either."

It was not the first time that she had denied him thus. One Sunday of last
year, when that painter had first come to Sorrento, Antonio had chanced
to be playing *boccia* with some other young fellows in the little piazza by
the chief street.

There, for the first time, had the painter caught sight of Laurella, who,
with her pitcher on her head, had passed by without taking any notice of
him. The Neapolitan, struck by her appearance, stood still and gazed after
her, not heeding that he was standing in the very midst of the game, which,
with two steps, he might have cleared. A very ungentle ball came knocking
against his shins, as a reminder that this was not the spot to choose for
meditation. He looked round, as if in expectation of some excuse. But the
young boatman who had thrown the ball stood silent among his friends, in
such an attitude of defiance that the stranger had found it more advisable
to go his ways and avoid discussion. Still, this little encounter had been
spoken of, particularly at the time when the painter had been pressing his
suit to Laurella. "I do not even know him," she said indignantly, when the

painter asked her whether it was for the sake of that uncourteous lad she now refused him. But she had heard that piece of gossip, and known Antonio well enough when she had met him since.

And now they sat together in this boat, like two most deadly enemies, while their hearts were beating fit to kill them. Antonio's usually so good-humored face was heated to scarlet; he struck the oars so sharply that the foam flew over to where Laurella sat, while his lips moved as if muttering angry words. She pretended not to notice, wearing her most unconscious look, bending over the edge of the boat, and letting the cool water pass between her fingers. Then she threw off her handkerchief again, and began to smooth her hair, as though she had been alone. Only her eyebrows twitched, and she held up her wet hands in vain attemps to cool her burning cheeks.

Now they were well out in the open sea. The island was far behind, and the coast before them lay yet distant in the hot haze. Not a sail was within sight, far or near—not even a passing gull to break the stillness. Antonio looked all round, evidently ripening some hasty resolution. The color faded suddenly from his cheek, and he dropped his oars. Laurella looked round involuntarily—fearless, yet attentive.

"I must make an end of this," the young fellow burst forth. "It has lasted too long already! I only wonder that it has not killed me! You say you do not know me? And all this time you must have seen me pass you like a madman, my whole heart full of what I had to tell you; and then you only made your crossest mouth, and turned your back upon me."

"What had I to say to you?" she curtly replied. "I may have seen that you were inclined to meddle with me, but I do not choose to be on people's wicked tongues for nothing. I do not mean to have you for a husband—neither you nor any other."

"Nor any other? So you will not always say! You say so now, because you would not have that painter. Bah, you were but a child! You will feel lonely enough yet, some day; and then, wild as you are, you will take the next best who comes to hand."

"Who knows? which of us can see the future? It may be that I will change my mind. What is that to you?"

"What is it to me?" he flew out, starting to his feet, while the small boat leaped and danced. "What is it to me, you say? You know well enough! I tell you, that man shall perish miserably to whom you shall prove kinder than you have been to me!"

"And to you, what did I ever promise? Am I to blame if you be mad? What right have you to me?"

"Ah! I know," he cried, "my right is written nowhere. It has not been put in Latin by any lawyer, nor stamped with any seal. But this I feel: I have just the right to you that I have to heaven, if I die an honest Christian. Do you think I could look on and see you go to church with another man, and see the girls go by and shrug their shoulders at me?"

"You can do as you please. I am not going to let myself be frightened by all those threats. I also mean to do as I please."

"You shall not say so long!" and his whole frame shook with passion. "I am not the man to let my whole life be spoiled by a stubborn wench like you! You are in my power here, remember, and may be made to do my bidding."

She could not repress a start, but her eyes flashed bravely on him.

"You may kill me if you dare," she said slowly.

"I do nothing by halves," he said, and his voice sounded choked and hoarse. "There is room for us both in the sea. I cannot help thee, child"—he spoke the last words dreamily, almost pitifully—"but we must both go down together—both at once—and now!" he shouted, and snatched her in his arms. But at the same moment he drew back his right hand; the blood gushed out; she had bitten him fiercely.

"Ha! can I be made to do your bidding?" she cried, and thrust him from her, with one sudden movement. "Am I here in your power?" and she leaped into the sea, and sank.

She rose again directly; her scanty skirts clung close; her long hair, loosened by the waves, hung heavy about her neck. She struck out valiantly, and, without uttering a sound, she began to swim steadily from the boat toward shore.

With senses benumbed by sudden terror, he stood, with outstretched neck, looking after her, his eyes fixed as though they had just been witness to a miracle. Then, giving himself a shake, he seized the oars, and began rowing after her with all the strength he had, while all the time the bottom of the boat was reddening fast with the blood that kept streaming from his hand.

Rapidly as she swam, he was at her side in a moment. "For the love of our most Holy Virgin," he cried, "get into the boat! I have been a madman! God alone can tell what so suddenly darkened my brain. It came upon me like a flash of lightning and set me all on fire. I knew not what I did or said. I do not even ask you to forgive me, Laurella, only to come into the boat again and not to risk your life!"

She swam on as though she had not heard him.

"You can never swim to land. I tell you it is two miles off. Think of your mother! If you should come to grief, I should die of horror."

She measured the distance with her eye, and then, without answering him one word, she swam up to the boat, and laid her hands upon the edge; he rose to help her in. As the boat tilted over to one side with the girl's weight, his jacket that was lying on the bench slipped into the water. Agile as she was, she swung herself on board without assistance, and gained her former seat. As soon as he saw that she was safe, he took to his oars again, while she began quietly wringing out her dripping clothes, and shaking the water from her hair. As her eyes fell upon the bottom of the boat, and saw the blood, she gave a quick look at the hand, which held the oar as if it had been unhurt.

"Take this," she said, and held out her handkerchief. He shook his head, and went on rowing. After a time she rose, and, stepping up to him, bound the handkerchief firmly round the wound, which was very deep. Then, heedless of his endeavors to prevent her, she took an oar, and, seating herself opposite him, began to row with steady strokes, keeping her eyes from looking toward him—fixed upon the oar that was scarlet with his blood. Both were pale and silent. As they drew near land, such fishermen as they met began shouting after Antonio and gibing at Laurella; but neither of them moved an eyelid, or spoke one word.

The sun stood yet high over Procida when they landed at the marina. Laurella shook out her petticoat, now nearly dry, and jumped on shore. The old spinning woman, who in the morning had seen them start, was still upon her terrace. She called down. "What is that upon your hand, Tonino? Jesus Christ! the boat is full of blood!"

"It is nothing, comare," the young fellow replied. "I tore my hand against a nail that was sticking out too far; it will be well to-morrow. It is only this confounded ready blood of mine, that always makes a thing look worse than it is."

"Let me come and bind it up, comparello. Stop one moment; I will go and fetch the herbs, and come to you directly."

"Never trouble yourself, comare. It has been dressed already; to-morrow morning it will be all over and forgotten. I have a healthy skin, that heals directly."

"Addio!" said Laurella, turning to the path that goes winding up the cliffs. "Good-night!" he answered, without looking at her; and then taking his oars and baskets from the boat, and climbing up the small stone stairs, he went into his own hut.

He was alone in his two little rooms, and began to pace them up and down. Cooler than upon the dead calm sea, the breeze blew fresh through the small unglazed windows, which could only be closed with wooden shutters. The solitude was soothing to him. He stooped before the little image of the Virgin, devoutly gazing upon the glory round the head (made of stars cut out in silver paper). But he did not want to pray. What reason had he to pray, now that he had lost all he had ever hoped for?

And this day appeared to last forever. He did so long for night! for he was weary, and more exhausted by the loss of blood than he would have cared to own. His hand was very sore. Seating himself upon a little stool, he untied the handkerchief that bound it; the blood, so long repressed, gushed out again; all round the wound the hand was swollen high.

He washed it carefully, cooling it in the water; then he clearly saw the marks of Laurella's teeth.

"She was right," he said; "I was a brute, and deserved no better. I will send her back the handkerchief by Giuseppe to-morrow. Never shall she set eyes on me again." And he washed the handkerchief with the greatest care, and spread it out in the sun to dry.

And having bound up his hand again, as well as he could manage with his teeth and his left hand, he threw himself upon his bed, and closed his eyes.

He was soon waked up from a sort of slumber by the rays of the bright moonlight, and also by the pain of his hand; he had just risen for more cold water to soothe its throbbings, when he heard the sound of someone at the door. Laurella stood before him.

She came in without a question, took off the handkerchief she had tied over her head, and placed her little basket upon the table; then she drew a deep breath.

"You are come to fetch your handkerchief," he said. "You need not have taken that trouble. In the morning I would have asked Giuseppe to take it to you."

"It is not the handkerchief," she said quickly. "I have been up among the hills to gather herbs to stop the blood; see here." And she lifted the lid of her little basket.

"Too much trouble," he said, not in bitterness—"far too much trouble. I am better, much better; but if I were worse, it would be no more than I deserve. Why did you come at such a time? If any one should see you? You know how they talk, even when they don't know what they are saying."

"I care for no one's talk," she said, passionately. "I came to see your hand, and put the herbs upon it; you cannot do it with your left."

"It is not worth while, I tell you."

"Let me see it then, if I am to believe you."

She took his hand, that was not able to prevent her, and unbound the linen. When she saw the swelling, she shuddered, and gave a cry: "Jesus Maria!"

"It is a little swollen," he said; "it will be over in four-and-twenty hours."

She shook her head. "It will certainly be a week before you can go to sea."

"More likely a day or two; and if not, what matters?"

She had fetched a basin, and began carefully washing out the wound, which he suffered passively, like a child. She then laid on the healing leaves, which at once relieved the burning pain, and finally bound it up with the linen she had brought with her.

When it was done: "I thank you," he said. "And now, if you would do me one more kindness, forgive the madness that came over me; forget all I said and did. I cannot tell how it came to pass; certainly it was not your fault—not yours. And never shall you hear from me again one word to vex you."

She interrupted him. "It is I who have to beg your pardon. I should have spoken differently. I might have explained it better, and not enraged you with my sullen ways. And now that bite—"

"It was in self-defense; it was high time to bring me to my senses. As I said before, it is nothing at all to signify. Do not talk of being forgiven; you only did me good, and I thank you for it. And now, here is your handkerchief; take it with you."

He held it to her, but yet she lingered, hesitated, and appeared to have some inward struggle. At length she said: "You have lost your jacket, and by my fault; and I know that all the money for the oranges was in it. I did not think of this till afterward. I cannot replace it now; we have not so much at home—or if we had, it would be mother's. But this I have—this silver cross. That painter left it on the table the day he came for the last time. I have never looked at it all this while, and do not care to keep it in my box; if you were to sell it? It must be worth a few piastres, mother says. It might make up the money you have lost; and if not quite, I could earn the rest by spinning at night when mother is asleep."

"Nothing will make me take it," he said shortly, pushing away the bright new cross which she had taken from her pocket.

"You must," she said; "how can you tell how long your hand may keep you from your work? There it lies; and nothing can make me so much as look at it again."

"Drop it in the sea, then."

"It is no present I want to make you; it is no more than is your due; it is only fair."

"Nothing from you can be due to me; and hereafter when we chance to meet, if you would do me a kindness, I beg you not to look my way. It would make me feel you were thinking of what I have done. And now good-night; and let this be the last word said."

She laid the handkerchief in the basket, and also the cross, and closed the lid. But when he looked into her face, he started. Great heavy drops were rolling down her cheeks; she let them flow unheeded.

"Maria Santissima!" he cried. "Are you ill? You are trembling from head to foot!"

"It is nothing," she said; "I must go home"; and with unsteady steps she was moving to the door, when suddenly she leaned her brow against the wall, and gave way to a fit of bitter sobbing. Before he could go to her she turned upon him suddenly, and fell upon his neck.

"I cannot bear it!" she cried, clinging to him as a dying thing to life—"I cannot bear it! I cannot let you speak so kindly, and bid me go, with all this on my conscience. Beat me! trample on me! curse me! Or if it can be that you love me still, after all I have done to you, take me and keep me, and do with me as you please; only do not send me away so!" She could say no more for sobbing.

Speechless, he held her a while in his arms. "If I can love you still!" he cried at last. "Holy Mother of God! Do you think that all my best heart's blood has gone from me through that little wound? Don't you hear it hammering now, as though it would burst my breast and go to you? But if you say this to try me, or because you pity me, I can forget it. You are not to think you owe me this, because you know what I have suffered for you."

"No!" she said very resolutely, looking up from his shoulder into his face, with her tearful eyes; "it is because I love you; and let me tell you, it was because I always feared to love you that I was so cross. I will be so different now. I never could bear again to pass you in the street without one look! And lest you should ever feel a doubt, I will kiss you, that you may say, 'She kissed me'; and Laurella kisses no man but her husband."

She kissed him thrice, and, escaping from his arms: "And now good-night, amor mio, cara vita mia!" she said. "Lie down to sleep, and let your hand get well. Do not come with me; I am afraid of no man, save of you alone."

And so she slipped out, and soon disappeared in the shadow of the wall.

He remained standing by the window, gazing far out over the calm sea, while all the stars in heaven appeared to flit before his eyes.

The next time the little curato sat in his confessional, he sat smiling to himself. Laurella had just risen from her knees after a very long confession.

"Who would have thought it?" he said musingly—"that the Lord would so soon have taken pity upon that wayward little heart? And I had been reproaching myself for not having adjured more sternly that ill demon of perversity. Our eyes are but shortsighted to see the ways of Heaven! Well, may God bless her, I say, and let me live to go to sea with Laurella's eldest born, rowing me in his father's place! Ah! well, indeed! l'Arrabiata!"

Selma Lagerlöf

THE OUTLAWS

A PEASANT who had murdered a monk took to the woods and was made an outlaw. He found there before him in the wilderness another outlaw, a fisherman from the outermost islands, who had been accused of stealing a herring net. They joined together, lived in a cave, set snares, sharpened darts, baked bread on a granite rock and guarded one another's lives. The peasant never left the woods, but the fisherman, who had not committed such an abominable crime, sometimes loaded game on his shoulders and stole down among men. There he got in exchange for black-cocks, for long-eared hares and fine-limbed red deer, milk and butter, arrowheads and clothes. These helped the outlaws to sustain life.

The cave where they lived was dug in the side of a hill. Broad stones and thorny sloe-bushes hid the entrance. Above it stood a thick growing pine-tree. At its roots was the vent-hole of the cave. The rising smoke filtered through the tree's thick branches and vanished into space. The men used to go to and from their dwelling-place, wading in the mountain stream, which ran down the hill. No one looked for their tracks under the merry, bubbling water.

At first they were hunted like wild beasts. The peasants gathered as if for a chase of bear or wolf. The wood was surrounded by men with bows and arrows. Men with spears went through it and left no dark crevice, no bushy thicket unexplored. While the noisy battue hunted through the wood, the outlaws lay in their dark hole, listening breathlessly, panting with terror. The fisherman held out a whole day, but he who had murdered was driven by unbearable fear out into the open, where he could see his enemy. He was seen and hunted, but it seemed to him seven times better than to lie still in helpless inactivity. He fled from his pursuers, slid down precipices, sprang over streams, climbed up perpendicular mountain walls. All latent strength and dexterity in him was called forth by the excitement of danger. His body became elastic like a steel spring, his foot made no false step, his hand never lost its hold, eye and ear were twice as sharp as usual. He understood what the leaves whispered and the rocks warned. When he had climbed up a precipice, he turned toward his pursuers, sending them gibes in biting rhyme. When the whistling darts whizzed by him, he caught them, swift as lightning, and hurled them down on his enemies. As he forced his way through whipping branches, something within him sang a song of triumph.

The bald mountain ridge ran through the wood and alone on its summit stood a lofty fir. The red-brown trunk was bare, but in the branching top rocked an eagle's nest. The fugitive was now so audaciously bold that he climbed up there, while his pursuers looked for him on the wooded slopes. There he sat twisting the young eaglets' necks, while the hunt passed by far below him. The male and female eagle, longing for revenge, swooped down on the ravisher. They fluttered before his face, they struck with their beaks at his eyes, they beat him with their wings and tore with their claws bleeding weals in his weather-beaten skin. Laughing, he fought with them. Standing upright in the shaking nest, he cut at them with his sharp knife and forgot in the pleasure of the play his danger and his pursuers. When he found time to look for them, they had gone by to some other part of the forest. No one had thought to look for their prey on the bald mountain-ridge. No one had raised his eyes to the clouds to see him practicing boyish tricks and sleep-walking feats while his life was in the greatest danger.

The man trembled when he found that he was saved. With shaking hands he caught at a support, giddy he measured the height to which he had climbed. And moaning with the fear of falling, afraid of the birds, afraid of being seen, afraid of everything, he slid down the trunk. He laid himself down on the ground, so as not to be seen, and dragged himself forward over the rocks until the underbrush covered him. There he hid himself under the young pine-tree's tangled branches. Weak and powerless, he sank down on the moss. A single man could have captured him.

Tord was the fisherman's name. He was not more than sixteen years old, but strong and bold. He had already lived a year in the woods.

The peasant's name was Berg, with the surname Rese. He was the tallest and strongest man in the whole district, and moreover handsome and well-built. He was broad in the shoulders and slender in the waist. His hands were as well shaped as if he had never done any hard work. His hair was brown and his skin fair. After he had been some time in the woods he acquired in all ways a more formidable appearance. His eyes became piercing, his eyebrows grew bushy, and the muscles which knitted them lay finger thick above his nose. It showed now more plainly than before how the upper part of his athlete's brow projected over the lower. His lips closed more firmly than of old, his whole face was thinner, the hollows at the temples grew very deep, and his powerful jaw was much more prominent. His body was less well filled out but his muscles were as hard as steel. His hair grew suddenly gray.

Young Tord could never weary of looking at this man. He had never before seen anything so beautiful and powerful. In his imagination he stood high as the forest, strong as the sea. He served him as a master and worshiped him as a god. It was a matter of course that Tord should carry the hunting spears, drag home the game, fetch the water and build the fire. Berg Rese accepted all his services, but almost never gave him a friendly word. He despised him because he was a thief.

The outlaws did not lead a robber's or brigand's life; they supported themselves by hunting and fishing. If Berg Rese had not murdered a holy man, the peasants would soon have ceased to pursue him and have left him in peace in the mountains. But they feared great disaster to the district, because he who had raised his hand against the servant of God was still unpunished. When Tord came down to the valley with game, they offered him riches and pardon for his own crime if he would show them the way to Berg Rese's hole, so that they might take him while he slept. But the boy always refused; and if anyone tried to sneak after him up to the wood, he led him so cleverly astray that he gave up the pursuit.

Once Berg asked him if the peasants had not tried to tempt him to betray him, and when he heard what they had offered him as a reward, he said scornfully that Tord had been foolish not to accept such a proposal.

Then Tord looked at him with a glance, the like of which Berg Rese had never before seen. Never had any beautiful woman in his youth, never had his wife or child looked so at him. "You are my lord, my elected master," said the glance. "Know that you may strike me and abuse me as you will, I am faithful notwithstanding."

After that Berg Rese paid more attention to the boy and noticed that he was bold to act but timid to speak. He had no fear of death. When the ponds were first frozen, or when the bogs were most dangerous in the spring, when the quagmires were hidden under richly flowering grasses and cloudberry, he took his way over them by choice. He seemed to feel the need of exposing himself to danger as a compensation for the storms and terrors of the ocean, which he had no longer to meet. At night he was afraid in the woods, and even in the middle of the day the darkest thickets or the wide-stretching roots of a fallen pine could frighten him. But when Berg Rese asked him about it, he was too shy to even answer.

Tord did not sleep near the fire, far in in the cave, on the bed which was made soft with moss and warm with skins, but every night, when Berg had fallen asleep, he crept out to the entrance and lay there on a rock. Berg discovered this, and although he well understood the reason, he asked what it meant. Tord would not explain. To escape any more questions, he did not lie at the door for two nights, but then he returned to his post.

One night, when the drifting snow whirled about the forest tops and drove into the thickest underbrush, the driving snowflakes found their way into the outlaws' cave. Tord, who lay just inside the entrance, was, when he waked in the morning, covered by a melting snowdrift. A few days later he fell ill. His lungs wheezed, and when they were expanded to take in air, he felt excruciating pain. He kept up as long as his strength held out, but when one evening he leaned down to blow the fire, he fell over and remained lying.

Berg Rese came to him and told him to go to his bed. Tord moaned with pain and could not raise himself. Berg then thrust his arms under him and carried him there. But he felt as if he had got hold of a slimy snake; he had a taste in the mouth as if he had eaten the unholy horseflesh, it was so odious to him to touch the miserable thief.

He laid his own big bearskin over him and gave him water, more he could not do. Nor was it anything dangerous. Tord was soon well again. But through Berg's being obliged to do his tasks and to be his servant, they had come nearer to one another. Tord dared to talk to him when he sat in the cave in the evening and cut arrow shafts.

"You are of a good race, Berg," said Tord. "Your kinsmen are the richest in the valley. Your ancestors have served with kings and fought in their castles."

"They have oftener fought with bands of rebels and done the kings great injury," replied Berg Rese.

"Your ancestors gave great feasts at Christmas, and so did you, when you were at home. Hundreds of men and women could find a place to sit in your big house, which was already built before Saint Olof first gave the baptism here in Viken. You owned old silver vessels and great drinking-horns, which passed from man to man, filled with mead."

Again Berg Rese had to look at the boy. He sat up with his legs hanging out of the bed and his head resting on his hands, with which he at the same time held back the wild masses of hair which would fall over his eyes. His face had become pale and delicate from the ravages of sickness. In his eyes fever still burned. He smiled at the pictures he conjured up: at the adorned house, at the silver vessels, at the guests in gala array and at Berg Rese, sitting in the seat of honor in the hall of his ancestors. The peasant thought that no one had ever looked at him with such shining, admiring eyes, or thought him so magnificent, arrayed in his festival clothes, as that boy thought him in the torn skin dress.

He was both touched and provoked. That miserable thief had no right to admire him.

"Were there no feasts in your house?" he asked.

Tord laughed. "Out there on the rocks with father and mother! Father is a wrecker and mother is a witch. No one will come to us."

"Is your mother a witch?"

"She is," answered Tord, quite untroubled. "In stormy weather she rides out on a seal to meet the ships over which the waves are washing, and those who are carried overboard are hers."

"What does she do with them?" asked Berg.

"Oh, a witch always needs corpses. She makes ointments out of them, or perhaps she eats them. On moonlight nights she sits in the surf, where it is whitest, and the spray dashes over her. They say that she sits and searches for shipwrecked children's fingers and eyes."

"That is awful," said Berg.

The boy answered with infinite assurance: "That would be awful in others, but not in witches. They have to do so."

Berg Rese found that he had here come upon a new way of regarding the world and things.

"Do thieves have to steal, as witches have to use witchcraft?" he asked sharply.

"Yes, of course," answered the boy; "everyone has to do what he is destined to do." But then he added, with a cautious smile: "There are thieves also who have never stolen."

"Say out what you mean," said Berg.

The boy continued with his mysterious smile, proud at being an unsolvable riddle: "It is like speaking of birds who do not fly, to talk of thieves who do not steal."

Berg Rese pretended to be stupid in order to find out what he wanted. "No one can be called a thief without having stolen," he said.

"No; but," said the boy, and pressed his lips together as if to keep in the words, "but if someone had a father who stole," he hinted after a while.

"One inherits money and lands," replied Berg Rese, "but no one bears the name of thief if he has not himself earned it."

Tord laughed quietly. "But if somebody has a mother who begs and prays him to take his father's crime on him. But if such a one cheats the hangman and escapes to the woods. But if someone is made an outlaw for a fish-net which he has never seen."

Berg Rese struck the stone table with his clenched fist. He was angry. This fair young man had thrown away his whole life. He could never win love, nor riches, nor esteem after that. The wretched striving for food and clothes was all which was left him. And the fool had let him, Berg Rese, go on despising one who was innocent. He rebuked him with stern words, but Tord was not even as afraid as a sick child is of its mother, when she chides it because it has caught cold by wading in the spring brooks.

On one of the broad, wooded mountains lay a dark tarn. It was square, with as straight shores and as sharp corners as if it had been cut by the hand of man. On three sides it was surrounded by steep cliffs, on which pines clung with roots as thick as a man's arm. Down by the pool, where the earth had been gradually washed away, their roots stood up out of the water, bare and crooked and wonderfully twisted about one another. It was like an infinite number of serpents which had wanted all at the same time to crawl up out of the pool but had got entangled in one another and been held fast. Or it was like a mass of blackened skeletons of drowned giants which the pool wanted to throw up on the land. Arms and legs writhed about one another, the long fingers dug deep into the very cliff to get a hold, the mighty ribs formed arches, which held up primeval trees. It had happened, however, that the iron arms, the steel-like fingers with which the pines held themselves fast, had given way, and a pine had been borne by a mighty north wind from the top of the cliff down into the pool. It had burrowed deep down into the muddy bottom with its top and now stood there. The smaller fish had a good place of refuge among its branches, but the roots stuck up above the water like a many-armed monster and contributed to make the pool awful and terrifying.

On the tarn's fourth side the cliff sank down. There a little foaming stream carried away its waters. Before this stream could find the only possible way, it had tried to get out between stones and tufts, and had by so doing made a little world of islands, some no bigger than a little hillock, others covered with trees.

Here where the encircling cliffs did not shut out all the sun, leafy trees flourished. Here stood thirsty, gray-green alders and smooth-leaved willows. The birch-tree grew there as it does everywhere where it is trying to crowd out the pine woods, and the wild cherry and the mountain ash, those two which edge the forest pastures, filling them with fragrance and adorning them with beauty.

Here at the outlet there was a forest of reeds as high as a man, which made the sunlight fall green on the water just as it falls on the moss in the real forest. Among the reeds there were open places; small, round pools, and water-lilies were floating there. The tall stalks looked down with mild seriousness on those sensitive beauties, who discontentedly shut their white petals and yellow stamens in a hard, leather-like sheath as soon as the sun ceased to show itself.

One sunshiny day the outlaws came to this tarn to fish. They waded out to a couple of big stones in the midst of the reed forest and sat there and threw out bait for the big, green-striped pickerel that lay and slept near the surface of the water.

These men, who were always wandering in the woods and the mountains, had, without their knowing it themselves, come under nature's rule as much as the plants and the animals. When the sun shone, they were open-hearted and brave, but in the evening, as soon as the sun had disappeared, they became silent; and the night, which seemed to them much greater and more powerful than the day, made them anxious and helpless. Now the green light, which slanted in between the rushes and colored the water with brown and dark-green streaked with gold, affected their mood until they were ready for any miracle. Every outlook was shut off. Sometimes the reeds rocked in an imperceptible wind, their stalks rustled, and the long, ribbon-like leaves fluttered against their faces. They sat in gray skins on the gray stones. The shadows in the skins repeated the shadows of the weather-beaten, mossy stone. Each saw his companion in his silence and immovability change into a stone image. But in among the rushes swam mighty fishes with rainbow-colored backs. When the men threw out their hooks and saw the circles spreading among the reeds, it seemed as if the motion grew stronger and stronger, until they perceived that it was not caused only by their cast. A sea-nymph, half human, half a shining fish, lay and slept on the surface of the water. She lay on her back with her whole body under water. The waves so nearly covered her that they had not noticed her before. It was her breathing that caused the motion of the waves. But there was nothing strange in her lying there, and when the next instant she was gone, they were not sure that she had not been only an illusion.

The green light entered through the eyes into the brain like a gentle intoxication. The men sat and stared with dulled thoughts, seeing visions among the reeds, of which they did not dare to tell one another. Their catch was poor. The day was devoted to dreams and apparitions.

The stroke of oars was heard among the rushes, and they started up as from sleep. The next moment a flat-bottomed boat appeared, heavy, hollowed out with no skill and with oars as small as sticks. A young girl, who had been picking water-lilies, rowed it. She had dark-brown hair, gathered in great braids, and big dark eyes; otherwise she was strangely pale. But her paleness toned to pink and not to gray. Her cheeks had no higher color than the rest of her face, the lips had hardly enough. She wore a white linen shirt and a leather belt with a gold buckle. Her skirt was blue with a red hem. She rowed by the outlaws without seeing them. They kept breathlessly still, but not for fear of being seen, but only to be able to really see her. As soon as she had gone they were as if changed from stone images to living beings. Smiling, they looked at one another.

"She was white like the water-lilies," said one. "Her eyes were as dark as the water there under the pine-roots."

They were so excited that they wanted to laugh, really laugh as no one had ever laughed by that pool, till the cliffs thundered with echoes and the roots of the pines loosened with fright.

"Did you think she was pretty?" asked Berg Rese.

"Oh, I do not know, I saw her for such a short time. Perhaps she was."

"I do not believe you dared to look at her. You thought that it was a mermaid."

And they were again shaken by the same extravagant merriment.

Tord had once as a child seen a drowned man. He had found the body on the shore on a summer day and had not been at all afraid, but at night he had dreamed terrible dreams. He saw a sea, where every wave rolled a dead man to his feet. He saw, too, that all the islands were covered with drowned men, who were dead and belonged to the sea, but who still could speak and move and threaten him with withered white hands.

It was so with him now. The girl whom he had seen among the rushes came back in his dreams. He met her out in the open pool, where the sunlight fell even greener than among the rushes, and he had time to see that she was beautiful. He dreamed that he had crept up on the big pine-root in the middle of the dark tarn, but the pine swayed and rocked so that sometimes he was quite under water. Then she came forward on the little islands. She stood under the red mountain ashes and laughed at him. In the last dream-vision he had come so far that she kissed him. It was already morning, and he heard that Berg Rese had got up, but he obstinately shut his eyes to be able to go on with his dream. When he awoke, he was as though dizzy and stunned by what had happened to him in the night. He thought much more now of the girl than he had done the day before.

Toward night he happened to ask Berg Rese if he knew her name.

Berg looked at him inquiringly. "Perhaps it is best for you to hear it," he said. "She is Unn. We are cousins."

Tord then knew that it was for that pale girl's sake Berg Rese wandered an outlaw in forest and mountain. Tord tried to remember what he knew of her. Unn was the daughter of a rich peasant. Her mother was dead, so that she managed her father's house. This she liked, for she was fond of her own way and she had no wish to be married.

Unn and Berg Rese were the children of brothers, and it had long been said that Berg preferred to sit with Unn and her maids and jest with them than to work on his own lands. When the great Christmas feast was celebrated at his house, his wife had invited a monk from Draksmark, for she wanted him to remonstrate with Berg, because he was forgetting her for another woman. This monk was hateful to Berg and to many on account of his appearance. He was very fat and quite white. The ring of hair about his bald head, the eyebrows above his watery eyes, his face, his hands and his whole cloak, everything was white. Many found it hard to endure his looks.

At the banquet table, in the hearing of all the guests, this monk now said, for he was fearless and thought that his words would have more effect if they were heard by many, "People are in the habit of saying that the cuckoo is the worst of birds because he does not rear his young in his own nest, but here sits a man who does not provide for his home and his children, but seeks his pleasure with a strange woman. Him will I call the worst of men."—Unn then rose up. "That, Berg, is said to you and me," she said. "Never have I been so insulted, and my father is not here either." She had wished to go, but Berg sprang after her. "Do not move!" she said. "I will never see you again." He caught up with her in the hall and asked her what he should do to make her stay. She had answered with flashing eyes that he must know that best himself. Then Berg went in and killed the monk.

Berg and Tord were busy with the same thoughts, for after a while Berg said: "You should have seen her, Unn, when the white monk fell. The mistress of the house gathered the small children about her and cursed her. She turned their faces toward her, that they might forever remember her who had made their father a murderer. But Unn stood calm and so beautiful that the men trembled. She thanked me for the deed and told me to fly to the woods. She bade me not to be robber, and not to use the knife until I could do it for an equally just cause."

"Your deed had been to her honor," said Tord.

Berg Rese noticed again what had astonished him before in the boy. He was like a heathen, worse than a heathen; he never condemned what was wrong. He felt no responsibility. That which must be, was. He knew of God and Christ and the saints, but only by name, as one knows the gods of foreign lands. The ghosts of the rocks were his gods. His mother, wise in witchcraft, had taught him to believe in the spirits of the dead.

Then Berg Reese undertook a task which was as foolish as to twist a rope about his own neck. He set before those ignorant eyes the great God, the Lord of justice, the Avenger of misdeeds, who casts the wicked into places of everlasting torment. And he taught him to love Christ and his mother and the holy men and women, who with lifted hands kneeled before God's throne to avert the wrath of the great Avenger from the hosts of sinners. He taught him all that men do to appease God's wrath. He showed him the crowds of pilgrims making pilgrimages to holy places, the flight of self-torturing penitents and monks from a worldly life.

As he spoke, the boy became more eager and more pale, his eyes grew large as if for terrible visions. Berg Rese wished to stop, but thoughts streamed to him, and he went on speaking. The night sank down over them, the black forest night, when the owls hoot. God came so near to them that they saw his throne darken the stars, and the chastising angels sank down to the tops of the trees. And under them the fires of Hell flamed up to the earth's crust, eagerly licking that shaking place of refuge for the sorrowing races of men.

The autumn had come with a heavy storm. Tord went alone in the woods to see after the snares and traps. Berg Rese sat at home to mend his clothes. Tord's way led in a broad path up a wooded height.

Every gust carried the dry leaves in a rustling whirl up the path. Time after time. Tord thought that someone went behind him. He often looked round. Sometimes he stopped to listen, but he understood that it was the leaves and the wind, and went on. As soon as he started on again, he heard someone come dancing on silken foot up the slope. Small feet came tripping. Elves and fairies played behind him. When he turned round, there was no one, always no one. He shook his fists at the rustling leaves and went on.

They did not grow silent for that, but they took another tone. They began to hiss and to pant behind him. A big viper came gliding. Its tongue dripping venom hung far out of its mouth, and its bright body shone against the withered leaves. Beside the snake pattered a wolf, a big, gaunt monster, who was ready to seize fast in his throat when the snake had twisted about his feet and bitten him in the heel. Sometimes they were both silent, as if to approach him unperceived, but they soon betrayed themselves by hissing and panting, and sometimes the wolf's claws rung against a stone. Involuntarily Tord walked quicker and quicker, but the creatures hastened after him. When he felt that they were only two steps distant and were preparing to strike, he turned. There was nothing there, and he had known it the whole time.

He sat down on a stone to rest. Then the dry leaves played about his feet as if to amuse him. All the leaves of the forest were there: small, light yellow birch leaves, red speckled mountain ash, the elm's dry, dark-brown leaves, the aspen's tough light red, and the willow's yellow green. Transformed and withered, scarred and torn were they, and much unlike the downy, light green, delicately shaped leaves, which a few months ago had rolled out of their buds.

"Sinners," said the boy, "sinners, nothing is pure in God's eyes. The flame of his wrath has already reached you."

When he resumed his wandering, he saw the forest under him bend before the storm like a heaving sea, but in the path it was calm. But he heard what he did not feel. The woods were full of voices.

He heard whisperings, wailing songs, coarse threats, thundering oaths. There was laughter and laments, there was the noise of many people. That which hounded and pursued, which rustled and hissed, which seemed to be something and still was nothing, gave him wild thoughts. He felt again the anguish of death, as when he lay on the floor in his den and the peasants hunted him through the wood. He heard again the crashing of branches, the people's heavy tread, the ring of weapons, the resounding cries, the wild, bloodthirsty noise, which followed the crowd.

But it was not only that which he heard in the storm. There was something else, something still more terrible, voices which he could not interpret, a confusion of voices, which seemed to him to speak in foreign tongues. He had heard mightier storms than this whistle through the rigging, but never before had he heard the wind play on such a many-voiced harp. Each tree had its own voice; the pine did not murmur like the aspen nor the poplar like the mountain ash. Every hole had its note, every cliff's sounding echo its own ring. And the noise of the brooks and the cry of foxes mingled with the marvelous forest storm. But all that he could interpret; there were other strange sounds. It was those which made him begin to scream and scoff and groan in emulation with the storm.

He had always been afraid when he was alone in the darkness of the forest. He liked the open sea and the bare rocks. Spirits and phantoms crept about among the trees.

Suddenly he heard who it was who spoke in the storm. It was God, the great Avenger, the God of justice. He was hunting him for the sake of his comrade. He demanded that he should deliver up the murderer to His vengeance.

Then Tord began to speak in the midst of the storm. He told God what he had wished to do, but had not been able. He had wished to speak to Berg Rese and to beg him to make his peace with God, but he had been too shy.

Bashfulness had made him dumb. "When I heard that the earth was ruled by a just God," he cried, "I understood that he was a lost man. I have lain and wept for my friend many long nights. I knew that God would find him out, wherever he might hide. But I could not speak, nor teach him to understand. I was speechless, because I loved him so much. Ask not that I shall speak to him, ask not that the sea shall rise up against the mountain."

He was silent, and in the storm the deep voice, which had been the voice of God for him, ceased. It was suddenly calm, with a sharp sun and a splashing as of oars and a gentle rustle as of stiff rushes. These sounds brought Unn's image before him.—The outlaw cannot have anything, not riches, nor women, nor the esteem of men.—If he should betray Berg, he would be taken under the protection of the law.—But Unn must love Berg, after what he had done for her. There was no way out of it all.

When the storm increased, he heard again steps behind him and sometimes a breathless panting. Now he did not dare to look back, for he knew that the white monk went behind him. He came from the feast at Berg Rese's house, drenched with blood, with a gaping axe-wound in his forehead. And he whispered: "Denounce him, betray him, save his soul. Leave his body to the pyre, that his soul may be spared. Leave him to the slow torture of the rack, that his soul may have time to repent."

Tord ran. All this fright of what was nothing in itself grew, when it so continually played on the soul, to an unspeakable terror. He wished to escape from it all. As he began to run, again thundered that deep, terrible voice, which was God's. God himself hunted him with alarms, that he should give up the murderer. Berg Rese's crime seemed more detestable than ever to him. An unarmed man had been murdered, a man of God pierced with shining steel. It was like a defiance of the Lord of the world. And the murderer dared to live! He rejoiced in the sun's light and in the fruits of the earth as if the Almighty's arm were too short to reach him.

He stopped, clenched his fists and howled out a threat. Then he ran like a madman from the wood down to the valley.

Tord hardly needed to tell his errand; instantly ten peasants were ready to follow him. It was decided that Tord should go alone up to the cave, so that Berg's suspicions should not be aroused. But where he went he should scatter peas, so that the peasants could find the way.

When Tord came to the cave, the outlaw sat on the stone bench and sewed. The fire gave hardly any light, and the work seemed to go badly. The boy's heart swelled with pity. The splendid Berg Rese seemed to him poor and unhappy. And the only thing he possessed, his life, should be taken from him. Tord began to weep.

"What is it?" asked Berg. "Are you ill? Have you been frightened?"

Then for the first time Tord spoke of his fear. "It was terrible in the wood. I heard ghosts and saw specters. I saw white monks."

"'Sdeath, boy!"

"They crowded round me all the way up Broad mountain. I ran, but they followed after and sang. Can I never be rid of the sound? What have I to do with them? I think that they could go to one who needed it more."

"Are you mad tonight, Tord?"

Tord talked, hardly knowing what words he used. He was free from all shyness. The words streamed from his lips.

"They are all white monks, white, pale as death. They all have blood on their cloaks. They drag their hoods down over their brows, but still the wound shines from under; the big, red, gaping wound from the blow of the axe."

"The big, red, gaping wound from the blow of the axe?"

"Is it I who perhaps have struck it? Why shall I see it?"

"The saints only know, Tord," said Berg Rese, pale and with terrible earnestness, "what it means that you see a wound from an axe. I killed the monk with a couple of knife-thrusts."

Tord stood trembling before Berg and wrung his hands. "They demand you of me! They want to force me to betray you!"

"Who? The monks?"

"They, yes, the monks. They show me visions. They show me her, Unn. They show me the shining, sunny sea. They show me the fishermen's camping-ground, where there is dancing and merry-making. I close my eyes, but still I see. 'Leave me in peace,' I say. 'My friend has murdered, but he is not bad. Let me be, and I will talk to him, so that he repents and atones. He shall confess his sin and go to Christ's grave. We will both go together to the places which are so holy that all sin is taken away from him who draws near them.'"

"What do the monks answer?" asked Berg. "They want to have me saved. They want to have me on the rack and wheel."

"Shall I betray my dearest friend, I ask them," continued Tord. "He is my world. He has saved me from the bear that had his paw on my throat. We have been cold together and suffered every want together. He has spread his bear-skin over me when I was sick. I have carried wood and water for him; I have watched over him while he slept; I have fooled his enemies. Why do they think that I am one who will betray a friend? My friend will soon of his own accord go to the priest and confess, then we will go together to the land of atonement."

Berg listened earnestly, his eyes sharply searching Tord's face. "You shall go to the priest and tell him the truth," he said. "You need to be among people."

"Does that help me if I go alone? For your sin, Death and all his specters follow me. Do you not see how I shudder at you? You have lifted your hand against God himself. No crime is like yours. I think that I must rejoice when I see you on rack and wheel. It is well for him who can receive his punishment in this world and escapes the wrath to come. Why did you tell me of the just God? You compel me to betray you. Save me from that sin. Go to the priest." And he fell on his knees before Berg.

The murderer laid his hand on his head and looked at him. He was measuring his sin against his friend's anguish, and it grew big and terrible before his soul. He saw himself at variance with the Will which rules the world. Repentance entered his heart.

"Woe to me that I have done what I have done," he said. "That which awaits me is too hard to meet voluntarily. If I give myself up to the priests, they will torture me for hours; they will roast me with slow fires. And is not this life of misery, which we lead in fear and want, penance enough? Have I not lost lands and home? Do I not live parted from friends and everything which makes a man's happiness? What more is required?"

When he spoke so, Tord sprang up wild with terror. "Can you repent?" he cried. "Can my words move your heart? Then come instantly! How could I believe that! Let us escape! There is still time."

Berg Rese sprang up, he too. "You have done it, then—"

"Yes, yes, yes! I have betrayed you! But come quickly! Come, as you can repent! They will let us go. We shall escape them!"

The murderer bent down to the floor, where the battle-axe of his ancestors lay at his feet. "You son of a thief!" he said, hissing out the words, "I have trusted you and loved you."

But when Tord saw him bend for the axe, he knew that it was now a question of his own life. He snatched his own axe from his belt and struck at Berg before he had time to raise himself. The edge cut through the whistling air and sank in the bent head. Berg Rese fell head foremost to the floor, his body rolled after. Blood and brains spouted out, the axe fell from the wound. In the matted hair Tord saw a big, red, gaping hole from the blow of an axe.

The peasants came rushing in. They rejoiced and praised the deed.

"You will win by this," they said to Tord.

Tord looked down at his hands as if he saw there the fetters with which he had been dragged forward to kill him he loved. They were forged from nothing. Of the rushes' green light, of the play of the shadows, of the song of the storm, of the rustling of the leaves, of dreams were they created. And he said aloud: "God is great."

But again the old thought came to him. He fell on his knees beside the body and put his arm under his head.

"Do him no harm," he said. "He repents; he is going to the Holy Sepulcher. He is not dead, he is not a prisoner. We were just ready to go when he fell. The white monk did not want him to repent, but God, the God of justice, loves repentance."

He lay beside the body, talked to it, wept and begged the dead man to awake. The peasants arranged a bier. They wished to carry the peasant's body down to his house. They had respect for the dead and spoke softly in his presence. When they lifted him up on the bier, Tord rose, shook the hair back from his face, and said with a voice which shook with sobs—

"Say to Unn, who made Berg Rese a murderer, that he was killed by Tord the fisherman, whose father is a wrecker and whose mother is a witch, because he taught him that the foundation of the world is justice."

Rudolf Eucken

BACK TO RELIGION

HE IS but a superficial observer of the times who can think that the movement of life today is altogether against religion, and that only the denial of religion has the spirit of the age with it.

For, certain as it is that blatant denial still holds the public ear and is more and more permeating the masses, yet in the work of the intellect, and likewise in the depths of men's souls, the case is different. Here, with ever greater vigor, is springing up the feeling that religion is indispensable, the yearning for religion. What is understood by religion is often anything but clear, and often very different from the traditional forms of religion; but the demand is unmistakable for more depth of life and for the establishment of profounder inner connections than our visible existence affords. In the spiritual life of the present day, molecular transformations are taking place, inconspicuous at first but constantly increasing, which will eventually burst upon our view, and which will necessarily provoke essential changes in the entire condition of life. Today this movement is still an undercurrent, and on the surface the tide flows in the opposite direction. But more and more the undercurrent is rising to the surface, and unless every indication fails, it will soon come into control.

The most fundamental reason for this tendency may be indicated by a single sentence. It is caused by the increasing dissatisfaction with modern civilization, or at least with those aspects of civilization which now occupy the surface of life. All the splendor of the external successes of civilization cannot hide the fact that it does not satisfy the whole man with his inner needs, and that the amelioration of the world around us which it has accomplished does not compensate for the inner emptiness of its excessive concentration of effort on the visible world, its secularization of life.

We moderns have set ourselves at work with all our might, have acquired technical perfection, have combined isolated achievements into great systems. By the increased efficiency of our labor we have increasingly subdued the world, and at the same time have imposed upon human society a far more rational form. But, while we have given every care and effort to the means and conditions of life, we have exposed ourselves to the risk of losing life itself, and while performing astounding external feats, inwardly we have become smaller and smaller. Our work has separated itself from our souls, and it now reacts overmasteringly upon them, threatening to absorb them utterly. Our own creations have become our masters and oppressors. Moreover, as the division of labor increases, work constantly becomes more specialized and engages an ever smaller part of each individual soul; the whole man comes less and less to activity, and we lose any superior unity of our nature. Thus more and more we become mere parts of a civilization-machine.

The dangers thus arising were not felt to be so serious a menace, so long as religion and a culture controlled by ideals kept before men's minds another conception of life. But now that these are weakened and repressed, this trend toward the visible world meets less and less resistance. Yet it is true that as a result of the same process the accompanying loss is at least clearly seen and keenly felt. The victory itself is thus calling forth a counter-movement, and the outer triumph, by letting us plainly discern the limits of human power, is being transformed into an inner defeat. An independence once gained for the spiritual life can be temporarily obscured, but not permanently destroyed. At one and the same moment the craving that life should have more soul and depth is expressing itself with elemental power, and, on the other hand, it is becoming clear that, if the All is without soul and no new spiritual world stands open before us, we humans, too, can have no souls. The result is that we are again driven into the path of religion, since without religion life cannot find the longed-for depth.

This craving for soul is accompanied by a craving for continuance and eternity.

Modernity has abandoned religion's mode of conceiving life and the world *sub specie aeternitatis,* has left eternity colorless and empty, in its uncurbed desire to plunge full into the current of the time, to uplift conditions here, and from this world to derive all its forces. In all this a special importance has attached to the idea of development. Instead of thinking their position to be fixed and unshakable by the appointment of a higher power, be it God or fate, men have come to think of our life as still in flux, and its condition as susceptible of measureless improvement; above all the immaturity and all the losses of the present has arisen the confident hope of a better and ever better future. Such a conviction has led men to devote endeavor entirely to the living present and carefully to adjust effort to the existing stage of evolution. That contributes great freshness and mobility to life; all rigidity is dispelled, all magnitudes become fluid, infinite increase multiplies the abundant forms.

Without in any wise attacking or disparaging all this, one's own experience of life yet makes it more and more clear that this trend has its dangers and limitations. To yield to the tendency of the times seemed at first to bring clea. gain, for a group of persistent convictions still maintained themselves and supplied to the movement a counterbalancing repose. More and more, however, the movement drew into itself these survivals; more and more exclusively it mastered all life. It constantly became more swift, more hurried, more agitated; the changes followed faster and faster, one moment crowded on another, and the present was reduced to a passing instant. But in this process it has become apparent that this passionate forward striving leaves no room for true life. And, further, all courage must needs perish, so soon as we are forced to the conviction that everything which we today revere as true, good, beautiful, is subject to change and may tomorrow become unstable, that what is today acclaimed "modern" may tomorrow be cast aside as obsolete. He who unreflectingly lives merely for the moment may in all seriousness look upon that moment as the acme of the whole; but he who looks a little farther cannot doubt that it will be no better with us than with those who went before us, and that the saying still holds which according to Indian doctrines the spirits of the dead cry to the living: "We were what you are; you shall be what we are." In fine, if life is all strung on the thin thread of successive moments, each crowding back its predecessor, so that when the moment vanishes all action at once sinks again into the abyss of nothingness, then, in spite of all the exciting activity of the moment, life becomes a mere shadow.

If only we were quite sure that all our pains and care and haste were bringing about progress for the whole of human life! But that, again, we are not. True, we are constantly advancing in exact science, as we are in the technical mastery of our environment; we are compelling the elements into our service; we are freeing our existence from pain and enriching it with pleasure. But are we by all that winning a closer connection with the depths of reality? Are we growing in spiritual power as in ethical sentiment? Are we becoming greater and nobler men? As life gains in pleasure, do our inner contentment and true happiness increase in due proportion? In truth, we are growing only in our relations to the world outside, not in the essence of our being; and hence the question is not to be evaded, whether the unspeakable toil of modern civilization is worth while. We work and work, and know not to what end; for in giving up eternity we have also lost every inner bond of the ages and all power of comprehensive view. Without a guiding star we drift on the waves of the time.

As soon as this becomes a fact of clear consciousness and individual experience, either all courage to live must collapse or we must again discover within our domain, and resuscitate, something durable, something eternal, to give us support against the flight of the moments and to permit us to work for durable aims. Otherwise, our life has no sense and no value. That a longing for such an eternity, for a superiority to mere movement, pervades our time, is revealed by many signs. But such a craving leads, if not directly to religion, yet near to religion, as the chief representative of eternal truth.

Again, men crave more love and more solidarity in the human race than modern civilization affords, and that, too, is driving men to religion. Christianity not only had made love the kernel of religion, but also, starting from a Kingdom of God, it had established an inner human solidarity and created an organization on a spiritual foundation. For the modern age, however, so far as it went its own way, other aims came to the front. The chief thing came to be the individual, his emancipation from all hindrances, the development of all his powers, their unlimited enhancement. In all departments of life the independent development of the individual is a chief trait of the modern world; each of the great civilized nations in its own way has contributed to it, according as each has found its high level in art and literature, in religion, or in political and social life. Now for a time this individualism did not come into collision with the old ideals, for the individual found the totality of a spiritual world present within him, so that each one in his proper station could make it his chief task to stamp his own peculiar form on this inner world and to render it his peculiar service. But the situation altered as soon as that world of the spirit faded and disappeared. With it vanished everything that inwardly united individuals and bound their souls together. One individual became inwardly indifferent to another, and the way was opened for a man to make his highest aim his own personal advancement and utmost selfish gain, in total unconcern for anyone else.

The same principles which govern individual conduct are extended to social groups and entire nations; self-interest is the single rule of action, the moral solidarity of mankind is relaxed and dissolved. The danger is imminent that the end may be a war of all against all (*bellum omnium contra omnes*). Undoubtedly the resulting rivalry and strife has effected much that is great; it has given life a thorough shaking up, and banished all idle repose. And on this new foundation cohesive forces are by no means lacking. Such a force in particular is Work, which with its growth to great combinations perfects organization, assigns to each single element a definite part, and binds them all firmly together. But such gearing together of performances by no means amounts to harmony of sentiment; if it did, the antinomies of the social question and our economic conflicts would be impossible. In truth, combination in work does not prevent wide divergence of conviction and opinion, or even mutual hatred and strife. Sects and parties are increasing; common estimates and ideals keep slipping away from us; we understand one another less and less, and are falling deeper and deeper into a confused Babel of tongues. Even voluntary association, that form of human unity peculiar to modern times, the free union of many individuals, unites more in accomplishment than in disposition, brings men together outwardly rather than inwardly. Thus, among the monstrous confusions of the present time the demand for stable connections grows insistent, connections which shall take concern both for the common weal and for the individual. If, however, this demand plants itself wholly on the basis of the visible world and denies everything invisible, it must inevitably assume the form of a harsh oppression and compulsion, for it can produce its effect not through conviction but solely through force. In the social-democratic movement of the present such a danger already shows itself in full distinctness. But while the modern man struggles with all his soul against such a compulsion, a solution of the entanglement is to be sought in no other direction than that of a recovery of inner human bonds and of recourse to an inner world, common to all, of convictions, faith, ideals. We need to upbuild humanity from within, and this cannot be done without a profound deepening of life, and this in turn is not possible without religion.

The fact that today, with the greatest abundance of external points of contact, we are internally getting farther and farther apart, necessarily leads to inner isolation. Amid the stupendous driving-gear the individual sees himself left to his own resources and completely indifferent to everyone else. Such isolation is painful, yes, unbearable, especially for finer natures. All the fulness of human activity, highly as it is to be prized, cannot make good the lack of inner union and essential love. It affords no sufficient counterweight for the self-seclusion of man in his special circle of interests, for the preponderance of selfishness. Yet this selfishness, which separates all from all, turns out to be too narrow for the man himself; irresistibly a longing arises for a greater harmony of our spirits and for a value for each individual that shall transcend himself. But how could such a longing push its way to victory against the indifference of nature and the corrupt doings of men, unless a kingdom of love, a world of love, come to man and lend him a value? But that is exactly what religion represented, and what it brought to mankind.

Soul, eternity, love,—these are not brought to us quickly and painlessly by the world about us; they require an inner elevation, they demand a new world. And beyond these individual aspects doubts are also awakened and transformations made necessary by the totality of human nature. It was a main point of religion, especially of the Christian religion, not to accept and recognize man as experience presents him, but to require of him a complete transformation, an inner re-birth. The modern age has more confidence in man, it awakens in him the consciousness of strength more than of weakness, it summons him to the full development of all his slumbering powers. And in fact it has been shown that man is capable of far more than he used to be given credit for, that he can actively put his hand to the world, and successfully strive to realize the rational and rationalize the real. While, however, man in the past thought highly of himself and bravely undertook high things, he formerly felt himself to be still living in the spiritual associations which he had inherited, as member of a Kingdom of God or as sharer in a world of reason; and this consciousness disciplined and enlarged his power. But these associations have gradually vanished; the tendency toward man has gradually passed into a rude opposition to any superhuman world, and constantly takes a more hostile attitude toward religion and toward any visible order. Characteristic of this is the well-known saying of Ludwig Feuerbach: "God was my first, reason my second, man my third and last thought." In contrast to such a conception of man, which limits him to himself alone, the saying of Hegel in his *Philosophy of History* has its truth: "The consequence of putting man into the highest place is that he holds himself in no esteem. For only with the consciousness that a higher being exists does man attain a standpoint which allows him true esteem."

It cannot be denied that by giving up all connection with an invisible world and by complete limitation to visible existence man has been growing smaller. First of all, his place in the sum of reality has been reduced. He is now a mere bit of nature, and cannot claim a superior position and a peculiar work. In contrast to the enormously expanded space and time which nature has opened to modern research, the whole human circle is shrinking into tiny littleness. Rightly did William James emphasize the fact that for one hundred and fifty years progress seems to have meant nothing but a continual magnifying of the material world and a steady diminution of the importance of man.

And not only has the external position of man grown worse, he has also retrograded internally. When man is limited to sensuous existence, he loses all motive and all capacity to raise substantially his spiritual level and to counteract with any vigor the petty, low, self-centred part of his own being. He has to accept what he finds in himself, and exclusively follow the impulses awakened in him by nature; all resistance to them necessarily seems folly. That was endurable while an optimistic point of view glorified man, and lent him greatness and dignity in his own eyes; it becomes intolerable as soon as a more candid consideration causes us to discern and recognize the limitations and defects of man, understood as a mere natural being. And it cannot be denied that the experiences of modern life have given decisive preponderance to this unfavorable estimate. Whereas the eighteenth century could not exert itself enough to exalt the dignity and greatness of man (*la grandeur de l'homme*), we of today, when we picture man to ourselves, are far more inclined to think of what is petty, low, self-centred, the "all-too-human"

(Nietzsche). And since we do not intend to yield without a struggle to this humiliation, we are developing a zealous endeavor to elevate man of himself, in his own sphere. Some hope to attain this by uniting individuals into great masses and considering those masses as the bearers of reason, in agreement with the doctrine set up by Aristotle of the accumulation of reason in the mass; such have a firm belief in the reason of the multitude. In exactly the opposite direction, others wish to exalt single eminent individuals as high as possible above the masses and to make them the centre of gravity of intellectual creation. Thus the former through aggregation, the latter through isolation, hope to be able to make more out of man. But, whatever relative justification these two tendencies may have, they do not reach the main goal. For by no readjustment within the human circle can greatness be given to man, if human nature is not capable of elevation from within, if man is a mere natural being. So we continued to press on to a mere human culture and civilization; we see through its inadequacy, and yet cannot emancipate ourselves from it or lift ourselves above it; we can neither discover new aims nor develop new powers other than those which it supplies. The fact, however, that, despite the vast amount of earnest work and the restless movement of today, we yet lack a satisfying aim for this work, an aim that ennobles and inspires the work itself,—that fact makes the present state of civilization absolutely intolerable. Man can bear much hindrance and hurt and not lose his courage; but he cannot endure to have his whole life aimless and meaningless. Just because our life is ever growing more intense and more laborious, we must unconditionally demand that it be given an aim and a meaning.

Therefore in all deeper souls today is stirring a demand for an inner uplift of human nature, for a new idealism. And this demand will necessarily have to seek an alliance with religion. No matter how many opponents religion may still encounter, nevertheless, stronger than all opponents, stronger even than all intellectual difficulties, is the necessity of the spiritual self-preservation of humanity and of man. Out of the very resistance to the menace of annihilation will proceed elemental forces,—which are the strongest thing in the world.

Thus, though it be through a course of hard fights and radical upheavals (as history indirectly tends to prove), religion will surely come to new ascendency. But the return to religion by no means signifies a return to the old forms of religion. Through modern culture too much in the condition of life has been changed for us to resume these forms unchanged. Religion will win back men's souls so much the sooner, the more energetically it harks back to its original sources, the more sharply it separates the temporal and the eternal in their own spheres, and so brings the eternal to new effectiveness and sets it in close and fruitful relation to the real needs of the present. The superiority of the eternal consists not in that it persists unchanged within time, but in that it can enter all times without losing itself in them, and from them all can elicit that particular portion of truth which their endeavor holds. "The old that ages, he must let go, who would hold fast the old that ages not" (Runeberg).

The fundamental mood of mankind today is essentially the reverse of what it was at the beginning of the modern period. At that time the freshness of new vital power lent a rose-colored hue to all reality, and it was possible to hope that an imminent culture would bring about the complete satisfaction of all man's spiritual needs. The experiences of the period have shown man his limitations; great complications have arisen, much unreason has become apparent in our circumstances, our ambition has encountered greater and greater obstacles. But the recognition of so much unreason in our world forces us to the following alternative: either we declare ourselves powerless against unreason,—then all the courage and strength of life must collapse and we succumb to pessimism; or, on the other hand, wrestling manfully, we gain a connection with an invisible world and the depths of reality, draw thence new power of life, and take up with new courage the fight against all unreason. That course will result in a well-founded and serious optimism, radically different from the superficial optimism of the market-place. The false optimism ignores complication and unreason, and hence inevitably loses all depth of life; the true optimism knows and appreciates these, but is not warped and deterred by them. It possesses a resource superior to every hindrance, and from opposition only gains new might and courage. I should like to think that such a genuine and well-founded optimism corresponds to the intrinsic nature of the American people. But without Religion genuine optimism is impossible.

Rudyard Kipling

THE WAY THROUGH THE WOODS

They shut the road through the woods
  Seventy years ago.
  Weather and rain have undone it again,
And now you would never know
There was once a path through the woods
  Before they planted the trees,
It is underneath the coppice and heath,
  And the thin anemones.
  Only the keeper sees
That, where the ring-dove broods,
  And the badgers roll at ease,
There was once a road through the woods.

Yet, if you enter the woods
  Of a summer evening late,
When the night-air cools on the trout-ring'd pools
  Where the otter whistles his mate,

(They fear not men in the woods
  Because they see so few)
You will hear the beat of a horse's feet
And the swish of a skirt in the dew,
  Steadily cantering through
  The misty solitudes,
  As though they perfectly knew
  The old lost road through the woods . . .
But there is no road through the woods.

THE STRANGE RIDE
OF MORROWBIE JUKES

Alive or dead—there is no other way.—*Native Proverb.*

THERE is no invention about this tale. Jukes by accident stumbled upon a village that is well known to exist, though he is the only Englishman who has been there. A somewhat similar institution used to flourish on the outskirts of Calcutta, and there is a story that if you go into the heart of Bikanir, which is in the heart of the Great Indian Desert, you shall come across not a village but a town where the Dead who did not die but may not live have established their headquarters. And, since it is perfectly true that in the same Desert is a wonderful city where all the rich money-lenders retreat after they have made their fortunes (fortunes so vast that the owners cannot trust even the strong hand of the Government to protect them, but take refuge in the waterless sands), and drive sumptuous C-spring barouches, and buy beautiful girls and decorate their palaces with gold and ivory and Minton tiles and mother-o'-pearl, I do not see why Jukes's tale should not be true. He is a Civil Engineer, with a head for plans and distances and things of that kind, and he certainly would not take the trouble to invent imaginary traps. He could earn more by doing his legitimate work. He never varies the tale in the telling, and grows very hot and indignant when he thinks of the disrespectful treatment he received. He wrote this quite straightforwardly at first, but he has touched it up in places and introduced Moral Reflections: thus:—

In the beginning it all arose from a slight attack of fever. My work necessitated my being in camp for some months between Pakpattan and Mubarakpur —a desolate sandy stretch of country as every one who has had the misfortune to go there may know. My coolies were neither more nor less exasperating than other gangs, and my work demanded sufficient attention to keep me from moping, had I been inclined to so unmanly a weakness.

On the 23rd December 1884, I felt a little feverish. There was a full moon at the time, and, in consequence, every dog near my tent was baying it. The brutes assembled in twos and threes and drove me frantic. A few days previously I had shot one loud-mouthed singer and suspended his carcass *in terrorem* about fifty yards from my tent-door, but his friends fell upon, fought for, and ultimately devoured the body: and, as it seemed to me, sang their hymns of thanksgiving afterwards with renewed energy.

The light-headedness which accompanies fever acts differently on different men. My irritation gave way, after a short time, to a fixed determination to slaughter one huge black and white beast who had been foremost in song and first in flight throughout the evening. Thanks to a shaking hand and a giddy head I had already missed him twice with both barrels of my shotgun, when it struck me that my best plan would be to ride him down in the open and finish him off with a hog-spear. This, of course, was merely the semi-delirious notion of a fever-patient; but I remember that it struck me at the time as being eminently practical and feasible.

I therefore ordered my groom to saddle Pornic and bring him round quietly to the rear of my tent. When the pony was ready, I stood at his head prepared to mount and dash out as soon as the dog should again lift up his voice. Pornic, by the way, had not been out of his pickets for a couple of days; the night air was crisp and chilly; and I was armed with a specially long and sharp pair of persuaders with which I had been rousing a sluggish cob that afternoon. You will easily believe, then, that when he was let go he went quickly. In one moment, for the brute bolted as straight as a die, the tent was left far behind, and we were flying over the smooth sandy soil at racing speed. In another we had passed the wretched dog, and I had almost forgotten why it was that I had taken horse and hog-spear.

The delirium of fever and the excitement of rapid motion through the air must have taken away the remnant of my senses. I have a faint recollection of standing upright in my stirrups, and of brandishing my hog-spear at the great white Moon that looked down so calmly on my mad gallop; and of shouting challenges to the camelthorn bushes as they whizzed past. Once or twice, I believe, I swayed forward on Pornic's neck, and literally hung on by my spurs —as the marks next morning showed.

The wretched beast went forward like a thing possessed, over what seemed to be a limitless expanse of moonlit sand. Next, I remember, the ground rose suddenly in front of us, and as we topped the ascent I saw the waters of the Sutlej shining like a silver bar below. Then Pornic blundered heavily on his nose, and we rolled together down some unseen slope.

I must have lost consciousness, for when I recovered I was lying on my stomach in a heap of soft white sand, and the dawn was beginning to break dimly over the edge of the slope down which I had fallen. As the light grew stronger I saw I was at the bottom of a horseshoe-shaped crater of sand, opening on one side directly on to the shoals of the Sutlej. My fever had altogether left me, and, with the exception of a slight dizziness in the head, I felt no bad effects from the fall over night.

Pornic, who was standing a few yards away, was naturally a good deal exhausted, but had not hurt himself in the least. His saddle, a favourite polo one, was much knocked about, and had been twisted under his belly. It took me some time to put him to rights, and in the meantime I had ample opportunities of observing the spot into which I had so foolishly dropped.

At the risk of being considered tedious, I must describe it at length; inasmuch as an accurate mental picture of its peculiarities will be of material assistance in enabling the reader to understand what follows.

Imagine then, as I have said before, a horseshoe-shaped crater of sand with steeply-graded sand walls about thirty-five feet high. (The slope, I fancy, must have been about 65°.) This crater enclosed a level piece of ground about fifty yards long by thirty at its broadest part, with a rude well in the centre. Round the bottom of the crater, about three feet from the level of the ground proper, ran a series of eighty-three semicircular, ovoid, square, and multilateral holes, all about three feet at the mouth. Each hole on inspection showed that it was carefully shored internally with drift-wood and bamboos, and over the mouth a wooden drip-board projected, like the peak of a jockey's cap, for two feet. No sign of life was visible in these tunnels, but a most sickening stench pervaded the entire amphitheatre—a stench fouler than any which my wanderings in Indian villages have introduced me to.

Having remounted Pornic, who was as anxious as I to get back to camp, I rode round the base of the horseshoe to find some place whence an exit would be practicable. The inhabitants, whoever they might be, had not thought fit to put in an appearance, so I was left to my own devices. My first attempt to 'rush' Pornic up the steep sand-banks showed me that I had fallen into a trap exactly on the same model as that which the ant-lion sets for its prey. At each step the shifting sand poured down from above in tons, and rattled on the drip-boards of the holes like small shot. A couple of ineffectual charges sent us both rolling down to the bottom, half choked with the torrents of sand; and I was constrained to turn my attention to the river-bank.

Here everything seemed easy enough. The sand hills ran down to the river edge, it is true, but there were plenty of shoals and shallows across which I could gallop Pornic, and find my way back to *terra firma* by turning sharply to the right or the left. As I led Pornic over the sands I was startled by the faint pop of a rifle across the river; and at the same moment a bullet dropped with a sharp *'whit'* close to Pornic's head.

There was no mistaking the nature of the missile—a regulation Martini-Henry 'picket.' About five hundred yards away a country-boat was anchored in midstream; and a jet of smoke drifting away from its bows in the still morning air showed me whence the delicate attention had come. Was ever a respectable gentleman in such an *impasse*? The treacherous sand slope allowed no escape from a spot which I had visited most involuntarily, and a promenade on the river frontage was the signal for a bombardment from some insane native in a boat. I'm afraid that I lost my temper very much indeed.

Another bullet reminded me that I had better save my breath to cool my porridge; and I retreated hastily up the sands and back to the horseshoe, where I saw that the noise of the rifle had drawn sixty-five human beings from the badger-holes which I had up till that point supposed to be untenanted. I found myself in the midst of a crowd of spectators—about forty men, twenty women, and one child who could not have been more than five years old. They were all scantily clothed in that salmon coloured cloth which one associates with Hindu mendicants, and, at first sight, gave me the impression of a band of loathsome *fakirs*. The filth and repulsiveness of the assembly were beyond all description, and I shuddered to think what their life in the badger-holes must be.

Even in these days, when local self-government has destroyed the greater part of a native's respect for a Sahib, I have been accustomed to a certain amount of civility from my inferiors, and on approaching the crowd naturally expected that there would be some recognition of my presence. As a matter of fact there was; but it was by no means what I had looked for.

The ragged crew actually laughed at me—such laughter I hope I may never hear again. They cackled, yelled, whistled, and howled as I walked into their midst; some of them literally throwing themselves down on the ground in convulsions of unholy mirth. In a moment I had let go Pornic's head, and, irritated beyond expression at the morning's adventure, commenced cuffing those nearest to me with all the force I could. The wretches dropped under my blows like nine-pins, and the laughter gave place to wails for mercy; while those yet untouched clasped me round the knees, imploring me in all sorts of uncouth tongues to spare them.

In the tumult, and just when I was feeling very much ashamed of myself for having thus easily given way to my temper, a thin, high voice murmured in English from behind my shoulder: 'Sahib! Sahib! Do you not know me? Sahib, it is Gunga Dass, the telegraph-master.'

I spun round quickly and faced the speaker.

Gunga Dass (I have, of course, no hesitation in mentioning the man's real name) I had known four years before as a Deccanee Brahmin lent by the Punjab Government to one of the Khalsia States. He was in charge of a branch telegraph-office there, and when I had last met him was a jovial, full-stomached, portly Government servant with a marvellous capacity for making bad puns in English—a peculiarity which made me remember him long after I had forgotten his services to me in his official capacity. It is seldom that a Hindu makes English puns.

Now, however, the man was changed beyond all recognition. Caste-mark, stomach, slate-coloured continuations, and unctuous speech were all gone. I looked at a withered skeleton, turbanless and almost naked, with long matted hair and deep-set codfish-eyes. But for a crescent-shaped scar on the left cheek —the result of an accident for which I was responsible—I should never have known him. But it was indubitably Gunga Dass, and—for this I was thankful —an English-speaking native who might at least tell me the meaning of all that I had gone through that day.

The crowd retreated to some distance as I turned towards the miserable figure, and ordered him to show me some method of escaping from the crater. He held a freshly-plucked crow in his hand, and in reply to my question climbed slowly on a platform of sand which ran in front of the holes, and commenced lighting a fire there in silence. Dried bents, sand-poppies, and driftwood burn quickly; and I derived much consolation from the fact that he lit them with an ordinary sulphur match. When they were in a bright glow, and the crow was neatly spitted in front thereof, Gunga Dass began without a word of preamble:—

'There are only two kinds of men, Sar. The alive and the dead. When you are dead you are dead, but when you are alive you live.' (Here the crow demanded his attention for an instant as it twirled before the fire in danger of being burnt to a cinder.) 'If you die at home and do not die when you come to the ghât to be burnt you come here.'

The nature of the reeking village was made plain now, and all that I had known or read of the grotesque and the horrible paled before the fact just communicated by the ex-Brahmin. Sixteen years ago, when I first landed in Bombay, I had been told by a wandering Armenian of the existence, somewhere in India, of a place to which such Hindus as had the misfortune to recover from trance or catalepsy were conveyed and kept, and I recollect laughing heartily at what I was then pleased to consider a traveller's tale. Sitting at the bottom of the sand-trap, the memory of Watson's Hotel, with its swinging punkahs, white-robed servants and the sallow-faced Armenian, rose up in my mind as vividly as a photograph, and I burst into a loud fit of laughter. The contrast was too absurd!

Gunga Dass, as he bent over the unclean bird, watched me curiously. Hindus seldom laugh, and his surroundings were not such as to move him that way. He removed the crow solemnly from the wooden spit and as solemnly devoured it. Then he continued his story, which I give in his own words:—

'In epidemics of the cholera you are carried to be burnt almost before you are dead. When you come to the riverside the cold air, perhaps, makes you alive, and then, if you are only little alive, mud is put on your nose and mouth and you die conclusively. If you are rather more alive, more mud is put; but if you are too lively they let you go and take you away. I was too lively, and made protestation with anger against the indignities that they endeavoured to press upon me. In those days I was Brahmin and proud man. Now I am dead man and eat'—here he eyed the well-gnawed breast bone with the first sign of emotion that I had seen in him since we met—'crows, and—other things. They took me from my sheets when they saw that I was too lively and gave me medicines for one week, and I survived successfully. Then they sent me by rail from my place to Okara Station, with a man to take care of me; and at Okara Station we met two other men, and they conducted we three on camels, in the night, from Okara Station to this place, and they propelled me from the top to the bottom, and the other two succeeded, and I have been here ever since two and a half years. Once I was Brahmin and proud man, and now I eat crows.'

'There is no way of getting out?'

'None of what kind at all. When I first came I made experiments frequently and all the others also, but we have always succumbed to the sand which is precipitated upon our heads.'

'But surely,' I broke in at this point, 'the river-front is open, and it is worth while dodging the bullets; while at night——'

I had already matured a rough plan of escape which a natural instinct of selfishness forbade me sharing with Gunga Dass. He, however, divined my unspoken thought almost as soon as it was formed; and, to my intense astonishment, gave vent to a long low chuckle of derision—the laughter, be it understood, of a superior or at least of an equal.

'You will not'—he had dropped the Sir after his first sentence—'make any escape that way. But you can try. I have tried. Once only.'

The sensation of nameless terror which I had in vain attempted to strive against, overmastered me completely. My long fast—it was now close upon ten o'clock, and I had eaten nothing since tiffin on the previous day—combined with the violent agitation of the ride had exhausted me, and I verily believe that, for a few minutes, I acted as one mad. I hurled myself against the sand-slope. I ran round the base of the crater, blaspheming and praying by turns. I crawled out among the sedges of the river-front, only to be driven back each time in an agony of nervous dread by the rifle-bullets which cut up the sand round me—for I dared not face the death of a mad dog among that hideous crowd—and so fell, spent and raving, at the curb of the well. No one had taken the slightest notice of an exhibition which makes me blush hotly even when I think of it now.

Two or three men trod on my panting body as they drew water, but they were evidently used to this sort of thing, and had no time to waste upon me. Gunga Dass, indeed, when he had banked the embers of his fire with sand, was at some pains to throw half a cupful of fetid water over my head, an attention for which I could have fallen on my knees and thanked him, but he was laughing all the while in the same mirthless, wheezy key that greeted me on my first attempt to force the shoals. And so, in a half-fainting state, I lay till noon. Then, being only a man after all, I felt hungry, and said as much to Gunga Dass, whom I had begun to regard as my natural protector. Following the impulse of the outer world when dealing with natives, I put my hand into my pocket and drew out four annas. The absurdity of the gift struck me at once, and I was about to replace the money.

Gunga Dass, however, cried: 'Give me the money, all you have, or I will get help, and we will kill you!'

A Briton's first impulse, I believe, is to guard the contents of his pockets; but a moment's thought showed me of the folly of differing with the one man who had it in his power to make me comfortable; and with whose help it was possible that I might eventually escape from the crater. I gave him all the money in my possession, Rs. 9-8-5—nine rupees, eight annas, and five pie— for I always keep small change as *bakshish* when I am in camp. Gunga Dass clutched the coins, and hid them at once in his ragged loin-cloth, looking round to assure himself that no one had observed us.

'*Now* I will give you something to eat,' said he.

What pleasure my money could have given him I am unable to say; but inasmuch as it did please him I was not sorry that I had parted with it so readily, for I had no doubt that he would have had me killed if I had refused. One does not protest against the doings of a den of wild beasts; and my companions were lower than any beasts. While I eat what Gunga Dass had provided, a coarse *chapatti* and a cupful of the foul well-water, the people showed not the faintest sign of curiosity—that curiosity which is so rampant, as a rule, in an Indian village.

I could even fancy that they despised me. At all events they treated me with the most chilling indifference, and Gunga Dass was nearly as bad. I plied him with questions about the terrible village, and received extremely unsatisfactory answers. So far as I could gather, it had been in existence from time immemorial—whence I concluded that it was at least a century old—and during that time no one had ever been known to escape from it. [I had to control myself here with both hands, lest the blind terror should lay hold of me a second time and drive me raving round the crater.] Gunga Dass took a malicious pleasure in emphasising this point and in watching me wince. Nothing that I could do would induce him to tell me who the mysterious 'They' were.

'It is so ordered,' he would reply, 'and I do not yet know any one who has disobeyed the orders.'

'Only wait till my servant finds that I am missing,' I retorted, 'and I promise you that this place shall be cleared off the face of the earth, and I'll give you a lesson in civility, too, my friend.'

'Your servants would be torn in pieces before they came near this place; and, besides, you are dead, my dear friend. It is not your fault, of course, but none the less you are dead *and* buried.'

At irregular intervals supplies of food, I was told, were dropped down from the land side into the amphitheatre, and the inhabitants fought for them like wild beasts. When a man felt his death coming on he retreated to his lair and died there. The body was sometimes dragged out of the hole and thrown on to the sand, or allowed to rot where it lay.

The phrase 'thrown on to the sand' caught my attention, and I asked Gunga Dass whether this sort of thing was not likely to breed a pestilence.

'That,' said he, with another of his wheezy chuckles, 'you may see for yourself subsequently. You will have much time to make observations.'

Whereat, to his great delight, I winced once more and hastily continued the conversation: 'And how do you live here from day to day? What do you do?' The question elicited exactly the same answer as before—coupled with the information that 'this place is like your European heaven; there is neither marrying nor giving in marriage.'

Gunga Dass had been educated at a Mission School, and, as he himself admitted, had he only changed his religion 'like a wise man,' might have avoided the living grave which was now his portion. But as long as I was with him I fancy he was happy.

Here was a Sahib, a representative of the dominant race, helpless as a child and completely at the mercy of his native neighbours. In a deliberate lazy way he set himself to torture me as a schoolboy would devote a rapturous half-hour to watching the agonies of an impaled beetle, or as a ferret in a blind burrow might glue himself comfortably to the neck of a rabbit. The burden of his conversation was that there was no escape 'of no kind whatever,' and that I should stay here till I died and was 'thrown on to the sand.' If it were possible to forejudge the conversation of the Damned on the advent of a new soul in their abode, I should say that they would speak as Gunga Dass did to me throughout that long afternoon. I was powerless to protest or answer; all my energies being devoted to a struggle against the inexplicable terror that threatened to overwhelm me again and again. I can compare the feeling to nothing except the struggles of a man against the overpowering nausea of the Channel passage—only my agony was of the spirit and infinitely more terrible.

As the day wore on, the inhabitants began to appear in full strength to catch the rays of the afternoon sun, which were now sloping in at the mouth of the crater. They assembled by little knots, and talked among themselves without even throwing a glance in my direction. About four o'clock, so far as I could judge, Gunga Dass rose and dived into his lair for a moment, emerging with a live crow in his hands. The wretched bird was in a most draggled and deplorable condition, but seemed to be in no way afraid of its master. Advancing cautiously to the river-front, Gunga Dass stepped from tussock to tussock until he had reached a smooth patch of sand directly in the line of the boat's fire. The occupants of the boat took no notice. Here he stopped, and, with a couple of dexterous turns of the wrist, pegged the bird on its back with outstretched wings. As was only natural, the crow began to shriek at once and beat the air with its claws. In a few seconds the clamour had attracted the attention of a bevy of wild crows on a shoal a few hundred yards away, where they were discussing something that looked like a corpse. Half a dozen crows flew over at once to see what was going on, and also, as it proved, to attack the pinioned bird. Gunga Dass, who had lain down on a tussock, motioned to me to be quiet, though I fancy this was a needless precaution. In a moment, and before I could see how it happened, a wild crow, who had grappled with the shrieking and helpless bird, was entangled in the latter's claws, swiftly disengaged by Gunga Dass, and pegged down beside its companion in adversity. Curiosity, it seemed, overpowered the rest of the flock, and almost before Gunga Dass and I had time to withdraw to the tussock, two more captives were struggling in the upturned claws of the decoys. So the chase—if I can give it so dignified a name—continued until Gunga Dass had captured seven crows. Five of them he throttled at once, reserving two for further operations another day. I was a good deal impressed by this, to me, novel method of securing food, and complimented Gunga Dass on his skill.

'It is nothing to do,' said he. 'To-morrow you must do it for me. You are stronger than I am.'

This calm assumption of superiority upset me not a little, and I answered peremptorily: 'Indeed, you old ruffian? What do you think I have given you money for?'

'Very well,' was the unmoved reply. 'Perhaps not to-morrow, nor the day after, nor subsequently; but in the end, and for many years, you will catch crows and eat crows, and you will thank your European God that you have crows to catch and eat.'

I could have cheerfully strangled him for this; but judged it best under the circumstances to smother my resentment. An hour later I was eating one of the crows; and, as Gunga Dass had said, thinking my God that I had a crow to eat. Never as long as I live shall I forget that evening meal. The whole population were squatting on the hard sand platform opposite their dens, huddled over tiny fires of refuse and dried rushes. Death, having once laid his hand upon these men and forborne to strike, seemed to stand aloof from them now; for most of our company were old men, bent and worn and twisted with years, and women aged to all appearance as the Fates themselves. They sat together in knots and talked—God only knows what they found to discuss—in low equable tones, curiously in contrast to the strident babble with which natives are accustomed to make day hideous. Now and then an access of that sudden fury which had possessed me in the morning would lay hold on a man or woman; and with yells and imprecations the sufferer would attack the steep slope until, baffled and bleeding, he fell back on the platform incapable of moving a limb. The others would never even raise their eyes when this happened, as men too well aware of the futility of their fellows' attempts and wearied with their useless repetition. I saw four such outbursts in the course of that evening.

Gunga Dass took an eminently business-like view of my situation, and while we were dining—I can afford to laugh at the recollection now, but it was painful enough at the time—propounded the terms of which he would consent to 'do' for me. My nine rupees eight annas, he argued, at the rate of three annas a day, would provide me with food for fifty-one days, or about seven weeks; that is to say, he would be willing to cater for me for that length of time. At the end of it I was to look after myself. For a further consideration—*videlicet* my boots—he would be willing to allow me to occupy the den next to his own, and would supply me with as much dried grass for bedding as he could spare.

'Very well, Gunga Dass,' I replied; 'to the first terms I cheerfully agree, but, as there is nothing on earth to prevent my killing you as you sit here and taking everything that you have' (I thought of the two invaluable crows at the time), 'I flatly refuse to give you my boots and shall take whichever den I please.'

The stroke was a bold one, and I was glad when I saw that it had succeeded. Gunga Dass changed his tone immediately, and disavowed all intention of asking for my boots. At the time it did not strike me as at all strange that I, a Civil Engineer, a man of thirteen years' standing in the Service, and, I trust, an average Englishman, should thus calmly threaten murder and violence against the man who had, for a consideration it is true, taken me under his wing. I had left the world, it seemed, for centuries. I was as certain then as I am now of my own existence, that in the accursed settlement there was no law save that of the strongest; that the living dead men had thrown behind them every canon of the world which had cast them out; and that I had to depend for my own life on my strength and vigilance alone. The crew of the ill-fated *Mignonette* are the only men who would understand my frame of mind. 'At present,' I argued to myself, 'I am strong and a match for six of these wretches. It is imperatively necessary that I should, for my own sake, keep both health and strength until the hour of my release comes—if it ever does.'

Fortified with these resolutions, I ate and drank as much as I could, and made Gunga Dass understand that I intended to be his master, and that the least sign of insubordination on his part would be visited with the only punishment I had it in my power to inflict—sudden and violent death. Shortly after this I went to bed. That is to say, Gunga Dass gave me a double armful of dried bents which I thrust down the mouth of the lair to the right of his, and followed myself, feet foremost; the hole running about nine feet into the sand with a slight downward inclination, and being neatly shored with timbers. From my den, which faced the river-front, I was able to watch the waters of the Sutlej flowing past under the light of a young moon and compose myself to sleep as best I might.

The horrors of that night I shall never forget. My den was nearly as narrow as a coffin, and the sides had been worn smooth and greasy by the contact of innumerable naked bodies, added to which it smelt abominably. Sleep was altogether out of the question to one in my excited frame of mind. As the night wore on, it seemed that the entire amphitheatre was filled with legions of unclean devils that, trooping up from the shoals below, mocked the unfortunates in their lairs.

Personally I am not of an imaginative temperament—very few Engineers are—but on that occasion I was as completely prostrated with nervous terror as any woman. After half an hour or so, however, I was able once more to calmly review my chances of escape. Any exit by the steep sand walls was, of course, impracticable. I had been thoroughly convinced of this some time before. It was possible, just possible, that I might, in the uncertain moon-light, safely run the gauntlet of the rifle shots. The place was so full of terror for me that I was prepared to undergo any risk in leaving it. Imagine my delight, then, when after creeping stealthily to the river-front I found that the infernal boat was not there. My freedom lay before me in the next few steps!

By walking out to the first shallow pool that lay at the foot of the projecting left horn of the horseshoe, I could wade across, turn the flank of the crater, and make my way inland. Without a moment's hesitation I marched briskly past the tussocks where Gunga Dass had snared the crows, and out in the direction of the smooth white sand beyond. My first step from the tufts of dried grass showed me how utterly futile was any hope of escape; for, as I put my foot down, I felt an indescribable drawing, sucking motion of the sand below. Another moment and my leg was swallowed up nearly to the knee. In the moonlight the whole surface of the sand seemed to be shaken with devilish delight at my disappointment. I struggled clear, sweating with terror and exertion, back to the tussocks behind me and fell on my face.

My only means of escape from the semicircle was protected with a quick-sand!

How long I lay I have not the faintest idea; but I was roused at the last by the malevolent chuckle of Gunga Dass at my ear. 'I would advise you, Pro-tector of the Poor' (the ruffian was speaking English) 'to return to your house. It is unhealthy to lie down here. Moreover, when the boat returns, you will most certainly be rifled at.' He stood over me in the dim light of the dawn, chuckling and laughing to himself. Suppressing my first impulse to catch the man by the neck and throw him on to the quicksand, I rose sullenly and followed him to the platform below the burrows.

Suddenly, and futilely as I thought while I spoke, I asked: 'Gunga Dass, what is the good of the boat if I can't get out *anyhow?*' I recollect that even in my deepest trouble I had been speculating vaguely on the waste of ammu-nition in guarding an already well protected foreshore.

Gunga Dass laughed again and made answer: 'They have the boat only in daytime. It is for the reason that *there is a way.* I hope we shall have the pleasure of your company for much longer time. It is a pleasant spot when you have been here some years and eaten roast crow long enough.'

I staggered, numbed and helpless, towards the fetid burrow allotted to me, and fell asleep. An hour or so later I was awakened by a piercing scream—the shrill, high-pitched scream of a horse in pain. Those who have once heard that will never forget the sound. I found some little difficulty in scrambling out of the burrow. When I was in the open, I saw Pornic, my poor old Pornic, lying dead on the sandy soil. How they had killed him I cannot guess. Gunga Dass explained that horse was better than crow, and 'greatest good of greatest number is political maxim. We are now Republic, Mister Jukes, and you are entitled to a fair share of the beast. If you like, we will pass a vote of thanks. Shall I propose?'

Yes, we were a Republic indeed! A Republic of wild beasts penned at the bottom of a pit, to eat and fight and sleep till we died. I attempted no protest of any kind, but sat down and stared at the hideous sight in front of me. In less time almost than it takes me to write this, Pornic's body was divided, in some unclean way or other; the men and women had dragged the fragments on to the platform and were preparing their morning meal. Gunga Dass cooked mine. The almost irresistible impulse to fly at the sand walls until I was wearied laid hold of me afresh, and I had to struggle against it with all my might. Gunga Dass was offensively jocular till I told him that if he addressed another remark of any kind whatever to me I should strangle him where he sat. This silenced him till silence became insupportable, and I bade him say something.

'You will live here till you die like the other Feringhi,' he said coolly, watching me over the fragment of gristle that he was gnawing.

'What other Sahib, you swine? Speak at once, and don't stop to tell me a lie.'

'He is over there,' answered Gunga Dass, pointing to a burrow-mouth about four doors to the left of my own. 'You can see for yourself. He died in the burrow as you will die, and I will die, and as all these men and women and the one child will also die.'

'For pity's sake tell me all you know about him. Who was he? When did he come, and when did he die?'

This appeal was a weak step on my part. Gunga Dass only leered and replied: 'I will not—unless you give me something first.'

Then I recollected where I was, and struck the man between the eyes, partially stunning him. He stepped down from the platform at once, and, cringing and fawning and weeping and attempting to embrace my feet, led me round to the burrow which he had indicated.

'I know nothing whatever about the gentleman. Your God be my witness that I do not. He was as anxious to escape as you were, and he was shot from the boat, though we all did all things to prevent him from attempting. He was shot here.' Gunga Dass laid his hand on his lean stomach and bowed to the earth.

'Well, and what then? Go on!'

'And then—and then, Your Honour, we carried him into his house and gave him water, and put wet cloths on the wound, and he laid down in his house and gave up the ghost.'

'In how long? In how long?'

'About half an hour, after he received his wound. I call Vishn to witness,' yelled the wretched man, 'that I did everything for him. Everything which was possible, that I did!'

He threw himself down on the ground and clasped my ankles. But I had my doubts about Gunga Dass's benevolence, and kicked him off as he lay protesting.

'I believe you robbed him of everything he had. But I can find out in a minute or two. How long was the Sahib here?'

'Nearly a year and a half. I think he must have gone mad. But hear me swear, Protector of the Poor! Won't Your Honour hear me swear that I never touched an article that belonged to him? What is Your Worship going to do?'

I had taken Gunga Dass by the wrist and had hauled him on to the platform opposite the deserted burrow. As I did so I thought of my wretched fellow-prisoner's unspeakable misery among all these horrors for eighteen months, and the final agony of dying like a rat in a hole, with a bullet wound in the stomach. Gunga Dass fancied I was going to kill him and howled pitifully. The rest of the population, in the plethora that follows a full flesh meal, watched us without stirring.

'Go inside, Gunga Dass,' said I, 'and fetch it out.'

I was feeling sick and faint with horror now. Gunga Dass nearly rolled off the platform and howled aloud.

'But I am Brahmin, Sahib—a high-caste Brahmin. By your soul, by your father's soul, do not make me do this thing!'

'Brahmin or no Brahmin, by my soul and my father's soul, in you go!' I said, and, seizing him by the shoulders, I crammed his head into the mouth of the burrow, kicked the rest of him in, and, sitting down, covered my face with my hands.

At the end of a few minutes I heard a rustle and a creak; then Gunga Dass in a sobbing, choking whisper speaking to himself; then a soft thud—and I uncovered my eyes.

The dry sand had turned the corpse entrusted to its keeping into a yellow-brown mummy. I told Gunga Dass to stand off while I examined it. The body —clad in an olive-green hunting-suit much stained and worn, with leather pads on the shoulders—was that of a man between thirty and forty, above middle height, with light, sandy hair, long moustache, and a rough unkempt beard. The left canine of the upper jaw was missing, and a portion of the lobe of the right ear was gone. On the second finger of the left hand was a ring—a shield-shaped blood-stone set in gold, with a monogram that might have been either 'B. K.' or 'B. L.' On the third finger of the right hand was a silver ring in the shape of a coiled cobra, much worn and tarnished. Gunga Dass deposited a handful of trifles he had picked out of the burrow at my feet, and, covering the face of the body with my handkerchief, I turned to examine these. I give the full list in the hope that it may lead to the identification of the unfortunate man:—

1. Bowl of a briarwood pipe, serrated at the edge; much worn and blackened; bound with string at the screw.

2. Two patent-lever keys; wards of both broken.

3. Tortoise-shell-handled penknife, silver or nickel, name-plate, marked with monogram 'B. K.'

4. Envelope, postmark undecipherable, bearing a Victorian stamp, addressed to 'Miss Mon——' (rest illegible)—'ham'—'nt.'

5. Imitation crocodile-skin notebook with pencil. First forty-five pages blank; four and a half illegible; fifteen others filled with private memoranda relating chiefly to three persons—a Mrs. L. Singleton, abbreviated several times to 'Lot Single,' 'Mrs. S. May,' and 'Garmison,' referred to in places as 'Jerry' or 'Jack.'

6. Handle of small-sized hunting-knife. Blade snapped short. Buck's horn, diamond-cut, with swivel and ring on the butt; fragment of cotton cord attached.

It must not be supposed that I inventoried all these things on the spot as fully as I have here written them down. The notebook first attracted my attention, and I put it in my pocket with a view to studying it later on. The rest of the articles I conveyed to my burrow for safety's sake, and there, being a methodical man, I inventoried them. I then returned to the corpse and ordered Gunga Dass to help me to carry it out to the river-front. While we were engaged in this, the exploded shell of an old brown cartridge dropped out of one of the pockets and rolled at my feet. Gunga Dass had not seen it; and I fell to thinking that a man does not carry exploded cartridge-cases, especially 'browns,' which will not bear loading twice, about with him when shooting. In other words, that cartridge-case had been fired inside the crater. Consequently there must be a gun somewhere. I was on the verge of asking Gunga Dass, but checked myself, knowing that he would lie. We laid the body down on the edge of the quicksand by the tussocks. It was my intention to push it out and let it be swallowed up—the only possible mode of burial that I could think of. I ordered Gunga Dass to go away.

Then I gingerly put the corpse out on the quicksand. In doing so, it was lying face downward, I tore the frail and rotten khaki shooting-coat open, disclosing a hideous cavity in the back. I have already told you that the dry sand had, as it were, mummified the body. A moment's glance showed that the gaping hole had been caused by a gunshot wound; the gun must have been fired with the muzzle almost touching the back. The shooting-coat, being intact, had been drawn over the body after death, which must have been instantaneous. The secret of the poor wretch's death was plain to me in a flash. Some one of the crater, presumably Gunga Dass, must have shot him with his own gun—the gun that fitted the brown cartridges. He had never attempted to escape in the face of the rifle-fire from the boat.

I pushed the corpse out hastily, and saw it sink from sight literally in a few seconds. I shuddered as I watched. In a dazed, half-conscious way I turned to peruse the notebook. A stained and discoloured slip of paper had been inserted between the binding and the back, and dropped out as I opened the pages. This is what it contained: *'Four out from crow-clump; three left; nine out; two right; three back; two left; fourteen out; two left; seven out; one left; nine back; two right; six back; four right; seven back.'* The paper had been burnt and charred at the edges. What it meant I could not understand. I sat down on the dried bents turning it over and over between my fingers, until I was aware of Gunga Dass standing immediately behind me with glowing eyes and outstretched hands.

'Have you got it?' he panted. 'Will you not let me look at it also? I swear that I will return it.'

'Got what? Return what?' I asked.

'That which you have in your hands. It will help us both.' He stretched out his long, bird-like talons, trembling with eagerness.

'I could never find it,' he continued. 'He had secreted it about his person. Therefore I shot him, but nevertheless I was unable to obtain it.'

Gunga Dass had quite forgotten his little fiction about the rifle-bullet. I heard him calmly. Morality is blunted by consorting with the Dead who are alive.

'What on earth are you raving about? What is it you want me to give you?'

'The piece of paper in the notebook. It will help us both. Oh, you fool! You fool! Can you not see what it will do for us? We shall escape!'

His voice rose almost to a scream, and he danced with excitement before me. I own I was moved at the chance of getting away.

'Do you mean to say that this slip of paper will help us? What does it mean?'

'Read it aloud! Read it aloud! I beg and I pray to you to read it aloud.'

I did so. Gunga Dass listened delightedly, and drew an irregular line in the sand with his fingers.

'See now! It was the length of his gun-barrels without the stock. I have those barrels. Four gun-barrels out from the place where I caught crows. Straight out; do you mind me? Then three left. Ah! Now well I remember how that man worked it out night after night. Then nine out, and so on. Out is always straight before you across the quicksand to the North. He told me so before I killed him.'

'But if you knew all this why didn't you get out before?'

'I did *not* know it. He told me that he was working it out a year and a half ago, and how he was working it out night after night when the boat had gone away, and he could get out near the quicksand safely. Then he said that we would get away together. But I was afraid that he would leave me behind one night when he had worked it all out, and so I shot him. Besides, it is not advisable that the men who once get in here should escape. Only I, and *I* am a Brahmin.'

The hope of escape had brought Gunga Dass's caste back to him. He stood up, walked about and gesticulated violently. Eventually I managed to make him talk soberly, and he told me how this Englishman had spent six months night after night in exploring, inch by inch, the passage across the quicksand; how he had declared it to be simplicity itself up to within about twenty yards of the river bank after turning the flank of the left horn of the horseshoe. This much he had evidently not completed when Gunga Dass shot him with his own gun.

In my frenzy of delight at the possibilities of escape I recollect shaking hands wildly with Gunga Dass, after we had decided that we were to make an attempt to get away that very night. It was weary work waiting throughout the afternoon.

About ten o'clock, as far as I could judge, when the Moon had just risen above the lip of the crater, Gunga Dass made a move for his burrow to bring out the gun-barrels whereby to measure our path. All the other wretched inhabitants had retired to their lairs long ago. The guardian boat drifted downstream some hours before, and we were utterly alone by the crow-clump. Gunga Dass, while carrying the gun-barrels, let slip the piece of paper which was to be our guide. I stooped down hastily to recover it, and, as I did so, I was aware that the creature was aiming a violent blow at the back of my head with the gun-barrels. It was too late to turn round. I must have received the blow somewhere on the nape of my neck, for I fell senseless at the edge of the quicksand.

When I recovered consciousness, the Moon was going down, and I was sensible of intolerable pain in the back of my head. Gunga Dass had disappeared and my mouth was full of blood. I lay down again and prayed that I might die without more ado. Then the unreasoning fury which I have before mentioned laid hold upon me, and I staggered inland towards the walls of the crater. It seemed that some one was calling to me in a whisper—'Sahib! Sahib! Sahib!' exactly as my bearer used to call me in the mornings. I fancied that I was delirious until a handful of sand fell at my feet. Then I looked up and saw a head peering down into the amphitheatre—the head of Dunnoo, my dog-boy, who attended to my collies. As soon as he had attracted my attention, he held up his hand and showed a rope. I motioned, staggering to and fro the while, that he should throw it down. It was a couple of leather punkah-ropes knotted together, with a loop at one end. I slipped the loop over my head and under my arms; heard Dunnoo urge something forward; was conscious that I was being dragged, face downward, up the steep sand-slope, and the next instant found myself choked and half-fainting on the sand hills overlooking the crater. Dunnoo, with his face ashy gray in the moon-light, implored me not to stay but to get back to my tent at once.

It seems that he had tracked Pornic's footprints fourteen miles across the sands to the crater; had returned and told my servants, who flatly refused to meddle with any one, white or black, once fallen into the hideous Village of the Dead; whereupon Dunnoo had taken one of my ponies and a couple of punkah ropes, returned to the crater, and hauled me out as I have described.

Giosué Carducci

LEVIA GRAVIA [1861–1871]

In an Album.

I SEE in memory your candid gaze,
   O children, and your face delights me now
   As once, and your untroubled, radiant brow;
      And my mind roams 'mid happy vanished days
When yet love seemed to me a heavenly thing,
And once again I hear the whispering
Of silken skirts on grass in the moonlight,
And breathe ecstatic murmurs in the night.

If a lone pilgrim in a valley dark,
Fearing the gloom that all about him lies,
And stones to trap his feet, life up his eyes
   To the hill paths whence he came down, and mark

His head yet circled with a parting ray,
He thinks upon the morning of his day,
And on his native land's new budded leaves,
And the paternal hearth on twilit eves.
Thus sighs my heart for green and sunlit peace
And tender winds and floating harmonies;
But in the whirlpool of the centuries
Life draws me still, where battle without cease
Undying passions, and from crumbling tombs
Sound words of wrath and trump of fiery dooms.
    But ye, oh heed them not: unspoiled and gay,
Pluck the fast fading roses while ye may.

IN THE ARNO VALLEY

NEVER do I behold you, Tuscan hills,
    Dear hills where my young muse first tried her wing,
    'Neath a clear sun that dappled shadows spills
Through laurel leaves on waters scurrying,
But my heart's lake with bitter tears o'erflows.
Silent is every other memory,
Since, while more proud thy jealous beauty grows,
Dread mount, my brother laid him down on thee.

Oh, what fond hopes thy swelling bosom bore!
How from the spring-tide that returns no more
We flew light-winged to meet a golden dawn!
'Mid idle studies now my days I pass
And futile dreams; but him in life's bright morn
Thy brown earth covers and thine emerald grass.

CARNIVAL

Voice from the Palaces

WHETHER in echoing vale,
    O fierce north wind, or forests wandering
    Sonorous, or pent up in cloisters dire,
The voice of human wail

Or of wild wounded beast the bellowing
Thou soundest on thy myriad-stringèd lyre,
I like thee well. And I delight in thee,
Stern winter throned aloft in majesty.

White flimsy mists absorb
The fading light, and melt into the sky
And snow-clad plain on the horizon dim.
The sun's subsiding orb
Flushes faint rose, and, like a human eye
Beneath shamed lids, lurks 'neath the vapours' rim.
Whisper of leaf, nor any note of bird,
Nor song of lass or wayfarer is heard,

Only the creaking shrill
Of branches crushed beneath their heavy pall
And splitting ice that twangs like a cracked lute.
Oh let Arcadia fill
The air with song and Zephyrus recall
With his sweet brood unto the fields. This mute
Chill desolation works to me more good.
Wake for me, Eurus, fire the sleeping wood.

Show me the radiant brow
And the enchanting promise of the spring
That fanned by thy swift pinions hourly grows.
Spread is the banquet now
Where on the face of beauty quickening
The bloom of an awakened ardour glows,
And from bright scattered locks and flowery wreaths
In newly-wafted scents young April breathes.

Voice from the Hovels

Oh would that with mine own
Life's blood I could revive thy members cold,
And give my life for thine, O son most dear!
My heart is like a stone,
My numbed arms can no more thy weakness hold,
And man is deaf, and God, He will not hear.
Oh my poor little one, thy tear-wet cheek
Rest on thy mother's; there thy comfort seek.

Not on his mother's breast
Thy brother ceased*; on bed of snow he lay,
And icy blasts stole his bewildered breath.
With unjust load oppressed

*While he was writing this poem, Carducci read in the Gazetta di Torino an account
of the death of a peasant boy, who perished of cold and hunger in the mountains near
Turin.

He followed in the dawn of his brief day
His cruel lords, and served them in his death;
And the relentless air and stubborn soil
Combined with man to bring him war and toil.
Through his poor sodden clout
The stinging sleet his tender body whipped.
He fell, and rose again, wan, weariful.
Hunger was wearing out
His strength, and on that woeful pass it gripped
And tortured him, till death came merciful.
Then, horrible and naked to the skies,
They brought and laid him 'neath his mother's eyes.

A juster law doth guard
The eagle on its peak from winter frore,
And in their pristine haunts have kinder lair
The tiger and the pard;
And warm soft kennels shelter and restore
The gorged hounds in the splendid palace there,
So near, while thou in this poor famished den
Diest frozen and forgotten, child of men.

Voice from the Banqueting Halls

Come pour the vintage old,
The vintage that the Rhine sustains and guards
With his tall coronet of castles crowned.
It sparkles red and gold.
Let's drink. In veins where the chill blood retards
Let's pour the quickening juice that in thy ground
The sun matures with temperate beam benign,
O France, fair land of heroes and of wine.

Then let the whirling dance
Snatch us into its maelstrom. Oh the wealth
Of rippling tawny tresses and of black!
Oh the bewildering trance
When breath mingles with breath, the luscious stealth
Of beauties half concealed, and blazèd track
Of eyes withdrawn, while through a thousand strains
Exasperated lust sighs and complains!

Oh with unsated lips
To brush a crimson-mantling cheek, and press
Against our heart a heart that's all afire,
And while the hot blood whips
To give free rein unto our secret stress,
Feel the sweet smart of unfulfilled desire,

And hold the cup, untasted and o'erbrimmed,
Whose promise disenchantment has not dimmed!

And of our wealth if some
Upon the necessary mob o'erflow,
And by our riches bounty has increase,
To us the praise shall come;
For the high justice that distributes woe
And pleasure of our piety has ease.
A favoured progeny, we, like the sun,
Merely by shining have our duty done.

Voice from the Garrets

We had nor sup nor crumb
Wherewith our meagre bodies to sustain.
Before the cheerless hearth and embers cold,
Pale with affright and dumb,
My mother sat, and her wide eyes of pain
Followed me. Many leaden hours had tolled
Haunted by that dull look of speechless woe
Ere I went out with weary steps and slow.

The moon like silvered rain
Poured through the wintry mists her pallid beams
Upon our squalid dwelling, and then slid
Behind the clouds again.
E'en so of my wan youth the fitful gleams
O'er my dark life 'mid thronging sorrows hid.
Methought I saw through the gaped mouth of hell
Daemonic leers, while on my heart there fell
A weight of doom like lead.
But more than these, famine my soul beset,
And on my aged mother's face that look.
I brought her sup and bread;
But hunger's pangs I felt no more; my wet
And heavy eyes no more the light could brook,
And on thy breast, O mother, my soul's shame
I hid, and the sharp grief that has no name.

Farewell, dim fantasies
About a holy love, and ye, O dear
Companions of this most unhappy maid!
To you the chastities
Of veils fond mothers moisten with a tear,
Dreams o'er a cradle hovering unafraid. . . .
I, scorned and uncompanioned, unabsolved,
Walk in the shadows' track and am dissolved.

Voice from Underground

O maiden, grieve not so!
O mournful mother, wherefore dost thou weep?
Hush thy poor little starveling's hungry fret.
Dost thou not see the glow
Of firelit windows in the shadows deep?
'Tis there our free land's honoured ones are met,
Scholars and magistrates and barons proud,
Soldiers and usurers, a merry crowd.

Thy youth's frail flower drooped,
O maiden vainly seeking through the land
The love and light each living soul must seek;
But in the dazzle looped
Of silks and gold that with her soft white hand
Yon countess gathers as she glides so sleek
Into the dance, it blooms. What matters more?
Wait now the prostitution at thy door.

The tears starvation froze,
O mother, in thy son's dim eyes, which thou
Hadst not the mournful joy to wipe away,
They wrought the gem that glows
In yon fine lady's burnished hair. See, now
Her cavalier so debonair and gay
Pours forth a torrent of vain words, and sips
Thy stolen honey from her painted lips.

Triumph, ye rich! Exult,
Ye mighty! Swollen wraiths! and when the sun
Shall drive the people to their daily task,
Show yourselves, and insult
With your proud pomps their pale starvation,
And, surfeited, in your fat fortunes bask.
Dream not the hour when at your gilded gate
Death shall come hammering and ruthless fate.

HOMER

AND ever as each fruitful spring is born
Unto thy song my soul returns, O thou
Most glorious ancient, from whose god-like brow
There spreads the radiance of eternal morn.

Sing to me of Calypso's island caves,
Of Sol's white daughter's mystic spells oh sing,
Of Nausicaa and her sire the king,
Whose cloak is blithely washed upon the waves.

Tell me . . . ah tell me not! Earth is become
The base tribunal of a court unclean;
Rulers are vile, the very gods are mean,

And if to-day unto our world didst come,
For thy dark steps there'd be no leader fond,
And none would give thee alms, O vagabond.

BY NIGHT

WHEN all about thy shadowy veils are thrown,
O black-haired night, earth's weary passions flee
And creeping sorrows. Thou dost call to me,
And my lone heart leans on thy bosom lone.

What tranquil promise to my hungry moan
Ease and fulfilment brings? What pinions free
Giv'st to dull thoughts that wandered listlessly
Upon the misty marge of the unknown?

O goddess night, I know not what this brief
And pensive presage bodes, in whose still deeps
Pain is forgot, and anger, fear and grief;

But this I know, that in thine arms I rest
E'en as a little child that sobs and sleeps
Upon its grandam's browned and aged breast.

Henryk Sienkiewicz

BARTEK THE CONQUEROR

MY HERO'S NAME was Bartek Slowik[1]; but owing to his habit of staring when spoken to, the neighbours called him "Bartek Goggle-Eyes." Indeed, he had little in common with nightingales, and his intellectual qualities and truly childish *naïveté* won him the further nickname of "Bartek the Blockhead." The last was the most popular, in fact, the only one handed down to history, though Bartek bore yet a fourth—an official—name. Since the Polish words "man" and "nightingale"[2] present no difference to a German ear, and the Germans love to translate barbarian proper names into a more cultured language in the cause of civilization, the following conversation took place when he was being entered as a recruit.

"What is your name?" the officer asked Bartek.

"Slowik."

"Szloik.[3] *Ach, ja, gut.*"

And the officer wrote down "Man."

Bartek came from the village of Pognenbin, a name given to a great many villages in the province of Poznań and in other parts of Poland. First of all there was he himself, not to mention his land, his cottage and two cows, his own piebald horse, and his wife, Magda. Thanks to this combination of circumstances he was able to live comfortably, and according to the maxim contained in the verse:

> To him whom God would bless He gives, of course,
> A wife called Magda and a piebald horse.

In fact, all his life he had taken whatever Providence sent without troubling about it. But just now Providence had ordained war, and Bartek was not a little upset at this. For news had come that the reserves would be called up, and that it would be necessary to leave his cottage and land, and entrust it all to his wife's care. People at Pognenbin were poor enough already. Bartek usually worked at the factory in the winter and helped his household on in this way; but what would happen now? Who could know when the war with the French would end? Magda, when she had read through the papers, began to swear:

"May they be damned and die themselves! May they be blinded!—Though you are a fool—yet I am sorry for you. The French give no quarter; they will chop off your head, I dare say."

Bartek felt that his wife spoke the truth. He feared the French like fire, and was sorry for himself on that account. What had the French done to him? What was he going after there,—why was he going to that horrible strange

[1]Nightingale.—TRANSLATOR.
[2]"Czlowiek" and "slowik."—TRANSLATOR.
[3]"Czlowiek" (man).—TRANSLATOR.

land where not a single friendly soul was to be found? He knew what life at Pognenbin was like—well, it was neither easy nor difficult, but just as it was. But now he was being told to go away, although he knew that it was better to be here than anywhere else. Still, there was no help for it;—such is fate. Bartek embraced his wife, and the ten-year-old Franek; spat, crossed himself, and went out of the cottage, Magda following him. They did not take very tender leave of one another. They both sobbed, he repeating, "Come, come, hush!" and went out into the road. There there they realized that the same thing which had happened to them had happened to all Pognenbin, for the whole village was astir, and the road was obstructed by traffic. As they walked to the station, women, children, old men, and dogs followed them. Every one's heart was heavy; but a few smoked their pipes with an air of indifference, and some were already intoxicated. Others were singing with hoarse voices:

> Skrzynecki[4] died, alas!
> No more his voice is heard;
> His hand, bedeckt with rings,
> No more shall wield the sword.

while one or two of the Germans from Pognenbin sang *Wacht am Rhein* out of sheer fright. All that motley and many-coloured crowd—including policemen with glittering bayonets—moved in file towards the end of the village with shouts, bustle, and confusion. Women clung to their "warriors' " necks and wept; one old woman showed her yellow teeth and waved her arms in the air; another cried: "May the Lord remember our tears!" There were cries of: "Franek! Kasko! Józek! good-bye!" Dogs barked, the church bell rang, the priest even said the prayers for the dying, since not one of those now going to the station would return. The war had claimed them all, but the war would not give them back. The plough would grow rusty in the field, for Pognenbin had declared war against the French. Pognenbin could not acquiesce in the supremacy of Napoleon III, and took to heart the question of the Spanish succession. The last sounds of the bell hovered over the crowd, which was already falling out of line. Heads were bared as they passed the shrine. The light dust rose up from the road, for the day was dry and fine. Along both sides of the road the ripening corn, heavy in the ear, rustled and bowed in the gentle gusts of wind. The larks were twittering in the blue sky, and each warbled as if fearing he might be forgotten.

At the station there was a still greater crowd, and more noise and confusion. Here were men called in from Krzywda Górna, Krzywda Dolna, from Wywlaszczyńce, from Niedola, and Mizerów. The station walls were covered with proclamations in which war was declared in the Name of God and the Fatherland: the *Landwehr* was setting forth to defend menaced parents, wives and children, cottages and fields. It was evident that the French bore a special grudge against Pognenbin, Krzywda Górna, Krzywda Dolna, Wywlaszczyńce, Niedola, and Mizerów. Such, as least, was the impression produced on those who read the placards. Fresh crowds were continually assembling in front of the station. In the waiting-room the smoke from the

[4]A popular song. Skrzynecki was a well-known leader in the Polish Revolution of 1830. —TRANSLATOR.

men's pipes filled the air, and hid the placards. It was difficult to make oneself understood in the noise, for every one was running, shouting, and screaming. On the platform orders were given in German. They sounded strangely brief, harsh, and decisive.

The bell rang. The powerful breath of the engine was heard in the distance coming nearer—growing more distinct. With it the war itself seemed to be coming nearer.

A second bell—and a shudder ran through every heart. A woman began to scream, "Jadom, Jadom!" She was evidently calling to her Adam, but the other women took up the word and cried, "Jada."[5] A shrill voice among them added: "The French are coming!" and in the twinkling of an eye a panic seized not only the women, but also the future heroes of Sedan. The crowd swerved. At that moment the train entered the station. Caps and uniforms were to be seen at all the windows. Soldiers seemed to swarm like ants. Dark, oblong bodies of cannon showed grimly on some of the trucks, on others there was a forest of bayonets. The soldiers had, apparently, been ordered to sing, for the whole train shook with their strong masculine voices. Strength and power seemed in some way to issue from that train, the end of which was not even in sight.

The reservists on the platform began to fall in, but any one who could lingered in taking leave. Bartek swung his arms as if they were the sails of a windmill, and stared.

"Well, Magda, good-bye!"

"Oh, my poor fellow!"

"You will never see me again!"

"I shall never see you again!"

"There's no help for it!"

"May the Mother of God protect and shelter you!"

"Good-bye. Take care of the cottage."

The woman in tears embraced him.

"May God guide you!"

The last moment had come. The whistle and the women's crying and sobbing drowned everything else. "Good-bye! Good-bye!" But the soldiers were already separated from the motley crowd, and formed a dark, solid mass, moving forward in square columns with the certainty and regularity of clockwork. The order was given: "Take your seats!" Columns and squares broke asunder from the centre, marched with heavy strides towards the carriages, and jumped into them. The engine, now breathing like a dragon and exhaling streams of vapour, sent forth wreaths of grey smoke. The women cried and sobbed still louder; some of them hid their eyes with their handkerchiefs, others waved their hands towards the carriages; sobbing voices repeated the name of husband and son.

"Good-bye, Bartek!" Magda cried from amongst them. "Take care of yourself!—May the Mother of God—Good-bye! Oh, God!——"

"And take care of the cottage," answered Bartek.

The line of trucks suddenly trembled, the carriages knocked against one another—and went forward.

"And remember you have a wife and child," Magda cried, running after

[5] "They are going." "Jadom" and "jada" are pronounced similarly.—TRANSLATOR.

the train. "Good-bye, in the name of the Father, the Son, and the Holy Ghost! Good-bye——"

On went the train, faster and faster, bearing away the warriors of Pognenbin, of both Krzywdas, of Niedola, and Mizerów.

II

Magda, with the crowd of women, returned crying to Pognenbin, in one direction; in the other the train, bristling with bayonets, rushed into the grey distance, and Bartek with it. There seemed to be no end to the long cloud of smoke; Pognenbin was also scarcely visible. Only the lime-tree showed faintly, and the church tower, glistening as the rays of the sun played upon it. Soon the lime-tree also disappeared, and the gilt cross resembled a shining speck. As long as that speck continued to shine Bartek kept his eyes fixed upon it, but when that vanished too there were no bounds to the poor fellow's grief. A sense of great weakness came over him and he felt lost. So he began to look at the sergeant, for, after the Almighty, he already felt there was no one greater than he. The sergeant clearly knew what would become of Bartek now; he himself knew nothing, understood nothing. The sergeant sat on the bench, and, supporting his rifle between his knees, he lighted his pipe. The smoke rose in clouds, hiding his grave, discontented face from time to time. Not Bartek's eyes alone watched his face; all the eyes from every corner of the carriage were watching it. At Pognenbin or Krzywda every Bartek or Wojtek was his own master, each had to think about himself, and for himself, but now the sergeant would do this for him. He would command them to look to the right, and they would look to the right; he would command them to look to the left, and they would look to the left. The question, "Well, and what is to become of us?" stood in each man's eyes, but he knew as much as all of them put together, and also what was expected of them. If only one were able by glances to draw some command or explanation from him! But the men were afraid to ask direct, as war was now drawing near with all the chances of being court-martialled. What was permitted and was not permitted, and by whom, was unknown. They, at least, did not know, and the sound of such a word as *Kriegsgericht,* though they did not understand it, frightened them very much.

They felt that this sergeant had still more power over them now than at the manœuvres in Poznań; he it was who knew everything, and without him nothing would be done. He seemed meanwhile to be finding his rifle growing heavy, for he pushed it towards Bartek to hold for him. Bartek reached out hastily for it, held his breath, stared, and looked at the sergeant as he would at a rainbow, yet derived little comfort from that. Ah, there must surely be bad news, for even the sergeant looked worried. At the stations one heard singing and shouting; the sergeant gave his orders, bustled about and swore, as if to show his importance. But let the train once move on, and every one, including himself, was silent. For him also the world now seemed to wear two aspects, the one clear and intelligible—that represented by home and family—the other dark, yes, absolutely dark—that of France and war.

He effectually revived the spirits of the Pognenbin soldiers, not so much by his personality, as by the fact that each man carried him at the back of his mind. And since each soldier carried his knapsack on his shoulder, with his cloak and other warlike accoutrements, the whole load was extremely heavy.

All the while the train was shaking, roaring, and rushing along into space. Now, a station where they added fresh carriages and engines; now another, where helmets, cannon, horses, bayonets, and companies of lancers were to be seen. The fine evening drew in slowly. The sun sank in a deep crimson, and a number of light flying clouds spread from the edge of the darkening sky across to the west. The train, stopping frequently at the stations to pick up passengers and carriages, shook and rushed forward into that crimson brightness, as into a sea of blood. From the open carriage, in which Bartek and the Pognenbin troops were seated, one could see villages, hamlets, and little towns, church steeples, storks—looking like hooks, as they stood on one leg on their nests—isolated cottages, and cherry orchards. Everything was passed rapidly, and everything looked crimson. Meanwhile the soldiers, growing bolder, began to whisper to one another, because the sergeant, having laid his kit bag under his head, had fallen asleep, with his clay pipe between his teeth. Wojtek Gwizdala, a peasant from Pognenbin, sitting beside Bartek, jogged his elbow.

"Bartek, listen!"

Bartek turned a face with pensive, wide open eyes towards him.

"Why do you look like a calf going to be slaughtered?" Gwizdala whispered. "True, you, poor beggar, are going to be slaughtered, that's certain!"

"Oh, my word!" groaned Bartek.

"Are you afraid?" Gwizdala asked.

"Why shouldn't I be afraid?"

The crimson in the sky was growing deeper still, so Gwizdala pointed towards it and went on whispering:

"Do you see that brightness? Do you know, blockhead, what that is? That's blood. Here's Poland—our frontier, say—do you understand? But there in the distance, where it's so bright, that's France itself."

"And shall we be there soon?"

"Why are you in such a hurry? They say that it's a terribly long way. But never fear, the French will come out to meet us."

Bartek's Pognenbin brain began to work laboriously. After some moments he asked: "Wojtek!"

"Yes?"

"What sort of people are these Frenchmen?"

Here Wojtek's wisdom suddenly became aware of a pitfall into which it might be easier to tumble head foremost than to come out again. He knew that the French were the French. He had heard something about them from old people, who had related that they were always fighting with every one; he knew at least that they were very strange people. But how could he explain this to Bartek to make him understand how strange they were? First of all, therefore, he repeated the question:

"What sort of people?"

"Why, yes."

Now there were three nations known to Wojtek: living in the centre were the Poles; on the one side were the Russians, on the other the Germans. But there were various kinds of Germans. Preferring, therefore, to be clear rather than accurate, he said:

"What sort of people are the French? How can I tell you? They must be like the Germans, only worse."

At which Bartek exclaimed: "Oh, the low vermin!"

Up to that time he had one feeling only with regard to the French, and that was a feeling of unspeakable fear. Henceforth this Prussian reservist cherished the hatred of a true patriot towards them. But not feeling quite clear about it all, he asked again: "Then Germans will be fighting Germans?"

Here Wojtek, like a second Socrates, chose to adopt a simile, and answered:

"But doesn't your dog, Lysek, fight with my Burek?"

Bartek opened his mouth and looked at his instructor for a moment.

"Ah! true."

"And the Austrians are Germans," explained Wojtek, "and haven't they fought against us? Old Świerszcz said that when he was in that war Steinmetz used to shout: 'On, boys, at the Germans!' Only that's not so easy with the French."

"Good God!"

"The French have never been beaten in any war. When they attack you, don't be afraid, don't disgrace yourself. Each man is worth two or three of us, and they wear beards like Jews. There are some as dark as the devil. Now that you know what they are like, commend yourself to God!"

"Well, but then why do we run after them?" Bartek asked in desperation.

This philosophical remark was possibly not as stupid as it appeared to Wojtek, who, evidently influenced by official opinion, quickly had his answer ready.

"I would rather not have gone myself, but if we don't run after them, they will run after us. There's no help for it. You have read what the papers say. It's against us peasants that they bear the chief grudge. People say that they have their eyes on Poland, because they want to smuggle vodka out of the country, and the Government won't allow it, and that's why there's war. Now do you understand?"

"I cannot understand," Bartek said resignedly.

"They are also as greedy for our women as a dog for a bone," Wojtek continued.

"But surely they would respect Magda, for example?"

"They don't even respect age!"

"Oh!" cried Bartek in a voice implying, "If that is so, then I will fight!"

In fact this seemed to him really too much. Let them continue to smuggle vodka out of Poland—but let them dare to touch Magda! Our friend Bartek now began to regard the whole war from the standpoint of his own interests, and took courage in the thought of how many soldiers and cannon were going out in defence of Magda, who was in danger of being outraged by the French. He arrived at the conviction that there was nothing for it but to go out against them.

Meanwhile the brightness had faded from the sky, and it had grown dark.

The carriages began to rock violently on the uneven rails, and the helmets and bayonets shook from right to left to the rhythm of the rocking. Hour after hour passed by. Millions of sparks flew from the engine and crossed one another in the darkness, serpentining in long golden lines. For a while Bartek could not sleep. Like those sparks in the wind, thoughts leapt into his mind about Magda, about Pognenbin, the French, and the Germans. He felt that though he would have liked to have lain down on the bench on which he was sitting, he could not do so. He fell asleep, it is true, but it was a heavy, unrefreshing sleep, and he was at once pursued by dreams. He saw his dog, Lysek, fighting with Wojtek's Burek, till all their hair was torn off. He was running for a stick to stop them, when suddenly he saw something else: sitting with his arm round Magda was a dark Frenchman, as dark as the earth; but Magda was smiling contentedly. Some Frenchmen jeered at Bartek, and pointed their fingers at him. In reality it was the engine scream-ing, but it seemed to him that the French were calling, "Magda! Magda! Magda!" "Hold your tongue, thieves," Bartek shouted; "leave my wife alone!" but they continued calling "Magda! Magda! Magda!" Lysek and Burek started barking, and all Pognenbin cried out, "Don't let your wife go!" Was he bound, or what was the matter? No, he rushed forward, tore at the cord and broke it, seized the Frenchman by the head—and suddenly——!

Suddenly he was sezied with severe pain, as from a heavy blow. Bartek awoke and dragged his feet to the ground. The whole carriage awoke, and every one asked, "What has happened?" In his sleep the unfortunate Bartek had seized the sergeant by the head. He stood up immediately, as straight as a fiddle-string, two fingers at his forehead; but the sergeant waved his hand, and shouted like mad:

"*Ach, Sie!* beast of a Pole! I'll knock all the teeth out of your head—blockhead!"

The sergeant shouted until he was hoarse with rage, and Bartek stood saluting all the while. Some of the soldiers bit their lips to keep from laugh-ing, but they were half afraid, too. A parting shot burst forth from the sergeant's lips:

"You Polish ox! Ox from Podolia!"

Ultimately everything became quiet again. Bartek sat back in his old place. He was conscious of nothing but that his cheek was swollen, and, as if playing him a trick, the engine kept repeating:

"Magda! Magda! Magda!"

He felt a heavy weight of sorrow upon him.

III

It was morning.

The fitful, pale light fell on faces sleepy and worn with a long, restless night. The soldiers were sleeping in discomfort on the seats, some with their heads thrown forward, others with their noses in the air. The dawn was rising, and flooding all the world with crimson light. The air was fresh and keen. The soldiers awoke. The morning rays were drawing away shadows and mist into some region unknown. Alas! and where was now Pognenbin, where Great and Little Kzrywda, where Mizerów? Everything was strange and different. The summits of the hills were overgrown with trees; in the valleys were houses hidden under red roofs, with dark cross beams on the white walls—beautiful houses like mansions, covered with vines. Here, churches with spires; there, factory chimneys with wreaths of purple smoke. There were only straight lines, level banks, and fields of corn. The inhabitants swarmed like ants. They passed villages and towns, and the train went through a number of unimportant stations without stopping. Something must have happened, for there were crowds to be seen everywhere. When the sun slowly began to appear from behind the hills, one or two of the soldiers commenced saying a prayer aloud. Others followed their example, and the first rays of splendour fell on the men's earnest, devout faces.

Meanwhile the train had stopped at a larger station. A crowd of people immediately surrounded it: news had come from the seat of war. Victory! Victory! Telegrams had been arriving for several hours. Every one had anticipated defeat, so, when roused by the unexpected news, their joy knew no bounds. People rushed half-clad from their houses and their beds, and ran to the post office. Flags were waving from the roofs, and handkerchiefs from every one's hands. Beer, tobacco, and cigars were carried to the carriages. The enthusiasm was unspeakable; every one's face was beaming. *Wacht am Rhein* filled the air continuously like a tempest. Not a few were weeping, others embraced one another. The enthusiasm animating the crowd imparted itself to the gallant soldiers, their courage rose, and they, too, began to sing. The carriages trembled with their strong voices, and the crowd listened in wonder to their unintelligible songs. The men from Pognenbin sang:

Bartosz! Bartosz! never lose hope!

"The Poles, the Poles!" repeated the crowd by way of explanation, and, gathering round the carriages, admired their soldierly bearing, and added to their joy by relating anecdotes of the remarkable courage of these Polish regiments.

Bartek had unshaven cheeks, which, in addition to his yellow moustache, goggle-eyes, and large bony form, made him look terrifying. They gazed at him as at some wild beast. These, then, were the men who were to defend Germany! He'd dispose of the French sure enough! Bartek smiled with satisfaction, for he, too, was pleased they had beaten the French. Now the French would not go to Pognenbin, they would not make off with Magda, nor capture his land. So he smiled, but as his cheek hurt him badly he made a grimace at the same time, and did certainly look terrifying. Then, displaying the appetite of a Homeric warrior, he caused pea-sausages and pints of beer to disappear into his mouth as into a vacuum. People in the crowd gave him cigars and pence, and they all drank to one another.

"There's some good in this German nation," he said to Wojtek, adding after a moment, "and you know they have beaten the French!"

But Wojtek, the sceptic, cast a shadow on his joy. Wojtek had forebodings, like Cassandra.

"The French always allow themselves to be beaten at first, in order to take you in, and then they set to until they have cut you to pieces!"

Wojtek did not know that the greater part of Europe shared his opinion, and still less that all Europe was together with him mistaken.

They travelled on. All the houses were covered with flags. They stopped a long while at several of the stations, because there was a block of trains everywhere. Troops were hastening from all sides of Germany to reinforce their brothers in arms. The trains were swathed in green wreaths, and the lancers had decorated their lances with the bunches of flowers given them on the way. The majority of these lancers also were Poles. More than one conversation and greeting was heard passing from carriage to carriage:

"How are you, old fellow, and where is God Almighty leading you?"

Meanwhile to the accompaniment of the train rumbling along the rails, the well-known song rang out:

> "Flirt with us, soldiers dear!"
> Cried the girls of Sandomir.

And soon Bartek and his comrades caught up the refrain:

> Gaily forth the answer burst:
> "Bless you, dears! but dinner first!"

As many as had gone out from Pognenbin in sorrow were now filled with enthusiasm and spirit. A train which had arrived from France with the first batch of wounded, damped, however, this feeling of cheerfulness. It stopped at Deutz, and waited a long time to allow the trains hurrying to the seat of war to go by. The men were marched across the bridge *en route* for Cologne. Bartek ran forward with several others to look at the sick and wounded. Some lay in closed, others in open carriages, and these latter could be seen well. At the first glance our hero's heart was again in his mouth.

"Come here, Wojtek," he cried in terror. "See how many of our countrymen the Frenchmen have done for!"

It was indeed a sight! Pale, exhausted faces, some darkened by gunpowder or by pain, or stained with blood. To the sounds of universal rejoicing these men only responded by groans. Some were cursing the war, the French and the Germans. Parched lips called every moment for water, eyes rolled in delirium. Here and there, amongst the wounded, were the rigid faces of the dead, in some cases peaceful, with blue lines round their eyes, in others contorted through the death struggle, with terrifying eyes and grinning teeth. Bartek saw the bloody fruits of war for the first time, and once more confusion reigned in his mind. He seemed quite stupefied, as, standing in the crowd, with his mouth open, he was elbowed from every side, and pommelled on the neck by the police. He sought Wojtek's eyes, nudged him, and said:

"Wojtek, may Heaven preserve us! It's horrible!"

"It will be just the same with you."

"Jesu! Mary! That human beings should murder one another like this! When a fellow kills another the police take him off to the magistrate and prison!"

"Well, but now whoever kills most human beings is to be praised. What were you thinking of, blockhead? Did you think you would use gunpowder as in the manœuvres, and would shoot at targets instead of people?"

Here the difference between theory and practice certainly stood out clearly. Notwithstanding that our friend Bartek was a soldier, had attended manœuvres and drill, had practised rifle shooting, had known that the object of war was to kill people, now, when he saw blood flowing, and all the misery of war, it made him feel so sick and miserable he could hardly keep steady on his legs. He was impressed anew with respect for the French; this diminished, however, when they arrived at Cologne from Deutz. At the Central Station they saw prisoners for the first time. Surrounding them were a number of soldiers and people, who gazed at them with interest, but without hostility. Bartek elbowed his way through the crowd, and, looking into the carriage, was amazed.

A troop of French infantry in ragged cloaks, small, dirty, and emaciated, were packed into the carriages like a cask of herrings. Many of them stretched out their hands for the trifling gifts presented to them by the crowd, if the sentinels did not prevent them. Judging from what he had heard from Wojtek, Bartek had had a wholly different impression of the French, and this took his breath away. He looked to see if Wojtek were anywhere about, and found him standing close by.

"What did you say?" asked Bartek. "By all the saints! I shouldn't be more surprised if I had lost my head!"

"They must have shrunk somehow," answered Wojtek, equally disillusioned.

"What are they jabbering?"

"It's certainly not Polish."

Reassured by this impression, Bartek walked on past the carriages. "Miserable wretches!" he said, when he had finished his review of the regulars.

But the last carriages contained Zouaves, and these gave Bartek food for further reflection. From the fact that they sat huddled together in the carriages, it was impossible to discover whether each man were equal to two or three ordinary men; but, through the window, he saw the long, martial beards and grave faces of veteran soldiers with dark complexions and alarmingly shining eyes. Again Bartek's heart leapt to his mouth.

"These are the worst of all," he whispered low, as if afraid they might hear him.

"You have not seen those who have not let themselves be taken prisoner yet," replied Wojtek.

"Heaven preserve us!"

"Now do you understand?"

Having finished looking at the Zouaves, they walked on. At the last carriage Bartek suddenly started back as if he had touched fire.

"Oh, Wojtek, Lord help us!"

There was the dark—nearly black—face of a Turco at the open window, rolling his eyes so that the whites showed. He must have been wounded, for his face was contorted with pain.

"What's the matter now?" asked Wojtek.

"That must be the Evil One, it's not a soldier. Lord have mercy on my sins!"

"Look at his teeth!"

"May he go to perdition! I shan't look at him any longer."

Bartek was silent, then asked after a moment:

"Wojtek!"

"Yes?"

"Mightn't it be a good thing to cross oneself before any one like that?"

"The heathen don't understand anything about the holy Faith."

The signal was given for taking their seats. In a few moments the train was moving. When it grew dusk Bartek continually saw before him the Turco's dark face with the terrible white of his eyes. Judging from the feelings which at the moment animated this Pognenbin soldier, it would have been impossible to foretell his future deeds.

IV

The particular share he took at first in the pitched battle of Gravelotte merely convinced Bartek of this fact—that in war there is plenty to look at, but nothing to do. For at the commencement he and his regiment were ordered to wait, with their rifles at their feet, at the bottom of a hill covered by a vineyard. The guns were booming in the distance, squadrons of cavalry charged past near at hand with a clatter which shook the earth; then the flags passed, then cuirassiers with drawn swords. The shells on the hill flew hissing across the blue sky in the form of small white clouds, then smoke filled the air and hid the horizon. The battle seemed like a storm which passes through a district without lasting long anywhere.

After the first hours, unusual activity was displayed round Bartek's regiment. Other regiments began to be massed round his, and in the spaces between them the guns, drawn by plunging horses, rushed along, and, hastily unlimbered, were pointed towards the hill. The whole valley became full of troops. Commands were now thundered from all sides, the aides-de-camp rushed about wildly, and the private soldiers said to one another:

"Ah! it will be our turn now! It's coming!"

Or inquired uneasily of one another:

"Isn't it time yet to start?"

"Surely it must be!"

The question of life and death was now beginning to hang in the balance. Something in the smoke which hid the horizon burst close at hand with a terrible explosion. The deep roar of the cannon and the crack of the rifle-firing was heard ever nearer; it was like an indistinct sound coming from a distance—then the mitrailleuse became audible. Suddenly the guns, placed in position, boomed forth until the earth and air trembled together. The shells whistled frightfully through Bartek's company. Watching, they saw something bright red, a little cloud, as it might be, and in that cloud something whistled, rushed, rattled, roared, and shrieked. The men shouted: "A shell! A shell!" and at the same moment this vulture of war sped forward like a gale, came near, fell, and burst! A terrible roar met the ear, a crash as if the world had collapsed, followed by a rushing sound, as before a puff of wind. Confusion reigned in the lines standing in the neighbourhood of the guns, then came the cry and command "Stand ready!" Bartek stood in the front rank, his rifle at his shoulder, his head turned towards the hill, his mouth set—so his teeth were not chattering. He was forbidden to tremble.

he was forbidden to shoot. He had only to stand still and wait! But now another shell burst—three, four, ten. The wind lifted the smoke from the hill: the French had already driven the Prussian battery from it, had placed theirs in position, and now opened fire on the valley. Every moment from under cover of the vineyard they sent forth long white columns of smoke. Protected by the guns, the enemy's infantry continued to advance, in order to open fire. They were already half-way down the hill and could now be seen plainly, for the wind was driving the smoke away. Would the vineyard prove an obstacle to them? No, the red caps of the infantry were advancing. Suddenly they disappeared under the tall arches of the vines, and there was nothing to be seen but tricolour flags waving here and there. The rifle fire began fiercely but intermittently, continually starting in fresh and unexpected places. Shells burst above it, and crossed one another in the air. Now and then cries rang out from the hill, which were answered from below by a German "Hurrah!" The guns from the valley sent forth an uninterrupted fire; the regiment stood unflinching.

The line of fire began to embrace it more closely, however. The bullets hummed in the distance like gnats and flies, or passed near with a terrible whiz. More and more of them came: hundreds, thousands, whistling round their heads, their noses, their eyes, their shoulders; it was astonishing there should be a man left standing. Suddenly Bartek heard a groan close by: "Jesu!" then: "Stand ready!" then again: "Jesu!" "Stand ready!" Soon the groans went on without intermission, the words of command came faster and faster, the lines drew in closer, the whizzing grew more frequent, more uninterrupted, more terrible. The dead covered the ground. It was like the Judgment Day.

"Are you afraid?" Wojtek asked.

"Why shouldn't I be afraid?" our hero answered, his teeth chattering.

Nevertheless both Bartek and Wojtek still kept their feet, and it did not even enter their heads to run away. They had been commanded to stand still and receive the enemy's fire. Bartek had not spoken the truth; he was not as much afraid as thousands of others would have been in his place. Discipline held the mastery over his imagination, and his imagination had never painted such a horrible situation as this. Nevertheless, Bartek felt that he would be killed, and he confided this thought to Wojtek.

"There won't be room in heaven for the numbers they kill," Wojtek answered in an excited voice.

These words comforted Bartek perceptibly. He began to hope that his place in heaven had already been taken. Reassured with regard to this, he stood more patiently, conscious only of the intense heat, and with the perspiration running down his face. Meantime the firing became so heavy that the ranks were thinning visibly. There was no one to carry away the killed and wounded; the death rattle of the dying mingled with the whizz of shells and the din of shooting. One could see by the movement of the tricolour flags that the infantry hidden by the vines were coming closer and closer. The volleys of mitrailleuse decimated the ranks; the men were beginning to grow desperate.

But underlying this despair were impatience and rage. Had they been commanded to go forward, they would have gone like a whirlwind. It was impossible merely to stand still in one spot. A soldier suddenly threw down his helmet with his whole force, and exclaimed:

"Curse it! One death is as good as another!"

Bartek again experienced such a feeling of relief from these words that he almost ceased to be afraid. For if one death was as good as another, what did anything matter? This rustic philosophy was calculated to arouse courage more rapidly than any other. Bartek knew that one death was as good as another, but it pleased him to hear it, especially as the battle was now turning into a defeat. For here was a regiment which had never fired a single shot, and was already half annihilated. Crowds of soldiers from other regiments which had been scattered ran in amongst and round theirs in disorder; only these peasants from Pognenbin, Great and Little Krzywda, and Mizerów still remained firm, upholding Prussian discipline. But even amongst them a certain degree of hesitation now began to be felt. Another moment and they would have burst the restraint of discipline. The ground under their feet was already soft and slippery with blood, the stench of which mingled with the smell of gunpowder. In several places the lines could not join up closely, because the dead bodies made gaps in them. At the feet of those men yet standing, the other half lay bleeding, groaning, struggling, dying, or in the silence of death. There was no air to breathe in. They began to grumble:

"They have brought us out to be slaughtered!"

"No one will come out of this!"

"Silence, Polish dogs!" sounded the officer's voice.

"I should just like you to be standing in my shoes!"

"Steht der Kerl da!"

Suddenly a voice began to repeat:

"We fly to thy patronage . . ."

Bartek instantly took it up:

"O holy Mother of God!"

And soon on that field of carnage a chorus of Polish voices was calling to the Defender of their nation, Our Lady of Czenstochowa:

"Despise not our petitions";

while from beneath their feet there came the accompaniment of groans: "Mary! Mary!" She had evidently heard them, for at that moment the aides-de-camp came galloping up, and the command rang forth: "Arms to the attack! Hurrah! Forward!" The crest of bayonets was suddenly lowered, the column stretched out into a long line and sprang towards the hill to seek with their bayonets the enemy they could not discover with their eyes. The men were, however, still two hundred yards from the foot of the hill, and they had to traverse that distance under a murderous fire. Would they not perish like the rest? Would they not be obliged to retreat? Perish they might, but retreat they could not, for the Prussian commander knows what tune will bring Polish soldiers to the attack. Amid the roar of cannon, amid the rifle fire and the smoke, the confusion and groaning, loudest of all sounded the drums and trumpets, playing the hymn at which every single drop of blood leapt in their veins. "Hurrah!" answered the Maćki.[6] "As long

[6]"Maćki"="Tommies."—Translator.

as we live!"[7] Frenzy seized them. The fire met them full in the face. They went like a whirlwind over the prostrate bodies of men and horses, over the wrecks of cannon. They fell, but they went with a shout and a song. They had already reached the vineyard and disappeared into its enclosure. Only the song was heard, and at times a bayonet glittered. On the hill the firing became increasingly fierce. In the valley the trumpets kept on sounding. The French volleys continued faster and faster—still faster—and suddenly—

Suddenly they were silent.

Down in the valley that old war dog, Steinmetz, lighted his clay pipe, and said in a tone of satisfaction:

"You have only to play to them! The daredevils will do it!"

And actually in a few moments one of the proudly waving tricolours was suddenly raised aloft, then drooped, and disappeared.

"They are not joking," said Steinmetz.

Again the trumpets played the hymn, and a second Polish regiment went to the help of the first. In the enclosure a pitched battle with bayonets was taking place.

And now, O Muse, sing of our hero, Bartek, that posterity may know of his deeds! The fear, impatience, and despair of his heart had mingled into the single feeling of rage, and when he heard that music each vein stood out in him like cast iron. His hair stood on end, his eyes shot fire. He forgot everything that had made up his world; he no longer cared whether one death was as good as another. Grasping his rifle firmly in his hands, he leapt forward with the others. Reaching the hill, he fell down for the tenth time, struck his nose, and, bespattered with mud and the blood flowing from his nose, ran on madly and breathlessly, catching at the air with open mouth. He stared round, wishing to find some of the French in the enclosure as quickly as possible, and caught sight of three standing together near the flags. They were Turcos. Would Bartek retreat? No, indeed; he could have seized the horns of Lucifer himself now! He ran towards them at once, and they fell on him with a shout; two bayonets, like two deadly stings, had actually touched his chest already, but Bartek lowered his bayonet. A dreadful cry followed—a groan, and two dark bodies lay writhing convulsively on the ground.

At that moment the third, who carried the flag, ran up to help his two comrades. Like a fury, Bartek leapt on him with his whole strength. The firing flashed and roared in the distance, while Bartek's hoarse roar rang out through the smoke:

"Go to hell!"

And again the rifle in his hand described a fearful semicircle, again groans responded to his thrusts. The Turcos retreated in terror at the sight of this furious giant, but either Bartek misunderstood, or they shouted out something in Arabic, for it seemed to him that their thick lips distinctly uttered the cry: "Magda! Magda!"

"Magda will give it you!" howled Bartek, and with one leap he was in the enemy's midst.

[7]The hymn in question was the national song, "Poland has not perished as long as we live," first sung by the Polish Legions under Napoleon; it won enormous popularity among the Poles, and is now the Polish national anthem.—M. M. G.

Happily at that moment some of his comrades ran up to his assistance. A hand-to-hand fight now took place in the enclosure of the vineyard. There was the crack of rifles at close quarters, and the hot breath of the combatants sounded through their nostrils. Bartek raged like a storm. Blinded by smoke, streaming with blood, more like a wild beast than a man, and regardless of everything, he mowed down men at each blow, broke rifles, cracked heads. His hands moved with the terrible swiftness of a machine sowing destruction. He attacked the ensign, and seized him by the throat with an iron grip. The ensign's eyes turned upwards, his face swelled, his throat rattled, and his hands let the pole fall.

"Hurrah!" cried Bartek, and, lifting the flag, he waved it in the air.

This was the flag raised aloft and drooping, which Steinmetz had seen from below.

But he could only see it for half a second, for in the next—Bartek had trampled it to shreds. Meanwhile his comrades were already rushing on ahead.

Bartek remained alone for a moment. He tore off the flag, hid it in his breast-pocket, and, having seized the pole in both hands, rushed after his comrades.

A crowd of Turcos, shouting in a barbarous tongue, now fled towards the gun placed on the summit of the hill, the Maćki after them, shouting, pursuing, striking with butt-end and bayonet.

The Zouaves, who were stationed by the guns, received the first men with rifle fire.

"Hurrah!" shouted Bartek.

The men ran up to the guns, and a fresh struggle took place round these. At that moment the second Polish regiment came to the aid of the first. The flag-pole in Bartek's powerful hands was now changed into a kind of infernal flail. Each stroke dealt by it opened a free passage through the close lines of the French. The Zouaves and Turcos began to be seized with panic, and they fled from the place where Bartek was fighting. Within a few moments Bartek was sitting astride the gun, as he might his Pognenbin mare.

But scarcely had the soldiers had time to see him on this, when he was already on the second, after killing another ensign who was standing by it with the flag.

"Hurrah, Bartek!" repeatedly exclaimed the soldiers.

The victory was complete. All the ammunition was captured. The infantry fled, and after being surrounded by Prussian reinforcements on the other side of the hill, laid down their arms.

Bartek captured yet a third flag during the pursuit.

It was worth seeing him, when exhausted, covered with blood, and blowing like a blacksmith's bellows, he now descended the hill together with the rest, bearing the three flags on his shoulder. The French? Why, what had not he alone done to them! By his side went Wojtek, scratched and scarred, so he turned to him and said:

"What did you say? Why, they are miserable wretches; there isn't a scrap of strength in their bones! They have just scratched you and me like kittens, that's all. But how I have bled them you can see by the ground!"

"Who would have known that you could be so brave!" replied Wojtek, who had watched Bartek's deeds, and began to look at him in quite a different light.

But who had not seen these deeds? History, all the regiment and the greater number of the officers. Everybody now looked with astonishment at this country giant with the flaxen moustache and goggle eyes. The major himself said to him, "Ah, you confounded Pole!" and pulled his ear, making Bartek grin to his back teeth with pleasure. When the regiment stood once more at the foot of the hill, the major pointed him out to the colonel, and the colonel to Steinmetz himself.

The latter noticed the flags, and ordered that they should be taken charge of; then he began to look at Bartek. Our friend Bartek again stood as straight as a fiddle-string, presenting arms, and the old general looked at him and nodded his head with approval. Finally he began to say something to the colonel; the words "non-commissioned officer" were plainly audible.

"Too stupid, your Excellency!" answered the major.

"Let us try," said his Excellency, and turning his horse, he approached Bartek.

Bartek himself scarcely knew what was happening to him: it was a thing unknown in the Prussian army for the general to talk to a private! His Excellency was the more easily able to do this, because he knew Polish. Moreover this private had captured three flags and two guns.

"Where do you come from?" inquired the general.

"From Pognenbin," answered Bartek.

"Good. Your name?"

"Bartek Slowik."

"Mensch," explained the major.

"Mens!" Bartek tried to repeat.

"Do you know why you are fighting the French?"

"I know, your 'Cellency."

"Tell me."

Bartek began to stammer, "Because, because——" Then on a sudden Wojtek's words fortunately came into his mind, and he burst out with them quickly, so as not to get confused: "Because they are Germans too, only worse villains!"

His Excellency's face began to twitch as if he felt inclined to burst out laughing. After a moment, however, his Excellency turned to the major, and said:

"You are right, sir."

Our friend Bartek, satisfied with himself, remained standing as straight as a fiddle-string.

"Who won the battle to-day?" the general asked again.

"I, your 'Cellency," Bartek answered without hesitation.

His Excellency's face again began to twitch.

"Right, very right, it was you! And here you have your reward."

Here the old soldier unpinned the iron cross from his own breast, stooped and pinned it on to Bartek. The general's good humour was reflected in a perfectly natural way on the faces of the colonel, the majors, the captains, down to the non-commissioned officers. After the general's departure the colonel for his own part presented Bartek with ten thalers, the major with five, and so on. Every one repeated to him smilingly that he had won the battle, with the result that Bartek was in the seventh heaven.

It was a strange thing: the only person who was not really satisfied with our hero was Wojtek.

In the evening, when they were both sitting round the fire, and when Bartek's distinguished face was bulging as much with pea-sausage as the sausage itself with peas, Wojtek ejaculated in a tone of resignation:

"Oh, Bartek, what a blockhead you are, because——"

"But why?" said Bartek, between his bites of sausage.

"Why, man, didn't you tell the general that the French are Germans?"

"You said so yourself."

"But you ought to have remembered the general and the officers are Germans too."

"And what of that?——"

Wojtek began to stammer a little:—"Well, though they may be Germans, you needn't have told him so, because it's always unpleasant——"

"But I said it about the French, not about them . . ."

"Ah, because when . . ."

Wojtek stopped short, though evidently wishing to say something further; he wished to explain to Bartek that it is not suitable when among Germans to speak evil of them, but somehow his tongue became entangled.

v

A little while later the royal Prussian mail brought the following letter to Pognenbin:

May Jesus Christ and His Holy Mother be praised.

DEAREST MAGDA! What news of you? It is all right for you to be able to rest quietly in bed at home, but I am fighting horribly hard here. We have been surrounding the great fort of Metz, and there was a battle, and I did for so many of the French that all the Infantry and Artillery were astonished. And the General himself was astonished, and said that I had won the battle, and gave me a cross. And the officers and non-commissioned officers respect me very much now, and rarely box my ears. Afterwards we marched on farther, and there was a second battle, but I have forgotten what the town was called; there also I seized and carried off four flags, and knocked down one of the biggest Colonels in the Cuirassiers, and took him prisoner. And as our regiment is going to be sent home, the Sergeant has advised me to ask to be transferred and to stay on here, for in war it is only sleep you do not get, but you may eat as much as you can stand, and in this country there is wine everywhere, for they are a rich nation. We have also burnt a town and we did not spare even women or children, nor did I. The church was burnt to the ground, because they are Catholics, and a good few people were roasted. We are now going on to the Emperor himself, and that will be the end of the war, but you take care of the cottage and Franek, for if you do not take care of it, then I will beat you till you have learnt what sort of a man I am. I commend you to God.

                                                      BARTLOMIEJ SLOWIK.

Bartek was evidently developing a taste for war, and beginning to regard it as his proper trade. He felt greater confidence in himself, and now went into battle as he might have gone to his work at Pognenbin. Medals and crosses covered his breast, and although he did not become a non-commissioned officer, he was universally regarded as the foremost private in the regiment. He was always well disciplined, as before, and possessed the blind courage of the man who simply takes no account of danger. The courage actuating him was no longer of the same kind as that which had filled him in his first moments of fury, for it now sprang from military experience and faith in himself. Added to this, his giant strength could endure all kinds of fatigue, marches and overstrain. Men fell at his side; he alone went on unharmed, only working all the harder and developing more and more into the stern Prussian soldier. He now not only fought the French, but hated them. Some of his other ideas also changed. He became a soldier-patriot, blindly extolling his leaders. In another letter to Magda, he wrote:

Wojtek is divided in his opinion, and so there is a quarrel between us, do you understand? He is a scoundrel, too, because he says that the French are Germans, but they are French, and we are Germans.

Magda, in her reply to both letters, set about abusing him with the first words that came into her head.

Dearest Bartek [she wrote], married to me before the holy Altar! May God punish you! You yourself are a scoundrel, you heathen, going with those wretches to murder half a nation of Catholics. Do you not understand, then, that those wretches are Lutherans, and that you, a Catholic, are helping them? You like war, you ruffian, because you are able now to do nothing but fight, drink, and ill-treat others, and to go without fasting and burn churches. But may you burn in hell for that, because you are even proud of it, and have no thought for old people or children. Remember what has been written in golden letters in the Holy Scriptures for the Polish nation, from the beginning of the world to the Judgment Day—when God most High will have no regard for sluggards,—and restrain yourself, you Turk, that I may not smash your head to pieces. I have sent you five thalers, although I have need of them here, for I do not know which way to turn, and the household savings are getting short. I embrace you, dearest Bartek.

MAGDA.

The moral contained in these lines made little impression on Bartek. "The wife does not remember her vows," he thought to himself, "and is meddling." And he continued to make war in his old way. He distinguished himself in every battle so greatly, that finally he came under still more honourable eyes than those of Steinmetz. Ultimately, when the shattered Polish regiment was sent back into the depths of Germany, he took the sergeant's advice of applying for leave to be transferred, and stayed behind. The result of this was that he found himself outside Paris.

His letters were now full of contempt for the French. "They run away like hares in every battle," he wrote to Magda, and he wrote the truth. But the siege did not prove to his taste. He had to dig or to lie in the trenches round Paris for whole days, listening to the roar of the guns, and often getting soaked through. Besides, he missed his old regiment. In the one to which he had been transferred as a volunteer, he was surrounded by Germans. He knew some German, having already learnt a little at the factory, but only about five in ten words; now he quickly began to grow familiar with it. The

regiment, however, nicknamed him "the Polish ox," and it was only his decorations and his terrifying fists which shielded him from disagreeable jokes.
Nevertheless, he earned the respect of his new comrades, and began little by
little to make friends with them. Since he covered the whole regiment with
glory, they ultimately came to look upon him as one of themselves. Bartek
would always have considered himself insulted if any one called him German,
but in thinking of himself in distinction to the French he called himself *"ein
Deutscher."* To himself he appeared entirely different, but at the same time
he did not wish to pass for worse than others. An incident occurred, nevertheless, which might have given him plenty to reflect upon, had reflection
come more easily to this hero's mind. Some companies of his regiment had
been sent out against some volunteer sharpshooters, and laid an ambush for
them, into which they fell. But the detachment was composed of veteran soldiers, the remains of one of the regiments of the Foreign Legion, and this
time Bartek did not see the red caps running away after the first shots. They
defended themselves stubbornly when surrounded, and rushed forward to
force their way through the encircling Prussian soldiery. They fought so desperately that half of them cut their way through, and knowing the fate that
awaited captured sharpshooters, few allowed themselves to be taken alive.
The company in which Bartek was serving therefore only took two prisoners.
These were lodged overnight in a forester's house, and the next day they
were to be shot. A small guard of soldiers stood outside the door, but Bartek
was stationed in the room under the open window with the prisoners, who
were bound.

One of the prisoners was a man no longer young, with a grey moustache,
and a face expressing indifference to everything; the other appeared to be
about twenty-two years of age. With his fair moustache scarcely yet showing,
his face was more like a woman's than a soldier's.

"Well, this is the end of it," the young man said after a while; "a bullet
through your head—and it's all over!"

Bartek shuddered until the rifle in his hand rattled; the youth talked
Polish.

"It is all the same to me," the second answered in a gruff voice; "upon my
word, all the same! I have lived so long, I have had enough."

Bartek's heart beat quicker and quicker under his uniform.

"Listen, then," the older man continued; "there is no help for it. If you are
afraid, think about something else, or go to sleep. Enjoy what you can. God
is my witness I don't care!"

"My mother will grieve for me," the youth replied low; and, evidently
wishing to suppress his emotion, or else to deceive himself, he began to
whistle. He suddenly broke this off, and cried in a voice of deep despair, "I
did not even say good-bye."

"Then did you run away from home?"

"Yes. I thought the Germans would be beaten, so there would be better
things coming for Poland."

"And I thought the same. But now——"

Waving his hand, the old man finished speaking in a low voice, and his
last words were overpowered by the roar of the wind. The night was dark.
Clouds of fine rain swept past from time to time; the wood close by was

black as a pall. The gale whistled round the corners of the room, and howled in the chimney like a dog. The lamp, placed high above the window to prevent the wind from extinguishing it, threw a flood of bright light into the room. But Bartek, who was standing close to it under the window, was plunged in darkness.

And it was perhaps better the prisoners should not see his face, for strange things were taking place in this peasant's mind. At first he had been filled with astonishment, and had stared hard at the prisoners, trying to understand what they were saying. So these men had set out to beat the Germans to benefit Poland, and he had beaten the French, in order that Poland might benefit! And to-morrow these two men would be shot! How was that? What was a poor fellow to think about it? But if only he could hint it to them, if only he could tell them that he was their man, that he pitied them! He felt a sudden catch in his throat. What could he do for them? Could he rescue them? Then he, too, would be shot! Good God! What was happening to him? He was so overcome by pity that he could not remain in the room.

A strange intense longing suddenly came upon him till he seemed somewhere far off at Pognenbin. Pity, hitherto an unknown guest in his soldier's heart, cried to him from the depth of his soul: "Bartek, save them, they are your brothers!" and his heart, torn as never before, cried out for home, for Magda, for Pognenbin. He had had enough of the French, enough of this war, and of battles! The voice sounded clearer and clearer: "Bartek, save them!" Confound this war! The woods showed dark through the open window, moaning like the Pognenbin pines, and even in that moan something called out, "Bartek, save them!"

What could he do? Should he escape to the wood with them, or what? All his Prussian discipline recoiled in aversion from the thought. In the Name of the Father and the Son! He could but cross himself before it! He—a soldier, and desert? Never!

All the while the wood was moaning more loudly, the wind whistling more mournfully.

The elder prisoner suddenly whispered, "That wind—like the autumn at home."

"Leave me in peace!" the young man said in a Pognenbin voice.

After a moment, however, he repeated several times:

"At home, at home, at home! God! God!"

Deep sighs mingled with the listening wind, and the prisoners lay silent once more.

Bartek began to tremble feverishly. There is nothing so bad for a man as to be unable to tell what is amiss with him. It seemed to Bartek as if he had stolen something, and were afraid of being taken in charge. He had a clear conscience, nothing threatened him, but he was certainly terribly afraid of something. Indeed, his legs were trembling, his rifle had grown dreadfully heavy, and something—like bitter sobs—was choking him. Were these for Magda, or for Pognenbin? For both, but also for that younger prisoner whom it was impossible to help.

At times Bartek fancied he must be asleep. All the while the storm raged more fiercely round the house, and the cries and voices multiplied strangely in the whistling of the wind.

Suddenly every hair of Bartek's head stood on end under his helmet. For it seemed as if somewhere from out of the dark, rain-clad depths of the forest somebody were groaning, and repeating: "At home, at home, at home!"

Bartek started back, and struck the floor with the butt end of his rifle to wake himself. He regained consciousness somehow and looked up. The prisoners lay in the corner, the lamp was burning brightly, the wind was howling —all was in order.

The light fell full on to the face of the younger prisoner—a child's or girl's face. As he lay there with closed eyes, and straw under his head, he looked as if he were already dead.

Never in his life had Bartek been so wrung with pity! Something distinctly gripped his throat, and an audible cry was wrung from his breast.

At that moment the elder prisoner turned wearily on to his side, and said, "Good night, Wladek." Silence followed. An hour passed.

The wind played like the Pognenbin organ. The prisoners lay silent. Suddenly the younger prisoner, raising himself a little by an effort, called, "Karol!"

"What?"

"Are you asleep?"

"No."

"Listen! I am afraid. Say what you like, but I shall pray."

"Pray, then."

"Our Father, Who art in Heaven, hallowed be Thy Name, Thy Kingdom come."

Sobs suddenly interrupted the young prisoner's words, yet the broken voice was still heard: "Thy—will—be—done!"

"Oh, Jesu!" something cried in Bartek. "Oh, Jesu!"

Impossible! He could stand it no longer. Another moment, and exclaiming, "Sir, I am only a peasant!" he had leapt with them through the window into the wood. Let come what may! Suddenly measured steps were heard echoing from the direction of the hall: it was the patrol, the sergeant with it. They were changing the guard!

Next day Bartek was drunk all day from early morning. The following day likewise. . . .

But fresh advances, fighting, and marches took place during the following days, and I am glad to say that our hero regained his equilibrium. A certain fondness for the bottle, in which it is always possible to find pleasure, and at times forgetfulness, remained with him after that night, however. For the rest, in battle he was more terrible than ever; victory followed in his wake.

VI

Some months had passed, and the spring was now well advanced. The cherry trees at Pognenbin were in blossom and the young corn was sprouting abundantly in the fields. One day Magda, seated in front of the cottage, was peeling some rotten potatoes for dinner, fitter for cattle than for human beings. But it was spring-time, and poverty had visited Pognenbin. That could be seen, too, by the saddened and worried look on Magda's face. Possibly in order to distract herself, the woman, closing her eyes, sang in a thin, strained voice:

> Alas, my Jasieńko has gone to the war! he writes me letters;
> Alas, and I his wife write to him,—for I cannot see him.

The sparrows twittered in the cherry trees as if they were trying to emulate her. She stopped her song and gazed absently at the dog sleeping in the sun, at the road passing the cottage, and the path leading from the road through the garden and field. Perhaps Magda glanced at the path because it led across to the station and, as God willed, she did not look in vain that day. A figure appeared in the distance, and the woman shaded her eyes with her hand, but she could not see clearly, being blinded by the glare. Lysek woke up, however, raised his head, and giving a short bark, began to grow excited, pricking up his ears and turning his head from side to side. At the same moment the words of a song reached Magda indistinctly. Lysek sprang up suddenly and ran at full speed towards the newcomer. Then Magda turned a little pale.

"Is it Bartek—or not?"

She jumped up so quickly that the bowl of potatoes rolled on to the ground: there was no longer any doubt; Lysek was bounding up to his shoulder. The woman rushed forward, shouting in the full strength of her joy: "Bartek! Bartek!"

"Magda, here I am!" Bartek cried, throwing her a kiss, and hurrying towards her. He opened the gate, stumbled over the step so that he all but fell, recovered himself—and they were clasped in one another's arms.

The woman began to speak quickly:

"And I had thought that you would not come back. I thought: 'They will kill him!' How are you?—Let me see. How good to look at you! You are terribly thin! Oh, Jesu! Poor fellow!—Oh, my dearest! . . . He has come back, come back!"

For one moment she tore herself from his neck and looked at him, then threw herself on it again.

"Come back! The Lord be praised! Bartek, my darling! How are you? Go indoors! Franek is at school being teased by that horrid German! The boy is well. He's as dull in the upper story as you are. Oh, but it was time for you to come back! I didn't know any more which way to turn. I was miserable, I tell you, miserable! This whole poor house is going into ruins. The roof is off the barn. How are you? Oh, Bartek! Bartek! That I should actually see you, after all! What trouble I have had with the hay! The neighbours helped me, but they did it to help themselves! How are you? Well? Oh, but I am glad to have you—glad! The Lord watched over you. Go indoors. By God, it's like Bartek, and not like Bartek! What's the matter with you? Oh dear! Oh dear!"

At that instant Magda had become aware of a long scar running along Bartek's face across his left temple and cheek and down to his chin.

"It's nothing. A cuirassier did it for me, but I did the same for him. I have been in hospital."

"Oh, Jesu!"

"Why, it's a mere flea-bite."

"But you are starved to death."

"*Ruhig!*" answered Bartek.

He was in truth emaciated, begrimed, and in rags—a true conqueror! He swayed, too, as he stood.

"What's wrong with you? Are you drunk?"

"I—am still weak."

That he was weak was certain, but he was tipsy also. For one glass of vodka would have been sufficient in his state of exhaustion, and Bartek had drunk something like four at the station. The result was that he had the bearing of the true conqueror. He had not been like this formerly.

"*Ruhig!*" he repeated. "We have finished the *Krieg*. I am a gentleman now, do you understand? Look here!" He pointed to his crosses and medals. "Do you know who I am? Eh? *Links! Rechts! Heu! Stroh! Halt!*"

At the word "*Halt,*" he gave such a shrill shout that the woman recoiled several steps.

"Are you mad?"

"How are you, Magda? When I say to you 'How are you,' then how are you? Do you know French, stupid? *Musiu, Musiu!* What is *Musiu*? I am a *Musiu*, do you understand?"

"Man, what's up with you?"

"What's that to you! *Was? Doné diner?* Do you understand?"

A storm began to gather on Magda's brow.

"What rubbish are you jabbering? What's this? Don't you know Polish? That's all through those wretches. I said how it would be! What have they done to you?"

"Give me something to eat!"

"Be quick indoors."

Every command made an irresistible impression on Bartek; hearing this "Be quick" he drew himself up, held his hand stiffly to his side, and, having made a half-turn, marched in the direction indicated. He stood still at the threshold, however, and began to look wonderingly at Magda.

"Well, what do you want, Magda? What do . . . ?"

"Quick! March!"

He entered the cottage, but fell over the threshold. The vodka was now beginning to go to his head. He started singing, and looked round the cottage for Franek, even saying "*Morgen, Kerl,*" although Franek was not there. After that he laughed loudly, staggered, shouted "Hurrah!" and fell full length on the bed. In the evening he awoke sober and rested, and welcomed Franek; then, having got some pence out of Magda, he took his triumphant way to the inn. The glory of his deeds had already preceded him to Pognenbin, since more than one of the soldiers from other divisions of the same regiment, having returned earlier, had related how he had distinguished himself at Gravelotte and Sedan. So now when the rumour spread that the conqueror was at the inn, all his old comrades hastened there to welcome him.

No one would have recognized our friend Bartek, as he now sat at the table. He, formerly so meek, was to be seen striking his fist on the table, puffing himself out and gobbling like a turkey-cock.

"Do you remember, you fellows, that time I did for the French, what Steinmetz said?"

"How could we forget?"

"People used to talk about the French, and be frightened of them, but they are a poor lot—*was?* They eat like hares into the lettuce, and run away like hares, too. They don't drink beer either, nothing but strong wine."

"That's it!"

"When we burnt a town they would wring their hands immediately and cry '*Pitié, pitié*,'[8] as if they meant they would give us a drink if we would only leave them alone. But we paid no attention to them."

"Then can one understand their gibberish?" inquired a young farmer's lad.

"You wouldn't understand, because you are stupid, but I understand. '*Donédipę!*'[9] Do you understand?"

"What do you mean?"

"Do you know about Paris? We had one battle after another there, but we won them all. They have no good commanders. So people said. 'The ground enclosed by the hedge is good,' they say, 'but it has been badly managed.' Their officers are bad managers, and their generals are bad managers, but on our side they are good."

Maciej Kierz, the wise old innkeeper of Pognenbin, began to shake his head.

"Well, the Germans have been victorious in a terrible war; they have been victorious—but I always thought they would be. But the Lord alone knows what will come out of it for us."

Bartek stared at him.

"What do you say?"

"The Germans have never cared to consider us much, anyhow, but now they will be as stuck-up as if there were no God above them. And they will ill-treat us still more than they do already."

"But that's not true!" Bartek said.

Old Kierz was a person of such authority in Pognenbin that all the village always thought as he did, and it was sheer audacity to contradict him. But Bartek was a conqueror now, and an authority himself. All the same they gazed at him in astonishment, and even in some indignation.

"Who are you, to quarrel with Maciej? Who are you——?"

"What's Maciej to me? It isn't to such as he that I have talked, you see! Why, you fellows, I talked, didn't I, to Steinmetz—*was?* But let Maciej fancy what he likes. We shall be better off now."

Maciej looked at the conqueror for a moment.

"You blockhead!" he said.

Bartek struck his fist on the table, making all the glasses and pint-pots start up.

"*Still, der Kerl da! Heu! Stroh!*"

"Silence, no row! Ask the priest or the count, blockhead."

"Was the priest in the war? Or was the count there? But I was there. It's not true, boys. They'll know now how to respect us. Who won the battle? We won it, I won it. Now they'll give us anything we ask for. If I had wanted to become a landowner in France, I should have stayed there. The Government knows very well who gave the French the best beating. And our regi-

[8]Polish "picie"=a drink.—TRANSLATOR.

[9]Polish *ç*=French *in*.—TRANSLATOR.

ment was the best. They said so in the military dispatches. So now the Poles will get the upper hand—do you see?"

Kierz waved his hand, stood up, and went out. Bartek had carried off the victory in the field of politics also. The young men remaining with him regarded him as a perfect marvel. He continued:

"As if they wouldn't give me anything I want! If I don't get it, I should like to know who would! Old Kierz is a scoundrel, do you see? The Government commands you to fight, so you must fight. Who will ill-treat me? The Germans? Is it likely?"

Here he again displayed his crosses and medals.

"And who did I beat the French for? Not for the Germans, surely? I am a better man now than a German, for there's not one German as strong. Bring us some beer! I have talked to Steinmetz, and I have talked to Podbielski. Bring us some beer!"

They slowly prepared for their carouse.

Bartek began to sing:

> Drink, drink, drink,
> As long as in my pocket
> Still the pennies chink!

Suddenly he took a handful of pence from his pocket.

"Beer! I am a gentleman now.—Won't you? I tell you in France we were not so flush of money; there was little we didn't burn, and few people we didn't put a shot into! God doesn't know which—of the French——"

A tippler's moods are subject to rapid changes. Bartek unexpectedly raked together the money from the table, and began to exclaim sadly:

"Lord, have mercy on the sins of my soul!"

Then, propping both elbows on the table, and hiding his head in his hands, he was silent.

"What's the matter?" inquired one of the drinkers.

"Why was I to blame for them?" Bartek murmured sadly. "It was their own look-out. I was sorry for them, for they were both my people. Lord! have mercy! One was as the ruddy dawn! Next day he was as white as linen. And even after that I still—— Vodka!"

A moment of gloomy silence followed. The men looked at one another in astonishment.

"What is he saying?" one asked.

"He is settling something with his conscience."

"A man must drink in spite of that war."

He filled up his glass of vodka once or twice, then he spat, and his good humour unexpectedly returned.

"Have you ever stood talking to Steinmetz? But I have! Hurrah! Drink! Who pays? I do!"

"You may pay, you drunkard," sounded Magda's voice, "but I will repay you! Never fear!"

Bartek looked at his wife with glassy eyes.

"Have you talked to Steinmetz? Who are you?"

Instead of replying to him, Magda turned to the interested listeners, and began to exclaim:

"Oh, you men, you wretched men, do you see the disgrace and misery I am in? He came back, and I was glad to welcome him as a good man, but he came back drunk. He has forgotten God, and he has forgotten Polish. He went to sleep, he woke up sober, and now he's drinking again, and paying for it with my money, which I had earned by my own work. And where have you taken that money from? Isn't it what I have earned by all my trouble and slavery? I tell you men, he's no longer a Catholic, he's not a man any more, he's bewitched by the Germans, he jabbers German, and is just waiting to do harm to people. He's possessed . . ."

Here the woman burst into tears; then, raising her voice an octave higher: "He was stupid, but he was good. But now, what have they done to him? I looked out for him in the evening, I looked out for him in the morning, and I have lived to see him. There is no peace and no mercy anywhere. Great God! Merciful God! If you had only left it alone—if you had only remained German altogether!"

Her last words ended in such a wail, it was almost like a cadence. But Bartek merely said:

"Be quiet, or I shall do for you!"

"Strike me, hit my head, hit me now, kill me, murder me!" the woman screamed, and stretching her neck forward, she turned to the men.

"And you fellows, watch!——"

But the men were beginning to disperse. The inn was soon deserted, and only Bartek and his wife, with her neck stretched forward, remained.

"Why do you stretch out your neck like a goose?" murmured Bartek. "Go home."

"Hit me!" repeated Magda.

"Well, I shan't hit," replied Bartek, putting his hands into his pockets. Here the innkeeper, wishing to put an end to the quarrel, turned out one of the lights. The room became dark and silent. After a while Magda's shrill voice sounded through the darkness:

"Hit me!"

"I shan't hit," replied Bartek's triumphant voice.

Two figures were to be seen going by moonlight from the inn to the cottage. One of them, walking in front, was sobbing loudly; that was Magda; after her, hanging his head and following humbly enough, went the victor of Gravelotte and Sedan.

VII

Bartek went home so tipsy that for some days he was unfit for work. This was most unfortunate for all his household affairs, which were in need of a strong man to look after them. Magda did her best. She worked from morning till night, and the neighbours helped her as well as they could, but even so she could not make both ends meet, and the household was being ruined little by little. Then there were a few small debts to the German colonist, Just, who, having at a favourable moment bought some thirteen acres of waste land at Pognenbin, now had the best property in the whole village. He had ready money besides, which he lent out at sufficiently high interest. He lent it chiefly to the owner of the property, Count Jarzyński, whose name shone in the "Golden Book,"[10] but who was obliged to keep up his house in a style of befitting splendour for that very reason. Just, however, also lent to peasants. For six months Magda had owed him some twenty thalers, part of which she had borrowed for her housekeeping, and part to send to Bartek during the war. Yet that need not have mattered. God had granted good crops, and it would have been possible to repay the debt out of the incoming harvest, provided that the hands and the labour were forthcoming. Unluckily Bartek could not work. Magda did not quite believe this, and went to the priest for help, thinking he might rouse her husband; but this was really impossible. When at all tired, Bartek grew short of breath and his wounds pained him. So he sat in front of the cottage all day long, smoking his clay pipe with the figure of Bismarck in white uniform and a cuirassier's helmet, and gazed at the world with the drowsy eyes of a man still feeling the effects of bodily fatigue. He pondered a little on the war, a little on his victories, on Magda— a little on everything, a little on nothing.

One day, as he sat thus, he heard Franek crying in the distance on his way home from school. He was howling till the echoes rang.

Bartek pulled his pipe out of his mouth.

"Why, Franek, what's the matter with you?"

"What's the matter?" repeated Franek, sobbing.

"Why are you crying?"

"Why shouldn't I cry, when I have had my ears boxed?"

"Who boxed your ears?"

"Who? Why, Herr Boege!"

Herr Boege filled the post of schoolmaster at Pognenbin.

"And has he a right to box your ears?"

"I suppose so, as he did it."

Magda, who had been hoeing in the garden, came through the hedge, and, with the hoe in her hand, went up to the child.

"What are you saying?" she asked.

"What am I saying? If that Boege didn't call me a Polish pig, and give me a box on the ears, and say that just as they have beaten the French now, so they will trample us underfoot, for they are the strongest. And I had done nothing to him, but he had asked me who is the greatest person in the world, and I had said it was the Holy Father, but he boxed my ears, and I began to cry, and he called me a Polish pig, and said that just as they have beaten the French . . ."

Franek was beginning it all over again, "and he said, and I said——" but Magda covered his mouth with her hand, and she herself, turning to Bartek, exclaimed:

"Do you hear? Do you hear? Go to the French war, then let a German beat your child like a dog! Curse him! Go to the war, and let this Swabian kill your child! You have your reward! . . . May . . ."

Here Magda, moved by her own eloquence, also began to cry to Franek's accompaniment. Bartek stared open-mouthed with astonishment, and could not bring out a single word, or comprehend in the least what had happened. How was this? And what of his victories? He sat on in silence for some moments, then suddenly something leaped into his eyes, and the blood

[10]List of Polish nobility.—M. M. G.

rushed to his face. With ignorant people astonishment, like terror, often turns
to rage. Bartek sprang up suddenly, and jerked out through his clenched
teeth:

"I will talk to him!"

And he went out. It was not far to go; the school lay close to the church.
Herr Boege was just then standing in front of the veranda, surrounded by a
herd of young pigs, to which he was throwing pieces of bread.

He was a tall man, about fifty years of age, still as vigorous as an oak. He
was not particularly stout, but his face was very fat, and he had a pair of very
protruding eyes, which expressed courage and energy.

Bartek went up to him very quickly.

"German, why have you been beating my child? *Was?*" he asked.

Herr Boege took a few steps backwards, measured him with a glance without a shade of fear, and said phlegmatically:

"Begone, Polish prizefighter!"

"Why have you been beating my child?" repeated Bartek.

"I will beat you, too, you low Polish scoundrel! I will show you who is
master here. Go to the devil, go to the law—begone!"

Bartek, having seized the schoolmaster by the shoulder, began to shake him
roughly, crying in a hoarse voice:

"Do you know who I am? Do you know who did for the French? Do you
know who talked to Steinmetz? Why do you beat my child, you cursed
Swabian dog?"

Herr Boege's protruding eyes glared no less than Bartek's, for Boege was
a strong man, and he resolved to free himself from his assailant by a single
blow. This blow descended with a loud smack on the face of the victor of
Gravelotte and Sedan.

At that the man forgot everything. Boege's head was shaken from side to
side, with a swift motion recalling a pendulum, but with this difference that
the shaking was alarmingly rapid. The formidable vanquisher of Turcos and
Zouaves awoke in Bartek once more. Boege's twelve-year-old son, Oscar, a lad
as strong as his father, ran in vain to his assistance. A short, but terrible
struggle took place, in which the son fell to the ground, and the father felt
himself lifted up into the air. Bartek, raising his hands, held him there, he
himself scarcely knew how. Unluckily the tub of dishwater, which Herr
Boege had been assiduously mixing for the pigs, stood near. Into this tub
Herr Boege now capsized, and a moment later his feet were to be seen projecting from it, and kicking violently. His wife darted out of the house:

"Help, to the rescue!"

The German colonists rushed from the houses near to their neighbour's
assistance. Some of them fell on Bartek and began to belabour him with
sticks and stones. In the general confusion which followed it was difficult to
distinguish Bartek from his adversaries: some thirteen bodies were to be
seen rolling round in a single mass, and struggling convulsively.

Suddenly, however, from out of this fighting mass Bartek burst forth like
fury, making towards the hedge with all his might.

The Germans ran after him, but an alarming crack was heard in the hedge
at the same moment, and Bartek's iron hands brandished a stout stick.

He returned raging and furious, holding the stick in the air; they all fled.

Bartek went after them, but luckily did not overtake any one. Thus his rage cooled, and he began to retreat homewards. Ah! if only it had been the French he had been facing! His retreat would then have made immortal history.

As it was, he was being attacked by about a dozen people who, when they had reassembled, set on him afresh. Bartek retired slowly, like a wild boar pursued by dogs. He turned round now and then and stood still: then his pursuers stood still too. The stick had earned their complete respect.

They threw stones at him, nevertheless, one of which wounded Bartek in the forehead. The blood poured into his eyes, and he felt himself growing faint. He swayed once or twice, let go the stick, and fell down.

"Hurrah!" cried the Germans.

But by the time they reached him, Bartek had got up again: then they held back. This wounded wolf was still dangerous. Besides, he was now not far from the first cottage, and some labourers could be seen in the distance hurrying to the battlefield at full speed. The Germans retired to their houses.

"What has happened?" inquired the newcomers.

"I have been trying my hand a bit on the Germans," Bartek answered. And he fainted.

VIII

It proved a serious affair. The German newspapers published flaming articles on the persecutions to which the peaceful German population was subjected at the hands of the barbarian and ignorant masses, who were roused by socialist agitation and religious fanaticism. Boege became a hero. He, the quiet, gentle schoolmaster, spreading the light of learning on the far borders of the empire; he, the true missionary of culture amid barbarians, had fallen a first victim to the riot. It was fortunate that there were a hundred million Germans to stand up for him, who would never allow . . . And so on.

Bartek did not know what a storm was brewing over his head. On the contrary, he was in good spirits; he was certain that he would win at the trial. For Boege had beaten his child, and had dealt him the first blow, and it had afterwards been he who had been attacked from behind! Surely he had a right to defend himself. They had also thrown a stone at his head—actually thrown it at him, who had been mentioned in the daily dispatches, who had won the battle of Gravelotte, had talked to Steinmetz himself, and received so many medals. It is true it never entered his head that the Germans did not know all this when they wronged him so greatly, any more than it occurred to him that Boege could substantiate his threat to Pognenbin that the Germans would now trample it underfoot in the same way in which they, the Pognenbinites, had so thoroughly beaten the French whenever they had had an opportunity. But as for himself, he was certain that public opinion and the Government would be in his favour. They would certainly know who he was, and what he had done during the war. If he was not a different man to what he thought him, Steinmetz would espouse his cause. Since Bartek was the poorer through the war, and his house in debt, they would, anyhow, not refuse to do him justice.

All the same, the police from Pognenbin rode up to Bartek's house. They had expected serious resistance, for as many as five appeared with loaded revolvers. They were mistaken; Bartek had not thought of offering any resistance. They told him to get into the carriage, and he got in. Magda alone was desperate, persistently repeating:

"Oh dear, what did you fight those French for? You will catch it now, poor fellow, that you will!"

"Be quiet, stupid!" Bartek answered, and smiled quite cheerfully to the passers-by as he drove along.

"I'll show then who it is they have offended!" he cried from the carriage.

And, covered with his medals, he drove along to the trial like a conqueror.

As a matter of fact, the trial went in his favour. The judge decided to be lenient under the circumstances: Bartek was only condemned to three months' imprisonment.

In addition to this he had to pay a fine of one hundred and fifty marks to the Boege family and "other injured colonists."

"Nevertheless the prisoner," wrote the *Posener Zeitung* in the Criminal Report, "showed not the slightest sign of contrition when the sentence was passed on him, but poured forth such a stream of invective, and began to enumerate his so-called services to the State in such an impudent manner, that it is surprising these insults to the court and the German nation," etc., etc.

Meanwhile Bartek in prison quietly recalled his deeds at Gravelotte, Sedan, and Paris.

We should, however, be doing an injustice in asserting that Herr Boege's action called forth no public censure. Very much the reverse. On a certain rainy morning a Polish Member of Parliament pointed out with great eloquence that the attitude of the Government towards the Poles had altered in Poznań; that, considering the courage and sacrifice displayed by the Polish regiments during the war, it would be fitting to have more regard for justice in the Polish provinces; finally, that Herr Boege at Pognenbin had abused his position as schoolmaster by beating a Polish child, calling it a Polish pig, and holding out hopes that after this war the incoming inhabitants would trample the native population under foot. The rain fell as the member was speaking, and as such weather makes people sleepy, the Conservatives yawned, the National-Liberals yawned, the Centre yawned—for they were not yet being faced by the "Kulturkampf."

Following immediately on this "Polish question" the Chamber proceeded to the order of the day.

Meanwhile Bartek sat in prison, or rather, he lay in the prison infirmary, for the blow from the stone had reopened the wound which he had received in the war.

When not feverish, he thought and thought, like the turkeycock that died of thinking. But Bartek did not die, he merely did not arrive at any conclusion.

Now and then, however, during moments, which science names *lucida intervalla*, it occurred to him that he had perhaps exerted himself unnecessarily in "doing for" the French.

Difficult times followed for Magda. The fine had to be paid, and there was nothing with which to pay it. The priest at Pognenbin offered to help, but it turned out that there were not quite forty marks in his money box. The parish of Pognenbin was poor; besides, the good old man never knew how his money went. Count Jarzyński was not at home. It was said that he had gone love-making to some rich lady in the Kingdom.[11]

Magda did not know where to turn.

An extension of the loan was not to be thought of. What else, then? Should she sell the horse or the cows? Meanwhile spring passed into summer, the hardest time of all. It would soon be harvest, when she would need money for extra labour, and even now it was all exhausted. The woman wrung her hands in despair. She sent a petition to the magistrate, recalling Bartek's services; she never even received an answer. The time for repayment of the loan was drawing near, and the sequestration with it.

She prayed and prayed, remembering bitterly the time when they were well off, and when Bartek used to earn money at the factory in winter. She tried to borrow money from her neighbours; they had none. The war had made itself felt all round. She did not dare to go to Just, because she was in his debt already, and had not even paid the interest. However, Just unexpectedly came to see her himself.

One afternoon she was sitting in the cottage doorway doing nothing, for despair had drained her strength. She was gazing before her at the golden flies chasing one another in the air, and thinking, "How happy those creatures are, they live for themselves and needn't pay"—and so on. After a while she sighed heavily, and a low cry broke from her pale lips: "Oh, God! God!" Suddenly at the gate appeared Just's long nose, and his long pipe beneath it. The woman turned pale. Just addressed her:

"*Morgen!*"

"How are you, Herr Just?"

"What about my money?"

"Oh, my dear Herr Just, have pity! I am very poor, and what am I to do? They have taken my man away, I have to pay the fine for him, and I don't know where to turn. It would be better to die than to be worried like this from day to day. Do wait a while longer, dear Herr Just!"

She burst out crying, and seizing Herr Just's fat, red hand, she kissed it humbly. "The Count will be back soon, then I will borrow from him, and give it back to you."

"Well, and how will you pay the fine?"

"How can I tell? I might sell the cow."

"Then I will lend you some more."

"May God Almighty repay you, my dear sir! Although you are a Lutheran, you are a good man. I speak the truth! If only other Germans were like you, sir, one might bless them."

"But I don't lend money without interest."

"I know, I know."

"Then write me one receipt for it all."

"You are a kind gentleman. May God repay you too in the same way."

"We will draw up the bill when I go into the town."

He went into the town and drew up the bill, but Magda had gone to the priest

---

[11]The Kingdom of Poland: the part of Central Poland that when this story was written was under Russian domination.

for advice beforehand. Yet what could he advise? The priest said he was very sorry for her; the time given for repayment was short, the interest was high, Count Jarzyński was not at home; had he been, he might have helped. Magda, however, could not wait until the team was sold, and she was obliged to accept Just's terms. She contracted a debt of three hundred marks, that is, twice the amount of the fine, for it was certainly necessary to have a few pence in the house to carry on the housekeeping. On account of the importance of the document, Bartek was obliged to sign it, and for this reason Magda went to see him in prison. The conqueror was very downtrodden, depressed, and ill. He had wished to forward a petition, setting forth his grievances, but petitions were not accepted; opinion in administrative circles had turned against him since the articles in the *Posener Zeitung*. For were not these very authorities bound to afford protection to the peaceful German population, who, during the recent war, had given so many proofs of devotion and sacrifice to the Fatherland? They were therefore obliged in fairness to reject Bartek's petition. But it is not surprising that this should have depressed him at last.

"We are done for all round," he said to his wife.

"All round," she repeated.

Bartek began to ruminate deeply on the circumstances.

"It's a cruel injustice to me," he said.

"That man Boege persecutes one," Magda replied. "I went to implore him, and he called me names too. Ah! the Germans have the upper hand now at Pognenbin. They aren't afraid of any one."

"Of course, for they are the strongest," Bartek said sadly.

"As I am a plain woman, I tell you God is the strongest."

"In Him is our refuge," added Bartek.

They were both silent a moment, then he asked again:

"Well, and what of Just?"

"If the Lord Almighty gives us a crop, then perhaps we shall be able to repay him. Possibly too the Count will help us, although he himself has debts with the German. They said even before the war that he would have to sell Pognenbin. Let us hope that he will bring home a rich wife."

"But will he be back soon?"

"Who knows? They say at the house that he will soon be coming with his wife. And directly he is back the Germans will be upon him. It's always those Germans! They are as plentiful as worms! Wherever one looks, whichever way one turns, whether in the village or the town—Germans for our sins! But where are we to get help from?"

"Perhaps you can decide on something, for you are a clever woman."

"What can I advise? Should I have borrowed money from Just if I could have helped it? I did it for a good reason, but now the cottage in which we are settled, and the land also, are already his. Just is better than other Germans, but he too has an eye to his own profit, not other people's. He won't be lenient to us any more than he has been lenient to others. I am not so stupid as not to know why he sticks his money in here! But what is one to do, what is one to do?" she cried, wringing her hands. "Give some advice yourself, if you are so clever. You can beat the French, but what will you do without a roof over your head, or a crust to eat?"

The victor of Gravelotte bent his head. "Oh, Jesu! Jesu!"

Magda had a kind heart; Bartek's grief touched her, so she said quickly: "Never mind, dear boy, never mind. Don't worry your head about it till it has healed up. The rye is so fine, it's bending to the ground; the wheat the same. The ground doesn't belong to the Germans; it's as good as ever it was. The fields were in a bad state before your quarrel, but now they are growing so well, you'll see!"

Magda began to smile through her tears.

"The ground doesn't belong to the Germans," she repeated once more.

"Magda!" Bartek said, looking at her with wide-open eyes; "Magda!"

"What?"

"But—because you are . . . if . . ."

Bartek felt deep gratitude towards her, but he could not express it

IX

In truth Magda was worth more than ten other women put together. Her manner towards Bartek was rather curt, but she was really attached to him. In moments of excitement, as, for example, in the prison, she told him to his face that he was stupid; nevertheless, before other people she would generally exclaim: "My Bartek pretends to be stupid, but that's his cunning." She used frequently to say this. As a matter of fact, Bartek was about as cunning as his horse, and without Magda he would have been unable to manage either his holding or anything else. Now, when everything rested on her honest shoulders, she left no stone unturned, running hither and thither to beg for help. A week after her last visit to the prison infirmary she ran in again to see Bartek, breathless, beaming, and happy.

"My word, Bartek, how are you?" she exclaimed gleefully. "Do you know the Count has arrived! He was married in the Kingdom; the young lady is a beauty! But he has done well for himself all round in getting her; fancy—just fancy!"

The owner of Pognenbin had really been married and come home with his wife, and had actually done very well by himself all round in finding her.

"Well, and what of that?" inquired Bartek.

"Be quiet, blockhead," Magda replied. "Oh! how out of breath I am! Oh, Jesu! I went to pay my respects to the lady. I looked at her: she came out to meet me like a queen, as young and charming as a flower, and as beautiful as the dawn!—Oh dear, how out of breath I am!"

Magda took her handkerchief, and began to wipe the perspiration from her face. The next instant she started talking again in a gasping voice:

"She had a blue dress like the cornflower. I fell at her feet, and she gave me her hand; I kissed it, and her hands are as sweet and tiny as a child's. She is just like a saint in a picture, and she is good, and feels for poor people. I began to beg her for help. May God give her health! And she said, 'I will do,' she said, 'whatever lies in my power.' And she has such a pretty little voice that when she speaks one does feel pleased. So then I began to tell her that there are unhappy people in Pognenbin, and she said, 'Not only in Pognenbin,' and then I burst into tears, and she too. And then the Count came in, and he saw that she was crying, so he just went and took her and gave her a little kiss. Gentlefolk aren't like us! Then she said to him, 'Do what you can for this woman.' And he said, 'Anything in the world, whatever you wish.'— May the Mother of God bless her, that lovely creature, may She bless her with children and with health! The Count said at once: 'You must be heavily in debt, if you have fallen into the hands of the Germans, but,' he said, 'I will help you, and also against Just.' "

Bartek began to scratch his neck.

"But the Germans have got hold of him too."

"What of that? His wife is rich. They could buy all the Germans in Pognenbin now, so it was easy for him to talk like that. 'The election,' he said, 'is coming on before long, and people had better take care not to vote for Germans; but I will make short work of Just and Boege.' And the lady put her arm round his neck, and the Count asked after you, and said: 'If he is ill, I will speak to the doctor about giving him a certificate to show that he is unfit to be imprisoned now. If they don't let him off altogether,' he said, 'he will be imprisoned in the winter, but he is needed now for working the crops.' Do you hear? The Count was in the town yesterday, and invited the doctor to come on a visit to Pognenbin to-day. He's not a German. He'll write the certificate. In the winter you'll sit in prison like a king, you'll be warm, and they'll give you meat to eat; and now you are going home to work, and Just will be repaid, and possibly the Count won't want any interest, and if we can't give it all back in the autumn, I'll beg it from the lady. May the Mother of God bless her. . . . Do you hear?"

"She is a good lady. There are not many such!" Bartek said at once.

"You must fall at her feet, I tell you—but if you don't I'll twist your head for you! If only God grants us a crop! And do you see where the help has come from? Was it from the Germans? Did they give you a single penny for your stupid medals? Well, they just gave you a crack on your head and nothing more! Fall at the lady's feet, I say!"

"I can't do otherwise," Bartek replied resolutely.

Fortune seemed to smile on the conqueror once more. He was informed some days later that for reasons of health he would be released from prison until the winter. He was ordered to appear before the magistrate. The man who, bayonet in hand, had seized flags and guns, now began to fear a uniform more than death. A deep, unconscious feeling was growing in his mind that he was being persecuted, that they could do as they liked with him, and that there was some mighty, yet malevolent and evil power above him, which, if he resisted, would crush him. So there he stood before the magistrate, as formerly before Steinmetz, upright, his body drawn in, his chest thrown forward, not daring to breathe. There were some officers present also: they represented war and the military prison to Bartek. The officers looked at him through their gold eyeglasses with the pride and disdain befitting Prussian officers towards a private soldier and Polish peasant. He stood holding his breath, and the magistrate said something in a commanding tone. He did not ask or persuade, he commanded and threatened. A member had died in Berlin, and the writs for a fresh election had been issued.

"You Polish dog, just you dare to vote for Count Jarzyński, just you dare!"

At this the officers knitted their brows into threatening leonine wrinkles.

One, lighting his cigar, repeated after the magistrate: "Just you dare!" and Bartek the Conqueror's heart died within him. When he heard the order given, "Go!" he made a half-turn to the left, went out, and took breath. They told him to vote for Herr Schulberg of Great Krzywda; he paid no attention to the command, but took a deep breath. For he was going to Pognenbin, he could be at home during harvest time, the Count had promised to pay Just. He walked out of the town; the ripening cornfields surrounded him on every side, the heavy blades hurtling one another in the wind, and murmuring with a sound dear to the peasant's ear. Bartek was still weak, but the sun warmed him. "Ah! how beautiful the world is!" this worn-out soldier thought.

It was not much farther to Pognenbin.

x

"The Election! The Election!"

Countess Marya Jarzyńska's head was full of it, and she thought, talked, and dreamt of nothing else.

"You are a great politician," an aristocratic neighbour said to her, kissing her small hands in a snake-like way. But the "great politician" blushed like a cherry, and answered with a beautiful smile:

"Oh, we only do what we can!"

"Count Józef will be elected," the nobleman said with conviction, and the "great politician" answered:

"I should wish it very much, though not alone for Józef's sake, but" (here the "great politician" crimsoned again with an "unpolitical" blush), "for the common cause. . . ."

"By God! A positive Bismarck!" cried the nobleman, kissing the tiny hands once more. After which they proceeded to discuss the canvassing. The nobleman himself undertook Krzywda Dolna and Mizerów (Great Krzywda was lost, for Herr Schulberg owned all the property there), and Countess Marya was to occupy herself specially with Pognenbin. She was all aglow with the role she was to fill, and she certainly lost no time. She was daily to be seen at the cottages on the main road, holding her skirt with one hand, her parasol with the other, while from under her skirt peeped her tiny feet, tripping enthusiastically in the great political cause. She went into the cottages; she said to the people working on the road, "God help you!" she visited the sick, made herself agreeable to the people, and helped where she could. She would have done the same without politics, for she had a kind heart, but she did it all the more on this political account. Why should not she also contribute her share to the political cause? But she did not dare confess to her husband that she had an irresistible desire to attend the village meeting. In imagination she had even planned the speech she would make at the meeting. And what a speech it would be! What a speech! True, she would certainly never dare to make it, but if she dared—why then! Consequently when the news reached Pognenbin that the authorities had prohibited the meeting, the "great politician" burst into a fit of anger, tore one handkerchief up completely, and had red eyes all day. In vain her husband begged her not to "demean" herself to such a degree; next day the canvassing was carried on with still greater fervour. Nothing stopped Countess Marya now. She visited thirteen cottages in one day, and talked so loudly against the Germans that her husband was obliged to check her. But there was no danger. The people welcomed her gladly, they kissed her hands and smiled at her, for she was so pretty and her cheeks were so rosy that wherever she went she brought brightness with her. Thus she came to Bartek's cottage also. Lysek barked at her, but Magda in her excitement hit him on the head with a stick.

"Oh, lady, my beautiful lady, my dear lady!" cried Magda, seizing her hands.

In accordance with his resolve, Bartek threw himself at her feet, while little Franek first kissed her hand, then stuck his thumb into his mouth and lost himself in whole-hearted admiration.

"I hope"—the young lady said after the first greetings were over—"I hope, my friend Bartek, that you will vote for my husband, and not for Herr Schulberg."

"Oh, my dear lady!" Magda exclaimed; "who would vote for Schulberg? Give him the ten plagues! The lady must excuse me, but when one gets talking about the Germans, one can't help what one says."

"My husband has just told me that he will repay Just."

"May God bless him!" Here Magda turned to Bartek. "Why do you stand there like a post? I must beg the lady's pardon, but he's wonderfully dumb."

"You will vote for my husband, won't you?" the lady asked. "You are Poles, and we are Poles, so we will hold to one another."

"I should throttle him if he didn't vote for him," Magda said. "Why do you stand there like a post? He's wonderfully dumb. Bestir yourself a bit!"

Bartek again kissed the lady's hand, but he remained silent, and looked as black as night. The magistrate was in his mind.

The day of the election drew near, and arrived. Count Jarzyński was certain of victory. All the neighbourhood assembled at Pognenbin. After voting the gentlemen returned there from the town to wait for the priest, who was to bring the news. Afterwards there was to be a dinner, but in the evening the noble couple were going to Poznań, and subsequently to Berlin also. Several villages in the electoral division had already polled the day beforehand. The result would be made known on this day. The company was in a cheerful frame of mind. The young lady was slightly nervous, yet full of hope and smiles, and made such a charming hostess that every one agreed Count Józef had found a real treasure in the Kingdom. This treasure was quite unable at present to keep quiet in one place, and ran from guest to guest, asking each for the hundredth time to assure her that "Józio would be elected." She was not actually ambitious, and it was not out of vanity that she wished to be the wife of a member, but she was dreaming in her young mind that she and her husband together had a real mission to accomplish. So her heart beat as quickly as at the moment of her wedding, and her pretty little face was lighted up with joy. Skilfully manœuvring amidst her guests, she approached her husband, drew him by the sleeve, and whispered in his ear, like a child, nicknaming someone, "The Hon. Member!" He smiled, and both were happy beyond words. They both felt a great wish to give one another a warm embrace, but owing to the presence of their guests, this could not be. Every one, however, was looking out of the window every moment, for the question was a really important one. The former member, who had died, was a Pole, and this was the first time in this division that the Germans had put up a candidate of their own. Their military success had evidently given them courage, but just for that reason it the more concerned those assembled at the manor house at Pognenbin to secure the election of their candidate. Before dinner there was no lack of patriotic speeches, which especially moved the young hostess who was unaccustomed to them. Now and then she suffered an access of fear. Supposing there should be a mistake in counting the votes? But there would surely not only be Germans serving on the committee! The older landowners explained to the lady the method of counting the votes. She had heard this a hundred times, but she still wished to hear it! Ah! and would it not make all the difference whether the local population had an enemy in Parliament, or someone to champion their cause? It would soon be decided—in a short moment, in fact—for a cloud of dust was rising from the road.

"The priest is coming! The priest is coming!" reiterated those present. The lady grew pale. Excitement was visible on every face. They were certain of victory; all the same this final moment made their hearts beat more rapidly. But it was not the priest, it was the steward returning from the town on horseback. Perhaps he might know something? He tied his horse to the gate post, and hurried to the house. The guests and the hostess rushed into the hall.

"Is there any news?—Is there any? Has our friend been elected?—What? —Come here!—Do you know for certain?—Has the result been declared?"

The questions rose and fell like rockets, but the man threw his cap into the air.

"The Count is elected!"

The lady sat down on a bench abruptly, and pressed her hand to her fast-beating heart.

"Hurrah! Hurrah!" the neighbours shouted. "Hurrah!"

The servants rushed out from the kitchen.

"Hurrah! Down with the Germans! Long live the member! And my lady the member's wife!"

"But the priest?" someone asked.

"He will be here directly," the steward answered; "they are still counting. . . ."

"Let us have dinner!" the hon. member cried.

"Hurrah!" several people repeated.

They all walked back again from the hall to the drawing-room. Congratulations to the host and hostess were now offered more calmly; the lady herself, however, did not know how to restrain her joy, and disregarding the presence of others, threw her arm round her husband's neck. But they thought none the worse of her for this; on the contrary, they were all much touched.

"Well, we still survive!" the neighbour from Mizerów said.

At this moment there was a clatter along the corridor, and the priest entered the drawing-room, followed by old Maciej of Pognenbin.

"Welcome! Welcome!" they all cried. "Well—what majority?"

The priest was silent a moment; then as it were into the very face of this universal joy he suddenly hurled the two harsh, brief words:

"Schulberg—elected!"

A moment of astonishment followed, a volley of hurried and anxious questions, to which the priest again replied:

"Schulberg is elected!"

"How?—What has happened?—By what means?—The steward said it was not so.—What has happened?"

Meanwhile Count Jarzyński was leading poor Countess Marya out of the room, who was biting her handkerchief so as not to burst into tears or to faint.

"Oh, what a misfortune, what a misfortune!" the assembled guests repeated, striking their foreheads.

A dull sound like people shouting for joy rose at that moment from the direction of the village. The Germans of Pognenbin were thus gleefully celebrating their victory.

Count and Countess Jarzyński returned to the drawing-room. He could be heard saying to his wife at the door, *"Il faut faire bonne mtne,"* and she had stopped crying already. Her eyes were dry and very red.

"Will you tell us how it was?" the host asked quietly.

"How could it be otherwise, sir," old Maciej said, "seeing that even the Pognenbin peasants voted for Schulberg?"

"Who did so?"

"What? Those here?"

"Why, yes; I myself and every one saw Bartek Slowik vote for Schulberg."

"Bartek Slowik?" the lady said.

"Why, yes. The others are at him now for it. The man is rolling on the ground, howling, and his wife is scolding him. But I myself saw how he voted."

"From such an enlightened village!" the neighbour from Mizerów said.

"You see, sir," Maciej said, "others who were in the war also voted as he did. They say that they were ordered——"

"That's cheating, pure cheating! The election is void—Compulsion!—Swindling!" cried different voices.

The dinner at the Pognenbin manor house was not cheerful that day.

The host and hostess left in the evening, but not as yet for Berlin, only for Dresden.

Meanwhile Bartek sat in his cottage, miserable, sworn at, illtreated and hated, a stranger even to his own wife, for even she had not spoken a word to him all day.

In the autumn God granted a crop, and Herr Just, who had just come into possession of Bartek's farm, felt pleased, for he had not done at all a bad stroke of business.

Some months later three people walked out of Pognenbin to the town, a peasant, his wife, and child. The peasant was very bent, more like an old man than an able-bodied one. They were going to the town because they could not find work at Pognenbin. It was raining. The woman was sobbing bitterly at losing her cottage, and her native place. The peasant was silent. The road was empty, there was not a cart, not a human being to be seen; the cross alone, wet from the rain, stretched its arms above them. The rain fell more and more heavily, dimming the light.

Bartek, Magda, and Franek were going to town because the victor of

Gravelotte and Sedan had to serve his term of imprisonment during the winter, on account of the affair with Boege.

Count and Countess Jarzyński continued to live in Dresden.

José Echegaray

THE STREET SINGER

CHARACTERS

ANGUSTIAS

PEPE, *her lover*

SUSPIROS, *a young girl*

COLETA, *a beggar*

PASSERSBY *and* TOWNSPEOPLE

The stage represents a square or street. There may or may not be trees; there may or may not be seats; there may or may not be lighted lamps. Several wine shops, lighted and standing open, may or may not be seen. The only thing which is essential is the wall of a house facing the front, or but slightly inclined to it, near the principal entrance used, so that the beggars and the singer may take their places against it.

The time is night.

COLETA, *fifty years of age, degraded, addicted to drink, a beggar by profession, and* SUSPIROS, *a girl of sixteen, attractive, soft-mannered, but sickly, who begs incidentally, are standing before the wall waiting to solicit alms.*

COLETA. Hello, Suspiros! Begging again to-night?

SUSPIROS. Yes, Señor Coleta. My stepmother made me. She says if I don't bring back two pesetas she'll give me a bigger cuff than she did yesterday.

COLETA. Did you get a good one yesterday?

SUSPIROS. Ay! Señor Coleta!

COLETA. You're not beginning to cry already?

SUSPIROS. If I didn't cry, I'd die of my troubles. My poor mother used to say that sighs are wings that you give to troubles and they fly away.

COLETA. Don't you want to lend me something?

SUSPIROS. What do you want me to lend you?

COLETA. Some of those lovely sighs of yours, which you say are wings. I might be able to use them.

SUSPIROS. Everybody has sighs of his own.

COLETA. I haven't; not if that's what they're like. When my troubles come, they come on all fours, like stray dogs. When I slip out of the tavern —just over there—and meet the police, my trouble is running; it's not flying. Never! That is—not flying with wings. Let me tell you, child, they say it is drink. Bah! They will say anything to ruin a man's reputation.

SUSPIROS. They'll ruin you any way they can.

COLETA. That's right. But to-night, when it's dark—you're not going to beg here?

SUSPIROS. I'm used to it; I'm not so much ashamed.

COLETA. But nobody goes by.

SUSPIROS. Ay! That's the reason I like it!

COLETA. You don't know how to beg.

SUSPIROS. Yes, sir, I know how to beg; the trouble is, people don't know how to give. I say: "A penny for my poor mother who is sick!" And you ought to see how sick she is! She died two years ago. Well, I get nothing. Or else I say: "A little penny for God's sake, for my mother, who is in the hospital, in the name of the Blessed Virgin! I have two baby brothers." No one gives either.

COLETA. They don't, eh? And how many brothers are you going to have to-night?

SUSPIROS. Ay, Señor Coleta! I had two and nobody gave me anything; I had three and they didn't give me anything. Last night I tried four and I got six pence, so to-night I mean to have five and see what they give me, or whether I just get the cuff from my mother.

COLETA. Just in the family, how many brothers have you, really?

SUSPIROS. Really, I had two. But they died—like my mother. Ay! They died because of the way my stepmother treated them—as she does

me; and I am dying! Listen! If I can make two or three dollars I am going to run away to Játiva, and live with my aunt.

COLETA. Listen! If I didn't have so much to do in the tavern over there —you know—I'd take you for my daughter, and then we could beg together. Because I know how to beg, with my education; but a man can't beg here; this place is a desert.

SUSPIROS. There was a new girl here last night. She looked like a lady, the way she was. She didn't sigh, though; she was crying.

COLETA. Well, if she can cry, I'll take you both for my daughters; I need a family. You with your sighs and she with her cries, and me with my poor old eyes, we'd do twenty *reals* a day and live like kings. It's a great life. I was a gentleman once; I was a school-teacher. Then I was an undertaker; Then I drove an ox-cart; and then—I didn't drive it; and here you have me.

SUSPIROS. I'd be better off with anybody else than my stepmother.

COLETA. That girl certainly did look like a lady.

SUSPIROS. That's why she was afraid to beg—she was ashamed.

COLETA. Was she? She stood here by the wall half an hour, glued to it; and then she went away without saying a word.

SUSPIROS. A good beggar ought to be able to do something; that's what I say. The old man who stands there with the violin, he makes a lot of money because he plays the violin. Take the little girl in the square— it's easy for her; she can sing. But you and I, we can't do anything. I wonder if she can—I mean that girl that was here last night?

COLETA. I think so. She began—like this—Ahem!—as if she was trying to sing.

SUSPIROS. No; she was crying. Between saying to herself, "I'm crying," and "I mustn't cry!" she gave such a gulp—

COLETA. She did? But then you saw what happened?

SUSPIROS. I? No.

COLETA. A young fellow came around the corner. He was pretty slick—yes, he was—and well dressed.

SUSPIROS. And he was generous and good! That's the man who gave me a handful of coppers and said, "I am sorry I can't give you any more!"

COLETA. Well, he said to me, "Get out of my way, damn you! You smell of wine." Lord, what does he expect a man to smell of when he's coming out of a tavern? People don't stop to think. And that wasn't the worst of it; what I smelled of was beer.

SUSPIROS. What did that gentleman want with the señorita?

COLETA. She saw him and ran away, like that!

SUSPIROS (*innocently*). I wonder why?

COLETA. Oh, I don't know. Though I was a teacher, I don't have to teach you. You will find out for yourself soon enough—when you get over these sighs.

SUSPIROS. Look! Look! There she comes now.

COLETA. That's her. Move up in the corner and give her room.

(ANGUSTIAS *enters at the rear.*)

ANGUSTIAS. Here it is. Here is where I stood last night. I am afraid—I am such a coward! But this time—I'll shut my eyes—I'll pretend that I am alone. I'll be blind—I must!—My poor mother suffering and dying so! And nothing in the house for to-morrow! How can I buy bread? How can I buy medicines? The doctor wants so many medicines. Prescriptions and pawn-tickets—I've nothing else in my pocket. Ah, at it, Angustias, at it! This is not begging. I can sing: I am not begging. People pay or don't pay, as they like. It's the same as if I were singing in a theater. An opera out-of-doors. Of course! I'll be a street singer. That's no disgrace; I am not afraid! I am not ashamed! What a coward I am! My mother would beg on her knees for me— and I can do as much for her!

(*She goes toward the spot where* COLETA *and* SUSPIROS *are waiting, but hesitates.*)

COLETA (*to* SUSPIROS). Here she comes.

SUSPIROS (*to* COLETA). Give her room.

COLETA (*to himself*). She'll sing to-night. I can see she's made up her mind to it.

SUSPIROS (*to herself*). She's made it up to cry till her heart breaks.

(ANGUSTIAS *takes her place in line with* COLETA *and* SUSPIROS, *standing with her back against the wall. A pause ensues.*)

ANGUSTIAS (*making an effort*). I can't—I can't sing—

COLETA (*to* SUSPIROS). She's beginning.

SUSPIROS. Beginning what?

COLETA. To sing.

SUSPIROS. To cry, I say.

COLETA. Humph! It's a sentimental song, take it from me, child.

ANGUSTIAS (*to herself*). If he comes again as he did last night, I can't do it.

SUSPIROS. Is the señorita going to sing?

ANGUSTIAS. Yes—I think so.

SUSPIROS. Something sad?

ANGUSTIAS. Very sad.

SUSPIROS. I love songs that make me cry.

ANGUSTIAS. So do I! Let us cry!

SUSPIROS. Are you ready to begin?

ANGUSTIAS. Yes. Let's begin.

COLETA. Hadn't you better clear your throat first?

ANGUSTIAS. No.

SUSPIROS. Don't keep us waiting then.

ANGUSTIAS. There's nobody here. Don't you see? There's nobody here.

SUSPIROS. There will be as soon as you begin.

COLETA. Take it from me, don't sing too good music; it's above the people's heads.

ANGUSTIAS (*passing her hand across her forehead*). It must be late—it must be very late—

COLETA (*assuming a grand air, about to pay a compliment*). The nightingales sang all night in my country when I was a boy.

SUSPIROS. When I was a little girl in Játiva the larks sang at daybreak.

COLETA. And daybreak is the end of the night.

SUSPIROS. And the beginning of the morning.

COLETA (*to* ANGUSTIAS; *he says this advancing a step*). So begin.

SUSPIROS. Begin.

ANGUSTIAS. Yes—thanks. Now we'll show them.

SUSPIROS. Stand close by me.

ANGUSTIAS (*indicating* COLETA). Is he your father?

SUSPIROS. Oh! He's Coleta. He has a good heart. And he's not drunk to-night.

ANGUSTIAS. Then I'll begin. (*She attempts to sing.*) My voice shakes.

COLETA. All the better. For the *tremolo,* it's better to have the voice shake.

SUSPIROS. Don't do that. (Then to ANGUSTIAS.) When you get through each verse, I'll go around and take up the money, if you want me to. I've a plate here my stepmother gave me.

COLETA. Yes! It's politer to beg with a plate.

ANGUSTIAS. It is? Thank you.

COLETA. And I'll go down the other side so that nobody escapes.

SUSPIROS. You'll see the pennies drop.

COLETA. And if that young fellow comes who was here last night, there'll be *pesetas* and *duros.*

ANGUSTIAS. What? Who did you say?

SUSPIROS. You know. The fellow who came when—when the señorita went away.

ANGUSTIAS. No! Have him hear me? Have him see me? I'd rather die first. No, no! Not to-night! I'll wait till to-morrow—to-morrow will do— (*Leaving the wall and coming forward.*)

COLETA. Here he is now.

ANGUSTIAS. Yes! It is he! Great Heaven!

COLETA (*to* SUSPIROS). She'll sing now.

(ANGUSTIAS *begins her song. Meanwhile* PEPE *enters. It is easy to see by his dress that he is a gentleman.*)

SUSPIROS (*to* COLETA). He's looking for her.

COLETA. They can sing a duet.

PEPE (*watching from the rear*). Yes, it is she. And it was last night. (*Coming forward.*) Angustias! Angustias!

ANGUSTIAS. What do you want?— Go away!—Let me be—

PEPE. Ah! it was you!—I knew it. I could not be deceived.

ANGUSTIAS. Leave me!—Leave me! —Great God! I am free.—Let me go!

PEPE. No! Wait! You cannot go without hearing me. Are you in such a hurry to go?

ANGUSTIAS. I cannot hurry enough.

PEPE. Have I hurt you so?

ANGUSTIAS. Was it a little?

PEPE. To love you with all my soul —was that to hurt you?

ANGUSTIAS. Love *me?*

568 *The Nobel Prize Treasury*

PEPE. Whom, then?

ANGUSTIAS. I found that out.

PEPE. You never found it out. Did I leave you, or was it you who sent me off? Tell me that—tell me the truth! Don't I always come back to you? All day long at your door, and all day long it is closed! All night long at your window, and all night long it is dark! I follow your steps when you go out, to see if I can put my feet where you have set yours; that is the only consolation you have left to me. And when I lose sight of you it seems as if my soul would rush out of my body after you; for the soul is lighter than the body, and can travel faster. My Angustias—for you were my Angustias—you were happiness to me!

ANGUSTIAS. You know how to talk. The more fool I, to have believed you at first! But since I believed you then, I cannot believe you now. No! though you were to do what you never do—speak the truth!

PEPE. Have I deceived you?

ANGUSTIAS. Do you ask me that?

PEPE. How?

ANGUSTIAS. In everything! Did you tell me who you were when you came to see me? No, you did not! You came to me as if you had been a man of my own class, a poor man who had to work for his living as I had for mine. And then what a game you played with my heart! Your cap and flannel shirt—Oh! they were honorable; yes, they were!—but they covered up a heart that was evil. You didn't wear a mask, for your face is a mask. It always is. Can you deny it? You can't deny it. Deny that you hid your position, your money, your name! Yes, your name! for it burns in my throat, it has been such a shame to me!

PEPE. I don't deny it. But if I had come to you in any other way—

you are so proud, so jealous—you would never have loved me.

ANGUSTIAS. How could you tell that I was so proud, before you knew me?

PEPE. Couldn't I see it in your face?

ANGUSTIAS. Proud, no; but honest —yes!

PEPE. I told you the truth at last.

ANGUSTIAS. At last? The truth? When I know it, and you know that I know it, why do you have to lie? You never told me the truth. I found it out! I found it out because God willed it so—He would not stand by and see a poor girl deceived. And He put you in my way and revealed you to me as you were—rich, deceitful, vain! Yes, a gentleman—without a particle of conscience!

PEPE. Angustias! Don't say such things!

ANGUSTIAS. Your memory is weak. One winter night, when it was dark —dark nights were not made for nothing—what have the nights done that they should be so dark?—well, one night I was in the heart of Madrid, delivering some work. When there is work to do, I work. You— when do you work? When you want to make people believe you! Well, I was passing the door of a theater—

PEPE. Angustias!

ANGUSTIAS. Do you remember? No, let me finish. Can't you see it? I can —I can see it as if it were happening now. I had to stop because a carriage drew up by the sidewalk—a carriage with two horses, a coachman and a footman. The footman opened the door, and with the door he took up the whole sidewalk so I couldn't pass; and I stood still. I waited to see the gentleman get out; and he got out. What clothes! How he did shine! A great fur coat, and the white bosom of his shirt was glistening in the fur. I had to laugh, he looked so

like my Pepe. "I am a fool," I thought
—and then I thought—I tell you I
am a fool! "No; Pepe would be
handsomer in clothes like those."
I thought so, because I loved you—
because I adored you—yes, I adored
you! My God! Love like that should
never die! The sun and the sky may,
and life itself go out, but not love—
no! For without love there is nothing!

(*She begins to cry.*)

PEPE. Angustias—let me explain.
You don't understand. There are
things in life—facts sometimes—
parents—and sometimes they don't
understand, either!

ANGUSTIAS (*interrupting*). There is
nothing to explain. Listen! Suddenly
you turned; that is, the gentleman
with the coat turned, and the white
bosom gleaming in the fur. Who
knows?—I may have ironed that
shirt myself. Well, he turned, and he
said to the footman, "Remember, at
twelve; be there!" Great God, what
a jump my heart gave! It was your
voice! Your voice! And what you
said to the lackey you had said to
me, oh, so many times! "Remember
—at twelve; be there!" I leaped forward; I couldn't hold back. I gave
a cry. I caught you by the arm—no,
not by the arm! What I caught was
the coat, not you. When you wore a
blouse I could touch you—I have,
so many times! But in that greatcoat,
my hand was lost in the fur and my
fingers couldn't reach you.

PEPE. No more, Angustias! No
more!

ANGUSTIAS. Why not? Wasn't it so?
I cried out: "Pepe, Pepe! Is it you?"
And you, with another cry, answered
"Angustias!" And the people stood
still in the streets and laughed. And
the lights of the theater beat on us
with a fierce burning glare. And I
blushed red, with shame—and I ran!

I got home, I don't know how—I
stumbled up the stairs, I threw myself into my mother's arms, and,
choking with tears, I cried out: "Pepe
is not Pepe! It is all over! He is rich!
He has a carriage!" "But you—you
have your honor," my mother said;
and, as I have no furs, her poor old
fingers sank deep into my arm. We
are poor—when we embrace our
embraces are real, body to body and
soul to soul. There come between us
no sables and no ermines.

PEPE. But the next day I came—

ANGUSTIAS. The next day my mother
saw you. "We live up too many flights
for you to climb to see my daughter,"
she said, "and my daughter would
have to go down too many if she
were to go to see you. Please don't
take the trouble."

PEPE. But I—

ANGUSTIAS. You said nothing. As
you were silent then, be silent now.
And remember to respect a woman.

PEPE. Angustias—

ANGUSTIAS. Not another word.

PEPE. Give me hope!

ANGUSTIAS. Hope? Have I hope?

PEPE. If, without thinking of hindrances, of anybody, of anything, I
said to you: "Be my wife!"

(*Seizing her hand.*)

ANGUSTIAS (*moved in spite of herself*). Is the pretense still on? Well!
—when you slip that ring on my
finger, we shall see whether the pretense is on.

PEPE (*endeavoring to remove the
ring*). At once.

ANGUSTIAS. No, not that bright one.
No; that costs too much! It sparkles
too brightly for a girl like me. I can't
afford to wear it. It would be a disgrace. It is for gentlemen like you.
I mean the other, the guard, the little
gold band that looks like a wedding-
ring. Don't say that I am proud. But
I can tell you this: My mother has

a ring like that, and though we are dying of hunger, she will carry it with her to her grave. Well, I shall be carried to mine with one like that—or without one! I have done with you.

PEPE. Angustias!

ANGUSTIAS. You may go! If you don't, I'll go myself—I'll run away—jump from the viaduct—kill myself!—

PEPE. I'll go, Angustias. I'll go—But, ah—who knows?—Good-by—Good-by.

(*He goes out.*)

ANGUSTIAS. I know! I know! He won't come back. Good-by! (*Various persons enter. As* ANGUSTIAS *begins to sing, they form a group about her.*) And now to sing—to earn money for my mother—to buy her medicines. To sing—though it tears out my throat! (*She goes up to the wall by* SUSPIROS *and* COLETA.) Here I am. I am ready now. I am going to sing.

(*She begins to try her voice.*)

COLETA (*to* SUSPIROS). Now she'll begin. Didn't I tell you that man would make her sing?

SUSPIROS. Keep quiet—I want to listen.

(ANGUSTIAS *begins to sing.*)

COLETA. Here come more people.

SUSPIROS. Go on! Go on! The flies flock to the honey.

(*The crowd grows greater as* AN-GUSTIAS *sings. The scene should be one of animation. Some applaud at appropriate moments; others shout out disconnected phrases such as* "Good!" "Brava!" "Olé for the street-singer!" "Encore!" "Encore!" "Another!" "Sing something lively!" "Something sad!" "Ole!" PEPE *returns. Little by little he draws nearer and mingles with the crowd, however without attracting attention.*)

PEPE (*to himself*). What is this?—Great God!—My Angustias!—Ah!—

No, no! Never!—Let them say what they will, I cannot—

SUSPIROS (*producing a tray*). Now leave it to me. I'll take up the money.

ANGUSTIAS (*supporting herself against the wall*). I can't sing any more. Do what you like.

SUSPIROS. Come on!—Oh, come on! Throw in the pennies—don't be stingy. It's worth it. I have seven little brothers—

(*She goes through the crowd passing the tray.*)

PEPE (*in a low voice*). Here—take this—

(*He throws in several duros, and the gold ring of which* ANGUSTIAS *spoke, along with them.*)

SUSPIROS. Ave María! What a lot of money! Goodness!—Duros! Look! Look! (*Running up to* ANGUSTIAS.) And a gold ring. He threw it in—the man who was here last night!

ANGUSTIAS. What? What's that you say? Ah! (*Seizing the ring.*) Yes, it is his! But where is he? (*Breaking through the crowd to find him.*)

PEPE (*rushing to meet her*). Here I am! Now come with me to your mother.

ANGUSTIAS. Swear to me by yours first, that you don't deceive me.

PEPE. I do; I swear it. Will you come? Do you want to?

ANGUSTIAS. What shall I do?

PEPE. Come.

SUSPIROS. Señorita, you forget the money—

PEPE. It's for you.

SUSPIROS. Hurrah! Now I can run away to Játiva.

COLETA. Promise me to let me buy your ticket.

ANGUSTIAS. My Pepe!

PEPE. This is the end of the song, for I am carrying off the Street Singer.

CURTAIN

Frédéric Mistral

THE MARES OF CAMARGUE

A HUNDRED mares, all white! their manes
Like mace-reed of the marshy plains
Thick-tufted, wavy, free o' the shears:
And when the fiery squadron rears
Bursting at speed, each mane appears
Even as the white scarf of a fay
Floating upon their necks along the heavens away.

O race of humankind, take shame!
For never yet a hand could tame,
Nor bitter spur that rips the flanks subdue
The mares of the Camargue. I have known,
By treason snared, some captives shown;
Expatriate from their native Rhone,
Led off, their saline pastures far from view.

And on a day, with prompt rebound,
They have flung their riders to the ground,
And at a single gallop, scouring free,
Wide nostril'd to the wind, twice ten
Of long marsh-leagues devoured, and then,
Back to the Vacarés again,
After ten years of slavery just to breathe salt sea.

For of this savage race unbent
The ocean is the element.
Of old escaped from Neptune's car, full sure
Still with the white foam fleck'd are they,
And when the sea puffs black from gray,
And ships part cables, loudly neigh
The stallions of Camargue, all joyful in the roar;

And keen as a whip they lash and crack
Their tails that drag the dust, and back
Scratch up the earth, and feel, entering their flesh, where he,
The God, drives deep his trident teeth,
Who in one horror, above, beneath,
Bids storm and watery deluge seethe,
And shatters to their depths the abysses of the sea.

THE COCOONING

WHEN the crop is fair in the olive-yard,
        And the earthen jars are ready
        For the golden oil from the barrels poured,
And the big cart rocks unsteady
With its tower of gathered sheaves, and strains
And groans on its way through fields and lanes:

When brawny and bare as an old athlete
    Comes Bacchus the dance a-leading,
And the laborers all, with juice-dyed feet,
    The vintage of Crau are treading,
And the good wine pours from the brimful presses,
And the ruddy foam in the vats increases;

When under the leaves of the Spanish broom
    The clear silk-worms are holden,
An artist each, in a tiny loom,
    Weaving a web of golden,—
Fine, frail cells out of sunlight spun,
Where they creep and sleep by the million,—

Glad is Provence on a day like that,
    'Tis the time of jest and laughter:
The Ferigoulet and the Baume Muscat
    They quaff, and they sing thereafter.
And lads and lasses, their toils between,
Dance to the tinkling tambourine.

Björnstjerne Björnson

SYNNÖVE'S SONG

OH, THANKS for all since the days long past
     When we played about on the purple heather!
     I thought that the merry times would last
Till we should grow old together.

I thought we should run on hand in hand
From the birches—and how we used to love them!—
To where the Solbakke houses stand,
And on to the church above them.

I waited many an eventide
And looked far off through the pines around me,
But shadows fell from the mountainside,
And you, oh you never found me.

I sat and waited, and often thought:
He'll surely dare it when dusk is falling.
But the twilight faded and then burnt out,
And the day was gone past recalling.

Poor eye, its wont it never forsook,
It never could get the trick o' turning;
It never knew anywhere else to look,
'Twas fixed in a deep-set yearning.

They tell of a place where peace may be:
It's in the kirk, as is rightly fitting.
But do not ask me to go and see—
He'd be right across from me sitting.

But still I know—and 'tis well and good—
Who let our farms be so near together,
And cut the opening in the wood
To look out on the bright spring weather.

But still I know—and 'tis right and fair—
Who built the kirk and its pointing spire,
And made the pews go pair and pair
Along the aisle to the choir.

BETWEEN THE BATTLES

A Play in One Act

CHARACTERS

KING SVERRE *of Norway, disguised as* EISTEIN, *a scout for the rival king Magnus.*

THORKEL, *spy for King Magnus (Once a rich landowner).*

HALVARD GJALA.

INGA, *his wife.*

EINDRIDE *and* ASLAK, *soldiers of King Magnus.*

GUDLAUG STALLAR, *and a number of "Birchlegs." (Birchlegs was the name given to King Sverre's soldiers who, because of poverty, wore the bark of birch trees in place of trousers. Later, when Sverre was victorious, this name became a title of honor.)*

SETTING: *A poor, smoky room. The main door has a large bolt. A low door to the right and two separate rooms on the left behind a bench. A spy-hole in the left wall. A fire is burning on the hearth.*

PLACE: *A log cabin on a Norwegian mountain.*

TIME: *About 1170.*

The stage remains empty for a while. HALVARD GJALA *and* EISTEIN *enter. Between them they hold* THORKEL. *All are heavily armed and dressed in winter clothes.*

HALVARD. This is my homestead. It's not built for banquets, you see. (*He and* EISTEIN *lead the old man to the fire. He removes the latter's clothing as well as his own. He hangs his weapons upon the wall.*)

THORKEL. It could be worse.

EISTEIN. It was right enough the last time I was here. It's no worse now.

HALVARD. It's bad weather outside,

tonight. (*To* THORKEL.) I'm surprised that an old man like you should be out in such weather.

THORKEL. It would have been just as well if I'd stuck in the snow. (*Warms himself.*)

EISTEIN. You should have told us so when we were pulling you out.

THORKEL. I didn't ask you to help me.

HALVARD. You must be in great trouble to talk that way.

EISTEIN. Don't remind us of such things. Better find us something to drink.

HALVARD. I'll call immediately.

EISTEIN (*aside*). Call? (*Apart, to* HALVARD.) If you're calling Inga, you'd better not call her by name.

HALVARD (*likewise, to* EISTEIN). Is he dangerous? Then I'd better not mention my own name.

EISTEIN. No, not dangerous. But a wise man must always be on his guard.

THORKEL (*aside*). I wonder what those two are talking about.

HALVARD. I'll follow your advice. (*Exit.*)

EISTEIN (*seating himself near* THORKEL). Well, old man, how are you?

THORKEL. Like a deer caught in the snow.

EISTEIN. Thaw yourself out by the fire—and have a horn of ale.

THORKEL. It will make me sleepy.

EISTEIN. No harm in that. We have the whole night before us. (*Stretches himself out upon the bench. Pause.*)

THORKEL. Were you out long before you found me?

EISTEIN. Not long.

THORKEL. You're a scout for the troops that came yesterday from the South?

EISTEIN. Yes.

THORKEL. What is your strength? About four hundred men, eh?

EISTEIN. Thereabouts.

THORKEL. Let's see . . . then altogether, King Magnus has about a thousand men here in the valley?

EISTEIN. Well, quite a force.

THORKEL. Sverre hasn't got that many together. I wish he were on the other side of the mountain.

EISTEIN. Yes . . . well, maybe . . . (*Pause.*)

HALVARD (*outside*). Hello! Answer me!

EISTEIN. Isn't his wife at home?

THORKEL. She can't have gone for a visit to the neighbors.

EISTEIN. Oh, no! On the mountain you've got to talk to yourself, if you want amusement.

THORKEL. Yes, and then there's no fear of slander.

HALVARD (*outside, calling from another side of the hut*). Come in . . . There are strangers here.

THORKEL. Isn't it true that a fox hides best when he's chased by a wolf?

EISTEIN. So you think Halvard has fled because of some crime?

THORKEL. Yes, for some such reason.

EISTEIN. His face disproves that. (*Testing the sword, aside.*) This sword has been used too rarely to be hung up like this.

THORKEL. It must be quite pleasant to live here like this, man-by-yourself-style.

EISTEIN. Yes, but you have to give up all contact with the world.

THORKEL. What do I care about the world?

EISTEIN. Serve your king!

THORKEL. For all I've gotten out of it! I've done more than my share. (*To* HALVARD *who enters.*) You were calmer when you went out.

(*Halvard comes forward without paying any attention to him.*)

EISTEIN. Well? (HALVARD *does not answer.*) What's the matter?

HALVARD. I've looked and looked—and I can't find her.

EISTEIN (*low*). Inga?

HALVARD. She's made the fire in here and in the other room. The cows have enough to eat in the stable. Either she's just left—or, she's figured on a long absence.

EISTEIN. Some accident?

HALVARD. I don't think so.

EISTEIN. What then *do* you think?

HALVARD. The worst. (*Sits down, covering his face with his hands.*)

THORKEL (*to himself, sleepily*). This mountain air isn't all they claim for it. (*Sleeps.*)

HALVARD. To have the courage to do such a thing! God! How I've been deceived!

EISTEIN (*approaches him*). Far from here? To King Magnus' men? The snow's very deep.

HALVARD (*gets up*). Why do you say that? (*Looks at him.*)

EISTEIN. It's not a trip for a woman.

HALVARD. Well, then, where can she be?

EISTEIN. Did she have some important errand?

HALVARD. How should I know?

EISTEIN (*meaningly*). Ask her.

HALVARD. Ask her? (*With a peculiar smile.*) No!

EISTEIN. So that's how it is! You're not on speaking terms. (*Pause.* HALVARD *bethinks himself of something. Is about to leave.*) Where are you going?

HALVARD. To Alf, our child.

EISTEIN. So there's a child?

HALVARD. Born last year.

EISTEIN. Then happiness will follow.

HALVARD. And she leaves him alone! Does a mother turn her back on her own child, especially when there's no one at home to keep an eye on him? No wonder I'm suspicious. (*He looks at* EISTEIN *as though awaiting an answer. Exit.*)

EISTEIN. Now I've learned that jealousy can find its way even into the hearts of two lonely people. Well, I suppose I must take a hand. (*Turns to* THORKEL.) The old man's asleep. Poor devil! There's not much to keep him awake. (*Nudging him.*) Go, lie down in the other room—and sleep soundly.

THORKEL (*awake*). Aren't you coming along?

EISTEIN. In the last seven or eight years I've grown accustomed to very little sleep. I sleep and wake any old time.

THORKEL. That's more than I can. (*Yawns.*) I'll take a nap till you call me. (*Remains standing by the door.*) But tell me first—where do you come from?

EISTEIN. I've told you. From the South.

THORKEL (*coming nearer*). It's surprising that a smart fellow like you should be only a plain soldier.

EISTEIN. Hmm . . . So long as the great lords rule over the king—they'll keep the best jobs for themselves.

THORKEL. Never a truer word said! It's only recently that a few people have gotten great power into their hands. You'll see, we'll soon have lots of little kingdoms as in the old days.

EISTEIN. Hmm . . . As long as King Magnus thinks only of obeying the Pope in Rome—just so long will the kingdom stay whole. But he'd better remember to welcome the Archbishop right well when he comes for a conference with a hundred armed men behind him. He'd better remember—and his mighty ones too—to rise, to kneel, to kiss the hem of the Bishop's cloth, and to pay him half of all the land's income —then the kingdom will hang together . . . for a while.

THORKEL. Yes. It must make every brave Norseman bitter to see the Priests and the Pope rule the ancient kingdom of King Harald. But, after all, King Magnus is a humane king. Good night, comrade-in-arms. (*He goes off into the next room to sleep.*)

EISTEIN (*alone*). Most of them are like that . . . Habit rules them . . . and neither Sverre nor Magnus . . . the humane king . . . Hmm . . . He does neither good nor bad. He gives them mead, and they, in exchange, give him their blood . . . King! Only he is king who has something to offer—something which impels him to become king. Harald was king—because he increased the kingdom . . . Haakon Adelstein was king—he built a stronghold of laws . . . The Olafs were kings—because they Christianized the land . . . Magnus the good was king—he freed it from a foreign yoke . . . God saw into their hearts and helped them bring it about. (*Looks upward, with folded hands.*) O Lord God!

(HALVARD *enters.*)

HALVARD. Am I disturbing you?

EISTEIN. Of course not. I've just sent the old man into the next room.

HALVARD. Good. Listen; while I was inside with the child a strange fear gripped me. Wherever she may be there's danger. The night is dark —the paths are deep with snow— and wild beasts are about . . .

EISTEIN. You think we ought to look for her?

HALVARD. Yes. And as soon as possible. I feel uneasy. God! If something were to happen to her.

EISTEIN. If she had the courage to try something, she'll have the strength to do it. She'll be here soon . . . (*He opens the spy-hole and looks out.*) Holy Olaf, here she is now!

HALVARD. Is she coming from the South?

EISTEIN (*lingering*). Yes.

HALVARD. Anybody else? (*Tries to glance out.*)

EISTEIN (*shuts the spy-hole quickly*). No! (*Aside.*) What does it mean? There are about ten or twelve armed men with her . . . And she's coming from the South . . . They must be Magnus' men.

HALVARD. You look worried. (*Tries to look out.*)

EISTEIN (*quickly*). Listen! She's taking off her snowshoes. (HALVARD *goes to the background and removes his weapons and clothing which he had put on to go look for* INGA. EISTEIN *looks out again.*) They're going around back to the stable. (*Closes the window*). We'll soon know what that means.

(INGA *enters.*)

INGA (*seeing* HALVARD). Home already? (*Looking about.*) No one else? (*Noticing* EISTEIN.) Oh, yes, there. . . . Oh . . . Eistein! A Magnus man.

EISTEIN (*grasping her hand*). Welcome, Inga!

INGA (*mechanically*). Welcome! (*Aside.*) I've made a terrible mistake. (*Anxiously approaching* HALVARD.) Good evening. (*He does not reply.*) Good evening, Halvard.

HALVARD. Good evening.

INGA. You're home early.

HALVARD. Earlier than you expected?

INGA. A welcome husband is never too early. (HALVARD *looks at her, but turns away.*) Halvard! (*He turns sharply away. Aside.*) Holy Mary, what's the matter? (*Aloud.*) Is Alf asleep?

HALVARD. His mother can tell you.

INGA. But I've just come in.

HALVARD. Yes, so I see.

INGA. Do you think a mother must be a slave to her child? You can wander about all day long—but I'm chained to the cradle. And it's so lively up here on the mountain! It's a wonderful life.

HALVARD. Inga!

INGA (*aside*). Holy Olaf! What have I said. I must talk to him, but I can't find words . . . I . . . (*To* EISTEIN.) Say something. (*He is silent.*) He, too? (*Looks at them. Starts to go.*)

HALVARD (*barring her way*). No! It's a slave's duty. I'll attend to our child. (*Starts to go.*)

INGA (*painfully*). Halvard! (*He remains standing.*) Halvard!

HALVARD (*coming a step nearer*). What were you going to say?

INGA. To say? . . . I wanted . . .

HALVARD (*softly*). Speak out, Inga! I'm listening.

INGA (*aside*). If I only could . . .

(*Aloud.*) Have you nothing to say to me?

HALVARD. Yes . . . so much . . . that the sun would be up before I was half through.

INGA (*coldly*). As much as that? Then let's wait as long as possible.

HALVARD. Until when?

INGA. Aye, it'll come soon enough. Things will begin to speak for themselves.

HALVARD. Have you seen to that?

INGA. Not I! Have you?

HALVARD. I?

INGA. Yes, you!

HALVARD. Well, then, I have.

INGA. Go ahead—laugh. I know when the tears will come.

HALVARD. And I know, too.

INGA. Well then, speak up!

HALVARD. No! Once I spoke a word too many.

INGA. You! I'd like to know when.

HALVARD. When I asked you to follow me here. Oh, how sorry I am I ever asked you! (*Exit.*)

INGA. Oh, God! We're farther apart now than ever before. I'd exchange places with any she-wolf hungrily stalking about in the snow. Help me now, Holy Sunniva; I'm so unhappy. (*Sinks down upon the bench.*)

EISTEIN (*approaches her*). I never expected to see you like this.

INGA. Leave me alone! You caused the trouble. You bedeviled him with delusions that disturbed our peace, and you gave him wicked counsel.

EISTEIN (*dryly*). Why not talk sense?

INGA. It's the truth. Ever since you told him of the fame to be gained in the dispute between the kings he's turned away from me. He has turned away from me and from his child to follow that scoundrel, that miserable monk Sverre.

EISTEIN. Scoundrel?

INGA. Yes! Didn't he burn down my father's homestead? Hasn't he killed the Jarl Earling and the bravest of the land? Since he took off his monk's cowl—where deviltry and corruption bred—there's wailing in every corner of the land. No need, now, to light bonfires to warn people that the enemy is coming. The whole country from Drontheim to Tunsberg's in flames. Everything is fuel for the flames—ships, palaces, everything. The noblemen and peasants, relatives and friends—even his own father—are part of this conflagration. (*Coming nearer.*) And is it for him that Halvard is to span his bow? No! I'd rather see his bow smashed to pieces, broken into splinters, crumbled to dust—rather . . .

EISTEIN (*interrupting*). Even Halvard?

INGA (*frightened*). What are you saying?

EISTEIN. Inga! Inga! You're about to destroy him.

INGA. I?

EISTEIN. Don't blame Sverre. You're talking about yourself. You're terrified at what you yourself have done.

INGA. What have I done?

EISTEIN. It will soon come out.

INGA. Well, now that you know, please help me!

EISTEIN. How can I help?

INGA. You brought discontent into this house—it is only right that you remove it. Halvard wasn't always like this.

EISTEIN. I know that. Last year I spent many pleasant hours up here.

INGA. And those hours in the evening in front of the hearth. (*Sighs.*) . . . They will never come back . . . One fine morning you came along . . .

EISTEIN. I came scouting for King Magnus.

INGA. So you said.

EISTEIN. From here one can survey the whole country below.

INGA. Unfortunately.

EISTEIN. And you received me hospitably. You showed me much kindness. I shall never forget it.

INGA. You brought us reports of the latest battles. I can still see him —there at the hearth—sitting breathlessly and drinking in your words. His silence spoke more than all your words. I understood the meaning of his silence. His thoughts were no longer of me . . . no, they were sweeping far, far away . . . and his eyes were bright. You monster! You saw all my sufferings—yet you stayed here and lured him away from me.

EISTEIN. Don't be hard on me, Inga. Tell me calmly just what happened after I left you.

INGA (*controlling herself*). Alf was born. For a short while after that, everything went well. Soon, however, your words came back to torment him. Each day he made longer trips . . . and in the evenings he became more and more silent. He put aside his work before he had even started. For hours he dreamed and sat sunk in thought . . . yearning to be with Sverre in the valley. He resented our being. Then I learned that Sverre's people had burned down my father's homestead.

EISTEIN. Those things are unavoidable in wartime.

INGA. Yes . . . but your ancestors weren't born under that roof— neither were his. Then I became really angry with Halvard . . . that he could still think of Sverre. But I sympathized and grieved for my poor father, for whom he had no feeling. Is that surprising? It was terrible for that old man; he had no home, no child. I had not been a good daughter to him.

EISTEIN. But Halvard must have understood your thoughts. Didn't he say anything?

INGA. He thought that I didn't love him any more. Great God! After all the things that I had done for his sake . . . and I . . . even I kept silent.

EISTEIN. How did you find out what he was thinking about?

INGA. He began to sing.

EISTEIN. Sing?

INGA. What he kept secret from me, he expressed in song. He sat near the well, working away at a new bow—and I, who was happy just looking at him, left the child and stole behind the bushes. Then I heard him singing . . . Great God! I'll never forget it!—"It's hard for the son of brave ancestors to sit silently by his wife's side and listen to the whirr of the spinning wheel, when swords are clashing all around; it's hard to span one's bow for hares and quacking ducks, when the war cries sound from the valley where booty and power are being divided. But it's harder still to lose the best part of your home and the peace in your own heart."

EISTEIN. That was a bad sign.

INGA (*after a short pause*). He sang a lot those days . . . and all the time I followed him and I discovered what was in his mind. But he could not learn my thoughts. Why was there no one to bring us together? Many's the time I took little Alf on my lap, turned his little face towards his father so that he should speak for me. But Halvard didn't understand. Even when the little one stretched out his hands and called "Daddy"—just as I had taught him —he didn't understand. (*Pause.*) I tried to let things speak for me. I made him a doublet—as best I could —and kept it hidden until the anniversary of our coming here. I counted the days. I placed it on his stool at table. He was touched when he saw it. Neither of us could eat anything. Tears filled my eyes and I had to turn away. There, right behind me, lay two new top coats—one for me and one for Alf. I turned to him . . . he was crying. I threw myself on his neck and we cried so long and so bitterly that Alf began to cry, too. But neither of us would ask the question, "Shall we stay here longer? If not, where shall we go?" He tore himself loose from me, took his bow and left—he didn't come back until the next morning. (*Pause. She sits down.*)

EISTEIN. Halvard's coming. (*She gets up.*)

HALVARD. I can't find the milk— Alf is awake and restless.

INGA. I'll go. (*Starts to go.*)

HALVARD. No, no! You stay here . . . I'll take care of the child. (*Searching about.*) You have other things to do.

INGA. What do you mean?

HALVARD. Well . . . You must have much to talk about. It's seldom that people come here with whom you can talk.

INGA. That's true. (HALVARD *is still searching.*) What are you looking for?

HALVARD. I told you. I'm looking for the milk.

INGA. The milk is on the top shelf in the other room. You must have passed by it over and over again.

HALVARD. It's quite possible. I have such a headache that I can hardly see anything.

INGA. You don't see much.

HALVARD. Sometimes I see too much. (*At the threshold he bumps against a shield which falls on the floor. He looks at it.*)

INGA. My father's shield!

HALVARD. Your father's?

EISTEIN (*quickly*). No, that's my shield!

INGA (*coming nearer*). And yet . . . it's so similar. (*Picks it up and scrutinizes it.*) It seems to me as if I'd often played with it . . . that cross there . . . the leather at the handle worn away . . . it's just as heavy. Oh, God! To think that father's hand may have touched it.

HALVARD (*who has watched her the whole time*). Do you hear? Do you see?

INGA (*letting the shield fall*). I seem to be back in the large room of my father's. Father! (*Stares at the shield, sunk in thoughts.*)

HALVARD. It is quite evident where her thoughts are. (*Exit.*)

INGA. Oh, it is so sad . . . so sad! (*Breaking out passionately.*) But rather than go on living like this— rather than see the word freeze upon the tongue before it is spoken . . . What have I done?

EISTEIN (*to her*). I'll help you . . . Tell me quickly—those men whom you brought here . . . are they Magnus' men?

INGA (*mechanically*). Yes.

EISTEIN. And you believed that they were Sverre's men?

INGA. I don't know what I believed. I can't think any more . . . my head . . . Sverre and his warriors are already in the valley . . . and Halvard is ready to join them. I hurried over to the other side . . . to Magnus' men . . . I'd rather have him and his followers captured . . . rather than be separated . . . (*Proudly.*) Do you understand?

EISTEIN. But he brought none of King Sverre's men along—and he doesn't intend to go away.

INGA. Neither you nor I can know anything about it. But this I do know, that Magnus' men have come too early . . . everything may be discovered. Try to get rid of them, do you hear. If he should see them, there won't be any more happy days here. Halvard will never understand that I did it only to reconcile him and my father . . . he doesn't even realize that he would kill me.

EISTEIN (*grasping her hand*). Be brave, Inga! If I were that scoundrel Sverre himself, I could not give you better counsel than I'm giving you now. Bring one of the men to me.

INGA (*mechanically*). Very well.

EISTEIN. To the others you will give mead . . . and bid them be quiet.

INGA. Yes. (*Exit.*)

EISTEIN (*alone*). Oh, this passion, this passion—it entangles more than Absalom's hair. I have had a glimpse into their souls. How changed everything is since last year. I feel as though I had just come from church. (*Quietly.*) Towards noon the battle will begin—I must arrange everything before then.

EINDRIDE (*entering*). Greetings! Are you Halvard Gjäla?

EISTEIN. No . . . Have a seat.

EINDRIDE (*sits down*). Thanks . . . I'm very tired . . . We had a hard trip.

EISTEIN. The weather is bad at this time of year.

EINDRIDE. Very bad. But it'll soon clear up.

EISTEIN. Yes . . . Stormy weather both in nature and in the land.

EINDRIDE. That's right. Who knows what the end will be.

EISTEIN. It doesn't look very promising.

EINDRIDE. It does not! As long as that devil Sverre lives . . .

EISTEIN. He was born in an evil hour.

EINDRIDE. Yes. God alone protects the land and the people. When the mighty quarrel, common folk suffer.

EISTEIN. Didn't you come on some errand?

EINDRIDE (*cautiously*). Perhaps . . . Who are you, if I may ask?

EISTEIN. If I'm not mistaken we both serve the same man. I'm one of King Magnus' men, scouting in the North, you see.

EINDRIDE. So . . . You're his man . . . he's a good master.

EISTEIN. A friendly king.

EINDRIDE. And the woman that brought us here was very friendly, too . . . She greeted us in the name of Halvard Gjäla.

EISTEIN. Halvard Gjäla?

EINDRIDE. Yes. He wants to please King Magnus and to accomplish something worthwhile for the cause. He thinks that's the way to become reconciled with his father-in-law.

EISTEIN. How?

EINDRIDE. He proposes to lure a couple of "Birchlegs" here . . . One of them is a chieftain. We are to capture them. See?

EISTEIN. A clever plan. How many men have you?

EINDRIDE. Twelve or thirteen.

EISTEIN. Too bad that the "Birchlegs" haven't come.

EINDRIDE. Yes, I know. But they'll come.

EISTEIN. I'm not so sure.

EINDRIDE. Damnation!

EISTEIN. What a trip for nothing!

EINDRIDE. Through snow and pitch-darkness. The others won't be very pleased.

EISTEIN. Think how the people in the camp will jeer. I can just imagine what that Einar Weiten will say.

EINDRIDE. That scoffer! Yes, he'll have something to say.

EISTEIN. Thirteen men went to the mountain—and all they caught was colds. They could have gotten them much more comfortably right here in the valley.

EINDRIDE. And that's not the half of it. The more I think of it, the angrier I get. I hate that fellow Halvard, and I hate his wife.

EISTEIN. And we shan't even get ransom-money for the prisoners.

EINDRIDE (*angrily*). And the ransom-money. He'll be sorry.

EISTEIN. The poor devil has nothing . . . it would be no use to kill him, if you can make it up some other way.

EINDRIDE. I don't understand.

EISTEIN. I have a plan if you'd care to listen.

EINDRIDE. Well?

EISTEIN. If you were to do—what Halvard was to have done . . . to lure a couple of "Birchlegs" here.

EINDRIDE. I don't see how.

EISTEIN. I do. You go down to Sverre's camp and ask for Gudlaug Stallar. Here is a ring . . . give it to him . . . and he'll act as your decoy.

EINDRIDE. But this ring . . .

EISTEIN. It's not mine . . . Just try it. I was out in a storm a few nights ago, you understand?

EINDRIDE. The devil! I could see right away that you weren't born yesterday.

EISTEIN. Well, you ask him in the name of the owner of the ring to hurry along with about ten men . . . He'll do it—and your journey will not have been for nothing.

EINDRIDE. I never expected to find such a clever plan in this place . . . yet . . .

EISTEIN. Sverre is not as far away as you think. Just a short distance . . . go straight ahead . . . and you'll be able to see his campfires.

EINDRIDE. As near as that? Our leaders ought to know of this.

EISTEIN. You can bring them the news yourself before the day's gone. And when you bring Stallar as prisoner—everyone will admit that

you've done a good day's work.

EINDRIDE. But . . . ten men . . . I think that . . .

EISTEIN. Too many, you think?

EINDRIDE. Especially when Gudlaug Stallar is with them . . . we must handle this thing very carefully.

EISTELN. But I'm here too.

EINDRIDE. Yes . . . I see that you're strong and trained in arms . . . still . . .

EISTEIN. You're forgetting Halvard. He's the best shot in the Westland . . . you know that he has no equal.

EINDRIDE. Is Halvard also with us?

EISTEIN. Before the "Birchlegs" reach the house, he will have brought down at least three.

EINDRIDE. Is he as good as that?

EISTEIN. He never misses.

EINDRIDE. Is that so?

EISTEIN. He can shoot a bird on the wing and a hare on the run.

EINDRIDE. So there's no danger?

EISTEIN (*laughing*). The worst that can happen is that he will dispose of too many and leave none for you.

EINDRIDE (*joining in the laughter*). Well then, I'll go down. I'll take the shortest path.

EISTEIN. Good luck.

EINDRIDE. Thanks. It makes me laugh . . . clever . . . clever.

EISTEIN. Try to catch a glimpse of Sverre himself.

EINDRIDE. That's exactly what I was thinking about. It can't do any harm.

EISTEIN. People say, though, that he's possessed by the devil.

EINDRIDE (*mysteriously*). Don't speak of it, comrade! My cousin saw him in the battle of Jlevold . . . They say he has a pair of eyes . . . brrr . . .

EISTEIN. So? Better hurry along, comrade.

EINDRIDE. Yes. Farewell.

(INGA *enters*.)

INGA (*holding him back*). Where are you going?

EINDRIDE (*in the door*). To Sverre.

INGA. To Sverre? (*To* EISTEIN.) What sort of a plan did you make?

EINDRIDE. The best I've ever heard. Make way for a traveler. (*Exit*.)

INGA. I have often wondered whether you really are a follower of Magnus.

EISTEIN. That's as may be.

INGA. Whoever you are . . . if it's in my power to reward you . . . I shall do so.

EISTEIN. It seems as though you knew what was going on.

INGA. I have an idea.

EISTEIN. Did you serve them?

INGA. Yes. But I don't think it was wise. They're making so much noise that Halvard will surely hear them.

EISTEIN. No danger in that.

INGA. You're in a good mood, it seems.

EISTEIN. Give me your hand.

INGA. Why? (*Obeys*.)

EISTEIN. A pretty hand.

INGA. It used to be even prettier.

EISTEIN. Your fate is written here.

INGA. Are you a fortune-teller?

EISTEIN. No . . . But everything seems to pass before my eyes.

INGA. Tell me—what do you see?

EISTEIN. I see . . .

INGA. Go ahead! I'm hemmed in on all sides by a towering wall. You can't realize how I yearn for light.

EISTEIN. Both your wishes will be fulfilled.

INGA. Which?

EISTEIN. To become reconciled with your father and with your husband . . . and to reconcile them with one another.

INGA. You knew that anyway—but when will it happen?

EISTEIN. Before the day is done.

INGA. I knew you were only joking.

EISTEIN. I see even more.

INGA. Tell me!

EISTEIN. Before the day is ended, all of you—you, little Alf, and your husband—will be gone from here to a new home.

INGA. If it were only true!

EISTEIN. . . . And you will reach a king's palace.

INGA (*quickly*). Not Sverre's?

EISTEIN (*letting her hand go*). Who knows? . . . I have prophesied.

INGA. No, I have no faith in you. I'm still standing here in the mountain-fog and staring ahead. I can't see a hand's-breadth away, and my heart is so heavy . . . O God, I wish I were dead!

EISTEIN. You're a child, Inga. You cannot mean that.

INGA. Yes. I mean it. Then—Halvard might understand me. Everybody . . . little Alf, my father . . . would be sorry for me . . . and I'd be so happy.

EISTEIN. One ray of light would evaporate all your sorrows like dew. Believe me, sorrow that finds an outlet passes quickly. An open wound is soon healed.

INGA. But I can't see the end.

EISTEIN. Your sorrow is not so great.

INGA. Is your own sorrow worse?

EISTEIN. No, not mine . . . I'm thinking of others!

INGA. Whom do you mean?

EISTEIN (*first to her, then almost to himself*). There are men who govern many people . . . who are the Pillars of the land. They must conceal their worries . . . even if they gnaw at their hearts. Even when within them they smart and bite, they must smile and they must jest. They must inspire courage . . . though they themselves have none.

There are noblemen who possess great store of good counsel for their country. But misunderstanding steps in, and to do good, they must resort to death and destruction. Yes, they are obliged to pour out a patient's heart's-blood in their intent to heal. I know a nobleman who was regarded as the savior of his country, but he was its curse. Terrified at his destiny, he fled from the stricken corpse-like faces that stared at him from all sides ... he would have fled even from his own fatherland, like a pariah ... if so many did not depend upon him and cling to him for help. So, Fate dragged him from one vale of blood to the next ... from one burning city to the next ... over corpses and smoking ruins ... and all hell was loosed about him. The devil walks by his side ... some even say that he is the devil himself. While they are butchering each other as cattle are butchered, he dare not lay his hand on anyone, lest he magnify his own unhappiness. Mass before the battle; mass after the battle ... he seeks to console and to heal ... to do good and to bring peace to all who seek it—but there is one to whom he can bring none—himself. Yet I know one who will endure despite all of hell's torments. He bites his lips and conquers all pain ... he spreads laughter and good cheer. And the more people fall around him, the more madly he laughs. And I know one, too, so masterful that he will endure until God and the people realize that he strove for the best.

INGA. Holy Sunniva!

EISTEIN. Ah, I forgot myself. I spoke foolishly ... and at a wrong time.

INGA. Tell me, you are not speaking of Sverre, are you?

EISTEIN. Sverre? No, he lives so much with himself that, of all those who surround him, very few know what he thinks or feels.

INGA. It seemed as though an avalanche had smothered me. My own worries seem to have been buried. (*Singing is heard.*)

EISTEIN. What's that? (*Singing continues.*)

INGA. Oh! That's the mead. Didn't I tell you? It wasn't wise. Now Halvard will know they're here.

HALVARD (*entering*). What's that noise? Has someone come to the mountain?

EISTEIN. Well, now the fat's in the fire.

INGA. God help us!

ASLAK (*calling into the room*). Give us more mead while we are waiting. (*Tries to enter.*)

HALVARD. Who are you? What do you want? Get out! I must see what the trouble is. (*Pushing the fellow out.*)

INGA. He'll find them ... and he'll think God knows what ... he'll throw me out of the house.

EISTEIN. You were so brave a few minutes ago.

INGA. I will get little Alf to help me ... I will go out to Halvard and speak to him ... He must listen to me ... Stranger, you have a kind heart—I know that—tell him what you know of me ... it's high time.

EISTEIN. Don't worry, little one. (*To* HALVARD *as he enters.*) Did you get rid of him?

HALVARD (*somberly*). Here's his sword.

EISTEIN. And where's he?

HALVARD. Dead.

EISTEIN (*aside*). That was not wise.

HALVARD. The fellow had the temerity to say ... (*Tries to smile*) but that was pure foolishness ...

that you had promised them in my name . . . that they would find here a leader of the "Birchlegs." No one can say such things and go unpunished . . . those were his last words.

INGA (*to herself*). Oh, God!

HALVARD. Trying to make me out a traitor. My worst enemy could not have attempted anything more evil. Yet, as I told you . . . it cost him his life. He'll tell no more lies.

INGA (*softly, almost kneeling*). Halvard!

HALVARD. No! No! Don't excuse yourself . . . I believe you . . . that's why I killed him. See . . . my sword is still bloody. (*Throws it to the ground.*) You could never do that much . . . No, because you love me.

(EISTEIN *goes into the other room where* THORKEL *is sleeping. Tumult outside, becoming louder and louder.*)

INGA (*upon her knees*). Halvard! Halvard! Listen to me!

HALVARD. There's no need, I tell you. None whatsoever.

INGA. By Holy Olaf, by Pious Sunniva, by all . . .

HALVARD (*darkly*). Don't swear!

VOICES. Dead! Is he dead? Killed! (HALVARD *arms himself.*)

INGA. If I could only fight!

VOICES. Let us in. (*They push against the door.*)

HALVARD (*draws the bolt*). No one enters.

VOICES. Open the door! (*Noise grows louder.*)

HALVARD. Look to yourselves, people! And why not? (*Tries to draw the bolt.*) Very well.

INGA (*springs up*). No! No! No!

HALVARD (*stops short*). Why do you stop me? What have I to live for?

INGA. If you wish to die—take me along.

HALVARD. What's that?

INGA. Take me along! I'm a thousand times unhappier than you. (HALVARD *stands there doubting.*) Try me . . . and you'll see.

HALVARD. No! No! I won't listen. (THORKEL *enters.*)

· INGA (*seeing* THORKEL). Father, father! God! You here?

THORKEL. Inga! My child! (*They embrace.*)

HALVARD. What? Inga's father?

EISTEIN. Yes. It's Thorkel. I knew you'd never seen him.

HALVARD. Now I understand . . . No, I don't even begin to understand.

INGA. You came just in time, dearest father.

THORKEL. It's thanks to this fellow that I found you. I knew you were somewhere on the mountain. Wherever I found a path, I followed it, looking for you. Oh, God! The pain you've caused me. I'll never let you leave me again!

INGA. Never, never! I'll never leave you again!

HALVARD. Ha! So, now we have the truth!

INGA (*on her knees*). Can you ever forgive me?

THORKEL. Yes, child. You can't realize how much I've missed you. But you look so unhappy . . . you've cried . . . your hair is disheveled. (*Fondles it.*) What's the matter, child? Oh, I understand. That scoundrel . . . I won't even mention his name.

INGA (*gets up*). Father! Father!

HALVARD (*stepping forward*). Here he is! Halvard is the man.

THORKEL. My savior of yesterday! You're too bad a man to have done such a good deed.

HALVARD. You think so?

THORKEL. But God has allowed me to save my child from your power.

(*Three knocks on the door.*)

A STRONG VOICE (*outside*). We have decided. If you don't open, we shall burn down the house.

HALVARD (*deciding*). Yes, I'll open. (EISTEIN *bars the door.*) Get away! You're in league with those outside. You've conspired with them. But you needn't have called so many . . . for . . . (*Places his hand upon his breast.*) It's already done. (*Tries to go out.*)

INGA (*clasping her father*). Hold him!

EISTEIN (*at the door*). You're not going outside. This is the time for all of you to stay here and to speak out.

ALL. Speak out?

EISTEIN (*horrified, to himself*). Silence is more deadly than words. (*Loudly and vigorously.*) Speak out, I say, you wretched men! Don't you see that God's judgment is upon you? The house is on fire and is burning. But by Saint Olaf I'll let it collapse before I let you out unless you speak and tell the truth.

HALVARD (*darkly*). We've kept silent so long—there is no use in speaking now . . . not in these last few minutes that remain.

EISTEIN. Think of Alf!

INGA.
HALVARD. } Alf! (*Both wish to go to him.*)

HALVARD. (*remains standing; pause*). Very well. One of us must live for the child. Listen, wife! For a long time I've sympathized with Sverre and his "Birchlegs." Many a night I've dreamed of winning fame and honor with him. And in the days I dreamed that too. But I'd never have drawn bow for him without your consent, not even when I could hear his men fighting and shouting near at hand. Never! Never! Do you hear? Yet you believed I would . . .

and you believed maybe even more . . . You thought of leaving me. Secretly you devised means. In silence you regretted the day you came here with me. You loved your father more than you loved me. I knew it, but I didn't have the courage to hear you say it. Now I've lived to see the day when I've both seen and heard it. I'd rather have waked in hell . . . I tell you that this one hour has torn all love from my heart. I curse the hour I first saw you. I'll blot out that memory among our enemies outside, or down yonder with King Sverre. There, they say, Death is a frequent guest. I'm going there now. (*Starts to go, turns to look at* INGA. *She remains immovable.*)

THORKEL. I'm a man of few words, but this I can tell you: his abuse means nothing. Come, my poor child! Bring your son along. Until now it has been his; now it shall be mine. (*Takes her by the hand and starts to leave.*)

EISTEIN. You shall not leave.

THORKEL. We'll see about that. (*Drawing his sword.*)

EISTEIN. Ask her if she wants to go with you.

THORKEL. That's my affair.

EISTEIN. Ask her! (INGA *is immovable as before.*)

THORKEL (*after a pause*). Answer, child! But let me tell you this—you choose now between me and him—and you choose for the last time . . . him or me!

INGA. You or him!

THORKEL. By Saint Olaf! Choose!

INGA. Very well, then. I love you both, that is the truth. I believed that I could make you friends . . . that's the crime I committed . . . but since I must choose . . . though I am driven away . . . though he seeks to die . . . Pious, sweet Sunniva . . . I can do no otherwise . . . I choose as I have chosen before, yesterday—today—and every day . . . I choose Alf . . . and you, strong, stern Halvard. (*Falls to her knees and clasps his feet.*)

HALVARD. Inga! (*He picks her up and embraces her.* THORKEL *drops the sword.*)

EISTEIN (*coming forward*). Now, that door is open. You can leave, you heartless old man, if you really are so . . .

INGA (*stretching out her hand to her father*). Father! Oh, father!
(*Clash of arms outside.*)

EISTEIN. Quiet! Listen!

HALVARD. I hear the clash of arms.

EISTEIN. They are here!

A STRONG VOICE (*outside*). Onward, warriors! Crusaders! Faithful men of Holy King Olaf!

THORKEL. Sverre's battle cry!

EISTEIN. It's Gudlaug Stallar's voice. (*Noise of battle during the entire following scene.*) The strong mead is doing its work. The enemy is drunk. They'll soon be beaten, and we shall be delivered.

INGA. Deliverance? Ah, I understand. You're not King Magnus' man. (*Full of misgivings.*) But who *are* you?

HALVARD. Who are *you?*

THORKEL. Yes. Who are *you?*

EISTEIN. Who am I? Some call me a cursed monk who has usurped many rights—some say I am the devil's companion—others say that I am the devil himself. Some, however, say that I am Sverre Sigurdson, rightful heir to the throne of Norway. Who is right?

ALL. King Sverre! (HALVARD *and* INGA *fall upon their knees.*)

EISTEIN. Up, children! This is no time for homage! (*Pointing to* THORKEL.) According to my old habit, I came here to scout. I met him and

I believed that in return for your hospitality I ought to bring him with me. I hope I've convinced you that the devil is not as black as he is painted. And between the battles we are not so terrible as during the battles.

INGA. My Lord the King!

SVERRE (*to* THORKEL). And you, old man. My people burned your homestead . . . There is a better one waiting for you a few miles north.

THORKEL. My king!

SVERRE. Take it as restitution. You are old and tired of warfare; take your daughter to you . . . (*to* INGA) and if I may . . .

INGA (*pushing* HALVARD *to him*). Take him. He must serve such a man.

(GUDLAUG STALLAR *and a few "Birchlegs" come in. Through the opened door, the glare of a blazing fire can be seen.*)

STALLAR. Greetings, my king!

SVERRE. Done already?

STALLAR. Finished.

SVERRE. Here are three or four men for my army—Halvard Gjäla.

STALLAR. You are heartily welcome.

SVERRE (*to* THORKEL). Your son-in-law will soon have a position worthy of your daughter. It will be best for all concerned . . . if you both surrender.

INGA }
HALVARD } Father!

THORKEL (*embracing them*). My children!

SVERRE. Hurry and get the child! (*Both parents exit*)

STALLAR. If we stay here much longer we'll burn.

SVERRE. You're right. Things are getting a little hot. Come!

CURTAIN

OVER THE LOFTY MOUNTAINS

EVER I wonder at what's to see
    Over the lofty mountains.
    Snow of course on all sides of me,
Pines with their dark green tracery,
Longing to get in motion;
When will they dare the notion?

Boldly the eagle wings his way
Over the lofty mountains,
Glad in the zest of new-born day,
Proving his strength in the perilous play,
Sinks when the mood comes o'er him,
Scans the dim coasts before him.

Apple tree, you've no urge to fare
Over the lofty mountains;
Clothing in leaves your branches bare,
Wait you will in the soft June air.
Birds in your shade are swinging,
Knowing not what they're singing.

He who has yeared for twenty years
Over the lofty mountains,
Knowing the while he's never more near,
He feels diminished year after year—
Harks what the bird is singing,
You are so jauntily swinging.

Birdie, what is it you come to find
Over the lofty mountains?
Better nesting you left behind,
Loftier vantage and scenes more kind.
Do you but bring the desire,
Not the wings, to go higher?

Oh, shall I never, never attain
Over the lofty mountains?
Shall their wall so impound my brain,
Something of snow-ice and awe remain
Barring the way till doom here,
Stifling me like a tomb here?

Out, I must out, must go far, far, far
Over the lofty mountains.
It cramps me, irks me, as here things are.
I am so young; let me seek my star.
Fiercely my soul is thirsting,
Here in these walls I'm bursting.

Some day, I know, I shall yet win past
Over the lofty mountains.
Have You above shut the door there fast?
But, God, though Your home will be good at last,
Keep the door-leaves a while unparted,
And let me stay eager-hearted!

THE FATHER

THE man whose story is here to be told was the wealthiest and most influential person in his parish; his name was Thord Overaas. He appeared in the priest's study one day, tall and earnest.

"I have gotten a son," said he, "and I wish to present him for baptism."

"What shall his name be?"

"Finn—after my father."

"And the sponsors?"

They were mentioned, and proved to be the best men and women of Thord's relations in the parish.

"Is there anything else?" inquired the priest, and looked up.

The peasant hesitated a little.

"I should like very much to have him baptized by himself," said he, finally.

"That is to say on a week-day?"

"Next Saturday, at twelve o'clock noon."

"Is there anything else?" inquired the priest.

"There is nothing else;" and the peasant twirled his cap, as though he were about to go.

Then the priest rose. "There is yet this, however," said he, and walking toward Thord, he took him by the hand and looked gravely into his eyes: "God grant that the child may become a blessing to you!"

One day sixteen years later, Thord stood once more in the priest's study.

"Really, you carry your age astonishingly well, Thord," said the priest; for he saw no change whatever in the man.

"That is because I have no troubles," replied Thord.

To this the priest said nothing, but after a while he asked: "What is your pleasure this evening?"

"I have come this evening about that son of mine who is to be confirmed to-morrow."

"He is a bright boy."

"I did not wish to pay the priest until I heard what number the boy would have when he takes his place in church to-morrow."

"He will stand number one."

"So I have heard; and here are ten dollars for the priest."

"Is there anything else I can do for you?" inquired the priest, fixing his eyes on Thord.

"There is nothing else."

Thord went out.

Eight years more rolled by, and then one day a noise was heard outside of the priest's study, for many men were approaching, and at their head was Thord, who entered first.

The priest looked up and recognized him.

"You come well attended this evening, Thord," said he.

"I am here to request that the banns may be published for my son; he is about to marry Karen Storliden, daughter of Gudmund, who stands here beside me."

"Why, that is the richest girl in the parish."

"So they say," replied the peasant, stroking back his hair with one hand.

The priest sat a while as if in deep thought, then entered the names in his book, without making any comments, and the men wrote their signatures underneath. Thord laid three dollars on the table.

"One is all I am to have," said the priest.

"I know that very well; but he is my only child, I want to do it handsomely."

The priest took the money.

"This is now the third time, Thord, that you have come here on your son's account."

"But now I am through with him," said Thord, and folding up his pocket-book he said farewell and walked away.

The men slowly followed him.

A fortnight later, the father and son were rowing across the lake, one calm, still day, to Storliden to make arrangements for the wedding.

"This thwart is not secure," said the son, and stood up to straighten the seat on which he was sitting.

At the same moment the board he was standing on slipped from under him; he threw out his arms, uttered a shriek, and fell overboard.

"Take hold of the oar!" shouted the father, springing to his feet and holding out the oar.

But when the son had made a couple of efforts he grew stiff.

"Wait a moment!" cried the father, and began to row toward his son. Then the son rolled over on his back, gave his father one long look, and sank.

Thord could scarcely believe it; he held the boat still, and stared at the spot where his son had gone down, as though he must surely come to the surface again. There rose some bubbles, then some more, and finally one large one that burst; and the lake lay there as smooth and bright as a mirror again.

For three days and three nights people saw the father rowing round and round the spot, without taking either food or sleep; he was dragging the lake for the body of his son. And toward morning of the third day he found it, and carried it in his arms up over the hills to his gard.

It might have been about a year from that day, when the priest, late one autumn evening, heard someone in the passage outside of the door, carefully trying to find the latch. The priest opened the door, and in walked a tall, thin man, with bowed form and white hair. The priest looked long at him before he recognized him. It was Thord.

"Are you out walking so late?" said the priest, and stood still in front of him.

"Ah, yes! it is late," said Thord, and took a seat.

The priest sat down also, as though waiting. A long, long silence followed. At last Thord said:

"I have something with me that I should like to give to the poor; I want it to be invested as a legacy in my son's name."

He rose, laid some money on the table, and sat down again. The priest counted it.

"It is a great deal of money," said he.

"It is half the price of my gard. I sold it to-day."

The priest sat long in silence. At last he asked, but gently:

"What do you propose to do now, Thord?"

"Something better."

They sat there for a while, Thord with downcast eyes, the priest with his eyes fixed on Thord. Presently the priest said, slowly and softly:

"I think your son has at last brought you a true blessing."

"Yes, I think so myself," said Thord, looking up, while two big tears coursed slowly down his cheeks.

Théodor Mommsen

CAESAR

THE new monarch of Rome, the first ruler over the whole domain of Romano-Hellenic civilization, Gaius Julius Caesar, was in his fifty-sixth year (born 12 July 102 B.C.?) when the battle at Thapsus, the last link in a long chain of momentous victories, placed the decision as to the future of the world in his hands. Few men have had their elasticity so thoroughly put to the proof as Caesar—the sole creative genius produced by Rome, and the last produced by the ancient world, which accordingly moved on in the path that he marked out for it until its sun went down. Sprung from one of the oldest noble families of Latium—which traced back its lineage to the heroes of the Iliad and the kings of Rome, and in fact to the Venus-Aphrodite common to both nations—he spent the years of his boyhood and early manhood as the genteel youth of that epoch were wont to spend them. He had tasted the sweetness as well as the bitterness of the cup of fashionable life, had recited and declaimed, had practised literature and made verses in his idle hours, had prosecuted love-intrigues of every sort, and got himself initiated into all the mysteries of shaving, curls, and ruffles pertaining to the toilette-wisdom of the day, as well as into the still more mysterious art of always borrowing and never paying. But the flexible steel of that nature was proof against even these dissipated and flighty courses; Caesar retained both his bodily vigour and his elasticity of mind and of heart unimpaired. In fencing and in riding he was a match for any of his soldiers, and his swimming saved his life at Alexandria; the incredible rapidity of his journeys, which usually for the sake of gaining time were performed by night—a thorough contrast to the procession-like slowness with which Pompeius moved from one place to another—was the astonishment of his contemporaries and not the least among the causes of his success. The mind was like the body. His remarkable power of intuition revealed itself in the precision and practicability of all his arrangements, even where he gave orders without having seen with his own eyes. His memory was matchless, and it was easy for him to carry on several occupations simultaneously with equal self-possession. Although a gentleman, a man of genius, and a monarch, he had still a heart. So long as he lived, he cherished the purest veneration for his worthy mother Aurelia (his father having died early); to his wives and above all to his daughter Julia he devoted an honourable affection, which was not without reflex influence even on political affairs. With the ablest and most excellent men of his time, of high and of humbler rank, he maintained noble relations of mutual fidelity, with each after his kind. As he himself never abandoned any of his partisans after the pusillanimous and unfeeling manner of Pompeius, but adhered to his friends—and that not merely from calculation—through good and bad times without wavering, several of these, such as Aulus Hirtius and Gaius Matius, gave, even after his death, noble testimonies of their attachment to him.

If in a nature so harmoniously organized any one aspect of it may be singled out as characteristic, it is this—that he stood aloof from all ideology and everything fanciful. As a matter of course, Caesar was a man of passion, for without passion there is no genius; but his passion was never stronger than he could control. He had had his season of youth, and song, love, and wine had taken lively possession of his spirit; but with him they did not penetrate to the inmost core of his nature. Literature occupied him long and earnestly; but, while Alexander could not sleep for thinking of the Homeric Achilles, Caesar in his sleepless hours mused on the inflections of the Latin nouns and verbs. He made verses, as everybody then did, but they were weak; on the other hand he was interested in subjects of astronomy and natural science. While wine was and continued to be with Alexander the destroyer of care, the temperate Roman, after the revels of his youth were over, avoided it entirely. Around him, as around all those whom the full lustre of woman's love has dazzled in youth, fainter gleams of it continued imperishably to linger; even in later years he had love-adventures and successes with women, and he retained a certain foppishness in his outward appearance, or, to speak more correctly, the pleasing consciousness of his own manly beauty. He carefully covered the baldness, which he keenly felt, with the laurel chaplet that he wore in public in his later years, and he would doubtless have surrendered some of his victories, if he could thereby have brought back his youthful locks. But, however much even when monarch he enjoyed the society of women, he only amused himself with them, and allowed them no manner of influence over him; even his much-censured relation to queen Cleopatra was only contrived to mask a weak point in his political position.

Caesar was thoroughly a realist and a man of sense; and whatever he undertook and achieved was pervaded and guided by the cool sobriety which constitutes the most marked peculiarity of his genius. To this he owed the power of living energetically in the present, undisturbed either by recollection or by expectation; to this he owed the capacity of acting at any moment with collected vigour, and of applying his whole genius even to the smallest and most incidental enterprise; to this he owed the many-sided power with which he grasped and mastered whatever understanding can comprehend and will can compel; to this he owed the self-possessed ease with which he arranged his periods as well as projected his campaigns; to this he owed the "marvellous serenity" which remained steadily with him through good and evil days; to this he owed the complete independence, which admitted of no control by favourite or by mistress, or even by friend. It resulted, moreover, from this clearness of judgment that Caesar never formed to himself illusions regarding the power of fate and the ability of man; in his case the friendly veil was lifted up, which conceals from man the inadequacy of his working. Prudently as he laid his plans and considered all possibilities, the feeling was never absent from his breast that in all things fortune, that is to say accident, must bestow success; and with this may be connected the circumstance that he so often played a desperate game with destiny, and in particular again and again hazarded his person with daring indifference. As indeed occasionally men of predominant sagacity betake themselves to a pure game of hazard, so there was in Caesar's rationalism a point at which it came in some measure into contact with mysticism.

Gifts such as these could not fail to produce a statesman. From early youth, accordingly, Caesar was a statesman in the deepest sense of the term, and his aim was the highest which man is allowed to propose to himself—the political, military, intellectual, and moral regeneration of his own deeply decayed nation, and of the still more deeply decayed Hellenic nation intimately akin to his own. The hard school of thirty years' experience changed his views as to the means by which this aim was to be reached; his aim itself remained the same in the times of his hopeless humiliation and of his unlimited plenitude of power, in the times when as demagogue and conspirator he stole towards it by paths of darkness, and in those when, as joint possessor of the supreme power and then as monarch, he worked at his task in the full light of day before the eyes of the world. All the measures of a permanent kind that proceeded from him at the most various times assume their appropriate places in the great building-plan. We cannot therefore properly speak of isolated achievements of Caesar; he did nothing isolated. With justice men commend Caesar the orator for his masculine eloquence, which, scorning all the arts of the advocate, like a clear flame at once enlightened and warmed. With justice men admire in Caesar the author the inimitable simplicity of the composition, the unique purity and beauty of the language. With justice the greatest masters of war of all times have praised Caesar the general, who, in a singular degree disregarding routine and tradition, knew always how to find out the mode of warfare by which in the given case the enemy was conquered, and which was thus in the given case the right one; who with the certainty of divination found the proper means for every end; who after defeat stood ready for battle like William of Orange, and ended the campaign invariably with victory; who managed that element of warfare, the treatment of which serves to distinguish military genius from the mere ordinary ability of an officer—the rapid movement of masses —with unsurpassed perfection, and found the guarantee of victory not in the massiveness of his forces but in the celerity of their movements, not in long preparation but in rapid and daring action even with inadequate means. But all these were with Caesar mere secondary matters; he was no doubt a great orator, author, and general, but he became each of these merely because he was a consummate statesman. The soldier more especially played in him altogether an accessory part, and it is one of the principal peculiarities by which he is distinguished from Alexander, Hannibal, and Napoleon, that he began his political activity not as an officer, but as a demagogue. According to his original plan he had purposed to reach his object, like Pericles and Gaius Gracchus, without force of arms, and throughout eighteen years he had as leader of the popular party moved exclusively amid political plans and intrigues—until, reluctantly convinced of the necessity for a military support, he, when already forty years of age, put himself at the head of an army. It was natural that he should even afterwards remain still more statesman than general—just like Cromwell, who also transformed himself from a leader of opposition into a military chief and democratic king, and who in general, little as the prince of Puritans seems to resemble the dissolute Roman, is yet in his development as well as in the objects which he aimed at and the results which he achieved of all statesmen perhaps the most akin to Caesar. Even in his mode of warfare this improvised general-ship may still be recognized; the enterprises of Napoleon against Egypt and against England do not more clearly exhibit the artillery-lieutenant who had risen by service to command than the similar enterprises of Caesar exhibit the demagogue metamorphosed into a general. A regularly trained officer would hardly have been prepared, through political considerations of a not altogether stringent nature, to set aside the best-founded military scruples in the way in which Caesar did on several occasions, most strikingly in the case of his landing in Epirus. Several of his acts are therefore censurable from a military point of view; but what the general loses, the statesman gains. The task of the statesman is universal in its nature like Caesar's genius; if he undertook things the most varied and most remote one from another, they had all without exception a bearing on the one great object to which with infinite fidelity and consistency he devoted himself; and of the manifold aspects and directions of his great activity he never preferred one to another. Although a master of the art of war, he yet from statesmanly considerations did his utmost to avert civil strife and, when it nevertheless began, to earn laurels stained as little as possible by blood. Although the founder of a military monarchy, he yet, with an energy unexampled in history, allowed no hierarchy of marshals or government of praetorians to come into existence. If he had a preference for any one form of services rendered to the state, it was for the sciences and arts of peace rather than for those of war.

The most remarkable peculiarity of his action as a statesman was its perfect harmony. In reality all the conditions for this most difficult of all human functions were united in Caesar. A thorough realist, he never allowed the images of the past or venerable tradition to disturb him; for him nothing was of value in politics but the living present and the law of reason, just as in his character of grammarian he set aside historical and antiquarian research and recognized nothing but on the one hand the living *usus loquendi* and on the other hand the rule of symmetry. A born ruler, he governed the minds of men as the wind drives the clouds, and compelled the most heterogeneous natures to place themselves at his service—the plain citizen and the rough subaltern, the genteel matrons of Rome and the fair princesses of Egypt and Mauretania, the brilliant cavalry-officer and the calculating banker. His talent for organization was marvellous; no statesman has ever compelled alliances, no general has ever collected an army out of unyielding and refractory elements with such decision, and kept them together with such firmness, as Caesar displayed in constraining and upholding his coalitions and his legions; never did regent judge his instruments and assign each to the place appropriate for him with so acute an eye.

He was monarch; but he never played the king. Even when absolute lord of Rome, he retained the deportment of the party-leader; perfectly pliant and smooth, easy and charming in conversation, complaisant towards every one, it seemed as if he wished to be nothing but the first among his peers. Caesar entirely avoided the blunder into which so many men otherwise on an equality with him have fallen, of carrying into politics the military tone of command; however much occasion his disagreeable relations with the senate gave for it, he never resorted to outrages such as was that of the eighteenth Brumaire. Caesar was monarch; but he was never seized with the giddiness of the tyrant. He is perhaps the only one among the mighty ones of the earth, who in great matters and little never acted according to inclination or caprice, but always without exception according to his duty as ruler, and who, when he looked back on his life, found doubtless erroneous calculations to deplore, but no false step of passion to regret. There is nothing in the history of Caesar's life, which even on a small scale can be compared with those poetico-sensual ebullitions—such as the murder of Kleitos or the burning of Persepolis—which the history of his great predecessor in the east records. He is, in fine, perhaps the only one of those mighty ones, who has preserved to the end of his career the statesman's tact of discriminating between the possible and the impossible, and has not broken down in the task which for greatly gifted natures is the most difficult of all—the task of recognizing, when on the pinnacle of success, its natural limits. What was possible he performed, and never left the possible good undone for the sake of the impossible better, never disdained at least to mitigate by palliatives evils that were incurable. But where he recognized that fate had spoken, he always obeyed. Alexander on the Hypanis, Napoleon at Moscow, turned back because they were compelled to do so, and were indignant at destiny for bestowing even on its favourites merely limited successes; Caesar turned back voluntarily on the Thames and on the Rhine; and thought of carrying into effect even at the Danube and the Euphrates not unbounded plans of world-conquest, but merely well-considered frontier-regulations.

Such was this unique man, whom it seems so easy and yet is so infinitely difficult to describe. His whole nature is transparent clearness; and tradition preserves more copious and more vivid information about him than about any of his peers in the ancient world, Of such a personage our conceptions may well vary in point of shallowness or depth, but they cannot be, strictly speaking, different; to every not utterly perverted inquirer the grand figure has exhibited the same essential features, and yet no one has succeeded in reproducing it to the life. The secret lies in its perfection. In his character as a man as well as in his place in history, Caesar occupies a position where the great contrasts of existence meet and balance each other. Of mighty creative power and yet at the same time of the most penetrating judgment; no longer a youth and not yet an old man; of the highest energy of will and the highest capacity of execution; filled with republican ideals and at the same time born to be a king; a Roman in the deepest essence of his nature, and yet called to reconcile and combine in himself as well as in the outer world the Roman and the Hellenic types of culture—Caesar was the entire and perfect man. Accordingly we miss in him more than in any other historical personage what are called characteristic features, which are in reality nothing else than deviations from the natural course of human development. What in Caesar passes for such at the first superficial glance is, when more closely observed, seen to be the peculiarity not of the individual, but of the epoch of culture or of the nation; his youthful adventures, for instance, were common to him with all his more gifted contemporaries of like position, his unpoetical but strongly logical temperament was the temperament of Romans in general. It formed part also of Caesar's full humanity that he was in the highest degree influenced by the conditions of time and place; for there is no abstract humanity—the living man cannot but occupy a place in a given nationality and in a definite line of culture. Caesar was a perfect man just because he more than any other placed himself amidst the currents of his time, and because he more than any other possessed the essential peculiarity of the Roman nation—practical aptitude as a citizen—in perfection: for his Hellenism in fact was only the Hellenism which had been long intimately blended with the Italian nationality. But in this very circumstance lies the difficulty, we may perhaps say the impossibility, of depicting Caesar to the life. As the artist can paint everything save only consummate beauty, so the historian, when once in a thousand years he encounters the perfect, can only be silent regarding it. For normality admits doubtless of being expressed, but it gives us only the negative notion of the absence of defect; the secret of nature, whereby in her most finished manifestations normality and individuality are combined, is beyond expression. Nothing is left for us but to deem those fortunate who beheld this perfection, and to gain some faint conception of it from the reflected lustre which rests imperishably on the works that were the creation of this great nature. These also, it is true, bear the stamp of the time. The Roman hero himself stood by the side of his youthful Greek predecessor not merely as an equal, but as a superior; but the world had meanwhile become old and its youthful lustre had faded. The action of Caesar was no longer, like that of Alexander, a joyous marching onward towards a goal indefinitely remote; he built on, and out of, ruins, and was content to establish himself as tolerably and as securely as possible within the ample but yet definite bounds once assigned to him. With reason therefore the delicate poetic tact of the nations has not troubled itself about the unpoetical Roman, and on the other hand has invested the son of Philip with all the golden lustre of poetry, with all the rainbow hues of legend. But with equal reason the political life of the nations has during thousands of years again and again reverted to the lines which Caesar drew; and the fact, that the peoples to whom the world belongs still at the present day designate the highest of their monarchs by his name, conveys a warning deeply significant and, unhappily, fraught with shame.

René Sully-Prudhomme

THE STRUGGLE

NIGHTLY tormented by returning doubt,
   I dare the sphinx with faith and unbelief;
   And through lone hours when no sleep brings relief
The monster rises all my hopes to flout.

In a still agony, the light blown out,
I wrestle with the unknown; nor long nor brief
The night appears, my narrow couch of grief
Grown like the grave with Death walled round about.

Sometimes my mother, coming with her lamp,
Seeing my brow as with a death-sweat damp,
Asks, "Ah, what ails thee, Child? Hast thou no rest?"

And then I answer, touched by her look of yearning,
Holding my beating heart and forehead burning,
"Mother, I strove with God, and was hard prest."

THE APPOINTMENT

Tis late; the astronomer in his lonely height,
Exploring all the dark, descries afar
Orbs that like distant isles of splendor are,
And mornings whitening in the infinite.

Like winnowed grain the worlds go by in flight,
Or swarm in glistening spaces nebular;
He summons one disheveled wandering star,
Return ten centuries hence on such a night.

The star will come. It dare not by one hour
Cheat Science, or falsify her calculation;
Men will have passed, but watchful in the tower

Man shall remain in sleepless contemplation;
And should all men have perished there in turn,
Truth in their place would watch that star's return

IF YOU BUT KNEW

IF you but knew the tears that fall
For life unloved and fireside drear,
Perhaps, before my lonely hall,
You would pass near.

If you but knew your power to thrill
My drooping soul with one pure glance,
One look across my window-sill,
You'd cast perchance.

If you but knew what soothing balm
One heart can on another pour,
Would you not sit—a sister calm—
Beside my door?

And if you knew I loved you well,
   And loved you too with all my heart,
You'd come to me, with me to dwell,
   And ne'er depart.

THE DEATH AGONY

YE WHO are watching when my end draws near,
   Speak not, I pray!
'Twill help me most some music faint to hear,
   And pass away.

For song can loosen link by link each care
   From life's hard chain,
So gently rock my griefs; but oh, beware!
   To speak were pain.

I'm weary of all words: their wisest speech
   Can naught reveal;
Give me spirit-sounds minds cannot reach,
   But hearts can feel.

Some melody which all my soul shall steep,
   As tranced I lie,
Passing from visions wild to dreamy sleep,—
   From sleep to die.

Ye who are watching when my end draws near,
   Speak not, I pray!
Some sounds of music murmuring in my ear
   Will smooth my way.

My muse, peer shepherdess! I'd bid you seek;
   Tell her my whim:
I want her near me, when I'm faint and weak
   On the grave's brim.

I want to hear her sing, ere I depart,
   Just once again,
In simple monotone to touch the heart
   That Old World strain.

You'll find her still,—the rustic hand gives
 Calm hopes and fears;
But in this world of mine one rarely lives
 Thrice twenty years.

Be sure you leave us with our hearts alone,
 Only us two!
She'll sing to me in her old trembling tone,
 Stroking my brow.

She only to the end will love through all
 My good and ill.
So will the air of those old songs recall
 My first years still.

And dreaming thus, I shall not feel at last
 My heart-strings torn,
But all unknowing, the great barriers past,
 Die—as we're born.

Ye who are watching when my end draws near,
 Speak not, I pray!
'Twill help me most some music faint to hear,
 And pass away.

THE SHADOW

WE WALK: our shadow follows in the rear,
 Mimics our motions, treads where'er we tread,
 Looks without seeing, listens without an ear,
Crawls while we walk with proud uplifted head.

Like to his shadow, man himself down here,
A little living darkness, a frail shred
Of form, sees, speaks, but with no knowledge clear,
Saying to Fate, "By thee my feet are led."

Man shadows but a lower angel who,
Fallen from high, is but a shadow too;
So man himself an image is of God.

And, may be, in some place by us untrod,
Near deepest depths of nothingness or ill,
Some wraith of human wraiths grows, darker still.

Biographical and Bibliographical Notes

Biographical and Bibliographical Notes

BENAVENTE, JACINTO (1866–   ), Spanish dramatist, wrote more than a hundred comedies and tragedies. His first books were dramatic sketches, a volume of poetry, and an essay which showed a keen understanding of women. Then Benavente turned to plays which broke sharply with the tradition of the previous Spanish winner of the Nobel award, Echegaray, in their realistic handling of characters and situations. A penetrating but gentle satire characterizes his work, which follows the dramatic tradition of Shakespeare and Molière, both of whom he translated into Spanish. His best-known plays are *The Governor's Wife, Saturday Night, Princess Bebé, Autumnal Roses, Brute Force,* and especially *The Evil Doers of Good, The Bonds of Interest,* and *The Passion Flower* (*La Malquerida*). Benavente won the Nobel prize in 1922.

BERGSON, HENRI (1859–1941), French philosopher, was the son of a Jewish merchant from Poland and an Englishwoman. Although born and brought up in Paris, he did not become a French citizen until he was grown up. Starting as an ardent disciple of John Stuart Mill and Herbert Spencer, he soon came to question their mechanistic concepts through his study of the quality and meaning of time. All of his work is concerned with revolutionary concepts of duration and motion, although he did not construct a complete philosophic system. He believed that each problem must be attacked individually from its own point of view rather than in reference to a preconceived, all-embracing framework of thought. The emphasis on intuition and mystical values accounted for much of his popularity, which developed for some years into a fashionable cult.

Bergson's most important books are *Time and Free Will, Matter and Memory, Creative Evolution, The Two Sources of Morality and Religion, Mind-Energy,* and *Laughter,* from which the selection of this volume is chosen. It displays Bergson's humor, his facility as a writer, and his appeal to the general reader, far greater than that of most philosophers. Bergson was elected to the French Academy in 1914 and won the Nobel prize in 1927.

BJÖRNSON, BJÖRNSTJERNE (1832–1910), Norwegian novelist, dramatist, poet, journalist, and orator, was long the "great man" of his country and the real creator of modern Norwegian literature. Coming from farmer and middle-class families, born in the mountains and brought up on the fjords, he always tried to fuse the diverse qualities and interests of the Norwegian people into one strong national character through a greater appreciation of their history and legends. He wrote his first newspaper article at the age of sixteen and for most of his life was an active journalist. Moving from literary and dramatic criticism to political and social articles, he was always a powerful voice on the side of liberal, progressive, democratic ideas. His connection with the theater began when he managed theaters in Bergen and Christiania, where he broke the hold of Danish literary tradition on Norway. His best-known plays are *The Bankrupt, Pastor Sang* (whose two parts are titled *Beyond Our Power* and *Beyond Human Might*), *Mary Queen of Scots,* and *Love and Geography,* the last a gay comedy. Björnson's first published work, however, was a little novel, *Sunny Hill,* followed by others such as *The Fisher Maiden, Arne, A Happy Boy,* and

Mary, most of them "peasant" novels. His many poems were so popular that he early became the great national poet of his country, loved for his personal lyrics as well as for his stirring patriotic songs, one of which became the Norwegian national anthem. Björnson was the third winner of the Nobel prize, in 1903.

BUCK, PEARL (1892–), American novelist, short-story writer, and biographer, spent many years of her life in China, where her father and mother were missionaries. Few non-Orientals have known and understood the Chinese as has Mrs. Buck, whose writings have brought that understanding to the rest of the world. *The Good Earth,* which won the Pulitzer prize in 1931, was the first novel of a trilogy about Chinese peasants, called *The House of Earth,* the second and third of which were *Sons* and *A House Divided.* Other novels are *East Wind: West Wind, The Mother, This Proud Heart,* and *The Patriot. The First Wife* and *Today and Forever* are volumes of short stories. Mrs. Buck also wrote biographies of her father and mother, *Fighting Angel* and *The Exile,* and translated into English the Chinese classic, *All Men Are Brothers.* She won the Nobel prize in 1938.

BUNIN, IVAN (1870–), Russian novelist, short-story writer, and poet, has lived in France since the Russian revolution of 1917. His first published works were poems and translations from the English, which won favorable critical attention but little popularity. His first novel, *The Village,* brought wide fame, and was followed by more poems and short stories, including *The Gentleman from San Francisco* (one of the stories included in this volume and specifically cited in his Nobel award in 1933). Other volumes of stories which have appeared in English are *The Elaghin Affair, The Dreams of Chang, Grammar of Love, The Cup of Life;* novels are *Mitya's Love* and *The Well of Days.*

CARDUCCI, GIOSUÉ (1835–1907), Italian poet, scholar, and orator, spent most of his life as professor at the University of Bologna. One of the foremost students of

Italian literature, he produced many volumes of literary history and criticism and definitive editions of early Italian authors, especially those of the Renaissance. An ardent nationalist, he was one of the most popular orators of his day, his speech on the death of Garibaldi being considered a masterpiece. But Carducci was primarily a poet, a master of satire, a skilled craftsman, keenly perceptive of beauty, full of love for the simple and natural things. Nine volumes of poems appeared during his lifetime, only some of which have been translated into English. Carducci won the Nobel prize in 1906.

DELEDDA, GRAZIA (1875–1936), Italian novelist and short-story writer, wrote almost entirely about her native Sardinia. Her first stories, written when she was only seventeen, showed that she was a natural storyteller, and she worked conscientiously to improve her writing, although never losing her simplicity of style. Action and violence fill many of the tales, although her most famous novel, *The Mother,* is a penetrating psychological study. Other novels are *After the Divorce* and *Ashes.* The Nobel prize came to her in 1926.

ECHEGARAY, JOSÉ (1832–1916), Spanish dramatist, did not take up writing until he was more than forty years old, when he had already achieved success and prominence in two other careers. A professor at the Madrid School of Civil Engineering, he entered politics after the revolution of 1868, was elected to the Spanish Cortes, made director of public works and Minister of the Interior. In 1874, however, two of his plays were produced with great success, and he thereafter devoted himself to writing. A somewhat tardy representative of the romantic school, his plots were strong and simple, his characters types rather than individuals. His best-known plays are *Folly or Saintliness* (also known as *Madman or Saint*), *The Great Galeoto, Mariana,* and *The Son of Don Juan.* In 1904 Echegaray shared the Nobel award with Frédéric Mistral.

EUCKEN, RUDOLF (1846–1926), German philosopher, studied ancient history and classical philology, but soon found that his chief interests lay in the field of philosophy, especially religious philosophy. A challenger of materialist concepts, he succeeded in reaching a wide popular public through his vigorous and idealistic approach to many of the problems that confront the ordinary man. Among his many writings are *The Fundamental Concepts of Modern Philosophic Thought*, *Can We Still Be Christians?*, *Christianity and the New Idealism*, *Knowledge and Life*, *The Truth of Religion*, *The Individual and Society*. Eucken was awarded the Nobel prize in 1908.

FRANCE, ANATOLE (1844–1924), French novelist, historian, short-story writer, and critic, was the son of a Parisian bookseller. His first published works were critical essays and poems and a few stories which failed to reveal the special quality of his style which was to make him widely read throughout the world. With *The Crime of Sylvestre Bonnard*, however, from which one of the selections in this volume is taken, he won his first popularity. This was followed by sentimental and charming memories of his childhood and by *Thaïs*, *At the Sign of the Reine Pedauque*, *The Red Lily*, and many other volumes of fiction and criticism which displayed his classical style, his sophistication, his love of beauty, and a gentle irony. But this calm and learned and witty side of France was only part of him, for he also battled alongside Zola in the Dreyfus case and fought intolerance and superstition and injustice with all his powers. This interest was revealed more strongly in later satirical novels such as *The Revolt of the Angels* and *Penguin Island*. His most important historical work was the monumental *Life of Jeanne d'Arc*. France received the Nobel prize in 1921.

GALSWORTHY, JOHN (1867–1933), English novelist and dramatist, was born into a very well-to-do family, attended Harrow and Oxford, was admitted to the bar but never practiced law. Instead, he went traveling about the world; on a sea voyage he became acquainted with one of the ship's officers, a Pole who showed Galsworthy the manuscript of a novel he was writing in English. The Englishman encouraged the

sailor, who later took the name of Joseph Conrad when the manuscript, *Almayer's Folly*, was published. This meeting began a lifelong friendship between two men destined to stand near the top in English literature. Galsworthy himself wrote for five years just to train himself, published his first four books under a pseudonym because they did not satisfy him. In 1906 the first novel of his greatest work, *The Forsyte Saga*, was published, *The Man of Property*, which displayed well the cutting satire with which Galsworthy pictures those of his own social class. His first play was *The Silver Box*. Others, motivated by Galsworthy's strong sense of social justice, included *Strife*, *Justice*, *The Skin Game*, and *Loyalties*. He continued to write novels of increasing popularity, but it was 1918 before he returned to the Forsyte family with the short piece, *Indian Summer of a Forsyte*, which was followed by *In Chancery* and *To Let*, which completed the saga itself. He continued to write about the younger generation of Forsytes in *The White Monkey*, *The Silver Spoon*, and *Swan Song*, which together are called *A Modern Comedy*. Galsworthy also wrote several volumes of essays, short stories, sketches, letters, and poems. He was offered a knighthood but refused it. The Nobel award came to him in 1932, with particular mention of *The Forsyte Saga*.

GIDE, ANDRÉ (1869–   ), French novelist, dramatist, and essayist, has been a center of controversy many times during his life, and is perhaps as important for his influence on other great writers as for his own work. Never troubled by inconsistencies and contradictions in his life or writings, he was actually proud of his uncertainties. The problems of personal freedom in complex men and women have been the subject of most of his novels—*The Counterfeiters*, *The Immoralist*, *Strait Is the Gate*, *The School for Wives*, and *Lafcadio's Adventures*. Always interested in social problems, he was mayor of a Normandy commune, a juror in Rouen (about which he wrote *Recollections of the Assize Court*), special envoy of the French Colonial Ministry (from which came his *Travels in the Congo*), and an ardent admirer of Communism, tempered by a disillusioning trip to Soviet Russia, as told in his *Back from the USSR.* Essays on Dostoievsky, Montaigne, Oscar Wilde, and Goethe show the breadth of his interests, as well as translations of Shakespeare, William Blake, and Rabindranath Tagore. His voluminous Journals have begun to appear in English. Representative pages from the first volume are included here. Gide won the Nobel prize in 1947.

GJELLERUP, KARL (1857–1919), Danish novelist, dramatist, and poet, was the son of a clergyman who planned to enter the church himself. But his reading of Darwin, Spencer, and Brandes helped turn him from religion to atheism. After marrying a German woman and living in Germany, he became a strong supporter of Germanic culture. His novel, *Minna,* is a tribute to his wife and is laid in Dresden, where he lived for many years, writing most of his books simultaneously in Danish and German. Like many European writers, he became interested in Buddhism and its doctrine of renunciation, as shown in his novel, *The Pilgrim Kamanita,* from which Gjellerup's selection in this volume is taken. He received the Nobel award in 1917, sharing it with a fellow Dane, Henrik Pontoppidan.

HAMSUN, KNUT (1859–   ), Norwegian novelist, poet, and dramatist, came from a peasant family. For years he tried a variety of jobs, being a clerk, a salesman, a cobbler, a teacher, and a writer for small-town papers. He made two trips to America, working at odd jobs and eventually achieving some success as a literary lecturer to Scandinavian groups in the Middle West. But he did not like America, and wrote a book to tell why—*The Cultural Life of Modern America.* In 1890 appeared his first novel, *Hunger,* a powerful psychological study which attracted wide attention. It ran counter to most current novels, which were concerned with social problems as opposed to those of the individual human being. Hamsun's interest in the individual, particularly the vagabond type, was carried forward in other novels, such as *Mysteries, Pan,* and *Wanderers,* and

in a few plays, which were unsuccessful on the stage. A volume of poems revealed one of the best lyric talents in Norwegian literature. Hamsun painted a broader social picture in three novels which marked the peak of his career—*Children of the Time, Segelfoss Town,* and *Growth of the Soil.* The last of these has been called the greatest of all "peasant novels," heroic in concept, simple and unaffected in manner, movingly beautiful in style. It was specially cited in the award of the Nobel prize to Hamsun in 1920; a selection from it is one of the Hamsun contributions to this volume.

HAUPTMANN, GERHART (1862–1946), German dramatist and novelist, was a poor student, a short-term farmer, an unsuccessful sculptor, before becoming an author. He experimented for many years before achieving any recognition which came with his play, *Before the Dawn,* the first of the naturalist dramas concerned with the impact of natural forces on human lives. In *The Weavers,* Hauptmann created a new dramatic form, featuring groups rather than individual leading characters. The same general technique was followed in *The Beaver Coat* and *Florian Geyer,* but Hauptmann then departed somewhat from naturalism in the dream-play *Hannele,* and even further in the fantasy which has been the most popular of his works, *The Sunken Bell.* Many other plays came from Hauptmann in the ensuing years, some in inspired verse, some naturalistic, some romantic— *Henry of Auë, Charlemagne's Hostage, Drayman Henschel, Rose Bernd, And Pippa Dances, The White Saviour, Till Eulenspiegel,* and others. Two great novels, *The Fool in Christ Emanuel Quint* and *The Heretic of Soana,* a travel diary, and many miscellaneous volumes bring his total works to more than sixty. Although much of this was of the first quality, it was for his contributions to the drama chiefly that he was awarded the Nobel prize in 1912.

HEIDENSTAM, VERNER VON (1859–1940), Swedish poet and novelist, spent ten years traveling after illness interrupted his schooling at sixteen. Soon after returning home he published his first book of poems, filled with color and vigor and a spirit of joy that won them wide popularity. In many critical essays he attacked the grim realism, the concern with serious social problems, that gripped all Scandinavian literature for many years; he called for a more purely Swedish literature with greater vitality and verve, more imagination and color. Later volumes of verse brought him the title of "Sweden's Laureate." At the same time he wrote historical fiction of great distinction, notably *The Tree of the Folkungs, Saint Birgitta's Pilgrimage,* and *The Charles Men* (from which one selection in this volume is taken), which glorified the heroic past of Sweden. Heidenstam was awarded the Nobel prize in 1916.

HESSE, HERMANN (1877–   ), German-born novelist and poet, has been a citizen of Switzerland since the World War I, when his opposition to the conflict won him enmity and accusations of treason. Before this he had become a popular author through his first novel, *Peter Camenzind. Demian,* one of the first and best novels based on psychoanalysis, so struck the right note at the right time that it was hailed by an entire generation emerging from the war in Germany as the perfect expression of their troubled souls. Hesse shared with many other European authors a great interest in mystical religions; he made a long trip to India to satisfy this interest and wrote a novel, *Siddhartha,* as a result. *Steppenwolf,* a strange experimental novel, condemns modern civilization as only a thin veneer over bestial human instincts. Several other Hesse novels of first importance have not yet been translated into English, nor have most of his poems. The selection for this anthology comes from *Demian,* the novel which has had the greatest influence of all his works. It soon will be reissued in America. The Nobel prize was awarded to Hesse in 1946.

HEYSE, PAUL (1830–1914), German novelist, short-story writer, and dramatist, came from a literary family, studied the classics, and specialized in Romance languages. Intending to enter academic life as a scholar and teacher, he nevertheless wrote a few stories and verses, among them the tale included here, *L'Arrabiata.* These won an offer of a position, with a lifelong honorarium, at the "literary" court of Maximilian II of Bavaria. He settled down in Munich to a life of great literary productivity, during which he wrote six long novels, several volumes of poetry, sixty plays (none successful on the stage), and more than a hundred novelettes, many laid in Italy, a country he always loved. The award of the Nobel prize in 1910 rescued Heyse from the oblivion into which he had fallen with the advent of the naturalistic and impressionistic schools of writing.

JENSEN, JOHANNES V. (1873–   ), Danish novelist, poet, and essayist, was born in Himmerland, the far-northern region of his country. His father was a veterinarian, and Jensen himself studied medicine, although he never became a doctor. His studies, however, gave him an interest in science which never left him and which has played an important part in much of his writing. His first great work, however, was *Himmerland Stories,* tales springing from his own countryside, like *Ann and the Cow* in this anthology. So simple and vigorous and alive were they that Jensen was hailed at once as an author of great originality. After some years of travel there came other volumes of tales and a historical novel, *The Fall of the King.* A trip to America, which amazed and delighted Jensen, brought forth more stories and poems. *Little Ahasuerus* is an example of these tales, and *At Memphis Station* a spirited and amusing example of the poems. Jensen's most ambitious work has been *The Long Journey,* which is the collective title given to six novels which delve into man's prehistoric past. Jensen has also written scientific essays and many volumes of what he calls "myths," a new form peculiar to him. Jensen won the Nobel prize in 1944.

KARLFELDT, ERIK AXEL (1864–1931), Swedish poet, occupied a position which made it almost impossible for him to win the Nobel prize in literature. He was elected to the Swedish Academy in 1904 and became a member of its Nobel Committee, which makes the awards, three years later. From 1912 until his death he was the permanent secretary of the Academy, and thus played a decisive part for many years in the naming of award winners. In 1920 the other members of the committee wished to give the Nobel prize to Karlfeldt, but he would not accept it. Only after his death, in 1931, was the award given to him; this possible violation of the terms of the Nobel will worried no one. Although Karlfeldt was little known outside Scandinavian countries, his gifts as a lyric poet were of the first order.

KIPLING, RUDYARD (1865–1936), English novelist, short-story writer, and poet, was born in India, the country with which much of his writing is associated. He learned to speak the native tongue along with English as a boy, and the spirit as well as the language of the country never left him. He went to school in England but at eighteen, when he was ready to enter the university, he returned to India and got a job on the *Lahore Civil and Military Gazette.* Here he became an experienced journalist and began to write short stories, chiefly about the three British soldiers who were later to appear in *Soldiers Three* and *Plain Tales from the Hills.* While in India he also published his first volume of poetry, *Departmental Ditties.* In 1889 he traveled to England by way of the United States, and from this trip came the travel volumes, *Letters of Marque* and *From Sea to Sea.* In London Kipling settled down to write, producing the novel, *The Light That Failed,* and the poems, *Barrack-Room Ballads.* He made a trip to the South Seas, and then lived in America for four years (his wife was an American), where he wrote *Many Inventions, The Jungle Books, The Seven Seas,* and *Captains Courageous.* He was back in England in 1896 but went off to report the Boer War. He was now wealthy and famous, a symbol of British imperialism and conservatism. The Nobel prize was given to Kipling in 1907 when he was forty-two years old, the youngest man ever to win the award.

LAGERLÖF SELMA (1858–1940), Swedish novelist and short-story writer, was born in Värmland, the district which has been the scene of most of her stories. Her first novel was her greatest and most successful, *Gösta Berling's Saga.* Based on old folk legends, it was a pure example of the storyteller's art at its best, warm, simple, personal, and poetic. Other important works are the novels *Jerusalem* and *The Ring of the Löwenskölds;* one of the world's best books for children, *The Wonderful Adventures of Nils;* two autobiographical volumes; and many collections of short stories. Selma Lagerlöf was the first woman to win the Nobel prize, which came to her in 1909.

LEWIS, SINCLAIR (1885–   ), American novelist and short-story writer, was born in Minnesota, graduated from Yale University, and worked for several years at editorial jobs in the book-publishing business. His early novels were of slight importance—*Our Mr. Wrenn, The Trail of the Hawk,* and *The Innocents.* His first serious work was *The Job,* but it was his next book, *Main Street,* which brought Lewis fame and popularity, and showed that he was one of the keenest observers and sharpest satirists American literature had developed. In a series of novels that followed he painted typical American figures, sometimes with acidity, sometimes with deep sympathy, and almost always with vigor and originality and entertainment. *Babbitt, Elmer Gantry, Arrowsmith, Dodsworth, Ann Vickers, Cass Timberlane,* and many others have showed ups and downs of importance and ability but consistent popularity. Sinclair Lewis won the Nobel prize in 1930, the first American to receive the award.

MAETERLINCK, MAURICE (1862–   ), Belgian dramatist, essayist, and poet, practiced law before becoming an author. When he was twenty-six, he went to Paris and became an important member of the new group of symbolist writers. A book of poems and a play achieved immediate success, which Maeterlinck augmented with a series of plays contrasting strongly with the social-problem dramas which had held the stage for a long time. *The Blind, The Intruder, Pélleas and Mélisande, Monna Vanna, The Blue Bird,* and others were concerned with the problems of the soul rather than those of the material world. Of great spiritual and idealistic strength, they proved popular and of profound influence on the theater. At the same time, Maeterlinck became interested in the study of insects and flowers, writing several popular books in this field, such as *The Life of the Bee, The Intelligence of Flowers,* and *The Life of the White Ant.* Maeterlinck has written essays on death, religious faith, the immortality of the soul, but it was chiefly for his contributions to the drama that the Nobel prize was awarded to him in 1911.

MANN, THOMAS (1875–   ), German novelist, short-story writer, and essayist, was the son of a wealthy merchant. He worked in the insurance business, then on the staff of the magazine, *Simplicissimus,* and began to write stories. He was twenty-five when he began his first great novel, *Buddenbrooks,* the story of a conservative and prosperous German family and its gradual disintegration. (The selection, *Little Hanno,* in this volume, is taken from *Buddenbrooks,* which received particular citation in the award of the Nobel prize to Mann in 1929.) He continued to write many stories, the best known of which—*Tonio Kröger, Death in Venice, Early Sorrow, Tristan, Mario and the Magician*—may be found in the volume, *Stories of Three Decades.* Thomas Mann has also written critical and political essays of wide influence, but his most important work has continued to be in the field of fiction. *Royal Highness* appeared in 1916, *The Magic Mountain,* one of the greatest modern novels, in 1924. Four volumes of his most ambitious work—the story of the Biblical Joseph—have appeared to date, *Joseph and His Brothers, The Young Joseph, Joseph in Egypt,* and *Joseph the Provider.* Mann left Germany with the coming to power of Adolf Hitler, living in Switzerland from 1933 to 1938, and in the United States, of which he has become a citizen, since that time.

MARTIN DU GARD, ROGER (1881–   ), French novelist and dramatist, saw his first two books, quite dissimilar, published in

1908. One was his doctoral thesis, an archaeological study, the other his first novel. Neither attracted much attention, but another novel, *Jean Barois,* won favorable comment. After service in the World War I, Martin du Gard settled down to the writing of his greatest work, a novel cycle in eight parts under the title, *The World of the Thibaults.* He is also the author of several plays for the experimental theater and some long stories, one of which is Martin du Gard's contribution to this volume. The Nobel prize came to him in 1937.

MISTRAL, FRÉDÉRIC, (1830–1914), Provençal poet and philologist, spent most of his life near the spot where he was born, not far from Avignon. The son of a farmer, he loved the speech and life of simple country people; as a student, he came to admire the old Provençal culture, which he wanted to revive by giving dignity to the native tongue in great poetry. A few others who shared his enthusiasm and beliefs gathered round him in a school which succeeded in doing what Mistral most desired. The chief work responsible for its success was his own epic poem, *Mireio,* from which the lyrics in this volume are selected. *Mireio* was a happy work about the people of Provence which revealed the beauties of their language and spirit. It was crowned by the French Academy, made into an opera by Gounod, and translated into many languages. Mistral wrote two other epics, many lyrics, memoirs, and a dictionary of his native tongue, which was mentioned, in addition to *Mireio,* in the award of the Nobel prize to him in 1904, when it was divided between Mistral and the Spanish dramatist, Echegaray.

MISTRAL, GABRIELA (1889–   ), Chilean poetess, whose real name is Lucila Godoy Alcayaga, was the daughter of a rural schoolmaster and minor poet, who left his home and family when his daughter was three years old. When Gabriela Mistral was fifteen, she came upon some verses of her father, which inspired her with the desire to write. Her first published works were sketches in prose, published in local periodicals. Meanwhile she was teaching school, and remained an active educator even after literary success came to her. This success came with the publication of her first book of poems, *Sonnets of Death,* inspired by a tragic love affair. The young man to whom she was engaged, finding himself in a difficult situation connected with his work, committed suicide. Her despair over this act is reflected in many of her poems, among them "The Prayer," which is printed in this volume. Her poetry reveals a deep religious feeling and a moving sadness, except for her verses for and about children. Gabriela Mistral held many important positions in Chile's Department of Education, spent two years in Mexico on an educational project, taught in the United States at Columbia, Vassar, and Middlebury. She was her country's representative on a committee of the League of Nations between the wars and has served in Chile's consular service in Brazil, Spain, and Argentina. In her writing she has been at home in many forms and techniques—as may be seen from the examples of conventional and free verse, as well as prose poems, contributed to this anthology. The Nobel prize was awarded to Gabriela Mistral in 1945.

MOMMSEN, THÉODOR (1817–1903), German historian and archaeologist, was born in Schleswig, studied at the University of Kiel, and devoted himself to the study of Roman law and antiquities. The Danish Government in 1843 gave him a grant for his first trip to Italy, where he began his study of Roman inscriptions. There were several plans afoot for the collecting of all existing inscriptions, but it was many years before the work was finally undertaken under Mommsen's supervision. Meanwhile he formulated the plan for such research and actually gathered all inscriptions from one town—a work which brought acclaim. But his political beliefs caused him difficulties, and when the revolution of 1848 came in Germany he lost his professorship and went to Switzerland for several years, where he worked on his great Roman history, which appeared in 1854 to 1856. A separate work, but in a sense a continuation of his *History of Rome,* was *The Roman Provinces under the Empire,* in 1884. Finally he returned to the gigantic

work of compiling Roman inscriptions, after which he wrote a *History of Roman Coinage* and analyses of Roman constitutional and criminal law. Rarely has any writer reached such pre-eminence in his field as that achieved by Mommsen, who towered above all others in his time. As his portraits of leading Romans have always been considered one of the best features of his history, his sketch of Julius Caesar has been chosen for this volume. Mommsen won the Nobel prize in 1902.

O'NEILL, EUGENE (1888–   ), American dramatist, was the son of a prominent actor who took him on many of his theatrical tours when he was young. One year at Princeton was enough college work for Eugene O'Neill, after which he worked as a secretary, prospected for gold in Central America (where he got malaria), and served as assistant manager of his father's acting company. But he was restless, and shipped as a seaman to South America, returned to try acting in America, took up newspaper reporting, and wound up with a physical breakdown. He started writing plays, studied in Professor G. P. Baker's famous 47 Workshop at Harvard, and finally became associated with the Provincetown Players in 1916, who produced some of his one-act plays. Then *Beyond the Horizon* achieved great success, won the Pulitzer prize, and made its author one of the most important American dramatists. This was followed by *Anna Christie, Emperor Jones, The Hairy Ape,* and others which were vivid, realistic, and powerful. But O'Neill continually strove for a deeper meaning, a broader significance, and in the plays which followed the symbolical grew in importance, the experimentation with new forms increased. Among the most important of his plays are *The Great God Brown, Lazarus Laughed, Desire Under the Elms, Marco Millions, Strange Interlude, Mourning Becomes Electra, Dynamo, Ah, Wilderness!,* and *The Iceman Cometh.* The Nobel prize was given to O'Neill in 1936; he was the second American to receive it.

PIRANDELLO, LUIGI (1867–1936), Italian playwright, short-story writer, and novelist, was born in Sicily. He began to write as a young man, in addition to teaching school, but was more than fifty years old before he achieved wide recognition. There is humor in almost everything he wrote, but humor with a bitter kernel and a deep significance. His first efforts were in the field of the short story, of which he wrote more than three hundred. He also produced several novels, among which may be mentioned *The Outcast, Shoot, The Old and the Young*. But his greatest success was in the drama. In 1921 his play, *Six Characters in Search of an Author*, was popular throughout the Western world. Other plays followed—*The Pleasure of Honesty, Right You Are if You Think You Are, As You Desire Me*, and *Henry IV* among them. The one-act play printed in this volume bears the unmistakable stamp of Pirandello, even to his love of unusual staging and deft tricks of the theater. He was awarded the Nobel prize in 1934.

PONTOPPIDAN, HENRIK (1857–1943), Danish novelist and short-story writer, came from a long line of clergymen, but decided to be a civil engineer. He gave up his studies, however, to become a teacher in his brother's school. At the same time he began writing, and soon was able to devote himself entirely to literature. He did not like the literary circles of Copenhagen, so settled down in the country, married a farmer's daughter, and came to know well and to love the simple country people and small villagers about whom he wrote most of his stories. In addition to several volumes of short stories, he wrote many novels, including three great novel cycles—*The Promised Land, Lucky Per*, and *The Kingdom of the Dead*. In these he pictured his countrymen in no favorable light; but despite his telling attacks on many Danish characteristics and institutions, he was always popular. Perhaps his public knew that Pontoppidan was often right; certainly they understood that his critical concern came from love and understanding. He shared the Nobel prize in 1917 with Karl Gjellerup.

REYMONT, LADISLAS (1867–1925), Polish novelist and short-story writer, grew up in great poverty on a poor farm near an ugly village in Russian Poland. He was long considered the utter failure of his large family, and he had little happiness or success until he broke away from them. In his youth the reading of books was his only real pleasure. He failed in numerous schools, was fired from one job after another. He spent a year wandering about Poland with a traveling theater troupe, worked in a railroad station—and kept on reading. Finally he went to Warsaw and, though almost starving, began to write. Slowly he won small success, which grew as he found himself in his stories of peasant life and novels of broad canvas. Early works such as *A Pilgrimage to Jasna Góra, The Comédienne*, and *The Promised Land* increased his fame, but the crowning work of his life was undoubtedly his novel cycle, *The Peasants*. The story included in this volume is a tale of this period, a grim and bitter anecdote about the poor peasants among whom he grew up. The Nobel prize was awarded to Reymont in 1924.

ROLLAND, ROMAIN (1866–1944), French novelist, playwright, and essayist, developed a great love for music when he was still a boy. At the university he specialized in history, but returned to music for his doctoral thesis, a history of the early opera in Europe. Meanwhile, however, he had begun the writing of plays, among which are *The Wolves, Danton, The Fourteenth of July, The Game of Love and Death*, and *Robespierre*. A short life of Beethoven, and lives of Michelangelo, Tolstoy, Gandhi and other figures he admired came from him, together with letters and essays during the World War I which called for peace and brought violent attacks against him as a traitor. But his greatest achievements were undoubtedly his novel cycles, of which *Jean-Christophe* is outstanding. The first important novel with a musician as its central character, it showed the artist's conflict with the world in which he lives. *The Soul Enchanted*, with a woman as the main character, was of great distinction but did not equal *Jean-Christophe*, which was particularly cited in the award of the Nobel prize to Rolland in 1915, when he was in the midst of his fight for peace and was being bitterly attacked.

SHAW, GEORGE BERNARD (1865–   ), Irish dramatist, did not like an office job when he was a young man, so left Dublin for London, where he did odd writing jobs and became music critic of the London *Star* under the name of Corno di Bassetto. Later he went to the *World* as music critic, became drama critic of *The Saturday Review*, and wrote book reviews. But his great interest at that time was radical politics. Shaw has always called himself a Socialist, though perhaps a highly individual brand. He was one of the founders of the socialist Fabian Society in 1884 and for many years was active in writing political tracts and making speeches. At the same time he started writing novels—*Cashel Byron's Profession*, *The Irrational Knot*, and *An Unsocial Socialist*. In 1904 his plays began to reach the stage, and by 1910 he was a great international success. Among his plays are *Arms and the Man*, *Candida*, *The Man of Destiny*, *Widowers' Houses*, *Mrs. Warren's Profession*, *The Devil's Disciple*, *Caesar and Cleopatra*, *Man and Superman*, *Major Barbara*, *The Doctor's Dilemma*, *Androcles and the Lion*, *Pygmalion*, *Back to Methusalah*, *Saint Joan*. Among Shaw's essays and works of non-fiction are *The Quintessence of Ibsenism*, *The Perfect Wagnerite*, *The Intelligent Woman's Guide to Socialism and Capitalism*. Witty, sure of his great ability, delighting in his role of difficult eccentric, Mr. Shaw is the only one of forty-two authors or their representatives who refused permission to reprint any writings in this anthology. He won the Nobel prize in 1925.

SIENKIEWICZ, HENRYK (1846–1916), Polish novelist and short-story writer, was the son of a well-to-do family in Russian Poland. After college, he wrote some critical pieces for periodicals and a story or two which showed no special ability. At thirty, he took a lengthy trip to the United States, writing travel letters to periodicals in Poland and obtaining ideas for some of his later short stories, among them the well-known *The Light-House Keeper*. Returning to Poland and to the writing of stories and novels, he quickly won great popularity with works about the people of his native land. He then wrote his great series of historical heroic novels about Poland—*With Fire and Sword*, *The Deluge*, and *Pan Michael*—glorifying Poland's struggle for independence in the seventeenth century. Another historical novel, *Knights of the Cross*, was laid in the thirteenth century, and the popular *Quo Vadis* was set in Nero's ancient Rome. Sienkiewicz also wrote fine psychological novels, *Without Dogma* and *The Polaniecki Family*. The Nobel prize was awarded to him in 1905.

SILLANPÄÄ, FRANS EEMIL 1888–   ), Finnish novelist and short-story writer, was of poor farmer stock, but his father was determined that he should have a good education. He studied natural history in Finland's capital, and at the same time became closely associated with a colony of artists in southern Finland, among whom was the great composer, Sibelius. But Sillanpää returned to his home without completing his university studies because he had decided to write. His short stories and articles brought him fame quickly. In 1916 his first novel was published, followed by more collections of short stories, his favorite medium. In 1919 the novel, *Meek Heritage*, established him as Finland's outstanding writer; the government recognized him by awarding him a pension for life. Other collections of stories were published regularly, and the novel, *The Maid Silja*, in 1931 spread his fame beyond the Scandinavian countries to the rest of Europe. But he was little known in America until he was awarded the Nobel prize in 1939.

SPITTELER, CARL (1845–1924), Swiss poet, essayist, and novelist, was one of the most original writers of our times. Apparently unaffected by literary trends, by warring schools of romanticists, realists, naturalists, or symbolists, he produced as his major work an epic poem dealing with the gods of ancient Greek mythology. *Olympian Spring* has been called by some an inspired work, a worthy successor to the *Iliad* and the *Divine Comedy;* other critics have decided that it was little more than a clever trick, though a huge one, written to prove that an epic in the classical tradition *could* be done. But the award of the Nobel prize to Spitteler in 1919 voiced the general acceptance of this poem as the sincere and often magnificent work of a poet of genius. Spitteler also wrote another epic poem on Prometheus, several novels, and many essays. In the last he showed a warm and happy and humorous personality and a keen mind.

SULLY-PRUDHOMME, RENÉ (1839–1907), French poet, was the first winner of the Nobel prize for literature, in 1901. Born in Paris, he thought for a time of entering a religious order, studied law and philosophy, and suffered an unhappy love affair which turned him to the writing of poetry. His first volume of verse was so immediately popular that he continued in the field of literature. In the classical tradition, his verse nevertheless had an emotional power which, though reserved and somewhat aloof, stirred his readers. Later, he wrote what he called "scientific-philosophic" poems in which he showed a keen comprehension of modern concepts that he wished to interpret through the medium of poetry.

TAGORE, RABINDRANATH (1861–1941), Bengalese poet, dramatist, and novelist, was born in Calcutta. The son of a wealthy Brahmin, he went to London to attend college, but instead of studying law, as he intended, he soon returned to India and began to write. His first book, published in 1878, was a long narrative poem. Other works soon followed this, chiefly poems or poem cycles. His plays and stories were really poems cast in different forms. In 1901 he founded a school in Bengal which became famous throughout the world and was always close to his heart. But he continued to write, to translate many works from Hindu into English, including his own. He was a talented musician and composed more than three thousand songs during his life. At sixty-eight he took up painting, and his canvases were exhibited in the principal cities of the world. In 1915 he was knighted, but renounced the title later in protest against British actions in India. The Nobel prize was awarded to

Tagor in 1913. His best-known works, *Gitanjali, Chitra, The Crescent Moon, The Gardener, The King of the Dark Chamber,* and others are collected in one volume of his poetic works. He also wrote essays and memoirs.

UNDSET, SIGRID (1882–   ), Norwegian novelist, was the daughter of a well-known archaeologist who died when she was only eleven years old, leaving the family in difficult circumstances. Sigrid Undset went to work in an office when she was sixteen, gaining experience later used in some of her modern stories. These attracted attention when they appeared, especially her collected stories, *The Happy Age,* and her first novels, *Jenny* and *Springtime.* Her first venture into historical fiction came in 1909 with a novel, *Gunnar's Daughter.* Then followed a period when she tried many different subjects and types of writing—stories, a retelling of the King Arthur legends, a study of the Brontë sisters, a volume of essays on women. Finally she returned to historical fiction with the trilogy, *Kristin Lavransdatter,* which appeared in 1920–22 and brought her fame throughout the world; she made her characters live and breathe despite the careful accuracy as to historical details which so often burdens the historical novel that pretends to genuine reincarnation of a long-past age. Her second great novel of medieval Norway was the tetralogy, *The Master of Hestviken,* from which the contribution to this anthology is selected. The Nobel prize was given to Sigrid Undset in 1928.

YEATS, WILLIAM BUTLER (1865–1939), Irish poet and dramatist, was born in Dublin and went to school there and in London. For three years he studied art—his father and brother were well-known painters—before deciding that he was a poet. His first verses and sketches appeared in Irish journals; then Oscar Wilde encouraged him to come to London, where his first book of verse was published in 1889, attracting the attention of critics and arousing a new interest in the renaissance of Celtic literature. Yeats himself was fascinated by the Irish spirit and its older literature, and next wrote a volume of Irish fairy tales and stories, an example of which, *The Wisdom of the King,* is included in this volume. More poetry and a verse drama, *The Countess Kathleen,* followed, together with a book of essays, *The Celtic Twilight.* His most famous verse drama, *The Land of Heart's Desire,* was acted in 1894 and published the following year. An increasing interest in the theater caused him to establish, with Lady Gregory, the Irish Literary Theater, which became the famous Abbey Theater. His first prose play was *Cathleen ni Houlihan,* and was followed by many other dramas in prose and verse—*The Pot of Broth, The King's Threshold, The Hour Glass, Shadowy Waters, Deirdre, The Cat and the Moon.* Many volumes of verse continued to appear, showing increasing strength and originality. Yeats also wrote essays, memoirs, and was active in Irish politics. He was awarded the Nobel prize in 1923.